PRINCIPLES OF
SCIENTIFIC SOCIOLOGY

PRINCIPLES OF SCIENTIFIC SOCIOLOGY

Walter L. Wallace

ALDINE PUBLISHING COMPANY

New York

Grateful acknowledgment is made to Random House, Inc., New York for permission to use the excerpt from p. 497 "Remembrance of Things Past," Vol. I, translated by C. K. Scott Moncreiff.

Aldine Publishing Company
200 Saw Mill River Road
Hawthorne, New York 10532

Library of Congress Cataloging in Publication Data
Wallace, Walter L.
    Principles of scientific sociology.

    Bibliography: p.
    Includes indexes.
    1. Sociology. I. Title.
HM51.W16 1983   301   83-11764
ISBN 0-202-30304-7
Printed in the United States of America
10 9 8 7 6 5 4 3 2

To
my dear
Sarane

Table of Contents

Acknowledgments

Six earlier efforts are brought together, revised, and expanded in this volume (see Wallace, 1966:8–17, 185–191; 1968; 1969:vii–xi, 1–59; 1971; 1975; and 1981). Neither they nor it could have been accomplished without a lot of help from my friends and colleagues. First among these is Alexander Morin, publisher of three of those earlier efforts and editorial consultant for this one. Alex read two drafts of the present book, made invaluable editorial suggestions, and gave strategic administrative support—for all of which he has my sincere thanks.

Marvin Bressler, Lewis A. Coser, Herbert Costner, Jonathan Turner, and Robin M. Williams, Jr. also read the manuscript in one or another version, and Sarane Boocock, Harry Bredemeier, Orville G. Brim, Jr., Hugh F. Cline, Howard Freeman, Margaret Gilbert, Michael Inbar, John I. Kitsuse, Michael Mulkay, Eleanor Sheldon, Conrad Snowden, Stanton Wheeler, and Margaret Wilson read various chapters. I am very grateful for their suggestions and encouragement. Several other colleagues at Princeton and elsewhere, including Alan Gewirth, Alex Inkeles, Robert Jastrow, George A. Miller, Walter J. Ong, Gilbert Rozman, Robert A. Scott, Paul Secord, Peggy Thoits, Charles Westoff, and Robert Wuthnow, were helpful in steering me to a particularly useful part of some relevant literature.

I am also grateful for the many stimulating responses of students in my courses over the years—especially at Princeton, but also at Northwestern, Columbia, Spelman, and in three summer seminars at Howard—and I regret that because of their number (and a memory that rarely fails to fail me) they must remain anonymous here.

Blanche Anderson and Cynthia Gibson (aided by Michelle Mistretta, Kim Naticzak, and Theresa Kuzianik) rendered an essential contribution by cheerfully and expertly typing tons of handwritten manuscript, and Cindy, in addition, helped immensely with the index. I also wish to thank Sheila Heller, managing editor at Aldine, for her expert and sympathetic handling of the publication of this book.

Finally, for help at crucial junctures in the past, Myrna Ingram Schuck, Sabra Holbrook, Gelolo McHugh, Lawrence Kamisher, Hylan Lewis, Raymond W. Mack, Orville G. Brim, Jr., Robert K. Merton, and Peter M. Blau, have my special gratitude.

Princeton, New Jersey
July, 1983

. . . . so that I spent my time running from one window to the other to reassemble, to collect on a single canvas the intermittent, antipodean fragments of my fine, scarlet, ever-changing morning, and to obtain a comprehensive view of it and a continuous picture.

Marcel Proust

1

General Introduction

This chapter outlines the book's objectives, its method, its contents, and some uses to which these contents may be put.

OBJECTIVES

Although they rely upon four very different traditions in sociology, Merton, Blalock, Luckmann, and Alexander all assess the present state of our discipline in roughly the same way, and all tell us to do roughly the same things to secure its future.

Merton's estimate is that "No one paradigm has even begun to demonstrate its unique cogency for investigating the entire range of sociologically interesting questions," and he warns against changing this situation: "it is not so much the plurality of paradigms as the collective acceptance by practicing sociologists of a single paradigm proposed as a panacea that would constitute a deep crisis" (1975:28, 29). Blalock's estimate points to the same facts but makes a different evaluation of them: "in many respects we seem badly divided into a myriad of theoretical and methodological schools that tend to oversimplify each other's positions, that fail to make careful conceptual distinctions, and that encourage partisan attacks"

(1979:881). Blalock's warning, predictably from the tone of this estimation, is different from Merton's:

> it is crucial that we learn to resist overplaying our differences at the expense of common intellectual interests. . . . We can ill afford to go off in our own directions, continuing to proliferate fields of specialization, changing our vocabulary whenever we see fit, or merely hoping that somehow or other the product of miscellaneous studies will add up (1979:881, 893).

Although they are indeed different, I believe these two warnings need not be antithetical; their reconciliation can be achieved by applying Blalock's plea for consensus at a more broadly encompassing level (i.e., the level of "common intellectual interests") than the level at which Merton's defense of dissensus is applied (i.e., the level of specific "paradigms" for investigating different "sociologically interesting questions"). The desirability of some such reconciliation is indicated by both Merton and Blalock. Thus, Merton warns that too much "theoretical pluralism" can be a bad thing: "full cognitive segregation [can set] in, with members of rival thought-collectives no longer making an active effort to examine the work of cognitively opposed collectives" 1981:vii), and he therefore asserts that "Sociological theory must advance . . . through special theories adequate to limited ranges of social data and through the evolution of a conceptual scheme adequate to *consolidate* groups of special theories" (1948:168). For his part, Blalock promises that even within the framework of unanimity which he urges us to create, "There will still be plenty of room for differences in terms of the kinds of propositions we wish to state and test, the assumptions we are willing to make, the problems we study, the courses of action we recommend, and the theoretical and ideological biases with which we operate" (1979:898). Thus, it is not the end of controversy but the systematization and specification of controversy within the bounds of an overarching consensus that seems to be the order of the day in Blalock's, as well as Merton's, eyes.

Luckmann, although an exponent of a different sociological tradition than either Blalock or Merton, nevertheless expresses a similar diagnosis and prescription when, speaking of a "crisis of social science," he says

> because every indication of the critical condition of the patient is attributed to a serious but localized infection (structural-functionalism, *structuralisme,* neopositivism, "critical theory," transformational grammar, symbolic interactionism, statistical historiography, ethnomethodology, etc.), the scattered symptoms are not recognized as forming part of a syndrome which has a single cause. . . . [I]n my view the solution to the crisis of social science lies in the formulation of a *mathesis universalis* appropriate to human affairs . . . [which can generate] a metalanguage into which the observational languages of the various social sciences could be translated (1978:237, 239; see also 244).

And most recently, Alexander urges that "evaluative criteria" in sociological debate

> must be expansive and inclusive. They must attempt to draw upon the full range of theoretical options presented by competing theories and to elaborate standards for evaluation that synthesize, as much as possible, the distinctive qualities embodied by each. Only then will one increase that consensus about evaluative standards which alone can diminish the "incompleteness of logical contact" (1982:115; Chapter 10 [footnote 11] examines how Alexander himself responds to this injunction).

We have, then, a call—issuing from quite different quarters—for a generalized disciplinary consensus, and for a metalanguage in which that consensus might be expressed.[1] The first objective of this book is to answer that call by setting forth a description of the content and form of sociology (and, to a lesser extent, of sociobiology) in which what I believe is our already existing, but still unrecognized consensus will be made explicit.

My argument, however, is not only descriptive of sociology; it is also broadly prescriptive. The second objective of this book, then, is to identify the several fronts on which we should move in order most rapidly to advance sociology as a scientific discipline. So interpreted, the principles set forth here identify points at which empirical research most needs new contributions from methodologists as well as theorists—that is, they try to say what we need to be able to measure about any social phenomenon that we wish to describe, explain, or predict from; what we need to be able to measure about the other phenomena that we call upon as explanatory of that social phenomenon or as consequences of it; the various causal connections between these two sets of phenomena that we need to be able to establish; and the procedural connections within and between pure sociology and applied sociology that we need to strengthen. We have, of course, a long way to go on all these problems. Their rigorous and systematically integrated formulation, however, may be the first step in mobilizing resources toward solving them.

METHOD

In pursuing the above objectives, my method is to infer how sociological analysis should be carried out by analyzing, critically and in detail, a variety of pub-

---

[1] This includes Mannheim, who says "An effort must be made to find . . . a common denominator for . . . varying perspectivistic insights" (1955:301); and also Stryker, who says

> without communication across specializations, there can be little common meaning to the label "sociologist," little shared sense of belonging to a common enterprise. This means distrust; it also means that the common core is emptied. . . . Our sociology is impoverished when that occurs (1982:iii).

lished cases showing how it has actually been carried out. I choose this method for two reasons. First, and obviously, it is always useful to take past experience explicitly and systematically into account when trying to improve a present condition; whether we end mainly in rejecting or mainly in accepting that experience, the improvement can be made more efficient because of it. And second, by relying on our *collective* past experience, we avoid the temptation to draw universalistic conclusions from the inevitably narrow, brief, and biased experience of only one person. Ideally, the authority for the principles inferred here should be demonstrably the entire discipline of sociology and most certainly not the author alone.

Consequently, I think the reader will find this book to be comprehensive of, and nonpartisan toward, all the various contending schools of thought in sociology (nonpartisan, that is, except for its classifying sociology as a natural science). This comprehensiveness and nonpartisanship produces here, I believe, a net of principles that catches virtually all the sociological fish so far hatched—whether they happen to be looked upon currently as small fry or big fry. Moreover, as I shall try to demonstrate, this same net catches virtually all the sociobiological fish as well, because the scientific analysis of social phenomena follows exactly the same general principles whether the objects of that analysis are human or nonhuman organisms. Note that the term "sociobiological" is used here to refer generically to all studies of social phenomena among nonhuman organisms—regardless of the kind of variables such studies call upon to explain these phenomena and regardless of whether the studies are more specifically designated as ethological, entomological, ecological, comparative psychological, behavior genetical, primatological, microbiological, marine biological, or whatever.[2]

As counterbalance to all this emphasis on comprehensiveness and nonpartisanship, however, let me hasten to add some words in defense of narrowness and partisanship. According to Mannheim (see 1955:80–81, 301–302), a double division of labor prevails in the scientific world: first, there is a competitive division of labor between partisans of different views—in which each partisan constantly challenges the others to develop their views to the fullest—and, second, there is a cooperative division of labor between all such partisans on the one hand and synthesizers on the other—in which partisans provide the views that synthesizers synthesize, and synthesizers then may provide the bases for new partisanships (see Chapter 10). In a word, then, if there were no partisans there could be no eclectics. Therefore, this book, although it is itself eclectic, constitutes no call to stamp out partisanship; quite the opposite.

Now as even this introductory chapter shows, part of my method here is to rely heavily on direct quotations from the relevant literatures. This reliance follows

---

[2] Wilson defines sociobiology both more narrowly (focusing on explanatory variables that Chapter 7 will call "existentially given"), and more broadly (including studies of human as well as nonhuman social phenomena), when he calls it "the systematic study of the *biological* basis of *all* social behavior" (1975:4, emphasis added).

from the fact that these literatures are the data for my analysis; that is, as indicated above, *I rely here on my observations of sociological analyses, and not on my observations of social phenomena.* As with all data, everything depends on the analyst's interpretation of them, and again, as always, it is incumbent upon the analyst to try to persuade readers that each such interpretation is both fair and sound (i.e., one that does not build its case on mere idiosyncrasies in the data, and one that the readers themselves would make). When dealing with data that are uniformly expository material presented in more-or-less ordinary language, I know of no better way to attempt that persuasion than to present the material itself, show how I interpret it, and let the reader decide on the spot. Note also that some of the material in question is so many-sided that it will have to be presented twice or more, in different interpretative contexts.

Surely someone will argue, however, that when it comes to evidence, published sociological analyses are not the place to look if what we really want to know more about and manage more effectively are actual social *phenomena* and not verbal *analyses* of such phenomena. Armchair sociologists, indeed, have been roundly condemned:

> Instead of systematically observing the process of interaction around them, as do ethologists, or immersing themselves in primary historical sources, as do historians; instead of living for extended periods in foreign cultures, as do anthropologists; these sociologists endlessly . . . rehash each others' recondite cognitions in an empirical near-vacuum (van den Berghe, 1975:14).

I hold, however, that the meaning of "systematically observing the process of interaction" is not unambiguous and deserves careful scrutiny somewhere away from the heat of data-collection—that is, back in the old armchair. I also hold that the attempt fully to immerse oneself in any single source, no matter how small, can totally absorb all the energies of any analyst. Weber says

> The absolute infinitude [of the successively and coexistently emerging and disappearing events in which life confronts us] is seen to remain undiminished even when our attention is focused on a single "object" . . . as soon as we seriously attempt an exhaustive description of *all* the individual components of this "individual phenomenon," to say nothing of explaining it causally (1949:72).

Furthermore, benefits of the division of labor extend even to the discipline that studies it—and rehashings, along with original hashings, may yield distinctive benefits for that discipline.

In pursuing my own particular rehashing of sociology, I have considered the three possible organizing themes mentioned by Nisbet: The first theme centers on "the thinkers themselves"; the second centers on "the system [or] the school"; and the third centers on "the ideas which are the elements of systems" (1966:3–4). Lovejoy, Nisbet says, argues that the "initial procedure" suggested by the third theme is "somewhat analogous to that of analytical chemistry. In dealing with the history of philosophical doctrines, for example, it cuts into the . . . individual systems, and . . . breaks them up into their component elements, into what may be called their unit-ideas" (1966:4). Nisbet follows this latter procedure, and, so do I—although the elements at which I arrive are far more elementary than Nisbet's.[3]

Thus, my overall method here, analogous in part to that of an analytical chemist or anatomist, is to dissect and schematize published analyses of social phenomena—analyses which must themselves represent schematizations of the vastly more complex analytical processes actually employed by their authors.[4] As a result of this *double* schematization, the actual substance and process of sociological analysis will appear in these pages as simpler, neater and trimmer, less subtle, less full of intuition (and flab) than it is, or can ever be, or should ever be. By conveying this appearance, however, I do not intend to derogate the artful features of scientific sociological analysis—no more than any sensible chemist intends to derogate cuisine or an anatomist, dance. I do mean, however, to pursue quite singlemindedly here the special benefits of decomposition and schematization—benefits that seem well-exemplified by the impact on teaching and research of several such attempts, ranging from Lavoisier's breakdown of all matter into a few chemical elements to Duncan's breakdown of occupational status into education and income.

CONTENTS

This book argues that sociology is, in its actual practice as well as its abstract design, one of the natural sciences—that is, much more akin to biology, chemistry, and physics than to philosophy, poetry, or religion—and everything in it should be regarded as explicating this view. Thus, the book addresses what makes scientific sociology "sociology," namely, its *substance* or empirical referents, in Parts I and II, and then addresses what makes scientific sociology "scientific," namely, its *form* or procedure, in Part III.

More specifically, Part I sets forth principles for specifying the empirical referents of sociological description. Here a generic definition of social phenomena is

---

[3] Nisbet identifies five pairs of "unit-ideas" as essential to sociology: community-society, authority-power, status-class, sacred-secular, and alienation-progress (see 1966:6).

[4] See Kaplan's distinction between "logic-in-use" and "reconstructed logic" (1964:8–11).

proposed, and that definition is then broken down into four components: social structure, cultural structure, spatial regularity, and temporal regularity. Part I also examines how each of these components may be hierarchically aggregated and how different levels in each such hierarchy may be determined.

Part II assumes the description, along lines indicated by Part I, of some social phenomenon of interest and sets forth principles specifying the empirical referents of sociological explanation of, and prediction from, that phenomenon. Here a generic typology of explanatory variables is proposed, along with a set of causal models whereby two or more such variables may be combined.

Part III sets forth principles, and some philosophical assumptions, pertaining to the general procedure followed by scientific sociology. Special attention is paid to the components of, and relations between, "pure" and "applied" science. As parts of pure science, I examine relations between observations, empirical generalizations, explanations, predictions, and tests of predictions; and as parts of applied science, I examine relations between plans, decisions, implementations, outcomes, and evaluations of outcomes—all with ample illustrations from the sociological and other relevant literatures. Part III closes with an examination of some philosophical premises on which procedure in all the sciences, regardless of their empirical referents, rests, and an examination of some leading objections to regarding sociology as a natural science—objections, therefore, to subjecting it to the indicated procedures and premises.

Three chapters introduce all the main ideas of this book: Chapter 2 introduces Part I and its ideas regarding the empirical referents of sociological description; Chapter 7 introduces Part II and its ideas regarding the empirical referents of sociological explanation and prediction; Chapter 13 introduces Part III and its ideas regarding general scientific procedure and its applicability to sociology. These main ideas are depicted at a glance in Figs. 2.1, 7.2, and 13.1

As that last paragraph implies, the structure of this book is largely hierarchical. This chapter stands alone at the most inclusive level of the hierarchy insofar as it offers a general introduction to the book's entire contents. At the next level are Chapters 2, 7, and 13—each of which introduces a part of the book's contents. And at the most detailed level there are Chapters 3–6, Chapters 8–12, and Chapters 14–16, which specify the contents of each of these parts.

Now although I believe the argument of this book can certainly be followed sequentially straight through from Chapter 1 to the end, its hierarchical structure permits other, perhaps more profitable and certainly more flexible, approaches. Thus, Chapters 2, 7, and 13 should be regarded as second-level extensions of the present chapter, and the reader is urged to examine these three next before dipping into the detailed chapters which they introduce. Readers with more specialized interests may wish to take other routes: After finishing the general introduction, those mainly interested in the application of scientific procedure to sociology may want to read Part III; others, mainly interested in sociological explanation, may

turn next to Part II, while still others, interested mainly in sociological description, may read Part I.

USES

There seem to be at least two kinds of uses to which the principles set forth
here may be put. One pertains to the understanding and teaching of sociology as
it has been practiced so far, and the other pertains to the creation of sociology as
it may be practiced in the future.

In the first kind of use, I include the encouragement that the principles set
forth here may give to eventual discipline-wide adoption of some broadly standardized sequence and content in the basic training of new recruits to professional
sociology—a sequence and content that, while not hindering the persistence of
existing intradisciplinary partisanships or the emergence of new ones, will help
establish a common, rigorous, and detailed universe of disputation and decision
among their proponents.

It follows, then, that the principles set forth here are aimed not only at restructuring how sociology is taught, but also at restructuring how sociology is fought
out between partisans of different sides in our on-going intradisciplinary controversies. Here this book offers ways of comprehending, within a single framework,
the essential nature of controversies between sociologists who favor, say, functionalism and those who favor conflict theory; between those who favor historical materialism and those who favor social actionism; between those who favor explanatory variables like ecology and genetics and those who favor variables like technology
and socialization; between those who see social phenomena as essentially changeful
and those who see them as essentially static; between those who see sociology as a
subfield of sociobiology and those who see the opposite relationship; between those
who see sociology as mainly a pure science and those who see it as mainly an
applied science.

The second kind of use includes the assistance that the principles set forth here
may give to the design of research which will be significantly more powerful,
replicable, and cumulative than in the past. Sociological research so far has rarely
been able to explain more than 60% of the variance in any social phenomenon,
and a major reason for this shortcoming may be that we have typically included in
any given equation only a few of the kinds of explanatory variables which, on
theoretic grounds explored in Part II, may actually be required. In addition, sociological research so far has suffered from the fact that social phenomena which, on
theoretic grounds explored in Part I, are quite different from one another are sometimes designated by the same term, and vice versa—with utterly devastating consequences for replicability and cumulation across such researches. The principles

set forth here are intended to help researchers produce more rigorously comparable descriptions of social phenomena, more complete explanations of such phenomena, and, consequently, predictions that have greater usefulness in solving not only the contemplative problems of scientific understanding but the practical problems of social betterment.

I believe Stinchcombe is right when he says "Theory ought to create the capacity to invent explanations" (1968:3, emphasis removed). And if one theory can create the capacity to invent one kind of explanation (e.g., functionalist, or conflict, or symbolic interactionist), then principles systematically derived from many theories should be able to create the capacity to invent *many* kinds of explanations. It is precisely this capacity, and further, the capacity to create many kinds of descriptions, many kinds of predictions, and indeed, many kinds of whole theories and whole researches in both pure and applied sociology, that this book is intended to enhance.

I
SOCIOLOGICAL DESCRIPTION

2

Introduction to Part I

Blumer puts the problem to which Parts I and II of this book are addressed as follows:

> there is a conspicuous absence of rules, guides, limitations and prohibitions to govern the choice of variables [in our field]. . . . [As a result,] current variable analysis in our field is operating predominantly with disparate and not generic variables and yielding predominantly disparate and not generic relations (1956:683, 685).

Parts I and II represent an effort to remedy this situation by setting forth guides (in Part I) to variables that can describe any social phenomenon in which the sociological analyst is interested, and (in Part II) to variables that can describe any phenomenon the analyst wishes to bring to bear upon that social phenomenon either as its explanatory cause or its predicted effect.

The rest of the present chapter, by way of introduction specifically to Part I, proposes a generic definition of social phenomena, describes its intended scope and limits of reference, derives from it the four components of every social phenomenon (i.e., social structure, cultural structure, spatial regularity, and temporal regularity) to which the rest of Part I is devoted, and examines some of the relevant sociological and sociobiological literature.

Before embarking on this effort, however, it is essential to note that no scien-

13

tific definition of any phenomenon should be regarded as more than tentative. This restriction follows from the scientific function of such definitions: at any given moment in the history of a science, they serve to point out the possible or actual existence of certain phenomena in which that science takes interest and to distinguish these phenomena from others. But as we come to understand and/or control more and more features of the phenomena in question, we revise our definitions of them. Thus, life itself now has a new definition at the hands of virology and genetic engineering, and death too has been redefined by electroencephalographs and heart-lung machines. In short, all scientific definitions of observable phenomena remain in continual touch with empirical and practical research—an interaction wherein definitions serve as running summaries of what we already understand and control about the world, and as moving springboards for future efforts to understand and control still more.[1] The scientific definition of a given phenomenon, therefore, should never be absolute and rigid, but always relative and modifiable; it should be appropriate to the stage which scientific understanding and control of the phenomena to which it points has attained at the time, and it should be discarded (or rather, traded-in) as understanding and control pass beyond that stage.

It is only with these qualifications in mind that the following definition is put forward.

A GENERIC DEFINITION OF SOCIAL PHENOMENA

Let us begin by noting that any phenomenon whatever may be defined as the regular coincidence of other phenomena. For example, water may be defined as the regular coincidence of hydrogen and oxygen, and each of the latter as regular coincidences of protons, neutrons, and electrons, and each of the latter as regular coincidences of quarks and gluons, and (undoubtedly) so on, to the limits of technologically augmented human sensory discrimination.

Accordingly, let us define a social phenomenon as an *interorganism behavior regularity*—that is, a regular coincidence of two or more organisms' behaviors—and let us propose this as a generic definition, applicable not only to sociology but to all the social sciences. The definition means that a social phenomenon may be said to exist if, and only if, at least one behavior of a given organism[2] is observed to

---

[1] Merton points to this interaction when he notes, on the one hand, that "Concepts . . . constitute the definitions (or prescriptions) of what is to be observed; they are the variables, between which empirical relationships are to be sought," and, on the other hand, that "the clarification of concepts . . . is a frequent result of empirical research" (1957:89, 115; see also 281–282).

[2] The problem of defining "organism" belongs to the discipline of biology; I, at least, am prepared to accept whatever definition is current there at any given moment (just as, presumably, biologists are prepared to accept whatever definition of "molecule" is current among chemists) in token of the hier-

be regularly accompanied in time and/or space by at least one behavior of at least one other organism. Thus, in order to identify a social phenomenon we need to observe that if organism A manifests a behavior, then organism B regularly (not necessarily always or everywhere, but satisfying some arbitrary criterion of relative frequency) manifests a behavior. B's behavior may be temporally or spatially ordered in any way with respect to A's behavior (i.e., at the same, or at a different, time and/or place); it may or may not be the same behavior throughout the regularity; and the behaviors in question may be literally anything within either organism's repertory. Note also that it is the regularity *between* different organisms' behaviors, and not the regularity *within* each organism's behavior, which is constitutive of a social phenomenon. Thus, in the manner of moiré patterns, the coincidence of a given behavior regularity in one organism with a different behavior regularity in another organism yields a third regularity, and although each individual organism's behavior regularity helps *explain* the third, it is only this third, coincident, regularity which is *defined* as social. This is exactly what Durkheim means when he says "society is not a mere sum of individuals. Rather, the system formed by their association represents a specific reality which has its own characteristics" (1938:103).

Here it must be added that it is always and only the *analyst* who decides what is and is not a social phenomenon, and who decides, therefore, which participants, behaviors, and regularities constitute that phenomenon. Certainly analysts may regard themselves as participants also, and certainly they are always at liberty to make their own identification of a social phenomenon contingent on its being so identified by someone else (say, its participants) whom they regard as authoritative. This requirement, however, is the analyst's choice—just as one might choose to require a certain kind of organism, or a certain kind of behavior, before certifying a phenomenon as "social" for the purposes at hand.

Thus, it suffices that *analysts* see an interorganism behavior regularity, whether the participating organisms see it or not. Clearly, if analysts only followed Blumer's injunction to "approach the study of group activity through the eyes and experience of the people who have developed the activity" (1956:689), much of that activity would not be defined as "group activity" by the people concerned[3] and so could not be analyzed sociologically at all (see Merton, 1948:166–167). In the end, of course, Blumer's injunction, and the method of *verstehen* (see Abel, 1948) for which it calls, both support the ethnocentrism implied by Hayek's view that

---

archic structure of scientific lexicons. "Behavior" may then be defined as any event perpetrated by, or occurring in, an organism.

[3] For example, Durkheim considered persons who committed suicide to have been members of societies which, judging by their own acts, they probably would have renounced. Spencer also considered conquered peoples to be members of the conquering societies—a membership they obviously disputed before conquest and probably continued to reject for some time thereafter.

> When we speak of man . . . . [i]t is not the lumps of flesh of a certain shape which we mean, nor any units performing definite functions which we could define in physical terms. . . . When we speak of man we refer to one whose actions we can understand (1973:67).

Designating the definition mentioned above as generic, core, or minimal, means that although analysts may not subtract elements from it, they remain free to add elements or restrictions: to specify certain organisms and not others, certain behaviors and not others, certain regularities and not others. Of course, the most far-reaching qualification of this sort is the traditional restriction of "sociological" attention to social phenomena among human organisms, so that the investigation of social phenomena among nonhuman organisms has been left, by sociology's default, to sociobiology. The generic definition of a social phenomenon as "interorganism behavior regularity" in no way rules out such special restrictions; it only asserts that they are indeed special rather than generic, and provides the criterion for systematically differentiating them.

Therefore, consider how the following examples of definitions of human (and, later, nonhuman) social phenomena from classical and modern sociological theorists come within the scope of this generic definition.

Classical Definitions

Marx says society is "The product of men's reciprocal action. . . . Society . . . expresses the sum of interrelations, the relations within which . . . individuals stand" (1978:136, 247), and he and Engels say "By social we understand the cooperation of several individuals, no matter under what conditions, in what manner and to what end" (1978:157). Durkheim says "in order that there may be a social fact, several individuals, at the very least must have contributed their action," and says, again, that a social fact is "every way of acting [which is general throughout a given society] . . . capable of exercising on the individual an external constraint" (1938:lvi, 13). Weber defines "social action" as having "subjective meaning attached to it by the acting individual (or individuals)" such that it "takes account of the behavior of others and is thereby oriented in its course" (1947:88), and defines a "social relationship" as "the behavior of a plurality of actors in so far as, in its meaningful content the action of each takes account of that of the others and is oriented in these terms" (1947:118). Simmel says "Society merely is the name for a number of individuals, connected by interaction" (1950:10).

All these definitions imply the generic one offered here, although it typically requires less than they, as befits any "generic" definition. Thus, Marx seems to require that the behavior in question must be cooperative,[4] and he, together with Simmel, requires behavioral reciprocation; Weber requires the coincidence of psychical (i.e., orientational) behavior as well as physical behavior; Durkheim seems to require more than two individuals, and also requires that the joint activity have a particular effect.[5] At the same time, however, none of these definitions (except Durkheim's) make the regularity component explicit and, in this respect, it requires more than they.

The situation is not much different, in these respects, when we consider the following modern definitions.

Modern Definitions

Davis omits mention of the behavioral and regular nature of "relations," but clearly specifies their interorganism character: "Like an organism, a society is a system of relations, but relations between organisms themselves rather than between cells" (1949:26). Blau and Scott's definition, on the other hand, specifies the behavioral and regular qualities but does not mention the interorganism quality of social phenomena: " 'Social organization' refers to . . . the observed regularities in the behavior of people . . ." (1962:2); and the same is true of Inkeles' definition: "When we say that there is a social system, we refer to the coordination and integration of social acts which permit them to occur in a way that produces order rather than chaos; and when we speak of 'order' we mean that events occur in a more-or-less regular sequence or pattern . . ." (1964:25). Schutz, too, omits mention of the "interorganism" requirements by declaring that "There will hardly be any issue among social scientists that the object of the social sciences is human behavior, its forms, its organizations, and products" (1953:26). At one point, not only does Homans require causation, rather than mere regularity, but he permits a single idiosyncratic event to be called "social": "social behavior is simply behavior in which the action of one man causes the action of another" (1974:77). However, Homans' view falls more in line with the generic definition proposed here when he omits mention of causation and also stresses the regularity component of social phenomena: "The usual descriptions of groups consist of statements of customs, that is recurrences, in human behavior at different places or at different

---

[4] We know, from all their writings on class struggle, that Marx and Engels did not intend to rule out conflict behavior. Indeed, their term "Zusammenwirken," here translated as "cooperation," may be rendered more literally and more inclusively as "joint activity." For the requirement of reciprocity, see Marx's letter to Annenkov, where society is called "The product of men's reciprocal action" (1978:136).

[5] At one point, Durkheim requires that a social fact be "capable of exercising on the individual an external constraint" (1938:13).

intervals" [1950:28]). Smelser provides an interesting example of seeming to deny outright the regularity component, without actually doing so. Thus, his first definition of a sociological dependent variable[6] cites "a *single* event (Why did violence erupt in the Congo when it did?)" (1968:8, emphasis added), but his illustration (i.e., violence in the Congo) implies that the "single event" was indeed composed of many events and that these events were at least spatially regular (i.e., in the Congo and not elsewhere)—and probably also temporally regular, insofar as the rest of Smelser's illustration (not quoted here) suggests postcolonial, and not colonial, or precolonial, violence in the Congo. Alexander's assertion that "Every social theory . . . [answers] the question of how a plurality of . . . actions become interrelated and ordered" (1982:90) seems to imply the generic definition of social phenomena put forward here—although he does not explicitly require that the "actions" in question must be those of at least two "actors."

Some examples that contain more than the proposed generic definition are given here: Parsons says "A social system consists in . . . individual actors interacting with each other . . . [i.e.,] actors who are motivated [by] the 'optimization of gratification' and whose relation to . . . each other is defined and mediated in terms of a system of cultural . . . symbols" (1951:5–6). This definition makes two requirements that are excessive for generic purposes: it requires "interaction" (thereby barring both one-way action and simple noncausal—spurious—coincidence from being called "social"), and it requires "motivation" and "symbols" (thereby barring both unconscious and nonsymbolic behavior from being called "social"). One of Merton's definitions of "group" also requires "interaction" ("the sociological concept of a group refers to a number of people who interact with one another in accord with established patterns" [1957:285]), but in his very next sentences Merton drops "interaction" in favor of the more ambiguous "relations": "This is sometimes phrased as a number of people having established and characteristic social relations. The two statements are . . . equivalent" (1957:285). In addition to this (or these) definitions, however, Merton proposes no less than twenty-six "properties" of groups—too many to examine in detail here but they all appear to refer, in various ways, to the components of the generic definition of social phenomena.[7]

It would certainly be difficult to prove beyond doubt, but I claim that all these definitions—classical and modern—are orbiting a common center of gravity which,

[6] The other two definitions include explicit mention of "regularities" and "patterns" (see Smelser, 1968:8).

[7] More specifically, it appears that the seventh, eighth, and tenth properties refer mainly to the "organisms" component; the first, second, fourth, sixth, ninth, eleventh, twelfth, thirteenth, fifteenth, seventeenth, eighteenth, twenty-sixth, and probably the sixteenth, refer mainly to the "behavior" component; and the third, fifth, fourteenth, nineteenth, twentieth, twenty-second, and twenty-fourth refer mainly to the "regularity" component. The twenty-third property seems to be a property of the group's environment rather than of the group itself, and the twenty-first and twenty-fifth seem to be properties of the relationship of the group to its environment (see Merton, 1957:310–324).

although not precisely indicated by any of them taken singly, is unambiguously revealed by them all taken together. It is this center of gravity that the generic definition proposed above seeks to express. However, there is obviously one requirement that several of the cited classical and modern definitions include but the proposed generic definition quite pointedly excludes. That requirement is "interaction" (and, in the case of Weber, "action"), and some justification for excluding it from the generic definition—though not from special definitions—is called for.

Interaction

In Chapter 12, I distinguish between different interpretations of "interaction": nearly simultaneous mutual influence (e.g., a handshake), and various speeds of sequential reciprocation (e.g., a conversation in which utterances alternate, quickly or slowly, between participants). In all interpretations, however, "interaction" between organisms A and B implies that each causes the other's behavior and that both jointly cause the social phenomenon in which they are participants. By requiring only a descriptive, conditional probabilistic, "regularity" of behavior between organisms, the proposed generic definition acknowledges that that phenomenon *may* be explained in this way, but acknowledges also that it may *not:* it may be explained by causes operating on each participant separately—either from inside or outside them—or, indeed, by causes emanating from sources randomly distributed throughout the universe, but the regularity would be no less "social" for that or any other explanation or prediction. Because I do not want to preempt any of these possible explanations by definitional fiat but want to leave them all for empirical investigation, I restrict the generic definition to "regularity" and bar the idea of interaction (as well as action and reaction) from that definition.

Thus, when Weber denies that the simultaneous opening of umbrellas by people caught in a sudden shower is social because the people are reacting to rain and not to each other (1947:113), he preempts scientific comparison of that hypothesis with others by defining social phenomena so as to rule it out from the start. Such comparison might well reveal, for example, that all but the first people to open their umbrellas during a shower (analogous, say, to all but the first physicians who adopt a new drug during an outbreak of disease[8]) are oriented to each other as well as (and even instead of) to rain. Such revelations, of course, can never occur if they are ruled out from the start by definition. But even should there be no such revelation—even if we should find that a given instance of umbrella-opening is really only a response to rain—still, equifinality (see Chapter 14) holds that any given outcome may be accomplished in several different ways, and there does not

[8] See Coleman et al. (1957).

seem to be any good reason to rule out the study of a particular instance of a given outcome just because it is not accomplished in some way that we happen to prefer.

Now, having tried to account for the exclusion of causal "action," "reaction," and "interaction" from the generic definition of social phenomena proposed here, let us examine the range of observations that that definition does include.

Scope of the Generic Definition

First, by referring merely to "organisms," the definition includes nonhumans (including micro as well as macro animals and plants), as well as humans. It therefore registers the fact that the way has always been more or less open to treating biological species as a variable rather than a constant in sociology, and thus open to a general, cross-species comparative, sociology that would be the conceptual peer of comparative psychology, comparative physiology, comparative anatomy, and genetics. Present-day sociology, therefore, should be regarded as a subfield of that future, more encompassing, comparative sociology inasmuch as sociology now concentrates almost entirely on social phenomena among only one species of animal.

In addition to including nonhuman organisms of whatever species, the generic definition of social phenomena proposed above includes aggregates or "collectivities" of any number of organisms (of a single or various biological species) as participants in social phenomena, provided only that there are identifiable behavior regularities within, and others between, such collectivities. Accordingly, I refer to "individuals" or "collectivities" (or simply "entities,"[9] as inclusive of both) as participants in social phenomena. Bearing in mind that the ultimate constituents of all entities in which sociology takes interest are individual living organisms, and noting also that the constituents of higher organisms seem themselves to have evolved from organisms that could at one time live independently of one another, it becomes reasonable to reverse the organismic analogy that "societies are like organisms" and suggest that "organisms are like societies"—a reversal made by Spencer himself ("every organism of appreciable size is a society" [1898:462]), and by Durkheim ("Not without reason has it been said that the self is itself a society, by the same right as the organism" [1938:3; see also xlviii]). In so doing, one would extend the potential relevance of sociological principles to biological disciplines in which they are now relative strangers.

---

[9] I avoid the term "actor" because the behavior selected for sociological analysis may be defined analytically as entirely psychical and therefore "thought" or "feeling" rather than "action." Even the Weberian and Parsonian definitions require the presence of physical behavior (see Weber, 1947:88; Parsons and Shils, 1951:53).

(As an aside, in this general context, it may also be asked how such principles pertain to the discipline often regarded as sociology's closest familiar, namely, social psychology. Insofar as social psychology represents "an attempt to understand and explain how the thought, feeling, and behavior of individuals are influenced by the actual, imagined, or implied presence of others" [Allport, 1968:3, emphasis removed; see also Krech, Crutchfield, and Ballachey, 1962:3; Brown, 1965:xx; Secord and Backman, 1974:1; and Hollander, 1976:31], that discipline is "social" only in the variables it selects as *explanatory* and not in the variables it selects *for* explanation. In this specific sense Allport is justified in claiming that "Social psychology is above all else a branch of general *psychology*. Its center of emphasis is the same: human nature as localized in the *person*" [1968:4, emphasis added]. However, given that Chapter 7 argues that sociology seeks not only to explain social phenomena but also to use social phenomena to explain other phenomena, it also seems fair to claim social psychology as a branch of sociology to the extent that it does the latter. The kinds of variables that social psychology typically employs to describe individual behavior are discussed in Chapter 8, and the kinds of variables it typically employs to explain that behavior are discussed in Chapters 9 and 10.)

Second, by referring simply to "behavior" the definition embraces literally *all* behavior—whether it be called "economic," "political," "educational," "religious," "cognitive," "affective," "attitudinal," "cooperative," "conflictful," or whatever. And most emphatically, both physical (roughly speaking, skeletomuscular, motor, or "body") behavior and psychical (roughly speaking, neuroendocrine, dispositional, or "mind") behavior are included, separately and in all their possible combinations. Thus, in contrast with Weber, it is not required (but it is permitted) here that physical behavior be "oriented" by psychical behavior,[10] or that it be psychically endowed with "meaning" by the manifesting entities, in order to constitute a social phenomenon. In contrast with Marx, it is not required (but it is permitted) here that psychical behavior be expressed in physical behavior in order to constitute a social phenomenon.[11] From the standpoint of the definition being offered here as generic and inclusive, the defining regularity between two or more entities may involve any variety of behavior described as physical on both sides, any variety described as psychical on both sides, any variety of one on one

---

[10] "Action is social insofar as, by virtue of the subjective meaning attached to it by the acting individual (or individuals), it takes account of the behavior of others and is thereby oriented to its course" (Weber, 1947:88). Parsons echoes this view by describing his own theoretic scheme as concerned with "acts," defined as "behaviors to which their authors and those who significantly interact with them attribute, in Weber's phase, a 'subjective,' which is to say cultural or symbolic, meaning" (1970:29).

[11] "From the start the 'spirit' is afflicted with the curse of being 'burdened' with matter, which here makes its appearance in the form of . . . language. Language is as old as consciousness, language is practical consciousness, as it exists for other men, and for that reason is really beginning to exist for me personally as well" (Marx and Engels, 1978:158).

side, and of the other on the other side, or any mixture of both on either or both sides.

Note, again, that *any* kind of behavior may be constitutive of social phenomena according to the generic definition. Parsons and Shils, in a more exclusive definition, argue that the "physics-chemical interchange between organism and environment . . . is not action, or behavior. . . . Action involves not a biochemical conceptual scheme but an 'orientational scheme' " (1951:542). Sorokin concurs in this exclusion: "stripped of their meaningful aspects, all phenomena of human interaction become merely biophysical phenomena and, as such, properly form the subject matter of the biophysical sciences" (1947:47). The present point of view, however, holds that *all* behavior (of course including subjectively meaningful behavior but not limited to it) falls within the scope of sociology. That organisms may blink, breathe, be born, die, fornicate, menstruate, believe, dream, open umbrellas, hunt, fish, rear cattle, and criticize together in time and/or space seems surely to provide foci for our disciplinary interest, whatever the limits of our personal specialties.

Third, the generic definition refers simply to "regularity" and thus requires, at minimum, only a nonzero probability of observing one organism's behavior conditional on observing at least one other organism's behavior.[12] The definition thus denotes merely a joint occurrence sometime and/or somewhere, such that interorganism behaviors may be regular—or "patterned," "structured," "organized," "ordered"—in time only (i.e., one organism's behavior may be observed regularly to precede the other's, or they may occur simultaneously), or in space only (i.e., the behaviors may be observed in some regular spatial relation, e.g., east-west, near-far, above-below, central-peripheral), or regular in both times and space (e.g., every July 4 in Boston, every July 14 in Paris, every Sunday in church). Because the regularities in question may be observed across any distance in space and/or time, some social phenomena may be described as extensive, sparse, or rare, while others may be described as concentrated, densely packed, or ordinary.

Note that in addition to being inclusive in all the senses just indicated, the generic definition proposed here is open. Thus, the questions of what constitutes an "organism" (Are viruses organisms? Will computerized robots, and other artificial—or other natural—entities eventually be regarded as organisms?); what constitutes an "inter"-organism versus an "intra"-organism phenomenon (Which sort of phenomenon occurs in colonial invertebrates like the Portuguese man-of-war?); and what constitues "regularity" (What level of conditional probability is satisfactory for a given purpose?) seem likely to be permanently moot questions. Their

[12] Weber grounds the definition of a social relationship and of social power in such conditional probabilities (1947:119, 152), and Parsons refers to a nonzero conditional probability as "factual order" ("The antithesis of [factual order] is randomness or chance in the strict sense of phenomena conforming to the statistical laws of probability" [1937:91]) and asserts that "a social order is always a factual order" (1937:92).

answers at any given moment seem only conventional working definitions that are always subject to debate and change.

Equivalent Formulations of the Generic Definition

The generic definition of social phenomena proposed above may be regarded as having three equivalent formulations, such that a social phenomenon may be defined as: *organisms* (and groups of organisms) between which behavior regularly occurs; *behaviors* (and groups of behaviors) regularly occurring between organisms; and *regularities* (and groups of regularities) in behaviors occurring between organisms. Thus, sociologists pursue interests in social *collectivities* when the organisms component is emphasized (here we employ concepts ranging from the two-organism "dyad" and larger "small groups" through crowds, publics, associations, communities, societies, groups of societies, and global society); interests in social *relations* when the behaviors component is emphasized (here we employ concepts like status, role, value, norm, conflict, exchange, communication, coercion, personal influence, etc.)[13]; and interests in social *stability and change,* and in social *location and spacing,*[14] when the component of temporal and/or spatial regularity is

[13] Durkheim expresses the difference between the first and the second interests when he notes that social and cultural phenomena "could be examined from two different points of view." One could study them as "a number of *actions* coordinated in view of a goal . . . . Or one might prefer to study the *entity* charged with accomplishing these actions" (1978:64, emphasis added). Levy's "distinction between concrete and analytic structures" seems to echo Durkheim—but with greater ambiguity, partly because Levy defines analytic structures only residually: "*Concrete structures* are . . . at least in theory capable of physical separation (in time and/or space) from other units of the same sort . . . [and include] membership units involved in social action . . . . *Analytic structures* are . . . not even theoretically capable of concrete separation from other patterned aspects of action ." Levy adds that "the economic and political patterns are analytic structures" (1952:88–89; for an interpretation of Levy's discussion similar to the present one, see Moore, 1978:338). Merton also draws the distinction between social collectivities and social relations when he defines a "group" as "a number of *people* having established and characteristic social relations," and then defines "social relations" as "patterned forms of social inter*action*" (1957:285, emphasis added).

[14] Reference here is to conventional physical space with its dimensions of length, breadth, and height. "Social" space is here constituted by organisms, behavior, and regularity dimensions and may thus be regarded as a "hyperspace" which includes another space (i.e., physical) in one of its dimensions. The general term "space" is taken to indicate an abstract concept applicable to the set of loci defined by the coordination of *any* two or more dimensions, and one's choice of dimensions is a matter of entirely arbitrary definition. Once the space is constructed, however, its usefulness becomes subject to other, nonarbitrary, criteria. What becomes crucial then is the ability of the space in question to order observations descriptively, to permit the application of explanatory-predictive principles to them, and to do all this in ways not inconsistent with other, better established, spaces and the principles applied to them. Therefore, no "ineluctability," no "reality," no "concreteness" can be inherent to any spaced whatever; all spaces (including physical space) have reality socially *conferred* on them (or revoked from them, or refused to them) by their perceived usefulness—which, of course, is always subject to influence and change.

emphasized (here we employ concepts referring to tempo, duration, and rhythm, to progress and retrogression, to cycles, evolution, decline, revolution, and catastrophe, and also to spatial longitude, latitude, zones, gradients, density, distance, and so on). Obviously, the equivalence of these different formulations lies in their adherence to the generic definition's requirement that we must observe organisms, behaviors, and regularities before claiming that we are studying social phenomena.

It should also be noted that in all its formulations the generic definition of social phenomena is equivalent to (more exactly, it is a specification of) a still more general definition, namely, that of "organization" per se.[15] Regarding the latter, Ashby says

> The hard core of the concept is, in my opinion, that of "conditionality." As soon as the relation between two entities A and B becomes conditional on C's value or state then a necessary component of organization is present. . . . [T]he converse of "conditional on" . . . occurs in mechanical forms, in hardware, when what looks like one machine proves to be composed of two (or more) sub-machines each of which is acting independently of the others. . . . If "conditionality" is an essential component in the concept of organization, so also is the assumption that we are speaking of a whole composed of parts (1968:108).

The three components of Ashby's concept of "organization" are "conditionality," "action," and "parts," and a reasonable reformulation of his definition of organization might be "interpart action conditionality"[16]—a close, but more general, conceptual parallel to the present definition of a social phenomenon as an interorganism behavior regularity.

PRIMARY DISTINCTIONS WITHIN EACH COMPONENT OF THE GENERIC DEFINITION

The generic definition of a social phenomenon as an "interorganism behavior regularity" clearly demarcates the central sociological subject matter from that of

---

[15] Compare this with Cohen's definition of "organization as an order of events conforming to a set of constitutive rules" (1959:479). On its face, this seems compatible with Ashby's definition—provided we regard a given degree of statistical "conditionality" as a kind of "constitutive rule." Cohen, however, requires the rule to be held by the participants ("we must use the participants' own criteria for defining that sort of game" [1959:475]), whereas Ashby rests the determination of that criterion with the analyst. Ashby's view is therefore more in accord with the one adopted here.

[16] At one point, Ashby himself comes very close to this formulation when he says that his "definition of organization . . . demands only that there be conditionality between the parts and regularity in behavior" (1968:111).

other sciences. That is, according to the generic definition, whatever phenomena involve only one organism (or no organisms), whatever phenomena are morphological and not behavioral, and whatever phenomena are unique or idiosyncratic— all such phenomena are excluded from the distinctively sociological subject matter.

More than that, however, the generic definition of social phenomena invites us to partition each of its components in order systematically to gain greater specificity within its framework. Thus, we traditionally partition the "organisms" component into human and nonhuman.

Human and Nonhuman Organisms

At this analytically portentous point, however, we confront Mead's claim that *"all* living organisms are bound up . . . in a complex of social interrelations and interactions upon which their combined existence depends" (1934:228, emphasis added); Allee's claim that *"no* living being is solitary, but . . . from the lowest to the highest each is normally immersed in some sort of social life" (1958:10; emphasis added); and Wilson's claims that "Thousands of . . . species are highly social" (1978:16), and that "Although the hundreds of the world's cultures seem enormously variable to those of us who stand in their midst, all versions of human social behavior together form only a fraction of the realized organizations of social species on this planet" (1978:18–19).

Eventually, then, sociological analysis (as distinct from social *anthropological* analysis) must investigate all interorganism behavior regularities, across all species of organisms, and pursue systematic comparisons between as well as within species. Thus, Allee argues that

> It is the viewpoint of general physiology that we cannot understand the working and the possibilities of the human nervous system . . . without study of the functioning of the nervous systems of many other kinds of animals. Similarly well-integrated information has been compiled concerning general and comparative psychology. From the same point of view some of us have been trying to develop a general sociology (1958:147–148).

Moreover, it should not go unnoticed that many social phenomena regularly include participants from more than one biological species: the social insects have their many symbionts (see Wilson, 1971:349–425); some eighty-two million dogs and cats participate in the American social system (*Time* magazine, December 7, 1981:72); and indeed all species participate in that all-embracing social phenomenon which ecologists call "the web of life."

At this point, it is essential to note Weber's admonition that "It is not the 'actual' interconnections of 'things' but the *conceptual* interconnections of *problems* which define the scope of the various sciences" (1949:68). Thus, if Allee's "general sociology" is eventually to come into existence we must first prepare its way conceptually—that is, by *defining* social phenomena in such a way as explicitly to permit their categoric presence in species other than our own, and also by *explaining* social phenomena with variables conceptualized so as to permit their categoric presence, too, for species other than our own. The generic definition of social phenomena set forth above and elaborated in the rest of Part I attempts to do the former, and Part II will attempt to do the latter.

However, my emphasis, throughout this book, on human organisms as participants in social phenomena will far exceed that on nonhuman organisms—not only because my own field of specialization is sociology rather than sociobiology, but also because to sociobiologists as well as to sociologists human social phenomena seem so much more complex, variable, and difficult to analyze that they deserve proportionately greater attention. Thus, it is not quite the case, as Wilson claims, that "the human brain is the most complex device that we know and the crossroads of investigation of every major natural science" (1978:204), for what is a still more complex device and still more of a crossroads of investigation must be that Device in which the individual human brain (and the rest of the individual human body—also a device of some complexity) is but a part, namely, human society. It is the immense complexity of this Device that most justifies Wilson's own claim that "the social sciences are potentially far richer in content [than biology]. Eventually they will absorb the relevant ideas of biology and go on to beggar them" (1978:13).

Physical and Psychical Behaviors

The next primary conceptual partitioning occurs in the "behavior" component of the generic definition, and distinguishes physical, skeletal muscular, or "body," behavior from psychical, neuroendocrine, or "mind," behavior.

Now the scientific opinion is certainly well established that all psychical behavior can, in principle, be reduced to physical behavior and it is not my intention here to challenge that reduction.[17] Sociological analysis, however continues to find the distinction between the two kinds of behaviors useful because, in our discipline at least, they still require quite different observational methods. By and large, as Mead indicates, sociological data on psychical behavior are produced by some variety of participant introspection: "The psychological datum is best defined," says

---

[17] One may well ask, however, if all psychical behavior reduces to physical behavior, to what does physical behavior reduce (there being no obvious logical reason why the reduction should stop at one point rather than another)?

Mead, "in terms of accessibility. That which is accessible, in the experience of the individual, only to the individual himself, is peculiarly psychological" (1934:5). As a result, under sociologically normal conditions, if we want to observe this type of behavior in the individuals we study, we typically have to *ask* them—in interviews or questionnaires. And even when "unobtrusive" measures are employed, we are forced to *infer* the psychical behavior (from physical traces thereof) without ever seeing it directly. On this point, Durkheim says "it is necessary . . . to substitute for the internal fact which escapes us, an external fact that symbolizes it, and to study the former through the latter" (1933:33). Homans elaborates by describing some of these "external facts":

> In deciding what sentiments a person is feeling, we take notice of slight, evanescent tones of his voice, expressions of his face, movements of his hands, ways of carrying his body. . . . Above all, we infer the existence of sentiments from what men say about what they feel and from the echo that their words find in our own feelings (1950:39).

Nowak has in mind the same difference between directly observing others' physical behaviors and indirectly inferring their psychical behaviors when he says

> The first [mode] of observing social phenomena . . . . is a purely external, "extrospective," observation, based solely on the registration of the external physical aspects of human behavior. . . . [In the second mode, the researcher gets to] the subjective, psychological side of human activities, to the motives underlying human behaviors, or the attitudes, perceptions, and actions of other persons, getting a grasp of the psychological consequences of particular social acts (1977:44–45).

In short, when a sociologist claims that others experience awe, embarrassment, excitement, affection, or hostility, or that they see, know, believe, dream, expect, or feel, none of these psychical behaviors can be directly pointed to in the sense that one can directly point to others' physical walking, talking, laughing, crying. Thus, although psychical behavior may indeed be reducible to physical behavior, and "mind" may therefore refer to the same phenomena as "body," the sociological methods for observing the two are quite different. As Feigl puts it, "the factual reference of [the two terms] may be the same while only their evidential bases differ" (1953:623). That evidential difference, however, remains crucial enough in sociological analysis to retain the conceptual and terminological distinction.

There is another reason for retaining that distinction. Chapter 13 will argue that all scientific analysis—in all fields, and in the commonsensical coping and curiosity of our everyday lives as well—pursues both practical control over the world and cognitive understanding of the world. We retain the distinction between body and mind because it conceptualizes the most immediate mechanisms through which that control and that understanding are possible for human beings. And note that body and mind in this sense can, in principle, exist separately—as seems clearly indicated by the prospect of behaviorally sophisticated robots, on the one hand, and artificial intelligence on the other. It is, of course, the marriage of a highly developed body with a highly developed mind that gives earthly dominance so far to humans, and may give still wider and longer-lived dominance to the artificially intelligent robots of a distant but likely future (see Chapter 11).

Spatial and Temporal Regularities

Finally, the primary conceptual partitioning of the "regularity" component distinguishes between regularities regarded as spatial from those regarded as temporal. Broadly speaking, in the spatial case the analyst is interested in *where* the designated organisms' behaviors coincide (e.g., in cities, in the West, at sea, in the air); in the temporal case, the analyst is interested in *when* they coincide (e.g., daily, on weekends, along about midnight).

Cross-classified, the above partitionings of the generic definition yield Figure 2.1—a simple but analytically crucial property-space purporting logically to exhaust all earthly social phenomena.

Regularity	Human		Nonhuman	
	Physical	Psychical	Physical	Psychical
Spatial	a	b	e	f
Temporal	c	d	g	h

Figure 2.1. Dimensions and components of social phenomena.

Consider, for the sake of simplicity, only the "human" side of Figure 2.1 (the same comments apply, in general form, to the "nonhuman" side as well). In cell (a) are located descriptions of social phenomena in which the behaviors of interest are regarded as physical, and the spatial aspect of the regularities is of primary interest (e.g., descriptions of students' talk and other actions in the classroom, rural-urban voting differences; suicide rates in France and Germany). In cell (b) are located descriptions of social phenomena in which the behaviors of interest are regarded as psychical, and the spatial aspect of the regularities is primary (e.g., descriptions of students' attitudes in the classroom; rural-urban political opinion differences; anomie in France and Germany). Descriptions of social phenomena in which the behaviors of interest are regarded as physical, and the temporal aspect of the regularities is primary are located in cell (c)—for example, descriptions of students' talk and other actions before, during, and after class hours, changes in voting patterns from early to late twentieth century, suicide rates during spring, summer, fall, winter. Descriptions of social phenomena in which the behaviors of interest are regarded as psychical, and the temporal aspect of the regularities is primary are located in cell (d)—for example, descriptions of students' attitudes before, during, and after class hours, political preference changes between early and late October, anomie during spring, summer, fall, winter.

Now consider certain pairings among these cells—pairings that yield the four most important of all sociological concepts (next to that of the generic social phenomenon itself, of course).

SOCIAL STRUCTURE, CULTURAL STRUCTURE, SPATIAL REGULARITY, AND TEMPORAL REGULARITY

In Figure 2.1, cells (a) and (c) indicate what we mean by human *social* structure, while cells (b) and (d) indicate what we mean by human *cultural* structure.[18] That is, the first pair of cells represent descriptions of people doing things together in space and/or time (i.e., interorganism physical behavior regularities), while the second pair represents descriptions of people perceiving, thinking, or feeling things

---

[18] I use the term "structure" in the simplest and most general sense of a whole composed of parts—no matter what the whole, or the parts, or their relations (provided that the latter are not entirely random). Thus, both abstract ideas (e.g., mathematics) and empirical phenomena (e.g., the solar system) may have structure—as may relations between abstract ideas and empirical phenomena (e.g., Kepler's mathematical descriptions of planetary motions). However, insofar as social phenomena are regarded here as *phenomena,* the terms "social structure" and "cultural structure" have empirical referents. Of course, whenever any phenomenon is actually perceived, a mental image or model of the phenomenon is formed which has its own structure. The relationship of the perceptual structure to the structure of the phenomenon being perceived (i.e., the validity and reliability of the former) is the ultimately insoluble problem to which scientific method is addressed (see Chapter 16). It is perhaps the logical independence of the structure of a phenomenon and the structure of a perception purporting to be its image that contributes to Lévi-Strauss' extreme view that " 'social structure' has nothing to do with empirical reality but with models which are built up after it" (1963:279). Giddens, in large part following Lévi-Strauss, also asserts that "structure does not exist anywhere in time-space . . . except in the form of memory-traces in the human brain," but he adds "and except insofar as it is instantiated in . . . acts" (1981:170). The addition, however, does not seem a significant differentiator between Giddens and Lévi-Strauss (compare Giddens, 1979:63) because Giddens' reference to "acts" (and "social system") as empirical phenomena ("instantiations" or "moments") in contrast with "structures" as abstract ideas closely parallels Lévi-Strauss' view that "social relations consist of the raw materials out of which the models making up the social structure are built, while social structure can, by no means, be reduced to the ensemble of the social relations to be described in a given society" (1963:279). In any event, Giddens concludes that "systems . . . have structures, or more accurately, have structural properties" (1979:66) and this is enough, in my view (though not in Giddens'), to call them "structures" for the same reason that one may call whatever has the properties of a house a "house" and whatever has the properties of a rose a "rose" (see Chapter 14).

together in space and/or time (i.e., interorganism psychical behavior regularities). This is the distinction Durkheim has in mind when he says

> Religious phenomena are naturally arranged in two fundamental categories: beliefs and rites. The first are states of opinion . . . the second are determined modes of action. Between these two classes of facts there is all the difference which separates thought from action (1965:51, see also 62, 121).

Now if we disregard the type of behavior involved in a given social phenomenon (i.e., whether it is physical or psychical) and focus on the type of regularity involved (i.e., whether it is spatial or temporal), two additional pairs of cells are derived. The first pair, cells (a) and (b), represent descriptions of what is somewhat misleadingly called human "ecology" (i.e., *spatial* regularities in interorganism behaviors), as Hawley indicates when he argues that the sociological specialty called human ecology is concerned with "the spatial pattern of the activities that make up a community" (1950:235). The second pair, cells (c) and (d), represent descriptions of what is usually called human social "change," "stability," and/or "process" (i.e., *temporal* regularities in interorganism behaviors). This is the distinction that helps specify that by "eating together" Moore must be referring not only to "timing" but also to spacing, when he says

> [C]lose timing extends far in human relations. Eating together, for example, not only has certain utilitarian advantages for those charged with the preparation of meals, but also has universal significance as symbolizing "solidarity" or friendship and equality. Physical [i.e., spatial—ed.] or temporal segregation in eating always symbolizes some kind of social gradation and social distance (1963a:46).

Notice, in connection with the distinction between social structure and cultural structure, that although the former is defined generically as *any* interorganism physical behavior regularity and although the latter is similarly defined as *any* interorganism psychical behavior regularity, whenever we seek to describe a *particular* social structure, or a *particular* cultural structure, we must designate the particular organisms, the particular behaviors, and the particular regularities of which that structure is actually composed. For example,[19] suppose we observed fourteen individuals who, for eight hours each day, five days a week, and always in the Western Electric Company's Hawthorne (Chicago) plant, engage in certain physical behaviors that we lumped together under the name "bank wiring." We could then call this particular social structure a "bank wiring" social structure, thereby

---

[19] The example is taken from Homans' description (see Homans, 1950: 48–80) of findings from Roethlisberger's and Dickson's 1939 study.

distinguishing it from other conceivable social structures, say, procurement, management, sales, service.

Looking more closely, suppose we observed that nine of these fourteen individuals regularly engage in an identifiable component of "bank wiring" behavior called "wiring," three other individuals engage in a component called "soldering," and the remaining two engage in a component called "inspecting." We could then identify these three interorganism physical behavior regularities as social substructures within the more inclusive "bank wiring" social structure.

Next, suppose we observed that the physical behaviors of three wiremen and one solderman are regular with each other (insofar as the latter only solder connections made by the former), and that the behaviors of the remaining wiremen and soldermen are similarly grouped. We could identify these three groupings, too, as social substructures ("soldering units")—ones that overlap the first.

If we observed that the physical behaviors of each of the two inspectors are regular with those of five wiremen and two soldermen, we could identify these two groupings as additional social substructures ("inspection units")—ones that overlap the above substructures and each other as well.

Furthermore, if we observed that certain of the fourteen individuals help each other, or trade jobs with each other, or play games, or get into arguments with each other more than with other individuals, we could, on these bases, identify a different set of social substructures (Homans calls them part of the "internal system") within the same bank wiring social structure.

There are three main points here: (1) The concept "social structure," while limiting our attention to *physical* behavior regularities between organisms, is still only a very general limitation which requires further specification.[20] The manner and extent of that specification ultimately depend upon the goals of the analysis being pursued at the moment—although Chapter 3 will go to some lengths to prevent it from becoming completely ad hoc. (2) Any social structure, in principle, may be decomposed into two or more mutually exclusive and/or overlapping, hierarchically and/or nonhierarchically ordered (see Chapter 6) substructures, sub-substructures, sub-sub-substructures, and so on.[21] (3) These points apply, of course, to cultural structure, and also to both spatial and temporal regularities.

[20] Homans' references to "friendships or antagonisms" are excluded from this discussion of social structure, insofar as he terms the latter *"emotional* relationships" (1950:69, emphasis added).

[21] Nadel may be construed as referring to the second point when he says

> We might describe subgroups as areas of bounded relationships. But inasmuch as they are also subdivisions of a wider collectivity and not isolated, self-sufficient units, the bounded relationships must themselves be interrelated. . . . The interrelation of subgroups is therefore only a special case of the relatedness or "orderliness" of relationships, and our definition of social structure both covers it and will logically lead us to it (1957:14).

Note, however, that in using only "subgroup" and "collectivity" rather than "substructure" and "structure" here, Nadel confounds his own assertions that "Subgroups . . . are made up of *people* in determinate, stable relationships," and that "We arrive at the [social] structure of a society through abstract-

Now, in order more fully to explicate the concepts social structure, cultural structure, spatial regularity, and temporal regularity, let us compare them with one another and take special note of the extent to which they are independently variable, analytically unequal, and causally asymmetrical. After that, we shall consider the combined forms "sociocultural" structure and "spatiotemporal" regularity, and then we shall see how the present conceptualizations—especially of social structure and cultural structure—derive from some that are already in the literature and depart from others.

Independent Variability

The distinction being urged here between social structure and cultural structure seems at first to be accepted by Nadel but is then unjustifiably rejected by him when he says

> [W]e have the execution of certain rights and obligations, that is, a *performance,* and [we also have] this set of rights and obligations embodied in a piece of *knowledge*—in a norm or prescription, or perhaps only in an image people carry in their heads. In brief, we have a rule and its application. It seems unnecessary if not illogical to give different names to these two "aspects"; for their coexistence is basic to every item of human acting that follows from rules (1957:29).[22]

However, once we realize that all phenomena *coexist* in the world (or coexist, at least, in the mind of their perceivers), it becomes apparent that mere coexistence cannot justify calling two things by the same name; only their *covariation* can do this—and, conversely, it is only the lack of covariation between things that justifies calling them by different names.[23] For example, it is only in recognition of certain ways in which dogs and cats covary that we call them both "mammals,"

---

ing . . . the pattern . . . of *relationships* obtaining [between people]" (1957:13, 12, emphasis added). It should also be noted that perhaps as a result of this confounding, Nadel, finally and most inexplicably, concludes that "it seems impossible to speak of social structure in the singular. Analysis in terms of structure is incapable of presenting whole societies; nor . . . can any society be said to embrace an embracing, coherent structure as we understand the term" (1957:153).

[22] Strictly speaking, of course, Nadel's last phrase here, "that follows from rules," renders his entire statement circular for, by definition, whatever physical behavior follows perfectly from psychical rules is perfectly correlated with these rules. In this case, and in this case only, it is indeed unnecessary and illogical to give different names to performance and image. That Nadel himself admits the correlation may *not* be perfect is indicated when he says "*if* the observed behavior and the rules about if fully tally, we shall be able to say that the structure abstracted conforms to the structure envisaged and believed in" (1957:140, emphasis added).

[23] The limiting case is where we regard coexistence as the most generalized covariation and take the latter as justification for the undifferentiated term "phenomena."

or "carnivores," or "pets"; but in other ways they do not covary and so we call them "dogs" and "cats," respectively.

In short, it is because "attitudes and overt behavior vary independently" (Merton, 1976:192) that it seems both logical and necessary to give them different names. Such independence, of course, means that if we know what certain organisms are jointly doing, we do not *thereby* know what (if anything) they are jointly thinking or feeling—and vice versa. For example, we might observe that the participants in one social phenomenon are doing the same things as the participants in another social phenomenon—say, showering each other with gifts—but in one phenomenon these acts may be accompanied by feelings of love while they may be accompanied by feelings of rivalry in the other. Similarly, we might observe two social phenomena in which the participants are thinking and feeling the same things but expressing them in radically different ways, or expressing them in one and not expressing them at all in the other.

Such independent variability is reflected in complementary ways by Homans' assertion that "an idea in the minds of members of a group . . . specifying what [persons should do] under given circumstances . . . is a norm only if any departure of real behavior from the norm is followed by some punishment" (1950:123)—thereby implying that the psychical idea need not be followed by the physical punishment—and by Becker's assertion that the labeling theory of deviant behavior emphasizes "the logical independence of acts and the judgments people make of them" (1973:186)—thereby implying that physical acts need not be followed by psychical judgments.

The same independence applies to spatial and temporal regularities, and justifies our calling them by different names. Thus, any given spatial regularity may occur at different times, and any given temporal regularity may occur at different places. Although Hawley asserts that "A temporal pattern is implicit in each and every spatial pattern" (1950:288), I hold that a given spatial pattern can be produced by impingements that have any temporal pattern or no temporal pattern at all, and vice versa. Thus, even if we can describe exactly the spatial pattern we are studying, we do not thereby know anything about the temporal pattern (or absence of pattern) that accompanies it, and vice versa. In both cases then—that is, in the case of social structure and cultural structure, and in the case of spatial regularity and temporal regularity—we have to find out empirically; we have to describe one structure or one regularity independently of the other and then measure (rather than assume) the area of overlap between them.

Analytic Inequality

If there is logical independence between social and cultural structures, and between spatial and temporal regularities, there is also analytic inequality between these two sets of social phenomenal components. Indeed, the reader will have noticed that I refer to social and cultural *structures* but spatial and temporal *regularities,* when both could well be called either, and I do so in recognition of this inequality—which may be described as follows.

Although relativistic physics regards space, time, matter, and energy as mutually interdependent, our more localized, macrophysical, and commonsensical sociological analysis looks upon space and time as the given, fixed, and passive dimensions or "setting" within which variably active matter and energy (including the body and mind behavior constituents of social and cultural structure) exist. Thus, we are apt to say that social and cultural structures exist *in* space and time, and not vice-versa, and therefore that social and cultural structures *have* spatial and temporal regularities, and not vice versa. The main consequence of this analytic inequality is the greater centrality of social and cultural structures to sociological analysis: that spatial and/or temporal regularities characterize social phenomena is sometimes only implicit in sociological analyses; that social and/or cultural structures characterize social phenomena is always explicit in such analyses.

Causal Asymmetry

So far as we know, only the physical behavior of any given person can directly influence (or be observed by) another person; psychical behavior cannot have such direct influence. Because there seems to be no evidence for telepathy (wherein the psychical behavior of one organism directly influences the psychical behavior of another) or psychokinesis (wherein the psychical behavior of one organism directly influences the physical behavior of another), we must assume that in order for one individual's psychical behavior to affect another individual, the former must translate that psychical behavior into physical behavior (a translation generally called "expression," "enactment," "externalization," "objectification," "realization," and the like) and the second individual must translate the other's physical behavior into his/her own psychical behavior (a translation generally called "receiving," and "interpreting"). Neither translation is required for one individual's physical behavior to affect another's.[24]

---

[24] This is the potentially revolutionary sociological import of ESP research (most of which must be included as would-be sociological research): Should ESP ever be placed on a firm evidential basis, interorganism causal symmetry between physical and psychical behavior would prevail. But so long as that evidential basis is absent, we must regard Durkheim's definition of social facts as "ways of acting, *thinking, and feeling, external to the individual,* and endowed with a power of coercion, by reason of which *they control him"* (1938:3, emphasis added) as empirically unfounded when taken literally. It should be noted, however, that Durkheim does not seem to intend this definition to be taken literally; he modifies it to refer not to thoughts and feelings but to their physical manifestations: "Social facts . . . qualify . . . as things. Law is *embodied* in codes; the currents of daily life are *recorded* in statistical figures and

There seem to be two profoundly important analytic significances of the causal asymmetry in question. First, whenever the communication of psychical behavior is to be explained, physical "gestures" and psychical "selection" and "interpretation" are central to that explanation. One variety of explanatory variable in sociology regards such gesturing, selection, and interpretation as primarily innate, and another variety regards them as primarily learned; I name these varieties "psychical contagionism" and "cultural structuralism" (the latter including symbolic interactionism), respectively, and discuss them both in Chapter 10. The second analytical significance pertains to differences in kinds of social structure and kinds of cultural structure. Let us see what this means.

In observing individual (and therefore also group) behavior, sociologists have never yet been far from the "everyday" observations that anyone can make. In the past, empirical sociology has been called an expensive and elaborate documentation of what everyone knows or could easily find out. Certainly, part of this allegation rested on the quality of relationships we have often found between variables, but that has been increasingly dispelled by the discovery of complex and counterintuitive relationships—thereby documenting the general nonspecificity and often contradictory quality of common sense. Another large part of the allegation, however, rests on the nature of the variables themselves. Durkheim warns us that "We need . . . to formulate entirely new concepts, appropriate to the requirements of science and expressed in an appropriate terminology" (1938:37), but insofar as such concepts refer to observables and insofar as our measurement of these observables remains essentially commonplace, the meanings of the concepts remain essentially commonsensical—however unexpected may be the relationships that we discover between them.

Undoubtedly, the main reason for this conceptual common sense is our very heavy reliance on field, rather than laboratory, observations—a reliance deeply rooted in ethicality as well as practicality. In making field observations, we cannot employ instruments equal to those of the laboratory physiologist or psychologist, and so, essentially, we rely only on our eyes and ears (more or less trained, but largely unaugmented technologically) and on our subjects' reports. The upshot is that we

---

historical monuments; fashions are *preserved* in costumes; and taste in works of art. By their very nature they tend toward an independent existence outside the individual consciousness" (1938:30, emphasis added). In addition, the causal asymmetry of physical and psychical behavior explicates the Thomases' famous aphorism: "If men define situations as real, they are real in their consequences." Of course, it is not the physical situations but the psychical *definitions* of those situations to which the Thomases intend to attribute constructed reality, and the immediate "consequences" of that reality can take place only within the person holding the definitions—although the person may or may not then act, physically, so as to bring about other, secondary, consequences for the external world. And, indeed, the context in which the aphorism appears makes this intention clear: In telling us about a prison inmate who "had killed several persons who had the unfortunate habit of talking to themselves on the street," the authors say that "From the movement of their lips he imagined that they were calling him vile names, and he behaved as if this were true. If men define situations as real, they are real in their consequences" (Thomas and Thomas, 1928:572).

are compelled to resort to what Chapter 14 will call "measurement by effect" (rather than "measurement by property") in order to be able to speak, for example, of differentiated "economic" and "political" social structures—that is, of social structures characterized by behaviors whose inferred effects are of these different kinds.

It should be clear, however, in light of the causal asymmetry discussed above, that we cannot treat the descriptive differentiation of physical and psychical behavior (and therefore social and cultural structure) in the same way. Thus, Chapter 3 will differentiate the physical behaviors of individuals and the social structures that derive from them according to their effects *between* as well as within individuals (e.g., an individual's physical behavior may nurture, or transport, or destroy other people), while Chapter 4 will differentiate psychical behaviors according to their effects *within* individuals only (e.g., an individual's psychical behavior may orient him/her cognitively, or cathectically, or conatively toward other people but that orientation, by itself, can have no effect on those people).

SOCIAL STRUCTURE PLUS CULTURAL STRUCTURE, AND SPATIAL REGULARITY PLUS TEMPORAL REGULARITY

Now, having sketched each component of social phenomena separately, let us consider their combination. Imagine one set of organisms whose physical behaviors always coincide but whose psychical behaviors never do, and another set whose psychical behaviors always coincide but whose physical behaviors never do. The first set would constitute a social phenomenon composed entirely of social structure and the second set would constitute a social phenomenon composed entirely of cultural structure. Certainly both situations are conceivable, but we need not go that far; we may simply imagine that, for any of a number of analytical and technical reasons, one social phenomenon is described entirely as social structure while another is described entirely as cultural structure. In short, it is possible that people may *actually* do things together without thinking anything together and vice versa, but even if they are actually doing things *and* thinking things together we may only be able (or only wish) to *describe* the things they are doing together without describing the things they are thinking together, and vice versa.

But suppose we want (and are able) to describe the things a given number of people are doing together and also the things they are thinking together. Still, the social and cultural structures thus described may or may not overlap substantively: people may collectively do one thing but collectively think another, or, to put this in terms that will be discussed in Chapters 3 and 4, the objects and referents of their social and cultural structures, respectively, may or may not be the same. Thus, the amount of substantive overlap between social and cultural structure may vary and this variation itself becomes an important element in sociological description and therefore in explanation and prediction as well. Therefore, when Sarbin argues that "[Role] connotes not only overt actions and performances but also covert expectations held by an observer, or by a group of observers" (1968:546), he implicitly defines not one but three descriptive concepts: social structural role-performances, cultural structural role-expectations, and role—the latter regarded as a variable area of overlap where the performed is expected and the expected is performed.[25]

So defined, then, "role" at the level of the individual has its counterpart in "institution" at the level of the social phenomenon in which the individual participates. Thus, Parsons and Shils define physical actions (the components of social structure, as defined here) as "institutionalized if the actors expect them to occur and there are cultural sanctions opposing nonconformity with expectation" (1951:40, emphasis removed; see also 191). Along the same lines, Parsons defines the process of "institutionalization" as consisting in "the integration . . . of values and norms with elements of the motivational systems of individuals in such ways as to define and support systems of social interaction" (1961:35). Blau defines institutionalization as "the emergence of social mechanisms through which social values and norms, organizing principles, and knowledge skills are transmitted from generation to generation" (1964:25). And Berger and Luckmann define institutionalization as a "reciprocal typification of habitualized actions by types of actors. . . . What must be stressed is the reciprocity of institutional typifications and the typicality of not only the actions but also the actors that constitute institutions are always shared ones" (1967:54). Goode introduces an additional element—namely, the "third party"—but the heart of his definition remains the combination of cultural structure with social structure: "status elements in all role relationships are . . . institutionalized, that is, normatively backed by 'third parties,' people in role relations with ego or alter" (1960b:250). It is noteworthy that Goode, alone of the theorists cited, explicitly refers to institutionalization as a continuous rather than a discrete variable (see Goode, 1960b:250).

Now let us add that institutionalization can occur through any of three processes: through cultural structure moving toward congruence with social structure (Marx holds mainly this view[26]); through social structure moving toward congru-

---

[25] Unfortunately, Sarbin goes on to identify "role" more with performances than with expectation when he says: "In general, the term 'role' continues to be used to represent the behavior expected of the occupant of a given position or status. . . . That is, interest is focused on what the occupant of a given position *does and says*" (1968:546, emphasis added).

[26] Marx and Engels claim that "The phantoms formed in the human brain are . . . necessarily, sublimates of their material life-process. . . . Morality, religion, metaphysics, all the rest of ideology and their corresponding forms of consciousness, thus no longer retain the semblance of independence. . . . Life is not determined by consciousness, but consciousness by life" (1978:154–155).

ence with cultural structure (Weber holds mainly this view[27]); or through both moving equally toward each other—and it is essential to bear in mind that these are descriptions, not explanations, of processes whereby the same outcome (an institution) can be accomplished.[28] That is, for example, cultural structure may move toward social structure more than the latter moves toward it either because social structure is causally more powerful than cultural structure (as Marx mainly believes) or because the cultural structure in question is under the influence of other causes that are not social structural—such as Blake and Davis have in mind when, in arguing against "the fallacy of normative determinism," they say "We are familiar with recognizing all sorts of *physical* and *environmental conditions* as causes of an individual's inability to meet normative demands" (1964:469).

Thus, from combinations of social structure and cultural structure, we conceptualize "institution," and "institutionalization."[29] Each should be regarded as interorganism behaviors possessing both temporal and spatial regularities, and therefore we should regard any of the above processes of institutionalization as capable of following evolutionary, cyclical, revolutionary, catastrophic, and other time paths, and we should regard any institution, for example, as capable of being distributed concentrically, radially, or otherwise, over space. Finally, of course, temporal and spatial regularities are capable of an overlap similar to that between social and cultural structure—such that one institution, for example, may occur (or be described as occurring) regularly in space but not regularly in time, and a third may occur regularly both in time and in space (i.e., spatiotemporally).

It seems essential to treat the overlaps between social structure and cultural structure, and between spatial regularity and temporal regularity, as variables that are to be explained (and not to be taken for granted) and to allow for the possibility of many different explanations of any given overlap. Thus, for example, though Merton says "of course social conflict cannot occur without a clash of values, norms, or interests variously shared by each of the social formations that are in conflict" (1975:38), I hold that to describe only the area of overlap between social structure

[27] Weber claims that "The magical and religious forces, and the ethical ideas of duty based upon them, have in the past always been among the most important formative influences on conduct"; that "To speak . . . of a reflection of material conditions in the ideal superstructure would be patent nonsense" when explaining the prevalence of Benjamin Franklin's business ideas in the backwoods of eighteenth-century Pennsylvania; and that in certain relations, "an influence of religious ideas on the material culture is really beyond doubt" (1958b:27, 75, and 283).

[28] Note also that the reverse of these same three processes apply to *de*institutionalization—that is, the diminution of overlap between social and cultural structure.

[29] Giddens' idea that

"Structure" . . . refers to rules and resources instantiated in social systems. . . . The "rules" involved here are social conventions, and knowledge of them includes knowledge of the contexts of their application. By resources I mean "capabilities of making things happen," of bringing about particular states of affairs (1981:170; see also 1979:65–69)

also seems, in part, to be an attempt to incorporate cultural structure (rules) and social structure (resources) in a single concept.

conflict and cultural structural clash inhibits analysts from paying attention to the variable extent to which these two may not overlap in different cases of social conflict. Further, I hold that to explain social structural conflict as due inevitably, or solely, to cultural structural dissensus[30]—or vice versa—(if that is what Merton means) inhibits analysts from considering the many alternative, and potentially complementary, causal variables to be examined in Part II.

The Complete Description of Social Phenomena

From all this, an important sociological principle emerges: In order to be complete, the description of any given social phenomenon should implicate all eight kinds of variables referred to in Fig. 2.1—albeit in varying degrees (such that some of them may not be observed at all in a given study or, being observed, may take effectively zero values). This conception of descriptive completeness in sociology will become an important consideration when, in the last chapter of this book, we examine the applicability of scientific procedures to sociology.

Other Conceptualizations of Social Structure and Cultural Structure

I have two main quarrels with other views of social structure and cultural structure. First, the two concepts are often intolerably vague and their contents are allowed to spill over into each other. Second, especially in the case of social structure (although, by implication cultural structure too, insofar as the term "structure" is at issue), the concepts have been restricted to phenomena exhibiting "stable" temporal regularities, thereby denying that changeful or short-term regularities can have "structure."

One can hardly doubt that the concepts (or at least the terms) "social structure" or "society" and "cultural structure" or "culture" are essential parts of the sociological stock-in-trade. However, in a fairly recent collection of essays devoted entirely to examining approaches to the study of social structure, one reads that "Most sociologists' concept of social structure is rich with connotations and implications, to which a single definition cannot easily, if at all, do justice. That is undoubtedly the reason that many choose to abstain from supplying a definition of the concept" (Blau, 1975:10), and in a presumably definitive encyclopedia article

---

[30] Coser, for example, claims that "The sociology of conflict must search for the structurally rooted interests and values that lead men to engage in conflicts with each other" (1975:214).

devoted to the subject one reads that "the concept 'social structure' is, paradoxically, so fundamental to social science as to render its uncontested definition virtually impossible" (Udy, 1968:489). Nadel tells us that "in anthropology, the very concept of social structure is still in a sense on trial" (1957:2), and most recently, Warriner says "Of all the problematic terms in the sociological lexicon, 'social structure' is perhaps the most troublesome. There is little agreement on its empirical referents and there are continuing arguments as to whether it is anything more than a metaphor for the analysis of social processes" (1981:179).

In short, we are told that when we talk about this concept that is so fundamental to us, we do not yet know, collectively, what we are talking about: the concept is so "rich" within the privacy of our individual minds as to be impoverished with respect to agreed-upon public content.

As one might expect, the situation is not much different with cultural structure. Thus, Gibbs, referring to what is almost certainly the single most important component in the sociological conceptualization of cultural structure, declares that "No particular generic definition of norms is widely accepted in the social sciences, and consensus is lacking as to the differentiation of types of norms" (1968:208). Geertz, too, indicates that "whether culture is patterned conduct or a frame of mind, or even the two somehow mixed together" (1973:10) is still a collectively unresolved definitional question (but compare Singer, 1968:540).

However, because sense-based intersubjective verification, and therefore constant pressure toward maximally unambiguous communication, is the prime requisite of natural science (see Chapter 16), several attempts to define and distinguish social structure and cultural structure have been made in sociology—however falteringly. I follow what I take to be their main thrust and try only to make that thrust more explicit, simple, and thoroughgoing.

Radcliffe-Brown says "We can define [culture] as the process by which a person acquires, from contact with other persons or from such things as books or works of art, knowledge, skill, ideas, beliefs, tastes, sentiments" (1965:4–5). Setting aside his assertion that culture is a process of individual acquisition (a process usually called "socialization"; see Chapter 8), Radcliffe-Brown's specification of shared psychical behaviors ("knowledge, skill, ideas, beliefs, tastes, sentiments") clearly accords with the definition of cultural structure being put forward here. Moreover, that list contrasts appropriately with his definition of social structure ("direct observation does reveal to us that . . . human beings are connected by a complex network of social relations. I use the term 'social structure' to denote this network of actually existing relations" [Radcliffe-Brown, 1965:190]). Thus (although his discussion of "social relations" implicates "interests" and "purposes" in ways that tend to compromise it), Radcliffe-Brown's distinction between culture and social structure seems generally to parallel the one being put forward here.

But perhaps the most important, most explicit, formulation of this distinction belongs to Kroeber and Parsons—a formulation of which Singer says:

In the United States the contrast between culture and social structure has symbolized the institutional rivalry between anthropologists and sociologists. Not until 1958 did the dean of American anthropologists, A.L. Kroeber, and the dean of American sociologists, Talcott Parsons, agree to sign a nonaggression pact in which both culture and society are recognized (1968:528).

In this "pact", Kroeber and Parsons agree that

it is useful to define the concept *culture* [as referring to] transmitted content and patterns of values, ideas, and other symbolic-meaningful systems. . . . On the other hand, we suggest that the term *society*—or more generally, *social system*—be used to designate the specifically relational system of interaction between individuals and collectivities (1958:583).

Parsons follows this with other, similar, statements (see Ogles et al., 1959; and also Parsons et al., 1951:7)—including this one:

The social system focus is on the conditions involved in the interaction of actual human individuals who constitute concrete collectivities with determinate membership. The cultural system focus, on the other hand, is on "patterns" of meaning, e.g., of values, of norms, of organized knowledge, and beliefs, of expressive "form" (1961a:34).

Unhappily, however, the distinction thus forcefully and repeatedly drawn is subtly abandoned when Parsons asserts that "the structure of *social* systems . . . *consists in* institutionalized patterns of normative *culture*" (1961a:36, emphasis added; see also 37, 43).[31] Similarly, after reading that "A social system is that aspect of action which is organized about the *interaction* of a plurality of human individuals," and that "A cultural system, on the other hand, is organized about patterns of the *meaning* of objects and the 'expression' of these meanings through symbols and

---

[31] Katz adopts Parsons' view ("when we are speaking of *expectations* we are describing the *structure* of social systems," and "the rules of chess *are* the structure of the game of chess" [1976:18, 56]. And as with Parsons, Katz seems subtly to confound definition with explanation—which may be somewhat excusable when dealing with a self-consciously invented "game" whose cultural structure "rules" may be known to have preceded and elicited (i.e., "defined") its social structure "moves," but not when dealing with other social phenomena where the reverse sequence can occur. Cohen, however, argues that both "games" and "the nongame activities of everyday life" are "defined by [their] respective constitutive rules"—although he admits that in "everyday life" the rules "may not command the same measure of agreement" as in "games" (1959:477). With this admission, Cohen implies that, according to Katz' criterion, there may be as many "structures" of a single social system as there are participants. Under those circumstances, having identified "structure" entirely with psychical expectations and finding these not to be shared at all, neither Parsons, nor Katz, nor Cohen could identify any "social" phenomenon whatever. The analyst who distinguishes social structure from cultural structure, however, might still identify such a phenomenon in social structure alone.

signs" (Parsons, 1967:141) (and even taking into account the ambiguity of "orga-nized about" and the physical behavior implications of "expression"), one fully expects Parsons to assign values to the cultural system—inasmuch as they confer ethical and aesthetic meaning on objects. Contrary to this expectation, Parsons first mentions values as one "level" of the structure of the *social* system (see 1967:141). And note that this is not because he is using here some special defini-tion of values which would justify regarding them as components of "interaction"; Parsons says "values *define* the desirable type of system of relationships," and says he conceives values to be "in Clyde Kluckhohn's phrase, *'conceptions* of the desir-able' " (1967:141, 143, emphasis added). What can Parsons be thinking?

The answer to that question begins by noting Parsons' second mention of values (initially under the slightly disguising term "patterns of evaluation" [see 1967:142] but then under the term "values" itself) as "components of the *cultural* system" (1967:143, emphasis added). Thus, values belong, in Parsons' view, to *both* the social system and the cultural system. How this comes to be is indicated by Par-sons when he refers to "the institutionalization of patterns of evaluation *from the cultural system to the social system* to constitute its topmost controlling component" (1967:142, emphasis added). At this point it becomes clear that Parsons confounds definition with explanation: it is because he is so strongly convinced that values, and the cultural system in general, *explain* ("control") the social system that he is seduced into overriding the distinction he himself draws between "interaction" and "meaning" by including values as parts of the *definition* of the social system. Par-sons expresses his enthusiasm quite unambiguously as follows:

> [S]ociety is *not understandable* apart from its relations to a cultural system. This is to say that the actions of individual persons in their capacities as members of a social system *must* be oriented in terms of the meanings of cultural symbols systems, of what is sometimes called patterns of culture (1973:35, emphasis added).

Obviously, to prefer one type of explanatory factor over others is anyone's prerog-ative but to include that same explanatory factor in defining the thing that is to be explained renders the explanation tautological.

Merton says "cultural structure may be defined as [an] organized set of norma-tive values . . . [while] by social structure is meant [an] organized set of social relationships" (1957:162).[32] Admittedly, it is circular to define "structure" as a

---

[32] Merton builds at least two other typologies on the physical-versus-psychical behavior distinction (although he does not cite these dimensions or relate them to the social-versus-cultural structure dis-tinction). One is a typology of members of an association according to "the degree of their *commitment* to the association . . . [by which] we mean the extent to which the association is important to members . . . [and according to the] degree of *participation* [by which] we mean the amount and character of actual agreement in the association's work" (1976:98, emphasis added). The other is a

"set of . . . relationships," and it is ambiguous to leave "social" undefined, but the contrast with "normative values" suggests that Merton has in mind the same distinction Kroeber and Parsons have in mind. But if that distinction is really what Merton intends, he falters when he says "Among the several elements of *social and cultural* structures, two are of immediate importance. . . . The first consists of *culturally* defined goals. . . . A second element of the *cultural* structure defines, regulates and controls the acceptable modes of reaching out for these goals" (1957:132; 133, emphasis added), and refers to "emphases upon cultural goals and institutional practices" as "two phases of the *social* structure" (1957:134, emphasis added; see also 159). And he falters again when he asserts that

> it is precisely [the] socially patterned differentiation of interests and values which leads structural analysis to hold that social conflict is not mere happenstance but is rooted in social structure (Merton, 1975:38).

Blau and Scott also seem to intend the distinction between social structure and cultural structure that I would make explicit here:

> Social relations involve, first, patterns of social interaction: the frequency and duration of influence between persons, the degree of cooperation, and so forth. Second, social relations entail people's sentiments to one another such as feelings of attraction, respect, and hostility. . . . These two dimensions of social organization—the networks of social relations and the shared orientations— are often referred to as the social structure and the culture, respectively (1962:4).

Blau seems to confirm this when he declares "I am a structural determinist, who believes that the structures of objective social positions among which people are

---

"typology of ethnic prejudice and discrimination" in which "the salient consideration" is the idea that "*conduct* may or may not conform with individuals' own *beliefs*" (1976:192, emphasis added). And of course, although there is considerable ambiguity in the way Merton develops the idea, his "social structure and anomie" hypothesis rests squarely on the distinction between physical-behavior-and-social-structure, on the one hand, and psychical-behavior-and-cultural-structure, on the other; "It is . . . my central hypothesis that aberrant behavior [is] a symptom of dissociation between culturally prescribed aspirations and socially structured avenues for realizing these aspirations" (1957:134). However, as a result of an ambiguity in Merton's handling of the concepts social and cultural structure (centering around his interchanging of "institutional means" and "institutional norms"), the typology he presents does not implicate social structure at all but is derived from two aspects of cultural structure only. Thus, when Merton says the innovation response "occurs when the individual has assimilated the cultural emphasis upon the goal without equally internalizing the institutional norms governing ways and means for its attainment" (1957:141), it is clear that his "central hypothesis" of dissociation between cultural structure and social structure is not reflected here; the only dissociation here is between goals and norms—two aspects of cultural structure. Although social structure is referred to in Merton's discussion ("The family, the school and the workplace" [1957:137], and "the class structure" [1957:145]), it is not given the systematic attention that cultural structure receives.

distributed exert more fundamental influences on social life than do cultural values and norms" (1977:x). But Blau falters when he says

> social structure . . . is rooted in the social distinctions people make in their role relations and associations with one another. These social distinctions give rise to differences in roles and positions, which in turn influence subsequent social intercourse. What is meant here by social structure is simply the population distributions among these differentiated positions (1977:4).

The rub here, of course, is that insofar as the making of a distinction is a psychical (cognitive) behavior, Blau's attributing the distinctions that define social structure to the participants in that social structure introduces cultural structure (i.e., "the social distinctions people make") as a necessary component of social structure.[33] That Blau intends to do this seems amply confirmed by his including among the "basic types of structural parameter" the following attributes of people: religion, ethnic affiliation, clan, marital status, political affiliation, national origin, socioeconomic origin and prestige (see 1977:8)—all attributes whose influence upon role relations seems to depend entirely on their meanings to participants.

Lenski refers, without explicit definition, to "sociocultural systems" and asserts they have "four basic components"—namely, "language, technology, social organization, and ideology" (1970:34). However, it is difficult to know what to make of this when Lenski claims that "Social organization is a rather general term that refers to *any* structured system of relationships among people" (1970:38, emphasis added)—thereby including both language and technology[34] under social organization.[35] But if we assume that Lenski, after all, does not really mean "any" relationships, but only physical behavioral ones, then at least the distinction between "social organization" and "ideology" reflects the social structure-versus-cultural structure distinction emphasized here.[36]

----

[33] Admittedly, however, Blau may mean that the psychical behavioral distinctions in question *cause,* rather than define, social structure ("these social distinctions *give rise to* differences in roles and positions"). If this is the case, however, then Blau does not here define social structure (i.e., those "differences in roles and positions" to which social distinctions "give rise") independently of its presumed causes. Blau is still more baffling with respect to his conceptualization of social structure. At one point he says "Social structure is an *abstraction,* of course, not an object that can be observed directly," but then, in the same paragraph, he refers to "the *empirically* related elements that compose the social structure," and to "the conceptually abstracted but still *observable* relations of elements [in a social structure]" (1977:244, emphasis added).

[34] Lenski defines "language" as "a system of symbols capable of transmitting and storing information. The core of every language is a system of spoken sounds. . . . These meaningful sounds are combined in customary ways which constitute the grammar of the language" (1970:35). He defines "ideology" as "a society's basic belief systems and their application to daily life" (1970:44). In both cases the implication of relationships between people seems clear.

[35] Lenski also implies here that a "system of relationships" can exist without being "structured," but because he does not define "system" or "structure" it is not clear what this implication can mean.

[36] I should also note the manner in which Lenski's definition of a "society" is incomplete according to Figure 2.1. Lenski begins by declaring that "a society is a *territorially* distinct organization . . .

Nowak distinguishes between social structure and culture when he asserts that "In the study of social structure. . . . [t]wo types of relations above all enter the picture here: relations of mutual interaction and interdependence and relations of inequality," and that "Culture . . . is a certain system of meaningful communications formulated in terms of various signs, verbal statements, etc." (1977:78, 88). This distinction seems in rough accord with the one proposed here except that I permit mere correlation and one-way action, as well as mutual interaction and interdependence, to come under the term "social structure," and I locate cultural structure in the psychical "meanings" that are shared between individuals whether these meanings are physically "communicated" or not.

A social-versus-cultural distinction, of course, is not always attempted; some analysts use one or the other term in the generic sense that includes both. Tylor uses "culture" in this way, calling it "that complex whole which includes knowledge, beliefs, art, law, morals, custom, and other capabilities and habits acquired by man as a member of society" (quoted in Kroeber and Kluckhohn, 1963:81). And it is little wonder that Lévi-Strauss, having accepted Tylor's broadly inclusive definition of "culture" (see 1963:18), then banishes "social structure" from the realm of empirical phenomena: "the term 'social structure' has nothing to do with empirical reality. . . . Therefore social structure cannot claim a field of its own among others in the social studies" (1963:279).

Linton, too, reflects Tylor's inclusive definition when he defines culture as "the sum total of ideas, conditioned emotional responses, and patterns of habitual behavior which the members of that society have acquired through instruction or imitation and which they share to a greater or less degree" (quoted in Kroeber and Kluckhohn, 1963:82). With similar sweep, Kroeber and Kluckhohn define culture as "patterns . . . of and for behavior acquired and transmitted by symbols . . . including their embodiment in artifacts," although they do give the term a focus similar to the definition proposed here when they say "the essential core of culture consists of traditional . . . ideas and especially their attached values" (1963:357). And Lynd, too, though a sociologist, says he uses "culture, . . . in the anthropologist's sense, to refer to all the things that a group of people inhabiting a common geographical area do, the way they do things and the ways they think and feel about things, their material tools and their values and symbols" (1946:19).

---

made up of animals of a single species" (1970:9, emphasis added), thereby seeming to limit society to a spatial regularity in some unspecified type of event. However, Lenski then promisingly says "To complete this definition, we must add three further criteria." The first of these criteria refers to a temporal regularity (duration) in social structure: "a society . . . [involves] relatively *sustained* ties of interaction among its members." The second criterion repeats the reference to social structure: "a society . . . [involves] a relatively high degree of *interdependence* among its members," and so does the third criterion: "a society is . . . characterized by a high degree of *autonomy*" from outside control (all quotations from Lenski, 1970:9, emphases changed). Lenski thus leaves out cultural structure in his definition of a society—although he does include "a system of rules and values" in discussing the "functional requisites" of a society, and also includes "ideology" among what he regards as "the basic components of sociocultural systems" (1970:44).

More recently, Geertz claims that neither thought nor culture is psychical in the sense in which I use that term here, but his defense of that assertion ends by negating it. Thus, Geertz asserts that "Though ideational, [culture] does not exist in someone's head" (1973:10); indeed, Geertz goes so far as to say no thought whatever goes on in the head (one wonders what does go on there): "thought does not consist of mysterious processes located in . . . a secret grotto in the head" (1973:362). Where, then, *is* thought located? "Thinking [is] basically a social act, taking place in the same *public* world in which other social acts occur" (Geertz, 1973:362, emphasis added). At this point, we see what Geertz is getting at: his view of thinking and culture as "public" "makes of the study of culture a positive science like any other . . . [as positive, indeed, as the sciences in whose provinces fall] the atomic weight of hydrogen or the function of the adrenal glands" (Geertz, 1973:362). Now it should immediately be acknowledged that the study of culture is regarded here, too, as a "positive" science (see Part III). The crucial difference is that in my view this positivistic character rests, in part, on the notion that certain physical (and, in this sense, "public") behaviors may be analytically designated as *indicators* of psychical behaviors and not on the notion that the former are conceptually *identical* to the latter.

That Geertz, too, in the end and despite himself, regards thought as existing "in someone's head" (and may then regard culture as existing in two or more someones' heads) seems clearly implied when, after declaring that "thought . . . [consists] of a traffic in significant symbols—objects in experience (rituals and tools; graven idols and water holes; gestures, markings, images, and sounds) upon which men have impressed meaning," he goes on to say

> The meanings that symbols, the material vehicles of thought, embody are often elusive, vague, fluctuating, and convoluted, but they are, in principle, . . . capable of being discovered through systematic empirical investigation—*especially if the people who perceive them will cooperate a little* (1973:362, emphasis added).

Thus, it is not the public "material vehicles of thought" that must be interrogated if we want to observe meanings; it is "the people who perceive them" who must be interrogated, and most significantly, it helps if those people "cooperate a little" in exposing their (after all) in-a-secret-grotto perceptions to public scrutiny.

Fine asserts that "The concept of culture generally has not proven useful as a significant variable in sociology because of difficulties associated with specifying its content and the population serving as its referent" (1979:733). After claiming that "a reconceptualization of the culture concept is desirable," Fine's own reconceptualization seems at first to adopt the focus on psychical behavior regularities between organisms that is emphasized here, but in the end, by accepting Herskovits' view, it lapses into the all-inclusive reference: "[Culture] is not interaction itself, but the content, meanings, and topics of interaction. In Herskovits' . . . definition: '. . . in the final analysis [culture] comprises the things that people have, the things they do, and what they think' " (1979:733). Fine and Kleinman confirm this all-inclusive reference: "We are not suggesting a dichotomy in which subculture refers to 'ideas' and social structure to 'behavior.' For our purposes, culture refers to ideas (values, norms) *and* practices (behavior) of some group of persons" (1979:3).

Udy prefers "social structure" to "culture" for the generic reference, calling it "the totality of patterns of collective human phenomena that cannot be explained solely on the basis of human heredity and/or the nonhuman environment," and specifically including within it "A *cultural* component comprising ideas (norms, values, beliefs) which are learned and shared by people and are transmitted symbolically from person to person" (1968:489). Let us also note what is perhaps the least frequent empirical referent of "social structure," namely, exclusively psychical behavior regularities. This may be the usage Leach has in mind: "A full description of the social structure would entail an analysis of all the rights and obligations which link all the offices and corporations in the system" (1968:485), but it is more certainly Tiryakian's usage when he defines "social structures as normative phenomena of intersubjective consciousness which frame social actions in social space" (1970:115).

One may well wonder how any *scientific* enterprise can possibly persist with such a fidgety intersubjective tangle crowding around its conceptual heart, and therefore crowding also around its explanatory and predictive heart—but it really is not as bad as it looks. When one notices how often sociologists put "social structure" first (but include "culture"), and how often anthropologists put "culture" first (but include "social structure"), a disciplinary preference emerges between two components of a single phenomenon. When one notices how often "interaction" or some other term denoting physical behavior is mentioned first in definitions of social structure, while "knowledge," "values," or some other term denoting psychical behavior is mentioned first in definitions of "culture," a forest (more exactly, two forests) begins to emerge from these trees. In short, it becomes clear that Kroeber and Parsons are right: with very few exceptions, both anthropologists and sociologists have long intended, wanted, implied, and very nearly explicitly stated, a distinction between those interorganism behavior regularities that consist of physical behaviors and those that consist of psychical behaviors. That distinction is what Figure 2.1 is meant to convey—along with the spatial-temporal distinctions, whose orthogonality to the first is essential.

In this connection it will be recalled that my second quarrel with other views of social structure and cultural structure centers on their denial that temporally changeful or short-term behavior regularities (whether physical or psychical) can have "structure." For example, Lipset says "The very concept of social structure

. . . as used by many sociologists refers to stable interrelations among parts of a system" (1975:172); Bottomore contrasts

> the opposition between structure and history—and between structural and historical modes of studying social life—namely, the contrast that can be drawn between society conceived as a fixed, stable, and persisting structure and society conceived as a process in which there is continual breakdown and renewal, development and decline, the disappearance of old forms and the creation of new ones (1975:159).

Laumann and Pappi define a "social structure . . . as a persisting pattern of social relationships among social positions" (1976:6);[37] Parsons declares that social structure "designates the features of the system which can, in certain strategic respects, be treated as constants over certain ranges of variation in the behavior of other significant elements of the theoretical problem" (1961a:36); and Homans says "As used by sociologists, 'structure' seems to refer first to those aspects of social behavior that the investigator considers relatively enduring or persistent" (1975:53). Homans adds that "Perhaps we should all adopt the rough distinction the French make between *structure* and *conjuncture*. . . . the former might be represented by a relatively enduring pattern . . . and the latter by the particular circumstances obtaining at a particular point in time" (1975:54).

Chapter 14 will argue that *unique* events (or rather, events in their unique aspects) are never, in themselves, of interest to natural science: although we are always interested in finding, say, a single bird, social revolution, or Loch Ness monster which is not classifiable under any known species, our specifically scientific side of that interest is grounded in the hope that the single instance is but the *first* instance and that we may find at least one other instance and so discover a new species, a new regularity, rather than merely a random aberration. On this ground, then, I too bar the "particular circumstances obtaining at a particular point in time [and/or space—ed.]." The problem, however, lodges in Homans' (and the others') requirement that "patterns" must be "relatively enduring" before they may be considered to be "structure." In my judgment, Radcliffe-Brown's view is better:

> There are some anthropologists who use the term social structure to refer only to persistent social groups, such as nations, tribes and clans, which retain their continuity . . . in spite of changes in their membership. . . . But I

---

[37] To define a *social* structure in terms of *social* relationships and *social* positions is doubly tautological, and although it is the notion of persistence to which I call attention here, it may be noted that tautology is further compounded when Laumann and Pappi define "A *social* relationship [as] any direct or indirect linkage between incumbents of different *social* positions," and describe "*Social* positions [as] arranged with respect to one another as a function of the pattern of *social* relationships directly and indirectly linking them" (1976:6, 7, emphasis added)—and all this without ever defining "social."

find it more useful to include under the term social structure a good deal more than this. In the first place, I regard as a part of the social structure all social relations of person to person. . . . Secondly, I include under social structure the differentiation of individuals and of classes by their social role. The differential social positions of men and women, of chiefs and commoners, of employers and employees, are just as much determinants of social relations as belonging to different clans or different nations (1965:191–192).

(It is essential to point out and reject, however, Radcliffe-Brown's confusing switch, in the last sentence here, from a descriptive concern with what social structure *includes* to an explanatory concern with what *determines* it.)

To be more explicit, the position I hold argues that as soon as we get beyond the unique and therefore instantaneous event, then duration, stability, persistence—and also spatial extension, distribution, and so forth—become empirically variable qualities of structures and not conceptually fixed criteria for structures. Chapter 5 will take up these and other related qualities of social and cultural structures.

Finally, in this chapter, let us examine the roles of the four main concepts that have been conceptualized above—especially social and cultural structures but also spatial and temporal regularities—in analyses of social phenomena among nonhuman organisms.

SOCIAL STRUCTURE, CULTURAL STRUCTURE, SPATIAL REGULARITY, AND TEMPORAL REGULARITY IN SOCIOBIOLOGY

Consider the titles of four books: "The *Social* Insects" (Wilson), "*Socio*biology" (Wilson), "The Evolution of *Culture* in Animals" (Bonner), and "Genes, Mind, and *Culture*" (Lumsden and Wilson). Let us see what distinctions are drawn here between "social" and "cultural."

Wilson defines the " 'truly' social insects" as possessing three traits: "individuals of the same species *cooperate* in caring for the young; there is a reproductive division of *labor* . . . [and] offspring *assist* parents during some period of their life" (1971:4, emphasis added)—thereby relying entirely on interorganism physical behavior regularities (in accord with the definition of social structure put forward in this chapter).[38] Wilson continues this reliance when he defines "society" as "a

---

[38] Compare Etkin's definition of groups as " 'social' when the members stay together as a result of their social responses to one another rather than by responses to other factors in their environment" (1964a:4), and Wynne-Edwards' definition of a "society" as "an organization capable of providing

group of individuals that belong to the same species and are organized in a *cooperative* manner" (1971:5, emphasis added), but modifies this, without explanation, when he goes on to claim that "Reciprocal *communication* of a cooperative nature is the essential intuitive [sic] criterion of a society" (1971:6, emphasis added; see also 1975:7, 595).

Now setting aside the undefended exclusion here of noncooperative (e.g., competitive, conflictful) behavior from society, the most important thing about this definition is its unresolved ambivalence regarding whether cooperation or communication is essential to society—an ambivalence that is repeated in Wilson's references to "The definition of a society as a cooperating group of conspecific organisms" but to "the bond of society [as] simply and solely communication" (1975:8), and to an "aggregation" as "a group of individuals of the same species . . . but not internally organized or engaged in cooperative behavior" (thereby implying that a society, by contrast, *is* engaged in such behavior), but to a society as "bounded by a zone of sharply reduced communication" (1975:9, 10).

The ambivalence here is not a trivial one, in my opinion, because whereas "cooperation" only implies joint physical behaviors—that is, *cooperation*—"communication" necessarily implies joint psychical behaviors: the physical "sending" of a "message" (i.e., a sign or symbol of the sender's psychical behavior) to another individual who, by "receiving" it, comes to "understand" the sender's psychical behaviors. This is why "information"—i.e., psychical behaviors including cognitive "beliefs," cathectic "feelings," and conative "behavior dispositions" about and toward the world—is almost universally considered to be the content of communication,[39] whereas constructive, destructive, and transportative physical behaviors like "mating," "nest-building," "killing," "capturing," "carrying," and the like are considered to be the content of cooperation. It follows that although cooperation can lead to communication, and communication can lead to cooperation, co-

---

conventional competition" (1962:14). Etkin's definition requires us to explain the phenomenon before defining it (i.e., we must know why its members stay together), and Wynne-Edwards' definition requires us to predict from the phenomenon before we can define it (i.e., we must know what it is capable of). Moreover, by limiting the acceptable explanations and predictions to what Part II will call social structuralistic variables, Etkin's definition rules out social phenomena that depend on *both* "responses to one another" and "responses to other factors in the environment," and Wynne-Edwards' definition slights organizations that are capable of providing outputs other than "conventional competition."

[39] Surprisingly, Wilson defines "biological communication" merely as "action on the part of one organism (or cell) that alters the probability pattern of behavior in another organism (or cell) in a fashion adaptive to either one or both of the participants" (1975:176; see also 10, 581). Again surprisingly, Wilson does not define "cooperation," and as a consequence of these two facts, it is not unreasonable to think his definition of "communication" *includes* cooperation and is perhaps even *synonymous* with cooperation. It is therefore possible that Wilson identifies communication as the "intuitive" criterion of a society because he sees no difference between communication and cooperation—in which case, however, "communication of a cooperative nature" is a tautology. Of secondary interest in the present context is Wilson's unexplicated ruling out of action that induces nonadaptive consequences (as, say, in a suicide pact) as "communication."

culturgens are labeled and swiftly juxtaposed to assemble and communi-
vastly more complex knowledge structures, such as narratives, instruc-
, and art. . . . Under the influence of the epigenetic rules, the cultur-
shared in such a manner will tend to possess similar core meaning and
voke similar behavior (1981:253, emphasis removed).

lture is redefined as *psychical* behavior only.

these unfortunately equivocal grounds, then, it seems fair to say that
and Lumsden) shares—eventually and on balance—the distinction being
ard here between social structure and cultural structure and applies it to
of nonhuman as well as human social phenomena.

et us consider Bonner, who, after acknowledging Wilson, and Dawkins,
provided a genetic "rationale . . . to explain a social existence", raises
ion: "If *social* behavior has a genetic basis, can *culture?*" (1980:29, em-
ded)—thereby implying a distinction between the two concepts. Let us
Bonner draws this distinction.

r says "Culture is [information] transmitted by behavioral rather than
neans," and "By culture I mean the transfer of information by behavioral
nost particularly by the process of teaching and learning. . . . [T]he stress
efinition is on the mode of transmission of the information rather than its
1980:4, 10). Note that both definitions, although they emphasize trans-
but in different ways: the first definition centers on the thing that is
ed and the second centers on the process of its transmission), mention
tion"—a psychical behavior—as the determining referent of culture.

g established this focus on the cultural structural component of social
na, Bonner then considers how "social existence . . . is related to cul-
980:29), and his conclusion is "one cannot have culture without social
n,"[41] and "Social existence is a necessary but not sufficient basis for cul-
80:29, 76). Now consider what Bonner means by "social." Actually Bon-
not define this term, but he does define "society": "An animal society is
group of intercommunicating individuals of the same species" (1980:76).
thing to notice here, of course, is that Bonner defines society in terms of
ication and that (assuming communication is defined as "the transfer of
ion by behavioral means") to this extent he therefore defines "society" in
he same terms as he defines "culture." Indeed, Bonner adds that "both
nd a social grouping[42] are *by definition* utterly dependent upon commu-

ue to Bonner's later conceptual confusion appears when he says this is "essentially true by
(1980:29) which suggests a *logical* identity between "culture" and "social interaction" rather
usal relation which is suggested by his statement that "Social existence is a necessary but
nt basis for culture" (1980:76).
Bonner's reference here to a *"social grouping"* rather than his previous reference to "social
—a switch of referent that seems facilitated by his initial, undifferentiated, reference to
ence."

operation may exist without communication—as
he notes that "the construction of termitaries, an
insects, is coordinated by the perception of work p
than by direct communication" (1975:12).[40]

If we take Wilson at his first word ("coopera
("communication"), and define these terms as abov
Wilson does indeed identify "social" phenomena an
terorganism *physical* behaviors. This inference seems
freely applies the term "social" to organisms not
psychical behavior, namely, "the colonial microc
(1975:383–396), but only begins to apply the term
ates with "culture") to species at the level of Monar
1975:168–172).

Now just as Wilson is ambiguous about "society
ambiguous about "culture"—but in a different way
and follow the anthropological tradition discussed e
they define culture "in the broad sense, to include t
structs and behaviors, including the construction ar
transmitted from one generation to the next by soc
Wilson, 1981:3), and define a "culturgen" as "the c
and as

> a relatively homogeneous set of artifacts, behav
> constructs having little or no direct correspondenc
> least share a consistently recurrent range of [functi
> a given polythetic set (1981:27).

Note that culture is defined here not only in terms
behavior regularities, but also in terms of physical beha
ical artifacts. However, true to Wilson's earlier referenc
ical whole invested in the brain" (1978:41, emphasis ad
of their book ("Genes, *Mind,* and Culture"), Lumsden
define both culture and culturgen in the direction of
forward here:

> Culture can be heuristically defined as the cognitiv
> of the totality of shared culturgens defined in this n
> symbolization are seen as devices for creating and
> more efficient processing, storage, and recall. Langu:

[40] See also his discussion of "a witless division of labor" among gree
themselves out of the sand and make their way to the sea (Wilson: 197!

nication" (1980:76, emphasis added), and asserts that "the very *characteristic* of [social] animals is a close system of communication between individuals" (1980:29, emphasis added). In the face of this conceptual circularity, what should we make of Bonner's emphatic assertion that "the social condition . . . [and] culture . . . are nevertheless quite separate phenomena" (1980:76)?

The answer seems to be that they are indeed separate phenomena in Bonner's eyes but the nature of their separateness can only be guessed at from the way he refers to them. For example, it will already have been noted that although he does not define the word, Bonner calls society "a *cohesive* group"—and when he says "A social existence merely provides the *togetherness;* the brain permits elaborate culture" (1980:82, emphasis added), one gets the impression that by "cohesiveness" Bonner means physical—rather than psychical—closeness. Similarly, when we read that certain bacteria "have become a social organism where all the cells *cooperate* to feed and then disperse" (1980:71–72, emphasis added), and that, in studying "social bacteria" and "social organisms," "our main concern . . . is *cooperation* between separate individual organisms" (1980:78, emphasis added), we have more clues pointing to the physical behavioral—rather than psychical behavioral—nature of "society," "social existence," and "social interaction" in Bonner's eyes.

In my view, then, Wilson, Lumsden, and Bonner all demonstrate that both social structure and cultural structure—in the senses set forth in this chapter—are among the descriptive foundations of studies of nonhuman social phenomena as well as of human social phenomena.

Among these foundations, too, are concepts of spatial and temporal regularities between the behaviors of different organisms. Thus, Bonner says

> For many vertebrates, a clearly defined territory for offspring rearing seems to be fundamental. This involves aggressive behavior of a great variety on the part of the male (and sometimes the female as well), usually of a ritual nature, but effective in defending an area that is the sole preserve of a mating pair (1980:90–91).

Wilson points to both temporal and spatial regularities: "The males and virgin queens of ants depart from the nests at certain hours of the day set by circadian rhythms," and "Each year ducks, geese, and swans migrate hundreds or thousands of kilometers . . . [while] each spring [Monarch butterflies] fly north and each fall south for distances of up to 1500 kilometers each way" (1975:141, 168).

With this introduction, let us now examine certain more specific principles governing the analysis of social structure in Chapter 3, cultural structure in Chapter 4, and spatial and temporal regularities in Chapter 5. Chapter 6 concludes Part I and its examination of principles of descriptive sociological analysis by discussing hierarchic structure in all four of these components of social phenomena.

3

Social Structure

This chapter attempts conceptually to differentiate components and kinds of social structure—defined generically as the regular coincidence of two or more individual organisms' physical behaviors. In order to do this, I try to specify (1) the kinds of physical behaviors that may be involved (e.g., constructive behavior toward nonliving things in the environment); (2) certain aggregates, within the same individual, of such behaviors (e.g., occupations); (3) certain aggregates, between different individuals, of such behaviors (e.g., the economic system); and (4) certain forms of the coincidence, between individuals, of these behaviors and their aggregates (e.g., cooperation, conflict, imitation, segregation).

In order to bring out the extent to which this proposed examination of social structure separately from cultural structure departs from other treatments in the literature of sociological analysis, let us consider some of the latter. Davis, for example, puts the case against separate examination in most extreme form:

> One thing should be clear. The social sciences are devoted to the study of mental rather than physical phenomena . . . No matter by what external indices we measure them or what instruments we apply, social phenomena are primarily mental phenomena and must be construed as such (1949:6).

Parsons shares this view:

society is not understandable apart from its relations to a cultural system. This is to say that the actions of individual persons in their capacities as members of a social system must be oriented in terms of the meanings of cultural symbol systems of what is sometimes called patterns of culture (1973:35).[1]

In the view proposed here, however, it is essential to acknowledge that individuals can do things together without feeling or thinking anything together; and they may feel and think things together without doing anything together. Chains and imprisonment constrain individuals' physical behavior to some uniformity but leave their thoughts and feelings variable; separate exposure to the same symbol (say, a cloth dyed red, white, and blue) constrains individuals' thoughts and feelings to some uniformity but leaves their physical behavior variable. It follows that if we know the nature of a given social structure, we do not thereby know anything about the cultural structure that may (or may not) accompany it—and vice versa. Only empirical investigation can tell which, if any, psychical behavior is associated with a given physical behavior—and vice versa.

Turning to concepts of somewhat narrower scope than are reflected in the two quotations above, Barber, after asserting that "human societies are dynamic systems in which differentiated activities and roles are valued in different degrees," describes social stratification as "the product of the interaction of social differentiation and social evaluation" (1957:1, 2, emphasis removed). I regard it as essential to distinguish between the *differentiation* of "activities and roles" and the way these activities and roles are socially (I would say "culturally") *evaluated*—and I include the former but exclude the latter from consideration in this chapter. In this, I follow the spirit of Durkheim's definition of the division of labor as simply "the sharing of functions up to that time common" (1933:276), with no mention of how these functions are evaluated.

I draw the same sort of distinction when Tumin defines social stratification as "the arrangement of any social group into a hierarchy of positions that are unequal with regard to power, property, social evaluation, and/or psychic gratification" (1967:12). This chapter includes "power" differences but excludes differences in "property" (insofar as property is "defined as *rights* over goods and services" [Tumin, 1967:12, emphasis added]), in "social evaluation," and in "psychic gratification," on the grounds that these are all cultural structural features. In short, the concept of "stratification" is included within the scope of this chapter so long as the rank-ordering in question is not regarded as being in the minds of the social participants

---

[1] On the other hand, Parsons also says "The social system is . . . essentially a network of *interactive* relationships" (1951:51, emphasis added), and only after saying "Reduced to the simplest possible terms . . . a social system consists in a plurality of individual actors *interacting* with each other," does he add "actors who are motivated . . . and whose relation to their situations . . . is mediated in terms of a given system of culturally structured and shared symbols" (1951:5–6, emphasis added).

under investigation, but in their physical behavior. Thus, insofar as "power" is generally defined as the physical bringing about of physical effects in some physical object, and insofar as one individual may bring about greater effects in a given object than another individual, such stratifications are included among the topics of this chapter; excluded are the many ways power may be evaluated by those who do and do not exercise it. So, when Parsons declares that "the point of view from which we approach the analysis of stratification prescribes that analysis should focus on the common value-pattern aspect" (1954:393), it is precisely this aspect and analysis that are excluded from present consideration. On the other hand, when Parsons says that "we have a class system . . . only insofar as the differentiations inherent in our occupational structure . . . [have] become ramified out into a system of strata, which involve differentiations of family living . . ." (1954:328–329)—and assuming that "occupational structure" and "family living" may be interpreted as entailing physical behavior and therefore social structure—it is just this conceptualization of "class" and "strata" that is included here.

Note that "property," in Tumin's sense, is excluded on the grounds of its implication of rights. But Parsons defines "possessions" as "situational *objects* . . . to which an actor (individual or collective) in a social system . . . has *in the institutionalized case* rights to their use, control or disposal" (1954:390, emphasis added)—thereby implying that some possessions are not institutionalized and not defended by rights and duties. Folk wisdom has it, indeed, that possession in this wholly physical, nonrightful, noncultural structural, sense, is nine-tenths of the (cultural structural) law. How, then, should we regard that aspect of possession which is not dependent on cultural structure in our present examination of social structure?

My answer hinges on the distinction between "possession," meaning the act of possessing (or of being possessed), and "possession," meaning the thing possessed. All the former are included—all acts of taking, or keeping, or relinquishing possession—as altogether physical and therefore (when shared) social structural,[2] but excluded are all things which are possessed (except insofar as they are not goods but services of others and may therefore enter into social structures of "dominance" and "oppression," as discussed below in connection with Fig. 3.3). The things that a person or group possesses (discussed in Chapter 11, under ecologism and technologism) may certainly have profound impacts on social structure (and, for that matter, also on cultural structure),[3] but they are not themselves social structural according to the definition set forth in Chapter 2.

[2] Note that Parsons insists that possession "is *always* a right or bundle of rights. In other words, it is a set of expectations relative to social behavior and attitudes. It is never as such a physical object." He goes on to acknowledge the involvement of physical behavior and physical objects in "possession," however: "It is true that physical objects 'change hands,' but in terms of the social system this is not the essential but a derivative phenomenon" (1951:119). See also his identification of "property" with "property rights" (1967:319).

[3] Parkin points specifically to the importance of these impacts when he argues that "The power and privileges emanating from the possession of wealth and capital are separate from those which stem

INDIVIDUAL PHYSICAL BEHAVIORS

Having thus set aside an otherwise confusing issue, let us take up the kinds of physical behaviors that can comprise social structures. This calls for developing a systematic conceptualization of the entire repertory of physical behaviors available to whatever sort of organism (in this case, human) participates in the social structure in question. How can this problem be approached?

Sociologists do not have at their disposal anything like the sophisticated instrumentation that experimental physiologists are able to use in the laboratory on one or two individuals at a time. In sociology—because of a typical reliance on field rather than laboratory settings, and because of the frequently large numbers of subjects involved—we do not usually differentiate behavior in terms of observable muscle flexions and extensions, blood pressure and pulse rate, caloric output, and the like,[4] and this inability imposes a profound limitation on the validity and reliability of all our behavior observations and descriptions. It is here that sociology most needs (but seems least likely soon to achieve) a technological revolution.[5] Meanwhile, we are forced to differentiate physical behaviors according to their large-scale, "naked-eye" effects or functions.[6] And note that we avoid explanatory tautology here by defining the behavior in question according to whether it is *already known* to have had the effect in question; we do not hypothesize that it *will be found* to have had that effect. Thus, the effect is regarded as though it were a constant epistemic property or extension of the behavior itself (see Chapter 14) rather than as an empirically variable outcome of the behavior.

Directions, and Objects, of Effects

With this understanding, we may now divide the concept "effect" into two dimensions: the direction or kind of effect, and the object or target of effect. In the "direction" dimension, let us distinguish between effects characterized as

---

directly from the division of labor. A model of class which addresses itself only to the latter is a lopsided one indeed" (1978:608).

[4] For an attempt to classify individual human behavior—albeit of "children under the age of twelve months"—without any special instrumentation and in field settings, see Jones and Woodson (1979). Here, more than 110 categories (including 11 different kinds of "attack" behavior) are employed, where the classificatory criteria are chiefly visible-to-the-naked-eye muscle flexions and tensions, as in the case of the category called "touch, hand on: S's hand contacts for a time any part of R with no or only very small nonrhythmical irregular movements" (Jones and Woodson, 1979:107).

[5] Conceivably, we might eventually employ some sort of choreographic notation together with computer-assisted videotaping for collecting, coding, and otherwise manipulating observations on the physical behaviors of large numbers of individuals simultaneously.

[6] Simmel explicitly shares this reliance when he says: "everything that is present in [individuals] in such a way as to endanger or mediate *effects* upon others or to receive such *effects,* I designate as the content, as the material, as it were, of sociation" (1950:40–41, emphasis changed).

building something up, effects characterized as moving something around, and effects characterized as breaking something down—that is, construction, transportation, and destruction functions.[7] Note that I have in mind the most situation-free, non-normative, strictly thermodynamic and mechanical meanings of these terms: by construction and destruction I simply mean, respectively, negentropic (derandomizing) and entropic (randomizing) effects, and by transportation, I mean moving or transmitting something from one spatiotemporal location to another. With respect to the "object" dimension, I assume the human individual can behave mainly toward him/herself or mainly toward his/her environment. If the latter, then the behavior can impinge mainly on other people there (and in turn, mainly on their bodies or mainly on their minds), or mainly on things there and mainly on living things there or mainly on nonliving things there). The cross-classification of these two dimensions, namely, direction of effect and object of effect,[8] is shown in Fig. 3.1.

Object of effect	Direction of effect		
	Construction	Transportation	Destruction
Self			
Body	————————— Self-nurturing —————————		
Mind	————————— Self-teaching —————————		
Other people			
Body	————————— Social structuring —————————		
Mind	————————— Cultural structuring —————————		
Things			
Living	————————— Domesticating, cultivating —————————		
Nonliving	————————— Extracting, fabricating —————————		

Figure 3.1. Typology of individual physical behaviors.

A Sociological Typology of Individual Physical Behaviors

Six broad sets of functional[9] descriptions of individual physical behavior, where each set comprises three subtypes, can be distinguished here. Within its chosen

[7] I include all maintenance functions under "construction" on the assumption that, given the second law of thermodynamics (the overall tendency of the universe to maximize entropy), some building up is always required to keep any phenomenon from naturally running down. It follows from the same law that any behavior which is constructive with respect to one object must be destructive with respect to some other, but the converse is not true: Some behaviors may conceivably be destructive of all objects, although no behavior can be constructive of all objects.

[8] These dimensions seem to correspond to, simplify, systematize, and interrelate the general idea behind what Murray and Kluckhohn simply list as some "vectors" of activity, on the one hand, and some "valued entities," on the other (see 1961:23).

[9] Note that I distinguish between "functional" and "functionalist"—the former merely refers to effects, while the latter hypothesizes that such effects operate, indirectly, as causes of their own repetitions (Chapter 9).

dimensions, the typology is intended to be logically exhaustive of individual phys-ical behaviors—although, of course, it is very short on detail.

The first two sets of behavior types shown here, called self-nurturing (or, broadly speaking, "hygiene") and self-teaching (or "learning"), are meant to be somewhat more inclusive than might appear at first glance. In the first place, of course, they include physical and psychical effects brought about in the individual by the in-dividual acting directly on him/herself. In addition, they include physical and psychical effects brought about in that individual by his/her being acted on by others, and similar effects brought about in the individual by his/her acting on others.

The grounds for including the latter two effects are Newton's first (inertia) and third (action-reaction) laws: for example, in order for individual B to be fed by individual A, the former must *stay put*—that is, offer physical inertia—and not bounce away at the first touch of spoon or cup, and in order for individual A to feed individual B the former must *push against* something (ultimately, under nor-mal circumstances, the earth) in proffering that spoon or cup. The same laws, of course, hold true for learning: in order for individual B to learn an idea from individual A, the former must *"attend"*—that is, his/her mind must offer psycho-physical inertia and not wander off in all directions, "aimlessly," upon presentation of that idea, and in order for individual A to teach individual B an idea, the former's mind must *concentrate*—that is, temporarily reject all other ideas in favor of propounding the idea in question.

Note that I have in mind here something much simpler and far more predict-able than what is usually meant by an individual's "response" to stimulus. For example, individual B's response to being fed or taught by individual A may be to bite A's hand *or* to say "Thank you," and individual A's response to feeding or teaching B may be to experience feelings of pleasure *or* resentment. All such re-sponses are problematic and contingent on circumstances. However, according to Newton's laws, neither the inertial resistance that B offers, nor the action-reaction pushing that A accomplishes, is problematic or contingent: they *must* occur as intrinsic parts of the feeding-and-being-fed, and the teaching-and-learning, pro-cesses.

In short, self-nurturing and self-teaching behaviors are necessarily involved in all three of the following cases: (1) the individual acts directly on him/herself; (2) the individual acts on other people (and things); (3) the individual is acted on by other people (and things). The importance of this conclusion will become apparent as we go along; among other things, it justifies conceptualizing an individual's social structural role-performance as including both what the individual does to other people (and things) and also what they do to him/her.

Self-nurturing behavior (or "hygiene") includes body-constructing behaviors (like eating, drinking, breathing, taking medication, exercising, and clothing and shel-tering oneself), body-destroying behaviors (like fasting, self-flagellation, taking poison, substance abuse, and the like), and body-transporting behaviors (like walking, swimming, running, rocking, and rolling). In the self-teaching (or "learn-ing") set are included behaviors like asking questions, reading, looking, listening, smelling, tasting, touching, taking notes. Through all such physical behaviors the individual's beliefs, desires, and skills are affected—some are constructed, some destroyed, some reinforced so that they may be carried in memory from one time and place to another.

The next two sets of descriptions shift the object of effect from the behaving individual him/herself to other people. Social structuring (broadly speaking, "nur-turing") behaviors include all physical behaviors described as affecting the bodies of other people—and therefore affecting the physical behavior regularities among them, and between them and the behaving individual. Here are located acts of physical assistance (including nutritional, medical, and dental) to others, acts of biological reproduction, acts that physically transport others from place to place, and acts that physically deprive, debilitate, torture, maim, imprison, banish, and kill others. Among these behaviors are ones often called physically "rewarding" and "punishing"—although one person's pleasure is sometimes another's poison because of the psychical behaviors to be examined in Chapter 4. Cultural structur-ing (broadly speaking, "teaching") behaviors include all those that are said to affect the minds of other people—and therefore to affect the psychical behavior regular-ities among them and/or between them and the behaving individual. All signaling behavior, all talking, teaching, indoctrinating, psychoanalyzing, threatening, promising, acting, writing, drawing, sculpting, performing, and publishing be-haviors—in short, all acts of communication—are located here.

The final two sets of descriptions shift the object of effect once again: away from people to "things." Among domesticating-cultivating behaviors are the selec-tive breeding and feeding of various species of plants and animals (including mi-croorganisms), the regular hunting, gathering, and harvesting of some and exter-mination of others, their transportation from one place to another, and their preservation from one time to another. Extracting-fabricating behaviors include those which exploit (and/or pollute) the nonliving "natural resources" and trans-form them into wealth—that is, tools and weapons—and waste.

Before comparing this typology with some more familiar concepts that are al-ready in the literature, a few comments on Fig. 3.1 are essential. First, and most essential and far-reaching of all, the analytical decisions made in describing behav-ior according to this (or any other) scheme are unavoidably arbitrary. One reason for this, of course, is that the indicated types of behavior are far more indistinct than their discrete naming suggests. The conceptual distinctions between what is the individual participant "itself" and what is "outside" it, between its "mind" and "body," between "people" and "things," and between their indicated sub-categories, are unavoidably vague and seem to grow more so with the development of scientific understanding and control. Consequently, the decision to describe a given physical behavior in any one of the ways indicated by Fig. 3.1 and not others seems doomed to remain arbitrary. Beyond this, there is a second reason why application of Fig. 3.1 requires arbitrary decisions: the effects of any given event (including individual human behavior) are in principle limitless—and, in addition, what is constructive behavior with respect to one object may well be destructive behavior with respect to another object, and transportative behavior with respect to still another. Therefore, when we characterize a behavior by some and not all of its limitless number and variety of effects, we make an unavoidably arbitrary decision in pursuit of given analytic purposes. As Chapter 16 will argue, however, we are protected against such arbitrariness degenerating into idiosyncratic, solipsistic, quirkiness by the insistence of scientific method on public declaration. Through public declaration of arbitrary decisions we assure the possibility of intersubjective testing to see whether the same results are obtained when the same decisions are made by others.

Second, and with continuing recognition of their arbitrariness, still finer distinctions may be drawn within each dimension (and therefore within each behavior type) shown in Fig. 3.1. Thus, we may distinguish, say, between cognitive, cathectic (including ethical and aesthetic), and conative components of mind; between skeletal, muscular, sensory, nervous, and visceral components of body; between plants and animals, and between microorganisms and macroorganisms among living things; between solids, liquids, gases, colloids, and plasmas among nonliving things (and, of course, we may draw still finer distinctions than these at any point we desire).

Finally, in keeping with the ability of Fig. 3.1 to sustain indefinitely finer detail, and also in keeping with the limitless number and variety of effects attributable to any given physical behavior, the variants of such behavior shown in Fig. 3.1 are meant to be combinable into any number of sequential chains and/or simultaneous clusters for descriptions of highly complex behaviors. For example, in referring to an individual's "occupation," we normally mean a complex of behaviors performed by that individual—a complex that stands in some stable causal relation to other complexes performed by other individuals, and that can be described in terms reducible to those shown in Fig. 3.1.

Other Typologies of Individual Physical Behavior

One important group of sociological descriptions of physical behavior is to be found in the several well-known lists of functional "prerequisites," "requisites," "imperatives," and "requirements," defined broadly as "things that must be done in any society if it is to continue as a going concern" (Aberle et al., 1950:100).[10]

---

[10] Aberle et al. (1950) refer to "prerequisites." Levy prefers "requisites": "A *functional requisite* . . . is a generalized condition necessary for the maintenance of the unit with which it is associated. . . ."

My justification for regarding such lists as functional descriptions of individual physical behavior[11] rests on three claims: First, getting things "done," and performing "functions," can only mean bringing about certain effects in the world,[12] and the agents for this doing and performing can only be society's participants. Second, the lists' emphasis on getting things *done,* as opposed to getting things thought, believed, or felt, implies physical behavior as the immediate focus—although that behavior is often required to affect psychical behavior, as in Parsons' "pattern maintenance" imperative which calls for "maintaining the stability of the patterns of institutionalized culture defining the structure of the system" (1961a:38), rather than calling simply for "patterns of institutionalized culture." Third, the lists are not represented as ethical injunctions that certain behaviors *ought* to be present; they are empirical conclusions that the behaviors in question actually *are* present (and were present, and will be present) in every persisting society—otherwise, the claim goes, those societies could not persist.

Indeed, it is only because a functional prerequisite, requisite, imperative, or requirement constitutes a functional description of physical behavior that it can be held to specify "things that must get done in any society." Thus, the latter claim, made explicit by all the lists mentioned, depends on the former claim, even though it remains only implicit in these lists.

We should not, however, expect such lists to include all possible physical behaviors because, by definition, the lists leave out whatever behaviors their authors regard as unnecessary for society—regardless of how widespread these behaviors may be in society. We shall shortly see which behaviors, specified in Fig. 3.1, these may be.

In a relatively early list (see Parsons, 1957:60–66), Malinowski describes the "instrumental imperatives of culture" as follows:

> (1) The cultural apparatus of implements and consumers goods must be produced, used, maintained, and replaced by new production. (2) Human behavior . . . must be codified, regulated in action and sanction. (3) The human material . . . must be renewed, formed, drilled, and provided with full knowledge of tribal tradition. (4) Authority . . . must be defined, equipped

(1952:62). Parsons and Smelser refer to functional "imperatives" as " 'problems' which must met adequately if equilibrium and/or continuing existence of the system is to be maintained" (1956:16). Merton refers to "the postulate of indispensability" as assuming that "there are certain *functions* which are indispensable in the sense that unless they are performed, the society (or group or individual) will not persist" (1957:33).

[11] Levy calls society (presumably, including all its functions and structures) "a system of *action in operation* . . ." and says that "the system involved consists of the uniformities observable in [the concrete *actions and interactions* of concrete individuals or groups of individuals]" [1952:113, 114, emphasis added]).

[12] Levy, for example, defines "function" as "a condition, or state of affairs *resultant* from the operation . . . of a structure" (1952:56, emphasis added), and Merton says "social function refers to observable objective *consequences*" (1957:24, emphasis added).

with powers, and endowed with means of forceful execution of its orders (1944: 125).[13]

The first "imperative" seems classifiable by Fig. 3.1 as domesticating-cultivating and extracting-fabricating behaviors, the second as chiefly social structuring and self-nurturing behaviors, the third as chiefly cultural structuring and self-teaching behaviors, and the fourth as a combination of cultural structuring (and self-teaching) and social structuring (and self-nurturing) behaviors.

The list of "functional prerequisites" put forward by Aberle et al. follows Malinowski's list by six years. Their first prerequisite ("provision for adequate relationship to the environment and for sexual recruitment") seems to combine references to domesticating-cultivating, extracting-fabricating, and social structuring behaviors. The second prerequisite ("role differentiation and role assignment") seems to refer to social structuring behaviors, insofar as "the systematic and stable division of activities" (1950:105) among different individuals in the environment is involved, while the third through seventh prerequisites ("communication," "shared cognitive orientations," "shared articulated set of goals," "the normative regulation of means," and the "normative regulation of affective expression") seem all to be cultural structurings because they call for physical behaviors that produce and maintain shared psychical behaviors among social participants. The eighth prerequisite ("socialization") specifies cultural structuring, insofar as "To each individual must be transmitted . . . the modes of dealing with the total situation" (1950:109). The last prerequisite is "the effective control of disruptive forms of behavior" and refers to social structuring (specifically, sanctioning) behavior since it involves "techniques for handling those who . . . use . . . disruptive means or are subject to . . . outbreaks" (1950:110).[14]

Note that both self-nurturing and self-teaching are omitted from this list—that is, the individual is regarded only as acting (as a part of "society") on others and not on him/herself. Thus, the list cites "the provision of adequate relationships to the environment," but it is "society" that does all the providing (as Aberle et al.

---

[13] Note the strong resemblance of Parsons' four "functional imperatives" (discussed below) to Malinowski's four "instrumental imperatives"—except that Parsons infuses three of his imperatives with cultural structuring behavior. Granting this difference, however, Parsons' "adaptive" imperative seems related to Malinowski's first imperative; Parsons' "integrative" imperative to Malinowski's second imperative; Parsons' "latency" imperative to Malinowski's third imperative; and Parsons' "goal attainment" imperative to Malinowski's fourth imperative. Note also that Malinowski says the "cultural responses to [his] imperatives" are, respectively, "1. Economics. 2. Social control. 3. Education. 4. Political organization" (1944:125). Parsons draws similar conclusions.

[14] Levy adds a tenth requisite, "adequate institutionalization," although he admits that there "may be a valid objection to its separate standing in the list of functional requisites" (1952:194), since it refers to "normative structures" already mentioned in other requisites (notably the third through fifth, and the sixth through eighth). Levy's tenth requisite may therefore be viewed as a kind of global reference to cultural structuring and self-teaching behaviors (and perhaps also to social structuring behaviors, insofar as "sanctions" are also said to be involved).

imply when they note that "A society . . . need not provide equally for the physiological needs of all its members" [1950:104]), and the list cites "socialization" but it is society that does all the socializing, for "*To* each individual must be transmitted . . . the modes of dealing with the total situation." In one sense, these omissions appear to be instances wherein lists of behaviors purported to be necessary do not include unnecessary, however widespread, behaviors. That is, it may be argued that the individual's acting upon his/her own body and/or mind is not a behavior which is necessary either to society or to the individual: admittedly, society requires living, behaving, individuals, but those individuals can be forcibly exercised and forcibly fed both food and orientations—almost entirely through the actions of others. Such relative absence of the individual's own action upon him/herself seems, indeed, to be the essential meaning of hospital "intensive care" in the body case and "brainwashing" and "hypnotic suggestion" in the mind case. In another sense, however, the omission of self-nurturing and self-teaching behaviors represents the less-excusable overlooking of Newton's first and third laws, mentioned above.

A further development, springing from Aberle's et al. list of functional prerequisites, seems especially noteworthy, in light of the arguments that functional imperatives are implicit descriptions of physical behavior and that such descriptions are essential to distinguish one social structure from another. Although Aberle et al. open their discussion of functional prerequisites with the declaration that "we are concerned with *what* must get done in society, not with *how* it is done" (1950:104), they close by claiming that their list of functional prerequisites "should be especially useful for constructing a general system of structural prerequisites that will tell us how the functional prerequisites may be met . . ." (1950:111). Levy, one of the authors of that suggestion, follows it up by advancing the concept of "structural requisite"—that is, "a pattern (or observable uniformity) of action (or operation) necessary for the continued existence of the unit with which it is associated . . ." (1952:63).[15]

Rephrased, Levy's argument is that certain behaviors ("structural requisites") have effects that are necessary for the performance of other behaviors ("functional requisites"), and the latter behaviors have effects that are necessary for the existence of "society."[16] Setting aside the explanatory import of this argument, the important thing for present purposes is that structural, as well as functional, requisites

---

[15] Merton argues against such structural requisites: "Once we abandon the gratuitous assumption of the functional indispensability of particular social structures, we immediately require some concept of functional alternatives, equivalents, or substitutes. This focuses attention on the range of possible variation in the items which can . . . subserve a functional requirement" (1957:52).

[16] It seems noteworthy that Aberle et al. explicitly restrict their prerequisites to societies ("the statement of the functional prerequisites of any social system . . . would be on too general a level for the present discussion" [1950:101]), while Parsons extends his imperatives to "all levels of organization and evolutionary development, from the unicellular organism to the highest human civilization" (1970:35). Levy (1952) seems to fall somewhere between these two extremes insofar as he sometimes speaks inclusively of "units" but sometimes exclusively of "societies."

specify behaviors by their effects or functions. Thus, when Levy proposes five "analytic structures" which he holds are "requisite" for any society,[17] they all reduce to physical behaviors that are comprehended by Fig. 3.1. A detailed examination of each of these structures would consume too much space here, so I content myself with the undefended, but (I believe) defensible, assertions that "solidarity," "role differentiation," "political allocation," and "integration" are all varieties of cultural structuring behaviors, and that "economic allocation" refers to domesticating-cultivating and extracting-fabricating behaviors.

Parsons' four "functional imperatives" comprise what is, perhaps, the best-known such list, although his many remarks about them are ambiguous. Nevertheless, it seems a fair guess that the pattern-maintenance and goal-attainment imperatives both specify cultural structuring behaviors insofar as "pattern-maintenance refers to the imperative of maintaining the stability of the patterns of institutionalized culture,"[18] and goal-attainment refers to the arrangement of goals "in some scale of relative urgency" and the creation of "motivation to contribute what is necessary for the functioning of the system." The adaptive imperative (defined as the provision of "disposable facilities," which are said to "involve control of physical objects, access to the services of human agents, and certain cultural elements") seems to refer to a combination of domesticating-cultivating, extracting-fabricating, social structuring, and cultural structuring behaviors. Finally, the integration imperative "concerns the mutual adjustments of [social] 'units' of subsystems from the point of view of their 'contributions' to the effective functioning of the system as a whole," and insofar as its "primary focus . . . is found in [the] system of legal norms and the agencies associated with its management," it seems that this imperative specifies cultural structuring behaviors but also implicates social structuring behaviors if the police force is included among its "agencies."[19]

---

[17] On the one hand, Levy argues emphatically *for* the likelihood of "concrete" structural requisites of *particular* societies: "If we define 'United States society' in sufficient detail to isolate its present form, then a particular form of family structure, several specific forms of predominantly economic structures, and several specific forms of predominantly political structures can be shown to be structural requisites of the society" (1952:199–200). But on the other hand, he argues *against* the likelihood of concrete structural requisites of *all* societies: "It is not . . . easy to show that a given functional requisite must be carried out in terms of any particular concrete structure" (1952:291). Undaunted by that difficulty, however, Levy suggests at least two concrete structural requisites of all societies: "It is possible that all . . . structures, both analytic and concrete, in any given society are either concrete subdivisions of, or analytically differentiated aspects of, the *family type structure* and one other. The one other concrete structure would be *some structure specifically interrelating different families*" (1952:203, emphasis added. On marriage as this structure, see Lévi-Strauss [1956], and on parenthood as a structure interrelating different generations of families through time, see Malinowski [1963]). Moreover, says Levy, "some concrete substructures of a society involving relationships between or among two or more generations must be sought in the analysis of any society" (1952:366); and "concrete structures involving only the members of one sex are usual, if not inevitable, in all societies" (1952:367).

[18] All quotations in this paragraph are from Parsons and Smelser (1956:17–18). For derivations of Parsons' functional imperatives from Bales' "interaction process categories" see Parsons and Bales, 1953.

[19] Turner and Maryanski go so far as to claim that description is the *only* utility of Parsons' functional imperatives: "as a method for describing social systems, Parsons' requisite functionalism can provide a valuable tool. As long as we do not aspire to use his conceptual categories as theoretical

Parsons also refers to four "mechanisms of social control" (i.e., compulsion—including coercion and inducement—support, permissiveness, and refusal to reciprocate), where only the first seems to refer to social structuring behaviors while the last three refer to cultural structuring behaviors [Parsons says they deal with "the subtler underlying motivational aspects" (1951:299)]. More recently, and in a similar vein, Parsons proposes a "paradigm of sanctions" that seems to cite social structuring behaviors ("inducement . . . backed by 'enforceability,' " and "activation of collective commitments, backed by contingent coercion") on a par with cultural structuring behaviors ("persuasion . . . backed by status-prestige," and "activation of value-commitments, backed by moral sanctions") (1968b:142).

Merton claims, at first, that the conception of functional requirements "remains one of the cloudiest and empirically most debatable concepts in functional theory," and that "As used by sociologists, the concept . . . tends to be tautological or *ex post facto*" (1957:52). However, without explaining his apparent change of opinion, Merton himself proposes four "functional requirements" of "democratic organizations." The first three of these requirements call for cultural structuring behaviors (i.e., providing for "ways to ascertain and record the will of the majority," "periodic audits of dissent as well as assent," and "a sufficient flow of organizationally relevant information . . . [to] the membership"), and the last is social structuring insofar as it implies the membership's ability to change leaders ("There must be provisions for accountability of policy-making representatives to the membership)." Merton then adds two other "functional requirements . . . for *any* form of effective organization" (emphasis added), namely, maintaining "a process of dynamic adaptation for coping with its environment . . . in order to acquire and use the resources needed to attain the goals of the organization" and "pacing and phasing of new organizational goals"—and these appear to refer especially, though perhaps not exclusively, to domesticating-cultivating and extracting-fabricating behaviors in the first instance and, again, to cultural structuring behaviors, in the second (see Merton, 1976:92–95).

Once again, unexpectedly, in light of his earlier insistence on "functional alternatives" as standing "In contrast to [the] concept of indispensable cultural forms (institutions, standardized practices, belief systems, etc.)" (1957:34), Merton goes on to propose four "structural components" of democratic organizations, three of which (despite his use of the more equivocal term "component" rather than "re-

---

explanations, his approach can provide guidance for those involved in describing social systems" (1979:136). Note, however, that Turner and Maryanski apply Parsons' functional imperatives to the description of "social systems" in general, rather than specifically to individual physical behavior and social structure (Turner and Maryanski do not distinguish between social structure and cultural structure); and note that by accepting the functional imperatives as "criteria for assessing the *importance* of structures and processes in all varieties of systems (1979:138, emphasis added), they assume that the "imperatives" are in fact imperative and therefore causally explanatory. Turner and Maryanski, despite themselves, therefore, seem covertly to "aspire to use [Parsons'] conceptual categories as theoretical explanations."

quirement") include the imperative "must": "The democratic organization provides for an inclusive electorate of members and for regularly scheduled elections"; "The democratic organization must provide for initiations of policy to come from elected representatives and to be evaluated . . . through recurrent elections of representatives"; "If it is to be effective as well as democratic, the voluntary association must provide organizational devices that enable executive action to work toward the association's goals"; and "Channels of communication [in the organization] must be open for a two-way flow of communication" (see Merton, 1976:95–97). Given Merton's discussion of these "components," it seems fair to say that the first and the third refer primarily to social structuring behaviors while the second and fourth refer primarily to cultural structuring behaviors.

Merton's distinction between "manifest" and "latent" functions is not included here as referring to physical behavior because it denotes two ways that a given physical behavior can be *imaged* in the minds of social participants: "Manifest functions are those objective consequences . . . which are *intended and recognized by participants in the system,*" and "Latent functions . . . [are] those which are neither intended nor recognized" (Merton, 1957:51, emphasis changed). The manifest-latent distinction, therefore, must be assigned to cultural structure rather than to social structure (see Chapter 4) while his distinction between functions and dysfunctions (mentioned below), of course, remains pertinent to social structure alone. This conclusion seems also to be what Levy has in mind when he says

> Concepts of latent, manifest [intended but unrecognized, and unintended but recognized functions] specifically focus attention on the point of view of the actor and involve the [assumption] that such actors . . . are capable of explicit thinking and observation . . . [while] concepts of function and structure in general . . . are concepts generally applicable to [phenomena that are not capable of explicit thinking and observation] (1968:26).

Levy confounds this view, however, when he indiscriminantly groups manifest, latent, unintended but recognized, and intended but unrecognized functions, along with "prerequisites . . . eufunction-dysfunction, eustructure-dysstructure, etc.," as various "forms of structural-functional analysis" (1968:28).

In presenting what amounts to be another set (incidentally, the smallest set) of functional requisites, Homans asks

> What does [the Bank Wiring] group need to have in order to keep going in its particular environment? It needs motives (sentiments) on the part of its members, jobs (activities) for them to do, and some communication (interaction) between them (1950:94).[20]

---

[20] Note that "action" (in the Newtonian rather than the Weberian sense) seems a more appropriate term than "interaction" because Homans does not require reciprocation (see Chapter 12).

Homans clearly has physical behaviors in mind when he tells us that "activity" refers "to movements of the muscles of men," and that "interaction . . . [refers] to the fact that some unit of activity of one man follows, or, if we like the word better, is stimulated by, some unit of activity of another" (1950:34, 36). Both activity and interaction, then, appear to encompass various combinations of domesticating-cultivating, extracting-fabricating, and social structuring behaviors.

"Sentiments," however, are another matter. Homans says "they all refer to internal states of the human body. Laymen and professional psychologists call these states by various names: drives, emotions, feelings, affective states, sentiments, attitudes" (Homans, 1950:37–38). Sentiments themselves are therefore, in our terms, psychical behavior (and, when shared, cultural structure) and do not come within the scope of Fig. 3.1. Their presence in Homans' scheme means that cultural structuring (and self-teaching) physical behavior is implied insofar as Homans claims that "activity" and "interaction" have effects on sentiment also.

Indeed, a special feature of Homans' scheme is its reliance on the likelihood that the same physical act will have multiple effects (and may therefore be classifiable in more than one of the categories shown in Fig. 3.1). Thus, he argues for "mutual dependence among activity, interaction, and sentiment" (1950:97)—which is to say the same act may count simultaneously as domesticating-cultivating and extracting-fabricating, and as social structuring, and also as cultural structuring. Thus, in indicating the simultaneous significances of the same act as both activity and interaction in the bank wiring room, Homans says "when a wireman had completed a level on one equipment he moved over to a second one, and that act was the signal for the solderman to begin soldering in place the connections of the first terminal. The wireman had interacted with the solderman . . ." (1950:101). In indicating the capacity of the same act to be simultaneously social structuring and cultural structuring Homans says "persons who interact frequently with one another tend to like one another" (1950:111). In indicating the capacity of the same act to be simultaneously domesticating-cultivating and extracting-fabricating and cultural structuring, Homans says "persons who feel sentiments of liking for one another will express those sentiments in activities . . . and these activities may further strengthen the sentiments of liking" (1950:118).

It should also be noted that Homans' classification of physical behaviors differs from other lists of functional imperatives insofar as he alone refers (perhaps because of his strong interest in individual psychology) specifically to self-nurturing and self-teaching behaviors:

A man feels hungry; he gets something to eat and his hunger disappears. If his activity does not result in his getting something to eat, new sentiments, which we call frustration, will be added to his original hunger, and we say that the activity was unrewarding or even positively punishing. He may then try a new one; if it ends in his getting something to eat, his hunger is allayed, and he will tend to repeat the activity the next time he feels hungry (1950:99).

In addition to all the above, more technically sociological, typologies we should also note some others of wider currency. Thus, one very common distinction is drawn between "economic" and "political" physical behaviors. Regarding economic behaviors, Marx says "the sum total of [the] relations of production constitutes the economic structure of society" (1978:4), thus downplaying relations of consumption[21]; and Weber says "the economic order is . . . the way in which economic goods and services are distributed and used" (1958a:181), thus downplaying the way goods and services are produced.[22] Together, however, these views seem to identify "economic" behavior with production, distribution and consumption, or what Fig. 3.1 refers to as domesticating-cultivating, extracting-fabricating, and self-nurturing behaviors of constructive, transportative, and destructive varieties.

Regarding "political" behavior, Weber identifies it not with goods and services (i.e., facilitators and enhancers of life) but with force and violence (i.e., inhibitors and terminators of life):

> We wish to understand by politics only the leadership, or the influencing of the leadership . . . of a state. . . . [And ultimately,] one can define the modern state sociologically only in terms of the specific means peculiar to it . . . namely, the use of physical force. . . . The state is considered the sole source of the "right" to use violence. Hence, "politics" for us means striving to share power or striving to influence the distribution of power, either among states or among groups within a state (1946:77–78, emphasis removed).

Engels makes the same point, although somewhat less explicitly than Weber, when he names as the second distinguishing characteristic of the state (after territoriality, an emphasis on spatial regularity in social phenomena) a

> special public power, [made necessary] because a self-acting armed organization of the population has become impossible since the cleavage into classes. . . . The people's army of the Athenian democracy was an aristocratic public power against the slaves, whom it kept in check, however, a gendarmerie also became necessary to keep the citizens in check. . . . This public power exists in every state; it consists not merely of armed people but also of material adjuncts, prisons, and institutions of coercion of all kinds (Marx and Engels, 1978:752–753).[23]

[21] This is not to say that Marx overlooks economic consumption—as witness his central discussion of "surplus value"—but it is secondary to and derivative from his definition of economic behavior in terms of *production.*

[22] Weber does not overlook economic production—as witness his discussion of "The systematic production of utilities through manufacture or transportation" (1947:168)—but Weber's emphasis remains on the *utilities* produced.

[23] Note that although Engels refers only to a *domestic* "gendarmerie," Weber, by referring to "the distribution of power . . . *among* states," also includes national armies among the instrumentalities of politics. No classical theorist, to my knowledge, refers to an *inter*national gendarmerie.

Comte argues that "The famous maxim of Hobbes, that government is the natural result of force, is the principal step that till now the positive theory of power made since Aristotle. . . . Social science would remain forever in the cloud land of metaphysics if we hesitated to adopt the principle of force as the basis of government" (1975:433).

Together, then, the nearly identical Weberian, Marxian, and Comtean views of political behavior[24] seem to identify it with what Fig. 3.1 calls social structuring behaviors (especially the destructive and transportative varieties) and their associated reactive self-nurturing behaviors.

A third, frequently mentioned, type of physical behavior is "educational" and "religious." Durkheim, for example, defines "education" as serving "to develop in the child a certain number of physical, intellectual, and moral states which are demanded of him by both the political society as a whole and the special milieu for which he is specifically destined" (1956:71). If we assign the development of "physical" states to social structuring behavior, then the development of "intellectual and moral" states may be regarded as consisting of cultural structuring behavior together with its associated reactive self-teaching behavior.

Durkheim also describes religious "rites" (which he calls "determined modes of [physical] action" [1965:51]) as identical to "moral practices," the objects of education, except that religious rites are addressed to a "different class of objects"—namely, the "sacred" rather than the "profane" (1965:51–52). Although this class of objects may be assigned certain physical representatives,[25] from a naturalistic standpoint the entire class exists only in the believer's mind. On this ground, then, religious physical behavior (i.e., "rites")—as well as more secular "educational" behavior—seems classifiable as cultural structuring behavior and its associated self-teaching behavior.

Finally, consider the physical behaviors called "sexual mating" and "biological

[24] Further on this point, note that Marx and Engels argue that state (political) power is usually exercised on behalf of a particular economic class: "the state is the form in which the individuals of [an economically] ruling class assert their common interests." But the state may also exist as an independent structure pursuing its own interests when "no one section of the population can achieve dominance over the others" (1978:187). In such unusual cases, "warring classes balance each other so nearly that the state power, as ostensible mediator . . . [can, for instance, play off] the proletariat against the bourgeoisie and the bourgeoisie against the proletariat" (1978:753–754)—an idea closely matching Simmel's picture of "Tertius Gaudens" (1950:154–169). Weber is less definite about what is usual and unusual in relations between the political state and economic classes, and argues that

> parties may represent interests determined through "class situation" or "status situation" and they may recruit their following respectively from one or the other. But they need be neither purely "class" nor purely "status" parties. In most cases they are partly class parties and partly status parties, but sometimes they are neither (1958a:194).

Both Marx and Engels, and Weber, however, agree that the state (and its participating political parties) may, at least on occasion, pursue interests independent of class interests and independent, indeed, of all interests except its own (see also Skocpol, 1979).

[25] There are "three classes of things which [totemism] recognizes as sacred, in varying degrees: the totemic emblem, the animal or plant whose appearance this emblem reproduces, and the members of the clan" (Durkheim, 1965:165).

reproduction." They may be regarded as combinations of highly specialized constructive social structuring and self-nurturing, and cultural structuring and self-teaching, behaviors directed, in mating, by adults toward one another, and in reproduction, by a mother toward the fetus and then by both parents toward the infant and the child. These are the physical behaviors implied by Marx and Engels' assertion that "from the very outset . . . men, who daily remake their own life, begin to make other men, to propagate their own kind: the relation between man and woman, parents and children, the *family*" (1978:156).

Note that I am not claiming that these societal subsystems (economic, educational, reproductive, etc.) consist *solely* of the indicated kinds of behaviors, but that these are the behaviors that must be present—regardless of what other behaviors are also present—in order to justify labeling a given subsystem by any of the indicated terms.

Destructive Physical Behaviors

It is especially noteworthy that none of the functional or structural requisites quoted above mentions the destructive side of the physical behaviors they include. On the surface, this may seem to follow from the express aim of their authors to say what must be done rather than what must not be done. But Simmel argues emphatically that destructive behaviors should be included among the things that must be done: "The solid organizational forms which seem to contribute to or create society, must continually be disturbed, disbalanced, gnawed-at by individualistic, irregular forces" (1950:315), and "negative and dualistic elements play an entirely positive role in [the] more comprehensive picture, despite the destruction they may work on particular relations" (1955:17). Similarly, Durkheim says that "To classify crime among the phenomena of normal sociology is not to say merely that it is an inevitable, although regrettable, phenomenon . . . it is to affirm that it is a factor in public health, an integral part of all healthy societies" (1938:67).

Spencer, too, asserts the inevitability of constructive and destructive behaviors, but he sees them as forming a sequence rather than coexisting simultaneously:

> [T]he direct effect of war on industrial progress is repressive. It is repressive as necessitating the abstraction of men and materials that would otherwise go to industrial growth; it is repressive as deranging the complex interdependencies among the many productive and distributive agencies; it is repressive as drafting off much administrative and constructive ability. . . . Warfare among men [however,] . . . has had a large share in raising their organizations to a higher stage. . . . War, in short . . . brings about a social aggregation which furthers that industrial state at variance with war; and yet nothing but war could bring about this social aggregation (1972:172, 168, 169).

Merton's distinction between constructive ("functional") and destructive ("dysfunctional") behaviors, while it does not assert their mutual necessity, does assert their widespread coexistence. Thus, Merton distinguishes between "functions . . . those observed consequences which make for the adaptation or adjustment of a given system; and dysfunctions, those observed consequences which lessen the adaptation or adjustment of the system" (1957:52).[26] Note that these two concepts share with functional requirements a determining reference to the effects of a given physical behavior, but there the effects are classified, not according to *what* they bear upon (i.e., their object), but *how* they bear (i.e., their direction). This is a dimension of the classification that the functional requisites consistently overlook.

In conclusion, then, Fig. 3.1 seems to subsume and make comparable a wide variety of descriptions of individual physical behavior. When we regard these descriptions as the most elemental behavioral units with which sociological analysis is concerned, they may be aggregated both within individuals and across individuals, thereby building up a hierarchy of concepts culminating in "society"—considered in its social structural aspect only, of course.

In their within-individual mode of aggregation, the behaviors shown in Fig. 3.1 may be used to characterize the different units that a single individual strings together into role-performances and sets of role-performances, and also they may be used to characterize the net outcome of one or more such role-performances by the same individual.

In their across-individuals mode of aggregation, the behaviors shown in Fig. 3.1 may be used to characterize not only the different units that different individuals contribute to some given net outcome of all their contributions, but also (as indicated above) to characterize that net outcome itself—as, say, "the economic system" or "the educational system", and so forth.

Let us examine more closely, then, the aggregation of unit behaviors within individuals first and then examine their aggregation across individuals.

WITHIN-INDIVIDUAL AGGREGATES OF PHYSICAL BEHAVIORS

Role-Performance

Consider one analyst's two contrasting definitions of "role." Parsons says "what the actor *does* in his relations with others seen in the context of its functional

---

[26] Admittedly, Merton's criterion of functionality is open to normative interpretations of what constitutes a worthy goal of "adaptation or adjustment." My definition of "construction" and "destruction" (in connection with Figure 3.1) shifts that criterion to probabilistic entropy. According to this criterion, analysts holding radically different moral values should, in principle, be able to agree on whether a given behavior has any variety of ordering, derandomizing, building-up effects on a given phenomenon or whether it tends to break the phenomenon down into statistically disordered, irregular, chaotic, parts. For discussions of entropy and negentropy, see Schrödinger (1968) and Brillouin (1968).

significance for the social system . . . [is what] we shall call his role" (1951:25, emphasis changed), but a few pages later Parsons also says "A role . . . is a section of the total *orientation* system of an individual actor which is organized about expectations in relation to a particular context" (1951:38). Thus also, Davis says "How an individual *actually performs* in a given position, as distinct from how he is supposed to perform, we call his role" (1949:90, emphasis changed), but Goode, who does not define "role" here, says a "role relationship" is "a set of mutual (but not necessarily harmonious) *expectations* of behavior between two or more actors" (1960b:248, emphasis added). And Nowak says "Roles . . . may be understood either as external prescriptions and expectations or as internal convictions held by their 'performers,' or else as the actual modes of behavior on the part of the latter when they perform the role [sic] in question" (1977:82). In one kind of definition, then, a "role" is said to be a variety of physical behavior and in another kind it is said to be a variety of psychical behavior.

There is, of course, a third kind of definition that regards a role as a substantive overlap between physical and psychical behavior—that is, things done that conform to things expected or prescribed. Thus, Linton says "When [a person] puts . . . rights and duties . . . into effect, he is performing a role" (1936:114); in yet another of his definitions, Parsons says "A role may . . . be defined as the structured, i.e., normatively regulated, participation of a person in a concrete process of social interaction" (1961a:42) (although on the very next page, Parsons reverses himself again and says "Structurally speaking . . . the role component is the normative component which governs the participation of individual persons in given collectivities" [1961a:43]); and Gross et al. say "[the concept 'role'] must include these three elements—social locations, behavior, and expectations" (1958:18).

Now inasmuch as this chapter is restricted to discussion of social structure and the physical behaviors of which it is composed, while the next chapter is restricted to discussion of cultural structure and the psychical behaviors of which it is composed, it behooves us stringently to divide the concept "role" into two logically independent components, namely, role-performance and role-expectation. As the quotations above suggest, to speak merely of "role" would perpetuate a crucial and insidious aspect of the already serious confusion between social structure and cultural structure, and it would unjustifiably take for granted that for every role-performance there is a role-expectation (and vice-versa).[27]

---

[27] Although Merton refers only to the "role-set" and does not distinguish between the role-performance set and the role-expectation set, he does clearly indicate that role-performance and role-expectation are independently variable ("role-performance [may differ] from the patterned expectations of the groups); that expectations for the same performed role may vary ("The individual . . . may . . . be readily subject to conflicting role-expectations"); and also implies that, "To the extent that the role-structure insulates the status-occupant from direct observation," performances by the same individual of the same role-expectation also vary (1957:320, 370, 374).

Accordingly, the following discussion concentrates on role-performances as components of social structure (not of cultural structure) and on those usages of "role" that appear to carry that referent rather than the referent of role-expectation. By an individual's role-performance we mean all of that individual's physical behaviors which have effects on a given object, plus (in line with the discussion earlier in this chapter) all of that object's effects on the individual. In short, an individual's role-performance in social structure is regarded here as object-specific doing and being done to. For example, an individual's role-performance vis-à-vis his/her child consists of all the things the individual does to the child plus all the things the child does to him/her, whether these things are prescribed, or expected, or not. Note that Fig. 3.1 indicates that the things one individual can directly do to another are social structuring and cultural structuring behaviors of constructive, transportative, and destructive varieties. Among cultural structuring behaviors, of course, I include those physical behaviors that are taken to be expressions of emotion insofar as they impinge on the other's mind (and also, by reaction, on one's own) to persuade him/her that we are, or are not, sincere and trustworthy. Goode almost makes this point when he says "Performances also include the appropriate emotional behavior (e.g., loving, reserved, or friendly)" (1960b:249); Fig. 3.1 of course, includes among performances only external manifestations and not the internal emotions themselves—which means that well-feigned emotions are as good, so far as cultural structuring performance is concerned (though not necessarily as far as self-teaching performances are concerned), as "genuine" expressions of actually felt emotions.

The next higher level concept in the within-participant aggregation of psychical behaviors is an adaptation of Merton's idea of the "role-set," which, for reasons just outlined, I partition into two ideas—the role-*performance* set and the role-*expectation* set—and consider the former in this chapter and the latter (except for a few quick remarks in the next paragraph) in the chapter that follows.

Role-Performance Set

Merton defines the role-set as

> that complement of role-relationships which persons have by virtue of occupying a particular social status. As one example: the single status of medical student entails not only the role of a student in relation to his teachers, but also an array of other roles . . . to other students, nurses, physicians, social workers, medical technicians, etc. (1957:369).

Accordingly, by an individual's role-*performance* set—in its most inclusive sense—I mean the totality of the physical behaviors that that individual performs toward and receives from all objects whatever. This most inclusive set may, of course, be broken down analytically into any number of smaller subsets—which Merton indicates by referring to the various "statuses" that an individual may "occupy" (concepts that I shall examine in a moment). Note that, as suggested above, role-performance set implies a role-expectation set (meaning, in its most inclusive sense, the totality of expectations regarding an individual's behavior toward all objects), or rather many role-expectation sets: one held by the individual him/herself, and the others held by people in the individual's environment. Once these components have been separated, relations of consonance, dissonance, or irrelevance between the many role-expectation sets and between each of them and given role-performance sets become analytically problematic issues.

Now consider what Merton means by "occupying" a "social status,"— that which, he says, enables a person to have a role set. Interpreting Linton as defining "status" as "a position in a social system occupied by designated individuals" (Merton, 1957: 368),[28] Merton argues that any given individual occupies many such positions and each position is associated with a role-set:

> for example . . . teacher, wife, mother, Catholic, Republican, and so on. We designate this complement of social statuses of an individual as his *status-set,* each of the statuses in turn having its distinctive role-set (1957:369–370).

In considering this picture, it is important to note that Merton defines a status as a "position in a social system," but then defines "position" only in terms of the role-set with which it is associated. On this basis, it seems fair to say that, for Merton, the two terms, status (or position) and role-set, refer to the same observable phenomenon: a social status *is* a role-set, and insofar as the individual's status-set is the set of all his/her role-sets, it, too, is a role-set—albeit the most inclusive one (i.e., it is the individual's role-*set* rather than one of his/her role-*sub*sets; Radcliffe-Brown refers to it as the individual's " 'social personality' "—that is, "the complex formed by all [the individual's] social relations with others" [1965:193]). Recalling that our emphasis here is restricted to physical performance and social structure, it seems fair to translate all this into the following conclusion: A status in social structure is observationally identical to some subset of an individual's role-performance set.

Why use two terms for the same observable phenomenon? The answer depends strictly on perspective: "role-performance set" calls attention to a set of performed

---

[28] Actually, Linton seems quite ambiguous and, in my judgment, even self-contradictory when, after saying "The polar positions in . . . patterns of reciprocal *behavior* are technically known as statuses" (thereby indicating a social structure referent), he goes on to say that "A status, as distinct from the individual who may occupy it, is simply a collection of *rights and duties*" (1936:113, emphasis added), and thereby indicates a cultural structure referent.

and received behaviors when seen in relation to the individual who performs and receives them, whereas "social status" calls attention to the same behaviors when seen in relation to the social structure (i.e., the *inter*organism behavior regularities), of which they are parts.[29] This is what we mean when we say a status is a position in a social structure, such as "cheerleader" (statuses are also describable in culture structure—for example, positions that agree with, dissent from, or are neutral toward a given idea [see Mannheim's discussion of ideologists, utopianists, and intellectuals, 1955]), and a role is the behavior manifested by occupants of that position, such as "leading cheers."

This perspective distinction between role-performance sets (or, as he calls them, "roles") and statuses seems clearly indicated by Levy, when he says

> [G]iven *role* as defined [according to Davis, as "the manner in which an individual actually carries out the requirements of his position"], there is no "social scientist role" or "warrior role" or "role of surgeon"; there are only roles of particular individuals who occupy the status (or position) of social scientists, warriors, or surgeons (1952:159).

Further: "If the term *role* is used consistently with its definition, then there can be no talk of people acting in terms of roles. Their actions are their roles" (Levy, 1952:159).[30] Goode also seems to have the perspective distinction in mind when he notes "if the analyst can speak of the position as existing even when no incumbent is in it (e.g., chief, messiah), he is more likely to speak of it as a 'status.' By contrast, he is more likely to use 'role' if the lack of an incumbent effectively ends that role relationship" (1960b:249).

It is because of this double pertinence of the same physical behaviors—that is, both to the individual participant in social structure, and to the social structure in which that individual participates—that the concepts "role" (more exactly, role-performance set) and "social status" are so closely linked together in sociological analysis: Merton asserts that "for some time now . . . it has been recognized that two concepts—social status and social role—are fundamental to the description, and to the analysis, of a social structure," and that "The patterned arrangements

[29] Parsons hints at this idea when he says the role is "the point of contact between the system of action of the individual actor and the social system. The individual then becomes . . . a composite of various action units which in turn are roles in the relationships in which he is involved" (1951:190). And, in a different way, so does Goode:

> The term "status" was used mainly in macrostructural analysis, the description of a total society in broad terms. . . . [but the term "role" is used mainly in] microstructural studies, that is, studies small sets of interrelationships. . . . [and in social psychology, with] its concern with "the" individual and its relative lack of concern with formal statuses (1960b:248).

[30] Unfortunately, from my point of view, Levy goes on to confound the statement that actions are . . . roles," when he says "roles involve *obligations, rights,* and *expected* performances of the individuals who hold them" (1952:159, emphasis added), although, admittedly, the word "involve" is ambiguous.

of role-sets, status-sets, and status-sequences may be held to comprise the social structure" (1957:368, 370). Parsons and Shils say (although with their customary uncertainty regarding the distinction between role-performances and role-expectations) "The social system is in a sense composed of a variety of roles or role expectations," and "A social system is a system of the actions of individuals, the principal units of which are roles and constellations of roles" (1951:92, 197). Nadel says the role concept "provides a concept intermediary between 'society' and 'individual.' It operates in that strategic area where individual behavior becomes social conduct" (1957:20, emphasis removed). And Goode says "The widespread notion that institutions are made up of roles . . . links a somewhat more easily observable phenomena, social behavior, to an important but less easily observable abstraction, social structure," and notes that analysts may trace out "the articulation between one institution or organization and another, by following the sequence of an individual's role performance and their effects on the role performances of other individuals with relation to different institutional orders" (1960a:483–484, 496).

Therefore, on this ground—that is, on the ground that social "statuses" are "role-performance sets" when seen from the perspective of social structure rather than that of individuals—let us shift now to the social structural perspective and consider the aggregation of physical behaviors, not within the same individual, but across different individuals.

ACROSS-INDIVIDUALS AGGREGATES OF PHYSICAL BEHAVIORS

Situses and Societal Social Structure

I have defined a "role-performance" as a within-individual behavior aggregate—that is, as the aggregate of a *single* individual's physical behavior insofar as it has effects on, and receives effects from, a single given object. However, when we consider the aggregate of *many* individuals' behavior insofar as it has effects on, and receives effects from, a single given object—that is, when we consider the across-individuals analog of role-performance—the term "societal (or community, organizational, etc.) subsystem or situs" seems appropriate. Thus, as indicated earlier, the "economy" subsystem or situs consists of the coincidence of many individuals' physical behaviors, centrally including those termed domesticating-cultivating and extracting-fabricating by Fig. 3.1.

Parsons expresses this general idea, and refers to three successively higher levels of physical behavior aggregates across different individuals—namely, "social interaction," "subsystems," and "complex social system" or "society"—when he asserts

that "all social interaction is bound to the physical task performance of individuals"; that "a complex social system consists of interdependent and interpenetrating
subsystems"; and that these subsystems must accomplish three things: "the maintenance of [the society's] patterns of institutionalized culture at the value level [our
cultural structuring—ed.], the integration of its system of differentiated norms
[cultural structuring, again—ed.], and the coordinated handling of external situations [our domesticating-cultivating and extracting-fabricating, and also, insofar
as external situations include external human societies, social and cultural structuring—ed.]" (1961a:45,44,46). Murphy and Morris refer to "situs" as a classification of occupations "in terms of primary work function" (1961:384; see also
Morris and Murphy, 1959:233), as do Broom and Selznick when they say "In
distinction to strata, equally valued categories may be identified by the term functional category or situs [and therefore] the occupational structure of a whole society
may be analyzed in terms of situses as well as strata" (1963:204).[31]

Figure 3.2 summarizes my arguments regarding within-individual, and across-
individuals, aggregates of physical behaviors and their relations by suggesting that
the elemental level of the individual hierarchy consists of unit behaviors (e.g.,
cultural structuring behavior) and its more complex levels consist of aggregates of
such behaviors called "role-performances" (e.g., "teaching"), and aggregates of the
latter called "role-performance sets" (e.g., interacting with students and with ad-
ministrators). The elemental level of the social structural hierarchy consists of statuses (e.g., "teacher," "student," "administrator") which are synonymous with
role-performance sets when these are viewed as attributes of social structure rather
than of its individual participants; the next level consists of aggregates of such
statuses called "situses" or social structural "subsystems"; the next level after that
consists of aggregates of such situses or subsystems, which are referred to as the
social structures of collectivities up to and including world society.

This conceptualization points to two broad classes of questions pertaining to
the descriptive analysis of social structures. One class focuses on the situses and
statuses of social structure, and the other focuses on the role-performance sets, role-
performances, and the unit physical behaviors of individuals. In the first class, we
ask How similar are situses across different social structures, and How similar are

---

[31] The term "situs" seems to have been used in sociological analysis first by Benoit-Smullyan, in
the following context:

> The basic term in the field of social differentiation and stratification is "social position" . . . the
> three chief criteria [of social position] in use are: relative position in a hierarchy, membership in
> a social group, and socially defined function in an organized group. Corresponding to these criteria
> are the three fundamental types of social position, which we propose to designate by the terms
> "status," "situs," and "locus," respectively (1944:151).

In this schema, *"locus,"* not "situs," is the term designating "function in an organized group." But
somehow Murphy and Morris, and Broom and Selznick, seem to have misconstrued Benoit-Smullyan
and I meekly follow them as having become more firmly established than Benoit-Smullyan's original
formulation.

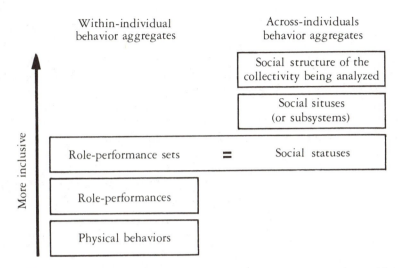

Figure 3.2. Within-individual, and across-individuals (social structure) aggregates of physical behaviors as overlapping hierarchies.

statuses across the same situses in different social structures? Whatever their success or failure so far, it is undoubtedly one aim of the lists of social structural universals (called functional and structural "prerequisites," "requisites," "imperatives," and "requirements") mentioned earlier to address these two crucial questions.

In the second class of questions, we ask how similar are the role-performance sets and role-performances of the same individual across different situses of the same social structure? A variety of analyses have been carried out with respect to this question: Lenski's concept of "status crystallization" (1954), Coleman's concept of community "polarization" (1955), Dahrendorf's concept of "superimposed contexts" (1959), Broom's concept of "status consistency" (1959), and Blau's concept of "consolidated parameters" (1977)—and, of course, their counterpart concepts (e.g., "status inconsistency," "intersecting parameters," etc.)—are all located here.

When it is noted that the same individual may have the same or different role-performance sets and role-performances within the same situs, we find that several analyses have attended to this possibility, too. Thus, an individual's "social mobility" implies dissimilar, but successive role-performance sets (statuses) within the same situs, while an individual's "status marginality" implies dissimilar, and simultaneous role-performance sets within the same situs. Mannheim relies heavily on both these concepts when he describes the emergence and social structure of the "free-floating" intelligentsia (1955); Weber relies on the notion of marginality when arguing that an elected official is "the 'servant' of those under his authority"

(1947:389); and Lipset relies on the notion of mobility when he complements Weber's argument by noting that "institutionalized democracy generally requires that the leader move from a high-status to a low-status position [upon electoral defeat]" (1954:121). As indicative of the possibility that both mobility and marginality may be eliminated, note Marx's argument that only when proletarians are so reduced (i.e., when each proletarian "has no chance of arriving at the conditions which would place him in the other class" [1978:200], and when "machinery increasingly obliterates all distinctions of labor, and nearly everywhere reduces wages to the same low level" [1978:480]), can they unite to overthrow the bourgeoisie. Not dissimilarly, Blau asserts that "The social distinctions implicit in consolidated parameters reinforce one another," and for those at the disadvantaged end of those parameters "The consolidation of severe inequalities produces a revolutionary situation" (1977:109, 240).

FORMS OF BETWEEN-INDIVIDUALS PHYSICAL BEHAVIOR COINCIDENCE

So far, I have focused on the kinds of physical behaviors that can be aggregated within and across individuals. Let us now see what forms the *coincidences* of such behaviors and their aggregates between individuals may take.

A Typology of Physical Behavior Coincidences Between Organisms

First, notice that two coincident physical behaviors may or may not be functionally the *same*. For example, both individual A and individual B may manifest, say, the same social structuring behaviors, but, on the other hand, A may manifest a social structuring behavior while B manifests, say, an extracting-fabricating behavior.

Second, the coincident physical behaviors may or may not be functionally *compatible* with each other in the environment which they share. For example, A may be constructing the same nonliving things that B is destroying. In a more abstract sense, my conception of "compatibility" derives from Boulding's definition: "Two positions are mutually incompatible if each excludes the other, that is, if the realization of either one makes impossible the realization of the other" (1962:4).[32]

---

[32] Note that this definition permits at least two types of compatibility: one where the realization of a given position is neither help nor hindrance but simply neutral toward the realization of another, and

Note that although Boulding does not say so, the incompatibility he defines is situationally determined: under different circumstances the same behaviors may be compatible (as when one's own running toward unlimited exits does not hinder anyone else's escape from disaster), or incompatible (as when the same running, but toward limited and closing exits, preempts others' escape). Beyond compatibility and incompatibility there is a further possibility: behaviors may be spatially and/or temporally (i.e., situationally) isolated from one another. With adequate isolation, behaviors that would otherwise be compatible or incompatible are neither; instead, they are merely separate. This appears to be the principle behind national boundaries, fences, prisons, training camps, "retreats," quarantines, isolation wards, honeymoons, and the uterus—among other things. It should be noted, however, that as Park and Burgess indicate, "Isolation . . . is *relative,* not *absolute*" (1921:226); at a high level of generality all human individuals share the same space (the earth, the solar system) and time (the past 50,000 years) but at the highest level of specificity, of course, none of us shares either the same space or time.

Now let us add a third dimension, namely, that there may or may not be equal causal *power* between the behaviors involved. Consider what is meant here by "power." "Power," says Weber, "is the probability that one actor within a social situation will be able to carry out his own will despite resistance" (1947:152; see also 1958a:180). In the present chapter, however, I bar both "wills" here: first, I bar reference to any participant's "will" on the ground that it implicates psychical behavior; and second, I bar reference to any probability that one participant "will" be able to accomplish something, on the ground that that probability is being used as a prediction of future observations rather than as a description of the relative frequency of past observations. Here are some obvious, but analytically crucial, implications of these two exclusions:

By excluding reference to a participant's will I permit power to be exercised independently of will, or intention, or recognition, or any other particular psychical behavior, on the part of either participant. For example, if in a crowded elevator one person accidentally steps on another's blue suede shoes, or if one person mistakes another for a burglar and fires a bullet into him/her, power (by my definition) has certainly been exercised, though without, and even against, the exerciser's will. And by restricting myself to observations rather than predictions, I imply that power heterogeneity in social structures can be strictly a matter of description—which may then become a basis for predicting future power (or loss, or increase, thereof), but which does not itself constitute such a prediction. Now, of course, both sociological analysts and social participants may attribute a predic-

a second where it is positively helpful. This important distinction will not be examined here, although Simmel seems to have had it in mind when he defines "society" in terms of three possibilities: "being with one another, for one another, against one another" (1950:43).

tion of future ("potential") power to those participants in whose behavior they have actually observed ("kinetic") power in the past, and so they may say that such participants "have" power in that predictive sense. My emphasis here on power as a description of already observed joint physical behavior is not intended to prevent such attributions, but specifically to identify them as predictions which, when made by the sociological analyst, are (like any other predictions) disconfirmable by future observations, and, when made by social participants, belong entirely to the realm of psychical behavior and cultural structure.

For some of the same reasons, I reject the many qualifications introduced when Parsons says

> Power . . . is generalized capacity to secure the performance of binding ob-
> ligations by units in a system of collective organization when the obligations
> are legitimized with reference to their bearing on collective goals and where
> in case of recalcitrance there is a presumption of enforcement by negative
> situational sanctions (1967:308, compare 298).

Thus, I would bar from the definition of power all references to "obligations," "legitimation," "goals," and "presumptions" (including threats) and relegate them to cultural structural features that are inessential qualifications of the one essential social structural element in Parsons' definition—namely, "capacity to secure . . . performance." And indeed, Parsons himself implies that this is the one essential when he says that when two power systems meet, "the use of *force* is the end of the line" (1967:277, emphasis added).

My definition of power, then, refers entirely to physical behavior and therefore social structure; it is the same as Lukes' definition when he says "The absolutely basic common core to all conceptions of power is the notion of the bringing about of consequences, with no restriction on what the consequences might be or what brings them about" (1978:634–635). However, although I do not restrict, I do classify what might be the consequences of power and what might bring them about. Power, as that concept is implied by Fig. 3.1, then, is the bringing about of any constructive, transportative, and/or destructive effect in self (body and/or mind), other people (bodies and/or minds), and/or things (living and/or nonliving)—with *social* power being restricted to one individual's power over other individuals and leaving out his/her power over nonpeople things and over him/herself except insofar as it is intermediate to power over other individuals.

Cross-classifying the concept of power equality-inequality between the behaviors of different participants with the sameness-difference, and the compatibility-incompatibility isolation, of those behaviors yields Fig. 3.3. Here nine forms of coincidence between the behaviors of different participants—and therefore nine forms of social structure—are systematically interrelated as follows.

"Unison" social structures include all those where the participants are doing the same things, causal power is equally distributed, and the behaviors are compatible. The Rockettes dancing chorus line approximates this case. Here I cite Tönnies' assertion, in his discussion of Gemeinschaft, that "Real helpfulness, mutual aid, and advancement exist in the purest form among brothers and sisters because they tend toward the same common activities" (1963:40). Here also is the basic idea behind Marx's image of "primitive communism," Durkheim's image of "segmental" social structure, Freud's image of the "primitive horde," Mead's image of "a situation where persons are all trying to save someone from drowning [and] there is a sense of a common effort in which one is stimulated by the others to do the same thing they are doing" (1934:273), and Simmel's remark that in human crowds "the individual, by being carried away, carries away" (1950:35).

"Imitation" social structures include those characterized by unison, but the unison has a leader. Platoons of marching soldiers, celebrants, or protestors—in each case under leadership—approximate this case. From the sociological literature, of

	A's and B's physical behaviors are:			
	Same		Different	
	Equal	Unequal	Equal	Unequal
Compatible	Unison	Imitation	Cooperation	Administration
Incompatible	Competition	Dominance	Conflict	Oppression
Isolated		Segregation		

Figure 3.3. Typology of between-individuals physical behavior coincidences.

course, we have Tarde's claim that "in sociology, the radiation of examples from [members of social classes] above to [members of social classes] below is the only fact worth consideration," and in future society, "whenever a happy initiative might show itself in the whole mass of humanity, its transmission by imitation would be almost instantaneous" (1968:188, 191). It should also be noted that despite Simmel's main emphasis on causal equality in superordination-subordination ["it conceals an interaction, an exchange of influences" (1950:186)] he also argues that "the superordination of one ruler is the cause of a commonness [among the ruled]" (1950:192; see also his discussion of the "mass" at 197–206). Merton mentions "role-models" (1957:302) and "influentials" as "individuals or groups [that are] taken as guides to behavior and evaluation in different social spheres" (1957:327–328), and I take these, too, as references to imitation social structures.

"Cooperation" social structures include those where the participants are doing different things, causal power is equally distributed, and the behaviors are compatible—indeed, they are complementary. A string, jazz, or barbershop quartet approximates this case. Mead's reference to "teamwork [where the individual] is doing something different from the others, even though what the others do determines what he is to do" (1934:273) may be cited here. Here, too, we have the basic idea behind Durkheim's "organized" social structure, Spencer's "industrial" social system, and Marx's (advanced, not primitive) "communism."

"Administration" social structures include those where cooperation is causally dominated by some participant or participants. A symphony orchestra almost epitomizes this case, and of course Weber may be cited for his definition of "legal authority with a bureaucratic administrative staff" wherein each official has "a specified sphere of competence" and "the organization of offices follows the principle of hierarchy; that is, each lower office is under the control and supervision of a higher one" (1947:330, 331). Marx, too: "All combined labor on a large scale requires, more or less, a directing authority, in order to secure the harmonious working of the individual activities. . . . A single violin player is his own conductor; an orchestra requires a separate one" (1978:385).

"Competition" social structures include those where the participants are doing the same things, causal power is equally distributed, but the behaviors are incompatible. Tennis tournaments and the baseball World Series approximate this case insofar as no ties are permitted in them. Durkheim notes that the "struggle for existence becomes more acute" the more given individuals engage in the same behaviors: "The judge is never in competition with the business man, but the brewer and the wine-grower, the clothier and the manufacturer or silks, the poet and the musician, often try to supplant each other. As for those who have exactly the same functions they can forge ahead only to the detriment of others" (1933:267). Park and Burgess also note that "It is a characteristic of competition, where unrestricted, that it is invariably more severe among organisms of the same than of different species" (1921:513)—a regularity Durkheim attributes to circumstance: "As long as [individuals] have more resources than they need, they can still live side by side, but if [they have too little resources,] war breaks out, and it is as violent as this insufficiency is the more marked" (1933:266).

At this point it seems useful to depart somewhat from the order in which I have been discussing the types of social structure shown in Fig. 3.3 and take up "conflict" social structure because it is so often discussed together with "competition." Thus, Simmel argues that "The pure form of the competitive struggle is above all not offensive and defensive . . . each competitor by himself aims at the goal, without using his strength on the adversary," while in conflict "victory over the adversary not only automatically secures, but itself is, the prize of victory" (1955:57, 58, 57). Similarly, Park and Burgess argue that "conflict or rivalry [is] *conscious* when competitors identify one another as rivals or as enemies" (1921:507); Boulding asserts that "conflict may be defined as a situation of competition in which the parties are *aware* of the incompatibility of potential future positions and in which each party *wishes* to occupy a position that is incompatible with the wishes of the other" (1962:5); and Coser defines social conflict as "a struggle over values and claims to scarce status, power, and resources in which the aims of the opponents are to neutralize, injure, or eliminate their rivals" (1956:8).

For my own part, however, I again emphasize the deliberate exclusion, from the present discussion of physical behavior and social structure, of all considerations of psychical behavior and cultural structure—and therefore of "aims," "consciousness," "awareness," and "wishes"—reserving them for examination in the chapter following this one. Once this exclusion has been made, it seems that we are left with only one specifically physical behavior distinction between competition and conflict: in competition, the participants are doing the same things—that is, moving in the same direction—but in conflict they are doing different things: the first is attacking the second and the second is attacking the first (or is defending itself).

It is also useful to discuss the next two types in Fig. 3.3, namely, "dominance" and "oppression" social structures, together insofar as they differ in the same way that "competition" and "conflict" differ. My reference to "dominance" relies heavily on the usage of that term in ethological studies such as is reflected in Etkin's statement that "precedence in competition assumed by an individual and acquiesced to by other members of the group is called 'behavioral dominance' " (1964:13), and in Wilson's remark that "the dominance of one member of a group over another [is] measured by superiority in aggressive encounters and order of access to food, mates, resting sites, and other objects promoting survivorship and reproductive fitness" (1975:11; see also 257).[33] Note that in these definitions, dominance social structure occurs among individuals who are all doing the same thing—that is, all seeking access to food, mates, resting sites, and so on. That their similar behaviors must be situationally incompatible if dominance social structure is to occur, however, is indicated by Schneirla, who asserts that "Describable dominance hierarchies appear under rather special conditions, particularly when groups of [individuals] are confined within a small space, when incentives (i.e., food and drink) are restricted in quantity or in accessibility, or when responsiveness is high . . . ." (1946:396)

In the literature devoted specifically to human social phenomena, the concept of "stratum," and especially "class," rests specifically on dominance, insofar as higher strata or classes are regarded as having more power and as securing for themselves a larger portion of given scarce resources than do lower ones. Note that dominance does not necessarily imply conflict or oppression.

"Oppression" social structures, however, include what Marx and Engels have in mind when they assert that "Hitherto, every form of society has been based . . . on the antagonism of oppressing and oppressed classes" (1978:483), and that oppression consists in institutionalized attacks by one class on the livelihoods, freedoms, and lives of another class. Note that here again power is unevenly distributed, as in the case of dominance social structure, but the participating indi-

---

[33] For present descriptive purposes, the behavior in question need not promote survivorship or anything else; only the behavioral superiority is essential.

viduals are manifesting different, rather than the same, behaviors—as in conflict, one is attacking the other and that other is defending itself, but the difference in power is clear and well-established.[34]

"Segregation" social structures include all those in which, by reason of temporal synchronization (e.g., use of the same athletic field for football, baseball, soccer, and track events—but at different times), or by reason of spatial coordination (e.g., use of the same time for medical, educational, military, manufacturing, and merchandising activities—but at different places), or distance in both respects, the behaviors of participants occur in situations so isolated as to make irrelevant their comparison with respect to sameness-difference of function and equality-inequality of power. Thus, Eisenstadt says the "pattern of segregative change" in traditional societies is characterized by among other things,

> a small degree of coalescence in the directions of change among tendencies toward restructuring the major components of the macrosocietal order [and] a low level of convergence among protest movements and between them and the more central political struggle (1978a:73).

Park and Burgess (with some editorial interjections on my part) point out interactions between this social structural form and others shown in Fig. 3.3:

> The first effect of the introduction of competition [and conflict—ed.] in any society is to break up all types of isolation and provincialism. . . . But as competition continues, natural and social selection come into play. Successful types [i.e., dominance and oppression social structures—ed.] emerge in the process of competitive struggle while variant individuals . . . withdraw or are ejected from the group. Exiled variants . . . under auspicious circumstances may in turn form a community [within which all of the remaining eight social structural forms—unison, imitation, cooperation, etc.—may then develop—ed.]. . . . The circle of isolation is then complete (1921:232).

Now, in conclusion regarding Fig. 3.3, the following points deserve some emphasis. First, the typology of forms shown in that figure is intended to complement the typology of contents of social structure discussed earlier in this chapter. Thus, any and all of the forms discussed may be used to describe social structures of any given content. That is, unison, imitation, cooperation, administration, competition, dominance, conflict, oppression, and, to a limited extent, segregation

---

[34] Gouldner identifies "exploitation" merely as referring to "a relationship in which unearned income results from certain kinds of unequal exchange" (1960:165), but when it is noted that his discussion of exploitation follows mention of "power disparities" as means of maintaining unequal exchanges, it seems reasonable to claim that he has in mind "oppression" social structure.

may all describe social structures of economic, political, educational-religious, biological reproductive, or whatever, substantive content.

Second, what may appear to be one form at a given hierarchic level of social structure may appear as quite another form at another level. And similarly, what may appear to be one form at a given moment may appear as another at some other moment. For example, a season's competition, such as between teams in a professional football league, may resolve into a sequence of two-team weekend conflicts and each such conflict may resolve into two sets of simultaneous cooperations at the team level and many sets of simultaneous conflicts at the player level. This means that when describing the form of social structures—no less than when describing their content—it is essential to declare the hierarchic level and the span of time and space to which the description pertains.

Finally, few empirically observable forms of physical behavior coincidences are likely to be pure types; mixed types seem likely to prevail in the forms as well as in the content of social structures. For example, as Simmel says over and over again, conflict is usually mixed with cooperation ("there probably exists no social unit in which convergent and divergent currents among its members are not inseparably interwoven" [1955:15]), and as Clark says, oppression is often mixed with segregation: " 'Ghetto' was the name for the Jewish quarter in sixteenth-century Venice. Later it came to mean any section of a city to which Jews were confined. . . . The dark ghettos [of America] are social, political, educational, and—above all—economic colonies" (1967:11).

SUMMARY

This chapter has tried to formulate some principles for describing social structure—defined as interorganism *physical* behavior regularities. Beginning with a typology of physical behaviors that an individual human being—or, in principle, any other living organism—can manifest (Fig. 3.1), I proposed the descriptive aggregation of such behaviors within the same individual into role-performances and then into role-performance subsets and sets—defined as all the physical behaviors that a given individual manifests toward and receives from any single object, in the first case, and toward some analytically selected set of objects, in the second.

At this point, the shift was made from the perspective of the individual participant in social structure to the perspective of the social structure in which he/she participates by arguing that role-performance sets and social statuses represent the same observations (i.e., aggregated physical behaviors of individuals) but seen from these two different perspectives (Fig. 3.2).

The perspective of social structure was then held to call for two kinds of descriptive principles. According to the first, different individuals' social statuses (their role-performance sets) may be *aggregated* into function-differentiated situses and the latter may then be aggregated into the social structure of an entire society (or of any social phenomenon of any size whatever). According to the second kind of principle, the regular temporal and/or spatial *coincidence* of two or more individuals' physical behaviors, role-performance, and role-performance sets (as well as of their aggregates, namely, two or more situses in social structure) may be described systematically (Fig. 3.3).

4

Cultural Structure

This chapter tries to do the same things for cultural structure that Chapter 3 tried to do for social structure. That is, it tries to specify (1) kinds of psychical behaviors; (2) certain aggregates, within the same individual, of such behaviors; (3) certain aggregates, across different individuals, of such behaviors; and (4) certain forms assumed by the coincidences, between individuals, of these behaviors and their aggregates.

INDIVIDUAL PSYCHICAL BEHAVIORS

Chapter 2 has argued that we cannot describe individual psychical behavior in the same terms with which we describe physical behavior because although the latter may have interindividual (as well as intraindividual) effects, the former can only have intraindividual effects. It follows that the inferral of "effects" or "functions" as means of differentiating among psychical behaviors must be given a more limited, exclusively intraindividual meaning than in the case of physical behavior. In acknowledging this distinction, it is customary to describe psychical behavior in terms of its "orientation" rather than its "function."

Within this generally established custom, I then partition "orientation" into two dimensions: the mode of orientation and the referent of orientation (corresponding to the direction and object of effect in the case of physical behavior).

Modes of Orientation

Let us begin by distinguishing between cognitive (believing), cathectic (desiring), and conative (behavior-readying) modes of orientation. Where I excluded such stratification variables as "prestige, "rights and duties," "expectations," and "psychic gratifications" from the chapter on social structure, I explicitly include them all in cultural structure. Thus, in cognitive orientations I include all existential beliefs—all beliefs about the way the world was, is, and/or will be—and therefore share Parsons' and Shils' view that "The cognitive mode . . . would include the 'location' of an object in the actor's total object-world, the determination of its properties and actual and potential functions, its differentiations from other objects, and its relations to certain general classes" (1951:59).

In cathectic orientations I include all desires, aversions (i.e., identifications of gratifying and aversive stimuli), and emotions—in short, "feeling."[1] Murray and Kluckhohn say

> certain specific objects, or kinds of objects, may become more or less enduringly attractive or repellent to the subject. In such cases, we say that the object has acquired a positive value, or positive cathexis, that is, the power to evoke affection and to attract; or that it has acquired a negative value or negative cathexis, that is, the power to evoke dislike (either antagonism, fear, or revulsion) (1961:11; see also Kluckhohn and others, 1951:395).

Similarly, Parsons and Shils define the "cathectic mode" of "motivational orientation" as involving "the various processes by which an actor invests an object with affective significance" (1951:59).[2]

---

[1] It should be especially noted that I do not here distinguish between desires and aversions that are "justified—'morally' or by reasoning or by aesthetic judgments" (Kluckhohn and others, 1951:396) and those that are not so justified, and therefore I do not distinguish between a "cathectic mode" and an "appreciative mode," where the latter implies the individual's commitment "to standards by which the appropriateness or consistency of the cathexis of an object or class of objects is assessed," standards which are independent of the desire or aversion itself (see Parsons and Shils, 1951:59–60; compare Habermas' distinction between "postulatory" and "critical" usages of language [1976:218]). Similarly, I do not distinguish here between cathexis and value as do Kluckhohn and others when they claim that "a cathexis is ordinarily a short-term and narrow response, whereas value implies a broader and long-term view" (1951:399). For my purposes, the only essential thing for a cathectic orientation is that it contain a desire and/or aversion, regardless of its origin, justification, scope, or consequence—although, of course, all of the latter may be employed in drawing finer distinctions among kinds of cathectic orientations.

[2] An essential difference between Parsons and Shils' conceptualization and my own is that the former distinguishes between "aspects of the actor's orientation . . . which are related to actual or potential gratification or deprivation of the actor's need-dispositions," and "aspects of the actor's orientation which commit him to the observance of certain norms, standards, criteria of selection" (1951:58, 59), respectively. This distinction leads Parsons and Shils to conceptualize what I regard as redundant sets of cognitive, cathectic, and conative orientations—that is, "three modes of *value*-orientation, which

In conative, behavior-readying or "predispositional" orientations I include two closely related psychical processes. The first involves adjusting cognitive and cathectic orientations into a personally acceptable correspondence—because what we believe and disbelieve about the world affects what we want and avoid in the world, and vice versa. The second process involves selecting the specific behaviors to be actually manifested in the cognized world toward the cathected ends—because every individual has some large repertory of possible behaviors and all of the behaviors in that repertory cannot be manifested at once. These are the processes Parsons and Shils seem to have in mind (although in reverse order, and they call the conative orientation "evaluative") when they say

> The evaluative mode [of motivational orientation] involves the various processes by which an actor allocates his energy among the various actions with respect to various cathected objects in an attempt to optimize gratification. Thus it would include the processes by which an actor organizes his cognitive and cathectic orientations into intelligent plans (1951:59, emphasis removed).[3]

Along the same lines, Murray and Kluckhohn list nine characteristics of "conation," all of which implicate some form of judgment and energy allocation. For example, the conating individual is said to "choose between alternative courses of action," "persist in the face of difficulties," "schedule and organize activities," "choose among the demands, claims, enticements, and suggestions that are made by other people," and so on (1961:25–26).

Now consider some examples in which cognitive, cathectic, and conative modes of orientation are mentioned together—albeit under varying rubrics and in varying order.

Homans, as noted in Chapter 3, builds his analysis of the human group, in part, on the concept "sentiment," defined as referring to "internal states of the human body. Laymen and professional psychologists call these states by various names: drives, emotions, feelings, affective states, sentiments, attitudes" (1950:37–38). Thus, Homans here concentrates on cathectic orientations, overlooking cognitive and conative orientations entirely. Homans' later and somewhat *ad hoc* introduction of the concept "norm," however, does implicate the latter two orientations ("A norm . . . is an idea in the minds of the members of the group . . . speci-

---

parallel the [three] modes of *motivational* orientation" (1951:60, emphasis added). I do not draw such a distinction here, but regard the desire to "observe certain norms" as a desire for a particular kind of "potential gratification," therefore regard "value-orientation" as subsumed by "motivational orientation," and both as subsumed by cathectic orientation.

[3]Note that according to the conceptualization being put forward here, conative orientation requires neither "optimization" of gratification (both maximization and minimization are entirely acceptable alternatives) nor "intelligent" plans (they may well be deemed "unintelligent" by some criterion).

fying what the members or other men should do, ought to do, are expected to do under given circumstances" [1950:123]), inasmuch as the recognition of "given circumstances" is cognitive, and the readying of "what the members or other men should do" is conative. All three orientations appear in Homans' discussion of "opinion" except that he calls the cognitive orientation "situation," the cathectic, again, "sentiment," and the conative "norm":

> Suppose . . . that one asks a design engineer to give his opinion on a certain subject. . . . His answer depends upon at least three factors that mutually reinforce one another. First, there is an *existing state of affairs . . . as this situation is seen by the person* of whom the question is asked. Second, there is the expression of a *sentiment* which inevitably expresses some degree of liking or disliking, favor or disfavor, approval or disapproval. . . . And third, there is some standard or *norm* on the basis of which the engineer decides whether he likes something or not. . . . When we are asked not only how we feel about something, but why we feel as we do, we refer to the norm (1950:409– 410, emphasis added).[4]

Parsons and Shils say "Action is organized by cognitive, cathectic, and evaluative modes of motivational orientation" (1951:72),[5] and their schema is close to mine except that (as indicated above) I call their "evaluative" mode conative, and hold that evaluation, properly so called, may be cognitive or cathectic.[6] Another of their statements comes still closer to my view except that I do not require conation to be "normatively regulated":

> The actor's system of orientations is constituted by a great number of specific orientations. Each of these "orientations of action" is a "conception" (explicit or implicit, conscious or unconscious) which the actor has of the situation in terms of what he wants (his ends), what he sees (how the situation looks to him), and how he intends to get from the objects he sees the things he wants (his explicit or implicit, normatively regulated "plan" of action) (1951:54).

Judging from this, although Parsons defines learning only as "that set of processes by which . . . new cognitive orientations, new values, new objects, new expres-

---

[4] Note that in Homans' illustration the engineer is being asked to make a physical, albeit verbal, reply to a verbal question. It therefore becomes apparent that the engineer's use of a norm involves not only the moral or other justification that Homans emphasizes, but a judgment and an allocation of energies to the verbal reply he actually gives rather than to others that he might have given. I therefore classify what Homans refers to as a "norm" as a conative orientation.

[5] Parsons and Shils also differentiate affect and cathexis: "*cathexis* is broader in its reference than the term *affect:* it is *affect plus object*. It is *object-oriented affect*" (1951:10).

[6] Parsons and Shils themselves argue that "Evaluation rests on standards which may be either cognitive standards of truthfulness, appreciative standards of appropriateness, or moral standards of rightness" (1951:5).

sive interests [are acquired by the individual]" (1951:203), he would almost certainly want to include new (conative) skills as well. And although Boocock says "The commonly recognized things that are learned in school are knowledge (history, mathematics, and so on) and skills (reading, writing, computing, and so on)," she also notes that "Sociologists have pointed out that schools teach other things as well" (1980:5)—most prominently, (cathectic) values.

Merton and Barber name the orientations "cognitive," "affective," and "conative" when they note that Eugen Bleuler

> identified three types of ambivalence: the emotional (or affective) type in which the same object arouses both positive and negative feelings . . . the voluntary (or conative) type in which conflicting wishes make it difficult or impossible to decide how to act; and the intellectual (or cognitive) type, in which men hold contradictory ideas (Merton, 1976:3).[7]

In this connection, we should note Merton's equifinal (see Chapter 14) argument that identical instances of racial and ethnic discrimination may be explained cognitively ("The employer . . . may discriminate against Negroes on the ground of the honest and ignorant conviction that they are inherently less intelligent than whites"), and/or cathectically ("discrimination is in part sustained by a socialized reward system . . . [and] by the direct gains to those who discriminate"), and/or conatively ("discrimination is sustained . . . also by cultural norms that legitimize discrimination" [1976:200, 201]).[8]

Finally, let us briefly cite Lenski, who names the cognitive, cathectic, and conative orientations "world view," "values," and "norms" and regards them as "elements" of the "ideology of a society" (1970:45); and Bourdieu, who names them "perceptions," "appreciations," and "dispositions" (1981:315).

Having considered all these substantively similar although terminologically different classifications of individual psychical behavior, let us note three other concepts that describe linkages between cognitive, cathectic, and conative orientations, on the one hand, and physical behaviors, on the other. In the cognitive-physical linkage we have visual, auditory, tactile, olfactory, and gustatory "perceptions," which imply both the physical behaviors of acquiring data through sensory organs and the psychical behaviors of selecting and preliminarily encoding the data

---

[7] They also speak, however, of ambivalence as comprising "mingled feelings, mingled beliefs, and mingled actions" (Merton, 1976:3). "Actions" are the confusing anomaly here: conative orientations are psychical behaviors that *ready* physical actions; they are not the actions themselves. It may also be noted that Merton derogates the "cognitive," "affective," and "conative" trichotomy (albeit under slightly different rubrics) when he criticizes Parsons for "resurrecting the ancient categories of cognition, volition, and affection. . . . One should be sensitive to the possibility that the elements in each of these spheres may be so heterogeneous as to put such general categories into serious question" (1948:167).

[8] Obviously, I assume "rewards" are cathected, and "norms" ready behavior.

thereby collected. In the cathectic-physical linkage we have the concept "drive," which implies both psychical desire and physical acts toward gratification. And in the conative-physical linkage we have linguistic, motor, and other "habits," which imply both psychical behavior-readinesses and the physical manifestations of those readied behaviors.

Referents of Orientation

As studies of sensory deprivation indicate, individuals cannot cognize, cathect, or conate in a vacuum; each mode of orientation must be directed toward some referent. In order to systematize such referents, I employ the same typology as was applied to the "objects" of physical behavior (see Fig. 3.1).[9]

In the only other sociological conceptualization of the possible referents of orientation of which I am aware, Parsons and Shils argue that

> A situation provides two major classes of objects to which the actor . . . may be oriented. These are either (1) nonsocial, that is, physical objects or accumulated cultural resources, or (2) social objects, that is, individual actors and collectivities. Social objects include the subject's own personality as well as the personalities of other individuals (1951:5)

and by "accumulated cultural resources" or "cultural objects," Parsons and Shils mean

> for example, laws, ideas, recipes . . . when these are taken as *objects* of orientation . . . [that is, when] the actor-subject sees these things existing outside of himself. The same laws and ideas may eventually become internalized elements of culture for the actor-subject; *as such* they will not be cultural objects but components of the actor-subject's system of action (1951:58).

This conceptualization, while it includes the same distinctions I do between self and other people, and between people and things, seems gravely and complicatedly flawed in at least one of its principal categories. In my view, "laws," "ideas," and "recipes," or other cultural phenomena can only exist internally, in the minds of individual organisms, and never outside such minds.[10] Of course, it may seem

[9] I regard orientations toward pure abstractions like "number" or "dimension" as directed toward one's own and others' minds.

[10] Parsons and Shils' conferral of external existence on ideas derives from their distinction between culture as an "embodiment in the orientation systems of concrete actors" and culture as "a body of artifacts and as systems of symbols" (1951:7). Thus,

that when we say "I got this idea from that book" we mean the idea was in the book. But what we really mean is that ideas already contained in our minds (as remembered perceptions, remembered systems of printed characters, and remembered rules of correspondence between these two) are stimulated to form new combinations when we perceive certain arrangements of such printed characters. The problem of deciphering "forgotten" languages and "secret" codes lies not in the characters laid on paper, stone, or clay but in our minds: we do not have the ideas which these characters can properly stimulate. However, having the necessary ideas is a matter of degree and not an all-or-nothing affair: if a given individual knows *anything* about a given idea or law, the idea or law is internal to the individual to the extent of that knowledge. As a result, in order for an idea or law to be internal to a given individual, I do not require that the idea be grasped "fully" (whatever that may mean) or that "intense guilt" (Parsons and Shils, 1951:8) be experienced when breaking the law. This first objection to Parsons and Shils' conceptualization extends, of course, to their assertion that ideas become social objects when internalized by self and others—thereby becoming part of "the subject's own personality as well as the personalities of other individuals." Thus, it seems reasonable to argue not only that ideas are always internalized, but that they become social only by coinciding across two or more individuals.

Returning, therefore, to the six types of objects of individual physical behavior presented in Chapter 3, and cross-classifying these with the cognitive, cathectic, and conative modes of orientation discussed earlier in this chapter, we have the typology shown in Fig. 4.1. By regarding as "referents" the same broad classification of phenomena that Fig. 3.1 regards as "objects," Fig. 4.1 suggests the capacity of human minds to know, to desire, and to mobilize action toward just those aspects of the world which our bodies are capable of physically manipulating—an important premise on which all the interdependences of thought and action, role-expectation and role-performance, and pure and applied science are founded.

---

symbols, being objectifiable in writing and in graphic and plastic representation, can be separated from the action systems in which they originally occurred and yet preserve intact the "way of orienting" which they represent; for, when they do happen to be oriented by an actor (to whom each element is meaningful), they will arouse in him the original complex manner of orientation (1951:160).

As a result, say Parsons and Shils, "unlike need-dispositions and role-expectations, the *symbols* which are the postulated controlling entities [in the case of culture] are not internal to the systems whose orientations they control" (1951:160). It is noteworthy, however, that Parsons' thought on this matter seems to undergo an evolution toward the conceptualization adopted here. Thus, Kroeber and Parsons, writing seven years later than Parsons and Shils, mute the inclusion of physical artifacts in culture when they restrict culture to "transmitted and created content and patterns of values, ideas, and other symbolic-meaningful systems as factors in the shaping of human behavior and the artifacts produced through behavior" (1958:582, 583). Parsons, writing alone, finally drops all mention of physical artifacts in defining culture: "The cultural-system focus . . . is on 'patterns' of meaning, e.g., of values, of norms, of organized knowledge and beliefs, of expressive 'form' " (1961a:34).

Referent of	Mode of orientation		
orientation	Cognitive	Cathectic	Conative
Self			
Mind	a	b	c
Body	d	e	f
Other people			
Mind	g	h	i
Body	j	k	l
Things			
Living	m	n	o
Nonliving	p	q	r

Figure 4.1. Typology of individual psychical behaviors.

Moreover, insofar as Fig. 4.1 identifies three different kinds of "meaning" with which individuals can endow six different components of the world, it explicates and expands Weber's claim that

> processes or conditions, whether they are animate or inanimate, human or non-human, . . . [possess] meaning if they [can] be related to action in the role of means or ends [and do not constitute] only the stimulus, the favoring or hindering circumstances (1947:93).

That is, assuming "ends" may comprise any or all of the six kinds of referents of cathectic orientation, and "means" may comprise any or all of the six kinds of referents of conative orientation, Figure 4.1 expands Weber's typology asserting that the six kinds of referents of cognitive orientation (which Weber apparently includes among "only the stimul[i]" of action and therefore claims are "devoid of meaning") can indeed possess meaning, and meaning precisely as the (cognized) "favoring or hindering circumstances" of action. It is for the conferral of this cognitive meaning of the world and its components that pure science is specialized, just as applied science is specialized for the conferral of conative meaning, while ethics and aesthetics are specialized for the conferral of cathectic meaning (see Part III).

A Sociological Typology of Individual Psychical Behaviors

Cells (a) through (f) classify ego's psychical behaviors of self-awareness, self-respect, and self-direction. And it is noteworthy that these categories do not include ego's direct reactions to others' thoughts and feelings about ego (by contrast, similar categories in Fig. 3.1 do include reactions to others' physical behaviors toward ego). This is because, as elaborated in Chapter 2, others' thoughts and feelings cannot impinge upon ego unless physically manifested or "expressed"— whereupon they become classifiable according to Figure 3.1 as behaviors physically received by ego, and therefore as self-nurturing and/or self-teaching behaviors. The latter categories (in both their proactive and reactive senses) are thus conceptualized as means whereby ego's psychical behaviors, toward him/herself and toward everything else, may be affected by others', and by his/her own, physical behaviors.

Cells (g) through (l) classify ego's beliefs about, appreciations and approvals of, and readinesses to behave physically toward, other people—that is, both true and false beliefs; both positive and negative appreciations, approvals, and attractions; and both propelling and restraining behavior readinesses.

Finally, cells (m) through (r) classify a similar set of beliefs, appreciations, approvals, attractions, and readinesses that have living and nonliving things as their referents.

Again, as with Fig. 3.1, I emphasize that all these categories are inevitably fuzzy around the edges and overlapping; that they are all liable to finer internal distinctions; and that they are capable of being aggregated analytically in two ways: both within the same individual and across different individuals.

WITHIN-INDIVIDUAL AGGREGATES OF PSYCHICAL BEHAVIORS

Norms

It will be recalled that Chapter 3 did not specify any particular way in which individual physical behaviors should be regarded as aggregated into a role-performance: a constructive behavior may just as easily be preceded, accompanied, or followed by a destructive behavior, as by a transportative, or another constructive, behavior in a given role. The constituents of role-*performances*, then, are individual physical behaviors in no necessary order or combination. Sociological convention seems to have it, however, that the constituents of role-*expectations* (i.e., prescriptions, proscriptions, and permissions) are "norms," and that although the referents of norms vary, each norm always combines cognitive, conative, and cathectic modes of orientation—as follows.

Consider the norm which may be formulated as "drivers should stop their cars at red traffic lights." Four kinds of expectations may be regarded as linked together in this and every other norm: there is an *actor* expectation ("driver"), a *situation* expectation ("at red traffic lights"), a *response* expectation ("stop car"), and a fourth, *consequence*, expectation is implied ("and you won't get a traffic ticket, or get hit by other cars, or run over anybody"). A norm thus combines elements of Fig. 4.1: the first two expectations are cognitive inasmuch as they contain existential beliefs; the third expectation is conative inasmuch as it readies a behavior; and the fourth expectation is cathectic inasmuch as it indicates a desirable goal. Norms, in short, tell us—in a single instruction—*who* should (or should not, or may) do *what* (physically and/or psychically), *how, when and where,* and *why.* Thus, the contrast that Knorr-Cetina draws between "a normative notion of social order" and a "cognitive" notion—such that in the former, "society is integrated by shared values and obligations," whereas in the latter, society is integrated by "language use and cognitive processes that represent and interpret the relevance of values and obligations" (1981:3; see also 7)—is rejected here in favor of a conceptualization of every norm as comprising cognitive as well as cathectic (and also conative) elements.[11]

As already indicated, any and all of the orientational referents shown in Fig. 4.1 may be implicated in a norm—that is, the actor expectation may refer to any combination of aspects of the self; the situation expectation may refer to any combination of aspects of other people and/or things; the response expectation may ready behavior toward aspects of the self, other people, and/or things; and the consequence expectation may indicate as desirable some state of aspects of the self, other people, and/or things.

It is essential to recognize that in describing a norm in this way I am referring only to expectations or "labels"; not actual actors or situations or responses or consequences but anticipatory mental images which serve as perceptual criteria for classifying actual observations when and if they are made. (Note also that I am not concerned here with how such expectations come into existence; that is an explanatory matter left for Part II.) The only existence of such expectations is within the individual participant's central nervous system or "mind," and that is all I am concerned with at present; the empirical accuracy and practical efficacy of their contents are other matters entirely.

---

[11] Knorr-Cetina also identifies the supposed normative-versus-cognitive cultural structural differences with a difference in the level and direction of explanatory variables (see Chapter 12): "The normative conception of order is at the same time a macrolevel conception of order," but "the cognitive turn [is] attributed to microsociological approaches" (1981:3); and

> Instead of being seen as a monolithic system which regulates individual action, order [in the cognitive notion] comes to be seen as an upshot of concrete, communicative interaction. . . . Social order is not that which holds society together by somehow controlling individual wills, but that which comes about in the mundane but relentless transaction of these wills (1981:7).

In my schema, however, both "values and obligations" and "cognitive processes" are psychical behaviors whose only locus is the mind of the individual participant; both can regulate individual action, and both may be influenced by the people—both singly and in various aggregates—in that individual's environment (see Chapter 10).

Other Conceptualizations of Norms

Before going any further with this conceptualization of norms, let me compare it with others that are already in the literature, and try to show how it subsumes and integrates them.

Parsons defines a norm as "a verbal description of the concrete course of action . . . regarded as desirable, combined with an injunction to make certain future actions conform to this course. An instance of a norm is the statement: 'Soldiers should obey the orders of their commanding officers' " (1937:75), thus explicitly mentioning only the response and actor expectations of a norm. However, in discussing this definition, Parsons implicates the consequence expectation when he identifies the term "normative" with the specification of "an end in itself" and says "When the question is raised as to why obedience is valued as a means it will lead . . . eventually [to] an ultimate end, whether it be military efficiency for its own sake or an indispensable means to other ends, such as material security" (1937:75). The situation expectation comes vaguely into the picture when Parsons remarks that the actualization of a norm "depends upon the effort of the individuals acting as well as upon the *conditions* in which they act" (1937:397, emphasis added). Oddly enough, in a later expression Parsons omits reference to the consequence expectation but includes the actor, situation, and response expectations: "normative expectations . . . define what people in various statuses and roles in one or more various senses, ought to do under various circumstances" (1968a: 323–324, emphasis removed). Parsons' most explicit and complete enumeration of the four norm expectations is found, however, in his description of the "action frame of reference": "The theory of action . . . conceives of . . . behaviors as oriented to the attainment of ends in situations, by means of the normatively regulated expenditure of energy," and "the frame of reference of the theory of action involves actors, a situation of action, and the orientation of the actor to that situation" (1951:53 and 56).

Only the renaming of the *"action* frame of reference" as the *"actor's* frame of reference,"[12] and specifically the actor's *normative* frame of reference, is needed to make the correspondence virtually complete.

Smelser, too, implicates the four norm expectations but in a manner that may not be immediately apparent. Thus, he defines values as "desirable end states which act as a guide to human behavior. . . . Norms . . . are more specific than values,

[12] That such a renaming would fully accord with Parsons' intentions seems indicated by his statement that a social scientist's view of "a case of suicide by jumping off a bridge" depends on knowing that *"the actor anticipates 'himself,* dead in the water' " (1937:734), emphasis added), and a similar statement that the ability to analyze "a man driving his automobile to a lake to go fishing" within the "action frame of reference" depends on knowing that "to be fishing is the 'end' *toward which our man's behavior is oriented'* (Parsons and Shils, 1951:53, emphasis added).

for they specify regulatory principles which are necessary if these values are to be realized" (1962:25, 27). Although Smelser seems here to omit actor and situation expectations, the omission is soon remedied:

> values and norms . . . supply certain general ends and general rules; they do not specify, however, who will be the agents in the pursuit of valued ends. . . . We have to specify, therefore, a third component which gives more detail to social action. . . . In dealing with this third component, we ask questions such as the following: Will economic processes be carried out by individual merchants and artisans, by small firms, or by gigantic corporations? . . . Most of what sociologists call "social organization" or "social structure" . . . is specified by this third component of "mobilization into organized action" (1962:27, 28).

It is essential to note that Smelser does not argue here that "mobilization" is, as one might otherwise expect, collective *physical* behavior (social structure). Instead, he argues that the latter *"is specified by"* mobilization, thereby making mobilization a type of collective *psychical* behavior (cultural structure) that names the "agents" (actors) who are to pursue (response) the specified values (consequences).

Smelser also mentions the situation expectations contained by norms but the mention is again somewhat deceptive. Thus, "situational facilities" are said to refer "to the actor's knowledge of the opportunities and limitations of the environment" (1962:28)—but note that Smelser does not argue, as one might expect, that situational facilities are *physical* phenomena; they are "the actor's *knowledge*" of such phenomena. On close examination, then, it appears that all four of Smelser's "components of social action" (i.e., values, norms, mobilization, and situational facilities) are normative and thus turn out to be virtually identical to the "action frame of reference" and therefore also to the four components of norms being set forth here.

Williams says "A norm is a rule, standard, or pattern for action. . . . Social norms are rules for conduct. The norms are the standards by reference to which behavior is judged and approved or disapproved. A norm . . . [is] a cultural (shared) definition of desirable behavior" (1968a:204)—thus leaving the actor expectation only implicit, omitting the situation expectation entirely, specifying the response expectation (as "conduct" and "behavior"), and only implying the consequence expectation (in the references to approval and disapproval). Homans, however, somewhat more explicitly indicates all four expectations when defining a norm as "a statement specifying how one or more persons are expected to behave in given circumstances, when reward may be expected to follow conformity to the norm and punishment deviance from it" (1974:97).[13]

---

[13] In an earlier attempt, Homans proposes a more complex definition where a norm is a psychical expectation plus a physical reaction: "A statement . . . is a norm only if any departure of real behavior from the norm is followed by some punishment" (1950:123).

Blake and Davis, similarly, define a norm as "any standard or rule that states what human beings should or should not think, say, or do, under given circumstances" (1964:456). Here, the actor expectation is indicated by "human being"; the situation expectation is indicated by "given circumstances"; the response expectation is indicated by "should or should not do"; and the consequence expectation is left implicit. It is especially worth noticing that Blake and Davis imply that a behavioral "standard or rule" must have a certain causal explanation (namely, learning) in order to be called a "norm";

> the intricate interactions of an ant colony or a beehive, like those of a prairie dog village, are governed mainly by instinctive reactions to natural and social stimuli. . . . In human groups, on the other hand, instinctive responses are channeled or even repressed by the enforcement of behavioral rules that are transmitted by symbolic communication. . . . Obviously, then, if the structure of human societies is to be understood . . . the normative aspect must be dealt with (1964:457).

In the view adopted here, a norm is a norm no matter what its explanation may be, and examination of the several variables that may causally explain norms is reserved for Part II.[14]

Moreover, in the view adopted here, a norm is a norm no matter what its effects may be; a norm, indeed, may have no measurable effects whatever (that is, none beyond those indicators necessary to observe it) and still be a norm. Because the causes and the effects of a norm are here regarded as explanatory rather than descriptive problems (and addressed in Chapters 8 and 10), Scott's view that "Normative statements are norms only when they have an effect on what somebody does" (1971:73) is rejected here.[15] The present view, instead, permits the existence of ineffective as well as effective norms and permits variability between extremes of each—a conceptual prerequisite for comparing the causal impact of norms with that of other variables.

Much closer to my own view are Wyer and Carlston, who, writing about the inference process that each individual performs, list

> five general classes of elements about which information may be available or about which judgments may be made. These elements comprise a prototypic

---

[14] Blake and Davis appear to confound their own assertion that norms cannot be instinctive when, after declaring that "If we forego the assumption that deviant motivation is to be found primarily in drives and glands, we can focus on sociological sources of deviant motives," the first source they mention rests on the implicitly instinctivistic claim that "individuals will *inevitably* react to conflicting intra- and interstatus demands with resentment and schemes for evading at least some responsibility" (1964:472, emphasis added).

[15] Scott also believes that "everything social is normative" (1971:75) and therefore adopts "normative determinism" as "a matter of definition" (1971:73). Such a priori explanatory exclusiveness is rejected here (see Part II).

social interaction situation in which one person or group responds in some fashion to another person, group, or object. . . . (1) *The actor.* Judgments of the actor may pertain to physical characteristics . . . , personality traits, abilities, motives, social groups to which he belongs, or social and vocational roles that he may occupy. (2) *The actor's behavior.* This behavior may be either overt . . . or subjective emotional reactions. . . . (3) *The recipient, or object of the behavior.* . . . (4) *The consequences* of the actor's behavior for either the actor himself or for the object. Judgments of consequences typically refer either to their desirability or their likelihood of occurrence. (5) *The situational context* in which the actor's behavior occurs (1979:9).

Once the third element is subsumed under the fourth ("consequence"), and conceivably also under the fifth ("situation"), we have exactly the four norm expectations set forth here.

Gibbs says "A norm is a belief shared to some extent by members of a social unit as to what conduct *ought to be* in particular situations or circumstances," and adds that "Everyday experience surely indicates that evaluations of conduct are conditional on characteristics of the actor, characteristics of the object of the act, and/or various situational considerations (e.g., time and/or place)" (1981:7, 12). Putting both comments together—and setting aside, for later discussion, Gibbs' requirement that a norm be "shared"—we therefore have another close approximation to the four norm expectations set forth here.[16]

Killian also comes close when he summarizes Turner's conceptualization of an "emergent norm" as including

A definition of what the situation is. . . . An indication of what sort of action is appropriate or inappropriate in this situation. . . . A set of justifications for both the constructed version of reality and of the actions defined as appropriate. . . . [and an] evaluation of population segments—potential actors—in relation to the situation as defined (1980:284)

—although the present conceptualization of a norm would specify "justifications" as cathected consequence expectations (see below), and specify that actors are "evaluated" not only in relation to the defined "situation" but also in relation to the "action" expectation and its "justification."

[16] The approximation is close, that is, assuming that by the "object" of the act Gibbs means the objective, or intended consequences, of the act and not merely the thing in which those consequences are to be realized. It should also be noted, however, that Gibbs confuses a norm—by his own definition, an internally held "belief"—with its externally observable indicator when he says "whatever else a norm may be, it is an *abstraction* from human events (necessarily the behavior of particular individuals" (1981:10). If a norm is regarded as a "belief" it is then no "abstraction from" human events or behaviors but itself *constitutes* such an event and such a behavior—although one that requires different observational procedures from those required for physical behaviors.

Now, because of its complementarity rather than its similarity or dissimilarity to these four expectational components of norms, let us consider the TOTE unit of behavior as proposed by Miller et al. These authors argue that the organization of an individual's behavior may be thought of as a sequence of four phases: First, the organism Tests "the input energies [of external and internal stimuli] against some criteria established in the organism." Second, the organism Operates or responds "if the result of the test [shows] an incongruity." Third, the organism Tests again to see if the incongruity still persists—and continues to Operate and Test, Operate and Test, until the incongruity has vanished. At that point, having exerted sufficient control over its environment and itself to create a new set of "input energies" which it takes to be congruent with the criteria established in the organism, "the organism Exits to another TOTE unit, Tests for a new incongruity, Operates, Tests, and finally Exits to the next TOTE unit, and so on" (see Miller et al., 1960:25–27).

The complementarity between the "TOTE" unit and what may be called the normative "ASRC" (Actor-Situation-Response-Consequence) unit may be summed up by saying that the former refers to phases in the developmental *form* of behavior, whereas the latter refers to components in the substantive *content* of behavior. More exactly, the TOTE unit conceptualizes the individual organism's process through time as cycling between psychical testing and physical operating behaviors (analogous to applied science, as described in Chapter 13), while physically carrying out or "executing" a psychical "plan." The ASRC unit, however, is confined to psychical behavior alone and conceptualizes the categories of substantive information the organism must have for recognizing, classifying, naming, and identifying something as testable at all (and if so, how and against what criteria) and as operable at all (and if so, how and with what anticipated results).

Thus, all four phases of the TOTE unit should be regarded as substantively problematic even when their form is taken for granted. Thus, not *all* conceivable "incongruities" must lead a given organism to respond by reducing them—or, indeed, to perceive them at all. Powers notes that "fast enough disturbances cease to be perceived, as the flickering of a movie fades and disappears when the projector is brought up to the proper speed" (1973:52–53), but what is "proper" speed for one organism (or one species of organism) may not be "proper" for another: what is defined as painful incongruity by one organism may well be defined as ecstatic congruity by another. Indeed, this is an inevitable consequence of all kinds of organismic differentiation—including the evolutionary kind. Even more fundamentally, however, the overwhelmingly vast number of incongruities necessarily go unnoticed because no finite organism can possibly have tests which detect them all. Just as clearly, not all conceivable operations or responses can have appreciable effects on a given incongruity: a pin cushion will not be sufficient to hammer nails into a two-by-four. It is just this kind of indispensable *substantive* information (i.e., about which tests and operations to apply to what, with what expected results, and when to stop operating and testing[17]) that norms supply.

Despite this difference in the referents of the TOTE unit and the ASRC unit, however, their complementarity (again, that between processual form and substantive content) makes many of the ideas of TOTE's inventors relevant to our own concerns.

Finally in connection with other views of the four norm expectations being proposed here, let us note how they underlie and explicate Matza's claim that "The major bases of negation and irresponsibility in law rest on self-defense, insanity, and accident" (1964:74). That is, if we ask why should these three, and not some other, claims form the bases in question, the answer lies in the nature of the norm expectations and their interrelations. Thus, a given *response,* having been committed by some individual and labeled as law-breaking by agents of social control, may be excused by the latter if the former can show (1) that the *situation* was such as normatively to justify the response in question, or (2) that the individual's *actor* expectation was adopted involuntarily—thereby rendering adoption of the other norm expectations equally involuntary, or (3) that the actual *consequence* of the response in question was normatively not to be expected (see Matza, 1964:76, 82, 85 for documentation of this interpretation).

Norm Accessing

In addition to conceptualizing a norm as a complex psychical behavior which, through interrelated actor, situation, response, and consequence expectations, combines cognitive, conative, and cathectic orientations toward any conceivable referent, I propose that this description of a norm also provides for its being accessed (i.e., brought to consciousness) by the individual holding it. Such accessing seems possible in four different ways: by calling for the norm by its actor expectation, by its situation expectation, by its response expectation, or by its consequence expectation. In other words, we seem to regard norms as though they were cross-filed or cross-indexed in four different ways within the mind of each participant in cultural structure.

One indexing files norms according to their *actor* expectation—such that when

---

[17] Thus, when Miller et al. ask "What is the 'stop rule' [for hammering]?," and answer that "the hammering continues until the head of the nail is flush with the surface of the work" (1960:33), they take for granted what I refer to here as the substantively variable consequence expectation of hammering norms. That is, according to *one* hammering norm the final consequence of hammering responses is certainly "head flush," but according to other hammering norms (containing other situation expectations), the final consequence may be "head one-quarter inch above surface," or "head one-sixteenth inch below surface," or "head driven to within an inch and one-quarter of surface and then bent over and driven into surface sideways."

they are called up at this address the individual forms an idea of the situations, responses, and consequences that he/she expects for given types of actors—including his/her own. Here is stored all our information about the kind of lives "burglars," "teachers," "students," "automobile mechanics," "Presbyterians," "widows," "Russians," and a host of other actor-types live. Another way of picturing the actor expectation file notes that it is made up of "role-expectation sets"—a concept derived from combining (1) the distinction proposed in Chapter 3 between role-performances and role-expectations, with (2) Merton's definition of a "role-set" as "that complement of role relationships which persons have by virtue of occupying a particular social status" (1957:369), and provided (3) that "a particular social status" is interpreted as an actor expectation and "role relationships" are interpreted as all the situation, response, and consequence expectations associated with that actor expectation.

A second indexing files norms according to *situation* expectation so that the individual can call up some idea of the actors, responses, and consequences that he/she expects for given situations. In a word, we more or less know what to expect in a prison, a school, a subway station, a sculptor's studio, or wherever: we have some idea (right or wrong) of who will be there, what they will be doing, when they will be doing it, and why.[18] Adopting Thomas' (1961) phrase, we may call this the "definition of the situation" mode of access or file, and in the spirit of that phrase we may call the first file (discussed just above) the "definition of the actor" file.

A third indexing files norms according to *response* expectation so that we have some expectation of the actors, situations, and consequences associated with given responses. In other words, using this mode of access, if I am told that a certain behavior occurred I can usually come up with a guess about whodunit, where, when, and why. Again in the spirit of Thomas' phrase, one might call this the "definition of the response" file.

Finally, a fourth indexing files norms according to *consequence* expectation so that we have some idea of why different people do the things they do in given situations. We might call this the "definition of the motivation" file.

What I have in mind by these cross-indexed files seems to be just what Powers means when, in more general terms, he distinguishes "associative addressing" from "location addressing" as methods of information storage and identifies the former with the human brain and the latter with most electronic computers: "In associative addressing, the information sent to the computing device's address input is

---

[18] Gouldner's distinction between "complementary and concrete status rights and duties" and "the generalized moral norm of reciprocity" (1960:170) depends entirely on which of two aspects of a given situation expectation are regarded as most salient to the behaving individual—that is, whether who is *present* in the situation, or what is being (or has been) *done* in the situation. Thus, "In the first case, Ego's obligations to Alter depend upon Ego's status vis-à-vis Alter; in the second case, Ego's obligations toward Alter depend on what Alter has done for Ego" (Gouldner, 1960:170).

not a location number, but a fragment of what is recorded in one or more locations in memory . . . . [so that] information may be retrieved from many locations, not just one" (1973:212–213). In any event, I hold that the posited cross-indexings of norms enable participants in a given cultural structure to construct facile and creditable answers not only to questions about the expected behavior of others but about their own expected behavior as well. Therefore, Just *who* do you think you are? Just *where* do you think you are? Just what do you think you are *doing?* Just what do you *want?* are the questions which—consciously or unconsciously, verbally or nonverbally, with casualness or urgency, good humor or hostility—we always mentally and sometimes verbally ask of others and of ourselves as we strive constantly to make sense out of the social world and ourselves in it. Norms seem to provide our basic guidelines in that ongoing construction so that it is never (under normal circumstances of both world and self) completely ad hoc, de novo, or idiosyncratic. As Nadel puts it, "We might say [the individual] carries a role map of his society in his head, indicating the way in which his role fits in amongst them" (1957:58)—or more exactly, given my parsing of "role" into role-expectation and role-performance, "indicating the way in which his role-expectation fits in amongst their role-expectations."

Note that at any given moment, of course, each participant in a cultural structure is apt to adopt certain actor expectations, certain situation expectations, and certain consequence expectations as descriptive of his/her own personal "identity" or "self," "life-space," "capabilities," and "aspirations-fears-conscience" (these concepts are discussed in Chapter 8, under slightly different rubrics). The "role map" of which Nadel speaks, then, is likely to be a polar projection with these *self-adopted* norm expectations at its center. The overall scope of the map, its detail, completeness, accuracy, rate and direction of change, may vary from person to person and from time to time as determined by age, socialization, education, access to media of mass communication, and the like.

Two other characteristics of norms should be noted. First, each norm expectation is variable in its specificity. Thus, Williams says "Norms are always to some extent both generalized and generalizable. They may refer to all human beings at all times and in all places, or they may refer only to a specific category of person in a specific type of situation" (1968a:205). At maximum generality norms become "morals" (e.g., "Everyone should everywhere and always do unto others as you would have them do unto you because this ensures peace and a clear conscience")[19]; at maximum specificity, norms become "techniques" (e.g., "Exposed

---

[19] Williams sees a continuum: "generalized norms . . . transcend the particular context and shade over by degrees into cultural values. . . . [Norms] are more specific and socially imperative than values or ideals" (1968a:206, 205; see also 1968b:284). Alexander seems to prefer exactly the opposite nomenclature when he says "Norms are the general conceptions of future expectations towards which action is directed. . . . Goals are the specific ends pursued in any given act, those ideal states which are pursued with reference to particular conditions" (1982:66). I prefer (1) to use "norm" to denote the

photographic film should only be removed from the camera in certain ways so that it will not be spoiled").[20] This implies, of course, that not only norms as entireties but each constituent expectation of a norm may vary in specificity—such that the actor expectation, for example, ranges from the most general "human being" or "living thing" designation to the usually unique combination of one's family name, given name, and nickname. At no conceivable level of expectational specificity and detail, however, is any actually observed actor, situation, response, or consequence ever indicated with perfect determinateness: the fathomless detail of perceived real life inevitably exceeds not only our most detailed descriptions (see Chapter 14) but, of course, also, and to a vastly greater extent, our most detailed and confident anticipations. As Goode puts it, "even when 'the norms of the society' are fully accepted by the individual, they are not adequate guides for individual action" (1960a:484); and Blake and Davis: "social norms are only approximations of how people should act. In specific situations, [specific] individuals must take many things into account [that are not specified by the norms]" (1964: 466).

Thus, in describing the process of learning to fly an airplane, Miller et al. argue that

> In order to be able to execute the [takeoff, flight, and landing] Plan . . . the aspiring aviator must find many small intercalated acts not specified in the instructor's original description of the Plan. The . . . instructor "knows" these intercalated acts because he knows how to fly, but they are locked in, implicit, tacit, rather than explicit and communicable (1960:83).

Moreover, Miller et al. argue, the "intercalated acts" are variable and equifinal (see Chapter 14).

> Once a strategy has been developed, alternative modes of action become possible, and we say that the person "understands" the job that he is to do. . . .

---

set of four expectations indicated above, and to treat its level of generality or specificity as a dimension of its more or less continuous variability, and (2) to use "value" or "goal" to denote (as discussed below) cathected consequence expectations of norms and therefore as potential components of every norm, regardless of its generality or specificity.

[20] At least three hypotheses may be found in the literature regarding determinants of the level of detail that is activated within a given individual. Davis argues for the power of formalization:

[N]o situation is completely defined in the sense that all the interaction is totally predictable. The nearest approach to total predictability is found in formal occasions, when the behavior is minutely regulated according to convention and when any deviation from the prescribed pattern is carefully avoided (1949:84–85).

And Homans argues that formalization is a function of group size: "The larger is the number of persons in contact with one another. . . . [the more] control becomes . . . external and formal. Persons must to a greater degree go by the rule, work by the book" (1974:364)—a point made earlier by Simmel: "the characteristics of the large group can, to a considerable extent, be explained as surrogates for the personal and immediate cohesion typical of the small group" (1950:96). Goode, however, argues for what is often associated with the absence of formality, namely, closeness: "individuals at some distance from us in the social network demand from us only a loose conformity; those who are closer define the norm itself more specifically and require a more specific performance (1960b:255, emphasis removed).

It is not necessary, fortunately, to know explicitly the rules that must be observed by a skillful performer—if it were, few of us would even be able to sit up in our cradles (1960:85, 87).

Second, each expectation contained by a given component of a norm (at whatever level of specificity) is apt to be associated with more than one expectation in the remaining components. Blake and Davis make a similar assertion: "The assumption that for each society there is one norm or one value regarding a given aspect of behavior is in most instances untrue" (1964:463). For example, the "student" actor expectation is associated with many situation expectations (e.g., lecture, library, examination, dormitory, etc.), and each of these situation expectations is associated with many response expectations, and each of these response expectations is associated with many consequence expectations.

Of course, the strengths of the associations at each point are not apt to be equal (Powers calls them "graded responses" [1973:214])—so that, for any given actor, we are likely to expect that some situations will be more common than others; some responses in those situations will be more common than others, and for each such response some consequences will be more common than others. This is what Becker has in mind when he says

A man who has been convicted of housebreaking and thereby labeled criminal is presumed to be a person likely to break into other houses. . . . Further, he is considered likely to commit other kinds of crime as well, because he has shown himself to be a person without "respect for the law" (1973:33).

It also seems to form the background for Berger's et al. similar reference to a "status-organizing process" (which might also, and perhaps better, be called a status-organi*zed* process) "by which differences in cognitions and evaluations of individuals, or social types of them, become the basis of differences in the stable and observable features of social interaction" (1977:3). The important point, however, is that the participant has more than one expectation in mind for every norm component, and thus norms can reduce but cannot eliminate the individual's cognitive, conative, and cathectic uncertainty.

For both these reasons, my image of norms does not regard the individual as mechanically calling them up as fixed and integrated wholes but as largely assembling them (or confirming their prior assembly) on the spot—that is, "ad hocing it"—under a variety of non-normative influences (see Part II), from more-or-less prefabricated and more-or-less connected actor, situation, response, and consequence expectation modules. As Hewitt and Stokes put it,

While it is clear that certain cultural elements are deeply internalized . . . relatively little of routine social action appears to be guided by deeply internalized normative structures. Man does not act like a well-programmed social robot; indeed, in much of everyday social action, variation from normatively prescribed behavior is statistically "normal" (1975:10, see also Berger et al., 1977:8–9).

And Miller et al. put it this way:

We do not mean that the Plan [i.e., the process whereby the organism controls the sequence in which its behaviors are performed] is stored in memory ready for execution down to the very last muscle twitch. Often it is a metaplan that is stored—a metaplan from which a large number of different Plans can be generated as they are needed. . . . For example, the Plan for reciting the alphabet is probably stored—memorized—directly, like any other motor skill. And so is the Plan for counting, at least through the first few hundred integers. But as the numbers begin to get large it is likely that we work in terms of a metaplan, a set of rules for generating $N + 1$ from N, rather than with a direct Plan for uttering the successive integers (1960:178).

Norm Limitations

As flexible and permissive as norms and their component actor, situation, response, and consequence expectations may be, however, this flexibility has limits. Although a given actor expectation may be linked to a variety of situation expectations, a variety of response expectations, and a variety of consequence expectations, it is not likely to be linked to *all* situation expectations, or *all* response and consequence expectations. Thus, some expectation linkages are more likely than others and the unlikely are, by definition, unconventional and may be prohibited to some degree ("We are not the sort of people who do that," or "Now is neither the time nor the place for that," etc.). Glassner and Berg, for example, argue that Jews avoid alcohol problems because they are normatively inhibited by (1) the actor expectation ("Defining alcohol problems as non-Jewish begins the cultural recipe for moderate drinking and excludes the entire group from eligibility for regular intoxication, while minimizing the possibilities for seeing alcohol use as related to one's problems"); (2) the consequence expectation ("Drinking practises . . . [emphasize] exclusion of substantive use of alcohol [i.e., to other than symbolic ends"]); (3) the response expectation; and (4) the situation expectation ("Moderate drinking and the association of alcohol with special occasions . . . is reinforced in adult peer groups through drinking with those who share these expectations and who punish and exclude others who do not" [1980:661]).

Role-Expectations

Following the identification earlier in this chapter of "role-expectation sets" with the norm-accessing actor expectation file, let us define a single role-expectation as two or more interconnected and observation-contingent norms in which the actor expectation (e.g., "automobile driver") remains constant. In Goode's terms, "the content of a given role [sic] is partly an organization of norms, that is a connection among several norms" (1960b:251, emphasis removed), and in Scott's, a "role" (sic) is "a collection of norms delimited by what a single actor may be expected to perform" (1971:85). Thus, a role-expectation, like a role-performance (see Chapter 3) is an aggregate or assembly of more elemental components. The manner in which such components are linked together, and the manner in which their linkages are contingent on observations, may be conceptualized, very roughly, as follows.

Given an actual situation that is "sensed" but not yet defined, the individual selects, from his/her full index of situation expectations, one expectation which provides a personally satisfactory definition of that situation. This definition enables the individual to "relate" to the situation by selecting, for him/herself, a relevant actor expectation. Selecting a situation expectation and an actor expectation for oneself also calls up (as indicated above) an associated range of response expectations, and each of these calls up a range of consequence expectations. When a given response expectation is selected and manifests itself in an observed response, the latter changes the situation in some way. This observed consequence is then compared with a consequence expectation selected from the range of such expectations associated with the now manifest response expectation, and the comparison yields a new situation definition. The latter calls up its associated range of response expectations; one of these is chosen and manifested—and so on.[21]

Now because the individual is pictured here as selecting, at several points, from a range of potentially appropriate expectations, the question of the criteria used in these selections arises. Parsons' pattern variables may be regarded as alternative criteria applicable to selection at two of these points—points that Parsons and Shils call "major dilemmas of orientation, a series of choices that the actor must make before the situation has a determinate meaning for him" (1951:76).[22] Briefly, the universalism-particularism and the quality-performance (ascription-achievement) pattern variables appear to be criteria for selecting situation expectations, and the

---

[21] Note that although this conceptualization interweaves role-expectations and role-performances (see Chapter 3), the analytic distinction between them remains clear.

[22] Parsons and Shils indicate that they have in mind consequence expectations as well as situation expectations when they add that "The objects of the situation do not interact with the cognizing *and cathecting* organism in such a fashion as to determine automatically the meaning of the situation" (1951:76, emphasis added).

remaining three pattern variables appear to be criteria for selecting consequence expectations—as follows.

Although the universalism-particularism pattern variable is formulated in an ambiguous way,[23] perhaps that ambiguity can be resolved by claiming that the universalism criterion instructs the individual to select a situation expectation on the basis of what is known about all individuals' experience with situations of this kind, and particularism says select one on the basis of one's own experience with situations of this kind. At this point, the quality-performance pattern variable is engaged, claiming that whether the criterion experience be universalistic or particularistic, the relevant aspect of that experience should pertain to the internal structure or "quality" of the situation, on the one hand, or to its external function or "performance," on the other.

Turning to the remaining three pattern variables, those which specify alternative criteria for selecting consequence expectations, it seems that affectivity-neutrality is pivotal here. Affectivity says draw the expectation in question from the subset that promises immediate gratification, while neutrality says draw it from the subset that promises no immediate gratification but which may contribute to some later gratification. Only if the immediate gratification subset is chosen are the specificity-diffuseness, and the self-collectivity, pattern variables called upon: Specificity says select a consequence expectation in which gratification will be focused on one or a few needs, while diffuseness says select an expectation in which gratification will be spread out over many or all needs. Whether specific or diffuse, however, to whom or what shall these gratifications go? Self answers this question by saying choose a consequence expectation in which the recipient of gratification is oneself alone, while collectivity says choose one in which the recipient is some group to which one belongs.[24]

Further, it may be argued that Parsons' "need dispositions" of the individual personality set forth categories of gratification for the self (response, approval, love, and esteem [see Parsons and Shils, 1951:116, 249]), and when we emphasize the "imperative" aspect rather than the "functional" aspect of his "functional imperatives" of the social system, they may be seen to represent categories of gratification for the collectivity (adaptation, goal-attainment, integration, and latent pattern maintenance and tension management [see Parsons, 1961a:36–41]). Finally, Par-

---

[23] Parsons and Shils say:

> In confronting any situation, the actor faces the dilemma whether to treat the objects in the situation in accordance with a general norm covering *all* objects in that class or whether to treat them in accordance with their standing in some particular relationship to him or his collectivity (1951:81).

It is, of course, one thing to define an object in relation to other objects, and quite another to define it in relation to oneself or one's group—but the two kinds of definition are not mutually exclusive (e.g., an apple may be both green in relation to other apples and mine in relation to me).

[24] For discussions on which this interpretation draws, see Parsons and Shils, 1951:76–91; Parsons, 1951:58–112; Parsons and Smelser, 1956:33–38; and Parsons and Bales, 1955: passim.

sons' analysis of masculine-feminine personality differences (see Parsons and Bales, 1955) conceptualizes two types of actor expectations.

Turner extends the range of alternatives for any given norm expectation indefinitely beyond any set number of categories when he argues that

> Interaction is always a *tentative* process, a process of continuously testing the conception one has of the role of the other. The response of the other serves to reinforce or to challenge this conception. The product of the testing process is the stabilization or the modification of one's own role. . . . The actor is not the occupant of a position for which there is a neat set of rules—a culture or set of norms—but a person who must act in the perspective supplied in part by his relationship to others whose actions reflect roles that he must identify (1962:23).

This, says Turner, is because "there is not just one role which enables an individual to interact in what is adjudged a consistent way with any given other-role. Roles are often comprehensive alternative ways of dealing with a given other-role" (1962:29).[25]

It should be noted that the idea of "alternative ways of dealing with a given other-role" points immediately to the idea of role-expectation ambivalence. This is what Merton and Barber have in mind when they say "sociological ambivalence refers to incompatible normative expectations of attitudes, beliefs, and behavior assigned to a status (i.e., a social position) or to a set of statuses in a society"; assert that "the core sense" of such ambivalence involves "socially prescribed ambivalence in a particular role, as, for example, in the therapist role of the physician which calls for *both* a degree of affective detachment from the patient and a degree of compassionate concern about him"; and conclude that "From the perspective of sociological ambivalence, we see a social role [i.e., cultural role-expectation—ed.] as a dynamic organization of norms and counter-norms, not as a combination of dominant attributes (such as affective mentality or functional specificity)" (Merton, 1976:6, 8, 17, emphasis removed). In a similar vein, Toby argues that the motivation to conform to a given rule as well as the motivation to deviate from it is ambivalent, and that therefore "If both conforming motivation and deviant motivation contain varying components of inclinations to conform to the rules and to violate them, most behavioral deviants are only slightly different from most behav-

---

[25] Turner argues for a particular decision-rule in choosing among such alternatives which he calls "the norm of consistency": "The basic normative element in role-taking-and-playing is the requirement that the actor be consistent—that his behavior remain within the confines of a single role" (1962:36). This, however, leaves open the question of the definition of "consistency", whether there is not just one definition but alternative definitions, and if so, whether some higher norm governs choice among alternative norms of consistency. For discussion of "prominence" and "salience" hierarchies of alternative role-expectations, as set forth by McCall, see Stryker, 1980:121–122.

ioral conformists in the organization of their personality systems" (1980:311).[26]

Further, regarding socialized role-expectations, when Brim says "There are three things a person requires before he is able to perform satisfactorily in a role. He must know what is expected of him (both in behavior and in values), must be able to meet the role requirements, and must desire to practice the behavior and pursue the appropriate ends" (1966:25), he cites both response and consequence expectations—leaving actor and situation expectations implicit. Brim also differentiates childhood and adult socialization in a way that argues for the capacity of the response (or "ability," "behavior") expectation to be inculcated independently of the consequence (or "motivation," "value") expectation:

> With respect to change, during the life cycle, the emphasis in socialization moves from motivation to ability and knowledge and from a concern with values to a concern with behavior. The highest priority in childhood socialization is . . . to take the basic desires of the infant and transform them . . . into desires for recognition and approval and finally to the pursuit of more specific cultural values. . . . The usual concern of adult socialization [involves assuming] . . . that the adult knows the values to be pursued in different roles, that he wants to pursue them with the socially appropriate means, and that all that may remain to be done is to teach him what to do (1966:25, 26).

And, complementing Brim's notion that socialization continues throughout the individual's life, Inkeles and Smith emphasize the malleability of the psychical behavior that results from childhood and adolescent socialization:

> No man need be limited to the attitudes, values, and modes of acting he develops in his early life. No matter how traditional his initial upbringing leaves him, his later-life experiences . . . may. . . . transform him from a highly traditional into a relatively modern man (1974:277).

Returning to role-expectations themselves, it should be emphasized that the norms comprising them may include expectations not only of physical behaviors, but of psychical behaviors and also expectations of the physical expression of those psychical behaviors. Thus, Williams says "There are norms for perceiving, feeling,

---

[26] Toby attributes the physical behavioral difference between conformists and deviants mainly to what is here regarded as another aspect of the individual's role-expectation (or more specifically, the individual's normative expectations)—namely, the extent to which he/she believes the physical behavior (response) in question is "legitimate" (i.e., not likely to elicit punishing consequences) for him/her as actor. Thus, Toby says "The greater its legitimacy, the more likely will [a given deviant behavior] be tried. Furthermore, the greater its legitimacy, the less likely will conforming members of the system react with moral indignation and thereby nip deviance in the bud" (1980:306). See the discussion of "conscience" in Chapter 8.

thinking, judging, evaluating, and acting" (1968a:205). Similarly, Goode says "Ego may fail in role performance by not carrying out the overt activities prescribed or by not feeling the prescribed emotions," and then goes on to distinguish between *"feeling* the prescribed emotions" and manifesting the prescribed *expressions* of emotions:

> Expressions of condolence are accepted as expressions of real sorrow or sympathy; salutations, gestures, the use of titles, and overt deference are accepted as indexes of real respect. Alter may, then, evaluate incorrectly the intensity [or the nature—ed.] of ego's real emotion (1960b:256).

Shott argues that emotional experiences are dependent on normative definitions of the situation:

> Social norms create pressures to establish the appropriateness of an emotion in a particular situation. . . . Within the limits set by their culture, people construct their emotions in a process requiring both internal cues indicating physiological arousal and definition of these cues (1979:1330).

In line, implicitly, with the conceptualization being put forward here of the four expectations that comprise every norm, Hochschild suggests that normatively prescribed feelings may vary, not only with the situation, but with the actor:

> Feeling rules reflect patterns of social membership. Some rules may be nearly universal, such as the rule that one should not enjoy killing or witnessing the killing of a human being, including oneself. Other rules are unique to particular social groups (1979:566).

Hochschild implies that normatively prescribed feelings may vary with the effect one desires to achieve—i.e., with the consequence expectation—when, in an illustration, she says that

> a young woman on the eve of her college graduation . . . could "pay" her parents in emotive display. . . . Going one step further, she could pay them with a gesture of . . . trying to feel. The most generous gesture of all is the act of successful self-persuasion . . . a deep acting that jells, that works, that in the end is not phony (1979:568–569).

Finally, note Gagnon and Simon's argument for the indispensability to sexual behavior of role-expectations that make a single, integrated "script" of otherwise ambiguous events occurring both inside and outside the participants:

Our use of the term *script* with reference to the sexual has two major dimensions. One deals with the external, the interpersonal—the script as the organization of mutually shared conventions that allows two or more actors to participate in a complex act involving mutual dependence. The second deals with the internal, the intrapsychic, the motivational elements that produce arousal or at least a commitment to the activity. . . . . Without the proper elements of a script that defines the situation, names the actors, and plots the behavior [and plots its expected consequences—ed.] nothing sexual is likely to happen (1973:20, 19).

Consequence Expectation as Value and as Validity-Check

Before ending this discussion of the conceptualization of norms being put forward here, special attention should be paid to the consequence expectation and to what I believe are implications in the sociological literature that it operates in two ways: First, when noticeably cathected by the individual, it encourages adoption of its associated actor and situation expectations and, when these are observationally verified, enactment of the associated response expectation. Second, whether noticeably cathected or not, the consequence expectation provides a built-in test of the accuracy of the individual's adoption and enactment of the other expectations, and therefore of the validity of the entire norm. In a word, the consequence expectation is regarded as serving both as a *value* operating before action to motivate it, and as a *test criterion* operating after action to assess and validate it.[27] Consider these two functions in turn.

VALUES

A value may be defined as any significantly cathected consequence that an individual expects to follow from or, once achieved, to be maintained by, specifiable responses in specifiable situations by specifiable actors. Note that this definition accords in important respects with Homans' views:

A man emits a unit of activity . . . and this unit is reinforced or punished by one or more units of activity he receives from another man or by some-

---

[27] Gibbs concentrates on these two functions of the consequence expectation, and then on some of the actual, physical, consequences themselves, when he says "A norm in the generic sense (i.e., encompassing all the various types of norms) involves: (1) a collective evaluation of behavior in terms of what it *ought* to be; (2) a collective expectation as to what behavior *will be;* and/or (3) particular *reactions* to behavior, including attempts to apply sanctions or otherwise induce a particular kind of conduct" (1965:589; see also 1968:208).

thing he receives from the non-human environment. . . . The *value* of the unit he receives . . . is the degree of reinforcement or punishment he gets from that unit (1961:39–40).

There is an important difference, however. Where Homans permits us to identify "reinforcement" and "punishment" with the *"activity [that an individual] receives* from another man or . . . from the non-human environment," the present definition identifies them both with a psychical behavior inside the individual him/herself—specifically, a cathected consequence *expectation*. Thus, an actual consequence is here regarded as reinforcing or punishing only if it has already been so defined within the individual's psyche.[28] To say that "help is a reinforcer, a reward, to Person" and that "a pigeon values grain highly" (Homans, 1961:43) is to say that certain expected consequences of certain of their respective expected responses in certain expected situations (including Person's and pigeon's states of deprivation) are positively cathected—presumably largely as a result of learning experiences in Person's case and genetic inheritance in pigeon's.

It should be emphasized that the present conceptualization identifies values with consequence expectations contingent on *the individual's own response expectations* (which are in turn, of course, associated with the individual's own actor expectations and situation expectations). Thus, for example, when someone says "I value that piano," the present definition implies that "valuing a piano" should be interpreted as referring to positively cathected expected consequences of the speaker's behaving toward the piano—that is, playing the piano, listening to someone else play the piano, touching the piano, looking at the piano, even merely thinking about the piano in its physical absence—in some range of expected situations. This means an individual (even one who adopts the actor expectation "pianist") may not value the piano as the object of *all* his/her expected responses, or as part of *all* his/her expected situations; and only those consequence expectations which a given individual positively cathects across all such expectations may properly be called "absolute" for that individual.

The same interpretation is indicated for value statements whose objects are more abstract—like "I value freedom," or "I value knowledge," or "I value the supernatural." That is, in all cases, what is being cathected are consequence expectations (and also the actual consequences themselves, when they satisfactorily conform to expectations) contingent on the speaker's own response expectations—given the actor and situation expectations associated with the latter. At the same time, however, it is important to say that although consequence expectations (whether cathected, as values, or not) are regarded here as *contingent* on response expectations and although the latter are regarded as *associated* with actor and situation expecta-

---

[28] Note that not only psychically defined "reinforcements" and "punishments" are capable of influencing behavior; birth, death, confinements, and other purely physical constraints also have this capability—a point made by Weber (see 1947:93–93), and developed systematically here in Part II.

tions, consequence expectations are not held to be the *same* as, or to *include,* the latter expectations. Thus, both Adler's view that "values and actions may safely be treated as identical" (1956:279), and Williams' view that "all values contain some cognitive elements" (1968b:283), are rejected here. Instead, I accept and extend into a conceptual principle what Williams proposes as only a methodological strategy when he says

> A sound general principle [in studying values] is to follow the dynamic course of sanctions wherever this may lead. Extremely close analysis of every detail of rewarding or punishing social consequences of a particular line of action typically will reveal important value data (1968b:285).

Consider some other conceptualizations of values. Parsons and Shils strive very hard to distinguish the "motivational orientation"—which, as we have already seen, includes a "cathectic mode"—from the "value-orientation" of the individual, arguing that whereas the cathectic mode of motivational orientation "involves the various processes by which an actor invests *an object* with affective significance," value orientation "refers to those aspects of the actor's orientation which commit him to the observance of certain *norms, standards, criteria of selection*" (1951:59; emphasis added). It should be clear that the former orientation subsumes the latter insofar as "norms, standards, criteria of selection" are also "objects" (indeed, Parsons and Shils call them "objects," albeit "nonsocial" ones [see Parsons and Shils, 1951:5, 58]) and insofar as the actor's "commitment" to them implies that he does indeed invest them with "affective significance."

In the end, however, despite their claim of "complex . . . *differences* between the [value] standards and the other classes of symbols" (1951:164, emphasis added), Parsons and Shils assert that value-orientations (or "standards") *include* two of the "other classes of symbols, namely, cognitive and cathectic classes: "It is, indeed, in the evaluative synthesis of cognitive and cathectic modes of orientation that the major lines of the patterns of value-orientation of a system of action emerge" (1951:164). They continue:

> The cognitive reference connects the orientation with the object world, particularly with respect to the anticipation of consequences, which flow from actual commitments to action and which might flow from hypothetical causes, which, because of these anticipated consequences, may indeed be rejected as alternatives in the situation of choice. . . . There is also the cathectic dimension, which has its meaning in terms of gratification-deprivation. Alternatives are selected with respect to their different consequences for the actor on this level (1951:164–165).

The chief difference between Parsons and Shils' view of values and the one proposed here is that where they regard values (or "value-orientations") as combinations of cognitive assessments and cathectic attachments, I regard values as cathectic attachments only. Therefore, insofar as "The cognitive reference connects the orientation with the object world" I reserve that reference for the situation expectation component of a norm, while reserving "the cathectic dimension" for the consequence expectation component.

Miller et al. seem ambiguous with regard to the location of values insofar as, after defining what they term the organism's "Image" as "all the accumulated, organized *knowledge* that the organism has about itself and its world" (1960:17, emphasis added)—which seems to incorporate what I refer to as the normative actor and situation expectations—they then include within that Image the organism's "*values* as well as his facts" (1960:18, emphasis added; see also 62, 116). The following explication, however, makes it clear that Miller et al. through an unusually broad definition of "knowledge," have in mind chiefly the consequence expectation as the locus of values:

> the elements with which the problem-solver seems to work are his perceptual image of the situation before he does anything, his imagination image of what the situation will be if he takes a particular course of action, his perception of the situation after he does something, his image of some ideal situation that he might hope to attain, etc. And each of these images must have some evaluation on a utility scale, and the decision to execute a particular Plan will depend upon the payoff function defined by these utilities (1960:174).

Thus, when Miller et al. say "In order to get [a list of nonsense syllables] memorized, a subject must have that mysterious something called an 'intent to learn' " (1960:129), I regard that "mysterious something" as cathexis conferred specifically on one or more expected consequences of such memorization—let us say, money, approval from the experimenter, and/or the personal satisfaction of achievement.

Blake and Davis, as we have already seen, define a norm as "any standard or rule that states what human beings should or should not think, say, or do under given circumstances" (1964:456), and they define values as "the goals or principles in terms of which specific norms are said to be desirable" (1964:456).[29] If we broaden "norms" in the latter definition to "behaviors" (thereby including thinking, saying, and doing), then we have substantially the view proposed here. Blake and Davis also argue that "Any theory of deviancy is faced with the fact that [an individual's] conscious motives (or desires) and behavior . . . may be either con-

[29] Blake and Davis are admittedly confusing as to how they regard values. Their claim that "A more satisfactory use of 'values' in sociological analysis is to abandon them as causal agents and to recognize them frankly as sheer constructs by which we attempt to fill in the subjective linkages in the analysis of social causation" (1964:461) overlooks that using values to "fill in . . . linkages in . . . social causation" seems equivalent to using them as "causal agents."

forming or deviant" (1964:468).[30] Here too we have substantially the present view of cathected normative consequence expectations (Blake and Davis' "motives" or "desires") and normative response expectations (Blake and Davis' "behavior"), although Blake and Davis do not acknowledge here that an individual's actor expectation and situation expectation may also be conforming or deviant—a point to which I return later in this chapter.

In addition, Blake and Davis argue that "The 'normative' . . . embraces the inner and outer compulsions (generally called 'sanctions') which tend to enforce conformity" (1964:457), and whereas I regard *outer* compulsions as physical behaviors and therefore social structural rather than cultural structural or normative (although the explanation of those physical behaviors may well be normative, as discussed in Part II), it is exactly those *inner* compulsions that I here refer to as significantly cathected, normative, consequence expectations. Blake and Davis' remark also leads me to point out that the idea of a cathected consequence expectation (i.e., a value) includes and goes beyond, the idea of an expectation of sanction, where the latter refers to a reward or punishment that is so intended by its giver and whose value is largely symbolic. Blake and Davis imply this reference when they list among "informal sanctions" an "approving or contemptuous glance, an encouraging or derisive laugh, a sympathetic or embarrassed silence," and among "formal sanctions" a "medal or a jail, an honorary dinner or an electric chair, a parade or a court-martial" (1964:465). As used here, the term "value" includes *all* significantly cathected consequence expectations, whether the expected consequence is intended by its giver or not and whether its expected effect is mainly symbolic or not.

VALIDITY

Among Parsons' pattern variables, affectivity-neutrality seems especially interesting in the present context because it suggests that expected consequences may or may not be cathected:

---

[30] It should also be noted that all of Blake and Davis' "five broad categories of inhibition to the acting out of deviant motivation in deviant behavior" find their basis in the present conceptualization of a norm as comprising actor, situation, response, and consequence expectations. Thus, the inhibiting "internalization of norms" depends on the individual's accepting only certain normative actor expectations for him/herself and rejecting others (Blake and Davis say the individual "asks 'Will I hate myself, if I do it?' "); the inhibiting "desire for approval," "anticipation of formal punishment," and "anticipation of nonreward" all depend on the individual's normatively expecting (desiring, anticipating) these consequences, and the inhibiting "lack of opportunity for deviant behavior"—insofar as such opportunity can be psychically defined by the individual—depends on the individual accepting certain normative situation expectations and not others.

No actor can subsist without gratifications, while at the same time no action system can be organized or integrated without the renunciation of *some* gratifications which are available in the given situation. The polarity of affectivity-neutrality formulates . . . this basic alternative (1951:60).

We may, however, put the matter continuously rather than dichotomously: the affectivity-neutrality pattern variable implies the possibility that cathexis is variably conferred on different consequence expectations, such that the individual may regard some as highly valuable or disvaluable and regard others as neutral or negligible in value. While they do not operate as motivators of behavior called for by the norm, the latter, value-neutral, consequence expectations operate as what might be called "technical" criteria against which that behavior is checked for validity.

Thus, by definition, an individual only knows whether something has gone right (or gone wrong) after the fact, that is, not when sizing up the situation and oneself, not when in the act of acting, but only afterward, when some expected consequence comes true or fails to come true. If it comes true, we proceed confidently and blithely; if it fails to come true (within the personal tolerance limits that make some people more patient and easier to satisfy than others), then, although we do not yet know *what* has gone wrong, we do know *something* has gone wrong, and we usually then begin searching to find out what it is. This validity-checking process seems to be what Miller et al. mean when they say the outcomes of tests tell the organism when to start and when to stop (and therefore when to correct or change) a response.

Thus, suppose someone is typing a letter. Everything goes along fine so long as the normatively expected (and cathected) little black marks appear in a certain order on the page. However, should any one of these thousands of normatively expected consequences of typists pressing the keys of typewriters not manifest themselves, good typists know instantly that something has gone wrong, check automatically for its source—perhaps first in their own response and then in situational features like paper, ribbon, electrical connection, and so on—correct that source, and move on.

The same validity-checking process applies to entire role-performance and role-expectation relations between individuals. Thus, suppose a "teacher" enters classroom situation and finding nothing amiss (i.e., finding the difference between the observed consequence and the expected consequence of his/her having crossed the classroom threshold to be negligible), calls to mind[31] the "lecturing" response expectation, glances at notes, and begins performing lecturing behavior. All this is observed by "student" who evaluates it as negligibly different from the normatively expected classroom situation. This evaluation then calls to student's mind

---

[31] Miller et al. say "When we have decided to execute some particular Plan, it is probably put into some special state or place where it can be remembered while it is being executed" (1960:65).

the "appear-calmly-attentive" response expectation and student then performs this behavior. Teacher observes this expected consequence of his/her lecturing performance and continues that performance. If, at some point, however, where teacher's normative response expectation—which, in general outlines, both teacher and student know—would call for, let us say, the phrase "in the future," teacher actually says "in the past," student may identify a significant difference between the observed and the normatively expected consequence of his/her calmly attentive-appearing behavior and begin to search for the source of this perceived difference. If this checking leads student to conclude that the source of the error most likely lies in teacher's actual response, and not in student's expectation, perception, or interpretation, student redefines situation as, perhaps, a "mistake," "joke," or "test" and, calling up normatively expected "questioning" response, raises hand. Teacher sees this raised student hand, evaluates the difference between the observed and the normatively expected consequence of his/her lecturing as significant, checks for source of error and, finding none, redefines situation as "uncertain," calls up normatively specified "acknowledge-student-question" response, suspends lecture, looks at student, and says "Yes?" with normatively expected consequence that student will lower hand and ask question or make comment. And so on.

At least two related points are important to add here. First, I assume that some discrepancy between normative expectation and actual observation is inevitable, but so long as these discrepancies are evaluated by the participant as negligible, the interaction proceeds smoothly and "uneventfully." Should any given discrepancy be evaluated by the individual as significant, however, error-checking and error-correcting behavior occurs. Second, I assume that all normative consequence expectations and all actually observed consequences are cathected, to some degree, by both participants. Although the teacher-student illustration deals only with consequence expectations and observations that are not apt to be strongly cathected (and therefore only with "errors"), other illustrations—say, teacher-student interaction regarding teacher favoritism or student plagiarism—would deal with more strongly cathected expectations (and therefore with "deviance"). In such cases, error-correction is apt to engage values and produce more or less powerful sanctions on one or both sides.

ACROSS-INDIVIDUALS AGGREGATES OF PSYCHICAL BEHAVIORS

So far we have referred simply to "norms" (and "values")—thereby implying, with Blake and Davis, that "A purely private, or individual, view of what people should do or think is a norm" (1964:456). But now the distinctively sociological question arises: Under what conditions may norms be called "social" (or more specifically, of course, "cultural structural"), in addition to being individual psychical behaviors? An examination of the sociological literature indicates that norms have been termed "social" according to at least two different criteria that may be called "reference-to-others" and "adoption-by-others."

In the first case, a norm has been termed "social" if its content refers or orients a given individual to other individuals—regardless of whether it is adopted by more than one individual; in the second case, a norm has been termed "social" if its adoption is common to two or more individuals—regardless of whether or not its content refers one individual to another. Reference-to-others is Weber's criterion of social action: "subjective attitudes constitute social action only so far as they are oriented to the behavior of others" (1947:112). According to this criterion, a norm through which one individual is oriented to the behavior of others would be social in its reference within that single individual, even when those others have no such orientation:

> Action is social in so far as, by virtue of the subjective meaning attached to it by the acting individual (or individuals), it takes account of the behavior of others and is thereby oriented in its course (Weber, 1947:88).

Adoption-by-others, however, is Durkheim's criterion:

> The totality of beliefs and sentiments common to average citizens of the same society forms a determinant system which has its own life; one may call it the *collective* or *common conscience*. . . . It is an entirely different thing from particular consciences, although it can be realized only through them (1933:79–80).

From the standpoint of the generic definition of social phenomena put forward in Chapter 2, only adoption-by-others is social; reference-to-others, insofar as it is solely intraorganismic, cannot be a social phenomenon in itself. At the same time, however, reference-to-others seems likely to *generate* social phenomena insofar as, by calling upon one individual to pay attention to another, it encourages the former to coordinate his/her behavior with the latter. It should be noted that reference-to-others may occur in any or all of the four normative expectations—so that when Weber requires social action to "take account" of the behavior of others, such account may be taken in the actor expectation (e.g., "teacher" implies other occupation titles), in the situation expectation (e.g., "classroom" implies "students"), in the response expectation (e.g., to "shake hands" implies another's hand), and/or in the consequence expectation (e.g., the norm may specify that the smiles of others or cries of others are to be expected).

Thus, an individual who holds a norm calling for reference-to-others seems likely eventually to adopt expectations of others that approximate the expectations those others have of themselves; furthermore, through the same process, each is likely to develop self-expectations that approximate the expectations that those others have of him/her. Considering the earlier discussion here of norm cross-indexing, each individual can develop a four-way index of norm expectations that is, in important respects, shared with other individuals. It is this shared norm index which provides the basis for "empathy—the sympathetic understanding of the lot of the other" (Merton, 1957:382); this index, one might indeed say, *is* empathy. It is also what Mead means by "taking the role of the other" (or, more exactly, taking the role-expectation of the other—since one may conceivably take on another's role-performance without taking on that other's role-expectation—and more flexibly, taking the actor, situation, response and/or consequence expectations of the other), and indeed the construction of a shared norm index is a central theme in Mead's work. Consider the difference he points out between play and the game:

> in the latter the child must have the attitude of all the others involved in that game. . . . Each one of his own acts is determined by his assumption of the action of the others who are playing the game. What he does is controlled by his being everyone else on that team, at least insofar as those attitudes affect his own particular response. We get then an "other" which is an organization of the attitudes of those involved in the same process (Mead, 1934:164).

Presumably (although Mead is not explicit on this point), play can be carried out without having the attitude of *all* the others involved; one can even play without having *any* such attitudes—especially if the objects of play are inanimate (but see Mead's curious footnote on taking the attitudes of inanimate objects toward oneself [1934:164]). The game, however, is a different matter. Apparently because it is a system of interrelated norms ("the game has a logic"), Mead argues that it can hardly be played without some shared comprehension of that system as a whole. In any case, his play-game distinction seems to have led Mead to propose an important addition to the Weberian reference-to-others idea, by suggesting that norms may specify orientations not only toward immediately particular others, but also toward "the generalized other"—that is, toward some internalized system of norms and role-expectations of which the given norm is a part. It is this shared system of psychical behaviors, this cultural structure, that enables one individual to have some idea of how other individuals regard him/her, what they expect of him/her, and what they are likely to do if those expectations are, or are not, met—and vice-versa. "Thus, both ego and alter know, or believe they know, what the other will, in fact, do in the situation" (Goode, 1960b:249; see Chapter 8).

It often happens, however, that a given norm index is shared only in part, such that two subgroups may hold certain sections of that index in common but not other sections. For example, both subgroups may have indexes in which the actor expectation "police officer" is present, but the situation, response, and consequence expectations associated with it may differ widely: one subgroup may expect the police to be courteous, helpful, and law-upholding while the other may expect them to be brutal, punitive, and law-breaking. To the extent that the two subgroups share the same norm expectations, norms, or norm-index, they are said to hold the same cultural structure (or "culture") and to the extent that they differ, they hold different cultural substructures (or "subcultures"). Moreover, to the extent that the two subgroups have different amounts of power (see Chapter 3) and the stronger negatively sanctions the weaker for its cultural substructure (as the stronger perceives that substructure), the latter is said to be "deviant."

Mention of deviant (and nondeviant) cultural substructures raises the more general question of how psychical behaviors may coincide between different individuals (including, of course, members of different subgroups).

FORMS OF BETWEEN-INDIVIDUALS PSYCHICAL BEHAVIOR COINCIDENCE

Let us begin, as when analyzing social structure, by noticing that two coincident psychical behaviors may or may not be the same. For example, individuals A and B may experience, say, cognitive orientation toward living things, but alternatively, A may experience a cognitive orientation toward living things while B experiences, say, a cathectic orientation toward his/her own body. In addition, we notice that the coincident psychical behaviors may be logically consistent, inconsistent, or irrelevant with respect to each other. Thus, the cognitive orientation of one participant may assert the existence of, say, a monument in Columbus Circle in New York City; a second participant's cognitive orientation may agree that such a monument exists, and specify that it honors the Battleship Maine; a third participant's cognitive orientation, however, may deny the existence of any such monument and insist, instead, that there is open meadowland in Columbus Circle; finally, a fourth participant's cognitive orientation may hold no belief about Columbus Circle at all and assert, for example, that there are holes in swiss cheese.

Cross-classifying the two indicated dimensions yields the property-space shown in Fig. 4.2.[32] These dimensions and categories apply not only to the four components of norms, but to entire role-expectations, definitions of the situation, and so on—in short, to entire norm-indexes as they may be coincident between two or more individuals.

---

[32] Merton refers to three of the types shown here: "almost any pair of statuses may . . . have conflicting requirements. . . . Other pairs may be mutually reinforcing . . . and still others may simply be neutral" (1957:383).

When participants hold "identical" orientations, we have cultural structural consensus, wherein the same orientation is held in common by different participants. This is what Durkheim has in mind when he speaks of "mechanical solidarity," defined as "a more or less organized totality of beliefs common to all the members of the group" (1933:129), and what Weber has in mind when he describes the reaction of "followers" to the "charismatic leader" (see 1947:358ff). In another, more recent reference to orientational relations of identity, Smelser argues that

> Before collective action [including unison and imitation social structures such as "panics," "crazes," and "hostile outbursts"—ed.] can be taken to reconstitute the situation brought on by structural strain, this situation must be made meaningful to the potential actors. This meaning is supplied in a generalized belief (1962:16),

| | A's and B's psychical behaviors are: | |
	Same	Different
Consistent	Identity	Complementarity
Inconsistent	Empty cell	Contradiction
Irrelevant	Neutrality	

Figure 4.2. Typology of between-individual psychical behavior coincidences.

and the latter belief is described as creating a " 'common culture' within which leadership mobilization, and concerted action can take place" (1962:82).

When participants hold substantively different but logically consistent orientations, a cultural structure of "complementarity" is produced (and it should be noted that the distinction between identity or consensus and complementarity specifies two different meanings of what is often loosely called "sharing"). Here we have individual B seeing, and/or wanting, and/or ready to do, something different from, but consistent with—often enhancing—what individual A sees, wants, and/or is ready to do. This orientational relation is what Durkheim seems to mean by "organic solidarity" which (although he never explicitly defines the concept) he contrasts with mechanical solidarity: "Whereas [mechanical solidarity] implies that individuals resemble each other, this type presumes their difference" (1933:131). Parsons also refers to complementarity relations: "an interaction system is characterized by a complementarity of expectations . . . [such that] . . . the attitudes of alter conform with the expectations of ego and vice-versa" (1951:252), and refers to socialization as a process of creating a "complementary role-expectation-sanction system" (1951:211), wherein "the roles of ego and alter are generally complementary and not identical. There is, therefore, an element of *common value* but equally an element of *differential applicability* of the common value element to ego and to alter" (1951:214). Similarly, Winch proposes a "complementary needs" theory in mate selection (1963:584–592) in contrast with the homogamy (i.e., orientational identity) theory espoused by Burgess and Locke (1953:369–370).

When participants hold substantively inconsistent orientations, a cultural structure of "contradiction" is produced—including "dissensus," "value-conflict," "conflicting interests," "conflicting expectations," and the like. Thus, Marx argues that

> The possessing class and proletarian class represent one and the same human self-alienation. But the former feels satisfied and affirmed in this self-alienation. . . . The latter, however, feels destroyed in this alienation. . . . Within this antagonism as a whole, therefore, private property represents the *conservative* side and the proletariat the *destructive* side (1978:133–134).

Merton also relies on the concept of cultural structural contradiction when he asserts that "The individual teacher [for example] may . . . be readily subject to conflicting role-expectations among his professional colleagues and among the influential members of the school board and, at times, derivatively, of the superintendent of schools" (1957:370), and sets forth several mechanisms for managing these orientational contradictions, for "otherwise the pressure to live up to all the details of all (and often conflicting) social norms would be literally unbearable" (1957:375).

Finally, when different participants hold orientations that are irrelevant to one another either logically or by virtue of being unrevealed to one another, a cultural structure of neutrality is present. And, to modify Merton's definition somewhat, "By neutral is meant only that the values and obligations of the respective statuses are such that they are not likely to enter into conflict [or complementarity, or identity—ed.]" (1957:383).

Luhmann argues for the essential role of neutrality cultural structure in sustaining social phenomena by avoiding the emergence of contradiction cultural structures when he claims that "There exists . . . in the communication process *thematization thresholds* [which control] negation potential" (1981:239). Luhmann conceives such thresholds as levels of participants' consciousnesses below which given orientations remain taken-for-granted, unnoticed, and neutral with respect to one another, and above which they become themes or topics of deliberate examination leading to their potential assessment as contradictory:

> Themes or topics are possible crystallization points for negations. . . . [and]—as Garfinkel has shown—thematizations that could push the taken-for-granted elements of everyday life and language into the zone of negatability are generally doomed to failure from the very start. They are simply not taken seriously or, if stubbornly insisted upon, lead to the termination of communication. . . . [Such thresholds are not only important in face-to-face interactions, but they] are also of importance for the system of society as a whole. They prevent the unhindered, thoroughgoing "legalizing" of all interaction systems

and thus, so to speak, defend the [autonomy of] functional areas or subsystems within the society (1981:238–239, 246).

Weber provides a complex but clear contrast between orientational relations of contradiction mixed with neutrality, on the one hand, and superordinate-subordinate complementarity, on the other, when he claims

> ethnic coexistences condition a mutual repulsion and disdain but allow each ethnic community to consider its own honor as the highest one; the caste structure brings about a social subordination and an acknowledgement of "more honor" in favor of the privileged caste and status groups (1958a:189).

When these four kinds of relations are cross-classified with the four norm expectations to which they may apply we have the possibility of relations of identity, complementarity, contradiction, or neutrality between the actor, situation, response, and consequence expectations of any two norms (and therefore at any point between any two role-expectations or role-expectation sets or at any point between any two entire norm-indexes). In short, people may hold the same opinions, complementary opinions, contradictory opinions, or irrelevant opinions about who should do what, when and where, and/or why. In these ways, people's opinions may conform to, or deviate from, each other's.

Cultural Structural Deviance and Conformity

It is important to indicate just which kind of deviance is being referred to here and which kind is not. As Gibbs points out, two different definitions of deviance may be found in the sociological literature. The first, "purely normative conception of deviance" defines it as "a type of behavior that is contrary to the norms of at least one particular social unit," and the second, "reactive conception of deviance," defines it as behavior toward which "someone reacts . . . in a distinctive way (e.g., punitively)" (Gibbs, 1981:22, 23). These are logically independent definitions insofar as punitive reactions may be levied against behavior that is not contrary to norms, and behavior that is contrary to norms need not be met with punitive reactions. Note, however, that the two definitions are not mutually exclusive—so that a given behavior may be described as deviant on *both* criteria.

The important distinction between the two definitions for present purposes is that insofar as "reaction" may refer to physical behavior alone (e.g., a punch in the mouth), the reactive definition does not specify the involvement of psychical behavior and is therefore not necessarily cultural structural. The "normative" definition, however, does explicitly refer to psychical behavior (i.e., comparison with a "norm") and thereby implicates cultural structure. It follows that, in the present chapter, devoted to defining cultural structure, reference is made only to the normative definition of deviance.[33]

Merton's typology of deviant and conforming behaviors is best known for its normative definition (Merton refers to "behavior deviating from prescribed patterns of conduct" [1957:131]) and provides an opportunity to trace some implications for that definition of the conceptualization of the four norm expectations set forth above. Although Merton argues that "attitudes and overt behavior vary independently" (1959:179), the key fact in his analysis of deviant behavior is his tacit assumption that attitudes and overt behavior do *not* vary independently and that, instead, a particular type of attitude is automatically expressed in a particular type of overt behavior. One manifestation of this assumption[34] occurs in Merton's description of "innovation," where he says "Great cultural emphasis upon the success-goal invites this mode of adaptation through the *use of institutionally proscribed but often effective means* of attaining at least the simulacrum of success—wealth and power," and then goes on immediately to add that "This response occurs when the individual has *assimilated the cultural emphasis upon the goal without equally internalizing the institutional norms* governing ways and means for its attainment" (1957:141, emphasis added). That is, the physical "use" of technological ("wealth") and social structural ("power") "means" is determined by the individual's having "assimilated" a certain cultural structural "goal" without "internalizing" certain cultural structural "norms." In short, Merton claims an individual's attitudes determine that individual's overt behavior, and certain kinds of attitudes (i.e., acceptance of both cultural goals and institutional norms, or nonacceptance of either one or both) automatically produce certain kinds of overt behaviors (i.e., kinds which an observer would identify as conforming or deviant).

I emphasize that the production of conforming or deviant overt behaviors is regarded by Merton as automatic once the right attitude configuration appears. For this reason, Merton does not investigate the conditions under which a given attitude is or is not expressed in a given overt behavior (Cloward [1959], and Cloward and Ohlin [1960] do investigate these conditions, under the rubric of "opportunity-structures"). Instead, because he takes the expression of attitude in overt behavior for granted, Merton's attention is drawn to the other end of the causal chain as he seeks determinants of psychical attitudes in physical social structure (or more exactly, as was discussed in Chapter 3, in the individual's role-performance set or

---

[33] However, to the extent that "reactions" include "labeling"—that is, a physical behavior explicitly symbolic of psychical behavior—and insofar as such labeling is held to explain the future behavior of the "deviant," it is discussed in Chapter 10.

[34] Only in describing "conformity" does Merton waver, and significantly, in his expression of this assumption. Thus he says "To the extent that a society is stable . . . conformity to both cultural goals and institutionalized *means* . . . is the most common and widely diffused" (1957:141, emphasis added).

social structural status—including the cultural structuring physical behavior that others direct toward that individual[35]). Thus, "Our primary aim," says Merton "is to discover how some social structures exert a definite pressure upon certain persons in the society to engage in nonconforming rather than conforming conduct." That the "pressure" in question is exerted on the persons' psychical attitudes and not on their physical bodies is indicated when Merton goes on to say "Should our quest be at all successful, some forms of deviant behavior will be found to be as *psychologically* normal as conformist behavior" (1957:132, emphasis added).

In summary, then, Merton implies a two-stage sequence (see Chapter 12) which underlies his analysis: given a focus on explaining rates, among individuals, of physical, overt behavior, (1) Merton explains such behavior with various configurations of physical, attitudinal behaviors; and (2) he explains differences in the rates of those configurations with differences in individuals' statuses in social structure.[36]

Thus, Merton's analysis holds that deviance in overt behavior is determined by prior deviance in attitudinal behavior, and indeed, he names the types of overt deviance after the attitudinal deviance that he takes for granted must cause them. Therefore, because they pertain directly to psychical behavior and cultural structure, let us examine the types of attitudinal configurations that Merton proposes.

Merton's typology, fundamentally, permutes two attitudes ("acceptance" and "rejection"[37]) held by an individual toward two other attitudes called "culture goals" and "institutionalized means" or "norms."[38] More fully and in terms set forth earlier in this chapter, Merton here employs cultural structural relations of identity and contradiction ("+" and "−") between one individual"s beliefs about *what* he/she should do ("institutionalized norms"), and about *why* he/she should do

[35] Merton briefly cites "The family, the school, and the workplace [as] the major agencies shaping the personality structure and goal formation of Americans" (1957:137), and also "mass communications" (1957:137), and "social class" (1957:145), as relevant social structures in this respect.

[36] It is probably in an attempt to differentiate clearly these two stages that Dubin proposes to "extend" Merton's typology by distinguishing between "behavioral" (i.e., physical) innovation and ritualism and "value" (i.e., psychical) innovation and ritualism (see Dubin, 1959:148–150). Merton welcomes this distinction (see Merton, 1959: 178–180).

[37] Merton's third attitude, designated "substitution" (±), combines " 'rejection of prevailing values and [acceptance] of new values' " (Merton, 1957:140).

[38] Merton is ambiguous in switching back and forth, without explication, between "institutional means" (i.e., physical, social structural, and, in the sense discussed in Chapter 11, technological ways of doing things) and "institutional norms" (i.e., cultural structural, prescriptive expectations regarding those ways)—an ambiguity that probably impelled Dubin's explicit distinction between these two concepts (1959:148–150). The terminological ambiguity here reflects an underlying explanatory ambiguity involving the part Merton proposes is played by (1) the individual's attitudinal "acceptance" or "rejection" of the normative (cultural structural) idea that certain goals and means are legitimate, and (2) the individual's "access" or lack of access to certain physical (social structuralistic and technologistic) means—whether the individual accepts such means as legitimate or not. The simplest way to resolve this ambiguity seems to be the two-stage explanatory sequence mentioned above plus the assumption, also mentioned above, that attitude is automatically expressed in overt behavior.

it ("cultural goals"), and the corresponding beliefs held by some other individual or group that the analyst accepts, for one reason or another, as standard.

The conceptualization of a norm put forward earlier here, as comprising actor and situation expectations, as well as response and consequence expectations, however, leads to asking how Merton disposes of the first two expectations. The answer is that he implicitly holds them constant by limiting his concern to "culturally defined goals [that are] held out as legitimate objectives *for all or for diversely located members* of the society" (1957:132, emphasis added), and by indicating that "To consider . . . several *spheres of conduct* would introduce a complexity unmanageable within the confines of this paper. For this reason, we shall be primarily concerned with economic activity . . ." (1957:140, emphasis added).[39]

The introduction of actor and situation expectations as variables in the typology, however, would take into account two considerations. First, the combinations of response and consequence expectations that Merton lists as deviant may conceivably be entirely conforming—for persons fitting certain actor expectations and confronted by circumstances fitting certain situation expectations (see, for example, Merton's own analysis of the innovation-encouraging norms governing scientific investigation, especially 1973:223–412). As Goffman says,

> there is hardly a social act that in itself is not appropriate or at least excusable in some social context. The delusions of a private can be the rights of a general; the obscene invitations of a man to a strange girl can be the spicy endearments of a husband to his wife; the wariness of a paranoid is the warranted practice of thousands of undercover agents (1971:356).

Similarly, Fishman says

> The same young man who sometimes says 'I sure hope yuz guys 'll shut the lights before leavin' also is quite likely to say, or at least to write, 'Kindly extinguish all illumination prior to vacating the premises'. It's all a question of *when* to say one and *when* the other (1972:48).

Erikson points to the situation-specificity of response expectations when he says "Behavior which qualifies one man for prison may qualify another for sainthood, since the quality of the act itself depends so much on the circumstances under

---

[39] In a not dissimilar omission, Hamilton and Rytina investigated whether "the notion that the punishment should fit the crime" is a norm, but although at one point in the study, they seem to have provided respondents with descriptions of kinds of perpetrators (actors), kinds of situations, and kinds of motives (cathected consequences), they do not specify how these descriptions were "manipulated" (1980:1125, n. 9) and they do not report the outcomes of such manipulations. Clearly, the conceptualization of a norm being put forward here would require such a report.

which it was performed and the temper of the audience which witnessed it (1966:5–6).

Second, introducing actor and situation expectations as variables in Merton's typology would bring out that deviance and conformity may apply not only to response and consequence expectations, but to actor and situation expectations as well.[40] There is the deviance of those who claim to be certified M.D.'s but are not, and the deviance of those who, awakening in the night, mistake their wives or husbands for burglars and shoot them. At least conceivably, the medical practice and professional goals of the non-M.D., as well as the sleepy shooting and its motive, may be normatively unimpeachable; it is the misrepresentation of actor, and the misconstrual of situation, that are deviant.

A further illustration (again, only partial and implicit) of theoretic reliance on the separable points of agreement, disagreement, and irrelevance mentioned above may be found in Merton and Barber's analysis of "sociological ambivalence." Although they do not differentiate the four possible foci of contradiction (actor, situation, response, and consequence expectations) when they define such ambivalence simply in terms of "conflicting normative expectations socially defined for a particular social role" (Merton, 1976:8), they do mention kinds of ambivalence that seem clearly (although only implicitly) to depend on such distinctions. One kind is described as "essentially a pattern of 'conflict of interests or of values,' " which I regard as disagreement about consequence expectations[41]; another kind is described as "the conflict between several roles associated with a particular status . . . [roles which] make competing demands for time, energy, and interest," and I regard that as disagreement about response expectations. Merton and Barber also assert that "people occupying different positions in a social structure will tend to differ in their appraisals of the same social situation," and, of course, I regard this as disagreement about situation expectations. Finally, they come close to citing disagreement about actor expectations in their reference to the "marginal man" but the reference is made in explicit connection with orientation "to differing sets of cultural values" (Merton, 1976:9, 10, 28, 12).[42]

---

[40] The same, of course, is true for Blake and Davis' version of a response and consequence expectation typology (which they call "the interrelations between conformity and deviancy on the one hand, and motives and behavior on the other" (1964:468)—a typology which seems to be exactly the same as Merton's, except Blake and Davis call "motives" what Merton calls "cultural goals," and they call "behavior" what Merton calls "institutionalized means."

[41] Merton and Barber point out that "different criteria of the effectiveness of professional work [may] be employed by professionals and their clients. . . . [that] laymen tend to appraise professional performance in terms of . . . whether it succeeds or fails to solve the problem. Professionals tend to judge performance in terms of what is accomplished in relation to what under the circumstances, could be accomplished" (Merton, 1976:28–29). All this refers to disagreement about the consequence expectation.

[42] The variability of response expectations by actor, situation, and consequence expectations seems to be what Erikson refers to somewhat vaguely as "deployment patterns" of deviant behavior (see 1966:27–29).

SUMMARY

This chapter has tried to formulate some principles for describing cultural structure—defined as interorganism *psychical* behavior regularities. Beginning with a typology of individual psychical behaviors (Fig. 4.1), three successively higher levels of within-individual aggregates of such behaviors were discussed: norms, role-expectations, and role-expectation sets. The double function of the normative consequence expectation—as a value and as a validity-check—was examined. Two senses (reference-to-others and adoption-by-others) in which norms have been regarded as not only individual phenomena but as social phenomena were discussed, and the forms that the regular coincidence of psychical behavior of any kind between different individuals (i.e., adoption-by-others) may take were outlined (Fig. 4.1), as were some of their implications for the description of deviance and conformity.

5

Spatial and Temporal Regularities

In this chapter I examine the last two components of social phenomena as defined in Chapter 2, namely, spatial and temporal regularities. It should be noted, again, by "regularity" I mean the conditional probability that the physical or psychical behavior of at least one organism will be observed, given that the physical or psychical behavior of at least one other organism is observed. It follows that all observations of two or more organisms behaving with some regularity in time and/or space—at whatever distances—are grist for the sociological mill, and so it is just as reasonable to speak of social phenomena (one-way) between protohumans who lived four million years ago and ourselves, or (two-way) between people on the moon and people on earth as between two people talking "face-to-face," dancing "cheek-to-cheek," or walking "hand-in-hand."

Now it may rightly be claimed that *all* organisms behave jointly with *some* regularity in time and/or space, and it follows, then, that *all* such joint behavior is, in principle, "social" according to the generic definition. Inevitably, however, in any given description the analyst explicitly or implicitly sets some criterion level of "regularity" below which the joint behavior in question will not be considered "social" for the purposes then at hand. It is essential to note, however, that that criterion level is a matter only of discipline convention and individual choice: some analysts will set the criterion level very high (they are interested in social phenomena that are "common," "everyday," or "everywhere"), and some will, with equal reason, set it very low (they are interested in "rare," "extraordinary," "deviant case" social phenomena).

As already indicated, the basic sociological distinction within the concept of "regularity" is drawn between temporal and spatial, and, as Hawley says, "space and time are separable from one another only in abstraction" (1950:288). The regularities that occur *in* time and *in* space, however, are quite clearly separable insofar as certain social phenomena may be observed virtually every*where* but only at certain times (e.g., most people sleep during the night and are awake during the day), whereas other social phenomena may be observed virtually every*when* but only in certain places (e.g., some big-city downtown movie houses and cafeterias stay open seven days a week, twenty-four hours a day—as does the clink in every town). Thus, some social structures, and some cultural structures, may be regular in time only; others may be regular in space only; still others may occur regularly at a given time *and* place, as is the case with meetings of the U.S. Congress, the Indianapolis 500, and the Wimbledon tennis championships.

Parsons refers to this empirical independence of temporal and spatial regularities, when he identifies two possible directions that subsystem differentiation may take [1]:

> The differentiation of the system may follow both temporal and, in the action sense, spatial patterns. The first we speak of as the differentiaton of *phases,* of system process, the second as differentiation of the *structure* of the system (1959:641).

Hawley implies the same independence when he notes that in "the temporal patterning of interdependent activities . . . each type of activity tends to occupy a particular place in the time span," but also "there is, of course, a division of labor in which a number of functions are carried on concurrently. . . . Such coordination is of vital importance, although it is often obscured by the preponderating rhythm of synchronous behavior" (1950:310). In other words, social structure or cultural structure differentiation may be accomplished by (1) a unit performing different physical or psychical behaviors within the same space but at different times, or (2) different units performing different physical or psychical behaviors at the same time, but within different spaces.

As a result of this independence, analysts may point to a distinctive spatial regularity, or to a distinctive temporal regularity, or to both, when identifying a certain kind of social phenomenon. Thus, on the one hand, Parsons stresses spatial regularity when identifying a "nation," claiming that it implies "a synthesis of

---

[1] Admittedly, Parsons' specification of spatial patterns "in the action sense" may refer to his posited "dimensions of action space" (originally goal achievement, expressive, adaptive, and integrative; see Parsons and Bales, 1953:88–90) rather than to the dimensions of physical space (length, breadth, height), but the fact that he explicitly distinguishes "structure" from "temporal . . . phases" seems to indicate he has physical space in mind.

citizenship and territoriality [which] is necessary because the individual is anchored in residential ties, even though there is high residential mobility, because work as well as residence is located physically, and because the availability of resources is territorially anchored" (1965:1011). On the other hand, however, Parsons stresses temporal regularity when identifying a social structure, claiming that "the concept of structure focuses on those elements of the patterning of the system which may be regarded as independent of the lower-amplitude and shorter time range fluctuations in the relation of the system to its external situation" (1961a:36).

In addition to the indicated empirical independence, however, there are certain strong conceptual parallels between spatial and temporal regularities—for example, between the rate at which between-individual coincidences of physical or psychical behaviors occur in time ("tempo") and their rate of incidence in space ("density"), and between a temporally recurrent set of coincidences (a "rhythm" or "cycle") and a spatially repeated set of coincidences (a "motif" or "pattern"). I rely on such parallels in the discussion that follows to make my description of dimensions of the two regularities conceptually parsimonious.

Before starting that description, however, two points should be stressed. First, the temporal and spatial regularities referred to here should be regarded as components of the description, not the explanation, of social phenomena. Blalock's interest, by contrast, is in explanation when he refers to the spatial or temporal location of an aggregate as "an independent variable" that does not itself affect the dependent variable but is taken as a "cause indicator of the unmeasured variables that are presumed to be the true causes of [the dependent variable]" (1979:889; see also 893); and Moore's interest is similarly in explanation when he argues that "a revolutionary break with the past" is a condition for the development of the democratic state (1966:431).

Second, regularity—whether spatial or temporal or both—is always and only in the eye of the beholder; different analysts may describe the regularity characterizing the same kind of events in radically different ways simply because their observations have different ranges or resolutions: what seems random over a narrow range of space and/or time, or at high resolution, may seem quite regular over a wide range or at low resolution. And once again, the "beholder" I have in mind here is always the sociological analyst, not the social participants whose interorganism behavior regularities the analyst is analyzing. Hall (1959) clearly has the latter, social participant, type of beholder in mind throughout his examination of how members of different societies define time and space. By contrast, the present chapter tries to systematize the way sociological analysts who adhere to natural science assumptions and procedures (among whom I include Hall) conceptualize spatial and temporal regularities in social phenomena—independently of how the participants in those social phenomena conceptualize these regularities, and independently of how such analysts conceptualize the latter conceptualizations.

DIMENSIONS OF SPATIAL AND TEMPORAL REGULARITIES

What are the dimensions of regularity in the coincidence of physical or psychical behaviors manifested by two or more organisms? First, there is the *placement*, in time and space, of the coinciding behaviors. Thus, the behaviors may be located, say, on land, at sea, and/or in the air, and they may occur at daybreak, noon, dusk, midnight, the winter solstice, the spring equinox, or whenever. Given what we may know about a particular kind of organism (for example, that it breathes through lungs, has no wings, does not have especially sensitive night-vision, and sleeps but does not hibernate), the spatial location and temporal occurrence of its behaviors will be crucial aspects of our description of the social phenomena in which it participates.

Second, there is spatial *attitude* and temporal *order*. That is, in the spatial case, the relevant behaviors may be observed in the same or different latitudes; in the same or different longitudes; in the same or different planes above or below sea level. The same dimensions also appear in more relativistic descriptions of one organism's behavior occurring "in front of or behind," "to the right or left of," and "above or below" another's. Thus, although all the players on a baseball team behave in the same plane above sea level (excepting, to the extent of a few inches, the pitcher's mound), infielders, outfielders, and batters behave in certain left-right, front-rear, and facing positions relative to one another. Burgess' conceptualization of concentric zones in a city (1961) exemplifies the analytic differentiation of social phenomena according to their spatial attitude.

In the temporal case, the one-dimensionality of time and the one-directionality of movement through time (as compared to the three-dimensionality of space and the multidirectionality of movement in space) means there are only three basic temporal *orders* (analogous to spatial attitude) that the behavior of one individual can take with respect to the behavior of another: the first individual's behavior can be located in the past, the present, or the future with respect to the second individual's behavior (i.e., it can occur before, during, or after the other's behavior).

Third, there is spatial *extension* and temporal *duration*. The duration and extension of a given social phenomenon may vary from momentary (e.g., a casual greeting on the street) to long-lasting (e.g., the four million year history of human social phenomena), and from spatially concentrated (e.g., sexual intercourse) to spatially extensive (e.g., Earth-to-Saturn-and-back human communication).

Melbin argues that the duration of certain human social phenomena is increasing in ways similar to prior increases in their spatial extension:

> Humans are sharing a trend toward more and more wakeful activity at all hours of the day and night. . . . [N]ight is a frontier, [and] expansion into

the dark hours is a continuation of the geographic migration across the face of the earth (1978:3).

Melbin argues, however, that there is a fundamental difference between temporal and spatial expansion, stemming from the one-dimensionality and the one-directionality of time mentioned above:

> What is the carrying capacity of the 24-hour day? What will happen when saturation occurs? Time . . . is unstretchable; we cannot do with it as we did with land by building up toward the sky and digging into the ground. Time is unstorable; we cannot save the unused hours every night for future need (Melbin, 1978:21).

Hawley points to a further and equally significant consequence of increases in the spatial extension and the temporal duration of social phenomena: "Whereas in the anarchy of a multiplicity of localized systems fatal errors could be made here or there without jeopardizing the survival chances of other systems, that can no longer be expected. The single world system has a limited tolerance for error" (1978:794).

Fourth, there is spatial *pattern* and temporal *rhythm,* where both terms refer to some repeated set of events: in the temporal case the set is termed a "phase," and in the spatial case it may be termed a "feature" (as of terrain). Thus, the Western urban week is a temporal cycle generally consisting of a five-day work phase and a two-day rest phase, and the Western urbanized area is a spatial pattern generally consisting of a central city feature and an urban fringe feature. Specifically regarding temporal rhythms, Moore notes that

> All enduring groups or social patterns exhibit characteristic rhythms. Even in those rare instances where a small group of persons is in "constant" interaction (or constant for the waking hours), the rhythms required for bodily functions, the ordering of the various collective activities in some sequence, impose a cyclical pattern of recurrence (1963b:47–48).

And Lynd says

> Many of the most acute problems in our culture derive from conflicts among rhythms, where the rhythms established in one institutional area of behavior coerce those in other areas (1946:43).

Rhythms and patterns may consist of any number, and any arrangement, of phases or features and their definition is a matter of analytic choice (although that choice is frequently conventionalized within a given sociological speciality at a given point in its history). Thus, for example, Hechter and Brustein argue that "three quite different types of social organizations coexisted in late medieval western Europe. These types—which we have termed the sedentary pastoral, petty commodity, and feudal modes of production—were found in specific regions of the continent and the British archipelago" (1980:1088); and McGranahan, examining "the spatial dimension of stratification," notes that "Low economic opportunities may be structured spatially in rural regions" (1980:323, 321).

Fifth, there is spatial *density* and temporal *tempo*. Sorokin notes that "Tempo should not be confused with rhythm. The same phonograph record with the same rhythms can be played at 78 revolutions per minute or at 156 revolutions per minute" (1947:690). And at one point, Parsons distinguishes between "structure" and "function" on the basis of tempo:

> Structure focuses on those elements of the patterning of the system which may be regarded as independent of the lower-amplitude and shorter time-range fluctuations in the relation of the system to its external situation. It thus designates the features of the system which can, in certain strategic respects, be treated as constants over certain ranges of variation in the behavior of other significant elements of the theoretical problem. . . . The functional reference, on the other hand, diverges from the structural in the "dynamic" direction (1961a:36).

So it is with density: The same spatial pattern may display greater or lesser density over any given space, just as the same rhythm may display faster or slower tempo over any given time span. Thus, gas stations, or families, or nations, may be spatially dense or dispersed, and, of course, social phenomena may have both fast tempo and high density, as Durkheim observed when he argued that "the progress of the division of labor is in direct ratio to the moral or dynamic density of society" (1933:259), and as Gove et al. imply when they conclude that

> overcrowding in the home . . . results in physical withdrawal, psychological withdrawal, a lack of effective planning behavior, and a general feeling of being "washed out". . . . The experience of crowding is related to poor social relationships in the home . . . [and to] poor social relationships outside the home. . . . In short, crowding does have substantial effects (1979:78–79; cf. Booth and Edwards, 1976).

Further, insofar as "distance" is a density variable in which only one spatial dimension (length, or breadth, or height) is involved, Hall's distinctions among the "intimate," "casual-personal," "social consultative," and "public" distances (roughly 6–8 inches, 30–48 inches, 7–12 feet, and 30–1500 feet between individuals, respectively) at which different social phenomena typically take place are relevant here (see 1972:140–148, and 1959:208–209).

Sixth, there is spatial *uniformity* and temporal *periodicity*. In these two dimensions, we are concerned with the degree to which the time or space occupied by each rhythm or pattern is constant; where it is not constant, the regularity is said to be nonperiodic or nonuniform. As Sorokin puts it, rhythms or patterns are periodic "when each complete rhythm ABC is of the same duration as measured by astronomical or watch time, say, one week; they are nonperiodic when the chronological duration of each complete rhythm ABC is different, as when ABC is completed in one hour on one appearance, and takes a week for completion on another appearance" (1947:681). It should be noted that temporal periodicities are often formally broken by nonperiodic intrusions such as holidays, and urban spatial uniformities are formally interrupted by boulevards, squares, monuments, parks, and the like. More informally, for industrial workers, "some variation in [periodicity] such as earning a brief respite by greater speed and 'working up the line,' may . . . occur" (Moore, 1963a:26), and, for city dwellers, shortcuts through alleys, hedges, and vacant lots may serve the same purpose with respect to spatial uniformity. Moreover,

> the very precision of temporal measurement, the elaborate specialization of temporal duties, and the orderly arrangements for synchronization . . . may give to the individual the negative power of mischievous disruption and some power of temporal strategies (Moore, 1963a:52).

The same seems true of the spatially disruptive power of individuals when spatial coordination (as in, say, a parade or a basketball game) is precise, elaborate, and orderly. It may be in answer to this enhanced disruptive power of the individual in modern society that deviations from formally set temporal and spatial regularities are made permissible only in "emergencies" or with a normatively acceptable "excuse" or "license".

The dimensions of spatial and temporal regularities in social phenomena are summarized in Fig. 5.1, and the general point should be made that "synchronization" in the temporal case, and "coordination" in the spatial case, are concepts referring to any of the above dimensions of regularities in the coincidence of two or more organisms' behavior. Thus, behaviors may be synchronized in their occurrence, order, duration, rhythm, tempo, and/or periodicity, and they may also be coordinated in their location, attitude, extension, pattern, density, and uniformity. Sorokin points out the analytical relativity of synchronism—but the same principle applies to spatial coordination: "If too short a time-unit is taken, say one-millionth part of one second, then factually all the sociocultural changes will be nonsynchronous. If a sufficiently large unit is taken, say one thousand years, then all sociocultural change will be simultaneous" (1941:69). Finally in this connection, we note Merton's implication of spatial coordination in his discussion of how one individual's role-activities may be insulated from observability by others (see 1957:319–322, 342–346, 374–376). This insulation may be said to center on not letting one's right hand know what one's left hand is doing—that is, a specifically spatial isolation of activity from would-be observers—and on this, Merton remarks that "the spatial distribution of the members of a group . . . is presumably related . . . to the observability of role-performance" (1957:322). The insulation, however, may also involve a temporal isolation of activity from would-be observers—letting bygones be bygones, letting the dead bury the dead, forgetting, destroying or falsifying records, and so on.

Whatever may be the particulars of temporal synchronization and/or spatial coordination of different individuals' behaviors, however, only three general classes of net effects may be imputed to them: either some given object (e.g., economic output) increases, decreases, or remains the same relative to some specifiable cri-

Definition	Spatial	Temporal
Placement of interorganism behavior	Location	Occurrence
Attitude and order of interorganism behavior	North-south; east-west; high-low	Past-present-future
Extent of interorganism behavior	Extension	Duration
Recurrent set of interorganism behaviors	Pattern	Rhythm
Rate of interorganism behavior recurrence	Density	Tempo
Regularity of interorganism behavior recurrence	Uniformity	Periodicity

Figure 5.1. Temporal and spatial regularity characteristics of interorganism behaviors.

terion. "Many hands make light work," and "Too may cooks spoil the broth" are folk-wisdom references to such incrementalizations and decrementalizations. Hawley is more specific when he writes of synchronizing simultaneously a number of individuals' behaviors "to come to fruition at moments which make for greatest efficiency" and also of a syncopated synchronization whereby "a species, by virtue of the periodicity of its activity, does not continuously use the part of the habitat it occupies, [leaving] a time-space for occupancy by other species" (1950:301, 291).

Now it is clear that social phenomena, especially human ones, are spatially and temporally complex, and to capture some of that complexity we pay attention to the regularities not just between individual participants but between subgroups. For example, of course, we are interested in the fact that people shop with certain spatial and temporal regularities in shopping malls, but we are equally interested in the fact that some of the same people work, again with certain spatial and temporal regularities, in offices, factories, and farms; that there appear to be spatial and temporal regularities, not only within but between, shopping and working; and that the latter regularities themselves change over time—say from winter to summer or from times of prosperity to times of recession. And, of course, we are interested not only in the social and cultural structures of prerevolution and post-revolution America, France, Russia, China, and Cuba, but also in the revolutions themselves—that is, in the regularity or phasing with which change from one relatively stable social and cultural structure to another is accomplished. The same goes for the regularity or boundary that separates one spatial zone from (or connects it to) another.

We are, in short, interested in regularities between regularities, and regularities between those regularities—and so on up to the overall global and human history regularities. As Bonner, citing Haldane's five hierarchic levels of process-time, puts it:

> Each of the processes considered is built up of a very great number of processes quicker than itself. A muscular contraction is the resultant of thousands of millions of molecular transformations. The growth of a limb is the resultant of thousands of millions of cellular divisions, and the acquisition of a skill is the resultant of millions of muscular contractions guided by the nervous system. A historical process is the outcome of millions of lives. An evolutionary process is the resultant of many historical processes (1980:57–58).

So let us consider some of the ways that sociology treats, first, regularities in temporal regularities (i.e., social change and stability), and then regularities in spatial regularities (i.e., social spacing).

SOCIAL CHANGE AND STABILITY

Static and Dynamic Models

Perhaps the most familiar terms in discussions of temporal regularity between regularities (whether the latter are themselves temporal or spatial) are "change and stability," "history," and "career." All such concepts imply a temporal succession of phases called "beginning," "middle," and "ending." That such phases are analytic creations enabling us to isolate an arbitrarily selected temporal regularity from a background teeming with all manner of other changes seems suggested by Nisbet:

> [I]t requires analysis and deduction . . . or metaphor, or analogy, to bind the plurality of observed changes into a single, ongoing process. And it requires still further analysis and deduction to reach the conclusion that this single ongoing process has beginning, middle, and end (1969:168).

Nevertheless, although all three phases seem implied by every notion of change, analysts often simplify even further and explicitly conceptualize only beginnings and endings.[2] Accordingly, we have comparative static, or static-equilibrium, models of change in which we are interested only in a beginning state (represented by a "before" observation) and an ending state (represented by an "after" observation). This simplification, obviously, can tell us whether a change has occurred, how much net change has occurred, and whether it is associated with changes in other variables, but it cannot tell us what path the change took through time (e.g., whether all the change occurred instantaneously, or whether it gradually increased, diminished, or oscillated across the entire before-after period). Only dynamic models that explicitly conceptualize middles as well as beginnings and endings can do this by filling in one or more observations between the before and the after observations.[3] Thus, Blalock says that in comparative static models,

> One assumes that if there is a once-and-for-all change in an exogenous variable, there will be a change in one or more endogenous variables, but the rates of change may not be measurable or of theoretical interest. In contrast, the study of dynamics is very much concerned with these differential rates of change (Blalock, 1969:138; see also Boulding, 1962:19).

Now it almost goes without saying that although every dynamic analysis of change and stability in social phenomena must, because it is a finite analysis, select some beginning, a middle, and some ending of that change or stability, whatever one analyst selects as beginning or ending, a second analyst may select as middle— thereby posing as a problematical *path* of change what the first analyst takes as the arbitrary boundary *points* of change. Thus, we may analyze the changes involved in group formation or the termination of social contacts, as well as in their maintenance and development, and in all these analyses our interests focus on the detailed paths of change and stability through time. Let us see how these paths may be described.

---

[2] And, of course, it is also possible to conceptualize only middles as being of interest. Gouldner describes this possibility when he suggests a contrast between evolutionism and functionalism in sociological theory such that the former expresses an abiding effort to explain beginnings and endings ("stages," "extinctions," etc.), whereas the latter abandons that effort in favor of explaining social phenomena with reference only to the present; not as "survivals" from some forgotten beginning, but as *currently* fulfilling an "ongoing usefulness" (1970:117–124). See also Merton's qualification of "the postulate of universal functionalism" (1957:30–32), and Moore's note that functionalism assumes that "social behavior . . . could be understood only within their setting or context, and not by the vain attempt to seek their first appearance" (1963b:7).

[3] It should be emphasized that the dynamic model does not require change to follow any particular path; it only argues the virtues of describing a *path* rather than merely a beginning and an ending. In short, analysts remain free to hypothesize with Moore, that "some kinds and degrees of change are universal in human experience" (1963b:1), or with Nisbet, that "change is . . . *not* 'natural,' *not* normal, and much less ubiquitous and constant. Fixity is" (1969:270).

Elementary Time-Paths of Change and Stability

Figure 5.2 graphically represents seven elementary paths of change: random, static, cyclical, evolutionary, revolutionary, devolutionary, and catastrophic.[4] In each graph, the horizontal axis is time and the vertical axis represents any social phenomenon in which we are interested. For example, the vertical axis may represent organic solidarity, group cohesiveness, population size, bureaucratization, personal freedom, modernization, anti-Semitism, racism, sexism, or whatever other social phenomenon whose time-path happens to be of interest.

RANDOM, STATIC, AND CYCLICAL PATHS

These three time-paths are grouped together because they share an absence of long-run change. They differ, of course, in their short-run implications: the static path is changeless in the short run as well as in the long run; the random path is aperiodically changeful in the short run; and the cyclical path is periodically changeful in the short run. Let us consider each of these in turn.

When change is described as "chaotic," "tumultuous," "anarchic," "haphazard," "disordered," and the like, random change is being referred to. This seems to be the picture Moore has in mind when he claims that

> European society took [the form of chaos] for a long time after the collapse of the Roman Empire. In the twentieth century large parts of China suffered from chaos during the warlord era. Many other examples of near anarchy exist, which is no novelty in human experience. Today it is the essence of the relationships among so-called sovereign states (1972: 151).

It should be noted that insofar as randomness is, by definition, *non*regularity, we are interested in it scientifically only as the limiting case that defines regularity and as the state from which regularity emerges and into which it disappears. This, of course, is as true for spatial randomness (discussed below) as for temporal randomness.

It should be noted, however, that what is often called "social disorganization" does not usually refer to randomness in the statistical sense in which I am using

---

[4] Lenski mentions some of these paths when he says "In addition to the two master trends of diversification and progress, there are . . . cyclical and semicyclical patterns, as well as certain static and regressive patterns" (1970: 110). I do not regard "diversification" as a time-path, but as a variable which itself can follow any of the given time-paths; this variable is treated as a causal model in Chapter 12.

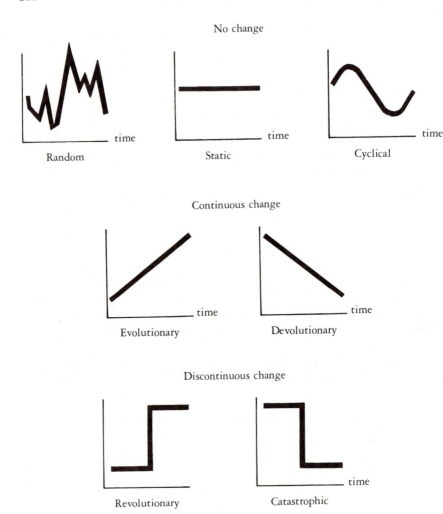

Figure 5.2. Elementary time-paths of stability and change.

the term here but more often represents an evaluative derogation of certain states of organization. Thus, Cohen defines "social disorganization" as *any* "interruption" in the " 'constitutive order of events'—an order conforming to the constitutive rules" (1959:476), as the participants themselves describe these rules. Cohen thereby permits a wide variety of possible social reorganizations to be defined as disorganization—as he himself tacitly admits when, after saying "If . . . a brawl develops in which all the players become involved, the game is disorganized," he adds that

"A brawl, in turn, can be regarded as a game subject to disorganization on its own terms" (1959:476).

In the second, static, time-path, we observe "a succession of identically similar states" (Boulding, 1962:20). In defense of such a succession as essential to human social phenomena, Nisbet claims that "change is . . . *not* natural, *not* normal, much less ubiquitous and constant. . . . Persistence in time is the far more common condition of things" (1969:270). It may be noted, however, that any such "normality of fixity" hypothesis must contend with the law of entropy that the normal dynamics of all things is change toward a state of maximum randomness or disorganization, which is the only state in which all dynamics cease. From the standpoint of this law, any "fixed" state of organization, whether social or other, is to be interpreted as change so slow as to be undetected, or as a local steady state maintained at the expense of an environment whose entropy thereby increases faster than it would otherwise. Within a closed universe, every environment must be eventually depleted, and every "fixed" state of organization must therefore eventually disappear. The impending exhaustion of fossil-fuel energy supplies is a case in point which is already having its changeful consequences for human social phenomena.

The third, cyclical, time-path implies regular oscillations, pulsations, fluctuations, rather than chaos or steadiness. Nisbet notes that for Plato,

> eternity is but an endless succession of [cycles]. Invariably one of these cycles is held to terminate in some great catastrophe, usually a flood . . . with but a handful of individuals left alive to commence the next cycle of civilization (1969:37).

Pareto expresses one cyclical theory of social history in claiming that "foxes" (bearing innovative instincts) and "lions" (bearing conservative instincts) alternate in dominating society (see 1935:1515–1518). Sorokin expresses a not-dissimilar theory in echoing the Biblical prediction of alternately "fat" and "lean" years:

> In varying degrees almost any family, business firm, and religious or political group, and even the state, at one period successfully adjusts its environment to itself, expands its needs and expenses, increases in size and influence, and subjugates its adversaries. Then it enters the "phase of adversity," when it must curtail its desires and expenses; retreat from previous positions; reinforce its self-discipline and self-control; and subsist with fewer means, vehicles, and members (1947:447).

Regarding the three sociocultural epochs he posits, Sorokin also claims cyclicality, arguing that they "have recurred in the same order: Sensate-Ideational-Idealistic, or what is the same, Ideational-Idealistic-Sensate" (1941:770).

Finally, Peterson and Berger's conclusion that styles in popular music in the United States between 1948 and 1973 underwent cycles consisting of "a relatively long period of gradually increasing concentration and homogeneity followed by a brief burst of competition and creativity" (1975:170) should be noted, as should Sykes' observation that "the prison appears to move in a cyclical rhythm from order to disorder to order; and riots . . . are a logical step in a pattern of repeated social change" (1965:110).

The next pair of time-paths (wherein regular long-run as well as short-run change is represented) may be viewed as analytic products of the decomposition of the cyclical time-path into an "up" phase and a "down" phase—whether these are called "evolutionary" or "revolutionary" and "devolutionary" or "catastrophic," respectively.

EVOLUTIONARY AND DEVOLUTIONARY PATHS

The basic idea represented in the evolutionary time-path (and here I include "growth") is continuous (or small discontinuous) increments in some variable over time—including, but not limited to, variables like "complexity," "adaptation," and "sophistication." The converse of evolution or "rise" is devolution or "decline," with its implication of continuous (or small discontinuous) decrements in some variable over time.

When a compound evolutionary-to-devolutionary sequence is formed, we have what Nisbet calls the "epic" model of social change—which he argues was derived historically from a more ancient model of recurrent cycles:

> In the Christian view . . . the cycle of genesis and decay is single, unique, never to be repeated. There is the one cycle of human existence that began in Adam, that will terminate sometime in the not distant future, and that is all (1969:70).

But it should be clear that the evolutionary and devolutionary time-paths may be joined together, not only in the "epic" sequence (with the devolutionary phase following the evolutionary one), but in the "renascence" sequence (with the evolutionary phase following the devolutionary one). The latter model seems to underlie the idea that Western European society declined and fell with the "barbarian" invasions of the Roman Empire and rose again in the fourteenth century with the Renaissance in Italy and elsewhere. Similarly, Marx and Engels view the invention of private property as signaling a long decline in the realization of human potential (i.e., a long rise in alienation), and the invention of historical materialism as signaling a renascence in that realization. All such "renascence" histories imply decay followed by resurgence, revival, resurrection, return, and may for this reason be contrasted with what Nisbet calls the "epic" career.

Perhaps it is unnecessary to add that, again, as one person's pleasure is another's poison, evolution from one viewpoint is necessarily devolution from some other. Thus the retrogression of homogeneity is a concept equivalent to the progress of heterogeneity, and the rebirth of a classical culture is a concept equivalent to the decline of medieval culture (whether any of these concepts is or was true is beside the point).

The final two time-paths shown in Fig. 5.2 are grouped together because although they share, with evolutionary and devolutionary paths, the representation of long-run change, they differ from the latter in the quality of that change. Revolutionary and catastrophic paths imply sharp, discontinuous changes instead of the smooth continuities implied by evolution and devolution.

REVOLUTIONARY AND CATASTROPHIC PATHS

Eisenstadt defines revolution as "encompassing the elements of totality of change, discontinuity, and novelty (and violence)" (1978b:3; compare 1978a:86); Skocpol describes social revolutions as "rapid, basic transformations of a society's state and class structure" (1979:4); and Tilly implies the same image of discontinuity and rapidity when he says that in social revolutions "Where there is a large transfer of power among classes, the particular coalition that gains power profoundly shapes the subsequent political development of the country" (1975:539)—but Tilly also strikes a properly relativistic note (which can be applied to the catastrophic path of change as well) when, after quoting one definition of revolution as " 'rapid, fundamental, and violent' " change, he says "Depending on how generously one interpreted the words 'rapid' and 'fundamental,' it would be easy to argue that no revolution has ever occurred" (1978:193).

Among sociological references to catastrophe, we have Durkheim's claim that "Whenever serious readjustments take place in the social order, whether or not due to a sudden growth or to an unexpected catastrophe, men are more inclined to self-destruction" (1951:246), and Sjoberg's definition of "disaster" as

a severe, relatively sudden, and frequently unexpected disruption of normal structural arrangements within a social system, or subsystem, resulting from a force . . . over which the system has no firm "control." For us the term catastrophe is synonymous with disaster (1969:357, emphasis removed).

Similarly, Thompson and Hawkes say disasters are "sudden and disruptive events that overtax the community's resources and abilities to respond, so that outside aid is required" (1969:268), and Erikson says "the two distinguishing properties of a disaster are, first, that it does a good deal of harm, and, second, that it is sudden, unexpected, acute" (1976:253).

Nisbet goes so far as to deny the significance of continuous change: "Change in any degree of notable significance is intermittent rather than continuous, mutational, even explosive, rather than the simple accumulation of . . . variations" (1969:281–282). And, relying on the knowledge that in a zero-sum game revolutionary ascent for one side is always catastrophic downfall for the other—and can lead to the winner redefining the game, or to the loser breaking it up—Marx and Engels assert the ubiquity of both kinds of change in human society:

> the history of all hitherto existing society is the history of class struggles.
> . . . [O]ppressor and oppressed stood in constant opposition to one another
> [and] carried on . . . a fight that each time ended, either in a revolutionary
> reconstitution of society at large, or in the common ruin of the contending
> parties (1978:473–474).

It should be noted that Marx and Engels regard this succession of small revolutions as incidental (one might call them epirevolutions) to the one master revolutionary time-path of human history. This path stretches from (1) the low-productivity and low-estrangement stasis of classless primitive communism, into (2) class society with its rising productivity, rising estrangement, and intensifying class conflict, through (3) the final and most intense class conflict of all—in which the proletariat overthrows the bourgeoisie, and (4) the high productivity and declining estrangement phase—called the socialist "dictatorship of the proletariat"—during which class society is dismantled and class conflict ended, to (5) classless advanced communism with its constantly accelerating productivity and absolute nonestrangement.

Rostow hypothesizes a very similar set of "five stages-of-growth" in societies (namely, "the traditional society, the preconditions for take-off, the take-off, the drive to maturity, and the age of high mass-consumption" [1960:4]),[5] except Rostow's set does not rest so heavily on materialistic explanatory variables, and does not implicate class struggle and a succession of small revolutions as necessary components (see Rostow, 1960:149–156).

It should be noted that revolutionary and catastrophic time-paths each contain an activation threshold at which the discontinuity (analytically defined as positive in the revolution case and negative in the catastrophe case) is turned "on," and a deactivation threshold at which it is turned "off." Thus, employing this imagery, Lumsden and Wilson say "the origin of euculture resembles the crossing of a

---

[5] Rostow himself compares his five "stages-of-growth" to a smaller set of four Marxian stages: "feudalism; bourgeois capitalism; Socialism; and Communism" (1960:145).

threshold," wherein "the steps leading to the threshold become increasingly un-likely and short-lived, but once the threshold is crossed evolution accelerates" (1981:327). And if we regard the crossing of a given threshold as nondeterminis-tic, then the threshold itself represents a "crisis"—a point at which the time-path established up to that point may turn in any of several different directions (see the discussion of equioriginality in Chapter 14).

Combination of Paths

There seem to be at least three ways that the time-paths discussed here may be combined: they may be serially linked to each other; they may be superimposed on each other; and they may be ordered hierarchically. Serial linkage between time-paths seems illustrated by the ideas (mentioned above) that "epic" (or rise-and-fall), and "renascence" (or fall-and-rise) paths are evolutionary and devolutionary paths linked in opposite sequences, and that the random, chaotic, path may be linked (both before and after, in the long run: "from dust, to dust") to any non-random path.

An example of superimposition of time-paths may be found in the idea, shared by V. Gordon Childe and W. F. Ogburn, among others, that each new revolution or invention in human history has taken place at a higher level than the previous one. The urban revolution was built upon the neolithic one; the use of iron and steel was added to the use of bronze, and so on. What is implied here is a repeat-edly revolutionary path superimposed on an evolutionary one. And evolutionary and devolutionary paths are superimposed in Spencer's argument that while the militant type of social and cultural structure gradually declines over the full course of human history, the industrial type gradually strengthens:

> In place of the doctrine that the duty of obedience to the governing agent is unqualified, there arises the doctrine that the will of the citizens is supreme and the governing agent exists merely to carry out their will. Thus subordi-nated in authority, the regulating power is also restricted in range. Instead of having an authority extending over all actions of all kinds, it is shut out from large classes of actions (1972:159–160).

Hierarchic ordering of time-paths of change and stability is exemplified in the idea that certain formal organizations such as business firms may sometimes be described as evolving while the society of which they are elements is described as static or even retrograde. Perhaps the most important case of hierarchic ordering of time-paths, however, lies in the notion of "progress" when it involves the for-mation, from units regarded as elemental, of aggregates of such elements—aggre-gates which then form aggregates, and so on up. For one example of the relationship of hierarchic order to progress, consider Leibnitz' opinion that " 'there always remain in the abyss of things slumbering parts which have yet to be awakened, to grow in size and worth, and in a word, to advance to a more perfect state. And hence no end of progress is ever to be reached' " (quoted in Nisbet, 1969:115). In other words, there exists a latent heterogeneity of "parts" within every manifestly homogeneous "thing" and the emergence of that heterogeneity constitutes progress. A similar idea is found almost two hundred years later in Spencer:

> this same evolution of the simple into the complex, through successive differentiations, holds throughout. From the earliest traceable cosmical changes down to the latest result of civilization, we shall find that the transformation of the homogeneous into the heterogeneous, is that in which progress essentially consists (1972:40).

And also, not long after, in Durkheim: "the more specialized the functions of the organization, the greater its development. . . . The division of labor in society appears to be no more than a particular form of this general process . . ." (1933:41). Seventy-five years later, we see it again in Parsons' assertion that

> The increasing complexity of systems . . . involves the development of subsystems specialized about more specific functions in the operation of the system as a whole, and of integrative mechanisms which interrelate the functionally differentiated subsystems (1966:24).

The notion of "social revolution" seems to represent a combination of superimposed and hierarchically ordered combinations of time-paths. Thus, when Skocpol defines social revolutions as *"basic"* as well as "rapid" (see above), she means that

> Social revolutions are set apart from other sorts of conflicts and transformative processes above all by the combination of two coincidences: the coincidence of societal structural change with class upheaval; and the coincidence of political with social transformation. . . . What is unique to social revolution is that basic changes in social structure and in political structure occur together in a mutually reinforcing fashion. . . . This conception of social revolution differs from many other definitions of revolution . . . [by identifying] a *complex* object of explanation of which there are relatively few historical instances (1979:4–5).

And when Eisenstadt says a revolution encompasses *"totality* of change" as well as "discontinuity," he seems to have in mind a similar superimposition and hierarchic ordering of time-paths followed by different societal components and different levels of those components: "The major distinctive characteristics of [modern] revolutions were the connections among the various associated movements of protest and between them and the central political struggle; their basic symbolism and its structural implications; and their structural consequences" (1978b: 173).

Sorokin sounds the note of eclecticism on which this discussion of models of social change may best be closed:

> the strictly cyclical (identically recurrent) conception of the sociocultural processes; the linear, in the sense of the nonexistence of any recurrent rhythms in the sociocultural processes; . . . the static conception that there is no change, and that the sociocultural world ever remains strictly identical with itself—all these conceptions are fallacious. The valid conception is that of an "incessant variation" of the main recurrent themes, which contains in itself, as a part, all these conceptions, and as such is much richer than any of them (1941:732).

SOCIAL SPACING

Elementary Patterns

We now turn to the spatial pattern corollaries of time-paths in social phenomena. Undoubtedly because the vast majority of human social phenomena until now have taken place at or near the surface of the earth, the most important conceptualizations of social spacing may be represented in only two dimensions (length and breadth) rather than in the three dimensions with which we shall ultimately have to deal. These conceptualizations are diagrammed in Fig. 5.3.

The first spatial pattern represented here, "random scatter," is implied by the idea of the residential or classroom "integration" of racial, gender, and ethnic groups. The second type, "homogeneous plain," is featureless in the sense that social phenomena are distributed homogeneously across it. Hawley illustrates this type when he says "the [concept of] region [refers to] an area of homogeneity in respect to physical features or human occupancy or both" (1950:260).

The third pattern may be called "latitudinal (longitudinal) belt," or "strip." In it, social phenomena are divided into two or more corridors. Bible, wheat, corn, sun, and sundry other "belts," as well as used-car, motel, honky-tonk, and other "strips," exemplify this type. When such differentiated lanes are overlaid at an angle to one another, we have a "grid," such as geographic longitude-latitude. Judging especially from the maps he shows, Hawley's "multicentered" or "multinucleated" pattern of communities refers to a grid, with "the interstices between centers and subcenters, and, in fact, within the centers themselves [constituting] areas of segregation, that is, areas which are internally homogeneous as to type of occupying unit" (1950:274).

The "concentric" spatial-pattern is exemplified by Weber's, von Thünen's, and

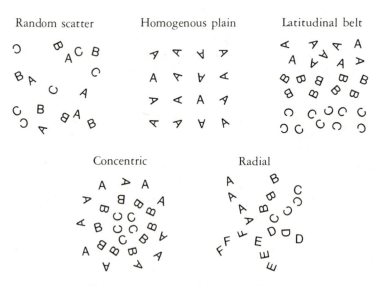

Figure 5.3. Typology of spatial distributions.

Burgess' images of land use in various parts of Europe and the United States (described in Hawley 1950:264–265), and summed up by Hawley: "A noticeable tendency appears for each class of land use to become segregated in a zone situated at an appropriate distance from the center. The resulting series of more or less symmetrical concentric zones represents in general outline a universal community pattern" (1950:264). More or less in this tradition, Wallerstein argues that

> By a series of accidents—historical, ecological, geographic—northwest Europe was better situated in the sixteenth century to diversify its agricultural specialization and add to it certain industries . . . than were other parts of Europe. Northwest Europe emerged as the core area of this world-economy. . . . Eastern Europe and the Western Hemisphere became peripheral areas. . . . Mediterranean Europe emerged as the semiperipheral area of this world economy (1979:18).

Finally, the "radial" pattern is illustrated by Hawley's conclusion that "the pattern of human settlement in its spatial arrangement resembles that of the wheel, or rather a series of wheels, with the essential features of center, spokes, and rims" (1950:234), or using a different metaphor, "the community tends to be star-shaped rather than circular in appearance" (1950:246).

Although the above illustrations focus on macrosocial phenomena (specifically, cities), others may be found in the literature of microsocial phenomena. For example, the four experimental "communications patterns" devised by Leavitt (1958) represent social phenomena spatial-patterns in the sense in which that term is being used here. As such, the "circle" is an instance of the concentric type, the "chain" is an instance of the latitude type, the "Y" is an instance wherein two latitude strips partially overlap into a grid, the "wheel" is an instance of the radial type, and one other pattern described by Leavitt (wherein each individual had equal access to and from every other individual), though not employed in the experiment, would have corresponded to the plain type.

Note that when we approach the boundary or transition between zones more microscopically, there seem to be at least five ways in which it may be described: as a continuous or diffuse "incline," with the incidence or character of social behavior in one zone gradually shading into the other; as a discontinuous or discrete "fault" between zones, with no shading; as an "undulation" of peaks and troughs; as containing "gates" through which some, but not all, social behavior from one or both zones can shade or pass into the other zone; or as a kind of "moraine" or random intermixture of the adjacent zones. It will be noted that the boundary between zones is itself a zone whose boundaries are, at higher resolution, themselves zones. It will also be noted that (with the exception of "gates") the ways just mentioned of describing such boundary spatial zones correspond to the time-paths of change (with the exception of "static") shown in Fig. 5.1—as seems fitting when the latter are regarded as descriptions of the boundary between the zone of the past and the zone of the future.

McKenzie's description of the smooth decline of traffic volume at various distances from Detroit's central business district (see Hawley, 1950:256) seems to illustrate the continuous transition case—although closer examination might well reveal a series of block-by-block discontinuities. Central city-suburb-satellite city-suburb-central city conglomerations illustrate the undulation of peaks and troughs, and all international borders are discontinuous with respect to certain social behaviors (e.g., military maneuvers, language, monetary currency use), but most are fitted with "gates" (e.g., diplomatic, espionage, immigration, and customs agencies) that control the passage of social behavior across them. Finally, the concept of a devastated but mutually patrolled "no-man's land," or "DMZ," between warring armies, and Burgess' (1961) concept of a "zone in transition," or "area of deterioration," between the downtown business zone ("Loop") and the "zone of workingmen's homes" which is constantly being invaded by both the latter zones, seem to exemplify the randomly interspersed type of boundary between spatial zones.

Just as the time-paths of change and stability discussed earlier are meant to be combinable into more complex images, so the patterns of spacing just discussed may also be combined. Once again, combination may be through contiguous linkages, overlays, or hierarchies. As an illustration of contiguous linkages, Hawley's discussion of the "multicentered community pattern" may be cited since it involves an image of "semi-independent communities scattered over the hinterland about a market center" (1950:270). Thus we have a central concentric-plus-radial zone surrounded by several similar but smaller zones, and each such zone is separated from the others by plains. Hawley also employs the overlay type of combination:

> In principle . . . the boundary of every community is determined . . . by the maximum radius of routine daily movement to and from a center. . . . On flat lands the shape of the area may tend toward circularity, especially where walking is the principal mode of travel. . . . [But] transportation combines with topography in the distortion of boundaries. . . . Movement invariably becomes channelized into routes or highways which take natural lines of least resistance, or in any event smooth the way and facilitate travel. . . . Radiating routes constitute lines of superior advantage along which units cluster and compete for sites. The interstitial areas between radial routes thus acquire uses different from those attracted to the lines of travel (1950:246 and 267).

The notion of hierarchic ordering of spatial-patterns is exemplified in the fact that city blocks (forming, roughly, a longitude-latitude grid) may be aggregated into larger, say, partly concentric and partly radial zones forming a city. Cities themselves may then be aggregated into, say, a concentric or "satellite" pattern extending across a very large region.

Although the spatial patterns of human social phenomena have been typically regarded, until now, as though they were only two-dimensional, certain exceptions are notable wherein a third, vertical dimension plays an important part. Thus we have Festinger's *et al.* concern with friendship between students living on different floors of the same building (1950:49–54), and Gouldner's discussion of differences in social phenomena between the mine and the surface at the Oscar Center plant of the General Gypsum Company (1954:154). Surely as we come to study human social phenomena that occur at significant distances above or below the Earth's surface (e.g., those involving mountaineers, balloonists, airplane pilots and passengers, astronauts, submariners, and deep sea divers), we shall have to utilize this dimension systematically in ways similar to those proposed by the ecologist Klopfer for the study of social phenomena among nonhuman animals:

> [C]onsider how space might be apportioned. We could make divisions with horizontal coordinates, producing layers at different altitudes to each of which a particular species [of animal] is relegated. This, in fact, is the situation among littoral and marine species. . . . Another possibility would be to divide a space with vertical coordinates, restricting some species to one area, others to another. This situation obtains where the distribution of species is determined by a geologic accident . . . finally, if our space is at all heterogeneous, we might divide it . . . into microhabitats. Thus, the portion of

the space atop the forest canopy might be reserved for one group, that close to the trunks of trees to another, and that beneath the bark to yet another (1962:52).

TYPES OF SOCIAL CHANGE AND SOCIAL SPACING COMBINED

When the spatial and temporal patterns discussed above are combined, we produce descriptions of social phenomena as "dispersing" or "concentrating" in space with the passage of time and as becoming more "long-lived" or more "short-lived" in time with change in space. Thus, on the one hand, we have descriptions of social phenomena (e.g., monotheism, the use of gunpowder) becoming "diffused" or "adopted" from some initial point or points in space randomly, concentrically, radially, or latitudinally outward, and on the other hand, we derive descriptions of social phenomena (e.g., human settlements) being "temporary" in one place but "permanent" in another. Moreover, the several spatial and temporal patterns enable descriptions to be specific about the manner of dispersal or concentration, permanency or transitoriness.

SUMMARY

This chapter has examined ways of describing spatial and temporal regularities in the coincidence of physical and/or psychical behaviors of two or more organisms. Although the empirical independence of spatial regularities and temporal regularities was affirmed, parallels between the concepts used to describe six dimensions of both kinds of regularities were proposed. Seven time-paths of change and stability in social phenomena and the components were proposed, as were five types of spatial distributions viewed from above, and five types viewed cross-sectionally across zones. End-to-end linkages, overlays, and hierarchic structure were discussed as ways of combining different time-paths or different spatial-patterns, and combinations of time-paths and spatial-patterns were also discussed.

6

Hierarchic Structure in Social Phenomena

The basic idea of hierarchic structure is the successive aggregation of elements into levels of greater and greater inclusiveness—as exemplified by the notion that under specifiable conditions two or more individual organisms may be described as a "small group," two or more small groups as an "organization" (or, under circumstances discussed in Chapter 4, an "institution"), two or more organizations as a "community," two or more communities as a "society," and so on. It should immediately be emphasized that I use the terms "aggregation" and "aggregate" in their generic references to any composite of parts, regardless of the nature of the parts and regardless of the relations between these parts—explicitly including the possibility of random relations. Thus, a "structure" (see Chapter 2) is a *kind* of aggregate wherein relations are nonrandom; a "system" is a more specific kind of aggregate wherein relations are nonrandom and causally interactive; a "living system" is a kind of aggregate wherein the parts are mainly organic and the relations are nonrandom and mainly interactive; and a "social system' is a kind of aggregate wherein the parts are living and the relations between them are nonrandom and mainly interactive.

Some examples of analytic reliance on hierarchic structure include: Nadel's reference to "Samuelson's suggestion that equilibrium processes should be visualized as being 'of quite different speed,' so that 'within each shorter run there is a still shorter run, and so forth in an infinite regression' " (1957:143); Kasarda's examination of "the structural implications of social system [i.e., population] size on

156

three levels of the social system hierarchy: the institutional, the communal, and the societal" (1974:19); Knorr-Cetina's reference to "levels of system formation and systems differentiation which start with interaction systems and end up with societal systems. . . . Thus neosystems theory arrives at a hierarchy of more inclusive systems" (1981:31); Eisenstadt's recognition of "the existence in any macrosocietal order of a multiplicity of levels of organizations, of social systems, and cultural traditions" (1978a:88); Wellman's assertion that "Not only individuals, but also clusters and collectivities, are linked through network ties. . . . A network of networks connects individuals, clusters, and collectivities in complex ways" (1979:1226); Merton's designation of the "complement of social statuses of an individual as his status-set, each of the statuses in turn having its distinctive role-set" (1957:370, emphasis removed); Collins' assertion that "All social reality . . . is microexperience; but there are temporal, numerical, and spatial aggregations of these experiences which constitute a macrolevel of analysis" (1981:99); Keyfitz' observation that "like historians, demographers assemble such elementary facts [as the 3.3 million American births in 1978] into larger entities, entities like the demographic transition, or the baby boom, or the presently rising mortality of the Soviet Union" (1980:180); Durkheim's claim that "A nation can be maintained only if, between the state and the individual, there is intercalated a whole series of secondary groups near enough to the individuals to attract them strongly in their sphere of action and drag them, in this way, into the torrent of social life" (1933:28);[1] and Granovetter's claim that "weak ties"[2] between components of the

---

[1] Durkheim clearly indicates the hierarchical character of this "series of secondary groups" when he argues that within every society having a high degree of functional differentiation and strong moral prescription of that differentiation, there should be organizations that are low on both these qualities, such that their members are "attracted toward each other under the influence of [their] likenesses . . . [and will] lead the same moral life together" (1933:14, 15). This, Durkheim tells us, is exemplified in the "occupational corporation," insofar as it would be found on the "common life" (1933:24) of members—that is, employees and employers alike—of the same occupation. However, within these functionally homogeneous corporations, Durkheim proposes that there should be functionally differentiated subgroups:

> if it is necessary that both [employers and employees] meet in the directing councils of the corporations, it is no less important that at the base of the corporative organization they form distinct and independent groups, for their interests are too often rival and antagonistic. To be able to go about their ways freely, they must go about their ways separately (1933:25).

One can easily imagine this series going all the way down to the individual. And at the top of this hierarchy, too, Durkheim implicitly unites all the moral prescriptions of difference under an umbrella prescription of sameness when he says that in societies in which differentiation is strongly prescribed "the common conscience is [not] threatened with disappearance. Only, it more and more comes to consist of very general and very indeterminate ways of thinking and feeling" (1933:172). It is only further evidence of the inconsistency of Durkheim's distinction between social structure and cultural structure, and of the greater emphasis he gives the latter, that he refers to the common *conscience* not disappearing, but does not mention common *labor* also not disappearing.

[2] Note that after defining an "interpersonal tie" as a "small-scale interaction" (1973:1361)—and therefore as social structural, according to my definition—Granovetter then specifies temporal regularity and cultural structural (as well as social structural) measures of its "strength": "the strength of a tie is a . . . combination of the amount of time, the emotional intensity, the intimacy (mutual confiding),

micro level can perform "Linkage of micro and macro levels" (1973:1377) and thereby integrate individuals into communities (and, presumably, communities into societies).

Note, however, that despite the explanatory implications of Durkheim's and Granovetter's arguments, hierarchic structure is here regarded as a purely descriptive concept, associated with no particular explanatory hypothesis or evaluative judgment. Thus, by itself, the concept does not imply that phenomena at more inclusive levels control, initiate, or sustain those at less inclusive levels, or vice versa; it does not imply that phenomena at middling (meso) levels dominate those at extreme (micro and macro) levels, or vice-versa; and it does not imply that phenomena at any level are "better" or "worse" than any other. (Inasmuch as the principle of hierarchic structure may be applied to anything, however, Chapter 12 will apply it to aggregative relations between causes and between effects—relations from which the principles of emergence and contextuality are derived.)

This chapter tries to explicate the concept of hierarchic structure, to demonstrate its consistently pivotal but too often unconscious and incomplete role in describing social phenomena, and to suggest ways of systematizing that role.

Simmel is my point of departure for identifying four variants of hierarchic structure in social phenomena. Next, the generic definition of social phenomena that was put forward in Chapter 2 will be combined with the principle of hierarchic structure and some descriptions of social phenomena (advanced by Parsons, Blau, Weber, and Marx) will be analyzed in light of that combination. Last, the principle of hierarchic structure will be applied to the description of complex social phenomena by taking into account the four variants of hierarchic structure that will now be discussed.

FOUR VARIANTS OF HIERARCHIC STRUCTURE

Simmel is expressly cognizant of the principle of hierarchic structure and the arbitrariness of all analytical truncations of that structure:

> It is . . . not true that reality can be attributed only to properly ultimate units, and not to phenomena in which these units find their forms. Any form (and a form is always a synthesis) is something added by a synthesizing subject. Thus, a conception that considers only individuals as "real" lets what

---

and the reciprocal services which characterize the tie" (1973:1361). Only Granovetter's omission of a spatial regularity (e.g., the number of different locations in which the interaction in question occurs) prevents his description and specification from covering all four of the components of social phenomena discussed in Chapter 2.

should be considered real get out of hand. It is perfectly arbitrary to stop the reduction, which leads to ultimately real elements, at the individual. For this reduction is interminable. In it, the individual appears as a composite of single qualities, and destinies, forces, and historical derivations, which in comparison to the individual himself have the same character of elementary realities as do the individuals in comparison to society (1950:7).

It is against the background of these views that Simmel's images of "concentric" and "juxtaposed" relationships between subgroups of a society may best be seen.

In the concentric relationship, the individual's "participation in the smallest of . . . groups already implies participation in the larger groups" (Simmel, 1955:147); participation in these groups implies participation in still larger groups; and so on up to the society as a whole. The picture is clearly hierarchic; Simmel describes a single nesting series of subgroups such that any given subgroup is composed of smaller subgroups (or, in the case of the smallest subgroup, individuals), and is also a member of a larger subgroup or group.

In the juxtaposed relationship, Simmel argues that the organizing principle is not one of successive whole inclusion of subgroups, but of chainlike sharing by one subgroup of another subgroup's members. Thus, a given individual "may belong, aside from his occupational position, to a scientific association, he may sit on a board of directors of a corporation, and occupy an honorific position in the city government" (1955:150)[3]; another individual may belong to the same scientific association but otherwise have a different set of subgroup memberships; a third individual may belong to the same board of directors but otherwise have still another set of memberships; and so on. The result, from the viewpoint of the subgroups, is linkage via shared membership rosters and I shall therefore refer to this relationship as concatenated.[4] Concatenated structure is the image underlying Merton's "status-set" and "role-set" (1957:368–384), and Blau's "multiform heterogeneity" (1977:83–90). Note that hierarchic and concatenated structures may coexist and be complementary, as Simmel indicates when he claims that "the individual *adds* affiliations with new groups to the singular affiliation which has hitherto influenced him in a pervasive and onesided manner" (1955:151, emphasis added).

Thus, in the hierarchic relationship, subgroups share their *membership*, as

---

[3] Note that Simmel's use of "may" here means that although the various subgroups *must* be overlapping in order to constitute a juxtaposed relationship, exactly which individual participants will manifest that overlap is to some extent indeterminate.

[4] I prefer "concatenated" to "juxtaposed" because the specifically chainlike (or better, chainmail-like) metaphor implied by concatenation seems to capture the linked positioning of subgroups that Simmel indicates better than "juxtaposition," which only indicates side-by-side positioning, without any necessary overlaps. Simmel elsewhere also discusses "mediated" relationships (see 1950:135), but this type appears to be concatenated structure again—that is, subgroups A and B share something (say, members or values) between them and subgroups B and C do likewise, but what is shared by A with B could not be shared by A with C nor could what is shared by B with C be shared by A with C.

subgroups, in the larger groups that they themselves constitute; in the concatenated relationship, subgroups share the *members* (whether these are regarded as smaller subgroups or as individuals) who constitute them. Now let us infer two other types of subgroup relationships which, although not mentioned by Simmel, complete the logical possibilities suggested by his conceptualization and help illuminate their joint implication.

The types in question may be called "integrated" and "independent." In the integrated case, subgroups share membership in larger groups and also share their own member elements. The extreme here is represented by Durkheim's concept of the primeval "horde" (1933:174–175) and by Tönnies' concept of "Gemeinschaft" (1957:37–42). In the independent case, subgroups share neither membership in larger groups nor their own member elements. This case seems represented by Tönnies' apocalyptic vision of the denouement of Gesellschaft (1957:228–235), by Sumner's separation of "in-group" and "out-group" (see Coser, 1978:297), and by Sorokin's notion of "independent congeries" (1947:58).[5] Figure 6.1 presents the integrated, hierarchic, concatenated, and independent subgroup relationships for direct comparison.[6]

The essential conclusion here, for present purposes, is that in all four relationships elements are aggregated into levels of greater inclusiveness, and it is on this ground that I regard them all as variants of hierarchic structure. One of these, however, is the pure type-case and is therefore called "hierarchic." Because this case epitomizes what all four variants have in common, let us concentrate on it first.

Before doing so, however, two points deserve special emphasis. First, Figure 6.1 and the following discussion refer only to hierarchic structure—that is, only membership or inclusiveness relations between elements and the aggregates which those elements, in turn, comprise—and not to the *coincidence* relations between the behaviors of different individuals (or more generally, different elements or aggregates at the same level) that were set forth in Chapters 3 and 4 or to the coincidence relations between regularities in those behaviors that were set forth in Chapter 5. Thus, note that Fig. 6.1 says nothing whatever about coincidence relations between the elements, or between the subgroups, or between the larger groups shown there (such relations would be represented by horizontal lines within levels rather than vertical lines between levels), just as Figs. 3.3 and 4.2 say nothing

---

[5] Sorokin, indeed, may refer to three of the four subgroup relationships shown in Figure 6.1: "the total sociocultural world appears as an enormous arena of millions of systems, now subordinated to one another and yielding sometimes the vastest supersystems; now coordinated with one another [as 'partners' without subordination of one to the other]; now being independent congeries in regard to one another" (1947:58).

[6] These four relationships should be regarded as ideal-typical, with many transitional points between types. Thus, subgroups may share few or many of their member elements and may share few or many of their memberships in higher groups.

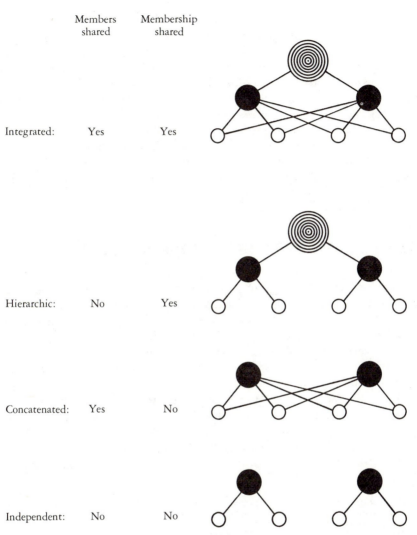

Figure 6.1. Hierarchic structure in social phenomena: Four types of subgroup (solid circles) relationships via shared members (open circles) and/or shared membership in larger groups (shaded circles).

about membership relations between individuals. The two sets of relations—that is, within-level coincidence and between-level membership—are intended to be complementary.

Second, note that hierarchic structure—defined in terms of aggregative relations, differs from simple ordinal stratification, as manifested in the levels of income, educational attainment, occupational prestige, and power (or, for that matter, age, height, and weight) that we often use to describe individuals. The difference is that ordinally higher levels *surpass* lower levels but they do not *include* them. For example, a college education surpasses a high school education but does not include two or more high school educations. Thus, when van den Berghe says "by hierarchy I shall mean a relatively stable rank order between co-specifics which determines preferential access to desirable resources, including the labor and sexual favors of co-specifics. Hierarchy is expressed through dominance and submission behaviors" (1974:780),[7] and when Wilson says "a hierarchy can be defined . . . as a system of two or more levels of units, the higher levels controlling at least to some extent the activities of the lower levels in order to achieve the goal of the group as a whole" (1975:11),[8] they both refer (despite their use of the term "hierarchy") to ordinal rather than hierarchic structure as these terms are used here.

THE PRINCIPLE OF HIERARCHIC STRUCTURE

A "hierarchy" may be defined as two or more levels in which elements at any given level are grouped into several aggregates and then these aggregates are treated as elements at the next higher level.[9] The principle of hierarchic structure states that any phenomenon whatever may be described as an element in a higher aggregate (which may itself be regarded as an element in some still higher aggregate) and also as an aggregate of lower elements (which may themselves be regarded as aggregates of still lower elements).

The distinction between "element" and "aggregate" is obviously crucial to this principle, and an "element" is defined as any concept or phenomenon treated as though it were homogeneous and indivisible, while an "aggregate" is defined as any concept or phenomenon treated as though it were heterogeneous and divisible. It is important to emphasize that it is one's "treatment" of a phenomenon and not

[7] van den Berghe probably means neither that hierarchy "determines" preferential access to resources, nor that hierarchy is "expressed through" dominance and submission behaviors, but rather that hierarchy *consists in* preferential access to resources and *is determined by* dominance and submission behaviors.

[8] The last phrase here, "in order to achieve the goal of the group as a whole" is clearly hypothetical rather than definitional.

[9] Simon provides the basis for this definition, although he uses more restricted descriptive terms (i.e., "system" and "interrelated") than I think are necessary: "By a hierarchic system, or hierarchy, I mean a system that is composed of interrelated subsystems, each of the latter being, in turn, hierarchic in structure until we reach some lowest level of elementary subsystem" (1965:64). Mesarovic's and Macko's definition, however, requires neither "system" nor "interrelationships" (but permits them, of course) and is thus more strictly in accord with the definition used here: "An object on a given stratum becomes a relation on a lower stratum and an element becomes a set. A subsystem on a given stratum is a system on the stratum below" (1969:34). And so is Grobstein's: "Hierarchical order refers to a complex of successively more encompassing sets" (1969:31).

what that phenomenon "actually is" (whatever that may mean) that counts. Thus, the very same phenomenon may be treated as an element in one analysis and as an aggregate in another. For sociological example, note that the individual organism is often treated as an element making up a larger aggregate in which the analyst is interested. In this tradition, Hawley argues that "life viewed ecologically is an aggregate rather than an individual phenomenon. The individual enters into ecological theory as a postulate and into ecological investigation as a unit of measurement" (1944:403).

But the individual may also be viewed as an aggregate composed of its own elements,[10] as Parsons suggests: "actors are conceived as systems: they are never oriented to their situations simply 'as a whole,' but always through specific modes of organization of independent components" (1960:471). Thus also, we find Adorno criticizing "empirical sociology" (i.e., chiefly survey research) for giving "primacy of significance to human beings as individuals, instead of defining socialized man today first and foremost as a moment—and, above all, the object—of the social totality." Empirical sociology, says Adorno, makes the error of regarding individually experienced "subjective facts [e.g., opinions, attitudes] as if these things existed in themselves and not, as they really are, reified" (1976a:242).[11] But in sharp contrast with this view, Collins argues that "only real people can do things. . . . 'Organizations,' 'classes,' or 'societies' never *do* anything" (1975:12), and insists that all such collectivities (presumably including the "social totality" to which Adorno refers) are mere "hypostatizations."

In short, one theorist may regard society as real and the individual as "reified," while another regards the individual as real and society as "hypostatsized." The principle of hierarchic structure, however, calls on us to regard no level as intrinsically any more or any less real than any other, to regard all designations of levels as hypothetical and not self-evident, and to seek empirical tests for them.

Micro Versus Macro Sociology

The view just expressed is not unanimously held among social scientists. There is, indeed, a continuing controversy on this issue, going under the general rubric

---

[10] Warriner properly (in my judgment) defends the position that "the group is just as real as the person, but . . . both are abstract, analytical units not concrete entities" (1956:550), but then goes on to confer concreteness on "the individual" rather than "the person": "it is only the individual, the biological structure, which we see directly, while the person is observed only through a series of actions and behaviors" (1956:552)—as if we do not observe the biological structure also only through a series of actions and behaviors.

[11] Note, however, that Adorno also says, in a paper originally published in the same year (1962) that "Societal totality does not lead a life of its own over and above that which it unites and of which it, in its turn, is composed. . . . System and individual entity are reciprocal and can only be apprehended in their reciprocity" (1976b:107).

of "methodological individualism versus methodological holism," and more specifically in our discipline, "micro versus macro sociology."

Before examining certain aspects of this controversy, however, it is important
to reiterate that the present context focuses on *description* only; the controversy itself
strongly implicates explanation as well, but consideration of this implication is
reserved for Chapters 7 and 12, on the grounds that explananda and explanantes
must be kept logically independent on pain of tautology. Thus, Brodbeck cor-
rectly, in my opinion, distinguishes between "descriptive emergence" and "explanatory emergence" and argues that

> Sometimes the phrase "methodological individualism" is applied both to the
> view that there are no undefinable group concepts and to the view that the
> laws of the group sciences are in principle reducible to those about individu-
> als. The former is a denial of descriptive emergence; the latter denies . . .
> explanatory emergence (1973b:309).

She concludes that "the denial of descriptive emergence does not entail the denial
of explanatory emergence" (Brodbeck, 1973b:310).

Consider, then, the purely descriptive implications of methodological individualism and methodological holism, and micro- and macrosociology.

Hayek argues in favor of the reality, exclusively, of the micro level:

> Social wholes are not given to us as what we may call "natural units" which
> we recognize as similar with our senses, as we do with flowers or butterflies,
> minerals or light-rays, or even forests or ant-heaps. . . . What we group
> together as instances of the same collective or whole are . . . classifications
> or selections of certain elements of a complex picture on the basis of a theory
> about their coherence. They do not stand for definite things or classes of
> things (if we understand the term "thing" in any material or concrete sense)
> but for a pattern or order in which different things may be related to each
> other—an order which is not a spatial or temporal order but can be defined
> only in terms of relations which are intelligible human attitudes (1973:46).

Popper takes a similar view: "most of the objects of social science, if not all of
them, are abstract objects; they are *theoretical* constructions. (Even 'the war' or 'the
army' are abstract concepts. . . . What is concrete is the many who are killed; or
the men and women in uniform, etc.)" (1973:71). Collins agrees: "Micro-sociology
has a strong claim to be considered the only directly empirical form of sociology,
with materials that are the only empirical reality there is" (1981:83); as does Duster in his reference to "microscopic work" as requiring "direct empirical observa-

tion" and to "macroscopic work" as requiring "less . . . direct observation of behavior. Economies and politics cannot be seen, as units, in motion. Rather, what we observe are national rates of employment, . . . summaries of voting trends . . . [etc.]" (1981:110–111).[12]

At the other end of the continuum from all these methodologically individual-istic views, Adorno (quoted in the preceding section) comes as close as I have seen to claiming that only macro social phenomena may be described as real. (Many analysts hold that macro social phenomena causally explain micro social phenom-ena, and many [including Ryder—quoted in Chapter 7] hold that macro social phenomena causally explain macro social phenomena, but in neither case are micro phenomena denied reality.[13])

There are at least two arguments against any position that confers reality, a priori, exclusively on any given level of phenomena. First, it seems most reason-able, in light of the presently unanimous conclusions of the nonsocial natural sci-ences (including physiology and psychology), to regard *all* phenomena—from the latest image of subatomic particles themselves up through individual organisms to the latest image of the universe itself—as "selections of certain elements of a com-

---

[12] It should be noted that methodological individualists frequently modify their otherwise exclusive conferral of reality on microphenomena with acknowledgments of the possible reality of macropheno-mena. Thus, Collins says "pure macro-concepts do exist in causal propositions and do survive micro-translation" (1981:99), and Harré says "there are some macro properties which are not susceptible to the standard epistemological criticisms" (1981:150,159). Harré claims that the macro properties in question are demographic, and although he refers only to sex ratio (see 1981:159), he may also have in mind population size—thus allying himself with Collins' claim that the "pure macro concepts" in question "are always some combination of number, time, and space applied to the micro contents of situations" (1981:99). In contrast with this view, I shall argue later in this chapter (also see Chapter 5) that there is nothing "purely" or intrinsically macro (or micro) about the concepts time or space—for example, seconds may be aggregated into minutes and minutes into hours—and it seems obvious that the same argument applies to number. What Collins seems to want to say, however, is better put by Knorr-Cetina: "[Collins'] aggregative hypothesis . . . says that macro phenomena are made up of *aggregations* and *repetitions* of many similar micro episodes" (1981:25–26)—which is the view adopted here except that the latter does not require the constituent "micro episodes" to be "similar," and thereby permits internal heterogeneity as well as homogeneity in macro phenomena.

[13] As will become clear later in this chapter, the micro-macro dichotomy is a gross but convenient simplification of hierarchic structures that may have any number of levels. Implicitly, Mandelbaum acknowledges this point:

it is assumed that all so-called "methodological holists" view a social system as an organic whole, the component parts of which are individual human beings. This is not necessarily the case. Some who reject methodological individualism would regard the component parts of a social system as being the institutions which comprise that system (1973b:237).

Harré provides a case in point:

Apart from the tendentious and highly problematic alleged attribute of "social class" there seem to be no person-constitutive relations which are of greater scale than can be found in institutions of the middle range (1981:147)

although one wonders how Harré regards the person-constitutive relations designated by "citizen" (member of a nation) and "human being" (member of a species).

plex picture on the basis of a theory about their coherence" (to use Hayek's phrase), or "theoretical constructions" (to use Popper's phrase). From this standpoint, an individual human being is *in principle* no more "concrete" or "real," and no less "rhetorical," than is "the working class," an "army," a "government," or a "nation" (see Chapter 14).

Second, *in practice,* the fact that our sensory perceptors are genetically pretuned to receive only certain kinds of stimuli in certain strengths does indeed force us, at least initially, to regard certain phenomena, like flowers and butterflies, as "natural units" but it has not prevented us from coming to recognize both micro phenomena like electrons and protons, and macro phenomena like galaxies and the universe itself as equally "natural"—despite the fact that they are entirely out of our direct sensory reach and require highly specialized observational instrumentation. Thus, "the indubitable fact," as Mandelbaum puts it, "that societal concepts are not capable of being 'pointed to,' in the sense in which we can point to material objects, or to the qualities or activities of these objects" (1973a:232) does not justify the claim that the latter objects "are the only empirical reality there is," or that they are the only ones on which we can make observations—when we appropriately modify our techniques and instrumentation of "pointing." The "national rates of employment, . . . summaries of voting trends . . . [etc.]" to which Duster refers are just such modifications—modifications which, by compiling many direct observations of behavior made by many different observers at different times and places, do indeed enable us to "see economies and polities, as units, in action." That is, if, as Knorr-Cetina says

> The "state" as circumscribed by a particular constitution can be seen as a highly simplified, large-scale abstraction. However, the concrete enactment of this abstraction . . . involves nothing larger in scale . . . than the situated *micro*interactions of members of congress and parliament, or of the people who frequent such localized government sites as the White House or 10 Downing Street (1981:38),

then some aggregate of observations taken on those "interactions" will constitute "seeing" the state, just as an aggregate of observations taken on the sun, planets, and their satellites, and so on, will constitute "seeing" the solar system. To be sure, we may not think the image formed of the state is as valid, reliable, or precise as the image formed of the solar system (because of more uncontrolled situational, technical, and motivational differences among observers of the state; see Chapter 16). In principle, however, the two images are no different insofar as they are both compiled from many observations taken by many observers with different techniques and motivations at different times and places.

Indeed, except for the multiplicity of observers (and the comfort of intersubjective verification; see Chapter 16), neither of these images is different in principle from what a single analyst does in "directly" observing even the simplest conversation between two people; that is, the individual analyst also forms his/her image of the conversation by compiling different perceptions made at different times and places, with different techniques, motivations, and so on.

Hierarchic Structure and the Generic Definition of Social Phenomenon

At this point it must be emphasized that the position that no level of social phenomena is, a priori, more real than any other is entirely compatible with the position (taken in Chapter 2) that social phenomena are defined generically as interorganism behavior regularities, and not as, say, interorganizational, or intersocietal behavior regularities.

In the first place, of course, the fact that a discipline takes phenomena of a certain kind, and a certain level, as its special focus in no way requires it to deny reality to all other phenomena; to do so, indeed, would be fatal to the discipline. In the second place, to say that the generic or minimal definition of social phenomena is "interorganism behavior regularities" does not prevent us from formulating any number of specific definitions within the boundaries of the generic one. Some of these specific definitions, as we have seen in the preceding three chapters, depend on drawing observable distinctions between *kinds* of organisms, kinds of behaviors, and kinds of regularities—distinctions which may be visualized as "horizontal." Other specific definitions, as the present chapter claims, depend on drawing observable distinctions between aggregation *levels* of organisms, behaviors, and regularities, distinctions which may be visualized as "vertical." Regarding the latter class of specific definitions, note that if sociology goes no further down the hierarchy of phenomena than whole organisms (and their behavior regularities), this in no way denies reality to lower levels (e.g., cells, organelles, molecules, atoms, and so on down); it merely declares a quite arbitrary, and perhaps only temporary, lower limit of disciplinary attention.

However, in declaring a lower limit we also declare a common denominator, that is, we declare the terms to which all specific definitions and descriptions of social phenomena must be reducible. That is to say, all definitions of concepts like social "groups," social "organizations," social "institutions," social "communities," "societies," and so on must be reducible to "interorganism behavior regularities" if their empirical referents are to qualify as social phenomena. And saying that such concepts must be so reduc*ible* does not mean they have to be so reduc*ed* in every case; shorthand notation is certainly admissible so long as we recognize it as such.

This view may seem to coincide with methodological individualism as ex-

pressed, say, in Watkins' statement that "According to [the principle of methodological individualism] the ultimate constituents of the social world are individual
people" (1973b:168). Similarly, Collins asserts that "the sum of all possible empirical evidence in sociology consists ultimately in a set of 'filmstrips' giving the
sensory and subjective experience, moment by moment, of every person who has
ever lived" (1981:99). There is an essential difference, however, between these
views and the generic definition of social phenomena put foward in Chapter 2.
This definition claims that the ultimate "constituents of the social world," and the
ultimate "empirical evidence in sociology," consists in *inter*individual behavior regularities and not in the behaviors or experiences of individual people. It is not
enough, according to this definition, to observe *individuals;* we must observe something going on *across* individuals. Collins' "set of 'filmstrips' " could not evidence
social phenomena unless we observed behavior regularities across such filmstrips,
and then *only* those interfilmstrip regularities (not necessarily the entire set of filmstrips) would constitute such evidence.[14]

Perhaps this is what Mandelbaum has in mind when he says "societal facts are
not reducible to the facts of individual behavior" (1973a:230; see also 223). Giddens, however, more clearly has it in mind when he says "social systems (and
overall societies as encompassing types of social system) consist of reproduced relationships between individuals and (or) collectivities" (1981:169), as does Knorr-
Cetina when she points out that "Micro-sociologies [in contrast with methodological individualism] do not turn to individuals, but to *interaction in social situations*
as the relevant methodological 'units' " (1981:8–9)[15]—although for reasons discussed in Chapter 2 the generic definition of social phenomena does not require
"interaction," nor does it require a specifically "social" situation; time and space
are enough.

Hierarchies: Real Phenomena Versus Heuristic Devices

Not only do I take no a priori position here regarding the reality of given levels
within a hierarchy, I also take no position regarding the reality of hierarchies
themselves. Here too there is controversy—between those who regard hierarchies
as (real) aspects of the way things exist independently of our observation of them,
and those who regard hierarchies solely as observers' (nominal) techniques for de-

---

[14] Collins' "set of 'filmstrips' " would be one *source* of such evidence (the other source being the
analyst's definitions of "behavior" and "regularity"), but they would not be the evidence itself.

[15] Knorr-Cetina goes on to confound a descriptive definition with an explanatory hypothesis (one
which will be called social structuralistic in Chapters 7 and 9): "Strictly speaking, the argument as to
a reality *sui generis* of social situations . . . require us to see the outcome of social action as tied to
particular *occasions* and to *other participants* in the situation" (1981:9).

scribing things. On the realistic side, Simon argues that "Scientific knowledge is organized in levels . . . because nature is organized in levels . . . and nature is organized in levels because hierarchic structures . . . provide the most viable form for any system of even moderate complexity" (1973:27). On the nominalistic side, Smith argues that "Nature itself comprises all levels and knows not our distinctions. . . . The new structures that seem to emerge as aggregates when seen on a larger scale are partly illusory: it is less a characteristic of the structure itself than of the limited resolution of our perception (whether visual or conceptual). Each 'level' is what we see at certain resolutions" (1969:80).

Neither side of the controversy over whether hierarchies are real or nominal[16] seems to deny the scientific utility of hierarchic concepts—even the nominalistic side recognizes their heuristic value—and my avoidance of the issue here is grounded on this common acceptance. Accordingly, it cannot be overemphasized that the principle of hierarchic structure is here regarded as setting forth neither the only way phenomena "are" (in some absolute, realist sense) nor the only way they can be described. Thus, Sorokin suggests three kinds of relations between social phenomena, only the first of which is explicitly hierarchic: "the total sociocultural world appears as an enormous arena of millions of systems, now subordinated to one another and yielding sometimes the vastest supersystems; now coordinated with one another [as 'partners' without subordination of one to the other]; now being independent congeries in regard to one another" (1941:58).[17] Similarly, Moore, inquiring "whether certain standard components of cultures and societies are especially autonomous," goes on to claim that "Although the evidence relating to . . . independent variability . . . is extremely sketchy, it does appear that aesthetic canons and forms provide one such manifestation and that strictly superempirical components of religious belief represent another" (1963a:75)—a hypothesis reminiscent of Durkheim's idea that religious "sentiments, ideas, and images . . . once born, obey laws all their own" (1965:471).

Obviously, what is needed in order to apply the principle of hierarchic structure to the description of social phenomena is a definition of whatever may be regarded as the most fundamental "elements" of such phenomena from which higher aggregates may be composed. For this, I turn to the generic components of social phe-

---

[16] One way of resolving the dilemma has been proposed most explicitly by Pattee, but adumbrated by Simon (1965). The latter points out that two kinds of self-descriptions are present within the living organism in the forms of DNA and RNA ("state descriptions"), and proteins ("process descriptions"). Pattee argues more generally that in certain inorganic as well as organic hierarchies, descriptions of their own behavior are formed, and that "Autonomous hierarchical function implies some form of self-representation. . . . We will have to learn how collections of matter produce their own internal descriptions" (1969:177). Such internal descriptions would seem to include culture in social phenomena; and culture may therefore be viewed as but one of a family of self-descriptions of complex systems.

[17] Simon, however, argues that "If there are important systems in the world that are complex without being hierarchic, they may to a considerable extent escape our observation and our understanding" (1965:72).

nomena set forth in Chapter 2 and propose that individual *organisms* may be aggregated and reaggregated into collectivities of increasing size and complexity[18]; individual physical and psychical *behaviors* may be aggregated and reaggregated into subsystems, systems, and supersystems of such behaviors; and individual spatial and temporal *regularities* may be aggregated and reaggregated into patterns of broader and more complex coverage, and longer and more complex duration.

Thus, we have what I shall call componential hierarchies, that is, hierarchic structure in each component of social phenomena taken separately. It is this conceptualization that points to general criteria for identifying substantively significant differences between levels.

Substantively Significant Levels

In a word, we know that a substantitively significant discontinuity (i.e., difference between levels) in any one of the componential hierarchies has been identified when that discontinuity is correlated with discontinuities in the other componential hierarchies.

This criterion of substantive significance in level distinctions rests on the claim that no phenomenon may be declared "real" until its boundaries have been confirmed in more than one of their properties (and also each property has been confirmed through more than one measurement procedure [see Campbell and Fiske, 1959]). Thus, Campbell quotes Rice to the effect that if a jazz concert patron visually sees a saxophone, " 'Corroboration would be required in the form of other sense impressions . . . emanating from or relating to the saxophone' " (1958:16) before the patron could safely say his/her vision of a saxophone is not an hallucination. Campbell concludes that

> for the more "real" entities, the number of possible ways of confirming the boundaries is probably unlimited. . . . "Illusions" occur when confirmation is attempted and found lacking, when boundaries diagnosed by one means fail to show up by other expected checks. . . . It might well be alleged that any scientifically useful boundary must be confirmable by at least two independent means (1958:23).

---

[18] This idea, applied to individual organisms and aggregates of organisms, is the basis of Laumann's and Pappi's discussion of "social networks":

[W]e propose to define a social network in its most general form as a set of nodes (e.g., persons) linked by a set of social relationships . . . of a specified type. In addition . . . we shall permit entities other than . . . "real" persons—for example, corporate actors, such as business firms, or aggregates of persons sharing a particular attribute, such as ethnic or class groups—to act as nodes (1976:18).

The pursuit of substantively significant discontinuities in the componential hierarchies of social phenomena, however, is persistently and seriously hampered (but not altogether prevented) by an inconsistency in the metrics applied to the various componential hierarchies. Thus, on the one hand, sociologists have long been unanimous in treating the individual human being as the irreducible element of the collectivity componential hierarchy—even though every one of us probably also accepts the view of the anatomical sciences that the individual human being may also be treated as an aggregate of smaller entities ranging from, say, the respiratory, digestive, nervous, and motor system level through the organ level to the cell, organelle, molecular, and so forth, levels. Moreover, we also seem to possess fairly wide consensus on units of the regularity hierarchy—received, in the main, from statistics, chronology, and geography.

However, we remain very far from agreement on the sociological units of physical and psychical behavior. As a result, one analyst may locate an interhierarchy correlation that other analysts find difficult to replicate partly because they may employ different units (and therefore describe different hierarchies of behavior). If sociological description, as well as the explanation that depends on it, is to become more testable, replicable, and cumulative, we must eventually remove the current metrical inconsistency between hierarchies by developing conventional behavior units just as we now accept conventional collectivity and regularity units.[19] Chapters 3 and 4 have tried to construct an elementary basis for progress in this direction.

Meanwhile, however, descriptive analysis in sociology continues to make progress despite this inconsistency, and generally takes (or should take) the form of searches for answers to three questions:

1. What are the behavior and regularity properties of collectivities at different levels? Most of the descriptive side of specialty literatures in sociology—those devoted to dyads, triads, and other groups, families, schools, social movements, organizations, bureaucracies, cities, communities, societies, and so on—addresses this general question. Here we want to know "what's going on," that is, we want to know the behaviors and their between-individuals coincidences (as discussed in Chapters 3 and 4), together with the spatial and temporal regularities characterizing such coincidences (as discussed in Chapter 5), that occur in these different collectivities.

2. What are the collectivity and regularity properties of social behavior at different levels? Here we inquire about the various collectivities that perform given behaviors at different times and places. We would like to know whether certain behaviors (any of those discussed in Chapters 3 and 4) are typically carried out by certain collectivities and with certain spatiotemporal regularities.

---

[19] A similar plea may be found in Adler (1960), except that he makes behavior the only unit measurement required in sociology. Other, more generalized pleas for measurement consensus may be found in Gibbs (1972), and Blalock (1979).

3. What are the behavior and collectivity properties of social regularities at different hierarchic levels? This question focuses attention on one of the least developed aspects of sociological description. Here we want to know whether certain temporal and spatial regularities are associated with certain collectivities and with certain behaviors. If a fast tempo (for example) is observed in a given behavior, we want to know whether we can expect that only small collectivities will be involved and whether only certain kinds of behaviors will be involved.

Needless to say, the identification of properties is an important variety of theoretic hypothesis and empirical research in every scientific field, and we may indeed think of all investigation into the properties of a given level in a given hierarchy as searches among conceptually related hierarchies for the empirical correlates of that level.

It follows that descriptive analyses of collectivities, behavior, and regularity componential hierarchies in sociology are highly interdependent and potentially self-correcting insofar as hypotheses concerning differences between levels in one componential hierarchy are testable against correlated differences in the other componential hierarchies. " 'What is the difference between an atom and a molecule? An atom interacts at one energy level and molecules interact at the other, and that is how we tell the difference' " (Simon, 1973:9, quoting Melvin Calvin). Similarly, Wilson points out that "What we call the 'natural interfaces' [between levels], are identifiable either by the occurrence of a steep decrement in the number or strength of linkages crossing them, as developed by Simon (1965) in the concept of near-decomposability, or through the existence of some form of closure" (1969:118).[20]

It appears, then, that our notions about collectivities of all kinds and at all levels are perpetually subject to revision by the correlated continuities and discontinuities that we discover between them, on the one hand, and behaviors and regularities, on the other. Similarly, our notions about behaviors undergo revision as we learn more about the collectivities that manifest them and the regularities with which they are manifested. Finally, our notions about regularities are revisable under the impact of new knowledge about the collectivities and behaviors that manifest them.

On the strength of this argument, the question of how many levels may properly be designated within any given componential hierarchy is here left open in order to permit one analyst to distinguish only micro and macro levels; another to

---

[20] Wilson also identifies two kinds of closure that correspond to the spatial and temporal types of regularities discussed here: "topological closure [involving] closed surfaces of a spatial neighborhood," and "temporal closure [involving] a neighborhood in time" (1969:54). He adds that "the properties of space and time are closure properties of structures, bringing to mind the basic idea of Leibnitz that space and time have no independent existence but derive from the nature of structures" (1969:55). The converse may also be true (i.e., entity and behavior structures may have no independent existence apart from space and time). In that case, structures, space, and time are all interdependent.

distinguish micro, meso, and macro levels; still another to distinguish ten or twenty different levels—all depending, first, on showing that the discontinuity between any two adjacent levels within the hierarchy of concern is empirically associated with a discontinuity in one or more of the remaining hierarchies, and second, on the precision required by the analysis, since greater precision is likely to require more levels.

At this point I have set forth, roughly, what may be regarded as a two-dimensional scheme in which the "horizontal" dimension consists of the components of social phenomena and the "vertical" dimension consists of the principle of hierarchic structure. Let us now see whether this scheme actually works for descriptive systematics, parsimony, and comparability by applying it to several images of social phenomena that are already in the literature. The first two images (set forth by Parsons, and Blau, respectively) will be seen to complement each other, and to illuminate related images described by Weber and Marx, respectively. Parsons and Blau both manifest interest in the physical behavior hierarchy but they each relate that hierarchy to a different one of the remaining componential hierarchies.

Parsons, Weber, and Social Action

Chapter 2 has already shown how Parsons first draws the distinction between social structure and cultural structure that I follow here and then reneges on that distinction by finally reducing "social system" to "cultural system." Suppose, however, we take Parsons at his first word and apply the social-cultural distinction strictly and consistently to the following description:

> The basic subsystems of the general system of action constitute a hierarchical series of such agencies of control of the behavior of individuals or organisms. The behavioral organism is the point of articulation of the system of action with the anatomical-physiological features of the physical organism and is its point of contact with the physical environment. The personality system is, in turn, a system of control over the behavioral organism; the social system, over the personalities of its participating members; and the cultural system, a system of control relative to social systems (1961a:38).

As just indicated, the first step in understanding this picture is to redraw Parsons' own distinction between "social system" and "cultural system." This serves as the basis for the second step: understanding the relationship to these systems, and to each other, of "behavioral organism" and "personality system."

Parsons provides one important clue in the following passage from a somewhat earlier publication:

A social system is a system generated and constituted by the interaction of two or more individual actors, whereas a psychological [i.e., personality] system is a system of action characterized by the fact that all the behavior belonging to it is behavior of the same living organism. . . . As a generalized mode of orientation, a cultural pattern is at least potentially applicable to more than one object and characteristic of more than one actor (1959:614, emphasis removed; see also 635, 645).

From this, it seems clear that in addition to the social-versus-cultural dimension, a second dimension is needed to describe logical relations between cultural system, social system, and personality system, such that the first two will refer to behavioral properties of *collectivities of several actors,* while the third will refer to psychical behavior properties of *one actor only.*

The "behavioral organism," however, presents a special interpretative problem. Here is what Parsons says:

The organism is that aspect of the physiologically functioning system which interacts directly with the personality and the other systems of action. . . . For many purposes, only part of the total concrete organism should be treated as part of the system of action. Later we will refer to this part as the "behavioral organism" (1959:615).

Note that of all the systems of the general system of action, only this one is not consistently called a "system" (except when it is significantly, though only momentarily, renamed the "behavioral-organic system" [1970:44], or the "physiological system" as against the "psychological system" [1959:632]). This terminological inconsistency is not trivial; it signals the conceptual problem: Does "behavioral organism" refer primarily to behavior or primarily to organism? If it refers primarily to behavior, then it is a system of action like the other systems of action (personality, social, and cultural), and we may then proceed to inquire about its distinctive kind of behavior. If it refers primarily to organism, then we are dealing with an entity in which a given kind of behavior may be problematic—that is, at any given moment the entity may or may not perform that behavior. In other words, if we read, literally, "behavioral *organism,*" then a specific kind of entity, not a specific kind of behavior, is indicated and the "behavioral organism" appears anomalous among the other systems of action. But if we read "organismic *behavior,*" then a specific kind of behavior is indicated, and the "behavioral organism" appears consistent with the other systems of action.

In trying to answer this question, note that in addition to writing, sometimes, simply of "organism," Parsons describes it (see above) as a *"part* of the total concrete organism," rather than, say, as a "behavior" or "process" of the total concrete organism. And, perhaps with some equivocation, he says, "The total concrete organism is not an action system in our sense" (1970:44). Such remarks seem to suggest an entity, rather than a behavior, referent. In apparent consistency with an entity referent, Parsons' definition of the personality system leaves no behavioral room for "behavioral organism": "The *total* system of behavior of one organism is its personality" (1959:645, emphasis added). On the other hand, Parsons argues forcefully that "*behavior* is the empirical subject matter of the theory of action. The properties of a behaving organism, independent of its behavior in actual situations, are of interest to that theory only insofar as they condition or are otherwise involved in the behavior" (1959:614, emphasis in the original). This suggests a behavioral rather than entity referent. The tendency toward a behavioral connotation also seems supported by Parsons' mention (quoted above) of that system as "physiological" (rather than anatomical).

Now suppose we somewhat arbitrarily resolve Parsons' ambiguity in favor of consistency with the other action systems and interpret "behavioral organism" to have a behavioral rather than entity referent—that is, as organismic *behavior*. Then Parsons' references to it as the "physiological system" in contradistinction with the "psychological system" seem clearly to indicate physical rather than psychical behavior.[21] On this basis, it immediately becomes clear that Parsons' "basic subsystems of the general system of action" describe the individual and society in terms of a two-level hierarchy of physical behavior ("behavioral organism" and "social system") and a two-level hierarchy of psychical behavior ("personality system" and "cultural system"), each implying a two-level hierarchy of entities (individual and collectivity).[22]

Thus interpreted,[23] Parsons' subsystems of action help illuminate the hierarchic

[21] Indeed, at one point, he does identify this system with "body" and the personality system with "mind" (Parsons, 1959:651).

[22] Note that Parsons and Shils are ambiguous in their definition of collectivity. On the one hand, they declare a collectivity to be a "social system" (1951:192) and assert that "the 'individual' actor as a concrete system of action is *not* usually the most important unit of the social system. For most purposes the conceptual unit of the social system is the role" (1951:190, emphasis changed). On the other hand, however, they distinctly imply that they do regard a collectivity as an aggregate of individual organisms when they say "A collectivity, as the term is used here, should be clearly distinguished from two other types of social aggregates. The first is a category of persons who have some attribute or complex of attributes in common . . . which [does] not involve 'action in concert'. . . . The second type of social aggregate is a plurality of persons who are merely interdependent with one another ecologically" (Parsons and Shils, 1951:193, emphasis removed). In a later publication, Parsons drops the "social system" interpretation of a collectivity and identifies it entirely with aggregates of organisms: "it is collectivities *composed of individuals* . . . in which the most important sociological interest lies" (1968:324, emphasis changed).

[23] This interpretation helps account for the rise in prominence, within Parsons' theory, of the concept "behavioral organism." The "action frame of reference" initially comprised only "three configurations" (personality, social system, and culture), wherein "personality" was ambiguously described as both a "system of orientation and motivation" and also a "physiological organism" (1951:7); as being, vaguely, "organized around the biological unity of the organism" (1951:75); and as being similar to social systems insofar as they—but not cultural systems—were said to be capable of physical behavior ("action") (1951:76). In 1959, however, Parsons stresses the separate introduction of "behavioral organism": It will be noted that, compared to previous publications, we speak of four rather than three primary subsystems of the general theory of action; the organism, in certain respects, has been added. . . . This represents a definite theoretical innovation" (1959:613). In 1970, he claims that this addition has "rounded out" the action frame of reference—although not for the reasons being stressed here,

components underlying the conceptualizations of "social action" and "social relationship" that are most essential to Weber's sociological theorizing. "Action is social," says Weber, "insofar as, by virtue of the subjective meaning attached to it by the acting individual . . . it takes account of the behavior of others and is thereby oriented in its course" (1947:88). Note that this definition is cast at the individual and not the collective level; it takes only one "acting" individual to constitute social action insofar as the other individuals—that is, the ones toward whom the first, socially acting, individual is oriented—may be oriented and behaving toward something else entirely. Note also that the definition requires both physical "acting" and psychical attachment of "subjective meaning" on the part of the first individual. It therefore seems fair to regard Parsons' "behavioral organism" and "personality system" as explications of Weber's definition of "social action."

Now let us note that from "social action" Weber constructs "social relationship": "the term 'social relationship' will be used to denote the behavior of a plurality of actors insofar as, in its meaningful content, the action of each takes account of that of the others and is oriented in these terms" (1947:118). Here Weber clearly refers to the collective level of physical and psychical behaviors when he indicates that "a plurality of actors" are both objectively behaving toward, and subjectively oriented toward, each other; and this image seems explicated by Parsons' "social system and "cultural system."

Note that the collectivity hierarchy is left only implicit in Parsons' description of the subsystems of action—although his occasional interpretations of the "behavioral organism" subsystem as an entity may well be signs of an irresolute awareness of the need to explicate that hierarchy. By contrast, Blau's discussion of "the division of labor and the distribution of power" (1977:185) includes clear and explicit emphasis on the collectivity hierarchy. This inclusion, however, is counterbalanced by an exclusion that Parsons would surely never tolerate: Blau drops the psychical behavior hierarchy from consideration.[24]

Blau, Marx, and the Division of Labor

Blau begins his discussion of the division of labor by asserting that "How society's work is organized can be looked at from two perspectives: that of the *occu-*

---

but because it enables him to identify that frame's now four subsystems with the four functional imperatives (see Parsons 1970:43–44). Parsons does not tell us *how* the addition enables him to make this identification, but considering the emphasis he gives to "a striking set of numerical relations" involving the number four (1970:38) it seems just possible that the presence of fourness in the form of both schemes is his principal criterion of substantive identity here.

[24] Blau says "I consider my focus on group structures and status structures, and explicitly not on culture [defined by Blau as "values and symbols, rules and myths"], to be in the tradition of Marx" (1977:16). In striking and unexplicated contrast, however, Blau also claims that "Value consensus is of crucial significance for social processes that pervade complex social structures" (1964:24).

pations among which work is divided, and that of the *organizations* among which work is divided" (1977:185, emphasis added). Although behavior and entity referents may seem to be indicated by "occupation" and "organization," that is not the case, as Blau immediately points out: "the term ['occupations'] is usually reserved for the distribution of [*individuals in*] *the labor force* among occupations, and it is used in this restricted sense here" (1977:185). Thus, by "occupations" Blau means not the *behaviors* performed but the *performers* of behaviors—the occupiers of occupations, so to speak—a reversal of meaning which is the converse of that in Parsons' "behavioral organism," as discussed above. We must therefore regard Blau's two "perspectives" on "How society's work is organized" as referring to two hierarchic levels of entities which can perform that work: individuals (i.e., "occupations") and collectivities (i.e., "organizations").

Now here is how Blau conceptualizes behavioral "work" itself. First, for Blau, as for Marx and Durkheim, "work" and "labor" clearly connote externalized, that is, *physical,* behavior (even where that behavior is only the expression of psychical behavior). Second, Blau differentiates two types of work: "The two major forms of division of labor are the subdivision of work into repetitive routines and its subdivision into expert specialties" (1977:188). Thus, eschewing the substantive distinctions in work (i.e., distinctions in *what* is done) that are implied by the behavioral notion of "occupations" (because he has already elected to use that term in the "restricted sense" quoted above), Blau employs a formal distinction in work (i.e., *how* it is done). The latter distinction hinges on defining as "routine" tasks that are "repetitive" (i.e., constant) over time and as "specialty" tasks that are "variable" over time (see 1977:187).

However, as information theory, linguistics, genetics, physics, astronomy, cytology—indeed, the entire corpus of natural science—seems to indicate, complex and specialized processes (not excluding the division of labor) may be usefully regarded as aggregates of shorter and simpler routines. Accordingly, Blau's "routinized" versus "specialized" distinction may be regarded as specifying a two-level hierarchy of behavior attributed to the social phenomenon called "the division of labor" such that that division is said to occur between elemental behavior "routines" or between complex aggregates of these routines, that is, "specialties."

Viewed in this light, it therefore appears that, in describing the division of labor, Blau implies two componential hierarchies whose levels are correlated: there is a two-level collectivity hierarchy (i.e., "occupations" and "organizations"), and by its side there is a two-level physical behavior hierarchy (i.e., "routines" and "specialties").

Although he does not say so explicitly, it seems that Blau believes these two hierarchies have undergone parallel evolutions from micro toward macro. Thus, he refers to "*modern* societies, where so much of the total work is carried out in large *organizations*" (1977:203, emphasis added; see also 197), and he refers to "*Earlier* industrial developments [as having] promoted large-scale *routinization*" (1977:194). Blau thereby implies that division of labor entities were once only (or mainly) individuals and the division of labor behaviors performed by them were once only (or mainly) routines; the modern division of labor, however, is between large organizations that perform specialties.[25] This hierarchic and evolutionary image helps illuminate an application of the principle of hierarchic structure to components of social phenomena which is central to the classical Marxian image of human history.

Thus, during what Marx calls "primitive communism," the individual was a generalist who produced all needed goods and services and was, in this behavioral sense, indistinguishable from the whole society. In terms of Fig. 6.1, the relationship, behaviorally speaking, was integration: the micro and macro entity levels encompassed the same macro range of behaviors; behaviorally, the individual was a little society and the society was a big individual.[26] With the development of handicrafts production, however, the individual became a behavioral specialist—producing only one commodity but producing that commodity in its entirety. That is to say, a meso level in the behavior hierarchy emerged and was allocated to the micro entity level. In the next, manufacturing, stage a meso-level entity (i.e., the factory, and more generally, the privately owned business firm) emerged and took over the meso-level behavioral specialties that had developed in the previous stage. To this end, however, the micro entity level was further downgraded to performing micro behavior.

Marx looks upon the successive demotion of individuals from behaviorally macro generalists, to meso specialists, and finally, to micro routinists as a central feature of the long but ultimately transitory process of individual "estrangement" and "alienation." The emergent meso-level factory and firm, however, does not seem to be regarded as transitory by him. Marx expects them to persist long after the proletarian revolution restores the individual to the generalist level by substituting machines for human beings in routines and specialties (a substitution already nascent, says Marx, in the present industrial stage of the division of labor),

[25] Blau also argues that "the trend has been toward increasing concentration of [power] in giant organizations, and their top executives" (1974:633), and that this concentration is "incompatible with democracy in the long run" (1977:241) because it endangers "the integration of the diverse parts in industrial society and the counteracting forces permitting gradual change in democracy . . . [and thereby threatens] to replace democratically instituted recurrent social change with alternate periods of social stagnation and revolutionary upheaval" (1974:633,634). In a similar line of argument, Coleman says of "corporate bodies" in modern society that "what was once a hard shell of protection for men, shielding them from the state and giving them the strength of collective action, has . . . come to develop power on its own" (1974:35) and to exert that power against individual freedom. Thus, both Blau and Coleman challenge and qualify Durkheim's hierarchic structural hypothesis that "A nation can be maintained only if, between the State and the individual, there is intercalated a whole series of secondary groups near enough to the individuals to attract them strongly in their sphere of action and drag them, in this way, into the general torrent of social life" (1933:28). Blau, and Coleman, assert that at least some of the secondary groups to which Durkheim refers may not maintain but destroy a democratic nation by emergent behavior regularities that do indeed drag individuals into the torrent of social life—but bind and drown them there.

[26] Durkheim, refuting this Marxian image, aptly says it portrays the individual as "an empire embedded within another empire" (1978:69).

and otherwise making it "possible for [the individual] to do one thing today and another tomorrow, to hunt in the morning, fish in the afternoon, rear cattle in the evening, criticize after dinner" (1947:22).

In differently partial but overlapping ways, then, Parsons and Blau (as well as Weber and Marx, their acknowledged intellectual forebears) illustrate the intersection of what this chapter terms the principle of hierarchic structure and the generic definition of social phenomena: Parsons concentrates on correlations between hierarchic levels in the psychical behavior and the physical behavior components of social phenomena, while Blau concentrates on correlations between hierarchic levels in the physical behavior component and the collectivity component of social phenomena.

It will certainly have been noticed that neither of the analyses examined above has explicitly involved the spatial or temporal regularity hierarchy, and indeed, sociological analyses that are complete in the sense of referring equally to all the componential hierarchies are, at best, rare. However, at least two theorists (Sorokin, and Moore) have written more extensively than others on the temporal regularity hierarchy and its relation to the other hierarchies; and two other theorists (Burgess, and Hawley) have written extensively on the spatial regularity hierarchy and its relations to the other hierarchies. Let us briefly scan their views.

Sorokin, Moore, and Social Dynamics

Sorokin declares his overriding interest in the temporal regularities of social life when he describes his four-volume principal work, entitled *Social and Cultural Dynamics,* as "an investigation of the nature and change, the dynamics of integrated culture: its types, its processes, its trends, fluctuations, rhythms, tempos" (1937:x). Elsewhere, he describes "dynamic general sociology" as an investigation of "(a) recurring social processes . . . (b) recurring cultural processes . . . (c) rhythms, tempos, periodicities, trends, and fluctuations in social and cultural processes in persons, and how and why persons change" (Sorokin, 1947:16). Accordingly, Sorokin proposes several hypotheses regarding relations between the temporal regularity componential hierarchy on the one hand and the behavior, and the collectivity, hierarchies on the other:

> the rhythms in the subsystems of a larger system tend to be shorter in their time duration than the rhythms of the larger systems; and the tempos of the succession of the phases in the rhythms of subsystems are faster than the tempos of those in the embracing systems. . . . Fluctuation of the value of certain stock-market shares tends to be faster and more erratic than that of all the shares registered on the stock market. The changes in the prosperity and depression of a certain industrial firm tend to be more frequent and abrupt

than in that of the whole economic system of the country. . . . Changes in methods, techniques, principles, and theories in one of the sciences are likely to be "speedier" than in those of the whole system of natural sciences (1941:385).

Moore says "Small-scale cycles and indeed most small-scale changes tend to be short-term ones, and with the exception of life cycles, long-term cycles tend to be large scale" (1963b:49)—although he does not indicate whether he has in mind different "scale" collectivities, or different "scale" behavior systems or both—and argues that "any combination of set time periods and set tasks necessarily has implications for the speed to be followed. The necessity is simply accentuated if different persons must be coordinated in sequence. . . ." (1963a:51). Referring specifically to the relation of behaviors in the family and other collectivities to temporal regularities, he asserts that

> The very continuity of urban life . . . implies that some people must be off-schedule with regard to the dominant temporal patterns. The need for protective and emergency services is never-ending. . . . For those workers, along with other "night-shift" workers [there is a] dilemma: either they must have a minimal relationship with their families and with other "normally" timed activities, or their families will be off-phase with the standard patterns of the community (Moore, 1963a:121)

Finally, note Moore's reference to relations between the collectivity, behavior, and temporal regularities, on the one hand, and spatial regularities on the other: "As one approaches the center of a city, the increasing concentration of persons in space appears to be matched by the increasing concentration of activities in time" (1963a:117), and with that let us move to a brief examination of some ideas of Burgess, and Hawley regarding the spatial regularity hierarchy.

Burgess, Hawley, and Social Spacing

Burgess proposes "a series of concentric circles [i.e., downtown business district at the center, zone in transition, zone of workingmen's homes, residential zone, and commuters zone] to designate both the successive zones of urban extension and the types of areas differentiated in the process of expansion" (1961:38)—thereby hypothesizing certain relations between collectivities, behaviors, and spatial regularities. And in a similar way, Zorbaugh argues for the existence of "natural areas" within a city: "The natural area . . . is a unit in the physical structure of the city, typified by a physical individuality and the characteristic attitudes, sentiments, and interests of the people segregated within it" (1961:193).

Hawley points out that Burgess' concentric zone scheme applies best to "local expansion [of the city] under the centralizing influences of steam and electric railway systems" (1971:99), and notes that prior to those technological inventions, other spatial regularities were evident in the American city. Thus, the early nineteenth-century city

> is more accurately described as cellular . . . [wherein] the urban agglomeration was a congeries of more or less self-contained districts or quarters, each with its own industries and shops and other institutions. . . . [But it was not until after 1850 that the] establishment of a steam railway terminal in the interior of the city, usually close by the piers and warehouses serving water carriers, set in motion a redistribution process that ultimately produced a well-defined centralization of activities. Public buildings, central offices, banks, services to business and industry, hotels, and retail and personal service establishments gathered about the terminal to take advantage of the quick communication with hinterlands and with other centers (Hawley, 1971:90, 91).

Hawley also argues that city expansion generally combined radial and concentric growth so that "the urban center tended to acquire a rather clear star-shaped configuration. Central growth followed radial growth as circumferential or "cross-town" street railway lines, intersecting radial lines, were built" (1971:95). At such intersections, secondary business centers developed, and "Lesser, or tertiary business districts were distributed over the entire built-up area at intervals of approximately three miles and interspersed among them were corner service centers comprising two or three stores each" (1971:95).

The outcome is a set of interrelated levels in the spatial regularity, behavior, and collectivity hierarchies, or, as Hawley himself puts it, we have

> a hierarchy in size distribution, in territorial spread, and in the variety of services offered. At the top was the central district, providing the maximum range of specialized as well as many standard services; the next echelon was formed of a small number of secondary centers offering fewer specialized services with a wide assortment of commonplace services; a third level was composed of many smaller subcenters dealing only in the most standardized goods; and finally there were a great many neighborhood outlets catering to the daily consumption needs of residents (1971:96).

Now, having tried to deal so far with only the simplest and most direct variant of hierarchic structure in social phenomena as that variant reveals itself in analyses of social collectivities, social behaviors, and social regularities, it is time to recall all four variants of that structure and take them explicitly into account.

COMPLEX SOCIAL PHENOMENA

All descriptions of complex social phenomena seem to hinge on identifying parts which are segregated from one another in certain respects and integrated with one another in certain other respects. For example, van den Berghe refers to social systems as consisting of "subsystems which are functionally unrelated and structurally discrete and disparate, but which are interlocked because they share certain elements in common" (1963:702), and Gouldner describes organizational structure as "shaped by a tension between centrifugal and centripetal pressures" (1959:423).

| Variants of hierarchic structure | Components of social phenomena | | | | |
| | | Behavior | | Regularity | |
	Collectivity	Physical	Psychical	Temporal	Spatial
Integrated	a	b	c	d	e
Hierarchic	f	g	h	i	j
Concatenated	k	l	m	n	o
Independent	p	q	r	s	t

Figure 6.2. Hierarchic structure and social phenomena.

It appears, then, that the concept of system complexity depends on the more elementary notions of differential hierarchic integration and independence among the various subsystems of the system. What exactly is meant by "differential hierarchic integration and independence"? Figure 6.2 provides the answer which is indicated by combining the generic definition of social phenomena with the principle of hierarchic structure.

Here I suggest that the hierarchic integration and independence of subsystems within a complex social phenomenon may take four principal forms, and that each form may be manifested at any of five points—thereby making it possible for two subsystems to be hierarchically related in one way at one point and another way at another point. By way of illustration, consider two classical views of different divisions of labor.

Durkheim's (1933) description of "lower" societies, with their "segmented" social structure (i.e., minimal division of labor) and "mechanical" cultural structure, may be interpreted as positing integrated relationships across all components. The emergence of "higher" societies, with their "organized" social structures (i.e., high division of labor) may then be interpreted as representing a shift to concatenated (i.e., product differentiation, process fragmentation, and exchange) relationships in the physical behavior component. At this point, it is important to note Durkheim's emphatic distinction (drawn explicitly only toward the end of his book and in the "Preface" to the second edition) between the "normal" and "abnormal" forms of societies in which this shift takes place.[27] The distinction emphasizes his belief that concatenated relationships in the physical behavior component cannot be self-sustaining but must be sustained by other relationships in other components.

Thus, in order to constitute the normal form, at least three hierarchic levels of psychical behavior relationships or cultural structure must be present (i.e., society-wide, occupation-wide, and job-specific levels of normative regulation—"organic solidarity"), and at least three hierarchic levels of collectivities (i.e., society as a whole, occupational "corporations," and individuals) must be correlated with them. In addition, Durkheim indicates that temporal and spatial regularities must be "coordinated" across physical behaviors, and the temporal and spatial regularity with which different individuals (and presumably also occupational corporations) come to perform such behaviors must be in accord with the distribution of "natural talent" among them (i.e., the division of labor must be "spontaneous" and "free").

In the abnormal forms, however, one or more of these mainly hierarchic relationships does not develop. Instead, they all tend toward independence (i.e., "anomie," selfish individualism, and "incoherence and disorder") and eventually drag physical relationships down with them.

Thus Durkheim describes three types of societies: one in which integrated relationships predominate in all components of social phenomena, a second in which concatenated relationships in one component are combined with hierarchic relationships in the others, and a third, degenerate, type in which the latter combination fails and all relationships deteriorate toward independence.

Where Durkheim refers to the appearance of that division in all realms of social life (with perhaps more emphasis on the economic realm), Weber's discussion of "legitimate authority" refers specifically to its appearance in the political aspects of life, that is, the division of labor between those who command and those who obey (1947:324–407, see also 124–132). A more important difference for present purposes, however, is that Durkheim stresses social structural concatenation between the physical behavior of one entity and the physical behavior of another, while Weber's stresses sociocultural cross-concatenation between the physical behavior of one entity and the physical behavior of another. Thus, Weber conceptualizes one individual's physical issuance of "commands" as belonging to the same sociocultural subsystem as another individual's psychical attribution of "legiti-

---

[27] For the principal causal model Durkheim uses to explicate the normal form of the division of labor, see Chapter 12.

macy" to those commands, and conceptualizes the second individual's physical "obedience" as belonging to the same sociocultural subsystem as the first individual's psychical imputation of its "right" to issue further commands.[28]

Together, then, Durkheim and Weber provide complementary illustrations of the flexibility offered by Fig. 6.2 and with that in mind I propose it as a property-space for devising, understanding, and comparing hierarchically complex sociological descriptions.

SUMMARY

This chapter has attempted to develop a "vertical" (between-level) relational complement to the primarily "horizontal" (within-level) relations that the preceding three chapters have discussed. Taking off from Simmel's description of "concentric" and "juxtaposed" subgroup relations, four variants of hierarchic structure were presented and the generalized principle of such structure was formulated. Hierarchic structure was claimed for each component of the generic definition of social phenomena (Chapter 2) and a general method for identifying levels in each hierarchy was proposed.

Descriptions of human society by Parsons, Blau, Weber, and Marx were examined in light of the combined generic definition of social phenomena and principle of hierarchic structure. Descriptions of hierarchic structure in temporal regularities by Sorokin, and Moore, were discussed—as were descriptions of hierarchic structure in spatial regularities by Burgess, and Hawley.

Finally, all four variants of hierarchic structure were applied to the generic components of social phenomena as ways of emphasizing hierarchic complexity in such phenomena.

---

[28] It may also be noted that where Durkheim's image of the "normal" division of labor portrays the equal subjection of all individuals and collectivities, and all physical behaviors, to the same society-wide level of the psychical behavior (i.e., normative) hierarchy, Weber describes an ultimate inequality in this respect. Thus, the individuals at the summit of legitimate authority only issue and never obey commands, while the individuals at the bottom only obey and never issue commands. Simmel proposes to remove this "onesidedness" with temporal and/or spatial alternation between an individual's issuing and obeying commands (1950:285).

II

SOCIOLOGICAL EXPLANATION AND PREDICTION

7

Introduction to Part II

Part I set forth a generic definition of social phenomena that requires two or more organisms behaving jointly; partitioned social phenomena into four components, namely, social structure, cultural structure, spatial regularity, and temporal regularity; and finally, specified that social phenomena and each of their components may be regarded as hierarchically structured.

To all these principles, essential for sociological analysis, I now add causation (and the equally essential logical procedures of subsumption, induction, and deduction [see Chapter 14]), because beyond describing social phenomena, sociological analysis strives also to understand the place of social phenomena in the causal, and the deductive, fabric of the entire world of human experience. We seek, in short, to explain and predict (and through the latter, to control) as well as describe.

Now social phenomena are, like everything else, effects of some phenomena and causes of others—and this is at least part of what Durkheim is attending to when he says "to explain a social fact it is not enough to show the cause on which it depends; we must also . . . show its function" (1938:97).[1] Consider, therefore, Fig. 7.1, which diagrams these relationships. Three propositions, set forth here, bear special emphasis:

---

[1] That Durkheim goes on to say the function in question must be "in the establishment of social order" is more restrictive than need be; we may also show its function in the establishment of social disorder—that is, its dysfunction.

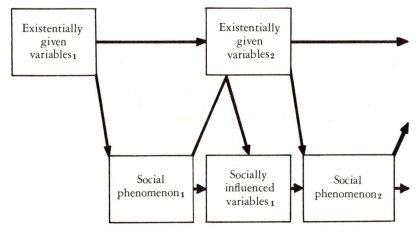

Figure 7.1. General causal model of sociological explanation and prediction.

1. Although the very first social phenomenon of any kind—which must have been coincidental, or nearly so, with the origin of life—could only have been "spontaneously generated" from existentially given variables alone, all subsequent social phenomena are partly (but not wholly) descendant from social phenomena that have preceded them. The latter is what Durkheim means when he says "all societies are born of other societies without a break in continuity" (1938:105).

2. Every social phenomenon can influence existentially given variables and make them into new socially influenced variables (e.g., first-growth trees can be cut down and made into paper).

3. Every social phenomenon can influence variables that come down to it as having already been influenced by other social phenomena and make them into its own socially influenced variables (e.g., old paper can be recycled).

To put these hypotheses another way: all the variables which can causally *explain* any given social phenomenon (except the first such phenomenon) are divisible into those regarded as existentially given and those regarded as already socially influenced. The variables which can be causally *explained by* the social phenomenon in question, however, are, by definition, limited to socially influenced ones—but these include some variables that have never been influenced by social phenomena before and others that have been influenced by social phenomena before.

This chapter will be mainly devoted to conceptual partitionings of existentially given and socially influenced variables, inasmuch as both types of variables can explain social phenomena and the latter can also be explained by social phenomena. As essential grounding for those partitionings, however, let us consider exactly what it is that we have to explain when we explain a social phenomenon. The answer to that question will give us the guiding principle of such partitionings.

THE TARGET OF SOCIOLOGICAL EXPLANATION

The central point is that in explaining any social phenomenon—that is, any interorganism behavior regularity—we need to explain only *one* organism's behavior (whether physical or psychical or both) at a time. To see why this is so, imagine any two individuals, anywhere, anytime. We may permit one of them, say individual A, to behave without any constraint whatever—that is, in any particular way, with any (or no) regularity whatever; we must, however constrain the other's behavior: B must behave regularly with respect to A's behavior if they are to constitute a social phenomenon. Even if A's behavior is completely irregular in itself, the regular coincidence of B's behavior with A's irregular behavior constitutes an interorganism behavior regularity (e.g., "milling," to use a term from the literature on crowd behavior). It is, therefore, the constraining of individual B's behavior into regularity with individual A's behavior—whatever the latter may be—that we have to explain.

Even in the more complex case of reciprocal interorganism behavior regularity, wherein B is constrained into behavior regularity with A and A is also constrained into behavior regularity with B (i.e., "interaction," including "conversation"), the explanatory problem is the same, only doubled. That is, we now have to explain the constraining of individual B's behavior *and also* the constraining of A's behavior. The same is true, of course, of the case in which A's behavior, and B's behavior, are each constrained not to coincide with the other's but to some third, common, regularity.

In all three cases, namely, constraint of B to coincide with A, constraint of B to coincide with A and of A to coincide with B, and constraint of B, and of A, to coincide at P, we have only to explain the constraining of one individual's behavior at a time (and it is essential to note that A's behavior and B's behavior may be under quite different sets of constraints and that the explanation of the social phenomenon constituted by their regular coincidence must take that into account).

In this way, although Chapter 2 has *defined* social phenomena as interorganism behavior regularities, and has therefore emphasized that the behavior regularities in question must occur between different organisms rather than within the same organism, the *explanation* of such social phenomena reduces to the explanation of each organism's behavior, taken separately.[2] Thus, Marx and Engels assert that "The social structure and the State are continually emerging out of the life process of definite individuals" (1978:154), and Weber says

> When reference is made in a sociological context to a state, a nation, a corporation, a family, or an army corps, or to similar collectives, what is meant is . . . only a certain kind of development of actual or possible social actions of individual persons (1968:14).

Although Durkheim takes the opposite view when he claims that "the determining cause of a social fact should be sought among the social facts preceding it and not among the states of the individual consciousness" (1938:110, emphasis removed), he later reverses himself: "society cannot exist except in and through individual consciousness" (1965:240; see also 253).[3]

It may also help to contrast the claim that the target of sociological explanation is the individual's behavior with two other claims: first, Homans' psychological reductionism, and, second, Ryder's demographic macroanalysis.

Homans says "We assume now, and we shall see the assumption borne out later, that . . . nothing emerges [in social behavior] that cannot be explained by propositions about the individuals as individuals" (1974:12), and "our general propositions will be individualistic and not holistic" (1980:19). Homans thus expresses what I take to be the common feature of our respective views. The crucial difference, however, centers on Homans' characterizing himself as a " *psychological reductionist*" (1974:12, emphasis added), and on his opinion that "Sociology . . .

---

[2] In this connection, note that when Parsons speaks of a "polarization" in "secular social thought," from the seventeenth century onward, "between 'individualistic' and 'collectivistic' references" (1961b:86), he seems to have in mind mainly an explanatory rather than a definitional "reference." This seems clear from his assertions that the individualistic "generalization about action in society . . . claims that, in the last analysis, the actions and decisions of individuals determine social structure and process," whereas "more 'collectivistic' social theories . . . [see the] collectivities of a society . . . interposed between the essential individual and the system of interactive rights and obligations in which he is involved" (1961b:86), and his judgment that "the individualistic strand is especially important in the attempts to formulate scientifically the determinants of social behavior" (1961b:87). Ekeh, however, seems to have in mind a definitional reference when he quotes, as "perceptive," the opinion that " 'in the United States . . . the idea that society is a body of individuals and that it has no existence of its own contrasts . . . with the French conception that first considers society as a whole' " (1974:10), but an explanatory reference when he says "The intervention of society in individual life is the credo of the collectivistic orientation in sociology; it is . . . the anathema of individualistic sociology" (1974:14). On the whole, however, it seems fair to say that Ekeh has the same explanatory reference in mind that Parsons has. In some contrast with both Parsons and Ekeh, however, it may be said that the view being set forth here combines a collectivistic definitional reference with an individualistic explanatory reference.

[3] As Parsons says, "Durkheim, starting from the 'collectivistic' end, was forced to consider the motivation of the individual, and eventually arrived at the concept of the internalization of normative culture" (1961b:96).

has already had its general propositions—or many of them—discovered for it by
. . . *psychology*" (1980:19, emphasis added). Not dissimilarly, Smelser insists that
"we as investigators endow [historical] facts with special *meanings for the historical
actors involved.* . . . [S]ystematic explanation requires some kind of meaning to be
endowed, or else we do not have an explanation" (1980:28, emphasis changed). In
contrast with Homans' narrowly psychological explanatory reduction and also with
Smelser's narrowly psychological explanatory requirement, later in this chapter I
introduce a classification of twelve types of sociological explanatory variables, all
of which seem necessary for a complete sociological explanation. This classification
identifies two types of explanatory variables that might well be linked to "individual psychology" and two that might be linked to "social psychology,"[4] but eight
altogether *non*psychological types are also identified. All twelve types, not just the
four psychological types, may be (and are) employed in "propositions about the
individuals as individuals" insofar as they all seek to explain social phenomena by
explaining the behavior of each participating individual.

At the other end of the spectrum from Homans, Ryder declares that "If one
begins with a macro question—why does one population have lower fertility than
it once did—it seems obvious that one must look for a macro answer," and "The
fundamental point is that fertility is a collective property and therefore calls for
explanation at the macroanalytic level in terms of other properties of the collectivity" (1980:200, 201). Ryder thereby seems to deny the conclusion reached above,
namely, that the explanation of *all* social phenomena, whether "macro" or "micro," must logically reduce to the explanation of individual behavior, and, by
insisting that macro questions have macro answers, implies that only micro questions can have micro answers.

In explicating this position, however, Ryder necessarily places the individual
squarely in the center of "macro" analysis—thereby making that analysis logically
dependent on analysis at the individual level. For example, in indicating how he
believes individual-level data should be employed in macro analyses, Ryder asserts
that the individual respondent should be thought of as "contributing a description
of her reproductive behavior to the construction of a macrodistribution, and [in-
dicating] the groups to which she belongs, and thus the aggregates for which it is
appropriate to construct such distributions," and goes on to add: "Given that
characteristics of individuals affect their behavior, it follows that the distribution
of individuals by any such characteristic, within a cohort, has influence on the
performance of the cohort aggregate" (1980:199). Thus, Ryder, after admitting
that despite the undoubtable fact, true by definition, that "The . . . distribution
of cohort members with respect to any characteristic . . . is the property not of
any individual element, but of the cohort to which the individual belongs"

---

[4] The two individual psychological variables will be called "instinctivism" and "enculturism," and
the two social psychological variables will be called "psychical contagionism" and "cultural structuralism" (see Fig. 7.2 and accompanying text).

(1980:199), the distribution itself is wholly determined (*logically,* not causally) by "the characteristics of individuals," then also admits that it is only to the extent that such individual characteristics[5] *causally* affect individuals' behavior that we are justified in claiming that the distribution (i.e., the statistical distribution) of individuals by any such characteristic has causal influence on the performance of the aggregate. Indeed, it follows from a conclusion reached in Chapter 2 that insofar as statistical distributions of any sort can only be descriptive ideas in the minds of analysts, no such idea, by itself alone (barring ESP and psychokinesis), can possibly affect any performance whatever—except that of the analyst in whose mind it exists.[6] Therefore, Ryder's notion that a statistical distribution "has influence on the performance of the cohort aggregate" appears defensible only as a conveniently brief, but possibly misleading, way of saying that factors operating in and on individuals have influence on those individuals' performances which may then be selected by an analyst for descriptive aggregation into an empirical generalization called "performance of the cohort." And at this point, Ryder's argument turns, despite itself, into the position being advocated here, namely, that the explanation of *all* social phenomena reduces to the explanation of individual behavior.[7]

To all this it is essential to add two further points with special emphasis: First, reducing the explanation of social phenomena to the explanation of individual behavior does not mean that for theoretical, methodological, and/or practical reasons we may not generalize across these individuals, their behaviors, and across their explanations in order to construct descriptions and explanations of more macro levels of social phenomena (see Chapter 6). As Hawley puts it, "To describe a population as consisting of so many individuals is no more a confession that the ultimate reality is the individual than is the measurement of a farm in acres of land an admission that only an acre is real" (1978:788–789), and as Watkins says,

> an individualistic explanation of a social event need not refer to specific individuals; it may be what I called an anonymous explanation: If I ask my stockbroker why De Beers shares have been rising and am told, "Because an increase is anticipated," I shall have been given an individualistic explanation although I have not been told anything about any particular share-holder (1973c:181).

Second, reducing the explanation of social phenomena to that of individual behavior does not mean that sociology is interested in explaining individual behavior as

---

[5] I construe "individual characteristics" as factors operating *on* as well as *in* individuals.

[6] It is otherwise, of course, with physical distributions—that is, distributions of matter and energy in time and space. These, according to physicalist natural science, are the *only* things that can influence performances or anything else.

[7] Taking a view similar to mine, Rosenberg and Pearlin assert that "it is imperative to understand how a demographic variable enters the individual's life, is converted into interpersonal experiences, is processed by a particular cognitive structure, and reflects the individual's relationship to his environment" (1978:72).

such. Instead, we select for sociological (rather than physiological or psychological) explanation only that part of individual B's behavior which, insofar as it coincides with A's behavior, helps constitute some social phenomenon in which we are interested.[8]

Before leaving this point it should be emphasized that although the generic *definition* of social phenomena proposed in Chapter 2 departs from that of methodological individualism (see Chapter 6), the target of *explanation* of social phenomena that has just been proposed clearly is in agreement with it. Thus, Watkins' definition of the "ultimate constituents of the social world" as "individual people who act" (1973b: 168) was rejected in Chapter 6, but his specification of the nature of attempts to explain that world is accepted here: "[The principle of methodological individualism] states that social processes and events should be explained by being deduced from (a) principles governing the behavior of participating individuals and (b) descriptions of their situations" (1973a: 149).

Reduction of the explanation of social phenomena to the explanation of individual behavior is a crucial step in constructing sociological explanations because it tells us exactly what kinds of explanatory variables to call upon—variables whose possible bearing on *individual* behavior is clearly specified. The next section of this chapter introduces a generic typology of such variables.

A GENERIC TYPOLOGY OF SOCIOLOGICAL EXPLANATORY VARIABLES

Let us assume, first, that an individual's behavior can be constrained mainly from inside or mainly from outside that individual; second, that internal constraints can be exerted mainly by the individual's own body or by the individual's own mind; third, that external constraints can be exerted mainly by people or mainly by things in the individual's environment; fourth, that external constraints may be attributed mainly to the bodies or mainly to the minds of people, and mainly to living things or mainly to nonliving things; and finally, that in any given constraint—whether internal or external—either the existentially given, "natural," component or the socially influenced, "artificial," component may be of primary analytical interest. When all these considerations are combined, the twelve

---

[8] Matters are quite different when, having described a social phenomenon, we do not want to explain it but want to use it to explain (i.e., predict) something else. That "something else" is then the target of explanation; the social phenomenon of interest is the arrow we shoot at it, and that arrow, according to the generic definition set forth in Part I, is not the regularity in any *individual* participant's behavior but the regularity between *different* participants' behaviors. It is only the influence of this latter regularity which can justify calling its outcome a "socially" influenced variable.

species of explanatory variables shown in Fig. 7.2 emerge. Let me quickly introduce them all before examining them more closely in the next four chapters.

"Materialism" emphasizes the explanatory power of those aspects of individual B's body which the analyst regards as innate (more precisely, genetically inherited) and as behaviorally consequential—including the gene itself, and, for all humans, anatomical features like large brain, binocular vision, primary and secondary sex characteristics, opposable thumbs, upright stature, and physiological features like aging, motility, and recurrent needs for oxygen, water, and food.

"Nurturism" emphasizes those aspects of individual B's body which the analyst regards as consequences of social influence—including the features mentioned under materialism as modified by the experience of, let us say, socially induced diet and fasting, exercise and sloth, and surgical modifications including amputations, grafts, bypasses, and transplants.

Locus of constraint on individual B's behavior	Origin of constraint on individual B's behavior	
	Existentially given	Socially influenced
Internal: in individual B's own		
Body	Materialism	Nurturism
Mind	Instinctivism	Enculturism
External: in individual B's environing		
People's bodies	Demographism	Social structuralism
People's minds	Psychical contagionism	Cultural structuralism
Living things ⎱ Nonliving things ⎰	Ecologism	Technologism

Figure 7.2. Typology of sociological explanatory variables.

"Instinctivism" emphasizes those aspects of individual B's mind which the analyst regards as innate, for example, linguistic "deep structure," intelligence and creativity falling within the distinctively human range, a similarly human capacity to experience certain emotions, and also whatever psychical drives or instincts may be regarded as innate.

"Enculturism" emphasizes those aspects of individual B's mind which are regarded by the analyst as consequences of social influence, for example, learned norms and values, language and other gestures, tastes, beliefs, hopes, fears, self, and conscience.

"Demographism" emphasizes those aspects of the bodies of people in individual B's environment which the analyst regards as existentially given, and includes the absolute number of such bodies and the distribution among them of features mentioned above in connection with materialism—especially age, sex, mortality, and physical mobility.

"Social structuralism" (including unison, exchange, conflict, and functionalist varieties) emphasizes socially influenced aspects of the physical behavior of people in B's environment—especially their role-performances as discussed in Chapter 3, and including aspects mentioned above in connection with nurturism.

"Psychical contagionism" emphasizes those aspects of the minds of people in individual B's environment which the analyst regards as existentially given—including the absolute number of such minds and the distribution among them of features alluded to above in connection with instinctivism, such as fear and dread, love and hope, excitement, attention, awe.

"Cultural structuralism" (including consensus, complementarity, dissensus, and symbolic interactionist varieties) stresses socially influenced aspects of the psychical behavior of people in individual B's environment—especially the role-expectations discussed in Chapter 4, and including aspects mentioned above in connection with enculturism.

"Ecologism" emphasizes those aspects of things (both living and nonliving) in individual B's environment which the analyst regards as existentially given, including sunlight, gravity, the motions of the moon and planets, the rotation of the Earth, climate, seasons, oceans, mountains, deserts, and also trees, viruses, bacilli, plankton, trout, termites, and tigers.

Finally, "technologism" emphasizes those aspects of things (again, both living and nonliving) in individual B's environment which the analyst regards as having been socially influenced, for example, houses, chairs, plows and axes, paper, computers, clothing, heart-lung machines, safety pins, guns, medicines, and also dairy cows, wheat, cotton, potatoes, thoroughbred horses, and microorganisms (like penicillin) whose growth patterns have been artificially modified. Clearly, both ecologism and technologism are divisible into types emphasizing aspects of living things, and aspects of nonliving things, respectively—thereby yielding a total of twelve types of explanatory variables.

Note that the property-space indicated by Fig. 7.2 is designed to be exhaustive of the world as we know it; every phenomenon so far known to humankind should be found in one or more of the cells of that property-space. Thus, although Katz claims there exist "factors *other* than sociological ones," and illustrates by arguing that "the prankster's choice of how to be funny on any particular occasion is apt to be influenced by his psychological disposition at the time, his physiological wellbeing, and his interactions immediately before arriving at the group on this particular day" (1976:20–21),[9] Fig. 7.2 rejects these exclusions and welcomes all the cited factors as perfectly legitimate sociological explanatory factors (i.e., instinctivistic and/or enculturistic in the first and third cases, and materialistic and/or nurturistic in the second). Indeed, to the extent that Fig. 7.2 succeeds in being exhaustive of the world, it implies that no factors whatever can be excluded a

---

[9] Note a similar exclusion, from the definition of social phenomena rather than from their explanation, by Parsons and Shils (1951:542)—discussed in Chapter 2.

priori from the sociological explanation of social phenomena. The world, in short, is as much a sociologist's oyster as anybody else's.

The Complete Causal Explanation of Social Phenomena

Thus, just as a complete *description* of any given social phenomenon should implicate—however equally—all the variables set forth in Fig. 2.1, so a complete causal *explanation* of such a phenomenon should implicate all the variables set forth in Fig. 7.2—even though the influence of some of them may not be measured at all in a given study or, being measured, may be found to be effectively zero. This conception of explanatory completeness in sociology, too, will become an important consideration when we examine the applicability of scientific procedures to sociology (see Chapter 16).

Variability in the Causal Contributions of Different Explanatory Variables

Turning this conception around, however, leads us to emphasize that although all the kinds of variables set forth in Fig. 7.2 must be implicated in any complete sociological explanation, the degree and manner of their implication may be expected to vary widely with the analyst's purpose, methods, and instruments, and with the type of social phenomenon he/she is trying to explain. Moreover, given the principles of equifinality and equioriginality (see Chapter 14), the contribution of each variable shown in Fig. 7.2 may even vary from one *instance* of the same type of social phenomenon to the next. Thus, as will be shown in Chapter 12, Durkheim (1951) argues that a given suicide rate (a kind of social structure, by the definition set forth in Chapter 2) may be influenced in exactly the same direction and degree (1) by "anomie" or too little normative regulation, (2) by "fatalism" or too much normative regulation, (3) by "egoism" or too little social interaction, or (4) by "altruism" or too much social interaction. This obviously complicates the problem of explaining a given change in suicide rate because, according to Durkheim's scheme, any of four possible single-factor explanations plus four possible two-factor explanations[10] may hold, and only empirical research

---

[10] The four possible two-factor explanations are anomie plus egoism, anomie plus altruism, fatalism plus egoism, and fatalism plus altruism. Durkheim, however, discusses only the first two combinations: "Two factors of suicide, especially, have a peculiar affinity for one another: namely, egoism and anomy," and "Anomy may likewise be associated with altruism" (1951:288). Durkheim also seems to discuss a third two-factor combination which I regard as logically impossible: "Finally, egoism and

in which all these alternative possibilities are investigated can tell us which explanation actually holds in a given case.

To make our explanatory problems still worse, I shall argue, in Chapter 12, that not only the *quantitative* contribution of each variable, shown in Fig. 7.2 may vary from one instance to the next of the same social phenomenon, but the *quality* of that contribution—that is, its sequential relation to the other variables also making contributions—may also vary.

In principle, then, different permutations of causal weights, and of causal positions, among the set of explanatory variables shown in Fig. 7.2 are believed capable of accounting for any given social phenomenon, and empirical research is believed capable of identifying the particular permutations that actually do prevail in a given case.

Not all of the variables shown in Fig. 7.2, however, may occupy any given position in such permutations; certain limitations in this respect derive from the nature of the variables in question, as follows.

Some Limitations on the Causal Positions of Different Variables

First, it should be noted that the internal variables (materialism, nurturism, instinctivism, and enculturism) are the only necessary *determinants* of B's behavior, and that when external variables are hypothesized, they can operate only through internal variables. This means that if we are interested in explaining B's participation in a social phenomenon with A, then the most proximate causes of that effect can only be internal variables—whatever other variables may operate to shape, activate, or direct these variables. Thus, as Watkins puts it,

> Speaking loosely, one can say that climate, famine, the location of minerals, and other physical factors help to determine history, just as one can say that

altruism themselves, contraries as they are, may combine their influence" (1951:289). Durkheim's phrase, "contraries as they are," surely expresses his hesitation with this combination of both too little and too much social interaction, and indeed, his discussion shows that he is not arguing for that combination after all:

> At certain epochs, when disaggregated society can no longer serve as an objective for individual activities, individuals . . . will nevertheless be found who, while experiencing the influence of this general condition of egoism, aspire to other things. . . . So *in thought they create an imaginary being whose slaves they become* and to which they devote themselves the more exclusively they are detached from everything else. . . . So they live a twofold, contradictory existence: individualists so far as the real world is concerned, they are immoderate altruists in everything that concerns this ideal objective (1951:289, emphasis added).

Thus, Durkheim's supposed combination of "egoism and altruism" actually combines too little *real* social interaction with too much *imaginary* social interaction.

alcohol causes road accidents. But speaking strictly, one should say that alcohol induces changes in people who drink it, and that it is the behaviour of alcohol-affected people, rather than alcohol itself, which results in road accidents (1973c: 179).

For similar (but unstated) reasons, perhaps, Alexander asserts that "the nature of action should be viewed as a generic, truly generalized, question. Every social theory, as Rex has argued, must contain an implicit conception of the 'hypothetical actor'." Alexander, however, overlooks both kinds of "body" variables shown in Fig. 7.1 (and does not distinguish between the two kinds of "mind" variables) when he narrows the sociologically relevant substantive content of the "hypothetical actor" to "motivation," and also says "the problem of action . . . directs attention to the nature of action's subjective component," and "The central question that every social theory addresses in defining the nature of action is whether or not—or to what degree—action is rational" (1982:72, 71, 72).

Second, the external-thing variables (ecologism and technologism) are the only necessary *contexts* or settings of B's behavior; all other variables must operate in their presence. This means that ecologistic and/or technologistic variables operate at all points of every causal image—that is, on every cause and every effect— whether they are explicitly specified there or not.

Third, the external-people variables (demographism, social structuralism, psychical contagionism, and cultural structuralism) are the only ones that are *not* necessary (either as determinants or as contexts) to explain B's behavior, but they are also the only ones in which individual A's (and/or other individuals') behavior plays a part, therefore the only ones that can account for the "socially influenced" aspects of B's internal variables. This means, obviously, that interactive causal images wherein A is hypothesized as influencing B's participation and B is hypothesized as influencing A's participation must include external-people variables in the explanation of each participation—although they may be different external-people variables in each case.

Other Subgroups of Explanatory Variables

Certain other subgroups among the variables shown in Fig. 7.2 should be mentioned, at least because their names are already familiar and when they are pointed out some of that familiarity may rub off on the typology as a whole.

First, as intimated earlier, Figure 7.2 specifies the content of variables often grouped together under the general heading "Nature," on the one hand, and "Artifact," on the other, and specifies the most direct relationships between them. Thus, the "natural" materialistic variables are the most direct raw materials for the "artifactual" nurturistic variables; the "natural" instinctivistic variables are the most direct raw materials for the "artifactual" enculturistic variables—and so on down the line.

Second, the groups of variables often called "physicalist" and "mentalist" (or, sometimes, "materialist" and "idealist" in their broad construals) are specified by Fig. 7.2 as including materialistic, nurturistic, demographistic, social structuralistic, ecologistic, and technologistic variables, on the one hand, and instinctivistic, enculturistic, psychical contagionistic, and cultural structuralistic variables, on the other.

Third, the explanatory variables often grouped together as "individual" and "society" are subdivided by Fig. 7.2 into materialistic, instinctivistic, nurturistic, and enculturistic variables, on the one hand, and demographistic, psychical contagionistic, social structuralistic, and cultural structuralistic variables, on the other hand. And when we speak, more inclusively, of "environment" (as contrasted with "individual" or "organism"), Fig. 7.2 specifies that ecologistic and technologistic variables are being added to "society" variables. Presumably, when Alexander says "I propose that. . . . action should be conceived as ordered both through internal and external structures" (1982:123), he refers to the "individual" and the "environment" groups of explanatory variables. (But, of course, when Alexander declares this manifestly explanatory proposition to be *"presuppositional"* and *"non*empirical" [1982:123, 115, emphases added]—i.e., a matter of faith not subject to observational and theoretical evaluation—the view taken here denies it such immunity.)

Fourth, what is often called genotypic "human nature" (or more broadly, any organism's "nature") is here partitioned into materialistic and instinctivistic variables; what might be called phenotypic "human nurture" (in the sense of genotypic nature plus the modifications of experience) is shown here as including nurturistic and enculturistic variables; the so-called "natural environment" is covered by ecologistic variables and the "man-made environment" is covered by technologistic variables; and lastly, the so-called "social environment" is shown as including demographistic, psychical contagionistic, social structuralistic, and cultural structuralistic variables.

Finally, it cannot be emphasized too strongly that the property-space shown in Fig. 7.2 is intended to be just as generic with respect to causal explanations of social phenomena as Fig. 2.1 is intended to be with respect to descriptions of social phenomena. That is to say, both property-spaces are intended to be applicable not only across all studies in sociology but across studies in all the social sciences— including sociobiology (provided, of course, that all references to "people" in Fig. 7.2 are generalized to "conspecifics" in order to include nonhuman participants). As there are "schools" in sociology that emphasize one or another subgroup of the generic explanatory variables, so there seems to be a clear, and broader, difference in emphasis between sociology and the other human-studying social sciences, on the one hand, and sociobiology, on the other.

Sociobiological Explanatory Variables

Wilson defines sociobiology as "the systematic study of the biological basis of all social behavior" (1975:4) and, according to Wilson, "biological basis," clearly means a combination of what Fig. 7.2 calls existentially given explanatory variables—that is, materialism, instinctivism, demographism, psychical contagionism, and ecologism—as follows:

> Ultimate causation consists of the necessities created by the environment: the pressures imposed by weather, predators, and other stressors, and such opportunities as are presented by unfilled living space, new food sources, and accessible mates. The species responds to environmental exigencies by genetic evolution through the anatomy, physiology, and behavior of the individual organisms (1975:23).

By contrast with sociobiology, sociology and the other social sciences have traditionally relied more on socially influenced explanatory variables—that is, nurturism, enculturism, social structuralism, cultural structuralism, and technologism. Wilson says "Sociology still stands apart from sociobiology because of its largely structuralist and nongenetic approach. It attempts to explain human behavior primarily . . . without reference to evolutionary explanations in the true genetic sense" (1975:4).[11] Bonner echoes these views—and, as we saw in Chapter 2, applies them more strictly to the cultural structural component of social phenomena—when he says

> the only way to improve [culture] is to select for gene changes that produce a generalized increase in the brain size. There is also an evolution of culture itself . . . but this nongenetical evolution can only make special kinds of changes, ones that are circumscribed by the power of the human brain; they cannot change the brain itself. Only genetical evolution can do that. . . . [S]ocial scientists . . . [however,] seek the causes of cultural evolution in the actions of man and in man's customs. . . . It is the very fact that the biol-

---

[11] Wilson goes beyond this descriptive, nonpartisan, statement to express favor for materialistic and instinctivistic explanatory variables when he declares "The accumulated evidence for a large hereditary component [in human social behavior] is more detailed and compelling than most persons including even geneticists, realize. I will go further: it already is decisive" (1978:19). This view is developed further in Lumsden and Wilson (1981) (see Chapter 8 here).

ogist and the social scientist are looking at different causes that makes it difficult for one to see the problems of the other (1980:194, 198).

I shall return to the first and last sentences in this quotation in a moment, but before that, it should be said that the explanatory contrast between sociology and sociobiology seems less sharp than the above comments by Wilson and Bonner make it out to be. As references throughout Part II to the relevant literatures will show, the difference is a matter of degree—a matter of relative emphasis rather than a dichotomy. Indeed, Wilson himself, despite his expressed desire "to reformulate the foundations of the social sciences in a way that draws these subjects into the Modern [neo-Darwinist biological evolutionary theory] Synthesis" (1975:4), acknowledges the greater importance of socially influenced explanatory variables in studies of human than of nonhuman social phenomena when he formulates the "autocatalytic theory" of "the origin [and, more to the point, the recent evolution—ed.] of human sociality" as follows:

> Big game hunting induced further growth in mentality and social organization that brought the hominids across the threshold into the autocatalytic, more nearly internalized phase of evolution. . . . What happened was that mental and social change came to depend more on internal reorganization and less on direct responses to features in the surrounding environment. Social evolution, in short, had acquired its own motor. When mankind has achieved an ecological steady state, probably by the end of the twenty-first century, the internalization of social evolution will be nearly complete (1975:574).[12]

Wilson continues:

> Although the evidence suggests that the biological nature of humankind launched the evolution of organized aggression and roughly directed its early history across many societies, the eventual outcome of that evolution will be determined by cultural processes brought increasingly under the control of rational thought (1978:116).[13]

And Bonner, too, admits that

---

[12] Engels seems to have the same idea in mind when he says

The further human beings become removed from animals in the narrower sense of the word, the more they make their history themselves, consciously, and the less becomes the influence of unforeseen events and uncontrolled forces on this history, and the more accurately does the historical result correspond to the aim laid down in advance (1968:353).

[13] It should be noted that Wilson takes this position in favor of the eventual causal dominance of socially influenced variables over existentially imposed ones (a position also reflected in his belief that "our descendants may learn to change the genes themselves" [1978:97]) in apparently oblivious contradiction of his arguments that "genes hold culture on a leash" and that "there is a limit to the amount of . . . cultural mimicry [of biological processes]" (1978:167, 33).

many human behavior patterns vary enormously in different societies; and there is every reason to believe that the role of cultural as opposed to genetic transmission of information plays an especially important part. . . . In cultural changes there is a great freedom for variation and transmutation that may not seriously upset the biological fitness, that is, the reproductive success of the individuals in any particular civilization (1980: 195–196, 198).

The difference between sociology and sociobiology in their relative emphases on existentially given and socially influenced explanantes is nevertheless important and should not be overlooked. It is an explanatory difference that seems traceable, at least in part, to the following subject-matter differences. First of all, whereas sociologists have typically studied social phenomena among members of a single species and have rarely bothered to make interspecific comparisons, sociobiologists have routinely compared social phenomena across two or more species (and when they have focused on some single species, our own species has unavoidably provided an implicit comparison with it). Now all scientific explanations of differences between two or more species have—since Darwin, and Wallace—successfully called upon existentially given variables like ecological niche, genes and gene mutation, and population (deme) size and density. Such variables, in short, have shown themselves highly capable of accounting for the origin of species—that is, the general differentiation of a single life form some three billion years ago into the more than 1.5 million species of life today. As a result, then, of their greater interest in interspecific comparisons, it makes sense that sociobiologists should pay more attention to existentially given explanatory variables than do sociologists.

This explanatory consequence of the intraspecific-versus-interspecific subject-matter difference between the two disciplines, of course, would apply regardless of which particular species were chosen by sociology, but there is a further consequence of sociology's having chosen *Homo sapiens* and not some other species.

The particular species whose social phenomena sociologists study happens to be the one whose members are most capable of modifying their own and others' minds and bodies without recourse to (and even in direct opposition to) existentially given variables. That is to say, biological evolution has produced, in this species, the existentially given capacity to work an indefinite number of variations on existential variables and, in this sense, transcend them. Inasmuch as sociologists focus on social phenomena among this particular species, it makes sense that they should pay more attention to acquired, socially influenced explanatory variables than do sociobiologists.

Thus, because their subject matters lead them in opposite directions with respect to explanatory variables, one might reach just the converse of Bonner's conclusion (quoted above): it may be the fact that the sociobiologist and the social scientist are looking at different *problems* that makes it difficult for one to see the causes emphasized by the other.

There seem to be clear circumstances, however, under which that mere difficulty becomes an outright rejection and they occur when either side asserts that the causes it emphasizes are the only or main causes that both sides should empha- size. Thus, social scientists are apt to reject biologists' claim that the same vari- ables that are successful in explaining differences *between* species must also be suc- cessful in explaining differences *within* a given species (e.g., between genders, races, class strata, age strata, ethnic groups, and ultimately individuals)—and es- pecially when the species in question is the one whose evolution, by the biologists' own account, has produced the most dramatically enhanced capacity for acquired modifications of mind and body. We are apt to argue, in this connection, that although it seems unquestionably true that between species (say, between a species of ant or ape and humans) "the only way to improve [culture]," as Bonner says, "is to select for gene changes that produce a generalized increase in the brain size," this may well not be the case within species. Here, acquired ways of improving culture (for example, inventing indefinitely enlargeable adjuncts for the brain such as books and computers) may prove most powerful, whereas a large generalized increase in brain size would necessitate large increases in the supporting skeleton, musculature, respiratory and digestive systems, and so on—and these, by uproot- ing the species from the ecological niche to which it has become adapted, and perhaps even making it unfit for any terrestrial niche at all, might easily result in extinction rather than improvement of the species and its culture.

For their part, biologists are just as likely to reject any claim from social sci- entists that the same variables that are most successful in explaining differences *within* species (the human one, in particular) must be most successful in explaining differences *between* (all) species. The fate of Lamarckianism-Lysenkoism in biology seems clearly to exemplify this rejection.

To avoid these interdisciplinary abrasions, perhaps sociology and sociobiology may best be regarded as complementary rather than competitive—each having its own distinctive subject-matter emphasis among those provided by the generic def- inition of social phenomena set forth in Part I, and each having its own distinctive emphasis among the explanatory variables set forth in Part II. Having argued in Chapter 2 that present-day sociology should be regarded as one subfield of a pro- jected future comparative sociology, I must now add that to the extent to which present-day sociobiology focuses on existentially given explanatory variables (and focuses on social phenomena among nonhumans), it, too, should be regarded as a subfield of that future comparative sociology. The implication and the opportunity seem clear: integration and division of labor between sociology and sociobiology, such that both human and nonhuman social phenomena will be studied under the same analytical principles. Such a detente could well enable the two disciplines maximally to inform each other without trying to colonize each other.

It is to this end that, in the five chapters to follow, illustrations of analytic application of each type of explanatory variable shown in Fig. 7.2 will be presented from the sociobiological, as well as the sociological literatures. In other words, having shown, in Part I, that the same subject matter principles apply to both literatures, I now wish to show that the same explanatory and predictive principles apply as well.

QUALIFYING COMMENTS ON THE TYPOLOGY

It is now essential to add certain qualifications to Fig. 7.2. First, I emphatically do not intend to make any assertions regarding the empirical *validity* of locating a given explanatory factor in this or that category; such validity is to be defended, at the time, and on the basis of the best available knowledge, by the analyst employing the factor. For example, Freud asserts that "aggression is an original, self-subsisting, instinctual disposition in man" (1962:69), and Marx and Engels assert that "the first fact to be established is the physical organization of [human] individuals. . . . The writing of history must always set out from these natural bases. . . ." (1947:7). I am not asserting here that aggression is *in fact* "instinctual," or that the physical organization of human individuals is *in fact* "natural." Instead, I am asserting that if Freud *regards* certain explanatory factors as instinctual, existentially given features of social participants' minds, then for him those factors fall within the category "instinctivism." If Marx and Engels *regard* certain other explanatory factors as natural, existentially given, features of social participants' bodies, then for them these factors fall within the category "materialism." The way in which the analyst *regards* phenomena is all I am concerned with; I do not pass judgment here on matters of empirical validity.

Second, the scope of each explanatory variable shown in Fig. 7.2 is meant to include whatever the values of the abstract dimensions which define it include and is not limited to the currently familiar connotations of the label arbitrarily given to it. For example, "materialism" here includes *all* existentially given characteristics of individual B's own body—no matter what these are thought to be now or in the future. The variable, as used here, is not limited either to that need for, and ability to produce, food, shelter, and clothing with which "materialism" is usually associated or to any of the other illustrative references made above or in Chapter 8.

Third, and as companion to this abstract inclusiveness, the distinctions shown in Fig. 7.2, like all distinctions, remain fuzzy at high resolution. This fuzziness holds here especially for the distinction between existentially given and socially influenced explanatory variables. Even those aspects of the participant's and others' bodies or minds which are now most authoritatively regarded as genetically inherited are, in all cases of sexual (rather than asexual) reproduction, the consequences of social influence. We are told that many aspects of things in the environment which may have seemed immune to social influence (e.g., climate, the atmosphere, the oceans, the moon, the planets) are not at all immune and are being, or may soon be, strongly influenced by us. Indeed, it seems a cliche nowadays to remark that throughout human history so far there has been a shift—uneven, halting, sometimes retrograde and, indeed, in the long run certainly only temporary—of causal weight in the explanation of human social phenomena from the existentially given variables toward the socially influenced variables. I include among the latter both intentionally modified variables (controlled results of the direct application of applied science) and unintentionally modified variables (uncontrolled side effects and long-run effects of that application).

Fourth, note that I refer here to *"isms"* rather than to whole explanations or whole theories, for example, "materialism" and "instinctivism" rather than to, say, Marx's and Freud's complete theories. Thus, I have in mind idealized explanatory variables, abstracted from their normal embeddedness in actual theories—much as, for similar purposes of focused examination, animals in a zoo have been taken out of their normal embeddedness in natural settings, given categoric names, and assigned to separate cages arranged according to abstract taxonomic criteria.

I make this abstraction because without exception, concrete, fully realized, sociological explanations (and predictions) include more than one variable, and sometimes employ complex causal images, to account for (or predict from) the particular social phenomena in which they are interested. This is so because almost every theorist knows well what other theorists are saying, and takes that polyphony into account while trying to lift his/her own voice to solo prominence above them. Thus, Marx and Engels, after having declared their own primary interest in "the physical organization of individuals" (i.e., materialism), immediately add "Of course, we cannot here go either into . . . the natural conditions in which man finds himself—geological, orohydrographical, climatic and so on" (1947:7), thereby acknowledging—though only as an aside—the ecologistic explanatory variables that other theorists regard as primary. I am not here mainly concerned with explicating complete explanations of social phenomena. Instead, I want to break all these complicated, variegated, wholes down into a few stock elements and thereby facilitate the creative recombination of such elements into new, and hopefully better, analyses.

Incidentally, let me confess that the names given to the explanatory variables shown in Fig. 7.2 are something of an embarrassment. I have found no other way, however, given that I would avoid coining altogether new names but insist that the base word of each name be immediately recognizable and evocative of its particular intended referent—even if much more than that referent is customarily connoted (as seems true for "matter" and "technology," especially), and even if the base word seems awkward when the suffix "ism" is added (as seems most true for "nurturism," "instinctivism," "demographism," and "enculturism"). After all, what I refer to as "materialism" here would, by any other name, have the same referent—as indicated not by its broader connotations in various literatures, but by the specification contained in the dimensions of the property-space shown in Fig. 7.2. It is this specification that is essential, and it is this specification that my discussion will seek to explicate and illustrate.

Last, note that all external-people variables seen from the standpoint of individual B are internal variables from the standpoint of individual A, and vice versa. Accordingly, demographistic and psychical contagionistic variables are identical to materialistic and instinctivistic variables, respectively, when the latter are attributed to people in B's environment. Similarly, social structuralistic and cultural structuralistic variables are identical to nurturistic and enculturistic variables, respectively, when they too are attributed to people in B's environment. The distinction between internal and external variables, however, permits the analyst to employ internal and external variables independently, in whatever combination seems to provide the most powerful explanation of the social phenomenon in question.

Let me also point out certain connections between the explanatory variables shown in Fig. 7.2 and the descriptive variables pertaining to aspects of individual physical behavior and of individual psychical behavior, shown in Figs. 3.1 and 4.1, respectively. Notice what all these have in common: the dimensions along their left sides are substantively identical. This means the same basic ontology underlies all our descriptive and explanatory variables—a distinctively *sociological* ontology that regards the world as composed entirely of the bodies and minds of people, and living and nonliving things (just as the ontology of modern chemistry, say, regards the world as composed entirely of a hundred odd elements, each composed entirely of protons, neutrons, and electrons).

Notice also how the dimensions along the top sides of Figs. 3.1, 4.1, and 7.2 differ, and how these differences enable the descriptive and explanatory variables of sociological analysis to be integrated within their shared ontology. Thus, in order to transform the existentially given aspects of people's bodies (the referents of materialism and demographism) into socially influenced aspects of those bodies (the referents of nurturism and social structuralism), the self-nurturing and social structuring aspects of human physical behavior must somehow be involved in producing that transformation—regardless of what other aspects of such behavior may also be involved. Similarly, in order to transform the existentially given aspects of people's minds (the referents of instinctivism and psychical contagionism) into socially influenced aspects thereof (the referents of enculturism and cultural structuralism), the self-teaching and cultural structuring aspects of human physical behavior must somehow be involved; and in order to transform the existentially given aspects of living and nonliving things in the environment (the referents of ecologism) into socially influenced aspects thereof (the referents of technologism), the domesticating-cultivating and/or extracting-fabricting aspects of human physical behavior must somehow be involved.

In short, the sociologically relevant causes of social phenomena have their own causes or sources: first, in whatever one chooses to regard as the ultimate origins of "existentially given" aspects of people and things, but second, and short of that ultimacy, in the behavior of human beings (which, of course, may then be influenced by the now socially influenced aspects of people and things to which that behavior has given rise).

Against the background of all these qualifications and elaborations, the next four chapters focus closely on different subsets of the explanatory variables shown in Fig. 7.2. Chapter 8 examines some classical and contemporary sociological and sociobiological analyses employing materialism, nurturism, instinctivism, and enculturism—that is, the subset of explanatory variables whose locus is inside individual B's own body or mind. Chapters 9 and 10 examine analyses employing demographism, social structuralism, psychical contagionism, and cultural structuralism—that is, the subset of variables whose locus is in the people in individual B's environment. Chapter 11 examines analyses employing ecologism and technologism—that is, the subset of variables whose locus is the things in individual B's environment.

MANY-VARIABLE CAUSAL MODELS

Although there are very many *main*-factor explanations and predictions in sociology, we have few if any *single*-factor explanations or predictions. Because it is therefore normal to combine two or more explanatory variables, the question arises whether any causal models recur in such combinations. Chapter 12 proposes a set of such models, all proceeding from the following assumptions.

Only four causal relations are possible between any two variables: The first influences the second (i.e., the balance of causes and effects between them favors the first); the second influences the first; they influence each other equally (either simultaneously or sequentially); neither influences the other. In each case, however, we may also wish to consider any of a potentially infinite number of variables that intervene (i.e., to facilitate, inhibit, amplify, terminate, or transform the flow of influence) between the original pair, and we may wish to consider any of a potentially infinite number of variables sharing a similar causal status (i.e., as co-cause or co-effect) with either of the original pair. These additional considerations increase the number of variables to be included in a given analysis, and they also increase the number of ways these variables may be related to each other. The most important of these ways is hierarchical, such that an aggregate of separate causes (or of effects) is often regarded as a new variable in itself which both "emerges" from their aggregation to operate on other variables in ways they never could, and also provides a new "context" within which they themselves are now constrained to operate. I propose a few simple models of testable relations within and between causal hierarchies.

8

Internal Variables

This chapter examines the four kinds of explanatory variables that are internal to individual B: materialism and nurturism focus on characteristics of individual B's body, while instinctivism and enculturism focus on characteristics of B's mind; materialism and instinctivism focus on existentially given or innate characteristics in their respective realms, while nurturism and enculturism focus on socially influenced or acquired characteristics in their realms.

MATERIALISM

What we look for in order to identify a given explanatory variable as materialistic is its reference to innate characteristics of individual B's body, interpreted behaviorally rather than anatomically. There seem to be two kinds of such characteristics—namely, needs and capabilities. Thus, materialism asserts the explanatory power of innate bodily input needs (say, for oxygen, water, food, constant and moderate body temperature, and the like), and it also asserts the power of innate bodily output capabilities (say, to move about on two legs, to vocalize, to grasp manually, and so on). Despite the currency of the term "drive," wherein both need and capability are merged into a need-to-exercise-a-capability-for-its-own-sake, it should be noted that needs and capabilities not only differ but may vary independently of one another. Thus, organisms may have needs that are not served by their own capabilities (the concepts of physical "dependency" and of psychical "love" express this), as well as capabilities that do not serve their own needs ("to err is human").

Marx and Engels state their version of the materialistic thesis as follows:

> the first fact to be established is the physical organization of [human] individuals . . . [because] men must be in a position to live in order to be able to make history. But life involves before everything else eating and drinking, a habitation, clothing, and many other things. The first historical act is thus the production of the means to satisfy these needs, the production of material life itself (1978:149, 155–56).

Notice that after referring, in a general way, to the "physical organization" of individuals, Marx and Engels go on to cite, separately, the needs side of that organization (i.e., the needs to eat and drink, to be sheltered and clothed), and then its capabilities side (i.e., the ability, in terms set forth in Fig. 3.1, to engage in domesticating-cultivating, and extracting-fabricating, physical behaviors). They go further, however, in asserting the independence of human producer capabilities from human consumer needs:

> [Human beings] begin to distinguish themselves from animals as soon as they begin to *produce* their means of subsistence, a step which is conditioned in their physical organization. . . . [An animal] produces only under the dominion of immediate physical need, whilst man produces even when he is free from physical need and only truly produces in freedom therefrom (1978:150, 76).

On this basis, then, let us summarize the role of the materialistic variable in Marx and Engels' theory: the general, undifferentiated materialistic explanatory factor underlies their hypothesis that social structure is causally dominant over cultural structure; the needs aspect of that factor underlies their hypothesis that the economic social structure is dominant over all other social structures of society, and the capabilities aspect of that factor underlies their hypothesis that economic production dominates the economic social structure. These hypotheses are expressed by Marx as follows:

> The sum total of . . . relations of production constitutes the economic structure of society, the real foundation, on which rises a legal and political superstructure and to which correspond definite forms of social consciousness. The mode of production of material life conditions the social, political, and intellectual life in general. It is not the consciousness of men that determines

their being, but, on the contrary, their social being that determines their consciousness (1978:4).

In contrast with Marx and Engels, Durkheim's use of the materialistic variable stresses its needs aspect rather than its capabilities aspect. Thus, where Marx and Engels regard human participants in social phenomena as potentially all-*producing*, Durkheim regards such participants as potentially all-*consuming*: our needs, says Durkheim, "are unlimited so far as they depend on the individual alone" (1951:247)[1]

More recently, both the needs aspect and the capabilities aspect of the materialistic variable underlie Wallerstein's assigning primary weight to the economy in explaining "the modern world system": "the defining characteristic of a social system [is] the existence within it of a division of labor such that various sectors or areas within are dependent upon economic exchange with others for the smooth and continuous provisioning of the needs of the area" (1979:5). Wallerstein adds that the significance of political struggles within national boundaries "can only be fruitfully analyzed if one spells out the implications of their organizational activity or political demands for the functioning of the world-economy" (1979:25), and, most importantly for his main argument,

> the only real social systems are, on the one hand, those relatively small, highly autonomous subsistence economies . . . and on the other hand, world-systems . . . [which] are defined by the fact that their self-containment as an economic-material entity is based on an extensive division of labor and that they contain within them a multiplicity of cultures (1974:348).

At least one other recent application of the capabilities aspect of the materialistic thesis deserves mention especially because the authors use it as one of the two key premises (the second premise is discussed below, under "instinctivism") in explaining human cognitive cultural structure. Berger and Luckmann declare that

> externalization as such is an anthropological necessity. Human being is impossible in a closed sphere of interiority. Human being must ongoingly externalize itself in activity. This anthropological necessity is grounded in man's biological equipment . . . [and these] biological facts serve as a necessary presumption for the production of social order (1967:52).

---

[1] The other materialist factor, namely, innate bodily capabilities, seems to play a shadowy role in Durkheim's analysis, emerging only when he hints that the physical act of committing suicide may be such a capability even though its specific instrumentalities are acquired (see 1951:290–294).

Admittedly, this may not be the most accessible of formulations but it seems to mean exactly what Marx and Engels mean when they say "man produces even when he is free from physical need" and that production "is conditioned by [his] physical organization"—that is, physical activity is a capability innate in human beings.

Three other recent applications of materialism stress the needs aspect: Wrong reaffirms its explanatory power at all levels of social entities, Homans applies it at the level of the small group, and Marcuse applies it at the societal level.

Wrong says "I think we must start with the recognition that in the beginning there is the body" (1961:191, emphasis removed); and asks

> what of desire for material and sensual satisfactions? Can we really dispense with the venerable notion of material "interests" and invariably replace it with the blander, more integrative "social values"? (1961:190).

Homans, reanalyzing Roethlisberger's and Dickson's (1939) study of work groups in a factory, says

> The Bank Wireman came to the Hawthorne plant in the first instance with certain motives. . . . They were working for money, money to get food, to support a family, to buy and keep a car, to take a girl to the movies (1950:94–95).

Although Homans adds that "the men must have had many other reasons for working at Hawthorne . . . [such as] a feeling that a man was not a fully self-respecting citizen unless he had a job," his concluding remark is clearly materialistic: "Man does not live by bread alone, but he lives by bread at least" (1950:95).

Marcuse declares his materialistic thesis in an apparent paraphrase of Marx and Engels when he says

> the only needs that have an unqualified claim for satisfaction are the vital ones—nourishment, clothing, lodging at the attainable level of culture. The satisfaction of these needs is the prerequisite for the realization of *all* needs, of the unsublimated as well as the sublimated ones (1964:5).

Apart from the materialistic capabilities and needs that are held to characterize all human beings (or, even more generally, all organisms) two, in particular, differentiate among such human beings in ways that appear to be causally very powerful; they are sex and age. Their sociological importance stems from the belief that males and females, and young people and old people, are directed by their genetic, anatomical, and physiological constitutions toward participations in social phenomena that are, to some extent, different. Let us briefly see what this means.

Sex Characteristics

After noting that "Males and females differ in every cell—every mammalian male cell has a sex-chromosomal component of XY and the female of XX" (1972:17), Hutt argues that these different genetic complements bring about the development of male and female gonads which, in turn, secrete male and female hormones. She continues:

> It is now quite clear that during a critical period in development the secretion of the male gonad organizes . . . the brain [especially the hypothalamus] according to a male pattern. . . . Because the hypothalamus is such an important control center . . . it is unlikely that other nonsexual functions controlled by the hypothalamus remain entirely unaffected by its differentiation according to sex (Hutt, 1972:41–42).

Similarly, Rossi argues that

> the reproductive and endocrine systems that underlie childbearing and lactation are functioning systems within the female throughout her life cycle, and to deny their significance to female psychology or to the organization of family systems is to devalue a central fact in human-species survival (1977:9).

Now because Rossi asserts that an explanatory perspective in which such variables are central "does not argue that there is a genetic determination of what men can do compared to women; rather, it suggests that the biological contributions shape what is learned, and that there are differences in the ease with which the sexes can learn certain things" (1977:4), she does allow that social and cultural structuralistic variables (see Chapters 9 and 10) may conceivably overcome the influence of sex-related materialistic variables—but only at great cost and without much stability:

> It is unrealistic to expect that we will achieve within a few generations a 50-50 distribution by sex in most human activities and occupations. It is doubtful that a unisex socialization alone can have that effect; it will require compensatory training of girls in some areas, boys in others. . . . For many generations to come, any slackening of institutional effort directed to compensatory training of the sexes will quickly be followed by a return to sex differentiation as a consequence of the [genetically determined] ease with which certain skills are learned by one sex and not by the other (1977:5, see also 18).

Age Characteristics

Moore, writing of what are here regarded as instinctivistic (see below) as well as materialistic variables associated with age, says

> Psychologists and scholars in various fields have observed pronounced changes in the behavior of the aging organism. Among these are deficits in sensation and perception, in muscular strength, in the ability to react quickly to stimuli and to respond by means of complex sensorimotor coordination, and among persons over 60, deficits in the ability to remember, learn, and respond with intelligence. To be sure, in our present state of knowledge, such behavioral changes . . . are difficult to interpret . . . [but] to the extent that such changes in behavior are inevitable among older people, a knowledge of them becomes crucial (1968b:241).

Materialistic Variables in Sociobiology

Materialistic variables play central roles in sociobiological explanatory analyses, where the existentially given (that is, naturally selected and genetically inherited) morphology and physiology of individual B's body (including its chromosomes and genes) is regarded as crucial. For example, Bonner emphasizes that culture "is mediated by the brain, and so there has been a selection pressure for a larger and more complex brain . . . [which has produced] a progression ultimately leading to culture" (1980:4), and again: "The first major step toward culture is the centralization of the nervous system and the formation of a brain" (1980:42). Wilson, however, being more concerned with the social structural than the cultural structural component of social phenomena, identifies "Four groups [that] occupy pinnacles [of social behavior] high above the others: the colonial invertebrates, the social insects, the nonhuman mammals, and man" (1975:379). Although Wilson thereby implies less overall emphasis on the brain as requisite for social phenomena, he does emphasize other materialistic variables. For example: "At the present time the key to [the societies of the ants, bees, and wasps] appears to be haplodiploidy, the mode of sex determination by which unfertilized eggs typically develop into males (hence, haploid) and fertilized eggs into females (hence, diploid)" (1975: 415). Of the nonhuman mammals, he says: "The key to the sociobiology of mammals is milk. Because [of it,] the mother-offspring group is the universal nuclear unit of mammalian societies" (Wilson, 1975:36).

Etkin points to three types of sexual dimorphism or secondary sex characteristics, and notes their impacts on social phenomena, when he says "it is an important general principle that the type of sexual dimorphism shown by a species correlates with the role of the sexes in courtship and parental activities" (1964b:114).

Regarding the explanatory bearing of age differences, Wynne-Edwards says that "one of the commonest determinants of status . . . is the age of the individual. In some species . . . the males, especially, continue to grow throughout their adult life, so that older adults are automatically stronger than their juniors and enjoy a higher social rank" (1968:156).

It should also be noted that Wilson points out the manner in which materialistic variables (especially when linked with instinctivistic ones) can become "*anti*social factors." Thus, when, through evolutionary sexual selection,

> the males become larger, more aggressive, and conspicuous by virtue of their exaggerated display behavior and secondary anatomical characteristic, [the] result is that the males are less likely to be closely integrated into the society formed by the females and juveniles. . . . Size dimorphism can also lead to different energetic requirements and sleeping sites, which have an even more disruptive effect (Wilson, 1975:36).

NURTURISM

What we look for in order to identify a variable as nurturistic are, as in the case of materialism, characteristics of the participant's body—behaviorally interpreted, of course—but here the socially generated or "nurtured" aspects rather than the existentially given or "natural" aspects of the characteristics are emphasized. Bonner gives some examples whereby human

> culture can . . . alter the body, the phenotype, physically. [These include] circumcision, ritual scars or tattoos, skulls flattened by binding during infancy, and innumerable others. [It] can even affect reproductive success, the most obvious case being castration to provide a class of eunuchs . . . or to provide adult male sopranos (1980:24–25).

The line between nature and nurture, however, is less of a razor's edge than these cases may suggest, and analysts often augment materialistic explanatory factors with nurturistic ones. Thus Marx and Engels, after asserting that "The writing of history must always set out from . . . natural bases [of the physical organization of human individuals]," immediately add "and their modification in the course of history through the action of men" (1978:150). After asserting that "The first historical act is . . . the production of the means to satisfy . . . needs [for food, shelter, and clothing], the production of material life itself," they go on to claim that "the satisfaction of the first need . . . leads to new needs; and this production of new needs is the first historical act" (1978:156; *two* first historical acts!).

It is Engels, however, who gives most ambitious classical expression to the nurturistic thesis:

> the human hand . . . has been highly perfected by hundreds of thousands of years of labor. . . . Thus the hand is not only the organ of labor, it is also the product of labor. . . . First labor, after it and then with it, speech— these were the two most essential stimuli under the influence of which the brain of the ape gradually changed into that of man. . . . Hand in hand with the development of the brain went the development of its most imme- diate instruments—the senses. . . . [Further, a] meat diet . . . had its greatest effect on the brain, which now received a far richer flow of the ma- terials necessary for its nourishment and development. . . . With all due respect for the vegetarians, man did not come into existence without a meat diet (1968:359, 363).

Engels' arguments pertain to the now-discredited heritability of socially influ- enced body characteristics but it seems clear that nonheritable changes in an indi- vidual's bodily health and longevity can be brought about by human intervention and that such changes may have an impact on the social phenomena in which that individual participates. For example, "although death is a biological process [i.e., an innate, materialistic, factor—ed.], how and when it occurs are conditioned by sociocultural and psychological factors [and becomes, thereby, a nurturistic fac- tor—ed.]" (Mechanic, 1978:179), and ill health and disease are similarly condi- tioned: "Innumerable studies indicate that . . . the poor have a greater prevalence of illness, disability, and restriction of activity because of health problems" (Me- chanic, 1978:198). Not only medical, but surgical modifications in the human body should be cited as nurturistic variables ("some forms of congenital heart dis- ease can be completely corrected by surgery" [Thomas, 1977:38])—including kid- ney, heart, and other transplantations—and, although still in their early stages, cloning and genetic engineering should be mentioned as responsibe for socially modified human bodies and therefore nurturistic explanatory variables.

Nutrition, of course, is a major generator of nurturistic variables. Thus, Berg quotes Orwell's claim that "changes of diet are more important than changes of dynasty or even of religion"; and, concentrating attention on the consequences of malnutrition for the economic situs of the social structure of nations, goes on to argue that the individual "man is the key to [national] development . . . and . . . among the factors affecting the human condition, food-nutritional adequacy is perhaps the major determinant" (1973:1, 5). Similarly, Suchman argues that "certain preceding variables such as social class or family eating patterns will affect the amount and types of foods offered the child. This will influence his resistance to disease-causing agents or his interest in exploring his environment, which, in turn, will affect his physical, social, and mental development" (1968:62).

In view of the above remarks, it hardly seems necessary to point out the close relationship between the nurturistic variables and the ecologistic and technologistic ones. The adjustment of nutrition and control of disease means management of living and nonliving things in the environment (e.g., food, bacilli, viruses, carcinogens) and that management is often achieved through manipulating other things in the environment (i.e., implements such as meat and potatoes, plows, penicillin, x-rays, lasers, surgical instruments, and the like).

Finally, it should be noted that any and all of the types of physical behaviors and their various role-performance aggregates (discussed in Chapter 3) may be regarded as existentially given and therefore as materialistic explanatory variables, or as socially influenced and therefore as nurturistic explanatory variables, or as some combination of both.

Nurturistic Variables in Sociobiology

Nuturistic variables appear repeatedly in sociobiological explanations of non-human social phenomena. Thus, Wilson cites the social "modification of body form" (1975:145) in certain insects as helping to explain their further social behavior:

> As populations of plague locusts grow dense making contacts among the individual hoppers more frequent, they pass from the solitary to the gregarious phase. The transformation takes place over three generations. . . . Locusts of the third generation belong to the fully gregarious form and are so different from their solitary grandparents that they can easily pass for a different species—and did, until the full life cycle was worked out by entomologists (1975:152).

Goetsch reports experiments which showed caste-determination among ants is a function of nurture:

> The experiments showed that if the larvae were fed plenty of insect meat during a certain sensitive or critical period . . . they suddenly began to grow quickly and develop into soldiers; but if they were given no meat during this period they became workers (1957:139).

Bonner concludes, referring not just to ants but to all social insects, that

> The evidence is overwhelming . . . that [among all but the stingless bees Meliponini] . . . caste differences are determined by external or environmental factors, that is by pheromones which are hormones passed between sepa-

rate individuals, or nutrition. There are no caste-determining genes other than for sex determination (1980:84).

And even regarding sex determination (albeit among fish, and although the mechanism of its accomplishment remains unknown), Warner reports that

> groups [of small fishes called cleaner wrasse on the Great Barrier Reef of Australia] are all female except for the largest individual. . . . If [this] male is removed or dies, an astonishingly rapid transformation occurs in the largest female. Within an hour she behaves like a male, defending [what is now her territory from males], and courting other females. A couple of weeks later her ovaries have completedly shifted to sperm production and "she" is now a fully functional male. . . . [It has also been shown that sexual replacement is quantitatively precise, so that] if nine males are simultaneously removed from a large group of bass, exactly nine females will change sex (1982:45–46).

Finally, Bonner cites laboratory evidence that social experience can induce physical changes in the animals' brains when he notes that

> young rats that had undergone a rigorous training program were compared anatomically with some deprived of the benefits of education. The trained animals shared a large increase in the number of connections between neurons in the cortical regions of the brain (1980:41).

INSTINCTIVISM

In order to identify a given variable as instinctivistic, we look for its reference to existentially given, innate, characteristics of individual B's mind. And in order to identify a variable as enculturistic we look for its reference to socially influenced, learned, characteristics of individual B's mind. I mention the latter kind of variable (on which the next section of this chapter will focus) here because classical expositions of instinctivistic variables set forth by Freud, Pareto, and Mead all implicate enculturistic variables as well—in different ways, of course. Let us scan these three expositions.

Although he gives somewhat different impressions elsewhere and is not altogether unambiguous even here, Freud, in *Civilization and Its Discontents* (his most sociologically relevant work), seems to claim that every human individual possesses two pairs of competing instincts.[2] One of these pairs calls for benefiting oneself,

---

[2] Simmel, too, speaks of an internal struggle between different innate psychical tendencies:

It is a trivial observation that the instinctive needs of man prompt him to act in these mutually conflicting ways: he feels and acts *with* others but also *against* others. A certain measure of the one

on the one hand, and injuring oneself, on the other; the other pair calls, similarly, for benefiting others and for injuring others. Freud seems to include both benefit instincts (i.e., to benefit oneself and others) when he refers to "the instinct of life" or "Eros," and seems to include both injury instincts when he refers to "the instinct of destruction" or "Death." He seems also to use "Death," however, for the drive to injure oneself as distinct from the drive to injure others (which he calls "aggression"), and to use "egoistic" for the drive to benefit oneself as distinct from the drive to benefit others (which he calls "altruistic" [see 1962:87–88]). Thus: "civilization is a process in the service of Eros, whose purpose is to combine single human individuals, and after that families, then races, peoples and nations, into one great unity, the unity of mankind" (and now Freud expresses his demurrer from Marx's, and Durkheims, position:) "Necessity alone, the advantages of work in common, will not hold them together." Freud continues:

But man's natural aggressive instinct, the hostility of each against all and of all against each, opposes this programme of civilization. This aggressive instinct is the derivative and the main representative of the death instinct which we have found alongside of Eros and which shares world-dominion with it. And now, I think, the meaning of the evolution of civilization is no longer obscure to us. It must present the struggle between Life and Death, between the instinct of life and the instinct of destruction, as it works itself out in the human species (1962:69.[3]

This struggle is carried out within, not between, individuals as a result of the modification society brings about in the individual's psyche in order to protect itself from the aggressiveness there:

His aggressiveness is introjected, internalized; it is, in point of fact, sent back to where it came from—that is, it is directed towards his own ego. There it is taken over by a portion of the ego, which sets itself over against the rest of the ego as super-ego, and which now [takes] the form of 'conscience'. . . . Civilization, therefore, obtains mastery over the individual's dangerous desire for aggression by . . . setting up an agency within him to watch over it like a garrison in a conquered city (1962:70–71).

In contrast with Freud, Pareto sees the most fundamental struggle that society establishes as occurring between, not within, individuals. In Pareto's view, individuals vary according to the relative strengths within them of different sides of at

---

and the other, and a certain proportion between them, is a purely formal necessity for man, which he meets in the most manifold ways (1955:155).

[3] In *Leviathan*, Hobbes prefigures the main ideas in Freud's *Civilization and Its Discontents* (see Hobbes, 1955:113, 210).

least the first of three instinctual dualisms. This dualism is between one "instinct" to create new things (represented by Class I residues) and another to preserve old things (represented by Class II residues). Pareto refers to individuals in whom the innovative side of this dualism is especially strong as "foxes" and to individuals in whom the conservative side is especially strong as "lions."[4] Pareto then argues that in order

> to prevent or restrict violence, the governing class [of a society may resort] to "diplomacy," fraud, corruption . . . [and] that sort of procedure comes to exercise a far-reaching influence on the selection of the governing class, which is now recruited only from the foxes, and the lions are blackballed. . . . So it comes about that the residues of Class I are intensified in the governing class, and the residues of . . . Class II debilitated [until, perhaps,] the subject class contains a number of individuals disposed to use force [i.e., lions] and with capable leaders to guide them, the governing class is . . . overthrown and another takes its place (1935:1515–1516).

Thus Pareto regards social history as a constant "circulation"—sometimes by peaceful, sometimes by violent, means—of individual "molecules" (to use his metaphor), bearing different but unchangeable instinctual charges.

To Pareto, society sets up no agency within the individual's psyche to *control* the instincts there, but Pareto does believe society provides rationalizations or "derivations" (see 1935:899)—roughly analogous to the Freudian "defense mechanisms"—whereby these instincts are *concealed* from direct view,[5] and although the need for derivations is instinctual (located in Class I residues), the specific kinds of derivations available to the individual at any given time and place are socially invented.

Where Freud divides the psyche into innate "id" and acquired "superego" (and "ego"), and where Pareto divides it into innate "instincts" (represented by "residues") and acquired "derivations," Mead divides it into innate "I" and acquired "me." To Mead, the I is both a perpetually unconventional psychical component

---

[4] The fox and lion metaphor appears earlier in Machiavelli (1940:64, 73), and the innovative-conservative dualism appears in Spencer ("That the aspiration after things as they should be, needs restraining by an attachment to things as they are, is fully admitted. The two feelings answer to the two sides of our present mixed nature" [1972:27]), and in Mannheim's pairing of "ideology" on the conservative side and "utopia" on the innovative side (see 1955:40, 192–193). The other two instinctual dualisms proposed by Pareto are between an instinct to behave physically and an instinct to behave psychically (Class III residues); and between an instinct to join with and serve others (Class IV residues) and an instinct to be separate from others and serve oneself (Class V residues). Pareto's Class VI residues representing the sex instinct, seem to be neither part of, nor to contain, a duality and, indeed, this class of residues seem to be a conceptual afterthought playing no role whatever in Pareto's analysis of society.

[5] Pareto may regard this concealment as an unintended by-product of "the human hunger for thinking [which] is satisfied in any number of ways; by pseudoexperimental reasonings, by words that stir the sentiments by fatuous, inconclusive 'talk'. So derivations come into 'being' " (1935:889).

that always injects an uncertain, novel, surprising, element into behavior and "gives the sense of freedom, of initiative" to participants in social phenomena (see 1934:173–178, 192–200), and also—when the I is "viewed as the biologic individual" (1934:175, n.12)—a reservoir of ten "groups of [innate] impulses" (see 1934:348–349). The me, however, is an acquired memory in which both the spontaneous impulse of the individual's own I, and also the inferred me's of others, are remembered: "The 'I' of this moment is present in the 'me' of the next moment. . . . It is what you were a second ago that is the 'I' of the 'me'," and "the 'me' is the organized set of attitudes of others which one himself assumes" (1934:174, 175).

Finally in this three-way comparison, it should be noted that in contrast with the first two theorists, Mead posits no fundamental struggle either within individuals' psyches (Freud) or between them (Pareto). Thus, Mead refers to the I and the me simply as "two distinguishable phases" of personality with no hint of conflict between them: "If [the self] did not have these two phases there could not be conscious responsibility, and there would be nothing novel in experience" (1934:178). Regarding conflict between individuals, Mead refers to "two attitudes [which] represent the most highly universal, and, for the time being, most highly abstract society" (1934:259), and neither of them smacks of aggressiveness: First, there are "such fundamental attitudes of human beings toward each other as kindliness, helpfulness, and assistance . . . [or] neighborliness," and second, "There is a participation in the attitude of need, each putting himself in the attitude of the other in the recognition of the mutual value which . . . exchange has for both" (1934:258).

Weber's reliance on instinctivistic variables seems best expressed in his declaration that "We are cultural beings endowed with the capacity and the will to take a deliberate attitude toward the world and to lend it significance" (1949:81, emphasis removed). That reliance continues (although less explicitly) into the distinctions he draws among four types of social action "according to its mode of orientation," insofar as one of these types, "affectual behaviors," is described as consisting in an "uncontrolled [i.e., instinctive—ed.] reaction to some exceptional stimulus" (1947:116). The weight of Weber's analysis, however, rests on the other three types of social action and their modes of orientation (i.e., Wertrationalität, Zweckrationalität, and traditional [1947:115–118])—all of which are described as, in various ways, socially influenced.

Finally, among classical expressions of the instinctivistic thesis, we should note McDougall's hypothesis that

> The human mind has certain innate or inherited tendencies which are the essential springs or motive powers of all thought and action, whether individual or collective, and . . . these [instincts] are the prime movers, the great motive powers, of human life and society (1914:19, 265).

More recently, in the continuing tradition of instinctivism and exemplifying the indefiniteness of the line separating it from materialism, we note that Wrong (who was cited above in connection with the latter, saying "in the beginning there is the body"), regards the factors he wishes to emphasize as "psychological variables" (1961:192). Homans too (also cited above in connection with materialism), asserts that "the general explanatory principles even of sociology are not sociological . . . but psychological" (1964:815), and that

> a tendency to imitate others is genetically inherited and not initially learned. . . . Some [human values] are innate—that is genetically determined and therefore shared by many men—. . . . Men could hardly have maintained pack behavior if they did not find social life as such innately rewarding (1974:24, 27).

Moreover, in a conclusion strikingly reminiscent of Freud, Homans says

> The trouble with civilized men is that they cannot live with the institutions they have themselves invented. . . . Sometimes the great rebellions and revolutions, cracking the institutional crust, bring out elementary social behavior hot and straight from the fissures . . . [but] the institutions the rebels invent . . . are just as apt to sacrifice something human as the institutions that preceded them . . . (1974:373).

Clearly, then, Homans argues that the innate psychical characteristics of *adults* influence the social phenomena in which they participate. Minsky, however, argues that the innate psychical characteristics of *infants* may influence the social phenomena in which they, and adults, participate:

> The [innate] internal communication mechanisms in the infant mind, at least at the higher level, may have enough uniformities to compel society, in subtle ways, to certain conformities, if social communication is to engage young children (1979:446).

In another recent use of an instinctivistic variable, Berger and Luckmann add to "externalization" (identified above as materialistic) the concept of "typification"—which they seem to regard as being just as much of a *mental* "anthropological necessity" as "externalization" is a bodily "anthropological necessity": "The reality of everyday life contains typification schemes in terms of which others are apprehended and dealt with in face-to-face encounters. Thus, I apprehend the other as 'a man,' 'a European,' 'a buyer,' 'a jovial type,' and so on" (1967:30–31).[6] As

---

[6] Note that I interpret typification per se (i.e., the "drive to typify"), and not its specific content (i.e., not the types "man," "European," "buyer," "jovial type," etc.) as instinctivistic.

the apparently innate psychical-physical link between typification and externalization Berger and Luckmann place "habitualization" ("any action that is repeated frequently becomes cast into a pattern which . . . is apprehended by its performer *as* that pattern" [1967:53]). In addition, they posit an innate need for consistency in psychical behavior that is not matched by a similar need for consistency in physical behaviors: "while performances can be segregated, meanings tend toward at least minimal consistency. . . . It is possible that this tendency to integrate meanings is based on a psychological need, which may in turn be physiologically grounded (that is, there may be a built-in 'need' for cohesion in the psychophysical constitution of man)" (1967:64; see also Berger, 1969:22).

van den Berghe asserts that "aggressiveness, hierarchy and territoriality are built into our in-born behavioral repertoire" (1974:778),[7] and argues that territoriality and hierarchy both inhibit and generate social structural aggression:

> Aggression is only suppressed so long as territoriality and hierarchy are tolerated by all parties concerned. Both territoriality and hierarchy, however, evoke challenge, as do other forms of privilege. . . . Territoriality and hierarchy . . . simultaneously cause and suppress aggression (1974:787).

Now although it is clear how van den Berghe believes territoriality and hierarchy *suppress* aggression ("territoriality . . . establishes monopoly rights over resources within a portion of usable space, and hierarchy . . . creates an order of precedence in access to, and distribution of, resources" [1974:778]), it is not so clear how they also *cause* aggression. It appears, however, that van den Berghe believes there is another innate, "natural," predisposition whose role in his analysis is left only implicit. Let us call this the predisposition to be "free." van den Berghe seems to believe it is activated—and violently so—by physical manifestations of the territoriality and hierarchy instincts[8]: "it is the nature of both boundaries and hierarchies that they are not suffered gladly. Both are violently challenged and no less violently defended" (1974:778).

Thus, although the details of his argument are not clear, it seems fair to say that van den Berghe leans heavily on one or more instinctivistic explanatory variables and comes close to a policy recommendation which is appropriate to that leaning when he reaches the following conclusion:

> Animal breeders have long known how rapidly controlled biological selection can modify a species. The spectre of eugenics conjures staggering ethical

---

[7] There is a persistent ambiguity in van den Berghe's analysis over whether and when "aggressiveness" (or "aggression"), "territoriality," and "hierarchy" signify psychical predispositions to behave or the physical behaviors themselves.

[8] Such manifestations, in turn, are activated by competition for the resources (both biological and "socially created") of life, and such competition is "aggravated" by population pressure (see van den Berghe, 1974:785–787).

problems, of course; but sticking our social scientific heads into the biological sand . . . is hardly a solution either (1974:788).

McDougall identifies "suggestibility" as a "general or nonspecific innate tendency" (1914:90) of individuals and notes that

> There was for some time a tendency to regard suggestibility as necessarily an abnormal condition. . . . But very quickly it was seen that there are many degrees of suggestibility, ranging from the slight degree of the normal educated adult to the extreme degree of the deeply hypnotized subject (1914:97).

We should especially note McDougall's distinction between "suggestibility" (an innate characteristic of an individual's psyche) and "suggestion" ("the process of communication between agent and patient which leads to the latter's acceptance of any proposition" [1914:97]). I follow this distinction here insofar as suggestibility is classified as an (intraindividual) instinctivistic variable while suggestion is treated as an (interindividual) psychical contagionistic variable and discussed separately, in Chapter 10. Thus, when Johnson and Feinberg say "Whether it is labeled contagion . . . social facilitation . . . or circular reaction . . . , nearly all students of collective behavior refer to a notion that individuals in the crowd situation are especially susceptible to the influence of others" (1977:508), they are referring to independently variable factors: First, there is the "susceptibility" that depends on factors *inside* individual B, and second, there is the "contagion" that depends on B receiving signals emitted by people *outside* B. It is essential to discriminate between these variables because equifinality (see Chapter 14) argues that the same social phenomenon may be explained by different combinations of susceptibility and contagion (e.g., high-low, low-high, medium-medium), and our explanations should discriminate among these combinations.

Parsons and Shils are quite circumspect about the way they regard innate psychical (and physical) needs, but it seems clear that when they say "We will use the term drives . . . to refer to the *innate* tendencies to orient and to act," and then claim that "A need-disposition represents the organization of one or more drive elements . . . [together with] cognitive and evaluative elements" (1951:111, 113, emphasis changed), they imply that the "need-dispositions for esteem, love, approval, and response" (1951:116) are at least partly instinctivistic.

Referring to much simpler, but still presumably instinctivistic, psychical needs—namely, for sleep, on the one hand, and for sensory stimulation, on the other, Scheff cites a report that the reactions of two individuals after 168 hours of continuous wakefulness contained "many elements which psychiatrists would describe as paranoid and depressive features," and cites other reports showing that "deprivation of sensory stimulation can cause hallucination and other symptoms" (1966:42).

Pertaining more to innate psychical capabilities than needs, Scarr and Weinberg conclude that

> intellectual differences among children at the end of the child-rearing period have little to do with environmental differences among families that range from solid working class to upper middle class. . . . From our data, it appears to us that . . . differences in family background that affect IQ are largely the result of genetic differences among parents, which affect their own status attainments and which are passed on genetically to their offspring, whose status attainments are subsequently affected (1978:691).

(Taylor denies this: "There is no hard and convincing evidence that the heritability of IQ is anywhere near substantial" [1980:206].)

Finally, we note that certain psychical behavior differences are claimed to be innately sex-, and age-linked. Maccoby and Jacklin argue that four, presumably innate, psychical sex differences are "fairly well established": "girls have greater verbal ability," "boys excel in visual-spatial ability," "boys excel in mathematical ability," and "males [sic] are more aggressive" (1974:351–352). After noting that "Few studies succeed in disentangling age changes in intelligence from related age changes (as in general health) or from societal trends (as in education)," Moore asserts that "When different age groups are compared at a given time, total intelligence test scores reach a peak in the late teens or early 20's and then decline with age," but "Analysis of test components indicates that scores for performance and reasoning are highest among the youngest adults, while scores for information and for verbal and numerical ability are highest at much later ages" (1968b:255).

Instinctivistic Variables in Sociobiology

Instinctivistic variables occupy an important place in analyses of nonhuman animal social behavior. Thus, Bonner cites the North American cowbird as possessor of "an inherited behavior pattern":

> A female [reared in isolation] will respond to the song of a male by immediately adopting a "copulatory posture." They will not give this response to the songs of other species. . . . This whole genetically determined transmission of song involving both the singing by the male and its reception by the female is in sharp contrast to the song transmission of many other birds where learning is also involved (1980:37–38; see also Klopfer, 1962:137).

Similarly, Wilson presents play as instinctive behavior that follows a distinctive developmental pattern: "animal play is not simply a melange of infantile behaviors. It progresses as part of the ontogeny, with specific patterns waxing and waning at different ages" (1975:167).

Wilson also expresses confidence in instinctivistic variables as applied specifically to human social phenomena: "innate censors and motivators exist in the brain that deeply and unconsciously affect our ethical premises; from these roots, morality evolved as instinct" (1978:5). Thus, Wilson claims,

> the mental processes of religious belief . . . represent programmed predispositions whose self-sufficient components were incorporated into the neural apparatus of the brain by thousands of generations of genetic evolution (1978:206).

Elaborating on these assertions, Lumsden and Wilson argue that through its influence over the mind "genetic natural selection operates in such a way as to keep culture on a leash" (1981:13), and in order fully to appreciate their argument as instinctivistic, the first thing to emphasize is the causal asymmetry that, despite protestations to the contrary, Lumsden and Wilson attribute to the relationship between genes and culture. Thus, although they assert that genes "keep culture on a leash," Lumsden and Wilson do not assert the converse; although they propose a "thousand-year rule" for the time it takes a new epigenetic rule to evolve and have an impact on culture, they propose no such rule for the time it takes a new culturgen to have an impact on epigenetic rules.[9] Although they propose a "gene-culture circuit"—wherein "the epigenetically guided actions of the individual members create the cultural patterns, but the patterns influence the actions and, ultimately, the frequencies of the underlying genes themselves" (1981:265)— and although they claim that "through euculture[10] [the highest level of culture] mankind has literally altered the form of organic evolution" (1981:325–326)— they also summarily assert that "The key element in the theory of gene-culture coevolution is the role of the epigenetic rules in culturgen choice" (1981:35).

[9] In fact, on this latter point, Lumsden and Wilson admit that

The crux [of the theory] is the manner in which selection operates on culture. . . . [S]ome culturgens undeniably provide superior genetic fitness over others. But how? . . . Until we have some answers, the feedback from culture to genes cannot be reliably investigated with the models of population genetics (1981:249).

It should be noted that Lumsden and Wilson claim "there is competition among the culturgens *recognized* as distinct alternatives within each culturgen category, and those most highly *valued* extinguish their competitors" (1981:305, emphasis added)—thereby implying that although *natural* selection may operate in the competition between "culturgen categories," some *other* selection (cultural?) operates in the competition within each category. Lumsden and Wilson do not explicate this point, nor do they say who does the "recognizing" of "distinct alternatives" and who does the "valuing" of such alternatives.

[10] See Lumsden and Wilson (1981:3); also see Wilson (1971:4–6) for discussion of "eusociality."

The second thing to emphasize is that although genes (classified earlier in this chapter as materialistic variables) play the initiating role in Lumsden and Wilson's theory,[11] primary explanatory weight is assigned to the instinctivistic derivatives of genes—namely, "epigenetic rules"—defined as

> the genetically determined procedures that direct the assembly of the mind, including the screening of stimuli by peripheral sensory filters, the internuncial cellular organizing processes, and the deeper processes of directed cognition. The rules comprise the restraints that the genes place on development . . . and they affect the probability of using one culturgen as opposed to another (1981:7).[12]

ENCULTURISM

By "enculturistic" explanatory variables I mean those whose referents are aspects of individual B's mind (whether regarded as conscious or nonconscious, voluntary or involuntary, rational or nonrational) which the analyst regards as socially influenced—that is, socialized or enculturated.

Habermas provides a sweeping but inconsistent appeal to enculturistic variables. Thus, after claiming that there exists an "evolutionary learning process of societies [which] is dependent on the competence of individual members" (a competence that individuals acquire "by growing into the symbolic structure of their social world") and that "the species is able to learn not only in the domain of technical knowledge . . . but also in the domain of moral-practical awareness that governs the development of structures of interaction," Habermas asserts that "Only with the help of [such] learning mechanisms can we explain why some societies find solutions to their problems at all" (1981:268, 272).[13] He then claims, how-

---

[11] Lumsden and Wilson argue that "Epigenetic rules are the outcome of specificity in cell structure, neuron circuitry, and the timing of hormone release, which properties are themselves more fundamental products of epigenesis at the cellular level" (1981:36). Compare Hutt's thesis (cited earlier in this chapter) regarding gender differences.

[12] A sociologist might wish for greater specificity from Lumsden and Wilson on at least two points: (1) What are the dimensions of the "populations" described as bearers of epigenetic rules; are they siblings only, or extended kin groups, or ethnic groups, or races, or only the entire human species? (2) What degree of selectivity is to be attributed to human epigenetic rules; what does it mean to say they are "selective to an intermediate degree" (Lumsden and Wilson, 1981:344). Perhaps, above all, a sociologist might want to see a larger explanatory role assigned in sociobiological studies to inclusive fitness, where inclusiveness extends outwardly from the individual, ultimately (in the case of the human species, at least) to the entire species, and to living things in general.

[13] Habermas also claims that without a "cumulative learning process . . . history could not be viewed as evolutionary or as a linear process" (1981:275), but in both these statements he ignores natural selection processes as fully capable of finding solutions and producing an evolutionary process—unless, of course, he regards natural selection as a "learning" process applicable not to individuals and thereby to individual societies but to the entire species of phenomena called "human society." Habermas is not clear on this point.

ever, that some societal problems have not only remained unsolved but have worsened—thereby implying that, in these respects at least, the societal learning process has been devolutionary rather than evolutionary and its individual participants have been enculturistically incompetent rather than competent:

> from the vantage point of moral standards applicable to both primitive and civilized societies, the form of exploitation necessarily practised in class societies must be judged as a regression in comparison with the moderate social inequalities possible in kinship systems (Habermas, 1981:275–276).

Note that enculturistic variables are pictured in Fig. 7.2 as the counterparts of nurturistic variables, in one respect, and as the counterparts of instinctivistic variables, in another respect, and that all three of these variables (plus materialistic ones) have their general locus of operation inside the individual social participant, and it is that locus of operation which is at the center of attention in the present discussion. I am not primarily concerned in this chapter with how that locus got to be what it is (except, of course, that it is in some way socially influenced)—or, to put it differently, I am concerned here with the socializees, and not with the socializers. This focus holds even though, as Goslin argues, in every socialization process involving interaction between a human socializer and a human socializee (i.e., excluding processes that only involve a socializee and some inanimate technological instrument such as a book or a TV screen), the minds of *both* become socially influenced thereby:

> Just as the learner is responding to stimuli from others around him, his responses constitute significant stimuli for those responsible for socializing him. To a variable but nonetheless considerable extent, therefore, the individual . . . becomes socializer as well as socializee (1969:5).

For present purposes this only means that I focus in this chapter on both participants as socializees only and not as socializers. The latter focus is reserved for Chapters 9 and 10, wherein social structuralistic and cultural structuralistic variables are examined.

The following discussion examines some complex enculturistic variables derived from the four norm expectations outlined in Chapter 4—thereby following up the claim made there that a norm's reference-to-others, while not *constituting* a social phenomenon, is likely to *generate* one. The variables in question are: "self" (a generalization across the individual's actor expectations), "conceptualizations of macro cultural and social structures" (generalizations across situation expectations), "role-expectations" (generalizations across response expectations), and "conscience" (a generalization across consequence expectations). We then examine two more elementary enculturistic variables—namely, "symbols" and "meaning."

Self

Mead argues that

> The self has the characteristic that it is an object to itself, and that character-
> istic distinguishes it from other objects and from the body . . . [It] is where
> one does respond to that which he addresses to another . . . where he not
> only hears himself but responds to himself as truly as the other person replies
> to him, that we have behavior in which the individuals become objects to
> themselves (1934:136, 139).

Put in terms set forth in Chapter 4, Mead here implies that the self consists in a
given individual taking the standpoint of one of his/her actor expectations and
then thinking about, speaking to, behaving toward him/herself as if he/she were
taking *another* of his/her actor expectations at the same time. Mead goes on to
argue that the self also requires knowledge of the actor expectations that pertain
to others (of course, along with the situation, response, and consequence expectations associated with those actor expectations): "little children play at being a
parent, at being a teacher. . . . These are personalities which they take, roles they
play, and in so far control the development of their own personality" (1934:153).
The final step is then:

> If the given human individual is to develop a self in the fullest sense, it is
> not sufficient for him merely to take the attitudes of other human individuals
> toward himself and toward one another . . . he must also . . . take their
> attitudes toward the various phases or aspects of the common social activity
> or set of social undertakings in which . . . they are all engaged. . . . What
> goes to make up the organized self is the organization of the attitudes which
> are common to the group (Mead, 1934:154–155, 162).

Thus Mead implies (again in terms set forth in Chapter 4) that the self is
constituted, in the end, not so much by reflexiveness among the several actor
expectations that individual B adopts for him/herself but by reflexiveness between
any or all of these and a generalization across all the other actor expectations attributed to all members of "the group" to which he/she belongs.

More recently, Turner seems to go only as far as Mead's first step in the construction of self—namely, reflexiveness between, and generalization across, the individual's own several actor expectations (and their associated situation, response,
and consequence expectations). Thus, Turner refers to "role-person merger"[14] (de-

---

[14] Turner avoids the term "self" because he believes that although "the terms 'self' and 'self-conception' are usually reserved for an object that resists strict compartmentalization by role-defining situa-

fined as "the attitudes and behavior developed as an expression of one role [being carried over] into other situations" [1978:1]) and permits several roles to become so "merged" or generalized—but not all equally so: "when a role is deeply merged with the person, socialization in that role has pervasive effects in personality formation. When there is little or no merger, role-socialization remains strictly compartmentalized" (1978:1–2). Accordingly, Turner says "In the broadest sense, the person consists of all the roles in an individual's repertoire. . . . [But the] person is best described in terms of the roles that are still played when not called for and that color the way in which other roles are played" (1978:2)[15]—although Turner does not say who is to judge whether a role is "called for" or not.

If Mead, and Turner, emphasize how the self is socially constructed, Garfinkel, and Goffman, examine certain circumstances in which it can be socially destroyed—and the latter also examines social protection against that destruction (a protection called "the mechanism of insulating role-activities from observability by members of the role-set" by Merton [1957:374]). Thus, Garfinkel, concerned with "the alteration of total identities," argues that "there is no society whose social structure does not provide, in its routine features, the conditions of identity degradation" (1956:420), and that "Moral indignation [as physically expressed in public denunciation] serves to effect the ritual destruction of the person denounced" (1956:421). Goffman, whose focus is not on public denunciation by others but rather on the private self-denunciation occasioned by discovering that one has been the victim of a confidence game, says that when such a victim gets the "sting" he

> finds that he has no defense for not being a shrewd man. He has defined himself as a shrewd man and must face the fact that he is only another easy mark. . . . This is a process of self-destruction of the self. . . . [But] the capacity of a person to sustain these profound embarrassments implies a certain looseness and lack of interpenetration in the organization of his several activities. . . . Lack of rigid integration of a person's social roles allows for compensation; he can seek comfort in one role for injuries incurred in others (1962:485, 500–501).

Finally, in connection with the self, we should note that Becker and Strauss' formulation incorporates phases of construction, maintenance, destruction, and reconstruction of the self within a single dynamic framework centering on occupational careers:

> A frame of reference for studying careers is, at the same time, a frame for studying personal identities. Freudian and other psychiatric formulations of

---

tion," such terms "are generally conceived subjectively, according to the arousal of self-feeling. . . . The idea of role-person merger is offered as a more behavioral complement to the subjective idea of self-conception" (1978:2–3).

[15] Stryker refers to "an image of the person as a structure of positions and roles which, internalized, is the self" (1980:79).

personality development probably overstress childhood experiences. . . . Yet central to any account of adult identity is the relation of change in identity to change in social position. . . . Hence members of structures that change . . . must gain, maintain, and regain a sense of personal identity. Identity "is never gained nor maintained once and for all" (1956:262–263).

Conceptualizations of Macro Cultural and Social Structures

Berger and Luckmann discuss situation expectations that refer to cultural structures ("legitimations," "symbolic universes") of high levels of generality, and Cicourel discusses situation expectations that refer to social structures ("macro-structures," "collective entities") of high levels of aggregation—as follows.

In the terms "reality" and "knowledge" Berger and Luckmann clearly refer to what Chapter 4 has called normative situation expectations: "The man in the street inhabits a world that is 'real' to him, albeit in different degrees, and he 'knows,' with different degrees of confidence, that this world possesses such and such characteristics" (1967:1). They then argue that "the objectivity of the institutional world, however massive it may appear to the individual, is a humanly produced, constructed, objectivity" (Berger and Luckmann, 1967:60).[16] The starting point for this construction, say Berger and Luckmann, is "the appearance of a third party" (especially an offspring) in an "ongoing social interaction between A and B," with the result that "For . . . children, the parentally transmitted world . . . confronts them as a given reality that, like nature, is opaque in places at least" and "Only at this point does it become possible to speak of a social world at all" (1967:58, 59).

Because there are many groups of parents-and-their-children, many different social worlds can be constructed—and further, "the degree of division of labor [implies] concomitant differentiation of institutions"—with the result that "The increasing number and complexity of [social worlds] make them increasingly inaccessible to outsiders. They become esoteric enclaves" (Berger and Luckmann, 1967:81, 87). To counteract this incipient cultural structural fragmentation, "legitimation," a more generalized level of normative situation expectation, is constructed:

---

[16] Berger and Luckmann's implication that the objectivity of the *non*institutional, "natural" world is *not* humanly constructed is rejected here (see Chapters 14 and 16). At first, Mannheim takes a position similar to Berger and Luckmann's implication ("natural science, especially in its quantifiable phases, is largely detachable from the historical-social perspective of the investigator" [1955:290–291; see also 49]), but changes his mind ("the natural sciences seem to be, in many respects, in a closely analogous situation [to that of the social sciences]" [1955:305]).

> Legitimation produces new meanings that serve to integrate the meanings already attached to disparate institutional processes. . . . [so that] the totality of the institutional order should make sense . . . to the participants in different institutional processes. . . . [Moreover,] the totality of the individual's life, the . . . passing through various orders of the institutional order, must be made subjectively meaningful (Berger and Luckmann, 1967:92).

There are "different levels of legitimation," however, and at the highest level, situation expectations take on dimensions so general as to become abstract "symbolic universes" which are

> bodies of theoretical tradition that integrate different provinces of meaning and encompass the institutional order in a symbolic totality. . . . [Here the] sphere of pragmatic application is transcended once and for all. Legitimation now takes place by means of symbolic totalities that cannot be experienced in everyday life at all. . . . On this level of legitimation, the reflective integration of discrete institutional processes reaches its ultimate fulfillment. A whole world is created. . . . The ultimate legitimation for "correct" actions . . . will then be their "location" within a cosmological and anthropological frame of reference (Berger and Luckmann, 1967:95–97).

The net result of this construction of successive levels of situation expectations is that "the reality of everyday life [becomes] ordered in terms of a hierarchy of realities, *ipso facto* becoming intelligible and less terrifying. . . . The entire society now makes sense" (Berger and Luckmann, 1967:98, 103).

Whereas Berger and Luckmann thus focus on constructed macro *cultural* structural elements in situation expectations, Cicourel focuses on similarly constructed images of macro *social* structural elements in such expectations:

> We must study the way human decision-making in complex micro-settings contributes to the creation of macro-structures by routine problem-solving activities necessary for the simulation or realization of basic organizational goals. These accomplishments presuppose a sense of micro-macro integration by the members of an organization and strategies for pursuing this integration (Cicourel, 1981:67).

The "macro-survey researcher," says Cicourel, makes "decisions that lead to distributions by income, education, social classes, occupational groups, and the like," and these decisions "create collective entities in the larger society regardless of whether these 'groups' have any coherent organized existence that can be studied by other means" (1981:65). Not only is it "macro-survey researchers" who create such macro situation expectations, but their creation is indeed "a routine feature of all cultural or social [sic] organization" (Cicourel, 1981:65), such that "Everyday settings . . . abound with highly organized ways of dealing with and producing macro-evaluations, reports, and summarizations of relentless micro-events" (Cicourel, 1981:66).[17] Starr shows in detail how the American medical profession— one such highly organized way—came to possess "The authority to . . . diagnose health or illness, to name diseases, and to offer prognoses" (1982:14).

Role-Expectations

Most definitions of "role" stress the behavior or responses deemed appropriate for a given actor in a given situation in pursuit of a given consequence (see Chapter 3). Taking into consideration the distinction between role-performance and role-expectation, then, the concept "role-expectation" may be said to stress the normative response expectation more than the actor, situation, or consequence expectation—such that the heart of the role-expectation concept seems to be *what* a given actor is expected to do and only secondarily where-and-when or why he/she is expected to do it. As Homans says, a "role" (sic) states "how persons are expected to *behave* and therefore . . . ought to *behave* in particular circumstances" (1974:335, emphasis added). One would hardly define a role-expectation as a statement of the *circumstances* under which persons are expected to behave in particular ways—although it is indeed this, too.

In addition, however, a role-expectation should be regarded as an aggregate or assembly of norms (as discussed in Chapter 4) such that an actor-in-role is expected to do this and also that and that—an aggregate that usually bears some summary rubric like "making a living," or "raising children,"or "celebrating communion," a rubric which also serves to emphasize the response expectations as salient.

Now any role-expectation which, like those just mentioned, implicates other actors will refer to them as part of its situation and consequence expectations, and therefore (as indicated in Chapter 4) a given individual is apt to learn others' role-expectations as well as his/her own. Thus, says Mead, "A child plays at being a mother, at being a teacher, at being a policeman; that is, it is taking different roles, as we say. . . . [The] roles which the children assume are made the basis for training" (1934:150). What Mead holds is thus trained into the individual is his/her "me":

[17] Knorr-Cetina calls Cicourel's the "representation hypothesis" of macro-phenomena; arguing that in its extreme version it "would have to deny the existence of a macro-order apart from the macro-representations [that are socially acquired by people] in micro-social action" (1981:40–41)—that is, apart from such enculturistic variables as normative situation expectations. It may be argued, however, that "micro-phenomena" seem no less constructed representations than are "macro-phenomena." Similarly, against Cicourel, it may be argued that individual entities like organisms or mountains seem no less "created" by no less "routine" features of social and cultural structure than are collective entities like social classes and occupational groups (see Chapter 6).

[The individual] can throw the ball to some other member because of the demand made upon him from other members of the team. . . . He has their attitudes, knows what they want and what the consequence of any act of his will be, and he has assumed responsibility for the situation (1934:175).

In this way, role-expectations become aggregates of interconnected norm expectations that, because they refer not only to individual B's own responses but to the responses of others, help explain B's participation in social phenomena with those others.

Conscience

The idea that one's conscience is causally derived from the same sources as one's self, and that, once formed, it can exert causal influence over one's social participation is classifiable, according to Fig. 7.2, as an enculturistic proposition. Just as the self may be considered a generalization across one's normative actor expectations, conscience may be considered a generalization across one's normative consequence expectations—differentially weighted, of course, by the cathexis with which one invests them. This view of conscience seems to be what Cohen has in mind when he says "To reap the rewards of the roles we have succeeded in claiming, we are willing to impose upon ourselves considerable sacrifice and self-discipline. These roles [sic] are, therefore, among the most potent mechanisms of social control" (1966:101).

Freud is a classical source for the argument that not only does civilization sublimate human aggressive instinct into individual personality and creativity, but it also sets up "an agency within [the individual's psyche] to watch over [that instinct]" (1962:71). This "agency" is conscience, and its punishing instrumentality is the sense of guilt. Similarly, Mead asserts that "The things one cannot do are those which everybody would condemn" (1934:168); but Mead goes on, less conservatively than Freud, to include in "everybody" not only the living but the dead and the yet-to-be-born:

A person may reach a point of going against the whole world about him; he may stand out by himself over against it. But to do that he has to speak with the voice of reason to himself. He has to comprehend the voices of the past and the future. That is the only way in which the self can get a voice which is more than the voice of the community (1934:168).

More recently, Scott defines conscience in terms of a generalized "dutiful condition or . . . the more general one of obligation," and guilt as that "aspect of 'conscience' " which is "the expectation of punishment when the individual is aware that he has violated a [specific] norm to which he has a learned commitment" (1971:124, 125). "[M]oral learning," Scott says, "entails the expectation of sanctions. . . . Guilt is a special case of the general expectation. The self-punishing aspects of guilt . . . derive from [the expectation of] external punishment" (1971:124).

In summary, then, from the normative actor, situation, response, and consequence expectations set forth in Chapter 4 certain preeminently enculturistic variables are derived at hierarchically higher levels of aggregation and generalization. Having examined these more complex enculturistic variables, let us acknowledge two of the more elementary ones, namely, symbols, and meaning.

Symbols

Mead argues that the world exists for us in ways that are determined by our psychical behavior: "The human animal is an attentive animal. . . . It is not simply a set of passive senses played upon by the stimuli that come from without. The organism goes out and determines what it is going to respond to and organizes the world" (1934:25). Most prominent among the stimuli to which the human organism gives its attention, according to Mead, are the gestures made by other human organisms: "When . . . that gesture means this idea behind it and it arouses that idea in the other individual, then we have a significant symbol," and "Symbolization constitutes objects not constituted before. . . . Language does not simply symbolize a situation or object which is already there in advance; it makes possible the appearance of that situation or object" (1934:45, 78).

More recently, Rose argues that "Man lives in a symbolic environment as well as a physical environment and can be 'stimulated' to act by symbols as well as by physical stimuli," and defines a symbol as "a stimulus that has a learned meaning and value for people" (1962:5, emphasis removed).

Meaning

But given that a world exists for us as a result of our selective attention and symbolizing, Weber argues that such a world can only have meaning as a result of further psychical behavior: " 'Culture' is a finite segment of the meaningless infinity of the world process, a segment on which *human beings* confer meaning and significance" (1949:81). In Weber's view, to confer meaning on something is to designate it as either a means or an end of human purposive behavior: "processes and conditions, whether they are animate or inanimate, human or nonhuman, are in the present sense devoid of meaning. . . . . if they cannot be related to action in the role of means or end but constitute only the stimulus, the favoring or hindering circumstances" (1947:93; see also 1949:52). The meaning that individual B attaches to a given social phenomenon is essential, in Weber's view, to explaining his/her participation (or nonparticipation) in it:

A correct causal interpretation of typical action means that the process which is claimed to be typical is shown to be both adequately grasped on the level of meaning and at the same time the interpretation is to some degree causally adequate. If adequacy in respect to meaning is lacking, then no matter how high the degree of uniformity and how precisely its probability can be numerically determined, it is still an incomprehensible statistical probability, whether dealing with overt or subjective processes (1947:99).

In the same tradition, when Parsons and Shils conceive of "the behavior of living organisms. . . . as oriented to the attainment of ends in situations, by means of the normatively regulated expenditure of energy" (1951:53), the "orientation" in question is the meaning (in Weber's sense) which the organism gives to its behavior. It is to various forms of "orientation" (including the pattern variables and need-dispositions) that Parsons and Shils assign primary causal weight in explaining social phenomena. Similarly, Stryker says:

Behavior is dependent upon a named or classified world. The names or class terms attached to aspects of the environment . . . carry meaning in the form of shared behavioral expectations that grow out of social interaction. From interaction with others, one learns how to classify objects . . . and in that process also learns how one is expected to behave with reference to those objects (1980:53–54).

Thus, if "self," "conceptualizations of macro cultural and social structures," "role-expectations," and "conscience" may be regarded as located at the top of the hierarchy of enculturistic variables, "symbols," and "meaning" may be located at its base, insofar as the latter constitute elements from which the former (as well as the four norm expectations, located at an intermediate level) are constructed.

Mead sums up the case for enculturistic variables at all hierarchic levels as follows:

A person is a personality because he belongs to a community, because he takes over the institutions of that community into his own conduct. He takes its language as a medium by which he gets his personality, and then through a process of taking the different roles that all the others furnish he comes to get the attitude of the community. . . . Such responses are abstract attitudes, but they constitute just what we term a man's character. They give him what we term his principles. . . . It is that which guides conduct controlled by principles, and a person who has such an organized group of responses is a man whom we say has character, in the moral sense (1934:162–163).

Enculturistic Variables in Sociobiology

Enculturistic variables, as already suggested in the discussion above of nurturism, appear frequently (and perhaps increasingly) in sociobiological explanations. For example, Wilson, noting that regional "dialects" often characterize the songs of male birds, argues that "the dialect is learned from the adult birds during rearing and before the young birds themselves attempt any form of song" (1975:157). Klopfer and Hailman summarize early research on imprinting:

In 1910 Heinroth announced an extraordinary discovery: young goslings follow the first relatively large moving object they see after hatching. The young geese subsequently follow the object in preference to anything else. Of course, in the wild, this object is usually the parent goose. Heinroth called this rapid fixing of social preferences "Prägung," the German term for impressing, as in stamping out a coin; Lorenz translated it *imprinting*. Lorenz further said that imprinting occurs rapidly, does not involve "rewards" as do usual kinds of learning . . . and lasts a lifetime (Klopfer and Hailman, 1967:49).

The social effects of imprinting are pointed out by Hess: "Imprinting refers to the primary formation of social bonds in infant animals. The nature of the first social experience that a young animal has is important in determining the character of the social behavior of that animal in its later and adult life" (1962:254.)

Wilson employs enculturistic variables[18] in explaining other social phenomena:

The social status of male Japanese and rhesus macaques is determined to a large degree by the rank of their mothers. The early social interactions of the monkeys and the way they respond generally to other troop members are influenced by this single circumstance. A lineage of success and failure might easily result . . . incorporating experiential and endocrine factors that remain to be fully analyzed (1975:153)

[18] Although Wilson defines "socialization" as "the sum total of all social experiences that alter the development of an individual" (1975:159), and therefore may not seem to draw the distinction made here between nurturistic and enculturistic variables, actually he does so when he distinguishes between "Morphogenetic socialization, for example caste determination," on the one hand, and "Learning of species-characteristic behavior," and "subculturation" on the other (1975:159).

and "When mother rats are psychologically stressed in certain ways, the emotional development of their descendants is altered for up to two generations. In other words, the future of an individual can indeed be influenced in the womb" (Wilson, 1975:152). Klopfer and Hailman point out that "young male rats reared with mature females failed to develop normal sexual responses. A pattern of play activity associated with females had apparently conditioned the young males so as to bar their recognition of females as sex-objects" (1967:149).[19] Marler and Gordon report on dietary socialization among macaques:

> Itani says that yearling macaques learn which plants are to be eaten by seizing and eating the food which their mother drops from her mouth. If they pick up something which their particular troop does not eat, the mother will snatch it away from them. By the age of two, he says, all young restrict their diet to the natural food of their troop without further prompting (1968:125–126).

Bartholomew notes a case in which the primary agents of socialization are peers rather than parents:

> The primary socialization of fur seal pups is to other pups, rather than to the adults of either sex. . . . [E]xcept for the first few days post partum the pups are only infrequently in contact with their mothers. Consequently, the pups are usually rebuffed in all their social contacts except with other pups. The social importance of pups to each other is further strengthened by their habit of spending most of the time together in the pup pods. . . . [A] social structure based in large measure on year class is maintained for the first several years of life by fur seals, particularly the males (1959:170).

Bonner stresses the importance of teaching (cultural structuralistic variables; discussed in Chapter 10) as well as learning, although he notes that learning can occur with no other teacher than the organism itself (see the reference to self-teaching in Fig. 3.1): "Perhaps the most primitive kind of teaching is self-teaching. It is the same thing as . . . trial and error learning" (1980:125).[20] By contrast, says Bonner, "the very fact that [the waggle-dance of the honey bee] is referred to as a language directly implies that teaching [as well as learning] is

---

[19] Mason finds a similar mating abnormality among socialization-deprived rhesus monkeys (see 1969), and Harlow finds childrearing abnormality among them as well (see 1965).

[20] Klopfer suggests the possible explanatory power of prenatal self-teaching:

> The schooling behavior of fish may depend on their aligning themselves tail-to-eye. During embryogenesis, the fish are curled within the fetal membranes with tail opposite eye. Perhaps, as Lorenz (personal communication) has jocularly suggested, it is the stimulation afforded by the slowly undulating tail during development that provides the basis for the responses that lead to schooling in the fry (1962:43).

involved" (1980:127). "Learning," Bonner argues, "came first during the course of evolution; complex teaching is a more recent invention and obviously basic to cultural evolution" (1980:114).

SUMMARY

This chapter has concentrated on the four types of explanatory variables internal to social participants. Materialistic variables were described as referring to innate characteristics of the participant's body, including both intake needs and output capabilities. Nurturistic variables were described as referring to the same characteristics as materialism, but in their socially influenced aspects. Marx and Engels are among the classical progenitors of materialism and nurturism. Instinctivistic variables include Freud and Pareto among their classical progenitors. Such variables refer to innate characteristics of the participant's mind—including instincts and other cognitive, cathectic, and conative dispositions presumed to be genetically determined. Enculturistic variables include Mead among their classical progenitors, and have the same empirical referents as instinctivistic variables but in their socially influenced aspects rather than their existentially given aspects. Six enculturistic variables were given special attention here: self, conceptualizations of macro cultural and social structures, role-expectations, conscience, symbols, and meaning.

9

External People Variables–Body

Chapter 7 argued that there are only two ways individual B's behavior may be constrained to constitute an interorganism behavior regularity with individual A: primarily through causes internal to individual B, or primarily through causes external to B. Accordingly, Chapter 8 examined four kinds of variables representing causes internal to B, and we now turn to variables representing causes originating with *people* external to B—namely, demographism and social structuralism (Chapter 9), and psychical contagionism and cultural structuralism (Chapter 10).

Note that, strictly speaking, what are here called "demographism" and "social structuralism" are both varieties of social structuralism broadly construed inasmuch as they both refer to interorganism physical ("body") behavior regularities—in their explanatory roles, of course. The terminological difference here acknowledges (1) the importance of the distinction between existentially given and socially influenced explanatory variables to sociological analysis, and (2) established usage in that analysis. The same applies to the terms ("psychical contagionism" and "cultural structuralism") used in the next chapter to designate interorganism psychical ("mind") behavior regularities—again, in their explanatory roles.

DEMOGRAPHISM

Figure 7.2 identifies demographistic variables as explaining B's participation in a social phenomenon with A by referring to causal influences impinging on B from existentially given physical ("body") aspects of people in B's environment—including, of course, A. Thus, demographism claims that social phenomena will be influenced by the absolute number of participants in them, by the existentially given physical needs and capacities of those participants, and by the extent to which dead and emigrated participants are replaced—hence the central demographistic variables are population size, age distribution, sex ratio, birth/death ratio, and immigration/emigration ratio. Demographism argues that such variables influence social phenomena in two ways: directly, insofar as different population characteristics imply different relationships (i.e., different social and cultural structures, and different spatial and temporal regularities) between participants in the social phenomenon in question, and indirectly, insofar as different population characteristics imply different relationships between the social phenomenon and its environment, and these relationships, in turn, imply different relationships between participants.

The group of sociological explanatory variables denoted by "demographism" should be distinguished from "demography." Hauser and Duncan say the latter includes both "demographic analysis" which is "confined to the study of components of population variation and change," and "population studies" which are "concerned not only with population variables but also with relationships between population changes and other variables—social, economic, political, biological, genetic, geographical, and the like" (1959:3). Similarly, Davis differentiates "population analysis" into "formal demography," including "not only the statistical measurement of a population's growth, its age-sex structure, and its fertility and mortality, but also the mathematical analysis of the interrelations among these," and "population theory" which interprets "the causes and consequences of demographic phenomena, a central question being the effect of population growth on the level of living" (1959:311–312). Demographism, as a substantive explanatory emphasis in sociology, is characteristic of what Hauser and Duncan call "population studies" and Davis calls "population theory," although, of course, these constantly draw upon "demographic analysis" or "formal demography" for deeper knowledge of their chosen explanatory variables—just as materialistic and instinctivistic explanations in sociology draw upon the disciplines of genetics, physiology, and psychology.

Note also that what holds for all the existentially given and socially-influenced pairs of variables shown in Fig. 7.2 holds here as well: Whenever a "demographistic" variable (including fertility, mortality, and mobility, or sex ratio, age structure, and emigration-immigration ratio) is regarded by the analyst as having been socially influenced (through, say, education, war, contraception, public health, or transportation technology), that variable becomes classifiable as "social structuralistic." Demographers, therefore, study the effects of social phenomena on erstwhile demographistic variables as well as the reverse, and when they do, they call, as do other sociologists, upon nurturistic, enculturistic, social structuralistic, cultural structuralistic, and technologistic variables to specify these effects.

Classical protagonists of the explanatory power of the absolute number of living human bodies in a given society (i.e., population size) include Simmel and Durkheim. Simmel emphasizes the direct effect of this population characteristic on social phenomena: "Where three elements, A, B, C, constitute a group, there is, in addition to the direct relationship between A and B, for instance, their indirect one, which is derived from their common relation to C" (1950:135)—thus, we have the possibility of C mediating conflicts between A and B, as well as participating in such conflicts through coalitions (see Simmel 1950:145–169), a possibility examined more recently and in detail by Caplow (1968). Thus, in general, "certain developments . . . can be realized only below or above a particular number of elements [and] certain other developments are imposed upon the group by certain purely quantitative modifications" (Simmel 1950:87).

More specifically, according to Simmel, differences in population size can explain certain social structural differences: for example, "it is often easier [for a ruler] to dominate a larger than a smaller group"; "A very large number of people can constitute a unit only if there is a complex division of labor"; "The principle of socialism—justice in the distribution of production and reward—can easily be realized in a small group and . . . can be safeguarded there by its members" (1950:205, 88). Simmel holds that population size can also explain certain cultural structural differences: "where large masses are indicated by political, social, or religious movements they are ruthlessly radical, and extreme parties overwhelm moderate ones. The reason is that large masses can always be animated and guided only by *simple* ideas" (1950:93). There are other consequences for cultural structure when a large population is made dense by a constricted spatial environment:

> Metropolitan life . . . underlies a heightened awareness and a preponderance of intelligence. . . . [Moreover, a money] economy and the dominance of the intellect are intrinsically connected. They share a matter-of-fact attitude in dealing with men and with things; and, in this attitude, a formal justice is often coupled with an inconsiderate hardness (Simmel, 1950:409–411, emphasis removed).

More recently, Blau takes an essentially Simmelian position—although Blau is more concerned with effects of different subpopulation sizes within the same social phenomenon, whereas Simmel is concerned with effects of the size of the overall population. Thus, Blau focuses on "the distribution of people among different positions and their social associations," and hypothesizes, to cite just two of many examples, that "For any dichotomy of groups, the mean number of intergroup associates is an inverse function of group size," and "The larger the difference in size between two groups, the greater is the discrepancy in the rates of intergroup associations between them" (1977:1, 21, 23). Another recent and Simmelian use of population size may be found in Berger and Luckmann, and where Blau is explicitly concerned with using this variable to explain "group structures and sta-

tus structures, and explicitly *not* . . . culture" (1977:16, emphasis added), Berger
and Luckmann *are* concerned with using it to explain culture. Thus, they argue
that

> As long as . . . institutions are constructed and maintained only in the in-
> teraction of [two participants, namely] A and B, their objectivity remains
> tenuous, easily changeable, even playful . . . [but with the] appearance of a
> third party . . . [the] institutional world . . . is now passed on to others.
> In this process institutionalization perfects itself (1967:58).

The question of increase, or more generally, change, in population size brings
us to variables pertaining to the replacement of population members. In its concern
with population replacement, demographism acknowledges the explanatory weight
and existential giveness of human biological reproduction, human locomotion, and
human death. These variables enable any given population to be over-replaced,
exactly replaced, or under-replaced with the passage of time—such that its size may
increase, remain constant, or decrease. Demographism argues that these different
possibilities will have different consequences for social phenomena in the population partly because they imply different relations among its members, and partly
because they imply different relations between those members and their natural
environments.

Malthus is a classical proponent of the indirect (i.e., via the nonhuman environment) effects of population replacement, arguing that they tend to overwhelm
whatever economically productive power a society may have, and thereby to bring
about debilitating social phenomena ranging from celibacy, poverty, negligent
childrearing practices, to wars and famines (see Malthus, 1933:11–14). And among
recent users of the Malthusian hypothesis is Davis, who argues that "human increase may be retarding the rise in level of living or thwarting it altogether," and
that that increase has brought "most underdeveloped countries . . . dangerously
close to making genuine economic development impossible for themselves"
(1976:273).

Weber is a classical proponent of the direct effect of population replacement on
relations between participants within society. Thus, speaking of the "routinization
of charisma" Weber argues that the

> interests of the members of the administrative staff, the disciples or other
> followers of the charismatic leader in continuing their relationship . . . be-
> came conspicuously evident with the disappearance of the personal charismatic
> leader and with the problem of succession, which inevitably arises. . . .
> [Therefore, the] problem of succession . . . is crucial (1947:364, 371).

More recently, and in the same vein, Ryder says

Any organization experiences social metabolism: since its individual components are exposed to "mortality," the survival of the organization requires a process of "fertility." The problem of replacement is posed not only for the total organization but also for every one of its differentiated components. The ineluctability of social metabolism is from one view a problem that any organization must solve in the interest of continuity and from another view a continual opportunity for adaptation and change (1964:461).

And Erikson attributes the catastrophic demoralization of survivors of the Buffalo Creek flood, in large part, to sudden demographic attrition: "the victims outnumbered the non-victims by so large a margin that the community itself has to be counted a casualty" (1976:202).

Age Distribution

A population that is not merely replacing but over-replacing itself through an excess of births over deaths will be a youthful population—that is, the younger age groups will be overrepresented in it—whereas a population that is underreplacing itself in this manner will be an older population. Populations with different age distributions are apt to manifest different social phenomena simply because their members are capable, for existentially given reasons, of doing, thinking, and feeling different things at different ages. For this reason, probably every long-established social phenomenon takes such innate age-related behavior differences into account in its social and cultural structures. Indeed, Riley and Waring argue that society may be thought of as "two fluid, shifting structures: an age structure of people and an age structure of roles . . . [wherein age] is not only a criterion for entering and leaving certain roles, but it also influences the nature of role prescriptions (norms as to what is expected), and the rewards or punishment allocated for role performance" (1976:358, 360). In such a situation, any change in replacement rates will have repercussions for every social and cultural structure in which age-grading is a factor. Thus, Waring argues that

When the fit between the cohort and the role system is poor . . . the customary orderly flow of cohorts becomes disordered. . . . Cohorts which are too large, for example, create a "people jam" at the entrances to the successive age grades they seek to occupy. Without intervention only some members of the cohort can experience the promised succession. The others risk role disenfranchisement. . . . By contrast, cohorts of insufficient size understaff existing role structures—and may ultimately threaten the survival of the population (1976:108, 112).

Waring cites two sets of societal responses to (i.e., consequences of) disordered cohort flow. One set involves changes in the number of age-graded statuses (Waring calls them "roles") through which cohorts flow at unchanged speed, and the other set involves changes in the speed at which cohorts flow through an unchanged number of age-graded statuses. In one case, the track is made longer or shorter; in the other case, the horses are made to run slower or faster. There are further social structural consequences of each: adding new statuses may divert resources from established ones ("A commitment to expansion of higher educational facilities for the numerous youth may be at the expense of providing ignored medical facilities for the old" [Waring, 1976:114]), and subtracting established statuses that are normally filled by one cohort may also result in subtracting statuses filled by another cohort: "For example, in response to recent declines in fertility, personnel requirements for obstetrical as well as educational services have been reduced" (Waring, 1976:115). In the second set of consequences, cohort flow may be accelerated or decelerated: "hospitals during the postwar years shortened the postpartum stay of new mothers in order to accommodate more"; and "In order to relieve doctor shortages . . . Congress offered financial incentives to medical schools to institute three-year training programs" (Waring, 1976:117).[1]

Waring also comments on some cultural structural consequences of cohort size:

> membership in a large cohort increases the motivation for deviance and membership in a small cohort increases the commitment to conformity. [Thus, among] young people in the large cohorts of the late 1960's . . . [the] motivation to drop out may have derived from a recognition . . . that "staying in" was not worth the "hassle." [However,] the small numbers of young adults in the 1950's [were characterized by] conformist behavior (1976:122–123).

In a similar argument, Davis claims that in order to absorb a suddenly increased number of youths

> an economy must expand rapidly. If it falters, large numbers become unemployed. If they attend school, they become a class of "educated unemployed." With youthful energy and idealism but no stake in the existing society, they are politically explosive, ready to follow any leader who promises a quick . . . solution (1976:277).

---

[1] We may regard these two sets of possible consequences of disordered cohort flow as equivalent insofar as acceleration over a sufficient number of cohorts may result in subtracting an age-graded role, and deceleration over a sufficient number of cohorts may result in adding an age-graded role. Waring suggests the latter case when she argues that the "retardation of cohort flow [via child-labor, and compulsory education, laws] eventuated in a new life stage between childhood and adulthood—adolescence" (1976:120).

Sex Ratio

Now it almost goes without saying that human biological replacement has so far been sexual and has, until recently, required that unique dyadic social phenomenon called "sexual intercourse" between fertile females and fertile males; only ants, bees, and wasps have approached self-maintaining all-female societies (none, of course, have approached self-maintaining all-male societies), and although they are all-female for most of their careers, there are always short periods during which males are present and reproductively active. It appears, however, that human technology (through sperm banks, *in vitro* conception and gestation, and cloning) has already conferred upon human society the ability, in principle, to do without reproductive sexual intercourse, and eventually to do without male and female parenting.

Until such time that that ability-in-principle is made manifest in practice, however, no human society can survive without fertile females and males. Thus, populations with different sex ratios are apt to manifest different social phenomena—if for no other reason than that males and females are innately capable of doing different things regarding the generation and early sustenance of infant recruits to that population.

Guttentag and Secord (unpublished) stress the existence of systematic variability in sex ratios at birth:

> Sex ratios at birth are *not* identical among different populations. Blacks, for example, have lower sex ratios at birth. . . . And we have found one ethnic group, the Orthodox Jews of Eastern Europe, with extremely high sex ratios at birth. . . . Sex ratios at birth also vary by socioeconomic class, approaching 110 for the highest levels, and falling to barely over 100 for the lowest levels.[2]

Regarding social and cultural structural consequences of sex ratio differences, Guttentag and Secord conclude that

> women in a high sex ratio society would be highly valued, would occupy and be satisfied with traditional roles such as wife and mother, that men would be committed to their families over long periods of time, and that a sexual morality would be imposed upon women. Low sex ratio societies would be

[2] Guttentag and Secord offer multiple explanations for low sex ratios at birth—chiefly poor nutrition and poor medical care—and in explaining the high sex ratio at birth among Orthodox Jews, Guttentag and Secord argue that "The only plausible explanation that we can find for the high sex ratios at birth among Jews is that they result from Jewish sex practices" which bear on "known physiological processes that would favor male conception."

sexually permissive for both men and women, women would be less valued, and men would have multiple or successive relationships with different women, either in marriage [or] out of it. . . . [Moreover, low sex ratios,] signifying a shortage of men, provide impetus for feminist movements. This is not to say that low sex ratios can bring movements about by themselves, but rather that they provide some facilitating conditions.

Finally in this discussion of sex ratio as a demographistic explanatory variable in sociological analysis, let us note that whereas Guttentag and Secord emphasize the social and cultural consequences of variation in the sex ratio (i.e., the size of a given male cohort relative to the size of a given female cohort), Oppenheimer emphasizes consequences of variation in the size of one female cohort relative to another female cohort, and relative to the economic demand for female workers, when she argues that partly because of "the secular decline in American fertility and, in particular, the low fertility of the 1930's [that] produced relatively small cohorts in women in their twenties in the 1950's and 1960's" (1973:956), the "supply of young women—those who would be most eligible for employment— underwent a sharp decline" just at the time "when the demand for female workers was rising steeply" (1973:954–956). This "has made possible the start of a transition in women's economic roles and with it the decline in normative restrictions against married women's working" (Oppenheimer, 1973:960).

Immigration/Emigration Ratio

Although physical locomotion is an existentially given characteristic of the human (and most other animal) species, all human individuals are not equally mobile. And although physical mobility is partly correlated with age and sex, it is by no means perfectly correlated with either. It follows that the migration of individuals to and from a given population is partly independent of their age and sex distributions—especially in the presence of highly developed technological means of transportation. Such migration is an important demographistic explanatory variable because it bears directly on the population size and replacement rates in different social phenomena. Davis indicates this importance when, after noting that "In the process of development, agrarian countries face a movement of something like sixty percent of their people from the country to the cities" (1976:278), he goes on to say

> Urban populations of the past usually failed to replace themselves because their deaths far exceeded their births. . . . Today . . . the cities of the Third World—thanks to modern public health—are growing rapidly by their

own excess of births over deaths. This means that they cannot absorb migrants as fast as the individualizing cities of the past could . . . [and in these] cities, rapid growth and poverty are creating history (1976:279–280).

Demographistic Variables in Sociobiology

Demographistic variables occur frequently in analyses of nonhuman social phenomena. For example, Wilson says

> The behavior of the society as a whole can be said to be defined by its demography. The breeding females of a bird flock, the helpless infants of a baboon troop, and the middle-aged soldiers of a termite colony are examples of the demographic classes whose relative proportions help determine the mass behavior of the group to which they belong (1975:14).

Among other social consequences of demographistic variables, Wilson notes the greater protection ("caterpillars in crowds were eaten much less frequently than solitary ones" [1975:43]), and the greater mating efficiency (the primary function of mating swarms among insects "is to bring the sexes together for nuptial displays and mating" [1975:57]), of larger population size. Wilson also reports on an experiment in which an effect of population size was tested:

> Archie Carr and his coworkers gained the impression that mass effort on the part of [green turtle] hatchlings is required to escape from the nests. They tested the idea by digging up clutches and reburying the eggs in lots of 1 to 10. Of 22 hatchlings reburied singly, only . . . 27 percent, made it to the surface. . . . When allowed to hatch in groups of 2, the little turtles emerged at [the rate of] 84 percent—and they journeyed to the water in a normal manner. Groups of 4 or more achieved virtually perfect emergence (1975:58).

Bonner points to some social effects of age and sex distributions:

> There are examples among bees and ants where a temporal or age difference between workers is used as a means of labor division. For instance, in honey bees it is known that the young workers stay in the hive and attend to housekeeping and brood care activities and as the worker ages she becomes a forager (1980:88).

Wilson also points to certain limits on the social benefits of larger population size when he says "Social insects and probably other highly colonial organisms have to contend with the 'reproductive effect': the larger the colony, the lower its rate of production of new individuals per colony member" (1975:36). Further,

> small group size and the inbreeding that accompanies it favor social evolution, because they ally the group members by kinship and make altruism profitable. . . . But inbreeding lowers the individual fitness and [thereby] imperils group survival. . . . Presumably, then, the degree of sociality is to some extent the evolutionary outcome of these two opposed selection tendencies (Wilson, 1975:80).

SOCIAL STRUCTURALISM

As we have just seen, the demographistic thesis emphasizes the explanatory power of physical characteristics of people in the participant's environment, including their absolute number and their distributions across such characteristics as age and mortality, sex and fertility, emigration and immigration—insofar as these characteristics are regarded as existentially given or innate to the people involved. In social structuralism, we encounter a complement of this demographistic thesis—insofar as it too emphasizes physical characteristics of the environing people—but here the characteristics of interest are socially influenced—or, more strongly, socially generated—as in the case of social class, nationality, gender (as distinct from sex), occupation, membership in voluntary associations, and the like.

Therefore, by "social structuralism," as an explanatory variable regarding social phenomena, I mean to indicate an emphasis on the socially generated physical behavior relations between the participant and others in that participant's environment. More precisely, social structuralism hypothesizes that B's participation in a social phenomenon with A may be explained by people in B's environment (including A) being in socially generated positions—by virtue, say, of wealth, or political power—physically to do certain things to B (called "social structuring" in Fig. 3.1) which influence B's social participation. This is what Merton refers to when he says he

> conceives of the social structure as active, as producing fresh motivations which cannot be predicted on the basis of knowledge about man's native drives. If the social structure retains some dispositions to act, it creates others. . . . [Moreover, the] social structure acts as a barrier or as an open door to the acting out of cultural mandates (1957:121, 162–163).

Comte is one progenitor of social structuralism: "every true social force is the product of a cooperation" (1975:420). Marx and Engels add that "with the division of labour . . . which is based on the natural [existentially given—ed.] division of labour in the family . . . is given simultaneously the distribution, and indeed the unequal distribution, (both quantitative and qualitative), of labour and its products, hence property" (1947:21), and Marx asserts his social structuralistic explanation of cultural structure as follows:

> The sum total of [the] relations of production constitutes the economic structure of society, the real foundations, on which rises a legal and political superstructure and to which correspond definite forms of social consciousness. The mode of production of material life conditions the social, political, and intellectual life process in general (1978:4).[3]

Durkheim would surely be listed among classical progenitors of social structuralism—especially for his argument that social structures may be too weak (i.e., "egoistic" [see Durkheim, 1951:202, 258, 299]) or too strong (i.e., "altruistic" [see Durkheim, 1951:221, 276]), and for either reason, their individual participants may voluntarily and permanently withdraw from them. (I examine Durkheim's concepts of "anomie" and "fatalism" in Chapter 10 as exemplifying his role as a classical progenitor of cultural, as well as social, structuralism.) Finally, Simmel, who hypothesizes different effects of "concentric" and "juxtaposed" group memberships (i.e., social structure), should be cited:

> [T]he objective structure of a society provides a framework within which an individual's noninterchangeable and singular characteristics may develop and find expression, depending on the greater or lesser possibilities which that structure allows (1955:150).

Four main varieties of social structuralism will be discussed here: unison, exchange, conflict, and functionalist. The first three of these argue that individual B will be influenced in different ways toward joining in a social phenomenon with A if the people in B's environment (including A) are doing the same things together, doing different and cooperative things together, or doing different but conflictful things together. The fourth, functionalist, variety incorporates features of all three other varieties.

---

[3] Engels, however, distinctly moderates this view by adding cultural structuralistic variables when he says

the reflexes of . . . actual [economic and political] struggles in the brains of the participants, political, juristic, philosophical theories, religious views and their further development into systems of dogmas, also exercise their influence upon the course of historical struggles and in many cases preponderate in determining their *form* (Marx and Engels, 1978:760).

Unison Social Structuralism

Of course, at the highest level of abstraction all physical behaviors are the same (i.e., they are all physical behaviors), and at the highest level of specificity they are all different (i.e., they each can be manifested once and only once, at one and only one place, by one and only one organism). It follows that the same social structure may be regarded as unison, on the one hand, or exchange or conflict, on the other, depending on the analyst's level of abstraction. Indeed, any given social structure may be regarded as having *both* qualities at the same time.

However, when the analyst compares two or more social structures with each other, one of them may display more sameness at a given level of abstraction than the others. Durkheim performs such a comparison when he contrasts "a social structure . . . to which mechanical solidarity corresponds," saying "What characterizes it is a system of segments homogeneous and similar to each other," with "the structure of societies where organic solidarity is preponderant." The latter societies, says Durkheim, "are constituted . . . by a system of different organs each of which has a special role, and which are themselves formed of differentiated parts" (1933:181). Similarly, Tönnies contrasts "Gemeinschaft" (the theory of which "starts from the assumption of perfect unity of human wills as an original or natural condition") with "Gesellschaft" (which "is to be understood as a multitude of natural and artificial individuals, the wills, and spheres of whom . . remain . . . independent of one another and devoid of mutual familiar relationships" [1963:37,76]).[4]

Segmental social structure, says Durkheim, generates mechanical solidarity (made manifest in "repressive" law) which demands that each individual participate in society in roughly the same way that every other individual participates (see Durkheim, 1933:68–79); and Tönnies refers to "Reciprocal, binding sentiment as a peculiar will of a Gemeinschaft" (1963:47). Thus, in our terms, unison social structuralistic variables are claimed to have explanatory power over individual B's social participation with A insofar as A is participating in a prior social phenomenon that exerts influence over B to manifest the same behaviors as A.

Exchange Social Structuralism

In the next two varieties of social structuralism, explanatory power is claimed for a prior social phenomenon that exerts influence over B to exchange behaviors

---

[4] Tönnies draws the distinction between social structure and cultural structure much less clearly than Durkheim—as exemplified by the former's reference to both "wills" and "spheres" (of activity).

with A. In what is usually called "exchange theory," emphasis falls on the benefits that B receives and that may be said to *induce* his/her participation, whereas in what is usually called "conflict theory" emphasis falls on the deprivations or injuries sustained by B and that may be said to *compel* his/her participation.

One classical expression of exchange social structuralism may be found in Spencer, who stresses the mediation by a third party of exchange between two original parties (thereby prefiguring Simmel's analysis of the triad):

> The organization of every society begins with a contrast between the division which carries on relations . . . with environing societies, and the division which is devoted to procuring necessaries of life. . . . Eventually there arises an intermediate division serving to transfer products and influences from part to part. And in all subsequent stages, evolution of the two earlier systems . . . depends on evolution of this additional system (1972:140; see also 1967:40–43 for Spencer's discussion of the mediating system, called "internuncial", between the governors and the governed of all three of the above systems).

But perhaps the most thoroughgoing classical expression of exchange social structuralism is Simmel's:

> All contacts among men rest on the schema of giving and returning the equivalence. . . . [S]ociety . . . always signifies that individuals are connected by mutual influence and determination. . . . To be true to this fundamental character of it, one should properly speak, not of society, but of sociation. Society merely is the name for a number of individuals, connected by interaction (1950:387, 10).

Exchange (or interaction), says Simmel, is omnipresent; we find it where we least expect it:

> Even in the most oppressive and cruel cases of subordination, there is still a considerable measure of personal freedom. . . . The super-subordination relationship destroys the subordinate freedom only in the case of direct physical violence. In every other case, this relationship only demands a price for the realization of freedom—a price, to be sure, which we are not willing to pay (1950:182).

Exchange is also present in hypnosis: "here, too, appearance shows an absolute influence, on the one side, and an absolute being-influenced, on the other; but it conceals an interaction, an exchange of influences" (1950:186). It is present in crowd behavior:

the individual feels himself carried by the "mood" of the mass, as if by an external force that is quite indifferent to his own subjective being and wishing, and yet . . . the mass is exclusively composed of just such individuals. . . . It conceals their own contributions from the interacting individuals. Actually the individual, by being carried away, carries away (1950:35).

It is present in secrecy: "the secret of a given individual is acknowledged by another . . . what is intentionally or unintentionally hidden is intentionally or unintentionally respected" (1950:330). It is present in social relations with strangers; "a special proportion and reciprocal tension produce the particular, formal relation to the stranger" (1950:408).

More recently, Homans, and Blau, have developed the exchange social structuralistic thesis further. Homans says

social behavior [is] an exchange of activity, tangible or intangible, and more or less rewarding or costly, between at least two persons. . . . [S]ocial behavior [is] true exchange, when the activity of each of at least two animals reinforces or punishes the activity of the other, and where accordingly each influences the other (1961: 13, 30).

Now Homans is especially "anxious to get motive into the system" (1961:13), and he does bring psychical behavior (cultural structure) in to the extent that "intangible" activity refers to it, and the identification of "reward," "cost," "reinforcement," and "punishment" all require it.[5] Thus, for Homans, it is not enough that the analyst observes two or more individuals or social structures exchanging physical behaviors; they must be observed exchanging physical behaviors whose values to each other are also known to the analyst. To this large extent, Homans' exchange social structuralism heavily implicates complementarity cultural structuralism,[6] discussed in Chapter 10.

[5] Homans defines the exertion of power of A over B entirely in terms of B's *psychical* behavior (i.e., B's cathectic evaluation of something as "rewards," and B's cognitive perception of B's "alternatives" and of net differences between B's and A's rewards); A need not behave at all, and B need not be physically influenced at all:

When A's net reward—compared, that is, with his alternatives—in taking action that will reward B is less, at least as perceived by B, than B's net reward in taking action that will reward A, and B as a result changes his behavior in a way favorable to A, then A has exerted power over B (1974:83).

Homans proposes an equally unusual definition of authority (see 1974:89-90).

[6] It also involves instinctivism and probably psychical contagionism. Thus, Homans, in describing "two kinds of norms," says "The first kind takes its origin from the fact that most members of a group tend under certain circumstances to behave in a particular way 'naturally.' They will behave that way without being told to do so and without any threat that they will be punished if they do not . . . [and] those who comply naturally with such norms will resent those who do not, if only because they are 'different,' and try to coerce them into compliance" (1974:98-99). The second kind of norm imposes that compliance on those who do not follow it "naturally."

Nevertheless, Homans' emphasis on the explanatory power of exchange structuralism seems clearly expressed: "we are less interested in the exchange itself than in what follows from it. . . . Suppose that a pair . . . have repeatedly entered into a particular kind of exchange. . . . [It] is almost inevitable that they will begin to enter into other kinds of exchange as well" (1974:57, 59), and these exchanges are apt to involve other participants. "The question then," says Homans, "is how the more complicated chains get established" (1974:358), and his answer to this question turns on three consequences of elementary exchange: (1) The establishment of norms; (2) the establishment of leadership as a permanent social status; and (3) the accumulation of capital (rewards)—all of which sustain complicated, long drawn-out, exchanges.

In declaring his own exchange social structuralism, Blau says

> Exchange is here conceived as a social process of central significance in social life. . . . Social exchange, broadly defined, can be considered to underlie relations between groups as well as those between individuals; both differentiation of power and peer groups ties; conflict between opposing forces as well as cooperation; both intimate attachments and connections between distant members of a community without direct social contacts (1964:4).

And where Homans, as we have seen, centrally implicates psychical behavior in all physical exchange, Blau says

> To be sure, each individual's behavior is reinforced by the rewards it brings, but the psychological process of reinforcement does not suffice to explain the exchange relation that develops. This social relation is the joint product of the actions of both individuals, with the actions of each being dependent on those of the other (1964:4).

Blau goes on to derive social integration, differentiation, opposition, legitimation, and value consensus from the social structure of exchange.

Like Homans, Bredemeier places psychical behavior near the center of exchange in his list of "eleven variables that the logic of exchange theory points to as controlling the probability that a person will engage in some action" (1978:428)[7]—that is, in our terms, eleven variables that can explain individual B's engaging in a social phenomenon with individual A. Five of these variables concern the rewards that A anticipates receiving as a result of such participation; five concern the costs that A anticipates; and one concerns the resources or ability that A anticipates being able to call upon in order to participate (see Bredemeier, 1978:428–429,

---

[7] It is not clear whether Bredemeier intends these to be exhaustive of all possible coordinative solutions, or to select only some possible solutions from the particular standpoint of "exchange theory."

who does not use the term "anticipates" but rather "perceives," "thinks," and "estimates"). It is his repeated emphasis on anticipations that deeply implicates psychical behavior in Bredemeier's discussion, but, like Blau, Bredemeier refers these anticipations back to the physical behavioral exchange itself, such that the latter becomes their explanatory cause: "the value to a person of an expected consequence of an act develops out of the person's previous interactions with environments . . . [and] it is out of exchange that inner controls become what they are" (Bredemeier, 1978:431–432).

Conflict Social Structuralism

"Conflict," say Mack and Snyder, "requires interaction among parties in which actions and counteractions are mutually opposed" (1957:218). The subsumption of conflict under exchange is thereby implied insofar as the latter includes the giving and receiving of any kind of physical behaviors and/or things, whereas the former is restricted to the giving and receiving of physical behaviors and/or things which, in Mack and Snyder's words, "are . . . designed to destroy, injure, thwart, or otherwise control another party or other parties" (1957:218).[8]

Among classical exponents of conflict social structuralism we have Spencer who, not unlike Simmel and Freud, attributes conflict to instinctivistic variables:

> To the end that [man] may prepare the earth for its future inhabitants—his descendants, he must possess a character fitting him to clear it of races endangering his life, and races occupying the space required by mankind. Hence he must have a desire to kill . . . [and] human beings are cruel to one another, in proportion as their habits are predatory (1972:18–19).

As a result, says Spencer, an

> important benefit bequeathed by war has been the formation of large societies. By force alone were small nomadic hordes welded into large tribes; by force alone were large tribes welded into small nations; by force alone have small nations been welded into large nations. . . . War, in short, in the slow

---

[8] When Mack and Snyder claim that "conflictful behaviors are . . . *designed* to destroy, injure [etc.]" they implicate intention—a psychical behavior—thereby permitting behaviors that do not *actually* injure to be called conflictful so long as they are so *intended*, and contradicting their assertion that "Conflict requires interaction . . . in which actions and counteractions *are* [actually] mutually opposed" (1957:218, emphasis added). Almost needless to say by now, I reserve the intention to injure for dissensus cultural structualism (discussed in Chapter 10) and assign only actual injury to conflict social structuralism.

course of things, brings about a social aggregation which furthers that industrial state at variance with war; and yet nothing but war could bring about this social aggregation (1972:169).

Whereas Spencer thus stresses the explanatory power of conflict between societies, Marx and Engels stress the power of conflict within societies: "The history of all hitherto existing society is the history of class struggles" (1978:473).

Simmel, who says "the instinctive needs of man prompt him to act in these mutually conflicting ways: he feels and acts *with* others but also *against* others" (1955:155), regards conflict as one phase of an endless oscillation with exchange (and perhaps unison):

> Both in succession and in the simultaneity of social life, [conflict and peace] are so interwoven that in every state of peace the conditions of future conflict, and in every conflict the conditions of future peace, are formed (1955:108–109).

Thus, says Simmel, "there probably exists no social unit in which convergent and divergent currents among its members are not inseparably interwoven. . . . Society . . . needs some quantitative ratio of harmony and disharmony, of association and competition, of favorable and unfavorable tendencies" (1955:15).

Coser examines a variety of propositions concerned with "those consequences of social conflict which . . . may, for example, contribute to the maintenance of group boundaries and prevent the withdrawal of members from a group" (1956:8). Thus, Coser hypothesizes that

> one reason for the relative absence of "class struggle" in this country is the fact that the American worker . . . is a member of a number of associations and groupings which represent him in diverse conflicts with different religious, ethnic, status and political groups. Since the lines of conflict between all these groups do not converge, the cleavage along class lines does not draw the total energies and allegiance of the worker into a single area of conflict (1956:76–77, see also Blau, 1977:260–268).

Dahrendorf asserts that "wherever there is social life there is conflict. . . . Not the presence but the absence of conflict is surprising and abnormal," and finds the origin of conflict in two phenomena which he regards as existentially given. First there is the shared psychical behavior (i.e., cultural structure) of cognitive uncertainty: "Because we do not know all the answers, there has to be continuous conflict over values and policies" (1958:127). And second, there is the shared physical behavior of superordination-subordination:

It may be possible to conceive of a society in which all differences of *income* and *prestige* are leveled and which is therefore "stratumless," but it is hardly possible to imagine a society in which there is no differentiation of roles in terms of legitimate *power*. Permanent anarchism is socially Utopian (Dahrendorf, 1959:219).

As a result, says Dahrendorf, the

differential distribution of authority invariably becomes the determining factor of systematic social conflicts in the traditional (Marxian) sense of this term. . . . Identification of variously equipped authority roles is the first task of conflict analysis (1959:165).

Not dissimilarly, Giddens claims that "Whereas in industrial society, class struggles center upon the appropriation of economic returns, in postindustrial society they concern the alienative effects of subordination to technocratic decisions" (1973:257).

Collins declares that "the only viable path to a comprehensive explanatory sociology is a conflict perspective," and asserts that "To be able to recognize competing interests as a matter of *fact* . . . is the essence of a detached position" (1975:21). And here is Skocpol's reliance on a conflict structuralism whose central participant is the state: ("We can make sense out of social-revolutionary transformations only if we take the state seriously as a macrostructure" [1979:29]):

The state . . . is fundamentally Janus-faced, with an intrinsically dual anchorage in class-divided socioeconomic structures and an international system of states. . . . State executives and their followers will be found maneuvering to extract resources and build administrative and coercive organizations precisely at [the intersection of these two conditions]. Here, consequently, is the place to look for the political contradictions that help launch social revolutions (1979:29, 32).[9]

FORCE AND VIOLENCE

Closely associated with conflict social structuralism are the concepts of force and violence, such that individual B is often said to have been influenced by force and

[9] Note Skocpol's unequivocal rejection of cultural structuralistic explanations of social revolutions: "any . . . consensual and voluntaristic conceptions of societal order and disruption or change are quite naive" (1979:16).

violence to participate in a given social phenomenon with individual A.[10] For example, when one person handcuffs or imprisons another person, the former prevents the latter's participation in some social phenomena and may also compel his/her participation in others. Let us see how such compellings may come within the scope of social structure as conceptualized here.

Briefly, "force," in its specifically sociological reference, may be regarded as any external physical behavior (see Fig. 3.1) that is applied—with or without the intermediary of animate or inanimate instruments (see Chapter 11)—to individual B's behavior. Typically, the direction of such force is regarded as at variance with individual B's own psychical disposition to behave (see Chapter 4), but that opposition is not necessary; individual B may conceivably want to do what he/she is also forced to do, and vice versa. "Violence," also in its sociological reference, may be regarded as any such force that is applied with high concentration in time and space to individual B's behavior—again, with or without technological instruments or "weapons." Typically, the direction of violent force is regarded as destructive rather than constructive or transportative but that does not seem necessary insofar as "revolutions" as well as "catastrophes," "booms" as well as "busts" (see Chapter 5), may be described as "violent." Thus, according to these definitions, not all force is violent although all violence is force because although force is a concept whose reference is social structural, violence is a concept referring to temporal and spatial regularities of fast tempo and high density (see Chapter 5) which may characterize that social structure.

By way of comparison, consider some other ways of conceptualizing force and violence. Graham and Gurr say

> "Violence" is narrowly defined here as behavior designed to inflict physical injury to people or damage to property. . . . "Force" is a more general concept: we define it here as the actual or threatened use of violence to compel others to do what they might otherwise not do. . . . Force necessarily involves the threat if not the actuality of violence; violence is forceful if it is used with the intent to change others' actions (1969:xxx).

Parsons says

> force is the use of control of the situation in which "alter" . . . is subjected to *physical* means to prevent him from doing something ego does not wish him to do, to "punish" him . . . or to demonstrate "symbolically" the ca-

---

[10] Note that at one point Weber asserts that "the concept 'law' will be made to turn on the presence of a group of men engaged in *enforcement*" (1947:128, emphasis added; see also 127 and 160), but at another point he says "every body of law consists essentially in a consistent system of *abstract rules* which have normally been intentionally established" (1947:330, emphasis added). Weber thus indicates both the social structural, and the cultural structural aspects of legal systems.

pacity of ego to control the situation. . . . I do not speak of the use of force unless the action . . . is "oriented" to an alter on whom it is expected to have an impact (1967:266).

Fanon refers to violence as involving the use of "bayonets," "knives," "guns," "electrodes," and, in general, the delivery of "blows" (see 1963:27–83). Himes asserts that "Most writers agree that violent conflict always leads to the injury or death of persons, the injury or destruction of human psyches, the disruption or destruction of material property" (1980:104).

Implicit in these views, and others like them, are at least four different assertions: that force and violence are *intention*-specific (they are "designed," and "used with . . . intent"); that they are *effect*-specific (they injure, kill, destroy, disrupt, prevent, punish); that they are *object*-specific (they take effect on people and property); and that they are *intensity*-specific (they involve large concentrations of energy delivered—with or without instruments—in small spatiotemporal compass). Ruling out intention (and threat) on the ground of its reference to psychical rather than physical behavior, and permitting force and violence to be exerted on people and all other living and nonliving things (whether "property" or not; see Fig. 3.1), and permitting the effects of force and violence to be constructive and transportative as well as destructive, we arrive at the definition set forth above, which assigns "force" to social structure and "violence" to the spatiotemporal regularity that may characterize it.

Functionalist Social Structuralism

I have left functionalist social structuralism for last in this discussion certainly not because it is any less important than unison, exchange, or conflict social structuralism but because it strives to embrace all three of these and to make sociological explanation isomorphic with a generalized "functionalism"—which Merton describes as an orientation "found in virtually all the sciences of man—biology and physiology, psychology, economics and law, anthropology and sociology" (1957:47; see also Buckley, 1957:236–240). Let us consider the principal arguments of functionalist social structuralism and see how exchange and conflict are implicit in them.

Functionalist social structuralism holds that in order to explain the persistence of a given social phenomenon, we must discover its function or consequence for (i.e., effect on) some social structure or structures whose feedback or reciprocation in eliciting a recurrence of, or in sustaining, the phenomenon in question is then taken for granted.[11] That is, if we want to explain B's continued participation in

[11] Because Chapter 3 has conceptually differentiated the physical behaviors that compose social structures according to their effects or "functions," it is especially important to note that that concep-

a social phenomenon with A, we have to show that that participation has consequences for A, or for other individuals, whose resulting influences on B are taken for granted. For example, if we demonstrate that voting (i.e., B's continuing to join with A in voting) has positive net consequences for a given system of government, functionalist social structuralism takes for granted that that system of government will, in its own interest, encourage voting. Because it takes that encouragement for granted, functionalist social structuralism can then regard the demonstration that voting has net positive consequences for the system as an abbreviated, shorthand, causal explanation of voting itself. By the same token, functionalist social structuralism accepts the demonstration that voting has negative net consequences for some other system of government as causal explanation for the absence of voting under that system.

It seems clear that the underlying assumptions of functionalist social structuralism are (1) that the persistence of any given social phenomenon is dependent on the persistence of other social phenomena; and (2) that other social phenomena sustain a given social phenomenon only insofar as it sustains them. Thus, if we are given observations on a total society, the functionalist social structuralistic thesis tells us to assume that each social phenomenon existing within it makes a net positive contribution to most other social phenomena in it (or at least to the most powerful of those phenomena), for only on condition of such contributions will those other social phenomena reciprocate—thereby continuing its existence to the extent that it helps to continue theirs.

Durkheim puts these assumptions as follows:

> the bond which unites the cause to the effect is reciprocal to an extent which has not been sufficiently recognized. The effect can doubtless not exist without its cause; but the latter, in turn, needs its effect. It is from the cause that the effect draws its energy; but it also restores it to the cause on occasion, and consequently it cannot disappear without the cause showing the effects of its disappearance. . . . Indeed, if the usefulness of a fact is not the cause of its existence, it is generally necessary that it be useful in order that it may maintain itself. . . . Consequently, to explain a social fact it is not enough to show the cause on which it depends; we must also at least in most cases, show its function in the establishment of social order (1938:95–97).

Note especially here Durkheim's distinction between the causes of a fact's *initial existence* and causes of a fact's *subsequent maintenance,* and his claim that functional

---

tualization does not necessarily imply tautology in functionalist explanations of such structures. Thus, for example, if we define an "economic" social structure as having a given level of constructive, transportative, and/or destructive effects on living and nonliving things in the environment (see Fig. 3.1), we may go on to hypothesize, without risking tautology, that such a structure (whether through its defining "economic" effects or other, ancillary, effects) performs functions for the society at large and other structures within it—thereby maintaining them—and these may then reciprocate by performing functions for the economic structure in question—thereby maintaining it.

social structuralism is limited to identifying the latter.[12] More specifically, Durkheim argues that

> to show how a fact is useful is not to explain how it originated or why it is what it is. . . . The need we have of things cannot give them existence, nor can it confer their specific nature upon them. It is to causes of another sort that they owe their existence (1938:90).[13]

In sum, then, Durkheim urges that the persistence (not the origin) of some (not all) social phenomena may be explained by their being reciprocated for their contributions to some larger social phenomenon of which they are parts. Now there are two aspects of this thesis: one aspect involves hierarchic causal structure (i.e., part-whole) and the other involves feedback or interaction causal structure (see Chapter 12 for general discussions of both kinds of causal structure). Note that neither necessarily implies the other; it is the decision to combine the two that best characterizes functionalist social structuralism—even though different theorists working in this tradition prefer to emphasize one causal structure or the other, as we shall now see.

PART-WHOLE RELATIONS

Among those emphasizing part-whole relations are Davis, who defines functional analysis as "the interpretation of phenomena in terms of their connection with societies as going concerns" (1959:760); and Merton: "the central orientation of functionalism [is] expressed in the practice of interpreting data by establishing their consequences for larger structures in which they are implicated" (1957:46–

---

[12] It has this limitation, that is, so long as the analysis is confined to *functions* (i.e., eufunctions). However, as soon as functionalist analysis incorporates an interest in *dysfunctions* (including under-functions and over-functions), this limitation disappears. Durkheim himself incorporates such an interest in his analyses of "abnormal forms" of the division of labor (1933:353–409), "abnormal forms" of crime (1938:66), and suicide as symptomatic of a "general contemporary maladjustment" (1951:37). See also Merton's analysis of dysfunctions of the social structural opportunities that are offered by the American economic system for the cultural structural goals that are taught by the American educational system, and vice-versa, as sources of "innovation," "rebellion," etc. (1957:131–160).

[13] Turner and Maryanski, in my judgment, misconstrue both Durkheim and functionalism when they attribute to Durkheim, and also assert in their own behalf, the following distinction: "Causal analysis asks: Why does the structure in question exist and reveal certain properties? Functional analysis asks: What need of the larger system does the structure meet?" (1979:17–18). This distinction ignores Durkheim's explicit designations of causal analysis as explaining how a phenomenon "originated" and functional analysis as explaining how a phenomenon "maintain[s] itself."

47).[14] In this tradition, Erikson interprets deviant behavior by establishing its consequences for the larger group:

> the confrontations which occur when persons who venture out to the edges of the group are met by policing agents whose special business it is to guard the cultural integrity of the community . . . demonstrate . . . where the line is drawn between behavior that belongs in the special universe of the group and behavior that does not (1966:11).

Erikson then asks whether the persistence of deviant behavior may be explained by its being constantly regenerated by the community of which it is a part: "Can we assume . . . that forces operate in the social structure to recruit offenders and to commit them to long periods of service in the deviant ranks?" (1966:13–14). Erikson answers affirmatively (however tentatively): "the deviant would appear as a natural product of group differentiation. He is not a bit of debris spun out by faulty social machinery, but a relevant figure in the community's overall division of labor" (1966:19).[15]

Closely related to their concern with social relations between part and whole, functionalists are also concerned with relations between part and part. Thus, Radcliffe-Brown asserts that "The function of any recurrent activity, such as the punishment of a crime, or a funeral ceremony, is the part it plays in the social life as a whole," but he also claims that "the function of a social activity is to be found by examining its effects upon individuals" (1965:180, 184). Thus, too, Davis says "functionalism is most commonly said to do two things: to relate the parts of society to the whole, and to relate one part to another" (1959:758, emphasis removed; see also Merton, quoted above). Similarly, Blau says "First, substructures are dependent on each other, which means that changes in one lead to changes in the others," and then he indicates, as "The second kind of interdependence," "the dependence of the substructures, not on each other, but on the larger social structure" (1964:302–303). Goode, too, says "functionalists emphasized . . . the unity

[14] Note that whereas Davis speaks of two-way *"inter*connections," Merton speaks here only of one-way "consequences *for.*" Merton's analysis of social structure and anomie (1957:131–160), however, manifests his concern with consequences *of* insofar as in this analysis he interprets data (on conforming and deviant behavior) as consequences of larger structures in which they are implicated.

[15] Both Merton's (discussed in Chapter 4) and Erikson's analyses of deviant behavior emphasize functionalist part-whole relations, but they each concentrate on a different phase of functionalist feedback relations (discussed below). In summary, Merton shows how the community generates deviant behavior in the first place, and how the form of that deviance varies with the community's "emphasis on institutionalized procedures for seeking these goals" (1957:139), while Erikson shows how deviant behavior, once generated, has positive functions for the community and how the substantive content of that deviance varies with the community's "unique identity" (see 1966:19–23). The two analyses are thus complementary.

of the entire social structure, and especially the interrelations among subgroups of the society or subareas of social interaction" (1973:72). Sztompka argues that "the core of functionalism is the systemic model of society" and identifies such a model with "a set of interconnections between [its] elements" (1974:56, 52). And finally, Moore says the functionalist "combination of differentiation and interdependence permits asking two related questions: how is the interdependence of units effected? What contribution do the parts make to the whole?" (1978:324).

FEEDBACK RELATIONS

If we ask about the nature of the causal "relations" and "interdependence" between parts and the whole and among parts of a whole, the functionalist answer is often said to rely on one-way "function" (Davis says functionalism sees "one part as 'performing a function for' or 'meeting a need or requirement of' the whole society or some part of it" [1959:758]). However, once we get firmly in mind that functionalist social structuralism aims at explaining the part that performs the function and not at explaining the part or whole for which the function is performed, then Gouldner's observation becomes crucial: "simply to establish its consequences for other social structures provides no answer to the question of the persistence of [the structure in question]. . . . To state the issue generally: the demonstration that A is functional for B can help to account for A's persistence only if the functional theorist tacitly assumes some principle of reciprocity" (1960:163).

In other words, if we want causally to explain A we have to show that causal influence *impinges on* A and not only that causal influence *emanates from* A. The latter demonstration can only be taken as explaining A if we assume that whenever A influences B, B automatically and unfailingly feeds back influence to A.

Once that assumption is made explicit, however, we immediately see that it is not always warranted; as Durkheim says, the effect restores energy to the cause only "on occasion." More generally, the influence B returns to A may be (1) variably commensurate with, and (2) variably synchronized with, A's effect on B. In addition to the concept of "returning good for ill" (i.e., benefit for injury), the concepts "over- and under-payment" indicate the first point, and several other concepts indicate the second: the term "survival"—in the sense of "holdover from the past"—may be applied to A if it once made a beneficial contribution to B, has now ceased making that contribution, but still receives support from B[16]; the term

---

[16] Merton says "a social survival . . . is, in the words of Rivers . . . 'a custom . . . [which] cannot be explained by its present utility but only becomes intelligible through its past history'" (1957:31). Note the unspoken implication here that past history makes the survival intelligible by revealing its past utility and that some sort of inertia leads the society as a whole to continue compen-

"investment" may be applied to the onset of support from B prior to the onset of contribution from A; and "prepayment" may be applied to the reverse sequence. Because functionalism takes all these problematics for granted and assumes the influence that B returns to A is both commensurate and synchronized with the function A has performed for B, Gouldner strongly criticizes "the functionalist polemic [for having] obscured [the problem of unequal exchanges] to the present day" (1960:165); and Merton criticizes the functionalists' "exaggerated 'postulate' to the effect that every custom . . . [presently] fulfills some vital function" (1957:32).[17]

If we set aside these questions of commensurateness and synchroneity of feedback, and bear in mind that all "feedback" is necessarily "feedforward" in time (see Chapter 12), we arrive at the following description of the central thesis of functional social structuralism: some social structure, A, causes another social structure, B, which then causes the recurrence of the first structure—call it A'. A' then causes B' which then causes A", and so on—where the social structures in question may be either parts of a social system or the system as a whole. This is simply an indefinitely extendable sequence of causes and effects, operating under the constraint that alternating members of the sequence (e.g., all the A's) are similar to each other—even indiscriminably similar to each other except for their temporal locations. When we ask how should the two sets of members of this causal sequence (i.e., all the A's, and all the B's) be named, we confront the problem of distinguishing between structures and functions.

STRUCTURES AND FUNCTIONS

Parsons seems to draw a clear causal distinction: "Functions are performed or functional requirements met by, a combination of structures and processes" (1970:35); thus, structures (and processes) are causes and functions are their effects. Levy, however, takes a different tack for, although he defines a function as "a

---

sating (or at least tolerating) the survival for that past utility. Gouldner, however, ignores the presumed past utility of a "social survival," concentrates only on its observed present nonutility, and therefore mistakenly defines it in terms of commensurateness rather than synchroneity: "a survival [is] . . . one of the limiting cases of reciprocity, that is one in which a pattern provides *nothing* in exchange for the benefits given it" (1960:165). Once we see what *kind* of limiting case a social survival is (i.e., one that in the past *did* provide something in exchange for the benefits given it), we can see the difference between it and another such case that Gouldner also discusses, namely, "exploitation"—where the pattern did not necessarily provide anything in the past.

[17] Note Durkheim's ambivalence regarding synchronization when, on the one hand, he claims that "An industry can exist only if it assumes some need. A function can be specialized only if this specialization corresponds to some need of society" (1933:272), and on the other hand, he claims that "a fact can exist without at all being [presently] useful. . . . There are, indeed, more survivals in society than in biological organisms" (1938:91).

condition or state of affairs, resultant from the operation . . . of structure through time" (1952:56; see also 1968:22)—thereby designating "structure" as cause and "function" as effect—he emphasizes the arbitrariness of these designations: "The same empirical phenomenon may be an example of either a function or a structure depending upon the point from which it is viewed" (1952:61; see also 1968:23). More recently Goode argues that

> in the actual usage of "structure and function" in the past, "functions" were usually effects, or consequences, while structures were independent or causal variables or behaviors. In any continuing analysis, however, it was always possible to challenge that independent or causal status and ask, with reference to any social pattern that was called a "structure" what caused *it* in turn, i.e., to view it . . . as a "function" of something [prior]. . . . How far one would go in such an alternation of focuses on structure and on function is perhaps a matter of intellectual taste (1975:68).

Levy's and Goode's views imply the following conclusion.

In the functionalist causal sequence described above—where A causes B and B causes A', and so on, and where all the A's are similar and all the B's are similar— either the A's or the B's may be called "structure" while the others are called "function"; the naming is arbitrary. A good analogy is a person walking: any given step by the left foot is similar to all other steps by that foot; each such step facilitates a different step by the right foot—any one of which, again, is similar to all other steps by the right foot, and the person does not favor either foot (i.e., parity is conserved between structure and function).

FUNCTIONAL PREREQUISITES, REQUISITES, AND IMPERATIVES

It should be noted that up to this point functionalist social structuralism has been treated as substantive only in a broad sense—that is, as claiming explanatory power merely for "social structure" without specifying what *kinds* of social structure. But if we should hypothesize that only a prior step by a left foot (and not, say, a nose twitch or an eye blink) can enable a step by a right foot, and perhaps also that only a prior step by a right foot can enable a step by a left foot, we then have the kind of hypothesis that produced the several lists of functional and structural "prerequisites," "requisites," and "imperatives" discussed in the context of description in Chapter 3. Such lists, in short, purport to tell us not only to look for the explanation of a given social structure in other social structures but they specify just *which* social structures (identified by their functions) to consider in this regard—just as, for example, Pareto's theory purports to specify just which instincts to consider.

IMPLICIT EXCHANGE AND CONFLICT

We are now in position to make two final points that were promised at the start of this section on functionalist social structuralism. First, when the feedback causal relations that functionalism takes for granted are made explicit, and when both function and feedback are of equal explanatory interest, we have exchange social structuralism—that is, the exchange of physical behavior between a part and a whole, or between one part and another part. Second, when we note Merton's argument against "The tendency to confine sociological observations to the *positive* contributions of a sociological item to the social or cultural system in which it is implicated," and the prominent place he gives to "dysfunctions"—"those observed consequences which lessen the adaptation or adjustment of the system" (1957:51)— it becomes apparent that exchanges between a part and the whole, or among parts, may involve dysfunctions (injuries), and therefore conflict.[18]

Thus, both exchange and conflict social structuralisms are clearly implicit in the emphasis that functionalism places on differentiated part-whole and part-part relations. But unison social structuralism is also implicit in the very notion of a "whole"—whose parts, however heterogeneous they may appear at high resolution, may also be regarded as homogeneous insofar as they all contribute to its persistence.

Other Varieties of Social Structuralism

Before leaving social structuralism, note that Fig. 3.3 has suggested not four (unison, exchange, conflict, and functional) but *nine* types of social structuralism (unison, imitation, cooperation, administration, competition, dominance, conflict, oppression, and segregation). However, if we grant that exchange and conflict social structuralisms represent explicated versions of functionalist social structuralism (as discussed above), then we may set the latter aside as having been incorpo-

---

[18] Merton says "dysfunction . . . implies the concept of strain, stress, and tension on the structural level" (1957:53), but he does not explicitly include conflict. More recently, however, Merton argues that "it is fundamental, not incidental, to the paradigm of structural analysis that social structures generate social conflict," and that the structural analysis he advocates "makes a large place for the structural sources and differential consequences of conflict, dysfunctions, and contradictions in the social structure" (1975:35,37). It is not clear to me just how Merton wishes to relate his "paradigm for *functional* analysis" (1975:50–54, emphasis added) to this "paradigm of *structural* analysis"—despite his remark that the latter "is deeply indebted to the classic mode of structural-functional analysis" (1975:36). His distinction between "manifest and latent levels [sic] of social structure as of social function" (Merton, 1975:36), however, suggests that the relationship would not be inconsistent with the conceptual symmetry between structure and function set forth on the preceding page.

rated by the first two. Regarding these types, it may be recalled that Chapter 3 suggested that the term "exchange" is often a general term for both cooperation and administration social structures while "conflict" is often a general term for competition, dominance, conflict (proper), and oppression social structures. This alerts us to the likelihood of subtypes of exchange social structuralism, and of conflict social structuralism, respectively. In addition, an earlier suggestion that "collective behavior" often covers both unison and imitation social structure, and that segregation social structure stands alone alerts us to still other subtypes of social structuralism that are not implied in unison, exchange, or conflict (or functional) social structuralism. Certain illustrations of such subtypes may be briefly cited.

Tarde has already been quoted in Chapter 3 to the effect that imitation social structures may virtually compel the participation of individuals. The following more recent reliances (the first one is only implicit) on imitation social structuralistic explanatory variables may also be cited. Archer and Gartner report that

> Most of the combatant nations in [our] study experienced substantial postwar increases in their rates of homicide. These increases did not occur among a control group of noncombatant nations. The increases were pervasive and occurred after large and small wars, . . . in victorious as well as defeated nations, in nations with improved postwar economies and nations with worsened economies, among both men and women offenders, and among offenders of several age groups. Postwar increases were most frequent among nations with large numbers of combat deaths (1976:961).

Phillips reports that

> motor vehicle accident fatalities increased markedly just after publicized suicide stories; . . . suicide stories about young persons tend to be followed by . . . crashes involving young drivers; conversely, suicide stories about older persons tend to be followed by . . . crashes involving older drivers; . . . [and] pure suicide stories and murder-suicide stories seem to trigger different types of crashes [such that] stories about murder and suicide tend to be followed by multiple-vehicle crashes involving passenger deaths, while stories about suicide alone tend to be followed by single-vehicle crashes involving driver deaths. . . . These findings indicate strongly that drivers of motor vehicles are affected by the processes of imitation, suggestion, and modeling (1979:1167; see also Phillips, 1974).

Finally in this connection, Spilerman implicates technologistic (see Chapter 11) as well as imitation social structuralistic variables when he says

> There is considerable evidence that skyjackings, prison riots, bomb threats and aggressive crimes of other sorts have been spread by television and the

other mass media. Indeed, a question which eventually will have to concern this nation is the determination of a policy to guide the reporting of destructive and potentially contagious events (Spilerman, 1976:790).

Durkheim's "organized" social structure should be noted as implying cooperation and administration. Dahrendorf implicates both dominance and conflict social structuralistic variables when he argues that "societies and social organizations are held together . . . by the coercion [dominance] of some others," and "We assume conflict is ubiquitous, since constraint is ubiquitous whenever human beings set up social organizations" (1958:127). And similarly, Tiryakian says "the social order is contingent upon the coercion [dominance] of the majority by the ruling minority's utilization of power facilities," and "the foundation of social order [is to be found] in the conflict between groups becoming ritualized" (1970:112, emphasis removed).

Weber attributes to administration social structure great explanatory power, claiming that "the purely bureaucratic type of administration organization . . . is, from a purely technical point of view . . . formally the most rational known means of carrying out imperative control over human beings" (1947:337). Freire argues for the explanatory power of oppression social structure when he asserts that "Once a situation of violence and oppression has been established, it engenders an entire way of life and behavior for those caught up in it—oppressors and oppressed alike" (1972:44). Fanon may be cited with reference to segregation social structuralism: "The colonial world is a world divided into compartments. . . . The zone where the natives live" and "the zone inhabited by the settlers . . . both follow the principle of reciprocal exclusivity" (1963:31–32). When such a segregation social structure is combined with an oppression social structure the result, Fanon says, is eventually a violent conflict social structure of reprisals and counter-reprisals between natives and settlers (see 1963:89).

Thus, it seems reasonable to suggest that, despite the greater currency of only unison, exchange, conflict, and functionalist social structuralism, others are also present in the literature.

Social Structuralism and Cultural Structuralism

Note that, in accord with the discussion of logical relations between social structure and cultural structure (considered as descriptive variables) in Chapter 2, demographistic and social structuralistic explanatory variables may or may not be linked, in a given analysis, with psychical contagionistic and cultural structuralistic explanatory variables. For example, exchange and conflict social structuralistic variables may either be offered alone, as strictly physical behavior explanations of a social phenomenon, or the analyst may also employ the further hypothesis that participants have some collective notion (whether innate or learned) of what constitutes "fairness," "value," "reward," "punishment," "threat," and so on. The latter, social-structuralism-plus cultural-structuralism, analytic linkage is often the case, as exemplified in the citations just above that implicate both imitation social structuralistic variables and cultural structuralistic "suggestion," "modeling," and "contagion."

Accordingly, the next chapter will examine (1) psychical contagionism as the variety of cultural structuralism (broadly construed—see the second paragraph of the present chapter) which is most often paired with demographism, (2) consensus cultural structuralism as most often paired with unison social structuralism, (3) complementarity cultural structuralism as most often paired with exchange social structuralism, (4) dissensus cultural structuralism as most often paired with conflict social structuralism, and (5) symbolic interactionism as most often paired with functional social structuralism.

Social Structuralistic Variables in Sociobiology

One of the purest examples of unison social structure anywhere is schooling in fish:

> At a distance, a fish school resembles a large organism. Its members, numbering anywhere from two or three into the millions, swim in tight formations, wheeling and reversing in near unison. . . . There is . . . no consistent leadership. When the school turns to the right or left, individuals formerly on the flank assume the lead (Wilson, 1975:439).

Wilson points out that this social structure constrains (by facilitating) individual participation by lending protection from predators, improved feeding ability, and energy conservation (see 1975:441–442).

Exchange social structuralism plays a secondary role to conflict social structuralism in sociobiological explanations. Thus, Darwinian evolution proceeds via natural selection, that is, survival of the fittest in competitive and conflictful (predator-prey) relations between individuals of the same, and different, species.[19] But although "It is part of our Darwinian heritage to accept the view that natural selection operates largely or entirely at two levels, discriminating on the one hand

---

[19] As Wilson puts it, "The pervasive role of natural selection in shaping all classes of traits in organisms can be fairly called the central dogma of evolutionary biology. . . . [Sociobiologists are convinced] that behavior and social structure . . . can be studied as 'organs,' extensions of the genes that exist because of their superior adaptive value" (1975:21–22).

in favor of *individuals* that are better adapted . . . and on the other hand between one *species* and another where their interests overlap and conflict" (Wynne-Edwards, 1962:18), selection is also held to operate at a level intermediate between the individual and the whole species; hence, *"group*-selection" (Wynne-Edwards, 1962:20, emphasis added).

It is only *within* such "groups" that sociobiologists are apt to give exchange social structuralism causal primacy. Wilson, indeed, as we have already seen (Chapter 2) defines society exclusively in terms of cooperation and does not even mention competition or conflict among the "most basic definitions [pertaining to] the properties of societies [considered holistically]" (see Wilson, 1975:7–11). Thus, Wynne-Edwards argues that unbridled competition among individual members of the same group works against evolution of the species as a whole because such competition would end by overconsuming the food on which the species subsists:[20]

> something must, in fact, constantly restrain [predators], while in the midst of plenty, from over-exploiting their prey. Somehow or other "free enterprise" or unchecked competition for food must be successfully averted, otherwise [over-consumption] would be impossible to escape: this could only result in lasting detriment to the predators and the risk, if they persisted in it, that the prey might be exterminated altogether (1962:8, emphasis removed).

Wynne-Edwards calls such a restraint on interindividual competition a "density-dependent convention . . . 'artifically' preventing the intensity of exploitation from rising above the optimum level" (1962:11), and cites the "territorial system" and "dominance" systems among many other instances of such conventions (see 1975:11–18; see also Etkin, 1964a:33).

What, exactly, is the sociobiological criterion for delimiting the "group" within which such cooperative restraints on competition can occur? Wilson supplies an explicit answer when, after asserting that "the central theoretical problem of sociobiology [is]: how can altruism, which by definition reduces personal fitness, possibly evolve by natural selection?" he says

> The answer is *kinship:* if the genes causing the altruism are shared by two organisms because of common descent, and if the altruistic act by one organism increases the joint contribution of these genes to the next generation, the propensity to altruism will spread through the gene pool (1975:3–4, emphasis added).[21]

---

[20] A crucial materialistic-ecologistic assumption here is that "in the great majority of species of animals . . . the critical resource, as far as population-density is concerned, is food" (Wynne-Edwards, 1962:4).

[21] Note that my interpretation of Wilson's remarks, which are explicitly about "altruism," as bearing on cooperation implies that (in contrast with what seems to be Wilson's view, at 1975:120–121)

—an answer that is reinforced by his definition of society as referring only to "individuals *belonging to the same species*" (1975:7, emphasis added).

Thus, sociobiological analysts, armed with natural selection as their "central dogma" (Wilson, 1975:22), rely most heavily on conflict social structuralism as its underlying mechanism. Having developed a conceptualization of a collectivity hierarchy whose units at any given level are differentiated on the basis of genetic kinship, such analysts now modify that reliance by acknowledging the possibility of exchange social structuralism as a major explanatory variable within such units.[22] Indeed, Wilson suggests that exchange social structuralism between normally competitive, genetically related, microorganisms constitutes one of the two, partly equifinal, ways that complex many-celled organisms originated:

> The achievement of the [colonial hydrozoans, including the Portuguese man-of-war] must be regarded as one of the greatest in the history of evolution. . . . They have created a complex metazoan body by making organs out of individual organisms. Other higher animal lines originated from ancestors that created organs from mesoderm, without passing through a colonial stage. The end result is essentially the same: both kinds of organisms . . . were free to invent large masses of complicated organ systems. But the evolutionary pathways they followed were fundamentally different (1975:386).

Regarding functionalist social structuralistic explanations in sociobiology, note that to explain the persistence or "survival" of a given social phenomenon by its "adaptive" significance (as sociobiologists almost always do[23]) is to invoke functionalism. Thus, when Bonner says "two kinds of adaptive or selective forces bring animals together into a society. One is kin selection. . . . The other selective force . . . [is the fact that] certain tasks can be performed by a group that would be impossible to achieve as separate individuals" (1980:97), he means, in short, that society is "functional" for kin selection and "communal task selection" and is thereby explained by them, or, in the greater schematic detail spelled out earlier in this chapter, he means that kin selection and communal task selection are two consequences of society A at time$_1$ that help cause society A at time$_2$, i.e., they cause the survival of society A from one time to the next.

I do not regard altruism as an all-or-nothing trait. Instead, I have in mind a continuum ranging from extreme egoism to extreme altruism with regard to any given benefit or injury. The exchange of benefits that is typical of exchange social structuralism (cooperation) may then be identified with some variable degree of altruism (i.e., some beneficence toward other at some cost to self).

[22] This modification seems to have emerged only recently in sociobiological analysis. Thus, Etkin says "It was difficult for theoretic evolutionists to see how cooperative behavior could develop very far in the face of [natural selection at the individual level]" (1964:7). Wilson credits Hamilton with having produced, in 1964, the theoretical basis for the concept "inclusive fitness"—a concept that recognizes the evolutionary advantage conferred by cooperation among kin.

[23] The partial exception seems to be the idea of "phylogenetic inertia," described by Wilson as being "similar to inertia in physics" (1975:32), that may permit a given social phenomenon (or any other biological feature—for example, the human appendix) to outlast its adaptiveness.

Finally, it should be noted that two concepts which figure very prominently in the sociobiological lexicon—namely, "dominance" orders or hierarchies, and "territoriality"—combine conflict and exchange social structuralistic variables with ecologistic variables. Although the ecologistic component will be discussed in Chapter 10, the conflict and exchange components should be pointed out here.

Thus, Wilson says "the dominance of one member of a group over another [is] measured by superiority in *aggressive* encounters and order of access to food, mates, resting sites, and other objects promoting survivorship and reproductive fitness" (1975:11, emphasis added), thereby giving conflict social structuralism a key place in this concept. Exchange social structuralism is also implicated, however, when Wilson notes that there are "advantages of being dominant" and also "compensations for being subordinate" (1975:287;291), including "direct incentive for subordinates to stay with their group" (1975:290). On the whole, however, Wilson concludes that "Sharing is rare among the nonhuman primates. . . . But in man it is one of the strongest social traits, reaching levels that match the intense trophallactic exchanges of termites and ants" (1975:551).

A sequence and interaction between conflict and exchange social structuralistic variables is indicated by Leyhausen's analysis of the modified dominance order he calls "brotherhood" among cats:

> In free-ranging tom-cats . . . after some initial fighting, those who pass the test . . . form a kind of order or establishment, ruling a great area in brotherhood. . . . [I]f, within the established neighborhood, there is a young tom just crossing the line from adolescence to maturity, [t]he established tom-cats of the vicinity, singly or in twos and threes, will come to his home and yell their challenge to him to come out and join the brotherhood, but first go through the initiation rites. . . . If the youngster lets himself be persuaded, hard and prolonged fighting ensues. . . . and after a year or so [of this], if he survives and is not beaten into total submission, he will have won his place within the order and the respect of the brethren (1965:255).

In a similar reference to sequence and interaction between conflict and exchange, but mediated by territoriality, Wilson says "Territoriality is a very special form of *contest* competition"—thereby giving conflict social structuralism a key place—but goes on immediately to say that the specialness of its form inheres in the fact that "the animal need win only once or a relatively few times," after which there emerges the "dear enemy" phenomenon: "A territorial neighbor is not ordinarily a threat. It should pay to recognize him as an individual, to agree mutually upon the joint boundary, and to waste as little energy as possible in hostile exchanges thereafter" (1975:268, emphasis added; see also 273).

Finally, let us note Wilson's argument that among ants the social structuralistic component of territoriality is a likely evolutionary precursor to slave-making (see Wilson, 1971:364), a phenomenon that may be regarded as oppression social structuralistic:

The slave raids are dramatic affairs in which the slave-making workers go out in columns, penetrate the nests of colonies belonging to other, related species, and bring back the pupae to their own nests. The pupae are allowed to eclose, and the workers become fully functional members of the colony. The workers of most slave-making species seldom if ever join in the ordinary chores of foraging, nest building, and rearing of the brood, all of which are left to the slaves (1971:358).

SUMMARY

This chapter has surveyed two sociological explanatory variables that claim causal power for physical behavior of the people in each participant's environment. Demographistic variables are the environmental counterparts of materialistic variables, and they refer to the absolute number of people in a given participant's environment, their existentially given physical capacities and needs, and the extent to which, when they die or move out of that environment, they are replaced there by newborns or immigrants. Social structuralistic variables are the environmental counterparts of nurturistic variables, and four major varieties of social structuralism (unison, exchange, conflict, and functionalist) were identified and explicated.

10

External People Variables–Mind

The two kinds of explanatory variables discussed in the preceding chapter locate the sociologically relevant causes impinging on individual B in the body behaviors of people in B's environment. The variables discussed in the present chapter locate these causes in the mind behaviors of people in B's environment.

PSYCHICAL CONTAGIONISM

Let us begin our examination of psychical contagionism (a term I prefer, for its greater inclusiveness, to "emotional contagionism" [see Park, 1972:20] and, for its greater specificity, to "social contagionism" [see Park and Burgess, 1921:874]) by trying to describe the distinction between it and demographism as clearly as possible. Our chief problem in this regard arises from the fact (discussed in Chapter 2) that, barring extrasensory perception, no mind behavior on the part of people in individual B's environment can influence B without first being "expressed" in body behavior. From this fact the question arises: How may psychical contagionistic variables be distinguished from demographistic variables if both types depend on observing innate body behavior?

The answer lies in the analyst's freedom arbitrarily to regard some body behaviors not primarily as such, but as observable indicators of otherwise unobservable mind behaviors. For example, as Nowak points out,

> When we say that someone is "running" we are using a term which is totally devoid of psychological meaning. . . . [But when] we say that someone is "fleeing" we are using a term which connotes two categories of elements— one indicating certain physical processes and the other certain mental traits which are to be sure, unobservable, but which can be deduced from the [physical] behavior of the individual, namely, the desire of the individual to remove himself from the vicinity of the object he perceives as a source of danger (1977:45).

That certain body behaviors may be regarded as existentially given expressions of particular psychical states seems clearly indicated when Homans suggests that crying is an innate human expression of grief (see 1961:381), when Melzack implies that laughing is an innate human expression of pleasure (see 1967:60–61), and when Clynes argues that

> [E]lemental units of expression. . . . turn out to underlie expression regard-less of the sensory modality in which they are expressed; thus, an expressive musical phrase, the tone of voice, a dance step, and an expressive touch par-take of similar . . . forms when seeking to express a particular quality. . . . The nervous system appears to be programmed in such a way as to be able to both produce and recognize these forms precisely. They thus represent win-dows across the separation between individuals and allow contagion of emo-tion to take place, and they provide emotional understanding of one another (1980:273).

In a word, then, demographism attributes individual B's social participation to people "doing" (in ways that are directly obervable) innate physical things in B's environment, while psychical contagionism attributes that social participation to people "thinking and feeling" (observable indirectly through arbitrarily designated physical indicators) similarly innate psychical things in B's environment. As we shall soon see, this distinction carries over to social structuralism and cultural structuralism, and in general we may say that demographism and social structur-alism together stress the explanatory power of what is often called the "social setting," while psychical contagionism and cultural structuralism together stress the power of the "cultural climate," in which individual B's social participation occurs. The important thing is that in the latter case what is taken to be the causally operative factors are the environing and shared psychical behaviors them-selves; the physical expressions of these behaviors—while essential to their com-munication—are regarded merely as their passive, incidental, and analytically dis-countable vehicles.

LeBon is a classical progenitor of psychical contagionism insofar as he asserts that the number of human minds (in certain of their innate aspects, and, presum-ably, as manifested in physical expressions) in individual B's environment will influence his/her own mind and his/her social participation. Thus, LeBon speaks of contagion which intervenes to determine the manifestation in crowds of their special characteristics, and at the same time the trend they are to take. . . . In a crowd every sentiment and act is contagious, and contagious to such a degree that an individual readily sacrifices his personal interest to the collective interest (1960:30).

As a result of this contagion, says LeBon, "A collective mind is formed, doubtless transitory, but presenting very clearly defined characteristics. The gathering has become . . . a psychological crowd. It forms a single being, and is subjected to the law of the mental unity of crowds" (1960:23).[1]

Durkheim, in a similar explanatory reliance on psychical contagionism and writing of what he takes to be the "life of the Australian [aborigine] societies," says that

When [members of such societies] are once come together, a sort of electricity is formed by their collecting which quickly transports them to an extraordinary degree of exaltation. Every sentiment expressed finds a place without resistance in all the minds, which are very open to outside impressions; each re-echoes the others and is re-echoed by the others. The initial impulse thus proceeds, growing as it goes, as an avalanche grows in its advance (1965:247).

Simmel, too, appeals to psychical contagionism when he argues that in crowds "the individual feels himself carried by the 'mood' of the mass, as if by an external force that is quite indifferent to his own subjective being and wishing" (1950:35). Weber implies a similar appeal in his description of "charisma" as a quality that leads its possessor to be "treated as endowed with supernatural, superhuman, or at least specifically exceptional powers or qualities" and elicits "complete personal devotion . . . arising out of enthusiasm, or of despair and hope"—with the result that "Charismatic authority is . . . specifically outside the realm of everyday routine and the profane sphere. . . . Charismatic authority is specifically irrational in the sense of being foreign to all rules" (1947:358, 359, 361). Note also that "affectual behavior," which, Weber intimates, is the characteristic response to charisma, "may, for instance, consist in an uncontrolled [i.e., existentially given—ed.] reaction to some exceptional stimulus" (1947:116).

More recently, Blumer's description of "circular reaction" indicates what is meant here by a psychical contagionistic explanatory variable. In circular reaction, says Blumer, "individuals reflect one another's states of feeling and in so doing intensify these feelings. It is well evidenced in the transmission of feelings and moods among people who are in a state of excitement" (1946:170). Then, by way of implying

---

[1] LeBon regards "contagion" as resulting from the innate "suggestibility" of the human individual. This seems to be an instinctivistic variable and LeBon therefore describes a causal model wherein psychical contagionistic variables add their value to instinctivistic ones in producing the social phenomenon of a crowd (see Chapter 12 for discussion of the value-added causal model).

that both the feelings and moods and the transmission thereof are existentially given or innate rather than socially learned, Blumer argues that

> One sees the process clearly amidst cattle in a state of alarm. The expression of fear through bellowing, breathing, and movements of the body, induces the same feeling in the case of other cattle who, as they in turn express their alarm, intensify this emotional state in one another (1946:170).

The crowd, says Blumer,

> is a means of . . . arousing strong collective feelings as in the case of enthusiasm, courage, and glee. . . . Students of the crowd are aware of an assortment of crowdlike phenomena of great importance, such as so-called "mass hysteria," manias, and mass fears (1957:131, 133).

Blumer argues that circular reaction is a powerful explanatory variable insofar as it produces social unrest ("It is only when restlessness is involved in circular reaction, or becomes contagious, that social unrest exists" [1946:172]), and "Social unrest may be regarded as the crucible out of which emerge new forms of organized activity—such as social movements, reforms, revolutions, religious cults, spiritual awakenings, and new moral orders" (1946:173).

And speaking of "crucibles out of which emerge new forms of organized activity," note that Rossi refers to the prenatal operation of psychical contagionistic variables when she says

> Ferreira found that the infants of high-stress mothers show more irritability, crying, irregular bowel movements, etc., than infants of low-stress mothers. . . . The study suggests, therefore, that prenatal environment includes more than simply food intake from the mother; it embraces the mother's attitudes and expectations concerning the child, in a process that probably involves the emotional state of the mother and its effects upon maternal body chemistry and, from there, on the nervous system of the fetus (1977:21).

Smelser, although he declares that "The defining characteristics of collective behavior do not lie in any particular kind of communication or interaction," and "The defining characteristics of collective behavior are not psychological" (1962:10, 11), goes on to say that in his analysis "We shall rely, however, on many psychological assumptions as we attempt to build determinate explanations of collective behavior. We shall assume, for instance, that perceived structural strain at the social level excites feelings of anxiety, fantasy, hostility, etc." (1962:11), and adds that "Panic can occur only if information, opinions, and emotional states can be communicated from one potential participant to another. Confusion and individual terror may arise in the face of danger, but not collective panic as we have defined it" (1962:139). Smelser is thus noncommittal as to whether the communication in question follows an innate format, but that possibility is certainly not ruled out.

Turner and Killian are similarly noncommittal when they say

> The form of behavior which has come to be designated as "milling" is the basis of social contagion and is the fundamental process through which a uniform mood and imagery is developed in a collectivity (1957:58).

Turner, however, differentiates three kinds of theories of collective behavior, and implies (through the idea that communications may be accepted uncritically) that the first kind assumes an innate communications format:

> Contagion theories explain collective behavior on the basis of some process whereby moods, attitudes, and behavior are communicated rapidly and accepted uncritically. Convergence theories explain collective behavior on the basis of the simultaneous presence of people who share the same predispositions and preoccupations. Emergent norm theories see collective behavior as regulated by a social norm which arises in a special situation (1964:384).[2]

Not dissimilarly, Marx distinguishes two "areas of interest" within the study of collective behavior. Although the first area (like Turner's "emergent norm" theories) seems to refer to cultural structuralistic variables (i.e., "the cultural processes involved in the development and communication of collective definitions"), the second area (i.e., "psychology states collectively experienced by individuals such as panic, hysteria, hypnotic states, visions, extreme suggestibility, and heightened emotion" [Marx, 1980:269]), refers to psychical contagionistic variables.

Not only is the study of "collective behavior" heavily reliant on psychical contagionistic variables,[3] but the study of "informal organization" seems similarly reliant—although much less explicitly so. For example, Barnard defines informal organization as being "without any specific conscious joint purpose" and as "indefinite and rather structureless" (1948:115). Similarly, Selznick says "informal patterns . . . arise spontaneously" (1948:27), and Blau and Scott characterize informal organization as "emergent" (1962:7). Thus, one gets the distinct impression that somewhere deep inside all these views there lodges the same psychical contagionism that informs the study of equally "indefinite," "spontaneous," "emergent" forms of collective behavior.

---

[2] Note that convergence theories also rely on psychical contagion insofar as " 'Nothing new [is] added to the crowd situation except *an intensification* of the feeling already present' " (Turner, 1964:388, quoting Allport, emphasis added); the "intensification" itself represents the contagion.

[3] Berk's argument against psychical contagionism as explantory of crowd behavior (1974) should be noted.

Psychical Contagionistic Variables in Sociobiology

As may easily be imagined, psychical contagionism is an important variable in explanations of nonhuman social behavior. Klopfer and Hailman, for example, discuss "displays" among nonhuman animals ("A behavior pattern whose primary biological function is communication is called a *display*" [1967:38]), and note that

> [C]lose observation by ethologists showed that courtship [displays] and vocal-izations serve many purposes, such as bringing mates together, stimulating hormonal flow necessary for reproductive activity, and assuring synchrony of the male and female in the breeding cycle (1967:38).

Wilson provides other instances of psychical contagionistic variables when he notes that "An alarm substance (*Schreckstoff*) is present in the skin of cyprinid minnows, catfish, and other . . . fishes. When a member of the school is injured, release of the material in the water causes the others to scatter" (1975:440), but that, on the other hand,

> Assembling signals serve . . . to draw societies into tighter configurations. . . . [Some] tropical fishes actually "summon" their young with a short lat-eral head movement, which appears to be a ritualized form of departure swim-ming. . . . [And among the social insects,] any well-nourished, fertilized queen attracts [with pheromones] a retinue of workers who tend to press close in with their heads facing her (Wilson, 1975:211–212).

Moreover, " '[T]he Fraser Darling effect,' defined as the stimulation of reproduc-tive activity at a social level beyond mere sexual pairing" (Wilson, 1975:41), seems likely also to refer to psychical contagionistic variables:

> Synchronized breeding, of unknown physiological origin . . . occurs in social ungulates. The reproductive cycle of the wildebeest . . . is characterized by sharp peaks of mating and birth. . . . [The] majority of births occur in the forenoon, in large aggregations on calving grounds usually located on short grass. . . . When a cow is thrown slightly out of phase, she is able to interrupt delivery at any stage prior to the emergence of the calf's head, thus giving her another chance to join the mass parturition (Wilson, 1975:42).

Finally, after noting Mead's remark that "it may be that there will be some way of discovering in the future a language among the ants and bees" (1934:235)— and indeed, von Frisch had already published his first paper on communication among bees 14 years earlier—we should cite Wilson's conclusion that "the waggle dance of the honeybee is an innate and "truly symbolical message that guides a complex response after the message has been given," and that that message (i.e., information about the path to a food source) is conveyed via a

> symbolic flight, with wings vibrating in nonfunctional manner and the abdomen also vibrating to add emphasis. [To symbolize direction, gravity] must replace the position of the sun since the bee is now in the darkened interior of the hive . . . [and] the duration of the straight run (or the duration of the wing buzzing, which is virtually the same thing) [symbolizes] the distance to the target or, more precisely, the effort expended to get there (1971:265).

Wilson also describes how the equally innate "buzzing dance" elicits swarming in bees:

> Just before the swarm occurs, most of the bees are still sitting idly in the hive or outside in front of the entrance. As midday approaches and the air temperature rises, one or several bees begin to force their way through the throngs with great excitement, running in a zig-zag pattern, butting into other workers, and vibrating their abdomens and wings. . . . The [buzzing dance] is swiftly contagious. . . . "The queen too has been aroused, and if she does not follow the swarming bees out at once she is badgered without interruption by bees buzzing and running until she has found the hive entrance and hurls herself into the swarm cloud." . . . The signal itself produces the same signal in others, with the result that a chain reaction and a behavioral "explosion" occur. Of course this is just the effect that is needed to ensure a simultaneous action by the ten thousand or more individuals who fly from the hive (1971:270–271).

Gould describes how such a swarm selects the site of its new hive:

> Scouts fly out in search of suitable cavities . . . [and on returning, they] advertise what they have found by means of the same dance used to communicate food location. . . . [E]ach scout makes its own evaluation [of its find] based on the cavity's size, exposure to sun, dryness, freedom from drafts, and so on [and] advertises its find with a degree of enthusiasm that reflects the site's quality as a potential dwelling. So far, this may sound like a forager bee reporting a flower patch, but now the scout will stop and watch dances indicating other sites. It will then fly out and visit them, perhaps also reinspecting its own discovery, then return to the swarm and dance for the best one. The bee has sampled the available locations, compared them, and come to a decision. When virtually all the scouts agree—that is, when all of the dancing indicates the same spot—the swarm will then be roused and led to the chosen cavity (1979:75; see also Wilson, 1971:269–270).

CULTURAL STRUCTURALISM

As suggested above, the distinction between social structuralism and cultural structuralism turns exactly on the same difference as that between demographism and psychical contagionism: when the analyst interprets a given socially influenced physical behavior (e.g., a raised arm or an utterance) as *only that* behavior, it is being regarded social structuralistically; when the analyst interprets that physical behavior (e.g., a "salute" or a "spoken word") as a *sign of psychical* behavior, the behavior is being regarded cultural structuralistically. In the first case, the behavior is treated as part of the social structure environing individual B; in the second case it is taken as indicative of part of the cultural structure environing him/her—and of course, the same behavior may be both social structural and cultural structural, as the practice of human sacrifice to the gods testifies.

Cultural structuralism, then, emphasizes the explanatory power of socially influenced psychical behavior relations among the people in individual B's environment—as those relations are indicated by gestural and other physical behavior which the analyst regards as their indicator.

Durkheim gives classical expression to cultural structuralism as well as social structuralism. Thus, he says

> morality is the least dispensable, the strictly necessary, the daily need without which societies cannot exist. . . . [The] anomic state . . . is the cause . . . of the incessantly recurrent conflicts, and the multifarious disorders of which the economic world exhibits so sad a spectacle. For, as nothing restrains the active forces and assigns them limits they are bound to respect, they tend to develop haphazardly, and come into collision with one another, battling and weakening themselves (1933:51, 2–3).

"Human passions," says Durkheim, "stop only before a moral power they respect" (1933:3), and "society . . . is the only moral power superior to the individual, the authority of which he accepts. It alone has the power to stipulate law and set the point beyond which the passions must not go" (1951:249). Therefore, says Durkheim, "Here . . . is a category of facts [i.e., social facts] with very distinctive characteristics: it consists of ways of acting, *thinking, and feeling,* external to the individual, and endowed with a power of coercion, by reason of which they control him" (1938:3, emphasis added).[4]

Simmel, another classical employer of cultural structuralism, argues that

---

[4] Note Durkheim's later explanation that these "ways of . . . thinking, and feeling, external to the individual" do not *directly* control the individual but only via expression in physical behavior and its artifacts: (see footnote 24, Chapter 2).

> The metropolis exacts from man . . . a different amount of consciousness than does rural life. . . . [Therefore] the metropolitan type of man . . . develops an organ protecting him against the threatening currents and discrepancies of his external environment which would uproot him. He reacts with his head instead of his heart. . . . The reaction to metropolitan phenomena is shifted to that organ which is least sensitive and quite remote from the depths of the personality. Intellectuality is thus seen to preserve subjective life against the overwhelming power of metropolitan life (1950:410–411).[5]

Weber, champions cultural structuralism over Marx and Engels' social structuralism:

> For those to whom no causal explanation is adequate without an economic (or materialistic as it is unfortunately still called) interpretation, it may be remarked that I consider the influence of economic development on the fate of religious ideas to be very important. . . . On the other hand, these religious ideas themselves simply cannot be deduced from economic circumstances. They . . . contain a law of development and a compelling force all their own (1958b:277–278).[6]

In cultural structuralism, as in social structuralism, four varieties are especially prominent in sociological explanations and, indeed, the varieties of cultural structuralism complement, and (as indicated in Chapter 9) are often paired with, those of social structuralism. Thus, in one variety of cultural structuralism (counterpart of unison social structure), *consensus* or identity characterizes the socially influenced mind behaviors of people in B's environment and B's social participation is held to be influenced by this consensus. In the second variety (counterpart of exchange social structuralism), *complementarity* is the determining characteristic; in the third (counterpart of conflict social structuralism), *dissensus* or contradiction is the characteristic. In the fourth, *symbolic interactionist,* variety (counterpart of functionalist social structuralism), the key characteristic is, again, feedback between part and whole or part and part (more specifically from the viewpoint of symbolic interactionism, between individual and society or individual and individual). Let us consider these four varieties in turn.

---

[5] Simmel may also be taken to imply cultural structuralistic explanations of conflict social structure (see Chapter 3) when (conceivably in an attempt to specify Marx and Engels' largely undifferentiated idea that proletarian "class consciousness" spurs the proletariat's overthrow of the bourgeoisie), he argues that "jealousy," "envy," and "begrudging" are different types of cultural structure that may lead to conflict (Simmel, 1955:50–51). In a similar attempt, Mannheim argues that "ideology" and "utopia" are cultural structures that help explain conflict (Mannheim, 1955:40).

[6] Just as Engels adds a measure of cultural structuralism to Marx and his social structuralism (see note 3, Chapter 9), so Weber moderates his own cultural structuralism:

> it is, of course, not my aim to substitute for a one-sided materialistic an equally one-sided spiritualistic causal interpretation of culture and of history. Each is equally possible, but each, if it does not serve as the preparation, but as the conclusion of an investigation, accomplishes equally little in the interest of historical truth (1958b:183).

Consensus Cultural Structuralism

Consensus cultural structuralism harks back at least to Comte: "the formation of any society, worthy to be so called, supposes a system of common opinions, such as may restrain individual eccentricity" (1975:228). Durkheim, too, exemplifies consensus cultural structuralism when he says "solidarity which comes from likeness [i.e., mechanical solidarity] is at its maximum when the collective conscience completely envelops our whole conscience and coincides in all points with it" (1933:130), as does Weber when he calls a social relationship "communal" if "the orientations of social action—whether in the individual case, on the average, or in the pure type—is based on a subjective feeling of the parties . . . that they belong together" (1947:136).

Weber's full treatment of consensus cultural structuralistic variables is more complex than this, however, insofar as he outlines a typology of such variables. The typology in question is founded on the proposition that " 'Culture' is a finite segment of the meaningless infinity of the world process, a segment on which *human beings* confer meaning and significance" (Weber, 1949:81), and on defining the conferral of meaning as the psychical act of relating something to "an intended purpose" and labeling it as "means or ends" in this respect (Weber, 1947:93). It is this psychical (and, when shared, consensus cultural structural) conferral of meaning that Weber believes orients physical behavior and thus explains social structure (see 1947:88).[7]

According to Weber, means and ends may be related to one another in rational or nonrational ways, and this is the primary distinction on which his typology of consensus cultural structuralistic variables—called "modes of orientation" (Weber, 1947:115)—rests. Nonrational orientations involve no choice by the actor; one particular means stands in fixed, invariant, taken-for-granted relationship to one particular end. Weber proposes two types of such orientations: The "traditional" orientation "is very often a matter of almost *automatic* reaction to habitual stimuli which guide behavior in a course which has been repeatedly followed," and the "affectual" orientation "may . . . consist in an *uncontrolled* reaction to some exceptional stimulus" (Weber, 1947:116, emphasis added).[8]

---

[7] Unfortunately, however, Weber also *defines* social phenomena in the same psychical and cultural structural terms that he *explains* it when he says "Action *is* social in so far as, by virtue of the subjective meaning attached to it by the acting individual (or individuals), it takes account of the behavior of others *and is thereby oriented in its course*" (1947:88, emphasis added). The first part of this sentence is definitional and the last part is explanatory.

[8] The difference between these two orientations seems to turn on whether the means-end linkage is socially influenced and thus acquired by the actor ("habitual"), or existentially given and thus innate to the actor (an "uncontrolled" reflex). For this reason, shared affectual orientation is psychical contagionistic rather than cultural structuralistic.

Rational orientations, according to Weber, always involve choice by the actor[9] and, logically speaking (given Weber's means-ends frame of reference and given the principles of equifinality and equioriginality discussed in Chapters 14 and 15), two kinds of choices are possible: choice among alternative means to a given end, and choice among alternative ends to be served by a given means. Contrary to expectation, however, the two types of rationality (Wertrationalität and Zweckrationalität) discussed as such by Weber do *not* correspond to these two kinds of choice. Consider Wertrationalität first; it seems clearly to be the case wherein the actor has a fixed end or value and chooses among various means to achieve it: Weber says Wertrationalität involves "the consistently planned orientation of [action's] detailed course" (1947:116) toward the value in question. Weber then goes on to say

> Examples of pure rational orientation to absolute values would be the action of persons who, *regardless of possible cost to themselves,* act to put into practice their convictions of what seems to them to be required by duty, honour, the pursuit of beauty, a religious call, personal loyalty, or the importance of some "cause" no matter in what it consists (1947:116, emphasis added).

In the phrase "regardless of possible cost to themselves," we have more than the simple notion of choice among alternative means toward a given end; we have a decision-rule for making that choice, and the rule is: Choose whichever means *maximizes the end in question,* regardless of the cost to other ends it might entail (treating "cost" as a function of both the net loss to a given end, and the importance of that end to the actor).

Now consider Weber's second type of rational orientation. Zweckrationalität is described as follows:

> Action is . . . *zweckrational* when the end, the means, and the secondary results are all rationally taken into account and weighed. This involves rational consideration of alternative means to the end, of the relations of the end to other prospective results of employment of any given means, and finally of the relative importance of different possible ends (Weber, 1947:117).

From this it appears that Zweckrationalität, no less than Wertrationalität, involves choice among a variety of means to a given end, but it is equally clear that a

[9] In his closest approach to a definition of "rationality" of which I am aware, Weber says "Where capitalistic acquisition is rationally pursued, the corresponding action is adjusted to calculations in terms of capital. . . . So far as the transactions are rational, calculation underlies every single action of the partners [to capitalistic enterprise]" (1958b:18, 19), and by "calculation" Weber seems to mean the comparison of alternative means to a given end (e.g., how to make a given amount of profit) and the comparison of alternative ends to which a given means may be put (e.g., how to spend a given amount of money).

different decision-rule is stated here, and the rule is: Choose whichever means *optimizes the end in question*—that is, choose the means that brings one maximally close to that end at minimal cost to other ends one might have.

Against what standard does the actor judge "the relative importance of different possible ends" and so compare the benefits and costs to different ends of choosing a given means? Weber's answer is clearly "self-interest" when he refers to " 'the exploitation of the opportunities of his situation in the self-interest of the actor' " as zweckrational (1947:121; see also 122, 123, 127). It should be emphasized that Weber seems to regard self-interest as an existentially given (materialistic-instinc-tivistic) variable, in contrast with the socially influenced (enculturistic) variables that he mentions in connection with Wertrationalität ("duty, honour, the pursuit of beauty, a religious call, personal loyalty, or . . . some 'cause' "). Both Wertra-tionalität and Zweckrationalität, then, emerge as consensus cultural structuralistic variables that involve fixed ends and alternative means; the differences between them are (1) they employ different decision-rules, and (2) they refer to existentially given, and socially influenced ends, respectively. A fully expanded typology of wertrational and zweckrational orientations, then, would consist of a fourfold cross-classification of such decision-rules and such ends, where (a) the rule for choosing among alternative means to different ends is maximization and the ends are exis-tentially given; (b) the rule is optimization and the ends are existentially given; (c) the rule is maximization and the ends are socially influenced; and (d) the rule is optimization and the ends are socially influenced.[10]

Finally, let us ask whether Weber considers the other general type of rational-ity—namely, that in which the choice is between alternative ends to be served by a given means. The answer is YES, but his discussion appears in a different context and he does not call it a type of "rationality." Thus:

> The question of what . . . is the cost of the use of the various possible technical means for a single technical end depends in the last analysis on their potential usefulness as means to other ends [i.e., opportunity costs—ed.]. This is particularly true of labour. . . . Economic action is primarily oriented to the problem of choosing the end to which a thing shall be applied; tech-nology, to the problem, given the end, of choosing the appropriate means (1947:162).

Renaming Weber's "economic action" "Mittelrationalität" (in order to conform terminologically to Weber's other two rationalities), and applying to it an appro-priately modified version of the cross-classification referred to above in connection with Wertrationalität and Zweckrationalität, we derive four subtypes of this ra-tional orientation too.

[10] Freud refers to (a) as the "pleasure principle" and to (b) as the wish for "security" (see 1962:23, 62). Other discussions of Weber's conceptualization of Wertrationalität and Zweckrationalität may be found in Parsons (1937:642–649); Parsons' editorial note number 38 to Weber (1947:116); and Blau (1964:5).

Thus, when fully explicated, Weber's typology distinguishes between two types of nonrational orientation and between two sets (consisting of four subtypes each) of rational orientations—any of which may be held in common by different individuals and thereby constitute consensus cultural structuralistic explanations of social phenomena (especially the social structure) in which these individuals participate.[11] By way of illustrating part of this typology and its explanatory role, Weber describes in *The Protestant Ethic and the Spirit of Capitalism,* how a traditional ori-

[11] So firmly committed is Alexander to cultural structuralistic (and enculturistic) explanations that he betrays his own call for "evaluative criteria" in sociology that are "expansive and inclusive" and that "draw upon the full range of theoretical options presented by competing theories" (1982:115, see Chapter 1). Thus, Alexander asserts that the "rational/nonrational dichotomy [in psychical behavior—ed.] . . . formulates one of the two most generalized and decisive questions in theoretical argument" (the other question is "how a plurality of . . . actions [so oriented] becomes interrelated and ordered"); and therefore "nonrationality presents an abstract presuppositional orientation in relation to which *every* social theory *must* take a position" (1982:89–90, 77, emphasis added). In simpler and more direct terms than he himself chooses, it seems Alexander would like to say rational action is determined by conditions external to the actor, whereas nonrational action is determined by conditions internal to the actor: "Since [rational] action is determined by calculations of efficiency vis-à-vis external conditions, the particular content of the ostensibly guiding [internal] norms becomes irrelevant"; and "Because the ideal reference [of nonrational action] is so explicitly preserved. . . . the internal voluntary aspect of human action is maintained and a purely deterministic perspective prevented" (1982:74, 76). However, able neither to deny nor differentiate the relevance of *both* external and internal conditions to both rational and nonrational action, Alexander is eventually reduced to a summary declaration of similarity between the latter two, together with a vague allusion to some "essential" difference between them (without specifying what he finally takes to be the nature of this difference): "from the multidimensional perspective advanced here, all action, both rational and nonrational, inherently involves the weighing of means and ends, norms and conditions. . . . [but] means and ends . . . can be interrelated in essentially different ways" (1982:80, 82). Now granted that Alexander thus does not succeed in drawing an explicit and consistent distinction between rational and nonrational action, why does he try to do so in the first place? The answer may be that given the centrality to him (as to Weber) of "action" in sociological theory, and given his (and Weber's) identification of action with a "subjective component" (Alexander, 1982:71), he would like the rational-nonrational distinction within that component to play the same consensus cultural structuralistic explanatory role that Weber does. That is, he would like shared rational subjectivity to explain the stable and routine features of human social phenomena, while shared nonrational subjectivity explains the unexpectedly changeful, "spontaneous" features of those phenomena. Thus, where Weber says "bureaucracy [rationally oriented—ed.] is fashioned to meet calculable and recurrent needs by means of a normal routine [wheras the] provisioning of all demands that go beyond those of everyday routine has had . . . a charismatic [i.e., nonrational—ed.] foundation" (1958a:245, emphasis removed), Alexander says, very similarly, "the logic of technical rationality leads theory to portray action as simply an adaptation to material conditions" whereas "the nonrational perspective on action emphasizes . . . [a] commitment to freedom" (1982:74, 76). The crucial difference, however, is that where Weber appeals to existentially given, automatic means-ends linkages in affectual orientation and charismatic authority, Alexander rejects this appeal (see 1982:80, 82, 85) because, for ideological reasons, he wants to associate nonrationality not with automatism but with voluntarism: "Without presupposing the existence of nonrational action, it is impossible to formulate the possibilities for voluntarism upon which all ideological arguments for increased freedom depend" (1982:89). Setting aside the fact that he clarifies neither "voluntarism" nor "freedom" here and so inhibits us from evaluating this assertion, one can only wonder what shared psychical mechanism for linking means and ends Alexander has in mind—what mechanism that is not existentially fixed and that also does not concern itself with efficiency or at least effectiveness (i.e., with whether or not the means serve the ends, in the actor's judgment). Indeed, absent such concern, "no matter how primitive [its] form" (Weber, 1958b:19), how would we ever identify anything as a "means"?

entation ("A man does not 'by nature' wish to earn more and more money, but simply to live as he is accustomed to live and earn as much as is necessary for that purpose" [1958b:60; compare 17]), when attacked by affectual orientation toward the charismatic figures Martin Luther and John Calvin ("In traditionally stereo-typed periods, charisma is the greatest revolutionary force" [1947:363]), gave way first to a wertrational and then a zweckrational orientation ("[When] affectually determined action occurs in the form of conscious release of emotional tension . . . it is usually well on the road to rationalization" [1947:116]; "the Puritan outlook . . . favoured the development of a rational bourgeois economic life" [1958b:174])—only to fall prey to a new traditionalism ("The people filled with the spirit of capitalism today tend to be indifferent, if not hostile to the church. . . . [The motive for] their restless activity . . . [is simply] that business with its continuous work has become a necessary part of their lives" [1958b:70]). It should be understood that each successive orientation here—traditional, affectual, wertrational, zweckrational, and back again to traditional—is regarded by Weber as a consensus cultural structure, while it lasts.

Mead proposes a typology of consensus cultural structuralistic variables that complements Weber's in at least three ways. First, where Weber holds that the human psyche confers meaning on an otherwise meaningless world, and that that conferral involves psychically designating something as "means" or "end" of hu-man conduct, Mead holds that

> the relationship between a given stimulus—as a gesture—and the later phases of the social act of which it is an early (if not the initial) phase constitutes the field within which meaning originates and exists. Meaning is thus a de-velopment of something objectively there as a relation between certain phases of the social act; it is not a psychical addition to that act and it is not an "idea" as traditionally conceived. . . . Awareness or consciousness is not nec-essary to the presence of meaning in the process of social experience. . . . [T]he locus of any given meaning is in the thing which, as we say, "has it" (1934:76, 77, 122).[12]

Although the two views are contradictory to the extent that one of them looks upon meaning as *given to* the world by human awareness and the other looks upon meaning as *in* the world independently of that awareness and by virtue of the temporal dimension of existence alone, they are compatible to the extent that the Weberian means-ends pair manifests the same temporal sequence as the Meadian gesture-completion pair, and the latter can manifest the same awareness as the former.

[12]Note, however, that Mead seems unaware that he contradicts this view and adopts Weber's means-ends meaning of meaning when he claims that "The meaning of a chair is sitting down in it, the meaning of the hammer is to drive a nail," and that the meaning of a house is "the use of it" (1934:104, 132).

Second, where Weber's image takes for granted that the thing to which meaning is given has already been perceived, Mead emphasizes that such perception is problematic insofar as the psyche must choose, from an infinite number and variety of potential stimuli, those few stimuli to which it will actually pay attention: "Our whole intelligent process seems to lie in the attention which is selective of certain types of stimuli. . . . The organism goes out and determines what it is going to respond to, and organizes that world" (1934:25).

Finally, where the primary distinction in Weber's typology is a formal one (i.e., it refers to the ways that means and ends can be connected—regardless of their substantive contents), the primary distinction in Mead's typology is substantive (i.e., it refers to the empirical referents of the stimuli to which the individual pays attention—regardless of how these stimuli are interconnected). Thus, Mead distinguishes between "mind" and "self" on the grounds that the former selects and organizes stimuli that are *external* to the individual, whereas the latter selects and organizes stimuli that are *internal*. Mead says, with respect to "mind," that

> We pick out an organized environment in relationship to our response, so that these attitudes . . . represent what exists for us in the world. . . . Mentality resides in the ability of the organism to indicate that in the environment which answers to his responses. . . . What we need to recognize is that we are dealing with the relationship of the organism to the environment selected by its own sensitivity (1934:128, 132).

With respect to "self," Mead says

> The self has the characteristic that it is an object to itself . . . [and it is where the individual] not only hears himself but responds to himself, talks and replies to himself as truly as the other person replies to him, that we have behavior in which the individuals become objects to themselves (1934:136, 139).

Further, as indicated in Chapter 8, Mead draws a secondary distinction between an existentially given component (the "I") and a socially influenced component (the "me") of the self. However, he does not so explicitly distinguish such components of mind, although his observation that

> The distinction of greatest importance between types of conduct in human behavior is that lying between . . . the conduct of the "biologic individual" and the conduct of the "socially self-conscious individual" . . . answers roughly to that drawn between conduct which does not involve conscious reasoning and that which does, between the conduct of the more intelligent of the lower animals and that of man (1934:347)

may certainly be so interpreted.

The hypothesis that consensus among "minds" explains social phenomena appears in Mead's assertion that "gestures . . . are significant symbols [required for thinking and for communication] because they have the same meanings for all individual members of the given society or social group" and in his subsequent proposition that "the complex co-operative processes and activities and institutional functionings of organized human society are . . . possible only insofar as every individual involved in them . . . can [through the use of significant symbols] take the attitudes of all other such individuals" (1934:47, 155).

Parsons and Shils are two more recent proponents of consensus cultural structuralism, asserting that

> A system or a subsystem of concerted action which (1) is governed by a *common* value-orientation and in which (2) the common values are motivationally integrated in action is . . . a collectivity. It is this integration of common values . . . which characterizes the partial or total integrations of social systems (1951:203, see also 192, 193, 220).[13]

And Parsons argues that "Stability of interaction . . . depends on the condition that the particular acts of evaluation on both sides should be oriented to common standards since only in terms of such standards is 'order' in either the communication or the motivational contexts possible" (1951:37).[14]

Complementarity Cultural Structuralism

Although, as we have seen above, Weber employs consensus cultural structuralistic variables in explaining the evolutionary and revolutionary changes leading to "bourgeois economic life," he relies on complementarity cultural structuralistic variables when explaining the stability of the "corporate group." Thus, Weber argues that the complementarity between shared beliefs in the "right" of those holding certain statuses (1947:328) and the "obligation" of those holding certain other statuses (1947:124) explains "imperative control"—defined as "the probability that a command with a specific content will be obeyed by a given group of

---

[13] van den Berghe, however, asserts that "the postulate of consensus . . . is logically gratuitous to functionalist theory, i.e., one could logically retain a functionalist model of integration while rejecting the consensus assumption" (1963:697), and although van den Berghe himself does not explain the latter comment, I hold the same view—as reflected in my separation of social structuralism from cultural structuralism—for reasons having to do with the principle of equifinality (see Chapter 14) and the distinction between social structure and cultural structure (see Chapter 2).

[14] Jacobs and Campbell (1961), however, conclude that the results of an experiment they conducted warn against overestimating the power of consensus cultural structure over certain variables that seem classifiable as instinctivistic.

persons" (1947:152). It is this complementarity cultural structure that forms the heart of Weber's conceptualization of bureaucracy as a "hierarchy" of offices whose "regular activities . . . are distributed in a fixed way as official duties" (1958a:197, 196) insofar as such "official duties" consist of rights to command and obligations to obey.

Mead, too, supplements consensus cultural structuralism with complementarity cultural structuralism. Thus, although he relies on consensus between A's mind and B's mind to explain the common, unison aspects of their activities together, in explaining the differentiated, cooperative aspects of these activities he relies on complementarity between A's mind and B's self, and between B's mind and A's self (so that the self of one is part of the mind of the other and vice-versa). In this way, each understands what the other is doing—despite the fact that they are both doing different things—and can adjust his/her behavior accordingly. Thus, Mead says "The individual experiences himself as such, not directly, but only indirectly, from the particular standpoints of other individual members of the same social group" (1934:138), and "[an individual must] take the attitude of other human individuals toward himself and toward one another within the human social process" (1934:154).

Simmel's complementarity cultural structuralism comes through clearly in his image of the role of complementary notions of values (i.e., in social exchange, individual B values what A can give him/her, and individual A values what B can give him/her). Simmel says

> Every exchange presupposes that valuations and interests have taken on an objective character. The decisive element is no longer the mere subjective passion of desire to which only fight is adequate, but the value of the object which is recognized by both sides and which, objectively unchanged, can be expressed by several other objects. Renunciation of the valued object, because one receives the value quantum contained in it in some other form, is the means, truly miraculous in its simplicity, of accommodating opposite interests without fight (1955:116).

Complementarity and reciprocity have been differentiated by Gouldner: "complementarity connotes that one's rights are another's obligations, and vice-versa. Reciprocity, however, connotes that each party has rights and duties" (1960:169). But because reciprocity, thus defined, is only mutual (or, one might say, complementary) complementarity, I regard the latter as fundamental and the former as derivative from it in the same way that the causal concept "interaction" is derivative from "action." Thus, one is not surprised to find Parsons (whom Gouldner says "centers his analysis on complementarity to the systematic neglect of reciprocity rigorously construed" [1960:168]) explicitly describing mutual complementarity or reciprocity as follows:

> What an actor is expected to do in a given situation both by himself and by others constitutes the expectations of that role. What the relevant alters are expected to do, contingent on ego's action, constitute the sanctions. . . . What are sanctions to ego are also role-expectations to alter, *and vice-versa* (Parsons and Shils, 1951:191, emphasis added).

In explicating his own mutual complementarity or reciprocity cultural structuralism, Gouldner claims that "A norm of reciprocity is no less universal and important an element of culture than the incest taboo," and describes that norm as making "two interrelated, minimal demands: (1) people should help those who have helped them, and (2) people should not injure those who have helped them" (1960:171). In Gouldner's view, the posited norm can explain not only the maintenance of social systems ("the norm of reciprocity is a concrete and special mechanism involved in the maintenance of any stable social system" [1960:174]), but its origin as well—although Gouldner is less explicit about the latter, saying only that "reciprocities processes . . . mobilize egoistic motivations [and bring one to the conclusion that] if you want to be helped by others you must help them" (1960:173), that is, you must make the first move.

Finally in this connection, note once more how closely consensus and complementarity cultural structuralism supplement each other. Thus, while Gouldner argues that reciprocity is mutual complementarity, he also argues that the norm which specifies that complementarity is "universal" and therefore consensual. Similarly, Berger and Luckmann use the term "institutionalization" to mean the achievement of cultural structural complementarity ("Institutionalization occurs whenever there is a reciprocal typification of habitualized actions by types of actors" [1967:54]), and they seem to use the terms "objectivation" and "legitimation" to mean the achievement of cultural structural consensuses about that complementarity. Thus:

> objectivity. . . . means that the institutions that have now been crystallized . . . are experienced as existing over and beyond the individuals who "happen to" embody them at the moment. . . . Only at this point does it become possible to speak of a social world at all . . . in a manner analogous to the reality of the natural world (1967:58, 59, see Chapter 13 for discussion of consensus as the only scientific basis for the perceived reality of the world);

and

> Legitimation . . . is best described as a "second-order" objectivation of meaning. Legitimation produces new meanings that serve to integrate the meanings already attached to disparate institutional processes (1967:92, see also the discussion in Chapter 8 of legitimations of legitimations).

Dissensus Cultural Structuralism

Marx and Engels assert the causal importance of socially generated dissensus between proletariat and bourgeoisie (and consensus among proletarians):

[The communists] never cease, for a single instant, to instill into the working class the clearest possible recognition of the hostile antagonism between bourgeoisie and proletariat, in order that . . . the fight against the bourgeoisie itself may immediately begin (1978:500).

But, of course, they also look forward to the eventual end of all such dissensus and the establishment of universal and permanent consensus—and they claim this consensus will then enable the construction of new social phenomena. In Marx's words,

consciousness is something that the world *must* acquire, like it or not. . . . Our whole task can consist only in putting religious and political questions into self-conscious human form. . . . Then it will transpire that the world has long been dreaming of something that it can acquire only if it becomes conscious of it (1978:15).

Somewhat differently, Mannheim relies (1) on dissensus cultural structuralism when arguing that "ideologies" (ideas that defend ruling groups against oppressed groups) and "utopias" (ideas that attack ruling groups on behalf of oppressed groups) intensify—and to this extent, explain—"political conflict" and a generalized "intellectual crisis" (see 1955:38–40); but (2) relies on consensus cultural structural structuralism when arguing that one outcome of this conflict and crisis is the emergence of the free intellectuals, a new social structural "stratum" bound together by "a consciousness . . . of their own general social position and the problems and opportunities it involves" (1955:160); and (3) relies on complementarity cultural structuralism when arguing that ideologists, utopianists, and free intellectuals all complement each other's ideas in the general pursuit of truth (see Mannheim, 1955:80–87).

Dahrendorf, a modern proponent of dissensus cultural structuralism, notes that "Consensus on values is one of the prime features of the social system [as described by Parsons]," and asserts that to dissensus cultural structuralists like himself, "It may be useful for some purposes to speak of the 'value system' of a society, but in the conflict model such characteristic values are ruling rather than accepted, at any given point of time" (1958:127). Dahrendorf, however, concludes on a Simmelian note: "As far as I can see, we need both models for the explanation of sociological problems. Indeed, it may well be that society, in a philosophical sense, has two faces of equal reality: one of stability, harmony, and consensus, and one of change, conflict, and constraint" (1958:127). Similar moderation is evident in Parsons and Shils, who, after asserting that "at almost all times the terms of exchange . . . have their roots in the generalized patterns of value-orientations widely shared in the society," go on to say "Even in a society in which the consensus on the generalized patterns of value-orientation . . . is great, it will still be insufficient for the maintenance of order. . . . Some sort of institutionalized mechanism is indispensable, and this is the function of authority" (1951:220).

van den Berghe regards consensus and dissensus cultural structuralism as close companions, respectively, of the "functionalist or 'structure-function' approach" ("The most important and basic factor making for social integration is value consensus" [van den Berghe, 1963:696]), and the "dialectic approach" (which studies "contradictions and conflicts between values, political or religious ideologies, and scientific or philosophical theories" [van den Berghe, 1963:699–700]). These efforts to link consensus and dissensus lead us toward symbolic interactionist cultural structuralism, which, as counterpart of functional social structuralism, includes consensus, complementarity, and dissensus cultural structuralism—plus feedback.

Symbolic Interactionist Cultural Structuralism

Chapter 8 has discussed self, conceptualizations of macro social and cultural structures, role-expectations, conscience, symbols, and meaning as key explanatory variables that enculturism attributes to individual B's mind. Symbolic interactionism explicitly includes all these variables, but it adds three specifications—all of which spring from its "interactionism," that is, its emphasis on individual B's physical (including gestural) relationship to other people in his/her environment: (1) Inasmuch as the empirical referents of all symbols and meaning (and therefore of all selves, conceptualizations of macro social and cultural structures, role-expectations, and conscience) are intrinsically indeterminate, they always require interpretation. (2) Interpretation is a matter of continual negotiation and renegotiation between individuals. (3) Negotiation may, at any given time, produce consensus, complementarity, or dissensus between individuals. Thus, Blumer says "We can and, I think, must look upon human group life as chiefly a vast interpretative process" (1956:686), and adds that

> human beings interpret or "define" each other's actions instead of merely reacting to each other's actions. Their "response" is . . . based on the meaning they attach to such actions. Thus, human interaction is mediated by the use of symbols, by interpretation, or by ascertaining the meaning of one another's action. . . . Through previous interaction [people] develop and ac-

quire common understandings or definitions of how to act in this or that situation. These common definitions enable people to act alike (1962:180, 187).

According to Mead, one of the individual's earliest experiences with interpreting and thereby internalizing the cultural structure around him/her is "play": "A child plays at being a mother, at being a teacher, at being a policeman; that is, it is taking different roles, as we say" (1934:150). A somewhat later and more complex experience of this kind is "the game":

> If we contrast play with the situation in an organized game, we note the essential difference that the child who plays in a game must be ready to take the attitude of everyone else involved in that game, and that these different roles must have a definite relationship to each other (1934:150–151).

Here we should note Lever's claim that

> some games . . . provide a highly complex experience for their young players while others do not . . . [and] the evidence of differential exposure to complex games leads to the conclusion that not all children will learn the same lessons. . . . One implication of this research is that boys' greater exposure to complex games may give them an advantage in occupational milieus that share structural features with those games (1978:473).

Goffman, and Becker, offer complementary perspectives on the lifelong process of interpreting and negotiating cultural structure. Goffman views this process mainly from the standpoint of the "self" who presents to others, and Becker sees it mainly from the standpoint of the "audience," or "society," that witnesses that presentation.

Goffman argues that "When an individual enters the presence of others, they commonly seek to acquire information about him or to bring into play information about him already possessed. . . . Informed in these ways, the others will know how best to act in order to call forth a desired response from him," but in giving (and giving off) this information, "we commonly find that the definition of the situation projected by a particular participant is an integral part of a projection that is fostered and sustained by the intimate co-operation of more than one participant," and Goffman calls such a "set of individuals who co-operate in staging a single routine" a " 'performance team' or, in short, [a] 'team' " (1959:1, 77–78, 79). He then adds:

> Since we all participate on teams we must all carry within ourselves something of the sweet guilt of conspirators. And . . . each team is engaged in

maintaining the stability of some definitions of the situation, concealing or playing down certain facts in order to do this (1959:105).

Goffman also points out role-expectation differentiation among members of a performance team:

> One often finds that someone is given the right to direct and control the progress of the dramatic action . . . [and] the director may be given the special duty of bringing back into line any member of the team whose performance becomes unsuitable (1959:97, 98).

If we continue to apply Goffman's dramaturgical metaphor, then Becker may be said to argue that deviance, like beauty, inheres not in the performer's performance but in the eyes of the beholding audience (that is, in their normative expectations; see Chapter 4):

> Social groups create deviance by making the rules whose infraction constitutes deviance and applying those rules to particular people and labeling them outsiders. . . . The deviant is "one to whom that label has successfully been applied; deviant behavior is behavior that people so label" (1973:9, emphasis removed).[15]

Society, according to Becker, is no more undifferentiated with regard to the production of its labels than is a team, to Goffman, in the production of a performance: "Rules are the products of someone's initiative and we can think of the people who exhibit such enterprise as moral entrepreneurs . . . [of which there are two] related species—rule creators and rule enforcers" (Becker, 1973:147).

Scheff, discussing a special type of deviance—namely, insanity—argues that the cultural structuralistic variable called "labeling," by conferring on an individual not only a normative actor expectation but also all the situation, response, and consequence expectations associated with that actor expectation (see Chapter 4), can powerfully affect the social phenomena in which that individual participates thereafter:

> In the crisis occurring when a residual rule-breaker is publicly labeled, the deviant is highly suggestible, and may accept the proffered role of the insane as the only alternative. . . . That is, when a residual rule-breaker organizes his behavior within the framework of mental disorder, and when his organization is validated by others, particularly prestigeful others such as physicians, he is "hooked" and will proceed on a career of chronic deviance (1966:88).

---

[15] Durkheim is an exact precursor of this view: "What confers [criminality] is not the intrinsic quality of a given act but that definition which the collective conscience lends them" (1938:70).

Similarly, Scott defends the thesis that "blindness is a learned social role" (1969:117) by arguing that the set of cultural structuralistic variables called "socialization" can influence "self," which can then affect the social phenomena in which the blind participate:

> The overpowering importance of [blindness organizations] in the socialization of the blind who are in [them] is demonstrated by looking at the blind who live outside [them]. These people . . . fail to display the attitudinal and behavioral patterns that so many insist they should have because they are blind. . . . [Blindness organizations] are active socializing agents that create and mold the fundamental attitudes and patterns of behavior that are at the core of the experience of being a blind man (1969:120, 121).

Finally, in this brief examination of symbolic interactionist cultural structuralism, consider its partial derivative, ethnomethodology: the study of the "methods" people (performers and audiences alike) use to generate "ethnicity"—that is, cultural structure. As Garfinkel puts it, "The study of common sense knowledge and common sense activities consists of treating as problematic phenomena the actual methods whereby members of a society . . . make the social structures of everyday activities observable" (1967:75). Thus, given that the meaning of any everyday symbolic communication is inevitably "indexical"—that is, highly dependent on context—rather than "objective" (or context free, a characteristic thought by Garfinkel to be present in scientific communication; see Garfinkel, 1967:4–5), and given that the context for any single symbol is always potentially infinite and therefore altogether ineffable, what Garfinkel wants to know is how participants indicate to each other which portion of that infinite context they intend to be taken into account in order to make a given symbolic communication make sense.

Essential to that indication, in Garfinkel's view, is not *what* is indicated but *how* it is indicated. That is, according to Garfinkel, no matter what a given participant indicates is the intended context for a given symbolic expression, that indication must be understandable by other participants as conforming to a rule which they recognize and honor:

> To see the "sense" of what is said is to accord to what was said its character "as a rule." "Shared argument" refers to various social methods for accomplishing the member's recognition that something was said-according-to-a-rule and not the demonstrable matching of subject matters (1967:30).

Such rules, Garfinkel argues, are specific to the social settings in which they apply: "Thus, a leading policy [of ethnomethodology] is to refuse serious consideration to the prevailing proposal that . . . rational properties of practical activities . . . be assessed . . . by using a rule or a standard obtained outside actual settings within which such properties are . . . used . . . by settings' members" (1967:33). Settings vary, of course, but they have one feature in common, according to Garfinkel: they all seek to maximize interindividual communication—symbolic interaction—and thereby to enhance negotiated consensus (i.e., intersubjective sense-based verification) regarding individual observations and interpretations:

> Exactly in the ways in which a setting is organized, it consists of methods whereby its members are provided with accounts of the setting as countable, storyable, proverbial, comparable, picturable, representable—i.e., accountable events (1967:75, 34).

The question now arises: According to what hierarchically higher, setting-free, metarules are such local, setting-specific, rules made? By what criteria do members of any given setting determine whether that setting is in fact "countable, storyable, proverbial," and so forth? Garfinkel's answer to this question is that there exists, in the conduct of everyday affairs, "a background of seen but unnoticed features of common discourse whereby actual utterances are recognized as events of common, reasonable, understandable, plain talk" (1967:41), and that all participants in human social phenomena are either born with or learn (Garfinkel does not say which) these background understandings. These are the universal metarules which make sense out of all local setting-specific rules:

> The anticipation that persons *will* understand, the occasionality of expressions, the specific vagueness of references, the retrospective-prospective sense of a present occurrence, waiting for something later in order to see what was meant before, are sanctioned properties of common discourse. They furnish a background of seen but unnoticed features of common discourse whereby actual utterances are recognized as events of common, reasonable, understandable, plain talk (Garfinkel, 1967:41).[16]

Central to these "background understandings," in Garfinkel's view, is the commandment that thou shalt trust others (and assume that others trust you), and

---

[16] Habermas proposes a related set of metarules: "[An] underlying consensus [on the basis of which speech acts are exchanged between persons] is formed in the reciprocal recognition of at least four claims to validity which speakers announce to each other: the comprehensibility of the utterance, the truth of its propositional component, the correctness and appropriateness of its performatory component, and the authenticity of the speaking subject" (1973:18). Not dissimilarly, Weiss and Bucuvalas argue that

> Decision-makers in federal, state, and local mental health agencies . . . invoke three basic frames of reference [in deciding whether to take a given social science research study into account in the work of their office]. One is the relevance of the content of the study to their sphere of responsibility, another is the trustworthiness of the study, and the third is the [policy] direction that it provides (1980:311).

believe that things are what they seem to be (a rule, incidentally, whose presuppositions must reduce to the presumed interchangeability of human analysts discussed in Chapter 16). In Garfinkel's words,

> Schutz proposed that for the conduct of his everyday affairs the person assumes, assumes the other person assumes as well, and assumes that as he assumes it of the other person, the other person assumes it of him, that a relationship of undoubted correspondence [exists] between the actual appearances of an object and the intended object that appears in a particular way. For the person conducting his everyday affairs, objects, for him as he expects for others, are as they appear to be (1967:50; see also 55–56, 272–277).

Cicourel outlines the problem ethnomethodology addresses, and its relationship to symbolic interactionism, when he says

> The actor must be endowed with mechanisms or basic procedures that permit him to identify settings which would lead to "appropriate" invocation of norms, where the norms would be surface rules and not basic to how the actor makes inferences about taking or making roles. The basic or interpretive procedures are like deep structure grammatical rules; they enable the actor to generate appropriate (usually innovative) responses in changing settings. . . . To the Meadian dialectic of the "I" and the "me" is added the explicit requirement that the actor must be conceived as possessing inductive (interpretive) procedures . . . (1974:27).

Cicourel says "Our present knowledge of the nature of interpretive procedures is sparse" (1974:52), but suggests four principles guiding such procedures: the reciprocity of perspectives, normal forms, the et cetera principle, and descriptive vocabularies as indexical expressions (see 1974:85–88; see also 34–35, 52–56).

Another Variety of Cultural Structuralism

Finally, in this examination of cultural structuralism, note that Figure 4.1 leads us to expect one additional variety—namely, *neutrality* cultural structuralism, the counterpart of segregation social structuralism—where one cultural structure is compartmentalized from another. And as summary exemplification of this variety, we find Kuper describing the "plural" society as

> in the strictest sense a medley of peoples, for they mix but do not combine. Each group holds by its own religion, its own culture and language, its own

ideas and ways. As individuals they meet, but only in the market place, in buying and selling (1969:10–11).[17]

Cultural Structuralism and Social Structuralism

As Figure 7.1 has suggested, social phenomena (unlike systems of nonliving components) are held to be partially self-determining in the sense that one inter-organism behavior regularity helps give rise to another. If this second interorganism behavior regularity is regarded as being very similar to the first, we say the social phenomenon in question is "maintaining" (or has "regenerated") itself; if it is somewhat dissimilar, we say the phenomenon is "modifying" itself; and if it is radically dissimilar (or if there is no second interorganism behavior regularity at all), we say the phenomenon has "terminated" itself. Whenever such claims are made, it is social structure and cultural structure—considered both as descriptive variables (see Chapters 2, 3, and 4) and as explanatory variables (discussed in Chapter 9 and in the present chapter)—that are regarded as performing this self-determining function, even though mediated by other socially influenced variables and assisted by the existentially given ones.

As a result, the following four kinds of hypotheses are common in sociological explanations:

1. Social structure generates cultural structure. Marx says "It is not the consciousness of men that determines their being, but on the contrary, their social being that determines their consciousness" (1978:4).
2. Cultural structure generates social structure. Weber says "The magical and religious forces, and the ethical ideas of duty based upon them have . . . always been among the most important formative influences on conduct" (1958b:27).
3. One social structure generates another. Durkheim says societies with "segmental" social structures evolve into societies with "organized" social structures (see 1933:185).
4. One cultural structure generates another. Durkheim says "from the moment when men have an idea that there are internal connections between things, science and philosophy are possible. Religion opened up the way for them" (1965:270).

---

[17] Kuper notes that "for Furnivall, who applied the concept to tropical societies . . . the political form of the plural society is one of colonial domination, which imposes a Western superstructure of business and administration on the native world, and a forced union on the different sections of the population" (1969:10). Social structural "domination," "business and administration," and "force," however, are all conceptually separable from cultural structural neutrality on grounds discussed in Chapter 2.

It is social self-determination hypotheses like (1) and (2) above (plus an underlying metaphysical presumption of symmetry) that seem best to account for the pairings noted in this chapter and the preceding one between the four main varieties of social structuralism, on the one hand, and the four main varieties of cultural structuralism, on the other.

Having said that, however, the functionalist-symbolic interactionist pair may be somewhat less obvious than the unison-consensus, exchange-complementarity, and conflict-dissensus (and the segregation-neutrality) pairs of social and cultural structuralisms, so it may not be amiss to point out that in addition to incorporating all the main varieties of their respective structuralisms, functionalism and symbolic interactionism both look upon social phenomena as self-determining, and complement each other's arguments in this respect. Thus, functionalist social structuralism argues that social phenomena are self-determining through what is *done* (i.e., through one individual or group doing something—performing a function—for another), whereas symbolic interactionist cultural structuralism argues that such phenomena are self-determining mainly through what is *thought and felt* (i.e., through one individual or group communicating—interacting symbolically—with another). The complementarity goes further: To functionalist social structuralism, psychical behaviors (norms and values) are necessary for the performance of functions, and to symbolic interactionist cultural structuralism physical behaviors (gestures) are necessary for the communication of thoughts and feelings.[18]

Cultural Structuralistic Variables in Sociobiology

The role of cultural structuralistic variables in explanations of nonhuman social phenomena is by no means as well-developed and differentiated there as in explanations of human social phenomena. This difference in explanatory prominence—together with a similar difference pertaining to enculturistic variables (see Chapter 8)—appears to be the most outstanding of all contrasts between explanations of human and of nonhuman social phenomena—and very probably will continue to be so.

Nevertheless, cultural structuralistic variables do appear in the latter—as Wilson's comment indicates:

---

[18] Giddens compares symbolic interactionism and functionalism along the micro-macro hierarchic dimension—although it is not clear whether he has a descriptive reference (see Chapter 6), an explanatory reference (see Chapter 12), or both, in mind:

> The territory that symbolic interactionism has staked out has been mainly that of "social encounters" in Goffman's sense: face-to-face interaction between individuals. A second, vying tradition, functionalism, has claimed the domain of institutional analysis (1981:167).

> Most tradition in the best investigated animals is concerned with . . . the tendency of individuals to return to the places used by their ancestors in order to reproduce, to feed, or simply to rest. Its most striking manifestation is in the fixed migration routes of birds and mammals (1975:168).

In the same vein, Klopfer notes that

> The gross features of community organization [among prairie dogs] are fixed and maintained by the clear-cut territorialism shown by the family units. . . . Unlike the situation in many other animal communities, as density rises above tolerable levels it is not the young animals that emigrate but the old ones. Thus, the fixity of the territorial boundary implies that there is a training of the young by their parents, a training that involves teaching the offspring the extent of the family territory (1962:139–140).

Marler notes the existence of traditional dialects among songbirds: "The tendency to learn songs from neighbours results in the development of local dialects in many species, including the blackbird, yellow bunting, song sparrow and the chaffinch" (1964:187). Sebeok reports on traditional signals among crows:

> Crows in this country are known to exhibit distinctive alarm notes inducing other crows to disperse, distress calls when caught, and assembly calls made when they sight a bird of prey or a cat. These calls were tape-recorded and, when played to wild crows in American woodland, elicited much the same reactions. When, however, these tape recordings were tested on crows in France, either there was no response or the French crows assembled where the Americans would have fled. Captive Pennsylvania crows respond "abnormally" to the calls of Maine crows and vice versa; but crows free to migrate between the two regions construct a dia-system which enables them to understand local dialects (1968:24).

Hooker reports that "the bullfinch [has] a family tradition in song, the young birds, singing like their parents and grandparents. This may be extremely important in maintaining social units" (1968:331), and that among a certain species of thrush, the ability to mimic sounds

> has been adapted for the maintenance of the pair-bond. The male of a pair sang a certain song motif which was never sung by the female until the male bird was removed. She would then sing the whole song of the male, which would have the immediate effect of recalling the male bird "as if by name," since there is nothing more stimulating to a mated male than to hear its own repertoire repeated in its own territory (1968:332).

Then there is the invention of sweet potato washing and wheat grain flotation by Imo, a 2-year old Japanese macaque, and the age-and-sex-differentiated diffusion of these inventions through her troop:

> By 1958, five years after Imo had invented it, potato washing was practiced by 80 percent of monkeys from 2 to 7 years of age. Older monkeys remained conservative; only 18 percent, all of them females, learned the behavior. . . . The pattern by which [the tradition of wheat grain flotation] spread through the troop resembled that for sweet-potato washing (Wilson, 1975:170).

Bonner also cites several different traditions among nonhuman animals, including "termiting" by chimpanzees, opening mussels by oyster catchers, hostility toward humans among African elephants, and opening of milk bottles by titmice in Britain (see Bonner, 1980:171–185).

SUMMARY

This chapter has surveyed two types of sociological explanatory variables that claim causal power for the psychical behavior of people in each participant's environment. Psychical contagionistic variables are the environmental counterparts of instinctivistic variables, and rely on the presumed innate abilities of individuals to send and receive messages of determinate content. Cultural structuralistic variables, the environmental counterparts of enculturistic variables, rely on the learned ability of individuals to send and receive such messages. Four major kinds of cultural structuralistic variables were identified: consensus, complementarity, dissensus, and symbolic interactionism. These cultural structuralisms were paired with unison, exchange, dissensus, and functionalist social structuralism.

11

External Thing Variables

In this chapter we come to the final pair (or pair of pairs) of sociological explanatory variables: ecologism and technologism. Here we find variables whose referents are outside the species *Homo sapiens* as well as outside the individual B. These variables refer, as Figure 7.2 indicates, to both living and nonliving things: animal, vegetable, and mineral; solids, liquids, and gases; space-time; the strong, weak, electromagnetic, and gravitational interactions. They refer to all these things in their "natural" state, in the case of ecologism, and to their "artifactual," "human-made," states in the case of technologism. The case for these two sorts of variables is summed up by Nowak: "Man lives in an environment of other people but he also lives in an environment made up of the material products of nature and his own activity, and these have a vital effect on social phenomena (1977:52).

ECOLOGISM

In order to qualify as "ecologistic," a variable must refer to some existentially given aspect of things (i.e., not people, but including living as well as nonliving "things") in individual B's environment. Thus, Hawley asserts that "The community . . . is in the nature of a collective response to the habitat; it constitutes the adjustment of organism to environment" (1950:37); and "human ecology . . .

302

refers to a concern with the processes and form of man's adjustment to environment. The community is a generalized form of that adjustment" (1971:11). Quinn says "No sociological study can be called truly ecological unless it uses certain aspects of environmental influence as principles of interpretation" (1939:163), and Duncan asserts that "man's morphological and intellectual capacity evolved under the pressure of a complex social and technical life that was initiated by ecological adaptations of his prehuman ancestors," and declares that "social institutions . . . do not themselves evolve, but rather adjust to new conditions either from environmental change or from technological development" (1964:48, 50).

At least two classical progenitors of ecologism should be cited. First, Ibn Khaldun, who argues that the social phenomenon called "civilization" varies with climate, so that "there is little civilization [near the equator]. There is a medium degree of civilization [farther away from the equator] because the heat there is temperate owing to the decreased amount of light. There is a great deal of civilization [still farther away from the equator] because of the decreased amount of heat there," but in the extreme north, "generation stops because of the excessive cold and frost and the long time without any heat" (1967:56). Moreover, says Ibn Khaldun, the natural fertility of the soil affects social phenomena:

> the inhabitants of fertile zones where the products of agriculture and animal husbandry as well as seasonings and fruits are plentiful are, as a rule, described as stupid in mind and coarse in body. . . . The frugal inhabitants of the desert and those of settled areas who have accustomed themselves to hunger and to abstinence from pleasures are found to be more religious and more ready for divine worship than people who live in luxury and abundance (1967:66–67).

Some 400 years later we have Montesquieu's different, but still ecologistic, conclusions:

> [G]reat heat enervates the strength and courage of men, and . . . in cold climates they have a certain vigor of body and mind, which renders them patient and intrepid, and qualifies them for arduous enterprises. . . . [F]ertile provinces are always of a level surface where the inhabitants are unable to dispute against a stronger power; they are then obliged to submit; and when they have once submitted, the spirit of liberty cannot return; the wealth of the country is a pledge of their fidelity. But in mountainous districts, as they have but little, they must preserve what they have. . . . It is, then, a more arduous, a more dangerous, enterprise to make war against them (1949:264, 272).

Two hundred years after Montesquieu, Park hypothesizes social effects of decline in the relative abundance of natural resources (including both nonliving and living things in the environment):

When the pressure of population upon the natural resources of the habitat reaches a certain degree of intensity, something invariably happens. In one case, the population may swarm and relieve the pressure of population by migration. In another . . . the pre-existing correlation of the species may be totally destroyed . . . [and when that happens, competition] operates in the human (as it does in the plant and animal) community to bring about and restore the communal equilibrium (1961:24, 25).

Park quickly grows more moderate with regard to humans:

man is not so immediately dependent upon his physical environment as other animals. . . . The exchange of goods and services has cooperated to emancipate him from dependence upon his local habitat. Furthermore, man has, by means of inventions and technical devices of the most diverse sorts, enormously increased his capacity for . . . remaking, not only his habitat but his world. Finally, man has erected upon the basis of the biotic community an institutional structure rooted in custom and tradition (1961:28).

Note even here, however, the persistent though implicit claim that if not "immediately" dependent, human beings are nonetheless *ultimately* dependent on the physical environment, and that human "customs and traditions" and "institutional structures" are based on the biotic community.

Ecologistic variables include four categories of existentially given living and nonliving things in the environment: (1) resources for, and (2) obstacles to, human life as they are distributed in (a) space and (b) time; and ecologism proposes that individual B can be causally influenced to participate (or not participate) in a social phenomenon with A by any and all of these factors. Hawley emphasizes the distribution of resources in space when he says

The study of territorially based systems . . . is known as human ecology. . . . [M]an relies on a great many things that are distributed over space: food, water, raw materials of all kinds. Were these necessities everywhere present in abundant supply, it is conceivable that the idea of space might never have occurred to man (1971:12).

Sopher also notes that the existentially given distributions of things in space can have causal impacts specifically on cultural structure:

Landmarks which may endure for long periods, as cultural markers of ethnicity go, can become, through their shared symbolic value, an especially powerful means of ethnic identification. In this way, the sense of place as home is expressed—be it for family, tribe, or nation (1973:107–108).

Similarly, Erikson, investigating the Buffalo Creek flood disaster, reports that "Along the entire length of Buffalo Creek, people continue to feel that they are lost in 'a strange and different place.' Part of the trouble is that the *terrain* is different. 'Amherstdale just doesn't look like it used to' " (1976:210, emphasis changed).

Finally, in connection with the existentially given spatial distribution of things, we should cite Lenki's argument that

> the ecology of a particular area has prevented potential recipients from adopting new technologies: much of sub-Saharan Africa, for example, seems to have been unsuited to the plow under preindustrial conditions.—The combination of poor soils and the presence of the tsetse fly (which severely limited the areas in which cattle and horses could be raised) virtually ruled out the use of the plow before the development of modern commercial fertilizers and chemical insecticides. . . .—The geographical concentration of simple societies in the modern world, with their concentration in deserts, rain forests, and arctic areas, is no mere accident of history, nor does it reflect some curious distribution of values (1975:147, footnote included).

But whatever space contains, time must also contain, and vice versa: whatever exists in space also exists at some time, and whatever exists in time also exists in some space. It follows that insofar as all things possess temporal as well as spatial limits, the way in which those things are distributed in time is an equally essential ecologistic variable. The distribution in time of the requisites for human life evokes in human behavior a constant sensitivity to the passage of time and to the periodicities, rhythms, durations, and tempos into which time may be divided. Thus, the existentially given diurnal, seasonal, annual, and other rhythms, as well as long-term trends in the distribution of things in the "natural environment" makes "Man . . . a time-bound creature" (Hawley, 1971:13) as well as a space-bound creature.

Further, as already indicated, the existentially given living and nonliving things distributed in the spatial and temporal environment of social participants present not only resources for human life but also obstacles to human life:

> Civilizations have retreated from the plasmodium of malaria, and armies have crumpled into rabbles under the onslaught of cholera spirilla, or of dysentery and typhoid bacilli. Huge areas have been devastated by the trypanosome that travels on the wings of the tsetse fly, and generations have been harassed by the syphilis of a courtier. . . . [And as for rats, they] destroy cultivated grains . . . destroy merchandise . . . poultry [and] enormous numbers of eggs. . . . [They] have gnawed holes in dams and started floods; they have started fires by gnawing matches; they have bitten holes in mail sacks and eaten the mail; they have actually caused famines in India by wholesale crop

destruction in scant years. They have nibbled at the ears and noses of infants in their cribs (Zinsser, 1967:6, 151).

Put them all together—all existentially given living and nonliving resources and obstacles as distributed in space and in time—and they spell "habitat" as a causal explanation for social phenomena: "the conception of the adjustment of man to habitat as a process of community development . . . is for human ecology the principal working hypothesis" (Hawley, 1944:405). In its fullest development, of course, this view asserts that not biology but ecology is destiny—a claim that seems increasingly well supported by the apparent predictability (in principle, and only in broad outlines and still incompletely) of sun, earth, life, sociality, intelligence, and all other phenomena, from the Macro-Habitat and its origin in the cosmic fireball 12 billion years ago.

Ecologistic Variables in Sociobiology

Not surprisingly, ecologistic variables play key roles in sociobiological explanations. For example, Wilson says "dispersed, predictable food sources tend to lead to territorial behavior, while patchily distributed sources unpredictable through time favor colonial existence. A second rule is that large, dangerous prey promote high degrees of cooperative and reciprocally altruistic behavior" (1975:34). Further, "In mammals the principal antisocial factor appears to be chronic food shortage" (Wilson, 1975:36), and in general, because "Social behavior, like all other forms of biological response, is a set of devices for tracking changes in the environment" (Wilson, 1975:144), "the form of social organization [among animals] and the degree of complexity of the society is strongly influenced by . . . the food on which it specializes, the degree to which seasonal change of its habitat forces it to migrate, its most dangerous predator, and so forth" (Wilson, 1975:37). Space and time in which to live and reproduce—and considered independently of their food and other contents—are crucial ecologistic variables that are often combined with demographistic variables to form "density" variables:

> [T]ransitions . . . occur in many vertebrate species from territorial to dominance behavior as the density passes a critical value. [But not] all density-dependent social responses consist of aggressive behavior. When populations of European voles (*Microtus*) reach certain high densities, the females join in little nest communities, defend a common territory, and raise their young together (Wilson, 1975:20).

At all times, materialistic variables—expressed as the genetically inherited bodily needs and capacities of the animals concerned—accompany ecologistic ones: "herbivores maintain the highest population densities and smallest home ranges, while top carnivores . . . are scarcest and utilize the largest home ranges" (Wilson, 1975:34).

Having discussed the conflict and exchange social structuralistic components of "territoriality" and "dominance" in the preceding chapter, let us now consider their ecologistic component. In this context, Schneirla relies on an ecologistic explanation for dominance: "dominance hierarchies appear . . . when groups of birds or primates are confined within a small space [or] when incentives (i.e., food and drink) are restricted in quantity or in accessibility" (1946:396). Similarly, Klopfer, after claiming that "space may be considered as restricting populations directly, by limiting nest or breeding sites or feeding territories, or indirectly, as the result of physiological responses to crowding" (1962:52), says

> A limited piece of land may be apportioned in one of two ways. The simplest method is to provide each individual with a discrete and exclusive chunk. . . . The second way . . . is to allow mutual use of a large area by a group of individuals and to establish social priorities within the group to determine the use of a particular spot at a particular time (1962:58, 60).

Regarding what he calls "the simplest method" of apportioning space, namely, territoriality, Klopfer asks "What . . . determines the size and shape of a territory?" and answers:

> In part, these factors depend on the particular kind of territory that is involved. According to some preliminary studies on Mantidae . . . there are at least some species for which the spacing is an immediate function of food supply. When mantids are deprived of food they become cannibalistic and intolerant of the proximity of a conspecific. Only when sated are they no longer spaced widely (1962:59).

TECHNOLOGISM

It should be apparent from its inclusion here, in this chapter devoted to "external thing" variables, that the present reference to "technology" is narrower than usual. Ordinarily, the term extends beyond socially influenced living and nonliving *things* (i.e., tools, machines, utensils, and instruments; draft, food, and experimental animals; cultivated grasses, fruit, and tubers, etc.) to the physical *techniques* and the psychical *knowledge* involved in constructing and operating these things.

Weber, for example, is maximally inclusive in this regard when he says "the term 'technology' applied to an action refers to the *totality* of means employed as opposed to the meaning or end to which the action is . . . oriented" (1947:160, emphasis added)—although he implicitly distinguishes among such means in noting that "the precision of [bureaucratic] functioning requires the services of the railway, the telegraph, and the telephone" (1947:339). Ogburn, who speaks of "material culture" rather than "technology," also includes techniques as well as tools when he claims that "material culture accumulates. The use of bone is added to the use of stone. The use of bronze is added to the use of copper and the use of iron is added to the use of bronze" (1933:73), and also says "Technology would encompass the making of a great variety of objects" (1957:8). White is similarly inclusive of techniques as well as tools: "The technological system is composed of the material, mechanical, physical, and chemical instruments, together with the techniques of their use, by means of which man . . . is articulated with his natural habitat"—although his next sentence emphasizes instruments rather than techniques: "Here we find the tools of production, the means of subsistence, the materials of shelter, the instruments of offense and defense" (1949:364). Duncan takes a similar view: "The concept of 'technology' in human ecology refers not merely to a complex of art and artifact whose patterns are invented, diffused, and accumulated . . . but to a set of techniques employed by a population to gain sustenance from its environment" (1959:682). Etzioni and Remp specify knowledge as well as tools and techniques: "We mean by technology a set or system of tools, techniques, and the knowledge their use requires" (1973:2), as does Lenski: "Technology refers to the information, techniques, and tools by means of which men utilize the material resources of their environment to satisfy their varied needs and desires" (1970:37). Bell is extreme in relegating tools to an altogether inessential role in technology and centering attention almost entirely on knowledge when he says "Technology . . . 'is the use of scientific knowledge to specify ways of doing things in a reproducible manner,' " and adds that "the organization of a hospital or an international trade system is a social technology, as the automobile or a numerically controlled tool is a machine technology. An intellectual technology is the substitution of algorithms (problem-solving rules) for intuitive judgments" (1973:29, emphasis removed). Finally, we note that Gouldner moves in the opposite (but no less extreme) direction from Bell by centering attention almost entirely on technique rather than knowledge and leaving out tools altogether: "technology per se is primarily a praxis . . . what 'technology' does is to present itself as a universal, all-purpose praxis, as a practice fit for the pursuit of any and all goals and as available to all and every group, whatever their goal" (1976:182)— although he does refer to "technological instruments," and "technological hardware" (1976:243, 246).

However, for reasons that must be clear by now, I assign all "knowledge" to cultural structuralism, and all "techniques," "use," and "making" to social structuralism—reserving only the socially influenced *things* themselves, the "tools," the "artifacts," the "instruments," the "domesticated" plants and animals, for technologism. I do this in exactly the same way and for exactly the same reasons that I reserve "habitat" for ecologism, and assign elsewhere the meaning its inhabitants may give to it and the physical behavioral adaptation they may make to it. Through these partitionings I intend logically to permit a variety of empirical possibilities: not only that the same thing may be made, used, and assigned meaning in widely different ways but also that the thing may influence social phenomena in ways entirely independent of how it is made, used, or understood. Thus, not only do I wish to allow for the possibility that climate, topography, radioactivity, predators, and prey may influence human social phenomena without human knowledge or techniques; I also want to allow that nuclear weapons can destroy the Tasaday as easily as Toronto; that an electric light bulb casts its light as far among the Nuer as among New Yorkers, and that, conceivably, human-made automatic machines may continue to function long beyond human memory of the knowledge and techniques that produced them. It is this independent explanatory capacity of socially influenced living and nonliving things[1] which Bell seems to identify as "technics," that is, "tools and things made by men yet given an independent existence outside himself" (1973:488) and as Nowak puts it:

> the difference between medieval handicraft and modern heavy industry cannot be reduced to differences between the value system and motivations of the persons living in these systems. . . . With the "same attitude towards work," the efforts of two different teams of workers whose factories differ as to how modern their equipment is, will lead to two very different results (1977:53).

The close relationship between ecologistic and technologistic variables should be emphasized. Indeed, the latter are only the former after they have been socially influenced: a farm is socially cleared, tilled, sowed, and harvested land; lumber is socially modified trees; the ports of London and New York City are socially modified estuaries; Wichita is a socially modified plain;[2] steel is socially modified iron ore and certain other chemicals; pasteurized milk and butter, steak, wool, silk, and scrambled eggs are socially modified products of socially modified animals; a functioning television set is a combination of socially modified metals, rare gases

---

[1] Here I take issue with Callon and Latour's remark: "What is a machine without an operator? Nothing more than a broken-down heap of iron" (1981:293)—unless it be admitted (1) that one machine may have another machine as its operator, and (2) that even a "broken-down heap of iron" may influence social phenomena in ways different from a vein of iron-ore in the earth. This does not mean, however, that, as Callon and Latour also claim, "If the machine can move, build, and repair itself, it must be a living thing" (1981:293:294).

[2] Note that this implies an important difference between the meaning of the term "ecology" when used by "urban ecologists" and when used in the present strict sense of *existentially given* things in the environment. According to the latter definition, most of what is called urban "ecology" should be classified as urban *technology*, to the extent that as the phenomena in question are regarded as socially influenced rather than existentially given.

and earths, electric currents, and so on. I regard instruments, then, as parts of the "natural" habitat that humans have converted into a socially cultivated and domesticated, extracted and fabricated, habitat. Components of this latter habitat may be classified in the same way as the first: into resources for human life and obstacles to human life, distributed in space and in time—all of which may influence B's participation in a social phenomenon with A.

Marx and Engels are undoubtedly the most outstanding classical proponents of technologism, alloyed, of course, with materialism, social structuralism, cultural structuralism, and instinctivism. Although they concentrate their attention on instruments of economic production (see 1978:especially 189–193, 345–351, 403–411), they also attend to other sorts of instruments—including instruments of exchange ("Money is the pimp between man's needs and the object, between his life and the means of life" [1978:102, emphasis removed]), instruments of destruction ("With the invention of a new instrument of warfare, firearms, the whole internal organization of the army necessarily changed . . . and the relations of different armies to one another also changed" [1978:204],[3] and instruments of ideational production ("The class which has the means of material production at its disposal, has control at the same time over the means of mental production" [1978:172]).

The great explanatory weight Marx assigns to technologistic variables seems most conclusively indicated by the fact that his major work is entitled not "Labor," or "The Class Struggle," (both titles would emphasize social structuralistic variables), or "Class Consciousness" (which would emphasize cultural structuralistic variables), but *Capital*—and Marx defines the latter in strictly technologistic terms:

> Capital consists of raw materials, instruments of labour and means of subsistence of all kinds, which are utilized in order to produce new raw materials, new instruments of labour and new means of subsistence. . . . [T]hese component parts of capital [are] creations of labour, products of labour (1978:207).

Engels concurs in this assignment of explanatory weight:

> Only at a certain level of development of the productive forces of society [including instruments of labor—ed.] . . . does it become possible to raise production to such an extent that the abolition of class distinctions . . . can be lasting without bringing about stagnation and even decline in the mode of social production (Marx and Engels, 1978:666).

---

[3] Sorel also observes that "Civil war has become very difficult since the discovery of the new firearms and since the cutting of rectilinear streets in the capital towns" (1950:94); and, earlier, Engels notes that by the late nineteenth century "the conditions of [class] struggle had essentially changed. Rebellion in the old style, street fighting with barricades, which decided the issue everywhere up to 1848, [became] to a considerable extent obsolete" (Marx and Engels, 1978:567).

Now two complementary claims of the Marxian view of the relationship between technologistic variables on the one hand and social and cultural structuralistic variables on the other seem especially crucial. First, it is claimed that for all their causal power, technologistic variables possess no causal *direction* of their own; they must get such direction from social and cultural structuralistic variables and may, therefore, bring death as easily as life. Thus,

> If machinery be the most powerful means for increasing the productiveness of labour . . . it becomes in the hands of capital the most powerful means . . . for lengthening the working-day beyond all bounds set by human nature. . . . The lightening of the labour, even, becomes a sort of torture, since the machine does not free the laborer from work, but deprives the work of all interest . . . it is not the workman that employs the instruments of labor, but the instruments of labour that employ the workman (Marx and Engels, 1978:404, 409).[4]

Second, it is claimed that for all their directorial capabilities, social and cultural structural variables possess very little causal *power* of their own; they must get such power from technologistic variables and may, therefore, be weak or strong. Thus, "Instruments of labor not only supply a standard of the degree of development to which human labor has attained, but they are indicators of the social conditions under which that labor is carried on" (Marx and Engels, 1978:346). Therefore,

> it is only possible to achieve real liberation in the real world by employing real means [and] slavery cannot be abolished without the steam engine and the mule and spinning jenny, serfdom cannot be abolished without improved agriculture (Marx and Engels, 1978:169).

We have, in short, a value-added and interactive causal model (see Chapter 12) in which social and cultural structuralistic variables create and direct technologistic variables, and the latter support and power the former, in a manner analogous to the organismic division of labor between the individual's mind and body. It is to the fullest possible development of this division of labor between humans on one side and machines on the other, rather than to the present division of labor among

---

[4] In a very similar vein, Marcuse says

Technics, as a universe of instrumentalists, may increase the weakness as well as the power of man. At the present stage, he is perhaps more powerless over his own apparatus than he ever was before. . . . Now automation . . . tends toward the point where productivity is determined "by the machines, and not by the individual output". . . . These changes in the character of work and the instruments of production change the attitude and the consciousness of the laborer. . . . Hatred and frustration are deprived of their specific target, and the technological veil conceals the reproduction of inequality and enslavement. . . . The slaves of developed industrial civilization are sublimated slaves, but they are slaves (1964:235, 28–29, 32).

humans (aided, of course, by machines) that Marx and Engels look as our ultimate destiny—a destiny toward which they believe human history so far has been struggling, in roughly the following way.

Humanity originated, according to Marx and Engels, in the paradise primeval. There, all individuals possessed and freely exercised their multiple capabilities and interests, and freely shared the products of these capabilities and interests with each other. But when instinctivistic and materialistic tendencies toward biological reproduction led to significant population growth, paradise proved primitive as well as primeval insofar as its instruments of production (its capital) as well as its social and cultural structures (its mode of production and its consciousness) were unable to sustain that growth without being transformed in fundamental ways.

So it came to pass that, in an epoch-making sacrifice of quality of life for quantity of life, humans turned their backs on paradise and began to shape their social and cultural structures into a vast pseudomachine called "the division of labor between people." In this pseudomachine, the mass of human beings came eventually to function as though they were its mindless levers, cogs, pistons, conveyor belts, nuts, and bolts—leaving only a small minority of individuals to function as its directing consciousness. Marx and Engels regard this division of labor between people—that is, between those who serve in the pseudomachine with their bodies and those who serve in it with their minds—as wholly unnatural and as the origin of all the horrors of class exploitation and class struggle to which written history bears witness.

The pseudomachine, though painful, is nevertheless the womb of human destiny. Two specializations that develop within it from the very beginning are (pure) science and (applied) engineering, and together they have invented *true* machines of ever greater power, efficiency, precision, and variety. As a result, Marx and Engels argue, it will soon become possible to turn over all economic production to the true machines and dismantle the pseudomachine once and for all—thereby substituting a new division of labor between people on the one hand and machines on the other for the old, transitional division of labor between people. Paradise will then be regained insofar as human beings will be restored to their unspecialized, unmechanical, unalienated, mutually sharing state. But a new paradise will also be gained insofar as the entire burden of physical production, so crippling and degrading to *people,* will have been transferred to *things* that are physically most capable, and ethically most worthy (*pace* Karel Čapek), of carrying this noisome burden. People will thereby be liberated to exercise fully and universally their distinctive, existentially given, capabilities for conscious direction of machines and to become, in Engels' words, "the real, conscious lord of Nature" (Marx and Engels, 1978:715). At this point, says Marx,

> Labour no longer appears so much to be included within the production process; rather, the human being comes to relate more as watchman and regulator to the production process itself. . . . He steps to the side of the produc-

tion process instead of being its chief actor. . . . The free development of individualities, and hence . . . the general reduction of the necessary labor of society to a minimum [will result] (1978:284–285).

Thus Marx foresees the automation and robotization of all such routine economic production as is currently performed by farms and factories.

More recently, Mitchie has the same general vision and foresees the end, through robotization, of at least one aspect of what Marx refers to as "alienation":

> One man, controlling a team of computer-driven assembly machines, might be able to assemble whole cars as an act of individual craftsmanship—instead of assembling one-thousandth of a car every few seconds as at present. This image can be enlarged. We can envisage the automobile craftsman being freed of the necessity to travel each day to his robotic workshop. Just as the office worker in the era of the universal computer network, so the factory worker may be able to ply his trade at home via high-speed video links and the rest of the apparatus of tele-operator technology (1974:198).

Very recently, indeed, a report to the Assembly of Engineering of the National Research Council is quoted as claiming that

> A new, highly dynamic period of CAM [computer-aided manufacturing] has begun in all the industrial countries" and by the year 2000 "the extent to which CAM principles are applied will be the determining factor of the status of a nation's industries". . . . Current technology points to the development in 10 or 15 years, the authors said, of the "metamorphic" robotic manufacturing system. Such a system would be taught the desired configuration of a finished or semifinished product, would itself determine the manufacturing sequence, would use the appropriate tools at appropriate stages, and would monitor its own performance. . . . "It is generally accepted in [Japan, the Soviet Union and Eastern Europe, and in the United Kingdom and Western Europe] that computer-aided manufacturing systems are the only way that nations that are relatively short . . . of highly skilled machining manpower can have hopes of remaining or becoming competitive in [the] world market [of the future]" (Schatz, 1982:4, 5, 11).

Inbar foresees the automation of a different kind of production, namely, the production of routine decisions, such as is currently performed by bureaucratic administrative organizations. Indeed, just as Marx may be said to regard a modern farm or factory as a social machine—that is, a primitive and makeshift machine whose chief working parts are people's bodily muscle power—Inbar says "a bureaucracy . . . may be conceived of as a social computer" (1979:13), that is, a primitive and makeshift computer whose chief working parts are people's mental symbol-manipulating power. Inbar argues that because "routinized decisions depend on very few variables and on simple heuristics, . . . for significant aspects of social life large-scale bureaucracies may be already functionally . . . machine-like and . . . autonomous" (1979:137, 196). Their outright computerization, Inbar argues, may be expected to have important social consequences:

> Thus, by the logic of its mode of operation, a computerized bureaucracy equalizes the treatment of the powerful and the powerless. Additionally, it removes the need to ask for services to which one is entitled, as if they were favors that a clerk, paid in part with one's tax money, might withhold or delay. Furthermore, it eliminates the kind of unreliability due to routine human errors. . . . [And when computerized bureaucracies] do make an error, it is likely to be a systematic one; as a consequence . . . an error of this type has at least the advantage of avoiding the individuation of the task and responsibility of redressing it. . . . Disregarding for the moment the impact of . . . computerization on the staff of a bureaucracy, this type of automation is likely to be regarded as a very dangerous development by various formal and informal elites; indeed, they stand to lose the measure of favoritism and human touch of which clerical bureaucracies are capable (1979:204).

Inbar, too, places human beings "to the side of the production process" as "watchmen and regulators," when he asserts that "In a computerized bureaucracy . . . one or more pools of experts or skillful decision-makers must . . . provide by their actual decision-making behavior the data needed for [programming the computer]," but he adds that such human experts will be necessary only "as long as the field of artificial intelligence has not made a currently unforeseen quantum jump beyond its present stage of development" (1979:205).

Others, however, do foresee the "quantum jump" to which Inbar refers. Thus, Jastrow says:

> I think it is reasonable to assume that human beings are not the last word in the evolution of intelligence on the Earth, but only the root stock out of which a new and higher form of life will evolve. . . . Powerful forces of evolution are at work—cultural rather than biological—that could lead to a more exotic form of life, evolved out of man, but the child of his brain rather than his loins. According to this vision, the new form of life is being created today in the laboratory of the computer scientist. It is an artificial life, made out of silicon chips rather than neurons. . . . In another 15 years or so— around 1995, according to current trends—we will see the silicon brain as an emergent form of life, competitive with man. . . . And what will happen then? What about the next century? And the century after that? There are no limits within sight for the rising curve of silicon intelligence (1981a:91, 144).

Jastrow offers two visions of such a future. There is, first, the possibility of artificial intelligences operating separately from human intelligences (" 'If we are lucky, they might decide to keep us as pets' " [1981a:144][5]), and second, the possibility of artificial intelligences into which human intelligences have merged:

> When the brain sciences reach the point of [thorough understanding of the electrical signals generated by the thinking and feeling human brain,] a bold scientist will be able to tap the contents of his mind and transfer them into the metallic lattices of a computer. . . . At last the human brain, ensconced in a computer, has been liberated from the weaknesses of the mortal flesh. The union of mind and machine has created a new form of intelligence. . . . [a form which] must be the mature form of intelligent life in the Universe (1981b:166).

Should either possibility come true, it is easy to imagine a superhuman social phenomenon such as McCorduck describes:

> When these machines [are talking to each other,] you might recognize them as Sam and George, and you'll walk up and knock on Sam and say, "Hi, Sam. What are you talking about?" What Sam will undoubtedly answer is "Things in general," because there'll be no way for him to tell you. From the first knock until you finish the "t" in about, Sam probably will have said to George more utterances than have been uttered by all the people who have ever lived in all of their lives. I suspect there will be very little communication between [such] machines and humans (1979:345–346).

One can also easily imagine a superhuman mode of scientific analysis such as Hogan describes:

> A man is aware of himself as existing in the localized region of space that is defined by the focal point of his senses. [A conceivable artificial intelligence, however,] will perceive the universe through billions of sensory channels distributed all over the surface of the Earth and beyond. On top of that, its "senses" [could] cover the whole spectrum from high-power proton microscopes in research labs to the big orbiting astronomic telescopes . . . from galactic gravity-wave detectors to the infrared sensors lowered into the ocean trenches. . . . [Such] an intelligence, controlling robot extensions, [could move] pieces of itself around in millions of places at one time [on Jupiter,] under the Arctic ice caps. . . . How can we even begin to imagine how an awareness as totally alien as that would perceive itself and the universe around it? (Hogan, 1979:65).

[5] It is Nietzsche's voice we hear, although Nietzsche certainly did not have in mind robots endowed with artificial intelligence when he wrote:

> All beings so far have created something beyond themselves; and do you want to be the ebb of this great flood and even go back to the beasts rather than overcome man? What is the ape to man? A laughingstock or a painful embarrassment. And man shall be just that for the overman: a laughingstock or a painful embarrassment (1954:124).

It is tempting to think that when we view pure and applied natural science as intrinsic parts of the universe as a whole, and therefore as instrumentalities whereby that universe evolves toward understanding and controlling itself (analogous to brain and limbs as instrumentalities whereby life has evolved toward understanding and controlling itself), Hogan's image may outline a likely next step in that titanic evolution (see the discussions of self-description and self-control in footnote 16 Chapter 6, and in the section on feedback causal models in Chapter 12, respectively).

To return, however, from speculation to an analytically more conservative vein, several other references to technologistic variables should be briefly cited. For example, Freud says "Man has, as it were, become a kind of prosthetic God. When he puts on all his auxiliary organs he is truly magnificent" (1962:38–39); Cardwell says "the clock and the printing press are . . . the twin pillars of our civilization" (1972:12); Hauser notes "Malraux's dictum that the painter is in love, not with landscape, but with pictures, that the poet cares nothing for the beauty of the sunset, but so much the more for the beauty of the verse, and that the musician is interested, not in the nightingale but in music" (quoted by Schneider, 1973:130); Weber says "the modern economic order . . . is now bound to the technical and economic conditions of machine production" (1958b:181); and Inkeles quotes Galtung as observing that " 'Technical-economic development is not reinforced by growing optimism, but rather seems to lead to growing skepticism and pessimism. . . . People living in the most developed countries . . . seem to reflect a feeling of being at the end of something, of moving into a corner, without any clear escape' " (1980:102)—or, as Weber puts it, "fate decreed that [care for external goods] should become an iron cage" (1958b:181).

Ogburn, a major proponent of technologism in sociology, argues that "material culture changes [i.e., changes in technologistic variables—ed.] force changes in other parts of culture such as social organization and customs," so that, for example, "the introduction of steam makes changes in home production, the growth of cities, changes in the position of women, new causes of war" (1933:196, 270). Similarly, Cottrell argues that technologistic variables determine the energy available to humans and "the energy available to man limits what he *can* do and influences what he *will* do" (1955:2). "The series," Cottrell says, "runs something like this:

> Increase in the use of high energy converters leads to the creation of large production units. This in turn requires concentration of control. The use of high energy technology also requires a tremendous increase in the specialization of labor, with increased development of specialized codes governing specific areas of performance (1955:227).

In the same tradition, Levy takes as "the measure of modernization the ratio of inanimate to animate sources of power," and asserts that "Modernization is a universal social solvent. The great social conquests, or cultural diffusions if one prefers, of the past have never had so broad and deep an impact on extremely general human lives and concerns" (1972:3, 5). White argues that "The primary role [in the 'system of culture as a whole'] is played by the technological system. . . . Man is an animal species, and consequently culture as a whole is dependent upon the material, mechanical means of adjustment to the natural environment" (1949:364, 365).

Freud foresaw technological manipulations of the mind (" 'The future may teach us to exercise a direct influence, by means of particular chemical substances, on . . . the mental apparatus' " [quoted in Habermas, 1971:247]), and both Keller and Firestone anticipate technological manipulations of sexuality. Thus, Keller says

> A number of already existing possibilities may give us a foretaste of what is to come. For example, the separation of conception from gestation means that motherhood can become specialized, permitting some women to conceive and rear many children and others to bear them without having to provide for them. Frozen sperm banks. . . . [and the] possibility to reproduce the human species without sexual intercourse . . . reduces a prime motive for marriage and may well dethrone . . . the heterosexual couple. . . . Even without such dramatic changes, already there is speculation that heterosexuality will become but one among several forms of sexuality [or on the other hand, quoting Leonard, that] "it will someday be possible to have a world with only one sex, woman, and thereby avoid the squabbles, confusions and headaches that have dogged this whole business of sex down the centuries" (1971:9, 11).

Firestone goes further when she says "the end goal of feminist revolution must be . . . not just the elimination of male *privilege* but of the sex *distinction* itself. . . . The reproduction of the species by one sex for the benefit of both would be replaced by (at least the option of) artificial reproduction" (1970:11–12).

A technologistic variable of wide explanatory importance is shelter, housing, the humanly built environment (including clothing—i.e., personally portable shelter). Thus, Festinger argues that

> Living in a house . . . means involuntary membership in a group. The decisions of the architect in designing the house, in laying out the site plan for a group of houses, and in deciding who will live in the houses determines to a large extent the nature of the group memberships which will be imposed upon the residents of the houses. When a person moves into a house, his social life and the group membership that will be attributed to him by outsiders will already have been determined to some extent by these decisions (1972:125, see also Festinger et al., 1950).

(Note, however, that as Chapter 13 will argue, it is not the psychical "decisions" but their physical *implementations* that make the indicated determinations.) In the same vein as Festinger, but speaking more qualifiedly of "influence" rather than "determination," Gutman argues that one of the "critical issues that today beset sociology is the study of the [built] environment" so that we can "understand the influence building has on behavior or its function in society" (1975:12). Gutman continues:

> Another set of issues revolves around determining the types of behivaior most likely to be influenced by the character of building. . . . [T]he effects that can be linked to architecture most directly, and that involve such matters as the relation of stair design to home accidents, are not very important [sic]. . . . [So that when sociologists] wonder about the effect of the environment, what they are really concerned with is its influence on family organization, social interaction, crime, delinquency, and the like (1975:13).

Accordingly, Gutman poses the applied science (see Chapter 15) question:

> [W]hat part can the physical environment play in resolving problems that emerge at the social system level? The tradition of human ecology is oriented in this direction and so, of course, is functional analysis in both sociology and anthropology. Neither of these traditions, though, has yet . . . addressed [these questions] to architecture (1975:14).

Alexander offers one answer to Gutman's question when he proposes "twelve specific geometric characteristics . . . [that,] when taken together define a housing pattern different from any available today" and that he believes will influence social phenomena in a desirable way (see 1972:421–431).

It should be noted that not only instruments of construction, transportation, and communication, but also instruments of destruction play essential (not to say vital) causal roles in social phenomena. Thus, we have not only the sudden impact of massed and centrally controlled armaments upon the social phenomena of nations at war but the generally slower and steadier social impact of weapons used against people during peacetime. For example,

> Although other weapons are involved in homicide, firearms are not only the most deadly instrument of attack but also the most versatile. Firearms make some attacks possible that simply would not occur without firearms. They permit attacks at greater range and from positions of better concealment than other weapons. They also permit attacks by persons physically or psychologically unable to overpower their victim through violent physical contact. It is not surprising, therefore, that firearms are virtually the only weapon used in killing police officers (Newton and Zimring, 1969:40).

Finally, in this written analysis of technologistic variables, we should take special note of Ong's claims that writing itself is "a technology—a matter of tools outside us" (1978:6), and that the effects of these tools on psychical behavior and therefore on cultural structure are quite different from those of the spoken word:

> Writing is an absolute necessity for the analytically sequential, linear organization of thought. . . . Without writing . . . the mind simply cannot engage in this sort of thinking, which is unknown in primary oral cultures, where thought is exquisitely elaborated, not in analytic linearity, but in formulary fashion, through "rhapsodizing," that is, stitching together proverbs, antitheses, epithets, and other "commonplaces" (1978:2; see also 1971:2).

In addition, Ong claims that because "an oral culture must maintain its knowledge by repeating it" (1978:3), "Originality threatens [such a culture with] disaster as it no longer need do when writing can store or 'park' knowledge outside the mind for any future use as needed, freeing noetic powers for pursuit of new thoughts" (1974:3; see also 1971:167, 255–283).[6] Similarly, Goody and Watt argue that in literate societies, people

> are faced with permanently recorded versions of the past and its beliefs; and because the past is thus set apart from the present, historical enquiry becomes possible. This in turn encourages scepticism; and scepticism not only about the legendary past, but about received ideas about the universe as a whole. From here the next step is to see how to build up and to test alternative explanations. . . . The kind of analysis involved in the syllogism, and in the other forms of logical procedure, are clearly dependent upon writing, indeed upon a form of writing sufficiently simple and cursive to make possible widespread and habitual recourse both to the recording of verbal statements and then to the dissecting of them (1972:353).

With similarly heavy emphasis on technologistic variables involved in communication, Gouldner argues that whereas the earlier technology of printing gave rise to the cultural structure feature called "ideology," the later technology of television tends to suppress that feature. Thus: "The culture of discourse that produces ideology was historically grounded in the technology of a specific kind of mass (or public) media, printing" (1976:39), but

> In contrast to the conventional printed objects central to ideologies, the modern communications media have greatly intensified the . . . multimodal character of public communication. . . . Television is a "you-are-there" par-

---

[6] Ong also implicates technologistic variables when he distinguishes between cultural structures whose orality is "primary" and those whose orality is "secondary": " 'primary orality' [is] the pristine orality of mankind untouched by writing or print . . . [whose] noetic processes . . . are formulaic and rhapsodic rather than analytic," whereas " 'secondary orality' . . . is the orality induced by radio and television [i.e., other technologistic variables—ed.], and it is by no means independent of writing and print but totally dependent on them" (1978:3; see also 1971:284–303).

ticipatory and consummatory activity. One is not commonly left with a sense that one needs to do something actively after a viewing. The viewing is an end in itself. . . . [The result is that there] is now a growing mass of the populace in advanced industrial countries who are incapable of being reached by ideological appeals and who are insulated from ideological discourse of any political persuasion (1976:168–169, 176).[7]

We should note that, in a strikingly parallel and earlier claim, Ong asserts that whereas the technology of printing gave rise to romanticism (see 1971: especially 264), the technology of television now suppresses it: "The Tokyo or Mexico City Olympics come on live television broadcasts into St. Louis, Boston, and Seattle. The cult of the exotic has proved self-defeating. All remoteness is naturalized now, including the four-billion-year-old rocks of today's recently visited moon" (1971:325). Similarly, Erikson notes that

> Today . . . we no longer parade deviants in the town square . . . but it is interesting that the "reform" which brought about this change in penal prac-tice coincided almost exactly with the development of newspapers as a me-dium of mass information. . . . [N]ewspapers (and now radio and television) offer much the same kind of entertainment as public hangings or a Sunday visit to the local gaol (1966:12).

Technologistic Variables in Sociobiology

Technologistic variables also appear among explanations of nonhuman social phenomena. Thus, Bonner says "animals . . . leave artifact messages. A simple example would be . . . a trail" (1980:133). And Wilson, although he rules out spider webs and wasp nests (and presumably therefore also the "trails" to which Bonner refers) as tools,[8] notes that

> On the Galapagos Islands, at least four species of Darwin's finches . . . use twigs, cactus spines, and leaf petioles to dig insects out of crevices in tree bark. . . . The sea otter . . . collects stones and shells from the ocean bot-tom, places them on his stomach while floating on his back at the surface,

---

[7] Note the contrast between Gouldner's claim that television leads to inactivity and Spilerman's claim (1976, quoted in Chapter 10) that it leads to activity.

[8] Wilson employs a much narrower definition of "tool using" than is advocated here when he refers to it as

the manipulation of an inanimate object, not manufactured internally by the organism, which is used in a way that improves the organism's efficiency in altering the position or form of some other object. Thus spider webs and wasp nests . . . are not tools (1975:172).

and uses them as anvils against which it pounds and cracks open mussels and other hard-shelled mollusks (1975:172).

That nests typically have profound consequences for social phenomena seems clearly indicated by Klopfer and Hailman's observation that

> A larger group of prairie dogs (within certain limits) is likely to fare better than a smaller group due to its having more burrows available when a predator threatens. . . . . Burrow construction, then, represents an important form of conditioning which is clearly better performed by several organisms than by isolates (1967:144).

The great communal nest-builders of the nonhuman animal world, however, are the social insects, whose nests often shelter millions of inhabitants and combine incubation and rearing of brood with cultivation and storage of food. Further, Wilson notes that "the complex architecture of the great nests of fungus-growing termites functions as an air-conditioning machine [wherein both temperature and carbon dioxide concentration are controlled]" (1975:60). Wallis describes the following case of age-graded and task-differentiated division of labor in fabricating nests by a species of East Indian ant:

> This species constructs nests by joining together the edges of leaves with the sticky silk extruded from their own larvae. In this way aerial chambers are formed. The larvae are held in the mandibles of the workers during silk extrusion. . . . [W]hen the nests are torn apart the workers separate into two groups. One group stations itself on the outside of the nest and draws the separated leaves together, holding them with feet and mandibles. The second group holds the larvae and moves them backwards and forwards within the nest, laying down a fine network of silk across the seam (1965:102).

Trail-making appears to be a close relative of nest-building, insofar as in both cases the contents of the space in which animals live is socially influenced and thereby reconstructed, with important consequences for social phenomena. Moreover, the social phenomena in question are often reproductive or economic in trail-making as in nest building. For example, Marler notes that:

> A solitary male bumble bee marks signposts along its track of the day by biting at leaves and twigs, so depositing scent from special glands in the mouth. The track is laid in a zone which varies with the species, either in the tree canopy, in small trees or shrubs, or near the ground. He then patrols the posted area for the rest of the day. If a queen bee looking for a mate should strike this trail, she will follow the scent signals, and so eventually meet the male (1964:154).

Wilson has shown that the trail made by fire ants contains information concerning the direction and distance of food supply (see 1971:255–256).

Wilson also describes the domestication of plants (more exactly, fungi) by leafcutter ants:

> As fresh leaves and other plant cuttings are brought into the nest . . . [first] the ants lick them and cut them into pieces 1–2 mm. in diameter. Then they chew the fragments along the edges until the pieces become wet and pulpy, sometimes adding a droplet of clear anal liquid to the surface. Then . . . they carefully insert the fragments into the substratum. Finally . . . the ants pluck tufts of [fungus] from other parts of the garden and plant them on [these fragments] (1971:41).

It is on the fungi thus cultivated that leafcutter ants live: the fungi "produce peculiar spherical or ellipsoidal swellings . . . which are plucked and eaten" (Wilson, 1971:43; see also Goetsch, 1953:75–80, and Morley, 1953:31, 87–88). There is also a description of domestication of animals (nonconspecifics) among yellow ants, wood ants, and others: "As aphids feed on the phloem sap of plants, they pass a sugar-rich liquid through their gut and back out through the anus in only slightly altered form. . . . It is no surprise, therefore, to find that ants . . . gather honeydew of all kinds . . . [and some] have developed the capacity to solicit the honeydew directly from the [aphids] themselves" (Wilson, 1971:419–420).[9] Goetsch says " 'we often see plant lice [aphids] protected by enclosures of earth and we see the ants defending their cattle [i.e., the aphids] from attack.' Both observations are accurate. . . . The yellow ants do in the strictest sense raise domestic animals" (1957:87; also see Morley, 1953:122).

SUMMARY

This chapter concludes my survey of explanatory variables in sociological analysis by focusing on variables that stress the causal power of nonhuman things external to the social participants themselves—in two words, "habitat," and "tools." Ecologistic variables refer to habitat and encompass its living as well as its nonliving components, while technologistic variables refer to tools and similarly encompass their living and nonliving components.

---

[9] Wilson adds:

When unaided by ants, the aphid disposes of the droplets by flicking them away with its hind legs or cauda or by expelling them by contracting its rectum or entire abdomen. The honeydew then falls upon the vegetation and ground below. . . . Sometimes honeydew accumulates in large enough quantities to be usable by man. The manna "given" to the Israelites in the Old Testament account was almost certainly [honeydew] (1971:419).

12

Many-Variable Causal Models

The general problem addressed by this chapter is: In what ways are *multiple* causes held to impinge upon a given social phenomenon that the analyst wishes to explain, and in what ways are *multiple* effects held to proceed from such a phenomenon? I emphasize the multiplicity of causes and the multiplicity of effects because so long as we are dealing with the causal relation of only one variable (whether cause or effect) to the social phenomenon of interest, the problem is simple: the linkage between them can only be singular and immediate. As soon as we consider two or more variables, however, we have to determine not only how these variables relate to the social phenomenon of interest but how they relate to each other as well. Thus, we may say, for example, that the relations of two or more variables to the social phenomenon of interest are "independent" of one another, or one may be "contingent" on the other; we may say their impingements are simultaneous, or sequential, and so on. This chapter inquires about the form of relations between variables that represent hypothesized causes and hypothesized effects of social phenomena. That is to say, the chapter examines some principles governing the way complex causal explanations and predictions are constructed from the elementary kinds of variables reviewed in the preceding five chapters.

For example, Tilly proposes one such complex causal explanation when he argues that "Collective action consists of people's acting together in pursuit of common interests. Collective action results from changing combinations of interests, organization, mobilization, and opportunity" (1978:7). First, of course, we have to set aside Tilly's tautological inclusion of one of his explanations ("interests") in the definition of collective action. Reserving "interests" for an exclusively explanatory role, then, it appears that Tilly uses this term to indicate both instinctivistic ("long run" interests) and cultural structuralistic ("short run" interests [see 1978:61]) variables; in "organization" he includes both cultural structuralistic ("how committed members are") and social structuralistic ("division of labor") variables (1978:7, see also 54); in "mobilization" he includes all the socially influenced variables shown in Fig. 7.2—i.e., "labor power, goods, weapons, votes, and any number of other things, just so long as they are usable in acting on shared interests" (1978:7); and in "opportunity" he includes the relationships, with respect to all the existentially given as well as the socially influenced variables, "between a group and the world around it" (1978:7).

Two broad groups of principles for combining the elementary kinds of variables shown in Fig. 7.2 will be set forth here: (1) principles pertaining to relations between causes or effects at *different* levels of a given hierarchy of causes or effects, and (2) principles pertaining to relations between causes or effects at the *same* level of a given hierarchy of causes or effects. The chapter ends by examining three interrelated theories by Durkheim, regarded as combinations of very simple elements.

It should be noted that throughout this chapter I am concerned only with the *order* in which multiple causes are held to impinge on, and the *order* in which multiple effects are held to proceed from, a given social phenomenon. I am not concerned here with what might be called the *quality* of that impingement or proceeding—for example, whether it is positive or negative. Regarding the latter question, Williams lists the following qualities of relationships which may operate, he says,

> more or less simultaneously [among] an interrelated set of independent variables: (1) both positive and negative linear correlations with dependent variables (2) both positive and negative curvilinear correlations with dependent variables (3) multiple collinearity among independent variables . . . (4) initial thresholds [below which a given independent variable shows no effect] (5) terminal thresholds [above which a given independent variables shows no effect] (6) reversals-of-effect at increasing or decreasing values of some independent variables in relation to some dependent variables (1976:320).[1]

HIERARCHICALLY STRUCTURED CAUSES OR EFFECTS

It will be recalled that Chapter 6 insisted on the purely descriptive character of the concept of hierarchic structure. Because that concept is abstract, content-free,

---

[1] It should be thankfully noted that Williams adds: "this devil's brew is not wholly unmanageable," and cites some instances of its having been managed.

and (in principle) may be applied to literally anything, it may also be applied to "causes" and "effects." Thus, although a causal hierarchy remains descriptive, what it describes in this case are aggregative relations between causes and between effects—or, more precisely, between phenomena explicitly regarded as one or the other. Hierarchic structure here is exemplified by the familiar analytic assumption that some appropriate aggregate of micro causes or micro effects (e.g., income, managerial status, property ownership, educational attainment) may be treated, at the meso level, as a single cause or single effect (e.g., social class), and that when this cause or effect is appropriately aggregated with others at a similar level (e.g., ascriptive status, or the aggregate of race, gender, ethnicity, and age), that aggregate may, in turn, be treated at the macro level as a single cause or single effect (e.g., overall status in the society at large). Causes or effects at levels higher than whatever the analyst regards as micro may often be termed "global" variables (when the nature of internal relationships within the aggregate is not specified), or "systemic" variables (when the internal relationships are specified as partly or wholly interactive).

Apart from the simplification that hierarchic causal structure obviously lends to explanations and predictions, the most important analytic feature of such structure is that the principles of "emergence" and "contextuality" derive from it. By emergence[2] I mean the hierarchically "upward" influence whose result is that an aggregate of causes or effects may constitute a new cause or new effect—and by contextuality I mean the hierarchically "downward" influence whose result is that an aggregate of causes or effects may constrain its own components to operate in ways they would not outside that aggregation.

Emergence and Contextuality

To illustrate the emergence case we have Durkheim's argument that

> Whenever certain elements combine and thereby produce, by the fact of their combination, new phenomena, it is plain that these new phenomena reside not in the original elements but in the totality formed by their union. The living cell contains nothing but mineral particles, as society contains nothing but individuals. Yet it is patently impossible for the phenomena characteristic of life to reside in the atoms of hydrogen, oxygen, carbon, and nitrogen (1938:xlvii).

[2] Nagel says "The doctrine of emergence is sometimes formulated as a thesis about the hierarchical organization of things and processes, and the consequent occurrence of properties at 'higher' levels of organization which are not predictable from properties found at 'lower' levels" (1961:366). Blau, however, defines "emergent properties" without explicit reference to hierarchic structure and therefore ambiguously when he says they are "essentially relationships between elements in a structure. The relationships are not contained in the elements, though they could not exist without them" (1964:3).

Similarly, Boulding argues that "atoms are an arrangement of protons and electrons, molecules of atoms, cells of molecules, plants, animals and men of cells, social organizations of men" (1968:5). Blau argues that "the concept of social exchange directs attention to the emergent properties in interpersonal relations and social interaction" insofar as "social exchange . . . cannot be accounted for by the psychological process that motivates the behavior of the partners" (1964:4). Gellner refers to an entirely quantitative emergence as many lower-level causes are aggregated into one higher-level cause:

> very small differences in individual conduct distributed irregularly over a large population may have important consequences for the society at large without being detectable individually. The argument in favour of "social facts" is historically connected with the presence of statistical regularities where none can be found at the molecular, individual level (1973:252).

To illustrate the contextuality case, we have Powers' picture of individual "human behavioral organization as it would exist after learning is essentially complete":

> This model consists of a hierarchical structure of feedback control organizations in which higher-order systems perceive and control an environment composed of lower-order systems. . . . Each level of organization but the lowest corrects its own errors by altering the definition of the reference condition [goal] for the level below (1973:78, 51–52).

Blau relies on the same principle, but applies it to behavioral organization between different individuals rather than within the same individual, when he describes "structural effects" in social phenomena:

> [If] it turns out that within each category of individuals [who are] about equally ready to talk about their problems those who belong to groups where frequent discussion is prevalent perform better than those in other groups, then it is demonstrated that the network of communication itself influences performance (1957:64).

Thus, an aggregate of working individuals may constrain the work of each individual participant in that aggregate. Similar findings are reported by sociobiologists. Chen, for example, finds that

> The amount of work accomplished is more when ants work in association than when they work in isolation. . . . The accelerating effect of association

is greater for the slow workers than for the rapid workers. The rapid co-worker has an accelerating effect, and the slow co-worker has a retarding effect, upon the work of an individual (1969:39–40).

Also relying on the principle of hierarchical contextuality, Laumann and Pappi claim that

> The hallmark of a network analysis . . . is to explain, at least in part, the behavior of network elements (i.e., the nodes) and of the system as a whole by appealing to specific features of the interconnections among the elements (1976:20).

If we ask what accounts for the emergence of a new cause or effect from the aggregation of old ones, and what accounts for the contextual constraint upon a single cause or effect by its being aggregated with others, the answers seem to be "structure," in the first instance, and "environment," in the second. That is, it is the relationships *internal* to the aggregate in question (i.e., its structure) that account for its manifesting a new cause or new effect, and it is the relationships *external* to the single cause or effect in question (i.e., its environment) that account for its operating under new constraints. Thus, on the one hand, Harré says that

> In the physical and biological sciences the existence of an emergent property is explained by introducing hypotheses of *structure*. . . . When iron molecules are brought together to form a key, the emergent property or power that the key has to open a lock is explained by the structure of the key, a structure which reflects a myriad relationships between individual iron molecules (1981:142–143).

On the other hand, after asking the contextuality question of "How are individuals influenced by having their being in collectives?" Harré says

> Some properties that are attributed to individuals are clearly constituted by virtue of that individual standing in a certain relation to some other. For instance though we say that this or that woman is a wife, that state is constituted wholly by virtue of the woman standing in the marriage relation to a husband (1981:145).

Finally on this point, it hardly needs emphasis that both emergence and contextuality are empirically problematic (new causes or effects do not always measurably emerge from the aggregation of old ones, nor are single causes or effects always measurably constrained by the aggregate of which they are parts), and non-deterministic (in any given aggregate, both higher- and lower-level elements are apt to retain some degree of autonomy from each other). Thus, referring back to Harré's examples: molecules of air cannot be aggregated into keys; a molecule of iron is probably no more constrained by being part of a key than by being part of a lock; and though she may become a wife, a woman does not thereby give up being a woman.

Now consider some appeals simultaneously to the principle of emergence and the principle of contextuality. Thus, Harré says "[there is a] place for hypotheses about the existence of macrosocial orders, having emergent properties by virtue of some structural feature of the total flux of intended and unintended consequences of interpersonal social actions," and "the macro-orders serve as selection environments exerting a diffuse influence upon the course of life" (1981:156, 158–159); and Bourdieu contrasts, on the one hand,

> a "structuralist" view which tends to see structural and morphological characteristics as . . . mechanisms capable of defining their own teleology and imposing it on their agents; and, on the other hand, an "interactionist" or psychosociological view which tends to see . . . practices as the product of the agents' interactions and strategies (1981:312).

Parsons, too, seems to have in mind both principles when he claims the cultural system, social system, personality system, and behavioral organism form a "hierarchy of controlling factors" when read in that order as if from the top down and a "hierarchy of conditioning factors" when read in reverse order as if from the bottom up (1966:28, 113, emphasis added; see also Turner and Maryanski, 1979:80–81).[3]

Now, having argued that relations between causes or between effects at *different* hierarchic levels may be categorized as emergence and contextuality, let us see how we may categorize causal relations between causes or between effects at the *same* hierarchic level.

RELATIONS WITHIN THE SAME LEVEL OF A CAUSAL HIERARCHY

In the most elementary sense, it seems that only the following causal relations are possible between any two causal variables at the same hierarchic level: The first

---

[3] Smelser, too, is concerned with the hierarchically upward and downward (i.e., conditioning and controlling) flow of influence: "The general principle for reconstituting social action is this: when strain exists, attention shifts to the higher levels of the components to seek resources to overcome this strain" (1962:67).

influences the second (i.e., the balance of causes and effects between them favors the first), the second influences the first, they influence each other equally, or neither influences the other. In each case, however, one may also wish to consider any of a potentially infinite number of variables that intervene causally (i.e., to facilitate, inhibit, or transform the flow of influence) between the original pair, and one may wish to consider any of a potentially infinite number of variables that share a similar status (i.e., as co-cause or co-effect) with either member of the original pair. Let us consider, then, the three basic types of models (and their most important subtypes) that may be applied to such an expanded roster of causal variables: the enumerative model, the sequential model, and the interactive model—as portrayed in Fig. 12.1.

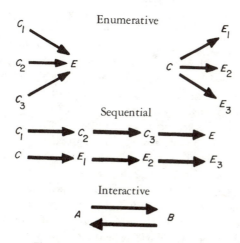

Figure 12.1. Basic types of causal models.

Enumerative

The first model is merely a list of causes of a given social phenomenon regarded as effect, or effects of that phenomenon regarded as a cause. Here the analyst only lists the relevant variables, without specifying their temporal order. Durkheim (1951) provides an example insofar as his four causes of suicide (egoism, anomie, altruism, and fatalism) are not temporally ordered. Now consider four important variants of the enumerative model.

CONVERGENCE AND CONTRIBUTION, DIVERGENCE AND DIFFERENTIATION

The variants in question describe *mutually exclusive,* alternative, causal paths leading to and from a given social phenomenon (i.e., convergence and divergence paths),[4] and *mutually complementary,* contributory or coalescing paths to it and distributory or "differentiation" paths away from it.

Ogburn provides an example of the convergence, all-roads-lead-to-Rome, model: "the same invention [does not demand] always the same cultural history. Two different cultural situations may result in the same invention or what appears to be the same invention" (1933:87). Gouldner's conception of "crisis" in Western sociology exemplifies the divergence, fork-in-the-road model: "The central implication of a crisis is not, of course, that the 'patient will die.' Rather, the implication is that a system in crisis may, relatively soon, become something quite different than it has been . . . it may change radically or may even fail to survive, in some sense" (1970:341, emphasis removed). Using a similar image, Eisenstadt and Curelaru say "the impact [of crises in sociology] might be productive *or* destructive" (1976:72, emphasis added). Inkeles employs both convergence and divergence models: "Convergence [among industrialized societies] is most dramatically and unambiguously illustrated by birth and fertility rates. . . . [for] it seems that the industrial nations are all converging on a condition of zero population growth by bringing the reproduction rate down to 1." On the other hand, however, "Divergence is most dramatically illustrated in the realm of production and the generation of physical wealth" (1981:14, 23).

The contributions, many-hands-make-light-work, model informs Durkheim when he says "different social causes of suicide . . . may simultaneously affect the same individual and impose their combined effects upon him" (1951:145). Durkheim also employs the differentiation model when describing the division of labor as "the sharing of functions up to that time common" (1933:276)—as do Marx and Engels when claiming that "the division of labor implies . . . the fact that intellectual and material activity . . . devolve on different individuals" (1978:159), where formerly both activities devolved on the same individual.

Sequential

In this second basic model (often called a causal "chain") a temporal order is specified among multiple causes and/or among multiple effects, thereby differen-

---

[4] See the discussion of equifinality and equioriginality in Chapter 14.

tiating them according to their proximity to the "final" effect or the "initial" cause on which the analysis focuses. For example, Douglas' analysis of religion proposes the following sequence: instinctivistic "yearning for rigidity" → social structuralistic "ritual" → cultural structuralistic "danger beliefs" → society. Thus, she claims "The yearning for rigidity is in us all. [Because it] is part of our human condition to long for hard lines and clear concepts," religious and other "ideas about separating, purifying, demarcating and punishing transgressions have as their main function to impose system on an inherently untidy experience." But since "it is a mistake to suppose that there can be religion which is all interior, with no . . . external signs of inward states," "rituals [generate] the necessary sentiments . . . to hold men to their roles"—and such sentiments prominently include "danger-beliefs . . . [i.e.,] threats which one man uses to coerce another [and] dangers which he himself fears to incur" (1969:162, 4, 62, 65, 3).

Note that a sequential causal model may be given the appearance of circularity, as when Homans says

> Assuming that there is established between the members of a group any set of relations satisfying the condition that the group survives for a time in its particular environment . . . we can show that on the foundation of these relations the group will develop new ones, that the latter will modify or even create the relations we assumed at the beginning, and that, finally, the behavior of the group, besides being determined by the environment, will itself change the environment (1950:91).

Homans himself seems to regret that his description "sounds circular" (1950:91), but he does not explain what is wrong with this circularity, and even confusingly reverses his argument and refers to "the problem of describing a cycle as a sequence of events" (1950:93), thereby implying that the difficulty lies with the sequentiality and not the circularity of his description. Insofar as causal circularity is sometimes called "feedback" (such that one might say, in the above propositions from Homans, that social behavior feeds back to the environment), let us turn to this causal model next. Brief discussions following that will examine, in turn, the diffusion/concentration, and value-added/value-subtracted causal models—also viewed as variants of the basic sequential causal model.

FEEDBACK: HOMEOSTASIS, EXPLOSION, AND COLLAPSE

The essential point here (already suggested in the discussion of functional social structuralism found in Chapter 9) is that the term "feedback" is somewhat misleading; the image it describes is always and necessarily "feedforward" in time.

That is, although we may speak of *spatial* circularity, we may not legitimately speak of *temporal* circularity because nothing acting in the present can affect anything in the past. Thus, when Stinchcombe says "By a functional explanation we mean one in which the consequences of some behavior or social arrangements are essential elements of the causes of *that* behavior" (1968:80, emphasis changed), we cannot take what he says literally. The only possible thing Stinchcombe can mean is that in a functional explanation the consequences of some given behavior are essential elements in the causes of the *next*, similar but not identical, behavior.

Indeed, Stinchcombe immediately (but unknowingly) abandons the impossible circularity of his own definition by substituting the prior *wanting* of a consequence for the later *occurrence* of that consequence: "When we say that someone wants a car, that generals want to win a war, that people generally do not want to be sick, and use this to explain their behavior, we are saying that the consequences of their behavior are its principle cause" (1968:80). Obviously, by this account, it is not the *actual* consequence—not the possession of the car, the winning of the war, the being not sick—but the anticipatory *wanting* of these things that Stinchcombe himself, in the end, believes causes the behaviors in question.[5] "Wanting," however, assumes there has been some prior experience with something similar to the wanted thing, and assumes also that that past experience is being fed forward in time to the presently behaving individual—through memory, if the experience happened to the individual, or through genes if the experience happened to the species—as motivations for the individual's behavior.

In order to derive a homeostatic or steady-state causal model from the general feedback model—explicated as above—we have to impose a special "equilibrating" restriction that may be described as follows: if most causal variables in a given sequence are positively related to their effects, at least one cause must be negatively related to its effect to an extent that more or less exactly counterbalances the others' net positive effects on some criterion effect—or vice versa (see Buckley, 1967:53; and von Bertalanffy, 1968:17). Figure 12.2 represents this sequence where the illustrative (because simple) case is that of room temperature, thermostat, and furnace.

Room temperature$_1$ — Thermostat call$_1$ + Furnace heat$_1$ + Room temperature$_2$

Figure 12.2. Homeostatic (negative feedback) causal model.

Here we see that a decrease in room temperature may lead to an increase in the thermostat's call for heat, leading to an increase in the furnace's output of heat.

---

[5] Similarly, Jeans argues that

If a student is working hard in the hope of passing an examination, it is argued that the present spell of hard work is the effect of a future cause, namely an examination which is to be held at some future date. But it is surely more true to say that the cause is not the examination—which after all may never take place . . . but the hope of passing the examination (1958:210).

The latter raises room temperature, which lowers the thermostat's call for heat, which lowers the furnace's output of heat, etc. In an ideal setup of this kind—one that has unlimited fuel and where the thermostat's calls for heat exactly anticipate the direction and amount of room temperature changes and exactly compensate for time-lags in the system—room temperature will remain constant within set tolerance limits: "The thermostat will maintain *any* temperature at which it can be set [because if the difference between an observed or recorded value of the maintained variable and its ideal value] is not zero the system moves so as to diminish it" (Boulding, 1968:7).

Applying the homeostatic negative feedback sequence to familiar human social phenomena, one could hypothesize that a decrease in the market supply of a given commodity may lead to an increase in its market price, which may lead to an increase in production of the commodity, a consequent increase in its market supply, a decline in its market price—and so on (for an analysis of heterosexual love that elaborates on this image, see Blau, 1964:76–85). Or one could hypothesize that a decrease in popular demonstrations against war may lead to an increase in wars, which may then increase popular dissatisfaction with them, leading to increased popular demonstrations against them, their subsequent decrease, etc.

In both of the latter cases, as in the room temperature-thermostat-furnace one, the sequence has been described as homeostatic—oscillating around some equilibrium point. In all three cases, however, the sequence can be transformed into one of explosion, or of collapse, by substituting positive for negative feedback. Thus, should the thermostat respond to high room temperature by calling for still more heat, or should an increase in market supply be met by increase in market price, or should increase in antiwar demonstrations be met by increase in wars, the process would become explosive (and should decrease be met by decrease, the process would become one of collapse or implosion).

Note that just as a single thermostat-furnace hookup may maintain any of a variety of temperatures and different thermostat-furnace hookups may therefore maintain different temperatures, just so, as Buckley says, "We have to be prepared for the possibility that a social system may generate and maintain deviant and disorganizing forces in just as 'automatic' a way as it generates mechanisms of conformity and organization" (1967:163; see also Durkheim, 1938:70–73; Merton, 1957:131–160; and Erikson, 1966:13–14, 19).

DIFFUSION AND CONCENTRATION

These variants of the basic sequential model combine it with variants of the basic enumerative model: the diffusion model represents a succession of differentia-

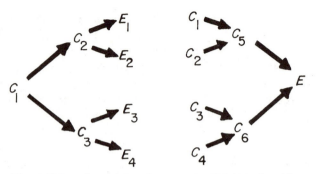

Figure 12.3. Diffusion (left) and concentration (right) causal models.

tion phases, while the concentration model represents a succession of coalescing phases. Figure 12.3 depicts both.

The diffusion model is illustrated by Ogburn's argument:

> The influence of an invention does not always end with its first derivative effects. For the derivative effect may become in turn a cause of a second derivative effect. Thus the loss of passengers on railroads because of the use of automobiles may lead to a reorganization of a railroad, and abandonment of short-haul tracks off the main line, or a modernization of equipment—all second derivative influences of the invention of the automobile. . . . The impact of an invention may continue through many derivatives (1957b:19–20).

A similar picture is presented by Wilson in describing the spreading consequences for a troop of Japanese macaques of their being provisioned with food on the beach by human observers:

> Young monkeys began to enter the water to bathe and splash, especially during hot weather. The juveniles learned to swim, and a few even began to dive and bring up seaweed from the bottom. One left Koshima and swam to a neighboring island. By a small extension in dietary opportunity, the Koshima group had adopted a new way of life (1975:171).

Lumsden and Wilson have the diffusion model in mind when they say

> it seems . . . likely that weak innate dispositions toward the adoption of one subset of culturgens out of a larger set available . . . can be amplified under certain conditions into much larger events in cultural evolution. For example, the relatively minor innate differences in early temperament in young boys and girls . . . are magnified into consistent role differences in all societies, including extreme male dominance in a few (1981:20; see also 110).

The concentration model is illustrated by Hart's idea of "invention by combination": "every invention consists of a new combination of old elements. For example, an airplane is a combination of a box-kite, a windmill, a gasoline engine, a pilot, and the atmosphere, each of these (except the atmosphere) being adapted by various modifications" (1957:48)—and each of which is a combination of prior inventions. A similar picture is presented by Campbell's description of ant, termite, and bee shelters (Campbell calls it an "apartment-house mode of living") as combining "a storable food supply and a full-time division of labor, including members who are fed rather than gathering their own food" (1965b:42–43). Concentration is also the causal model adopted in Eisenstadt's concept of "coalescent change" among the different institutions and collectivities of a given society (see 1978a:90; 1978b:80).

VALUE-ADDED/VALUE-SUBTRACTED

In this complication, two or more causal sequences interweave such that a sequence of effects is brought about by one or more sequences of causes. In the value-added model, the final effect is "built-up," "shaped," or "put together" by causes occurring in a particular sequence. In its converse (let us call it the "value-subtracted" model), that process is reversed and the final effect is created by "deprogramming," "dismantling," or "purification"—that is, by successively stripping away extraneous effects—through the impingement of a particular sequence of causes, as shown in Fig. 12.4. In each case, the operation of a given cause is dependent on all the causes before it having operated in their proper sequence. Figure 12.4 may be read, in the value-added direction, as follows: Given an initial phenomenon as effect E_1) of some prior and analytically extraneous cause, the first cause (C_1) produces E_2 from E_1; C_2 then produces E_3 from E_2, and C_3 finally produces E_4 from E_3. The same diagram may be read as value-subtracted when the C_1, C_2, and C_3 sequence reduces rather than elaborates on each successive E. Smelser relies on the value-added causal model (and of all the analysts mentioned here, he is the only one who does so by name) as mainstay of his theory of collective behavior: "Many determinants or necessary conditions, must be present for any kind of collective episode to occur. These determinants must combine, however, in a definite pattern" (1962:14; see also LeBon's very similar discussion of "remote factors" and "immediate factors" in determining the opinions and beliefs of crowds, 1962:80).

Ogburn uses a value-added model when he asserts that

> machines employing the wheel can not be constructed or invented until the existing culture has achieved the wheel. Similarly certain technical develop-

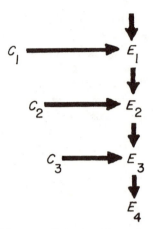

Figure 12.4. Value-added (value-subtracted) causal model.

ments could hardly occur without the knowledge of smelting iron. . . . The underlying cultural achievements necessary for the construction of a modern printing press, may conceivably run into the thousands or indeed millions (1933:82).

Lenski argues that a prehistoric social structuralistic variable (big-game hunting) added its value directly to prior social structuralistic variables, as well as indirectly (via natural selection) to materialistic and instinctivistic variables, in helping to determine the evolution of human social phenomena:

> big-game hunting seems to have strengthened the relatively weak social bonds among males and between males and females, thus supplementing the already strong primate bonds among females and between females and their offspring. In addition, many scholars now believe that the rise of big-game hunting played a critical role in the growth of the hominid brain and in the development of speech. If all this is true, there has never been a more critical development in human history from the standpoint of impact on social structure (1975:144).

Hogan presents a value-added image of the process of growing-up in the present-day United States:

> the passage to adulthood is achieved in a socially prescribed manner when a man first finishes his formal schooling, next becomes financially independent through employment at a full-time job, and finally forms his own family of procreation through marriage. . . . [A] disorderly sequencing of life cycle events is viewed as disrupting the natural harmony between a man's own life

style and the institutional structure which provides the social context in which he lives (1978:385).

Westoff and Rindfuss present a combination of technologistic (sex control technologies), social structuralistic (use of such technologies), and cultural structuralistic (women's preferences regarding the sex of their children) variables in a combined multiple contributions and value-added image that predicts damped oscillations—that is, a cyclical time-path where the amplitude of cycles devolves (see Chapter 5)—in the sex ratio at birth:

> If effective sex control technologies were rapidly and widely adopted in the United States, the current sex preferences of married women indicate that the temporary effect would be a surplus of male births in the first couple of years. This would be followed by a wave of female births to achieve balance, and the oscillations would eventually damp out. Ultimately, under conditions of sex predetermination, the sex ratio would be similar to the existing natural sex ratio at birth of 105 (1974:636).

Several examples of value-subtracted or purification causal models may be cited. One is present in Marx and Engels' claim that "the estrangement, the alienation of the worker" (1978:73), having been harmfully value-added to the worker's innately human "species character" (1978:76) by class society, must eventually be value-substracted from it—thereby enabling the worker to regain his/her species character in pure form and, with the aid of advanced technology, to become "conscious lord of Nature" (1978:715, see also Chapter 11 here). Another may be found in Freud's opinion that " 'As we analyze [the torn mind of the neurotic patient] and remove the resistances, it grows together; the great unity which we call his ego fits into itself all the instinctual impulses which before had been split off and held apart from it' " (quoted in Habermans, 1971:233). A third is present in Berger's definition of "secularization":

> By secularization we mean the process by which sectors of society and culture are removed from the domination of religious institutions and symbols. . . . [S]ecularization manifests itself in the evacuation by the Christian churches of areas previously under their control or influence—as in the separation of church and state (1969:107).

And Goffman provides a fourth in his description of how "the [mental hospital] prepatient starts out with at least a portion of the rights, liberties, and satisfactions of the civilian and ends up on a psychiatric ward stripped of almost everything" (1961:140). Goffman also indicates that such severe value-subtraction may lead to a crisis (see the discussion of divergence causal models above) from which the patient may either undergo a new value-additive process or remain in a "stripped" state:

> In the usual cycle of adult socialization one expects to find alienation and mortification followed by a new set of beliefs about the world and a new way of conceiving of selves. In the case of the mental-hospital patient, this rebirth does sometime occur. . . . [but sometimes the] moral career of the mental patient . . . can illustrate the possibility that in casting off the raiments of the old self—or in having this cover torn away—the person. . . . can learn, at least for a time, to practise before all groups the amoral arts of shameless-less (1961:169).

Finally, in this connection, note that value-added and value-subtracted models are further specified by "thresholds"—discontinuities in the difficulty of producing a given cause (i.e., its scarcity) in the sequence that builds up toward some looked-for, "final" effect. Every cause in the sequence, of course, crosses a threshold to the extent that its scarcity differs from that of the causes preceding and following it, but some differences may be large enough, by some arbitrary criterion, to call discontinuities.

There are two kinds of thresholds (corresponding to the revolutionary and cat-astrophic time-paths and the two fault spatial discontinuities discussed in Chapter 5): there is the threshold represented by the cause that begins a segment of the overall sequence whose component causes are scarcer than those of the segment *preceding* it, and there is the cause that begins a segment of causes that are scarcer than the segment *following* it. In the first case, crossing the threshold is like climb-ing up a cliff to a plateau or "ceiling"; in the second case, it is like falling off a cliff to a "floor." When both cases are combined (that is, when a given cause begins a segment that is scarcer than the one that follows it as well as the one that precedes it), we speak, appropriately, of getting "over the hump."

Rostow employs the value-added model with an over-the-hump threshold in his analysis of stages in economic history. Thus, after placing the many different so-cieties of the "pre-Newtonian world" in "a single category [called 'traditional so-ciety'] on the ground that they all shared a ceiling on the productivity of their economic techniques," he argues that "the take-off awaited not only the build-up of social overhead capital and a surge of technological development in industry and agriculture, but also the emergence to political power of a group prepared to re-gard the modernization of the economy as serious, high-order political business" (Rostow, 1960:5, 8). The beginning of take-off itself

> can usually be traced to a particular sharp stimulus . . . [which] may take the form of a political revolution . . . [or] a technological (including trans-port) innovation . . . [or] a newly favorable international environment. . . . [or] a challenge posed by an unfavorable shift in the international environ-ment (Rostow, 1960:36).

Whatever the stimulus, take-off itself follows a rapid diffusion, multiplier model:

> During the take-off, new industries expand rapidly, yielding profits a large
> proportion of which are reinvested in new plant; and these new industries, in
> turn, stimulate, through their rapidly expanding requirement for factory
> workers, the services to support them, and for other manufactured goods, a
> further expansion in urban areas and in other modern industrial plants (Ros-
> tow, 1960:8).

After take-off, "there follows a long interval of sustained if fluctuating progress,
as the now regularly growing economy drives to extend modern technology over
the whole front of its economic activity"; and, finally, "Some sixty years after take-
off begins (say, forty years after the end of take-off) what may be called maturity
is generally attained" (Rostow, 1960:8, 9).

Inkeles provides an illustration of the threshold-to-ceiling causal model when
he argues that

> Thresholds evidently exist with regard to the effectiveness of school systems.
> Once an essentially modern school system is in place, and certain basic stan-
> dards for facilities, books, and teacher training are achieved, further invest-
> ment to increase the expenditure per pupil seems not to produce any signifi-
> cant improvement in the academic performance of students taking standardized
> tests (1981:17).

He also provides an illustration of the threshold-to-floor model: "a nation may
move rapidly from high to low death rates for children 5–14 years of age, but
. . . once the rate is down to 50 per thousand, further reduction is very difficult
to achieve" (Inkeles, 1981:18).

Interactive

The interactive causal image represents two-way, mutual, influence between
variables such as Kleck exemplifies when describing "a deadly circularity of gun
ownership and homicide, homicide pushing up gun ownership and gun ownership
at the same time pushing up homicide . . . crime is a cause of gun ownership
just as gun ownership is a cause of crime" (1979:908). The interactive causal image
is, therefore, an enumerative or a sequential image that has been complicated by
reciprocation—such that, in the extreme case, one variable influences another and
that other simultaneously influences the first variable.

As we move away from that hypothetical extreme of perfect simultaneity, however, the lag between the phase in which the first variable influences the second and the phase in which the second variable influences the first increases. Thus, Homans includes a noticeable but brief lag between phases when he says "Perhaps the simplest example of interaction . . . is two men at opposite ends of a saw, sawing a log. When we say that the two are interacting [we mean] that the push of one man on the saw is followed by the push of the other" (1950:36). It does not take much modification to use Homans' example as illustrating an interaction phase-lag: simply noting that the push of one man influences the *pull* of the other is enough to reduce the lag to the time it takes the push to travel the length of the saw. But what happens when phase-lag increases beyond that between the push of one man on a saw and the push of another; what happens when it increases to minutes, hours, months, years, centuries, millennia, and longer?

First, of course, at the millennia-and-longer end we may simply never find out that what appears to fit only a one-way enumerative or sequential image really fits an interactive image better. Down toward the years-months-hours-minutes end, where interaction is clearly noticeable, special mechanisms may come into play that reduce the effect of phase-lag by stabilizing or otherwise preparing the first variable (e.g., individual A) so that it is more receptive to influence from the second variable (e.g., individual B), when that variable does emit its influence, than it would otherwise be after the lag. Memory, of course, is such a mechanism, and so are writing (for example, A's carbon copy of a letter sent to B), money, warehouses, trust, and the consequence expectation of cultural norms (see Chapter 4).

Social structuralism in sociology, especially its exchange and conflict varieties, relies most heavily on the interactive causal image, and both Spencer and Simmel should be cited as mentioning phase-lag mechanisms when they refer to the role, in interaction, of the intermediary or go-between (the "distributive" and "internuncial" systems in Spencer's case, and the "mediator" and "arbitrator" in Simmel's case).

DIALECTICAL

The dialectical causal model incorporates with the interactive model certain features of the enumerative and sequential models, as indicated in Fig. 12.5. Here, one phenomenon, called "synthesis," differentiates into two mutually contradictory phenomena called "thesis" and "antithesis," and after a period of increasingly intense interaction the latter two coalesce into a new synthesis, which then differentiates into a second interactive thesis and antithesis—and so on. Marx and Engels' argument exemplifies this image: "The history of all hitherto existing society is the history of class struggles. . . . [Here,] in a word, oppressor and oppressed

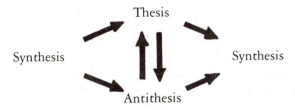

Figure 12.5. Dialectical causal model.

stood in constant opposition to one another [and] carried on . . . a fight that each time ended, either in a revolutionary re-constitution of society at large, or in the common ruin of the contending classes" (1978:473–474).

Note that the dialectical causal image is usually teamed with a two-phase temporal regularity (see Chapter 5) such that the phase during which thesis and antithesis coalesce is regarded as rapid and revolutionary, while the phase during which thesis and antithesis interact is regarded as slow and evolutionary. In the short-run, then, the dialectical process takes on the aspect of a series of positive steps in an overall evolution. However, that that series is to be regarded as only one half of a longer-run cycle that includes a series of negative steps in an overall devolution is also proposed by Engels:

> Nevertheless, all that comes into being deserves to perish. Millions of years may elapse, hundreds of thousands of generations be born and die, but inexorably the time will come . . . when gradually even the last trace of organic life will vanish; and the earth, an extinct frozen globe like the moon, will circle in deepest darkness and in an ever narrower orbit about the equally extinct sun, and at last fall into it. . . . And what will happen to our solar system will happen sooner or later to all the other systems of our cosmic island, will happen to those of all the other innumerable cosmic islands, even to those the light of which will never reach the earth while there is a living human eye to receive it (1968:354).

Engels speculates that such long-run cycles (some modern opponents of the permanently-expanding-universe theory would call them "oscillations") should be regarded as an *endless* series insofar as

> the incandescent raw material for the solar systems of our cosmic island was produced in a natural way . . . the conditions of which, therefore, must be reproduced by matter, even if only after millions and millions of years, more or less accidentally, but with the necessity that is also inherent in accident. . . . It is an eternal cycle in which matter moves . . . [and] with the same iron necessity with which it will again exterminate on the earth its highest

creation, the thinking mind, it must somewhere else and at another time again engender it (1968:355, 356–357).

Now, by way of brief illustration of how a few of the causal models discussed above may be combined, consider the theories contained in Durkheim's three main works, which are descussed below.

DURKHEIM'S COMBINATIONS OF CAUSAL MODELS AND THE VARIABLES THEY CONTAIN

Figure 12.6 summarizes the single overall causal model to which *The Division of Labor in Society, Suicide,* and *The Elementary Forms of the Religious Life* each make distinctive contributions, as follows: (1) *The Division of Labor* hypothesizes a mutually sustaining interaction between social structure and cultural structure at the societal level; (2) *Suicide* hypothesizes that these structures form a context for, and thus influence, individuals' psychical behaviors (which then influence their physical behavior); and (3) *The Elementary Forms* hypothesizes that social structure and cultural structure at the societal level emerge from, and are thus influenced by, individuals' physical behaviors (which are, in turn, influenced by their psychical behaviors). In a nutshell, then, Durkheim's overall causal model argues for the integration of society and for the integration of the individual with society.

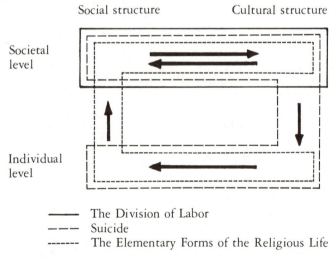

— The Division of Labor
--- Suicide
------ The Elementary Forms of the Religious Life

Figure 12.6. Overall causal model of Durkheim's three main works.

The Division of Labor In Society

Underlying the first work mentioned above is the causal model portrayed in Fig. 12.7.

Here Durkheim uses an enumerative causal model, citing a demographistic variable (population increase) and an ecologistic one (natural resource relative decline) as contributing causes of increased social structural competition, and then employs a causal sequence leading to an increase in the division of labor.[6] Thus:

> If work becomes divided more as societies become more voluminous and denser, it is . . . because struggle for existence is more acute. . . . As long as [two organisms] have more resources than they need, they can still live side by side, but if their number increases . . . war breaks out. . . . It is quite otherwise if the co-existing individuals are of different species or varieties. As they do not feed in the same manner, and do not lead the same kind of life, they do not disturb each other. . . . Men submit to the same law. In the same city, different occupations can co-exist without being obliged mutually to destroy one another, for they pursue different objects (1933:266–267).

What was the state of society, however, before that population increase and mutual competition? Durkheim calls its social structure "segmental" and says "What characterizes it is a system of segments homogeneous and similar [in function] to each other" (1933:181; see also 174), and calls its cultural structure "mechanical solidarity"—saying it "comes from a certain number of states of conscience which are common to all the members of the same society" (1933:109). These two,

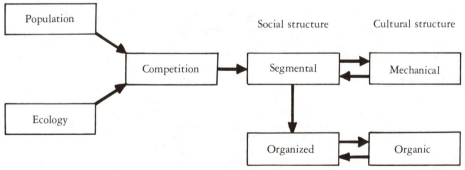

Figure 12.7. Principal causal model of Durkheim's *The Division of Labor in Society*.

[6] In his only definition of "the division of labor" in the book of that title, Durkheim says only that it "consists in the sharing of functions up to that time common" (1933:276), and centers his definition of "function" on "movements . . . of the organism" (1933:49). On this admittedly slender basis, it seems fair to characterize the division of labor as social structural.

segmental social structure and mechanical solidarity cultural structure,[7] sustain each other so long as population and natural resources remain in balance and at low levels.

When the population increase and consequent competition mentioned above add their value to the homogeneity of segmental social structure, division of labor increases and a new, "organized" (Durkheim, 1933:302), social structure is the result—characterized by "a system of different organs each of which has a special role, and which are themselves formed of different parts" (1933:181). This new social structure then produces a new cultural structure called "organic solidarity." Here, Durkheim says whereas in mechanical solidarity "the proper duty of man is to resemble his companions, . . . in [organic solidarity] his nature is, in large part, to be an organ of society, and his proper duty, consequently, to play his role as an organ" (1933:403).

Note that although Durkheim emphasizes the social structuralistic hypothesis that the division of labor initiates solidarity, he also puts forward the cultural structuralistic hypothesis that solidarity, in return, sustains the division of labor. Thus, "Though normally the division of labor produces social solidarity, it sometimes happens that it has different, even contrary results" (1933:353), and when that happens, only "abnormal forms" of the division of labor can result (see 1933:351–395). Normally, however, social structure of a certain sort, and cultural structure of an appropriately corresponding sort, form an interacting system— stable until unbalanced by exogenous demographic and/or ecological shocks.[8]

Suicide

Having developed this model of society, Durkheim next seeks to demonstrate, among other things,[9] that structures at that level have contextual consequences for behavior at the individual level. This is in line with his conviction that "social facts . . . [are] endowed with a power of coercion, by reason of which they control [the individual]" (1938:3).

---

[7]Unfortunately, Durkheim repeatedly confuses social structure and cultural structure and refers to the division of labor not only as an aspect of the former but as an aspect of the latter as well. For example, he asserts that "It is the division of labor which, more and more, fills the role that was formerly filled by the common conscience" (1933:173; see also 41, 129, 131, 147). But this is a profoundly misleading statement given the underlying schematics of Durkheim's theory: it is organic solidarity (and not the division of labor which produces that solidarity) that "fills the role that was formerly filled by the common conscience"—or more exactly, by mechanical solidarity.

[8]Other interpretations of Durkheim's *The Division of Labor* may by found in Parsons (1937:308–324); Lukes (1975:147–178); Coser (1977:129–132); and Turner and Maryanski (1979:18–21).

[9]In *Suicide,* Durkheim seems also to be pursuing two other problems that derive from his discussion of "Abnormal Forms" of the division of labor (see 1933:353–388): (1) Can abnormality result from excess as well as deficiency?, and (2) Can social structure and cultural structure operate independently in generating abnormality?

Note, therefore, that Durkheim defines suicide as a "case of [individual] death" resulting from an act of "the [individual] victim himself" (1951:44), and declares that his aim is to "determine the nature of the *social* causes, how they produce their effects, and their relations to the *individual* states associated with the different sorts of suicides" (1951:52, emphasis added).

It is true that Durkheim employs data on the "social suicide *rate*" only, and argues that "this total is not simply a sum of independent units, a collective total, but is itself a new fact *sui generis*" (1951:46). He does this, however, not because he wants to explain these rates as such, but because he wants to explain the individual acts of which they are composed by social causes, and these causes, he argues, can only be discerned in aggregate data.[10] His rhetorical question is clearly indicative:

> But is the fact [suicide] thus defined of interest to the sociologist? Since suicide is an individual action affecting the individual only, it must seemingly depend exclusively on individual factors, thus belonging to psychology alone. Is not the suicide's resolve usually explained by his temperament, character, antecedents, and private history? (1951:46).

In *Suicide,* Durkheim answers that although it may be usually so explained, it *need* not be so explained and that there are indeed societal-level social structural and cultural structural explanations for individual acts of suicide—explanations which Durkheim indicates by the names he gives to what he calls his "aetiological" (1951:147) types of suicide.

Durkheim says many, sometimes confusing things about these types of suicide (egoistic, anomic, altruistic, and fatalistic) but his most informative statements are those in which he compares two or more types. Thus, in comparing egoistic and anomic suicide, he asserts that

> both spring from society's insufficient presence in individuals. But the sphere of its absence is not the same in both cases. In egoistic suicide it is deficient in truly collective *activity*. . . . In anomic suicide, society's influence is lacking in the basically individual *passions,* thus leaving them without a check-rein (Durkheim, 1951:258, emphasis added).[11]

---

[10] Durkheim argues that rates perform the same function in survey designs as random assignment to treatment and control groups in experimental designs: "Since each [rate] contains all the individual cases indiscriminately, the individual circumstances which may have had a share in the production of the phenomenon are neutralized and, consequently, do not contribute to its determination" (1938:8). Note, therefore, that Durkheim does not want to explain *particular* individual acts—one person's suicide is as good as another's for his purposes.

[11] Durkheim is certainly less than consistent regarding the distinction between egoistic and anomic suicide—precisely because he does not rigorously differentiate between social and cultural structure. Thus, in discussing egoistic suicide, Durkheim stresses mainly collective activity: "for a group to be said to have less common life than another means that it is less powerfully integrated. . . . It is more unified and powerful the more active and constant is the intercourse among its members. . . . So we

In order to make clear the kind of "check-rein" he has in mind, note Durkheim's remark that "the force [that constrains the passions] can only be moral. . . . Physical restraint would be ineffective; hearts cannot be touched by physico-chemical forces. . . . The appetites can be halted only by a limit they recognize as just" (1951:248–249)—thereby portraying the "check-rein" in question as the same as that "completely moral" phenomenon to which he refers in *The Division of Labor* as "social solidarity," or, in our terms, cultural structure. Further, inasmuch as Durkheim's mention of "collective *activity*" as the referent of egoism recalls his mention of "function" and "movement" as characterizing the "division of labor," it seems proper to conclude not only that anomie refers to too little cultural struc-ture (i.e., too few psychical behavior regularities between participants in society), but also that egoism refers to too little social structure (i.e., too few physical behavior regularities between participants in society).

Durkheim devotes only thirteen lines, and these only in a footnote, to fatalistic suicide[12]:

> there is a type of suicide the opposite of anomic suicide, just as egoistic and altruistic suicides are opposites. It is the suicide deriving from excessive reg-ulation, that of persons with futures pitilessly blocked and passions violently choked by oppressive discipline (1951:276).

This is a crucial description, however, because having differentiated the quality of egoistic suicide from that of anomic suicide, Durkheim here indicates that al-truistic and fatalistic suicides are simply their respective quantitative extremes, and so completes the picture: fatalism represents excessive collective regulation of the passions (i.e., too much cultural structure); anomie represents deficient collective regulation of the passions (i.e., too little cultural structure); altruism represents excessive collective activity (i.e., too much social structure); and egoism represents deficient collective activity (i.e., too little social structure).

reach the general conclusion: suicide varies inversely with degree of integration of the social groups of which the individual forms a part" (1951:202, 209). Then Durkheim proceeds apparently to confound all this by referring to egoism as the individual's *"personality"* tending to surmount the collective *person-ality"* and the "individual *ego* asserting itself to excess in the face of the social *ego*" (1951:209, emphasis added). Similarly, in discussing anomie, Durkheim stresses mainly collective *conscience* as regulatory of individual passions, but also implicates collective activity in references to expressions of "public opin-ion," "reproof" of those who do not live according to such expressions, "law," and so on (see 1951:248–250).

[12] This represents a near-oversight on Durkheim's part, arising from the fact that he does not consistently bear in mind the distinction between social structure and cultural structure. Had he done so, once he identified deficiencies in *both* (as "egoism and anomie"), his attention would have been drawn to excesses in *both*. The anomaly here is compounded by the imbalance between thirteen lines given to fatalistic suicide and a full chapter given to altruistic suicide, when, considering his avowed concern in this analysis with "contemporary" (1951:37) societies and considering his association of abnormalities of deficiency rather than excess with such societies (see 1933:353–395), Durkheim should have given equally secondary roles to them both.

Finally, it is important to note Durkheim's claim that the social causes of suicide do not operate directly on the individual's physical behavior in the act of suicide but on his/her psychical disposition (i.e., "resolve"—see the quotation above) to behave in that manner. Durkheim does not discuss how individuals might come by the cognitive knowledge of how to commit suicide (although he does suggest how they might come by the technological instruments for doing so—see 1951:292). Instead, he assumes that whoever develops the cathectic "resolve" to commit suicide automatically manifests the appropriate physical behavior.

The enumerative (contributions) and sequential model, combining social structuralistic and cultural structuralistic explanatory variables, that is implied by the above interpretation of Durkheim's *Suicide* is shown in Figure 12.8.[13] Note that although it is acknowledged here that Durkheim's theory refers to four kinds of suicide, only two variables explain them all (compare Johnson, 1965), and the effect of each variable depends upon its position on a continuum that ranges from extreme excess to extreme deficiency—such that moderation in both variables would produce the lowest levels of suicidal resolve.[14]

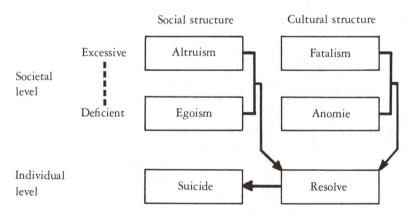

Figure 12.8. Principal causal model of Durkheim's *Suicide*.

[13] This figure contrasts sharply with Durkheim's own schematization of egoistic, altruistic, and anomic suicide (see 1951:293) in two respects: (1) Fig. 12.8 includes fatalistic suicide and Durkheim's schema does not (the latter is thereby incomplete, according to Durkheim's own expressed judgment—see 1951:276); and (2) Fig. 12.8 classifies "social types of suicide" by variations in their *social causes,* while Durkheim's schema classifies them by variations in the *"individual forms* assumed."

[14] The moderationist claim of *Suicide* (i.e., that the best society has neither too much nor too little social structure and cultural structure) is central to Durkheim's theorizing. He heralds this theme in *The Division of Labor:* "pleasure accompanies neither the very intense states of conscience, nor those very feeble. . . . Pleasure is, then, situated between these two extremes . . . human experience sees the condition of happiness in the *golden mean"* (1933:235, 237), and reiterates part of it in *The Elementary Forms:* "a very intense social life always does a sort of violence to the organism, as well as to the individual consciousness, which interferes with its normal functioning" (1965:259).

Durkheim's causal model in *Suicide* ends with an individual-level behavior; he is not concerned here with tracing the effects of individual behavior on social and cultural structure at the societal level. In fact, as we have already seen, he asserts that "suicide is an individual action affecting the *individual only.*" Durkheim's last major work, however, prominently includes an analysis of the effects of individual-level behavior on societal structures.[15]

The Elementary Forms of the Religious Life

As we have already seen in Chapter 2, Durkheim puts the distinction between social structure and cultural structure as follows:

> Religious phenomena are naturally arranged in two fundamental categories: beliefs and rites. The first are states of opinion, and consist in representations; the second are determined modes of action. Between these two classes of facts there is all the difference which separates thought from action (1965:51).

Because Durkheim immediately confounds this distinction by making "rites" designate, not physically manifested action, but psychically conceived rules ("rites are the *rules* of conduct which *prescribe* how a man *should* comport himself in the presence of . . . sacred objects" [1965:56, emphasis added]), we are left with only "beliefs" as clearly and consistently cultural structural in Durkheim's view. On the side of social structure, we have Durkheim's concept of the "concentration" of individuals and of their interactions—and it is this variable which gives rise to cultural structure (i.e., "beliefs") in much the same way that "dynamic density," and the division of labor, give rise to "social solidarity" in the *The Division of Labor*. Thus, referring to Australian aborigines, Durkheim says

> Sometimes . . . the population concentrates and gathers at determined points for a length of time varying from several days to several months. . . . When they are once come together, a sort of electricity is formed by their collecting which quickly transports them to an extraordinary degree of exaltation. . . . So it is in the midst of these effervescent social environments and out of this effervescence itself that the religious idea seems to be born (1965:246–247, 250; see also 470).[16]

[15] Other interpretations of Durkheim's *Suicide* may be found in Parsons (1937:324–338); Lukes (1975:205–222); and Coser (1977:132–136).

[16] Durkheim here prefigures Simmel's remark that in a crowd "the individual, by being carried away, carries away" (1950:35).

In other words, Durkheim holds that demographistic and ecologistic variables combine to activate psychical contagionistic variables, which then produce "the religious idea"—that is, sacred beliefs. In this way, members of a clan, by cognitively accepting the same species of animal as their sacred totem, "consider themselves united by a bond of kinship . . . [and] recognize duties towards each other . . . such duties as aid, vengeance, mourning, the obligation not to marry among themselves, etc." (1965:122), and recognize as sacred not only "the totemic emblem, the animal or plant whose appearance this emblem reproduces [but also] the members of the clan" (1965:165). These beliefs constitute individual morality and this morality in turn leads individuals to behave in certain ways—that is, not only to "recognize" duties but actually to carry them out—and it is the collective aggregate of those behaviors that constitutes the periodic reconcentration that regenerates religious beliefs, and so on.

Thus, almost explicitly acknowledging the emergence of structures at the societal level from the aggregation of individual behaviors, Durkheim says "The collective force is not entirely outside us; it does not act on us wholly from without; but rather, . . . society cannot exist except in and through individual consciousness" (1965:240), and therefore

> We now see the real reason why the gods cannot do without their worshippers any more than these can do without their gods; it is because society, of which the gods are only a symbolic expression, cannot do without individuals any more than these can do without society (1965:389).

Moreover, mindful that "if left to themselves, individual consciousnesses are closed to each other," Durkheim asserts that individuals "can communicate only by means of signs which express their internal state. . . . It is the appearance of [signs] that informs individuals that they are in harmony and makes them conscious of their moral unity" (1965:262), and with this remark heralds symbolic interactionism (see Chapter 9).

Although Durkheim's effort to "bring the individual back in" appears to be the main relevance of *The Elementary Forms* to his overall causal imagery (Fig. 12.6), it has two other relevances as well. First, by way of following up the idea expressed some 10 years earlier in his "Preface to the Second Edition" of *The Division of Labor* that

> A nation can be maintained only if, between the State and the individual, there is intercalated a whole series of secondary groups near enough to the individuals to attract them strongly in their sphere of action and drag them, in this way, into the general torrent of social life (1933:28),[17]

[17] Durkheim hints at this idea in *The Division of Labor* itself (see 1933:187, 190).

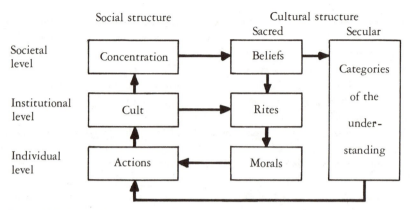

Figure 12.9. Principal causal model of Durkheim's *The Elementary Forms of the Religious Life.*

Durkheim "intercalates" the "cult" and "rites"[18] between the societal and individual levels of social structure and cultural structure, respectively. Second, *The Elementary Forms* specifies the role of religious cultural structure in the genesis of "the categories of the understanding: ideas of time, space, class, number, cause, substance, personality, etc." (1965:21–22)—that is, the social construction of reality, profane as well as sacred, physical as well as social.[19] When these features are added, we have the causal model shown in Fig. 12.9.[20]

SUMMARY

This chapter has concluded Part II and its examination of explanatory sociological analysis by considering various ways of combining two or more variables as

---

[18] Durkheim defines the cult as

> a system of diverse rites, festivals, and ceremonies which all have this characteristic, that they reappear periodically. They fulfill the need which the believer feels of strengthening and reaffirming, at regular intervals of time, the bond which unites him to the sacred beings upon which he depends (1965:80).

—and note Durkheim's stress on temporal periodicity in this interorganism behavior regularity. Insofar as a single society or tribe may have more than one cult, the cult assumes a meso-level location as do "rites," insofar as there may be several rites associated with a single belief. ["It is possible to define the rite only after we have defined the belief" (Durkheim, 1965:51).]

[19] Weber, too, causally derives a secular cultural structure (the spirit of capitalism) from a sacred one (the Protestant ethic) (1958b).

[20] Note that the complementarity between Durkheim's *Suicide* and his *Elementary Forms* suggested here is matched by the more recent one between the "anomie" theory of individual reactions to societal behavior (see Merton, 1957:131–160) and the "labeling" theory of societal reactions to individual behavior (see Kitsuse, 1962, and Becker, 1973:177–208). Other interpretations of Durkheim's *The Elementary Forms* may be found in Parsons (1937:411–450); Lukes (1975:462–474); Coser (1977:136–140); and Turner and Maryanski (1979:21–26).

they bear upon a given social phenomenon of interest (more specifically, of course, as they bear upon individual B)—either as causes or as effects of that phenomenon.

The relationship of the principles of emergence and contextuality to hierarchic structure among causes and among effects was discussed. Next, three basic models of relations between causes, or between effects, at the same hierarchical level— namely, enumerative, sequential, and interactive—were set forth. Convergence and contribution, divergence and differentiation, were presented as subtypes of the enumerative model; feedback, diffusion/concentration, and value-added/value-subtracted were presented as subtypes of the sequential model; and the dialectic was presented as a subtype of the interactive model which incorporates elements of the sequential and enumerative models as well.

Finally, three of Durkheim's theories were analyzed in terms of the basic models.

III

SCIENTIFIC PROCEDURE

13

Introduction to Part III

Parts I and II have tried to offer systematic answers to the question What are the distinctive empirical referents of scientific sociology? Part III addresses questions having to do with the overall methods and philosophical premises that scientific sociology shares in common with all other natural sciences, and closes with a discussion of some leading objections to regarding sociology as scientific and therefore to applying these methods and premises to it.

It is indeed high time to consider methodological questions, too, because contrary to Durkheim's belief that "Before inquiring into the method suited to the study of social facts, it is important to know which facts are commonly called 'social' " (1938:1), I hold that it is method, and method alone, that permits us to know which facts are called "social," or "biological," "chemical," "astronomical," "physical," "metaphysical," or whatever—whether in common, scientific, or any other parlance.

That is to say, it is only our way of perceiving, thinking, and communicating that creates the world as humanly experienced out of a substratum whose existence seems logically necessary but whose "real" nature is permanently and utterly unknowable. "The mind makes the world in which it lives," says Wilson:

> Of the near infinity of stimuli that impinge on the body moment by moment, the sense organs select only a minute fraction to relay to the central nervous system; these messages are transmitted by the afferent nerves and by the as-

355

sociated relays of the central nervous system, which codify the information by reissuing impulses according to rules built into the structure and arrangement of their respective neurons. Each organism therefore creates an *Umwelt* within the brain, a highly imperfect monitoring device by means of which it picks its way through the real world (1971:197)

Human ways of perceiving, thinking, and communicating certainly seem socially generated in part, and so there are many such ways and they change perceptibly. But (and this much I hold with the sociobiologists) whatever remains distinctively human about all those ways seems existentially imposed via the genetic inheritance of the species. The fact that we are *human*—with all the generalized but not unlimited methods implied by our possession of relatively large forebrains, primary reliance on visual stimuli, six or seven other sensory modalities, opposable thumbs, heels, verbal communication, and so forth, and that we are not, say, oysters, eagles, amebas, or baboons—must make a very significant difference in what we experience of the world. Still more fundamentally, Jeans argues that

> the world of man lies just about half-way [in a hierarchy of physical entities] between the world of the electron and the world of the nebulae . . . [and although] all objects are governed by the universal laws of physics . . . one aspect of these laws is all important for the electron, another for man-sized objects, and yet a third for the movements of the nebulae. . . . We may conjecture that a denizen of the world of the electron might vigorously challenge [propositions based on observations of the man-sized world.] . . . Our own minds [therefore] contribute something to the nature they study (1958:42, 47, 71).

The fact that we are *only* human, and not vastly superior intelligences such as seem likely to exist in other parts of the universe—that, too, must make a very significant difference in what we experience of the world. Finally, the fact that some of us humans are sociologists who look upon our discipline as a natural science, and that we are not, say, priests dispensing blessings or mystics seeking salvation must also make for a difference—surely a very small one relative to that between the average oyster and the average human, but a difference nonetheless.

In a word, then, although we cannot know the ultimate nature of the stream into which we dip, we do know that what we come up with depends on whether we use a bucket, cup, spoon, or net.

Nevertheless, I have waited to take up the methodological (or as one might call them, because they are so general, the "metamethodological" or simply "procedural") principles that scientific sociology has in common with all natural sciences until now for two reasons. First, these principles might well seem intolerably abstract unless viewed against the more concrete background of the empirical referents of sociology that have been discussed in Parts I and II. Second, many of the issues underlying the principles to be set forth here properly belong not to sociology but to the philosophy of science—a discipline with which I can claim only an amateur's familiarity. I therefore tread here much more diffidently than in the realms of sociological subject matter but with no less (and in some ways much deeper) interest—for here reside the most fundamental and most awesome of all questions pertaining to human existence, let alone scientific sociology.

Let us now turn, therefore, to an overview of Part III and its focus on the general methodological or procedural principles of scientific sociology. As an essential preliminary, however, let me try to make clear exactly which kind of "procedure" is referred to here and which kind is not referred to.

Because sense-based intersubjective verification is indispensable to every natural science, such sciences are unavoidably collective endeavors. It follows that every scientific analyst necessarily works in social, cultural, spatial, and temporal relations with others whom we may call, broadly speaking, his/her co-workers. However, analysts also work in certain physical, ideational, and evaluative relations with their subject matter—moving it around, observing it, conceptualizing it, explaining it, etc. Thus we have two types of procedures that pertain to scientific analysis: those employed in analysts' relations with their co-workers, and those employed in analysts' relations with their subject matter.

Viewed from this perspective, Merton may be interpreted as citing four norms governing co-worker procedures (which he calls "institutional imperatives"): "universalism, communism, disinterestedness, organized skepticism"; and two norms governing subject matter procedures (which he calls "technical norms"): "The technical norm of empirical evidence, [which] is a prerequisite for sustained true prediction; [and] the technical norm of logical consistency [which is] a prerequisite for systematic and valid predictions" (1973:270; see also 1949:164).[1]

Mulkay, too, draws the distinction I have in mind when he differentiates the "social norms" and the "cognitive/technical norms" of science—arguing that the former constitute "vocabularies which are employed by members in negotiating meanings for their own and their colleagues' actions,"[2] while the latter "refer to the whole range of research methods, techniques, criteria of adequacy, established bodies of knowledge, and so on, in so far as they are employed as resources for judging knowledge claims and scientific competence" (1979:93, 94).[3]

---

[1] Actually, by the criterion distinction between procedures toward co-workers and procedures toward subject matter, Merton's "organized skepticism" pertains more to the latter than the former: "organized skepticism . . . [is the] temporary suspension of judgment and the detached scrutiny of beliefs in terms of empirical and logical criteria" (1973:277). Universalism, communism, and disinterestedness, however, seem clearly to pertain to procedures toward co-workers.

[2] For a similar view, see Mills (1940).

[3] It seems possible that Stehr (1978) has the same distinction in mind when he distinguishes between the "social and cognitive norms of science," but he does not define either "social" or "cognitive"—an important matter when (if we substitute "cultural" for "social") there can be considerable overlap between the two. However, when Stehr criticizes "the bifurcation of theory and inquiry into the social and cognitive norms of science" on the ground that "Few analyses [have taken seriously Merton's] observation that 'methodological canons are often *both* technical expedients and moral compulsives' " (1978:179), he tacitly identifies "cognitive norms" with "technical expedients" and "social norms" with "moral compulsives." This, of course, implies a very different distinction from the one being advanced here.

The discussion throughout Part III (with the exception of Chapter 16) pertains only to subject matter procedures.

SUBJECT MATTER PROCEDURES OF SCIENTIFIC ANALYSIS

Figure 13.1 outlines the subject matter procedures of scientific analysis that Part III will set forth. In this diagram, scientific analysis is portrayed as consisting of eight information elements (represented in ovals), whose transformations into one another (represented by arrows) are systematically regulated by twelve sets of techniques (represented in rectangles) and two value elements (represented in diamonds).

Three brief illustrations may help put some recognizable flesh on these schematic bones. Before turning to these illustrations, however, it is important to note that the procedure of scientific analysis, as represented in Figure 13.1, is endless. Each step presupposes that all the others have been taken before it—presumably at lower levels of understanding and control. Thus, although one may *consciously* start a given analysis by making certain predictions, one always has in mind (as largely unconscious background assumptions) certain prior explanations, empirical generalizations, tests, outcomes, implementations, and so on (see Gouldner, 1970:31–35). When one emphasizes that the analyst's *prior* levels of understanding and control, upon which he/she constructs an analysis, are indeed "lower" than the levels at which that analysis is *aimed* (and which, when successful, it produces), it becomes apparent that the endlessness of scientific procedure is better represented as two connected spirals (another double helix)—thereby avoiding tautology by appealing to "progress." It should be noted that, in sharp contrast with this cyclical and processual image, Alexander proposes a linear and nonprocessual (albeit "two-directional") "continuum of scientific thought" that ranges from one pole which he calls, variously, "the empirical observational world," the "empirical environment" of scientific thought, and the "physical environment of science (empirical)," to another pole variously called "the non-empirical metaphysical" world, the "metaphysical environment" of scientific thought, and the "metaphysical environment of science (nonempirical)" (see 1982:2, 3, 40; the differences among these various rubrics are not explicated, nor is Alexander's placement on the continuum of various "contemporary theoretical debates" in sociology).[4]

---

[4]One of Alexander's main points is that a methodology for the metaphysical end of this continuum should be developed to a degree matching that for the empirical end:

   If the nature of social science is to be properly understood, and its true potential fully achieved, the careful attention to methodological rules for induction from empirical observation must be

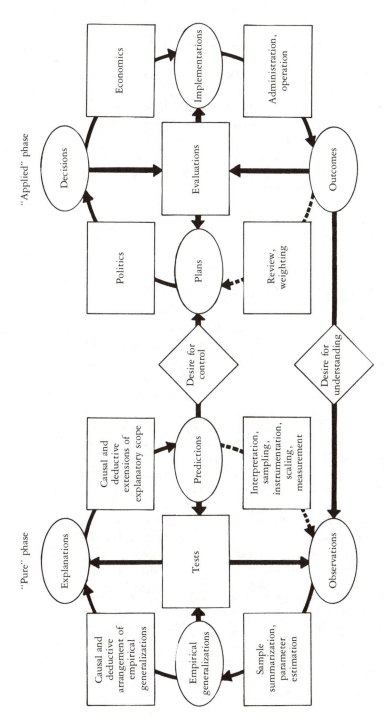

Figure 13.1. The procedures of scientific analysis.

The endlessness of scientific procedure means that it has no "natural" starting point or end point. One need not start (consciously) a given scientific analysis with observations; one may start with a prediction, an empirical generalization, an explanation, an outcome, an implementation, a plan, a decision-to-implement. Moreover, one need not start with an information element; one may start with a method element. That is, one may have a test procedure, or a sampling technique to try out, some economic resources to spend, some political power to wield or political fences to mend, some control-values or understanding-values to pursue, and so forth. Thus, scientific analysis is represented here as open to a variety of equally fruitful starting points (and also open to the same variety of fruitful end points).

Against this general background, let us now turn to some illustrations of Fig. 13.1.

The First, Partly Imaginary, Illustration[5]

Suppose that, being of sound and wondering mind, we have developed a curiosity (i.e., a "desire for understanding") about what makes people commit suicide. Or suppose that, being of warm and humanitarian mind, we have become alarmed (i.e., developed a "desire for control") over the fact that some people commit suicide and we want to find out if anything can be done about it. From the first starting point we consciously begin our analysis by making some observations—more systematically than before—on suicides and the conditions under which they seem to occur and not occur. We would then aggregate these observations into empirical generalizations, and then arrange these into a first-approximation explanation. Let us suppose that that explanation claimed individuals are pressed to commit suicide by extreme levels in certain social and/or cultural conditions, and that they are restrained from committing suicide by moderation in these same social and/or cultural conditions. Suppose also that we identified the extreme, suicidogenic, conditions in question as follows: When social interaction (or "collective activity") frequencies are very high, or very low, the condition may be called "altruism," or "egoism," respectively; and when cultural normative "regulation"

matched by an effort to create a "theoretical methodology" than can explain [sic] the opposing [sic] movement from more general principles (1982:33).

Although Alexander does not propose the components which he believes such a "theoretical methodology" should comprise, Fig. 13 and its discussion in Chapters 14 and 15 suggest that at least one set of such components (called here "causal and deductive extensions of explanatory scope," "interpretation, sampling, instrumentation, scaling, measurement") has already been created—and is, indeed, already in widespread use.

[5] Only "partly" imaginary, insofar as it is based on the pure analytical ideas, and the applied analytical implications, of Durkheim's *Suicide* (1951).

is very strong, or very weak, the condition may be called "fatalism," or "anomie," respectively.[6]

At this point, what we want to do is find out if this first-approximation explanation is actually true, and if not, how we should change it to make it more true. In order to do that, we have to derive predictions from the explanation (predictions that say if this explanation is true, when you look at such-and-such you will also find such-and-such) and we have then to develop new empirical generalizations, based on new observations, that are made especially for comparison with these predictions.

Thus, suppose we predicted that if the fatalism-anomie part of our explanation is true, when we look at very young husbands as a group (on the assumption that they tend to be subjected to expecially strong normative controls), and Protestants as a group (on the assumption that they tend to be subjected to especially weak normative controls), we shall find that larger proportions of these groups than of others commit suicide. In order to test this prediction, we have to make all of its terms ("suicide," "very young," "husband," "Protestant"), and all of our samples, instrumentation, and measuring scales, as precisely replicable as possible—that is, rigorously uniform across all *our* own observations and rigorously communicable to other analysts so that they may make *their* own observations. Then, taking all these replicability restrictions into account, we have to make new observations and construct new empirical generalizations from them in, again, replicable ways. Once these generalizations have been constructed, we compare our predictions to them in order to test the extent to which the latter fit the facts. From this test we draw conclusions that confirm, deny, or suggest modifications in our explanation and/or in the observations from which the criterion empirical generalization was constructed—depending on which one (explanation or observations) holds more of our confidence.

Finally, to the extent to which our tests confirm our explanations, we conclude that we understand the part that extremes of social interaction frequency and of cultural normative regulators play in causing suicides. At that point, our original curiosity subsides somewhat and we may move on to analyze the effect of some other phenomenon on suicide.

But I have grossly abbreviated one step in the above process—namely, the generation of new observations based on a prediction—so let us look more closely at what is involved here. The illustration above (and the dotted arrow from predictions to observations, in Fig. 13.1) suggests that the generation of new observations designed to produce an empirical generalization which can test the accuracy of a prediction requires us to interpret (operationalize) the prediction, devise or select measuring instruments, sample the phenomena that are to be observed, devise or select measurement scales, and finally, take measurements. A more detailed

---

[6] See Chapter 12 for discussion of this interpretation of Durkheim's *Suicide*.

statement of what is required, however, would include plans of various ways (including alternative interpretations, instrumentations, scales, samples, and measurings—and their relative costs and benefits) through which the required new observations could be generated; a decision (based on the distribution of political power among the sponsors and scientists involved) to select one or more of these ways; implementation (based on the availability of economic wherewithal in the society as a whole, and the specific budgeting of the project) of the selected way or ways; and finally, the administration and operation of the implementation so as actually to collect the projected new observations. Thus, the dotted arrow in Fig. 13.1 from predictions to observations in the "pure" phase of scientific analysis is shorthand for the more detailed progression from plans to decisions to implementations to outcomes in the "applied" phase. In this more fully explicated way, then, "pure" scientific analysis always involves some "applied" scientific analysis.

Now let us consider the second possible starting point of analysis mentioned above, where we have become alarmed about suicide—let us say, among students and faculty at a particular university—and we want not so much to understand it as to do something about it. The first thing to note here is that in order to do anything about something, we have to foresee it. We can do nothing about the past, and we can only survive the present. Thus, foresight is necessary (though not sufficient, of course) for control, and in order to foresee something we must explain it in at least a rudimentary sense.[7] Obviously, the need for foresight is as clear in the case of preventing, as ensuring, given events. Thus, all legal and medical preventive steps (e.g., setting bail, committing the insane, quarantining the contagious, vaccination, antiseptic procedures, etc.) rest on predicting what the world would be like with and without them.

Having foreseen the event of interest, one further step is prerequisite to undertaking to do something about it: we must evaluate it as desirable or undesirable (rather than merely interesting or uninteresting in the cognitive sense) and therefore warranting human control. In short, it is the desire for some predicted phenomenon to occur or not to occur that transforms a pure science *explanandum* into an applied science *desideratum*.

Therefore, the "alarm" mentioned above must be directed toward predicted,

---

[7] It may appear that "extrapolative" or "straight-line" predictions do not rest on explanations, but they do—albeit very general ones. Thus, when we predict that tomorrow's weather will be more like today's than the weather five days ago, we rely on the explanatory hypothesis that day-to-day meteorological changes depend on a close continuity—rather than, say, a periodic discontinuity—of causal forces, whatever the latter may be. But when we predict that tomorrow's weather will be more like the weather twelve months ago than that six months ago, we rely on the hypothesis that yearly meteorological changes depend on periodic discontinuities in causal forces, again, whatever the latter may be. Reversing the explanatory hypotheses would revise the predictions. Thus, Popper argues summarily that "In order to deduce predictions one needs laws and initial conditions; if no suitable laws are available or if the initial conditions cannot be ascertained, the scientific way of predicting breaks down" (1961:205).

future, suicides—rather than directed toward past or present suicides—if it is to lead to a deliberate effort to do something about them. Given such alarm, then, we would probably begin (again, "begin" in the conscious, deliberate, sense) by constructing some alternative plans for diminishing the number of predicted future suicides. Let us say two plans are considered: one to put bars on all windows above the first floor, and another calling for all students and faculty members to have their heads examined. University politics will determine which (if any) plan is finally settled on, and university economics (i.e., budgeting) will determine whether, and if so how, the chosen plan is implemented.

Let us say the head-examinations plan is decided upon (as being not such a bad idea all around) and actually carried out. What we want to do next is determine whether this implementation works, and if not, what we have to do to make it work. In order to do that, we must observe its actual outcomes and compare them with the anticipated outcomes that originally led us to decide in its favor. On the results of that comparison we then evaluate the implementation (and the plan on which it was based) as adequate or inadequate. Then, to the extent that we evaluate the implementation and plan as adequate, our original alarm about suicide turns into satisfaction that we have successfully reduced its rate.

Here too I have grossly abbreviated one step in the above process—that is, the generation of plans from observed outcomes via review and weighting, as represented in Fig. 13.1 by a dotted arrow. A more precise tracing of the path from outcomes to plans would note that "review and weighting" is shorthand for: (1) the generation of empirical generalizations from observed outcomes, (2) the generation of explanations from empirical generalizations, and (3) the generation of predictions from explanations. Of course, it is possible that this process could turn up the altruism-egoism-fatalism-anomie explanation mentioned above, and we might then be deflected from both our earlier plans (bars on windows and head examinations) toward an attempt to manipulate the social and cultural conditions under which the students and faculty in question live.

Thus, pure scientific analysis is inevitably involved in applied analysis, just as applied analysis is inevitably involved in pure analysis. The only thing that enables us to tell one from the other is a differential emphasis on prospective product or goal—as between understanding of the world and control over the world—and the resulting differential investment in the procedures shown on the two sides of Fig. 13.1. In apparent accord with this view, Freeman and Sherwood distinguish between applied and pure analysis by contrasting the opinion that "the social scientist should direct his work toward the solution of contemporary social problems"[8] with the opinion that "the primary goal of social science is the discovery and

---

[8] Freeman and Sherwood do not discuss the matter, but obviously both the definition of a contemporary social "problem" and the definition of what constitutes a "solution" to such a problem are moot questions that implicate ethical and/or aesthetic values.

verification of principles of social behavior, whether or not they are immediately useful in programs to improve social life and social conditions" (1970:1), and their distinction properly rests on a difference in goals and not means:

> Social-policy research generally is no different from other types of social and psychological investigations, either in terms of the empirical perspective of the researcher or the research principles and techniques which guide him. It is in the selection of the problems and the goals of the research that social-policy research is distinguished from so-called "pure" research (Freeman and Sherwood, 1970:2).

To this I must add, as mentioned above, that that primary difference in "problems and goals" entails an important secondary difference in relative emphasis on the procedural elements shown in Fig. 13.1. Thus, of all the features mutually implicated in them both, pure science gives most emphasis to explanation (as the central feature of understanding) and applied science gives most emphasis to implementation (as the central feature of control). In a word, pure science strives to *discover why things exist;* applied science strives to *invent things that work.*

It follows that applied science concentrates on the most powerful and robust causal relationships in which deliberate human manipulation can play a part and only reluctantly explicates the exact process and conditions involved in that relationship. *That* something works is always the important thing to applied science, not *why* it works; applied science typically becomes interested in why something works when it does *not* work and has to be fixed. By contrast, pure science is always interested in why things exist (whether their existence is construed as "working" or not) and therefore it always extends its efforts beyond the search for powerful and robust causal relationships in which deliberate human intervention can play a part to fully explicating, for their own sake, the myriad complex, weak, contingent, and beyond-human-intervention relationships that often interpret and condition—and therefore help explain—the powerful, robust, and manipulable ones. As a result,

> The true outlooks of the scholar-scientist and of the practical men of affairs who surround the world of science tend to be different. The former works in a long, leisurely world in which the hands of the clock crawl slowly over a vast dial; to him the precise penetration of the unknown seems too grand an enterprise to be hurried. . . . The practical man of affairs, on the other hand, works by a small time-dial over which the second-hand of immediacy hurries incessantly. "Never mind the long past and the infinite future," insists the clattering little monitor, "but do this, fix this—now, before tomorrow morning" (Lynd, 1946:1–2; see also Katz, 1976:4).

The Second Illustration

Merton provides an instance of the sociological analyst repeatedly moving back and forth, within a single analysis, between pure and applied phases. Starting in the pure phase, Merton argues that "attitudes and overt behavior vary independently" (1976:192) and, on this basis, he develops a descriptive "typology of ethnic prejudice and discrimination" specifying four types of individuals: "unprejudiced nondiscriminator," "unprejudiced discriminator," "prejudiced nondiscriminator," and "prejudiced discriminator" (1976:192). Then, arguing that "Those who practice discrimination are not people of one kind," Merton moves into the applied phase of analysis: "And because they are not all of a piece, there must be diverse social therapies, each directed at a given type in a given social situation" (1976:199; emphasis removed). After proposing different plans or "social therapies" for the unprejudiced discriminator, the prejudiced nondiscriminator and the prejudiced discriminator, Merton returns to the pure phase in order roughly to assess the prevalence of these different types of individual in Far South and New England communities ("It is safe to assume that communities and larger areas vary in the proportion of these several types" [1976:208]), and in different social classes, on the assumption that plans or therapies are to be determined and implemented on a community and/or a class basis.

Merton closes the formal part of his paper by coming back once again to the applied phase of analysis and calling for social indicators of ethnic prejudice and discrimination ("An inventory to determine the relative proportions in various areas of the four prejudice-discrimination types; Within each area, an inventory of these proportions among the several social classes, major associations, and nationality groups; [and] Periodic audits of [all] these proportions" [1976:210]), and for evaluation research ("Continuing studies of the consequences of various programs designed to promote ethnic equities, thus reducing the wastage presently entailed by well-intentioned, expensive, and ineffectual programs" [1976:210]). In an Appendix entitled "A Formal Note on the Use of Paradigms in Qualitative Analysis" (1976:210–216), Merton returns principally, and yet again, to the pure phase of analysis but closes with a long quotation from Raymond Firth ending with this reference to both pure and applied analysis: " 'A focus on the world of ideas should complement, not replace, a focus on the world of action' " (1976:216).

The Third Illustration

An empirical generalization is declared the starting point of the final illustration of Fig. 13.1 to be cited here: "Strong individual and aggregate level correlations between poverty and official measures of crime are perhaps among the most firmly established of social science empirical generalizations" (Berk et al., 1980:766).[9] Noting that "the precise mechanisms linking poverty to crime remain elusive . . . [There are several] plausible theoretical explanations, but, to date, the empirical tests have proved equivocal," the analysts choose a sociologically modified economic explanation emphasizing that " 'the decision to commit an illegal act is reached via an egocentric cost-benefit analysis' " and also emphasizing that the value of "legitimate employment [is not] exclusively as a source of income" but includes social prestige, self-respect, and the like. From this explanation they predict that, among men and women who are about to be released from state prisons, their number of subsequent arrests for property crimes will be reduced by receiving modest amounts of money as unemployment benefits, and having job placement and counseling services leading to actual employment in legitimate jobs.

At this point, the analysts turn to an experimental design requiring them "to manipulate at least some of the important causal variables in a manner that . . . would permit one to determine whether change in a prospective causal variable in fact preceded change in an outcome of interest." Having thus entered the realm of applied sociology, the analysts construct a plan in which two causal variables (number of weeks of money payments, and number of weeks of employment) would be manipulated in various ways.

The politics leading to decisions regarding which, if any, combination of these ways would be implemented had, in large part, already been accomplished ("the beginnings of the . . . experiments can be found in the Manpower Development and Training Act of 1962"), and the economics leading to implementation were accomplished by a Department of Labor grant to the analysts plus the regular budgets of the state employment offices that administered and operated the payment and job placement services.

Outcomes showed that both payments and number of weeks legitimately employed significantly reduced number of arrests, and the favorable comparison of these outcomes with the original decision to implement the plan in question confirmed both plan and implementation, such that "a good case can be made for implementing [on a nationwide scale] the policy as tested."[10] In addition, the outcomes were fed back to pure sociology as observations leading to empirical generalizations whose comparison with the original predictions confirmed "the ability of a blend of theory from economics and sociology to explain at least some of the sources of variation in criminal behavior. For ex-offenders at least, unemployment and poverty do cause crime on the microlevel."

Finally, it should be noted that the analysts in this research are attentive to the

---

[9] All subsequent quotations in this illustration are drawn from Berk et al. (1980).

[10] Rossi says "We believe the results justify attempting to set up a benefit system—the 'severance pay' model, as we have called it—that does not have a severe work disincentive built into it" (1980:900).

scientific requirement of replication: "the experiment was conducted independently in two states [Texas and Georgia]. This means, that if one state is taken as the initial site, the other state can be taken as replication."

Against the background, then, of Fig. 13.1 and the above illustrations, it seems fair to argue that scientific analysis strives to achieve understanding of the world *and* control over the world, as intrinsically inseparable goals.

When we ask, By what criteria are we to recognize understanding and control?, Fig. 13.1 provides the following answers: (1) As natural scientists we regard *understanding* of a certain set of event-observations (i.e., a particular empirical generalization) as having been produced when, after predicting a second set of event-observations on the basis of an explanation developed for the first set, we compare the prediction with an actual set of new event-observations and find the two sets satisfactorily congruent. We then reason that that congruence confirms, first, the validity of the explanation from which the prediction was derived and, second, the adequacy of the observations from which the empirical generalization was derived. We conclude that we understand the now-confirmed observations in question as instances of what we already knew, namely, the now-confirmed explanation. (2) As natural scientists, we say that *control* over a certain set of event-observations has been produced when, having decided to manipulate that set through a particular planned implementation, we compare the outcomes of the implementation as actually operated with the outcomes we originally wanted (and decided) to produce and find them satisfactorily congruent. We reason that that congruence confirms, first, the effectiveness of the implementation by which the outcomes were produced, and second, the validity of the plan on which that implementation was based. We conclude that we now control the outcome event-observations in accord with our prior decision.

IMAGINARY AND ACTUAL ANALYSES, AND INDIVIDUAL AND COLLECTIVE ANALYSES

The procedures outlined in Fig. 13.1 and illustrated above may be carried out (1) in imagination only or in imagination first and then in actuality, and (2) by individuals separately or by individuals separately and also collectively. Cross-classification of these two dichotomies yields four ways in which the procedures in question may be carried out: in imagination and by individuals only; in imagination only and by a collectivity; in actuality and by individuals only; and in actuality and by a collectivity. The last combination is the only one that is normally termed "scientific," but imaginary performance of the procedures, and their performance by separate individuals, both play important roles in producing that collective actualization.

Performance in Imagination: Insight, Foresight, and Ideology

Marx says: "the architect raises his structure in imagination before he erects it in reality. At the end of every labour-process, we get a result that already existed in the imagination of the labourer at its commencement" (1978:344). When such imaginings, trials, or "thinkings-through," sometimes running several times through the entire analysis—correcting, adjusting, adding, retracting—seem suddenly to lock into consistency with everything else one knows, the analyst is said to have experienced "insight." Thus

> Archimedes, while wholly absorbed in [the problem of how to be certain that an equal weight of silver had or had not been substituted for gold in a crown made by a craftsman for the prince of Syracuse] took a bath one day, and noticed that as he immersed himself in the tub, the water spilled over. This observation led him to the desired discovery, and he was so overcome by joy that he rushed out of the bath and, running naked throughout the house, he began shouting that he had discovered what he had sought, which in Greek is *Eureka, Eureka* (I have found it, I have found it) (Taton, 1962:75).

On the other hand, when an analyst—knowing, through training and/or experience, what comes next in the analysis—prepares for future steps while carrying out present steps we say he/she has "foresight." Thus, foresightful social planners, knowing in advance that politics and budgeting will determine whether the plan they construct will be implemented, "usually spend a great deal of their time seeking support and legitimation. [And, indeed, some] planners maintain that the planning process must begin with legitimation" (Freeman and Sherwood, 1970:5).

One variety of imaginary trial that seems to combine both insight and foresight (whether accurate or not) is ideology. As Rule says,

> What we mean by a political doctrine or philosophy . . . is not simply a set of value affirmations. When we speak of such positions, we mean to suggest both sets of ideas concerning what is ultimately good in social life *and* a series of *empirical propositions* on how societies work (1978a:73).

Thus, an ideology (and also an utopia [see Mannheim, 1955:40, 192–193]) may be regarded as an imaginary trial that embraces (with varying degrees of communicability, logical rigor, and empirical verifiability) all the elements of scientific analysis shown in Fig. 13.1—including both its pure and applied phases.

In order to be regarded as scientific, however, all imaginary trials (including ideologies) must be brought out of that realm into actual fact. As Marx puts it,

"Man must prove the truth, i.e., the reality and power, the this-sidedness of his thinking in practice" (1978:364), and Merton notes that

> Intuition, hunch, and guess may, and often do, orginate ideas, but they do not provide a sufficient basis for choosing among ideas. Logical analysis and abstract reasoning interlock with empirical inquiry and it is only when the results of these two prove consistent that contemporary scientists consider them to be an authentic part of validated scientific knowledge (1973:164).

Thus, after racing around the house for a while, Archimedes cooled off, dried off, and settled down to actualize his insight: "It is said that . . . he ordered two masses of the same weight as the crown, one of gold and one of silver, which he then plunged into a vessel of water . . ." (Taton, 1962:75), and so on. In this way, Archimedes eventually reached the applied science evaluation that "the worker [who had made the crown] had clearly been a swindler" (Taton, 1962:75), and also discovered the pure science principle of specific gravity.

It should be clear even from Archimedes' ordering "two masses of gold and silver" that actualization is more costly than imagination: the cost difference in time, energy, money, and so on, between imagining, say, a test of hypothesis, a decision, or an implementation, and actually constructing them is apt to be huge. The dangers are apt to be vastly different, too, between, say, imagining atomic power plants and actually building and operating them. Insofar as scientific analysis requires actual performance of the procedures shown in Fig. 13.1, the greater costs and greater risks inherent in such actualizations are prime sources of scientific carefulness as manifested in unremitting pressures toward procedural exactness, uniformity, and deliberateness—those pressures, indeed, which are the justifications for calling scientific fields "disciplines."

Care, however, is not enough; communicability is also required, and this demand originates in the fact that every scientific analysis is a collective, and not merely an individual, activity. Let us see what this means.

Performance by the Individual: Common Sense

Everybody constantly carries out the procedures shown in Fig. 13.1: that is, all living human individuals make observations and empirical generalizations, formulate explanations and predictions about these observations and generalizations, carry out tests of their predictions, and revise their explanations and observations—thereby achieving some understanding of the world. All living human individuals, having predicted events to which they attach positive or negative value, make plans, reach decisions about which—if any—means of control to employ, carry out, and implement that decision, observe outcomes of that implementation (which become new observational sources of understanding), carry out tests to see if these outcomes match what they had in mind when they made the decision in the first place, and finally, use that match or mismatch to revise their implementation and their plans—thereby achieving some control over the world. Individuals, in short, are *curious* about the world and *cope* with the world.

This, again, is the theoretical (rather than methodological) significance of the distinction between psychical behavior and physical behavior that was drawn in Chapter 2. In short, despite all their interdependence, we identify "mind" as the chief mechanism of curiosity and the pursuit of pure science, and "body" as the chief mechanism of coping and the pursuit of applied science. It is also useful to reiterate here that the distinctions drawn in Chapter 4 between cognitive, cathectic, and conative mind orientations have added further detail to this picture by suggesting that the pure phase of scientific procedure constitutes an elaboration of the cognitive orientation; the applied phase comprises not only actual physical behavior but an elaboration of the conative orientation which prepares and directs that behavior; and the desires for understanding and control constitute the driving cathectic orientations of the pure and applied phases, respectively.

Analysis that we call "scientific," then, is only the common sense environment-exploring (i.e., world-understanding) and self-preserving (i.e., world-controlling) activity of every living individual human being—indeed, of every living individual organism—made into a collectively shared activity through which each individual participant requires sense-based[11] intersubjective verification of his/her own conclusions. Thus, when I ask "Do you see what I see?" and "Can you do what I can do?" and make my confidence in the veracity of what I myself think I see and do dependent on your answers,[12] and when you reciprocate in like manner, we have transformed our separate common sense analyses into a single, collective, *scientific* analysis.

In sharp contrast, then, with Sztompka's opinion that "scientific results are objective if and only if they are true" (1979:220–221), I hold that we cannot know "truth"—or, more precisely, that if we did know truth, we could not know that we knew it. I therefore agree with Schutz's more relativistic, and above all more social and historicist, view that "objects and their aspects [which are] actually known by me and potentially known by you [are apprehended] as everyone's knowledge. Such knowledge is conceived to be objective and anonymous"

---

[11] "Sense-based," in order to rule out purely abstract ratiocinations and purely imaginational speculations as bases for intersubjective agreement, because that way lies dogma and the *"folie à deux"* Scheff describes as occurring "when the delusions and hallucinations of [one individual are] accepted by the other" (1966:42).

[12] Kaplan says "I ask 'Do you see what I see?' to help decide whether what I see is to be explained by self-knowledge or by knowledge of the presumed object" (1964:128). The necessary assumptions about "you," "I," "see," and "object" that underlie this question are discussed in Chapter 16.

(1953:9);[13] with Popper's view that "the objectivity of scientific statements lies in the fact that they can be intersubjectively tested" (1961:44, emphasis removed); and therefore with Kaplan's summary statement that "The intersubjective becomes the mark of objectivity" (1964:128). It is just this distinctively scientific requirement of sense-based intersubjective verification which underlies Merton's observation that

> The institution of science reinforces, when it does not create, [a] deep-rooted need for validation of work done. . . . Science is a social world, not an aggregate of private, solipsistic worlds (1976:44–45).

The question then arises: Why on earth would I want to make my confidence in what I myself see with my *own* eyes and do with my *own* hands depend on what you tell me about what *you* see and do? After all, two heads can be much worse than one—and Simmel even claims they are typically so when he quotes Schiller to the effect that " 'Seen singly, everybody is passably intelligent and reasonable, but united into a body, they are blockheads' " (1950:32). You and I, in short, could be merely confirming each other's errors and thereby socially constructing a "reality" that leads us both further and further away from ultimate reality, whereas one or both of us might reject those errors if left alone. What, then, justifies the distinctive, essential, and invariant reliance of natural science on intersubjective verification?

I believe the answer to this question lies in the fact that although the naturalistic working assumption regards the world as subject, *in principle*, to human understanding and control (see Chapters 1 and 16), we know the human species is finite and we believe the world is infinite. It follows that, *in practice*, even if human understanding and control should continue to increase by leaps and bounds throughout the entire lifespan of the human species, that understanding and control can never be perfect. This is why Mannheim, who argues, on the one hand, that the synthesizer of many ideas (i.e., the compiler of intersubjective verification) can discover "the approximate truth . . . [and can come] closer to reality," nevertheless warns that the exact truth and ultimate reality can never be attained, and so "the only adequate synthesis would be a dynamic one, which is reformulated from time to time" (1955:84, 151). Because of this fearful conviction, we know the world must remain to us permanently mysterious, permanently dangerous, permanently and utterly dreadful—capable, at any moment and without the slightest warning, of upsetting all our applecarts.

---

[13] Note, however, that Schutz believes disinterestedness or value-freedom, not intersubjective verification, differentiates common sense from science: "All science presumes a special attitude of the person carrying on science; it is the attitude of the disinterested. In this manner it is distinguished above all from the attitude of the person who . . . has an eminently practical interest in [the world]" (1978:138). The idea of a "disinterested" or "value-free" scientist is rejected later in this chapter and in Chapter 16.

Thus, natural scientists, perhaps more than some others (certainly more than those who believe their private ecstacies reveal ultimate reality and their prayers and rituals exert control over it), are permanently *afraid* because we know that "every scientific statement must remain *tentative for ever*" (Popper, 1961:280). Thus, it is not certainty or safety that we seek in numbers, for we know full well there is no certainty or safety under any conditions whatever (Kafka tells us "There is infinite hope, but not for us"); what we seek in numbers is only the comfort of company. That is, even if intersubjective verification were actually dragging us closer and closer to some sudden and unimaginable doom, we cannot know it—at least not until the last moment. What we can know, however, is that for better or worse, for richer or poorer, we are not alone.[14]

Natural science, then, is the systematic displacement of existential fear and trembling by sociability. As Festinger et al. argue in a related connection, "if everyone in the whole world believed something there would be no question at all as to the validity of this belief" (1964:28). From the physicalist's standpoint, of course, the mere absence of *question* about the validity of a belief does not make that belief valid (you can fool all the people some of the time, and there can be no guarantee that you can't fool all the people all the time), but it does reassure the believers, who, whistling together in the dark, cling to the faith that "If more and more people can be persuaded that the system of belief is correct, then clearly it must, after all, be correct" (Festinger et al., 1964:28).

For this reason, then, sense-based intersubjective verification is the hallmark of natural science. Clearly, however, in order to "make my confidence in the veracity of what I myself think I see or do dependent on your answer to [my] question" I have to be confident that you are indeed answering *my* question. That is, I have to be sure that we both mean the same things by "see," "do," "what," "you," and "I" because if not, I would be foolish to trust your answer. Consequently, I will go to great lengths to specify precisely what I mean by my question, and if we are reciprocating you will also go to great lengths to specify what you mean by your answer, and so the specifications will go, back and forth, as we strive to negotiate the least ambiguous common understanding that we can, given our resources of language, time, energy, and patience. Thus, insofar as every scientific analysis requires intersubjective verification, every such analysis calls for the most rigorously determinate communicability of conclusions and therefore of all the procedures leading to those conclusions.

Although Habermas is explicitly concerned (as we shall see in Chapter 16) with the intersubjective verification of values rather than cognitive beliefs ("The question is . . . whether we choose what we want for the purpose of the pacification and gratification of existence. . . . [T]he solution demands [an] unrestricted communication about the goals of life activity and conduct" [1970a:119–120]), his

---

[14] At least we do not *seem* to be alone (see the tentative rejection of solipsism in Chapter 16).

views of the communication conditions for the former seem applicable to the latter as well:

> The dialogue-constitutive universals [of language—including personal pronouns, interrogative, imperative, and assertive formators, modal formators, and the like] at the same time generate and describe the form of intersubjectivity which makes mutuality of understanding possible. Communicative competence is defined by the ideal speaker's mastery of the dialogue-constitutive universals, irrespective of actual restrictions under empirical conditions (1970b:369, see also 1979:29).

But in order actually to achieve intersubjectivity, Habermas argues, a social structure of (ideally) perfect freedom and perfect equality must prevail between such communicatively competent participants:

> Pure intersubjectivity is determined by a symmetrical relation between I and You (We and You), I and he (We and they). An unlimited interchangeability of dialogue roles demands that no side be privileged in the performance of these roles: pure intersubjectivity exists only when there is complete symmetry in the distribution of assertion and dispute, revelation and concealment, prescription and conformity, among the partners of communication (1970b:371).

Such social structural symmetries would seem clearly to combine one of Simmel's proposed solutions to the problem of manifest contradiction between social freedom and social equality—namely, the "temporal alternation" of superordinate and subordinate statuses (1950:285 see also 65–67)—with Merton's claim that "universalism" and "communism" are parts of the (cultural structural) "ethos of modern science" (1973:270). But above all, they underscore the central importance of scientific method and instrumentation, and of the various efforts to control for values, in pursuing that intersubjective verification which is essential to natural science (see Chapter 16).

PURE AND APPLIED PHASES OF SCIENTIFIC ANALYSIS

As Fig. 13.1 and its illustrations have indicated, Part III of this book rests on the claim that all scientific analysis (including sociological analysis, as conceived here) pursues both practical control over the world and cognitive understanding of the world. This, in a nutshell, appears to be the import of a great many remarks in the philosophical, as well as the social science, literatures. For example, White-head says

> Science is a river with two sources, the practical source and the theoretical source. The practical source is the desire to direct our actions to achieve predetermined ends. . . . The theoretical source is the desire to understand. . . . [And] I most emphatically state that I do not consider one source as in any sense nobler than the other, or intrinsically more interesting (1967:103–104).

And Weber says:

> One does [science], first, for purely practical, in the broader sense of the word, for technical, purposes: in order to be able to orient our practical activities to the expectations that scientific experience places at our disposal. . . . [But secondly,] the academic man . . . maintains that he engages in "science for science's sake" and not merely because others, by exploiting science, bring about commercial or technical success and can better feed, dress, illuminate, and govern (1958a:138).

In accord with these opinions and others like them (see, for example, Comte, 1975:21, 321; Hempel, 1965:333; Malinowski, 1961:4–5; Lynd, 1946:115–116; and Sztompka, 1974:8, 1979:173) scientific procedure is here regarded as composed of two different but intimately connected phases: (1) "pure," "descriptive," "basic," or "theoretical" analysis—whose desired product is the *understanding* [15] of phenomena—and (2) "applied," "engineering," "normative," or "practical" analysis—whose desired product is the *control* [16] of phenomena. It follows that the cul-

---

[15] By "understanding" I mean the parsimonious, intersubjectively verified, symbolic representation of the sensuously experienced world. This definition is at once similar to, more specific, and more general, than Bell's definition of "knowledge" as "a set of organized statements of facts or ideas, presenting a reasoned judgment or an experimental result, which is transmitted to others through some communication medium in some systematic form" (1973:175). With my own definition of understanding I wish to (1) specify parsimony as the organizing principle for the statements in question—a specification not evident in the idea of "knowledge"; (2) specify the transmission of such statements to others as not an end in itself but as a means to the end of intersubjective verification; (3) specify that the statements in question must symbolize human sensuous experience with the world—otherwise, from the point of view of science they are not "factual"; and (4) permit that symbolization to take any form—whether reasoned, experimental, systematic, or not—so long as it is intersubjectively (and sensuously) verified.

[16] By "control" I mean the purposive, intersubjectively verified, physical manipulation of the sensuously experienced world. This definition is at once similar to, more specific, and more general, than Etzioni's: "We [define] control as the process of specifying preferred states of affairs and revising ongoing processes so as to move in the direction of these preferred states" (1968:45). My own definition (1) specifies the dependency of control on intersubjective verification; and (2) specifies that the "states of affairs" in question must be sensuously experienced.

mination of the pure science phase—the thing we strive most to verify intersubjectively there—is an *explanation,* which is a psychical behavior (idea) in symbolic representation; whereas the culmination of the applied science phase is an *implementation,* which is a physical behavior (manipulation) in concrete manifestation. Thus, the procedures of scientific analysis comprise interdependent cultural structural and social structural components (see Chapter 2).

Before going any further, let us pause to consider why these definitions rely on *desired* product rather than actual product. Merton's argument is relevant here; he draws a sharp distinction between the "personal intent" and the "cultural consequences" of "basic research"—although he includes them both among the "components" of such research:

> Basic research discovers uniformities in nature and society and provides new understanding of previously identified uniformities. This conception departs from a prevailing tendency to define basic research in terms of the aims or intent of the investigators. It is a functional, not a motivational, definition. It refers to what basic research objectively accomplishes, not to the motivation or intent of those engaged in that research (1963:87).[17]

When we note that much research "objectively" *fails* to discover uniformities and fails to provide new understanding (just as much research fails to "achieve practical outcomes in new ways" [Merton, 1963:87]), it appears that Merton must be referring only to successful research. Why, however, should we deny the name "basic" to unsuccessful research (especially inasmuch as our assessment of a given research's success may change, and even the most successful research is unsuccessful in some respect and to some degree)? Because I have not found a satisfactory answer to this question, the definitions of pure and applied phases of scientific analysis that I put forward here hinge on the intentions or desires that motivate them—regardless of whether these desires are at any point declared satisfied or frustrated, successful or unsuccessful.

It should be emphatically added that I do not claim that pure scientists must be motivated *exclusively* by the desire to understand something (nor exclusively by the desire to control something, if they are applied scientists), nor do I claim that *all* analysts working on a given analysis must be motivated by either or both the indicated desires: the desire for personal fame and fortune is probably the most consistently powerful of motivations for scientists (see, for example, Merton, 1973:281–412), and certainly the desired product of a given analysis may be kept secret from most of the participating analysts. What I do claim, however, is that

---

[17] Merton, however, abandons this clearly functionalist definition of basic research for a subtly intentionist definition of applied research when he says: "we can distinguish applied research from basic as that which makes use of existing knowledge, fundamental or empirical, *to* achieve practical outcomes in new ways" (1963:87, emphasis added).

the one or more *directing* analysts of every scientific project must be motivated to *some* degree (however small or large) to achieve understanding and/or control, regardless of what desired products motivate the other participating analysts and regardless of what other desires also motivate the directors. This seems to be the sense in which scientific analysis should be regarded as an activity having its own distinctive goals or purposes that prevail regardless of the extent to which they are successfully reached.

Actual success in reaching either goal (and the degree of that success), however, is stepping-stone to success in reaching the other: actual understanding begets actual control, and more control begets more understanding; the more we understand about the world (including social phenomena) the more we can control it, and the more we control it, the more we can understand it.

To get this whole positive feedback process started, we need only stumble, accidentally, on some understanding or on some control; either will suffice. Thus, "It may be that in certain spheres of knowledge, it is the impulse to act which first makes the objects of the world accessible to the acting subject, and it may further be that it is this factor which determines the selection of those elements of reality which enter into thought" (Mannheim, 1955:4). Thus also, "Rocks were thrown, arrows fired from bows, and guns and cannon constructed before the science of ballistics was mastered" (Bauer, 1968:4), and "scientific medicine does not *always* wait upon certain knowledge of causes before experimenting with remedies. Indeed, thoroughly effective treatments sometimes long precede understanding; many proven techniques are in widespread use even though we haven't the foggiest idea of why they work" (Cohen, 1966:38–39). Similarly,

> Edison's work on "etheric sparks," which led to the development of the electric light and generated a vast new revolution in technology, was undertaken outside the theoretical research in electromagnetism and even in hostility to it. . . . . Edison, as one biographer has written, lacked "the power of abstraction" (Bell, 1973:20).

On the other hand, the pure science of astronomy developed quite far before the telescope—a way of exercising control over the phenomena which it studies (i.e., electromagnetic radiation reaching the vicinity of the Earth[18])—was invented, and "the further development of electrodynamics [beyond Edison], particularly in the replacement of steam engines, could only come from engineers with formal training in mathematical physics" (Bell, 1973:20). So the whole process of scientific analysis can start, and has started, in its pure phase or in its applied phase.

[18] Jeans points out that "Bertrand Russell considers it as incorrect to say that you see a star when you only see the light from it as to say that you see New Zealand when you see a New Zealander in London" (1958:87).

Once started, however, the process is sustained by the mutual contributions that pure and applied science make to each other. Let us now consider the nature of these contributions.

Contributions of Applied Science to Pure Science

Merton argues that "the applied researcher is continuously engaged, *nolens volens*, in testing the assumptions contained in basic theory" (1949:179). More specifically, we may say that applied science contributes the bases for making judgments of the reliability and validity[19] of pure science because it is only by pursuing control over the world—only by physically positioning ourselves and others within the world, and/or positioning the world around us—that we can discover whether we have found a regularity, explained it in a regular fashion, and tested that explanation in a logically appropriate way.

Thus, Horkheimer says

> Every datum depends not on nature alone but also on the power man has over it. Objects, the kind of perception, the questions asked, and the meaning of the answers all bear witness to human activity and the degree of man's power (1972:244).

Kaplan argues that

> An observation in science is first of all something done, an act performed by the scientist. . . . Scientific observation is deliberate search, carried out with care and forethought, as contrasted with the casual and largely passive perceptions of everyday life. It is this deliberateness and control of the process of observation that is distinctive of science. . . . Above all, "observation" means that special care is being taken: the root meaning of the word is not just "to see," but "to watch over" (1964:126–127).[20]

---

[19] Stouffer provides a concise idea of the meaning of these two terms: "By reliability is meant: Does [a given] index measure *something* consistently? By validity is meant: Granted that the index measures something consistently, is it really describing what we think it is describing?" (1962:265). Riley tacitly extends "reliability" to other information elements besides measurements (observations) when she refers broadly to "results": "reliability is defined as the extent to which [two or more researchers studying the same phenomenon and using the same or comparable methods] obtain the same results" (1963:73). Campbell applies "validity" to explanations and predictions, as well, when he distinguishes two varieties:

> First, and as a basic minimum, is what can be called *internal validity:* Did in fact the experimental stimulus make some significant difference in this specific instance? The second criterion is that of *external validity, representativeness, or generalizability:* To what populations, settings, and variables can this effect be generalized?" (1957:297).

[20] Kaplan's emphasis here on deliberate control as the main difference between scientific observation and everyday perception seems related to his distinction between what he calls "knowing something

The "controlled experiment," indeed, remains the ideal research design in pure science precisely because it is *controlled* and constitutes our closest approach so far to determining the occurrence of a particular event (i.e., the experimental stimulus or independent variable) so as to isolate its influence on another event (i.e., the response or dependent variable). As Campbell says, "no . . . true experiments are possible without the ability to control [the experimental variable or stimulus event], to withhold it from carefully randomly selected respondents while presenting it to others" (1957:307). Of course, however, experimental design must remain forever only an approximation to absolute human control; being of the cosmos and not above it, we can never be in full control of ourselves—never mind anything else. So, because we can never entirely control anything, we can never know for sure that anything will or will not occur, and because we can never know for sure that anything will or will not occur we can never entirely control anything. These two impossibilities writhe intertwined at the very bottom of that existential fear and trembling, mentioned above, from which all natural science arises; the controlled experiment, however, constitutes our most direct assault on them both.

Experimental designs, then, yield maximum understanding because they exert maximum control. Other nonexperimental designs (Campbell optimistically calls them "pre-experimental"), however, are also in widespread use—especially in fields like astrophysics (where our control is, and must certainly remain, severely limited) and also in fields in which human beings are the subjects and ethics prohibit using that control where we might have it. The essential characteristic of all such nonexperimental designs is that they require less control over the world than do experimental designs and as a result, in them, "there are [several] categories of extraneous variables left uncontrolled which thus become rival explanations [of an observed difference in a given independent variable]" (Campbell, 1957:298). We may thus summarize the first dependence of pure science on applied science as follows: without some control over the world, we can have neither reliable nor valid understanding of the world.

A second main dependence of pure science on applied science involves the latter's increasing pressure for precision in estimating the costs, direct effects, side effects, and long-run effects of given implementations. Thus, Coleman argues that when the results of pure sociology are used by applied sociology,

> The cost of incorrect results is high, both to the researcher and to society. It is high to the researcher because, since the results . . . are likely to be

---

and having an experience of it." Kaplan says, "It is one thing to know that the day is warm, and another to feel its warmth. Though the cognitive process itself is an experience, as richly concrete as any other, *what* is known is something abstract, formulable in a proposition . . . [and] no limited set of propositions can exhaust the content of an experience of the situation" (1964:208). Thus, the natural sciences should not be misconstrued; they seek only knowledge, not the re-creation of experience. The latter pursuit falls to the arts, lucid dreams, and an increasing variety of chemical, electrical, hypnotic, and other stimulations of the brain.

harmful to some interests there will very likely be reanalysis and attempts at replication of results. It is high to the society because of the incorrect social policies that may be guided by these results. . . . [Therefore] the more stringent requirements of social policy will force—and to some degree have already forced—the development of more powerful analytic tools that will benefit other research in the discipline (1976:256–257, emphasis removed).

Rossi argues, similarly, that "Applied social research often demands greater technical skills than does basic research," and notes "the predominance of quantitative empirical researchers in [the applied researcher] group," and that "one of the most important contributions of applied research has been to technical developments in research methods" (1980:896, 894). "New Methodologies," says Rossi, "have been invented, old ones adapted to new problems; and interdisciplinary transfer of ideas has been accelerated through the critical evaluation of applied research" because "the critical process for applied work is more timely and more intense, characteristics . . . which are more productive of relatively rapid progress in technical and conceptual quality" (1980:896–897).Finally, and perhaps most important of all, we should note that it is

a major function of applied research . . . to provide occasions and pressures for interdisciplinary investigations and for the development of a theoretic system of "basic social science" rather than discrete bodies of uncoordinated specialized theory (Merton, 1949:171, emphasis removed).

And so, Katz argues,

The applied scientist . . . does not mind being eclectic: the engineer who designs a bridge considers tensile strength of the material he has to work with; soil and rock conditions; type and amount of traffic that will pass over the bridge; weather conditions during the process of erecting the bridge and later upon the building material [etc.]. . . . In this respect he differs from the analytic scientist, who feels it is difficult to say anything until "extraneous" variables are controlled or, at least, until the various kinds of forces that are at work have been disentangled (1976:103).

It is often precisely at the junctures created by applied science between two or more existing pure sciences that new pure sciences arise—as seems exemplified by pharmacology and the impetus it gave to the rise of biochemistry and biophysics, and also by the impetus given to the rise of political economy and sociology by the applied science demands of state management during the transition in Western Europe from feudalism to modernism.

Contributions of Pure Science to Applied Science

If we ask what essentials does the pure phase of science contribute to its applied phase, there seem to be at least four answers.

First, pure science contributes the intersubjectively verified predictions which applied science then strives to realize or avoid. It may be useful also to consider just why predictions (rather than, say, empirical generalizations or explanations) are necessary to achieve control, the objective of applied science. As briefly suggested earlier in this chapter, although we can readily manipulate our *memories* of the past, "the past" itself is beyond all manipulation. Indeed, it is just this exemption-in-principle from causal influence that differentiates the past from the present and future. But what must we do in order to manipulate the present or the future? Because there seem to be absolute limits on the speed with which any causal influence can be propagated, we always have to launch our influence ahead of the time we want it to take effect so that (like trap-shooting, or catching a fly ball) the influence and its target will reach the same place at the same time. Hence, every deliberate manipulation of the present or future world requires a prediction—however unconsciously made—of the future, and therefore, says Comte, "The importance we attach to theories that teach the laws of phenomena, and give us the power of prevision, is chiefly due to the fact that they alone can regulate our otherwise blind action upon the world" (1975:321).

Second, pure science identifies humanly manipulable points of intervention in the processes that produce the predicted event—that is, it assesses the practicability of bringing about the desired outcome in the target event, given the tools at hand. This entails reviewing the causal model (or, assuming equifinality—discussed in Chapter 14—the several causal models) that predicts the event of interest in order to find one or more variables to which available forms of human intervention might be applied. "For want of a nail, the shoe was lost/For want of a shoe the horse was lost/For want of a horse the rider was lost" suggests a diffusion causal model (Chapter 12) in which the efficiency of human intervention to save the rider was highest early in the process but intervention would still have been effective later in that process.

Third, pure science presses applied science for precisely measurable outcomes when the latter are incorporated as pure science observations. Thus, pure science wants to know not only *that* a given implementation outcome occurs, but precisely how often, under precisely what conditions, and with precisely what consequences it occurs. This is because, fourth, pure science requires that the general features of a given observation be distinguished from its idiosyncratic features in the interests of devising empirical generalizations, explanations, and predictions of ever-wider range (see Chapter 14). The latter enable applied science to anticipate the likely side effects, and long-run effects of manipulating the particular case in hand.[21]

UNDERSTANDING OF WHAT? CONTROL OVER WHAT?

Lynd says

> If nobody goes about endlessly counting throughout a lifetime the number of particles of sand along infinite miles of seashore over all the coasts of the world, why is this? Because there is no point to it, no need to complete this particular aspect of the jigsaw puzzle of the unknown (1946:183).

One may well quarrel with the finality of Lynd's declaration that there is no point and no need for this or any other possible item of understanding or control, but one can hardly quarrel with the observation that at any given time and place natural science pursues the understanding, and the control, of some things and not others.

What guides this selectivity—apart, of course, from our relatively fixed, species-inherited, "hardware" which permits us to perceive, conceive, and manipulate the world only in those ways we call "human"—is our more variable cathectic "software": our nonscience values (see Chapter 4).

It is essential to distinguish *non*-science values from science values.[22] By science values, I mean the desirability of understanding in general and of control in general; by non-science values I mean (1) the desirability of other general states vis-à-vis the world (such as ignorance, appreciation, or horror, on the one hand, or passivity, avoidance, or play, on the other) that compete with the desirability of understanding and control; and (2) the desirability of certain specific objects of understanding and control (such as international peace, and domestic tranquility)

---

[21] On the ground that "theory" belongs to pure science insofar as it is a wholly psychical (ideational) behavior, while "empirical research" implicates more physical (manipulation) behavior and therefore connotes more elements of applied science, the above discussions may be compared to Merton's views on "the bearing of sociological theory on empirical research" and vice versa (see 1957:85–117).

[22] Popper distinguishes between what he calls *"extra-scientific problems,"* for example, problems of human welfare or . . . of national defense; or . . . of an aggressive nationalist policy; or of industrial expansion; or of the acquisition of personal wealth," and "extra-scientific interests," on the one hand, and "the purely scientific interest in truth," on the other (1976:96). I reject this distinction on two grounds: (1) I regard applied science as no less scientific than pure science, and (2) "truth," to my ear, has a more strongly realist ring than "understanding," by which I mean to imply a stronger measure of phenomenalism than of realism. Polanyi uses this term too, but he also manifests the same derogation of applied science and the desire for control that Popper does, when he says "Scientific inquiry is motivated by the craving to understand things" (1969:120).

that supplement the general desirability of understanding and control by selecting their targets.

In this view, then, the relation of science to values is a complex one: Science *has* its own values, *rejects* other values that contradict these, *ignores* other values that are neutral toward them, and *relies upon* still other values to give them direction (see Fig. 4.1 for the typology that underlies this analysis).

I shall not examine here the role of competing, or irrelevant, non-science values but perhaps the role of object-specifying non-science values (called throughout the rest of Part III simply "values") may be clarified by examining a controversy in which that role is at confused issue.

Popper argues (as I have, earlier in this chapter) that "the objectivity of science is not a matter of the individual scientists but rather the social result of their mutual criticism," and that objectivity therefore "depends, in part, upon a number of social and political circumstances which make this criticism possible" (1976:95). Popper seems to specify the nature of these "circumstances" when he says

> Objectivity can only be explained in terms of social ideas such as competition (both of individual scientists and of various schools); tradition (mainly the critical tradition); social institution (for instance, publication in various competing journals and through various competing publishers; discussion at congresses); the power of the state (its tolerance of free discussion) (1976:96).

Popper also notes that although "such details as the [particular] social or ideological habitat of the researcher . . . tend to be eliminated in the long run, . . . admittedly they always play a part in the short run" (1976:96). Therefore, says Popper,

> Our motives and even our purely scientific ideals, including the ideal of a disinterested search for truth, are deeply anchored in extra-scientific and, in part, in religious evaluations. Thus the "objective" or the "value-free" scientist is hardly the ideal scientist. Without passion we can achieve nothing— certainly not in pure science (1976:97).

But Popper flatly contradicts all his expressions of belief in the "anchoring" of science in "extra-scientific" values (thereby providing the ground for Adorno's opposition[23]) when he declares that "an objective science must be 'value-free'; that is, independent of any value judgment" (1976:91), and claims that

[23] Adorno says sociology is necessarily

a critique of [its] object . . . [because] no matter how instrumentally the . . . [procedures of science] are defined, their adequacy for the object is still always demanded. . . . In the method, the object must be treated in accord with its significance and importance, otherwise even the most

> As in all other sciences, we are, in the social sciences, either successful or unsuccessful, interesting or dull, fruitful or unfruitful, in exact proportion to *the significance or interest of the problems* we are concerned with. . . . In all cases, without exception, it is *the character and the quality of the problem* which determine the value, or the lack of value, of a scientific achievement (1976:88–89, emphasis added).

As though "significance," "interest," "character," and "quality" inhered *in* the problem rather than being conferred *on* the problem by "social and political circumstances," "social ideas," "the social or ideological habitat of the researcher"— in short, by values.[24]

Popper, of course, recognizes the contradiction (although he calls it a "paradox" and says he does not regard it as very important) and claims it

> disappears . . . if we replace the demand for freedom from attachment to all values by the demand that it should be one of the tasks of scientific criticism to point out confusions of value and to separate purely scientific value problems of truth, relevance, simplicity, and so forth, from extra-scientific problems (1976:97–98).

However, merely *separating* values to which one is attached, obviously, cannot produce freedom from them, and therefore, because he goes no further than this, Popper does not resolve the contradiction at all. We are left believing that Popper holds both that science must be *free* of values, and also that it must be *attached* to the same values.[25]

A simple resolution, however, does seem to reside in the argument put forward above which differentiates among values in a different way from Popper and permits science, like any other sociocultural substructure of a society, to adhere to its own distinctive values while rejecting some other values, ignoring others, and (again, like any other sociocultural substructure) depending upon still others.

---

polished method is bad. . . . [Therefore,] if its concepts are to be true, critical sociology is, according to its own idea, necessarily also a critique of society (1976b:114).

In other, perhaps plainer, words: by deciding to study one object and not another, and by deciding to use one method in that study and not another, we necessarily imply an evaluation of the objects chosen and rejected (see also Sztompka, 1979:209–210).

[24] Popper says this while making the point that "objectivity in the social sciences is much more difficult to achieve (if it can be achieved at all) than in the natural sciences . . . [because] only in the rarest of cases can the social scientist free himself from the value system of his own social class and so achieve even a limited degree of 'value freedom' and 'objectivity' " (1976:91). But this is clearly contradicted by another statement only a few pages later in the same essay: (1) "it is just as impossible to eliminate [extra-scientific interests] from research in the natural sciences . . . as from research in the social sciences" (Popper, 1976:96).

[25] As corollary to this contradiction, we are also left believing that Popper holds both that objectivity (i.e., "truth, relevance, simplicity, and so forth") can be achieved *without* intersubjectivity, "mutual criticism," and the "social and political circumstances which make this criticism possible," and also that it can *never* be so achieved.

Other Views of the Relationship Between Pure and Applied Science

The schematic image of relations between pure and applied science presented in Fig. 13.1 and discussed above may be further elucidated by comparing it with others in the sociological literature. MacRae specifies certain qualities of applied science with which I agree, but he is not explicit about the qualities of pure (or "basic") science and their connections to, as well as differences from, applied science:

> The concepts and variables of applied science differ from those of basic science in three ways. In applied science (1) The dependent variable is a valuative one. (2) The independent variables . . . are expected to relate to action that influences the realization of the value in question; (3) Applied research often involves a repeated alternation between action and the monitoring of a valuative dependent variable (1976:281).

Coleman differentiates pure and applied science in the same general way that I do ("I will call the research that is designed to advance knowledge in a scientific discipline 'discipline research' and will call the research designed as a guide to social action 'policy research' " [1972:2]), but he goes on to counterpose the two researches in ways that drastically minimize their interdependence: "[Disciplinary] values do not recognize the existence of action, nor even the world of action—except as subject-matter for study—but only of knowledge" (1972:14), and "Discipline research resides wholly within the world of the discipline and is subject only to this latter set of values" (1972:10).

Scott and Shore also argue for roughly the same difference between "the academic's world" and the "policy-maker's world" that I do ("The academic sociologist's main goal is to further understanding about society; the policy-maker's goal is to initiate programs of social action in order to change society" [1979:224]), but like Coleman, they minimize interdependence between the two "worlds" when they "reject as misleading the notion put forth by some that most pure research has some practical utility and that most applied research has interesting theoretical implications" (1979:53), and when, most inexplicably of all, they assert that "research carried out in accordance with disciplinary [i.e., pure science] standards is unlikely to result in causal explanations" (1979:227). For my part, I hold, first, that all intersubjectively verified pure research either has had, now has, will have, or at the very least can have, practical utility (and also that all intersubjectively verified applied research either has had, now has, will have, or can have theoretical utility). The fact that a given item of pure research has not *yet* had practical utility does not mean that it will or can have none. Indeed, Taton claims that "the theoretical discoveries which have had the richest results in the applied field have often been those which in their original form had appeared to be the most abstract, and [the] furthest removed from all concrete consideration" (1962:31).

Second, I hold that research carried out according to "disciplinary" standards is, in fact, the *only* research that can result in causal explanations. Here I agree with Campbell when he says

> naturalistic observation of events is an intrinsically equivocal arena for causal inference, by qualitative or quantitative means, because of the ubiquitous confounding of selection and treatment. Any efforts to reduce that equivocality will have the effect of making conditions more "experimental." "Experiments" are, in fact, just that type of controlled observational setting optimal for causal inferences (1975a:7).

Merton gives an example:

> it may be found that provision for several rest periods in an industrial plant reduces labor-turnover, raises employee morale, etc. The plant manager who finds that this program "works" may see no occasion for further research. . . . [But the] fact remains that he has not yet identified the critical variable in this result: was it that rest-periods reduced fatigue? Or was it, possibly, that the degree of managerial concern with employees' problems (as symbolized by rest-pauses) was the decisive variable?. . . . Unless the crucial theoretical variable . . . can be identified, there is no basis for assuming that the same results will be obtained on other occasions (1949:179).

Moreover, I hold that the policy-maker's sense of causation is no different from the pure scientist's sense except that the former is apt to want a stronger and more robust effect, and the latter is apt to want stronger and more precise intersubjective verification, to justify inferring its presence.

Rossi denies "formal difference" between pure and applied sociology, while upholding an environmental difference:

> There are no formal differences between "basic" and "applied" research or between "research as such" and "evaluation research". . . . Whatever differences there are between pure research and evaluation research . . . lie in the kinds of organizational contexts in which typically the one or the other type of research is carried out and in the relationship among researchers, those who provide the funds for research, and the audiences to which findings are directed (1979:97).

Mulkay also argues against formal difference between pure and applied research ("The intellectual procedures adopted in pure and applied research are frequently indistinguishable and the scientific results often identical" [1977:95]), and in favor of an environmental difference:

> from a sociological perspective the distinction is *not* between types of science or between types of motive, but between the social contexts in which research is undertaken. [Participants in pure research] are expected, indeed, they are constrained, to pursue research topics on the basis of their scientific significance. The audience for results consists of other researchers who are working upon the same or related problems and who judge the adequacy of the results by means of scientific criteria. . . . [Participants in "applied research"] are expected to produce results which have useful practical consequences. Furthermore, the main audience for these results is composed of nonresearchers (1977:95).

Now there seem to be two separate questions raised by Rossi, and Mulkay: one is whether there are any differences in procedure or purpose between pure and applied science; the other is whether there are any differences in their organizational or social environments. While I certainly do recognize the environmental differences to which Rossi, and Mulkay, point, I argue that these differences are determined by more fundamental differences of purpose and procedure—a view which Mulkay, in spite of himself, seems implicitly to support when he claims applied research is *"expected* to produce results which have useful practical consequences." Indeed, I argue that even should all environmental differences of organizational setting, funding relationships, and audience be removed, the differences (and linkage) between the purposes and procedures of pure research, on the one hand, and applied research, on the other, would persist. Alexander takes the next step and argues that those differences *should* persist (although unfortunately he does not say the same thing about their linkages): "If the integrity of both kinds of thinking, the normative and the cognitive, is to be presumed, it is precisely [the distinction between facts and values, theory and practice] which must at all costs be maintained" (1981:283).

Finally, let us note that the relationship between pure and applied science (or between "theory and praxis")—together with the nature of the communication required for intersubjective verification of the conclusions of such analysis—has occupied much of Habermas' attention, although it must be admitted that his style of expression is not exactly transparent. Thus, Habermas seems to have in mind both the distinction between pure and applied science and their interdependence when, after distinguishing "between communication (which remains embedded within the context of action) and discourses (which transcend the compulsions of action)," he goes on to say that "The interests which direct knowledge presume the unity of the relevant system of action and experience vis-à-vis discourse; they retain the latent reference of theoretical knowledge to action by way of the transformation of opinions into theoretical statements and their reformation into knowledge oriented toward action" (1973:19–20). In a comment generally reminiscent of Fig. 13.1, he argues that "In [an industrially advanced society], science, technology, industry, and administration interlock in a circular process. In this process the relationship of theory to praxis can . . . assert itself as the purposive-rational application of techniques assured by empirical science" (1973:254). Habermas then adds, however, as I would not (inasmuch as I stress the contributions of applied to pure science just as much as those of pure to applied) that "The social potential of science is reduced to the powers of technical control—its potential for enlightened action is no longer considered. . . . Emancipation by means of enlightenment is replaced by instruction in control over objective or objectified processes" (1973:254–255).

SUBSTANTIVE INTERRELATIONSHIPS

Because this chapter introduces Part III, dealing specifically with scientific procedure, I have stressed *formal* interrelationships among the components shown in Fig. 13.1 up to this point. It is important to note, however, the way in which the *substantive content* of each component may also be related to that of every other component. Indeed, when we speak of different scientific "disciplines" as wholes, we mean that analyses carried out within any given one of them are closely related to each other substantively. Thus, biochemistry, physics, and economics investigate different phenomena and therefore have their own substantively distinctive observations (made via their own distinctive instrumentation, scaling, and measurement techniques), their own empirical generalizations, explanations, and predictions. Similarly, on the applied side, genetic engineering, electronics, and business are characterized by substantively distinctive plans, decisions, implementations, and outcomes—and the politics, economics, and administration involved in producing them take such substantive differences into account.

Scientific disciplines are, in a word and by definition, more-or-less integrated substantively, and this integration manifests itself in each information component of scientific procedure. Moreover, within each scientific discipline, the "subfields," "specialties," and individual "research reports" that comprise it also possess substantive integration—albeit of successively narrower focus—and at the level of broadest focus, there is also substantive integration insofar as all the natural sciences share common interest in the world as sensually experienced and intersubjectively communicable.

Thus, we seem to have a rough hierarchy of substantive interests, such that each level is more-or-less integrated within itself across all the information components shown in Fig. 13.1. Such substantive integration seems to be what Kuhn has in mind when he refers to disciplinary "paradigms" as "accepted examples of actual scientific practice—examples which include law, theory, application, and instrumentation together—[that] provide models from which spring particular coherent traditions of scientific research" (1970:10). This may also be what Lakatos has in mind when he refers to "scientific research programmes" as telling us "what paths of research to avoid . . . [and] what paths to pursue," and, while citing specific cases like "Newton's programme" and "Einstein's programme," also claims that "Even science as a whole can be regarded as a huge research programme" (1978:47 ff).[26]

It should be emphasized, however, that although a given discipline, or subfield, or specialty, or individual research report may be substantively integrated within itself and across some or all the relevant components of Fig. 13.1, it is not likely to be the exclusive creator or possessor of a given observation, empirical generalization, explanation, or prediction—or the exclusive participant in a given plan, decision, implementation, or outcome. That is, the substantive content of every information component shown in Fig. 13.1 is apt to carry relevance across multiple subfields, multiple specialties, and/or multiple research reports. As a result, the latter will be linked together substantively at one or more of the points shown in Fig. 13.1. It is just this multiple and variable linkage that is referred to when we say, for example, that social psychology is more closely related to sociology than to geology but less closely related to sociology than to psychology.

In summary, the picture I want to suggest of substantive interrelationships across the full range of natural science disciplines, subfields, specialties, and research reports represents these interrelationships as (1) a multidimensional and constantly changing lattice having a roughly hierarchic structure in which (2) the nodes within the lattice at which the various disciplines are, at a given moment, substantively related (and within each discipline the nodes at which the various subfields are substantively related; and within each subfield the nodes at which the various specialties are related; and within each specialty the nodes at which the various research reports are related) are one or more of the information components shown in Fig. 13.1, and (3) the possible forms of being "related" are given by the typology of psychical behavior coincidences shown in Fig. 4.1, namely, identity, complementarity, contradiction, and neutrality.

Against the preceding background and outline, let us turn to a closer examination of each element portrayed in Fig. 13.1—bearing in mind that no attempt will be made to be comprehensive in that examination. Attention will focus on those aspects of each element that seem most relevant to specifically sociological analysis and that contribute most to the substantive principles of that analysis as developed in Parts I and II.

[26] Lakatos' notion of "scientific research programmes" seems conceptually heterogeneous insofar as it includes, without explicit distinction, (1) substantive laws (divided into a "hard core" and a "protective belt"—see Chapter 14), (2) a procedural plan including unspecified "successive links" and "steps," and also (3) normative injunctions (called the "negative heuristic" and the "positive heuristic") not to attack the laws in the hard core and to build up laws in the protective belt (see Lakatos, 1978:47 ff).

14
Pure Science

This chapter covers the following information elements (and their associated techniques and information transformations), as shown in Fig. 13.1: *Observations* and *empirical generalizations* try to discover what exists in the world as humanly experienced; *explanations* try to discover why it exists; *predictions* try to discover what will exist; and *tests* try to assess the accuracy of predictions and therefore the truth of explanations and the believability of observations.

We begin by examining three kinds of referents of observations, and then discuss the derivation of generalizations across such observations, and the way such empirical generalizations are constructed and how they set the limits of explanations. Next, we consider explanations and predictions, and the two principles (causation and subsumption) on which they both rest. The roles of these principles in discriminating between theories and models during what Kuhn has called the "normal" and "crisis" phases of scientific development, and in extending the scope of any given explanation or prediction, are discussed. The chapter closes with some procedures involved in testing predictions.

OBSERVATIONS

By an "observation" I mean the outcome of comparing sensory perceptions of some kind to some prior, standardizing, scale. In "measuring," the scale is numerical,[1] but in other kinds of "observing" the scale may include nominal concepts like "society," "behavior," "organism," and so forth. When no substantively applicable scale is available—as when a person is deaf or colorblind or unfamiliar with the concept "society" or cannot read a sphygmomanometer—no observation of the indicated kind can be made. Without observations, of course, no communicable, intersubjectively verifiable, empirical descriptions can be made. Thus, the scale we use is a crucial determinant of our descriptions—and these, in turn, are crucial determinants of our empirical generalizations, which are necessary contributors to explanations and predictions. It is for this reason that Parts I and II of this book were devoted to explicating the most important substantive concepts in sociology, for these concepts represent the scales that enable us to make distinctively sociological observations and to communicate descriptions of these observations to one another.

The scales used in empirically delimiting a given phenomenon may be differentiated according to the kind of data to which they refer. One scale may be *epistemic* and refer to properties of the phenomenon in question;[2] a second may be *genetic* and refer to presumed causes of the phenomenon; and a third may be *functional*[3] and refer to its presumed effects. For example, we may identify and

---

[1] Stevens defines measurement as "the assignment of numerals to objects or events according to rules" (1946:22; see also Torgerson, 1958:13).

[2] Northrop says "when [one] interprets the yellow . . . disc in the blue sky as a sign of the presence of a three-dimensional object called the moon, an epistemic correlation has occurred. The two-dimensional, directly inspected, circular colored patch is conceived as correlated with one hemisphere of the three-dimensional, astronomical body" (1959:119–120). Although Northrop uses this example to show that "an epistemic correlation joins a thing known in the one way to what is in some sense that same thing known in a different way" (1959:119), what was essential about an epistemic correlation for my purposes is the relationship it asserts between two or more properties of a phenomenon (e.g., circularity and sphericity in the case of the moon)—whether these properties are at any given time and place "known in the same way" (whatever that means) or not. Note that the epistemic or property criterion is itself a kind of functional or effect criterion, but the effects of concern are strictly limited to those occurring in some specialized observation instrument. Thus, the properties of a phenomenon (e.g., its height, weight, color, duration, or probability of occurrence) are its observed effects on some yardstick, weight scale, colorimeter, clock, counter, etc.—including the unaided human eye, ear, nose, finger, or tongue—however crude, or sophisticated, such instruments may be. The functional criterion may, in turn, be described as a type of epistemic criterion wherein the properties are not observed in specialized measuring instruments but in other phenomena (to which such instruments are, however, applied in assessing the change in their properties). Thus, the difference between the two criteria may be exemplified as follows: the *effect* of a fire engine on a fire is to help reduce the dimensions of the fire's properties—that is, to "put it out"—but the color *property* of a fire engine has the effect of making our retinas register "red."

[3] Geuss' appeal to "epistemic properties," "functional properties," and "genetic properties" to characterize "ideology in the perjorative sense" (1981:13) is related to my own appeal to these criteria in complicated ways. The complications may be suggested by the facts that he calls all three criteria "properties" and combines them all, indiscriminately, in setting forth "ideology in the descriptive sense" (1981: especially 10–11). Blalock's analysis appears similar but not the same as my own, when, after asking "How do we get a theoretical handle on . . . diverse behaviors [of individuals] so as to group them into a much smaller number of conceptual ones?" (1979:883)—and assuming that by "getting a theoretical handle on" he means only "define empirically," not "explain"—he indicates

measurably differentiate houses according to their size and shape, color, composition, contents, locations, and so forth, or we may identify and differentiate houses according to the purposes, fabricators, fabrication processes, and the like, that cause them to exist, or we may identify and differentiate houses according to what they do—for example, provide shelter for humans, for nonliving human artifacts, for living human artifacts, and so forth, of various kinds and numbers.

Consider, for a more sociological example, Durkheim's and Weber's definitions of social phenomena. Durkheim first defines a "social fact" by its effects: "A social fact is every way of acting, fixed or not, capable of exercising on the individual an external constraint," and then goes on, apparently unaware of the difference, to define a social fact by its properties: "or again, every way of acting which is general throughout a given society . . ." (1938:13). Weber eschews property criteria altogether and concentrates on defining "social action" by its causes—especially its causing intention or "orientation." Thus, "Action is social," Weber says, "in so far as, by virtue of the subjective meaning attached to it by the acting individual (or individuals), it takes account of the behavior of others and is thereby oriented in its course" (1947:88).

Homans follows Durkheim's reliance on effect criteria: "social behavior is simply behavior in which the action of one man causes [i.e., has an effect on] the action of another" (1974:77), and also on definition by property: "The usual descriptions of groups consist of statements of . . . recurrences, in human behavior at different places or at different intervals" (1950:28). Parsons, however, follows Weber's reliance on cause criteria when, in setting forth the "theory of action," he declares that "any behavior of a living organism might be called action; but to be so called, it must be analyzed in terms of the anticipated states of affairs toward which it is directed . . ." (1951:53).

Note that the three kinds of observation criteria just mentioned vary independently of each other: Whatever has the properties of a social phenomenon (or a house, or anything else) may have variable causes and variable effects; whatever

---

four strategies, all of which rely on theoretical assumptions that usually remain implicit: (1) a linkage is assumed between the behavior and some motivational state, which usually appears in the theoretical definition [of the behavior]; (2) there is an assumed causal linkage between the behavior and some consequence, which is an integral part of the definition [of the behavior]; (3) the behavior is defined in terms of some general social standard with which it is compared; and (4) there is an assumed linkage between the behavior and other variables that cause this behavior to be repeated, with replication being an essential component of the definition (1979:883).

Empirical definition on the basis of Blalock's first assumption is, in my view, genetic; the second assumption is functional; and the third assumption is epistemic. (Although Blalock is noncommittal regarding the nature of the "general social standard," his illustrations [1979:886–887] seem clearly to indicate what I refer to here as properties.) Blalock's discussion of measurement on the basis of his fourth assumption is ambiguous. He seems clearly to indicate only his second (functional) assumption in his illustrative definition of "reinforcing behaviors as those that are followed by later instances of the behaviors they are supposed to reinforce" (1979:887), but replications can, in principle, be just as easily observed on the basis of the first (cause) or third (property) assumption. In short, I do not regard Blalock's fourth strategy as independent of the first three.

possesses the causes attributed to a social phenomenon may have variable properties and variable effects; and whatever possesses the effects attributed to a social phenomenon may have variable properties and variable causes. As a result, we have a choice: we may require that one, two, or all three criteria be met—giving increasing specificity to the observation with each additional criterion—so that in the third, fully combined form, we would restrict ourselves to the claim that only something having such-and-such properties, *and* such-and-such causes, and *also* such-and-such effects should be considered a social phenomenon, or a house, or whatever.

Of course, every use of the cause criterion, and the effect criterion, is risky: we must have strong theoretical grounds for believing that the causes and effects we impute to, and therefore regard as indicating, the phenomenon in question are actually and unexceptionably associated with that phenomenon; otherwise, our observations and descriptions will be inconsistent. We must be careful not to explain the phenomenon with the same causes, or predict the same effects of the phenomenon, as we have used in defining it; otherwise, the explanation or prediction will be tautological. The property criterion is risky too—we must beware of other phenomena mimicking the phenomenon in question by displaying some of its properties—but the risks seem less here because the causal inferences are fewer. Thus, the general natural science preference is for epistemic criteria, reserving genetic criteria and functional criteria for identifying homologs and analogs, respectively, of a given property-identified phenomenon.

Torgerson says "measurement pertains to properties of objects, and not to the objects themselves. . . . [A] stick is not measurable in our use of the term, although its *length, weight, diameter, and hardness* might well be" (1958:14). When we apply the epistemic criterion, then, a phenomenon—any phenomenon and, of course, including a social phenomenon—should be regarded as an assertion of association between two or more properties.[4] Indeed, our sense organs seem to receive information only on properties (brightness, shape, color, texture, weight, odor, taste, sound, amount of electrical charge, temperature), and not on "things." The observation of any "thing," then, constitutes an assertion that two or more such properties are associated.[5]

---

[4] Cohen and Nagel say "All observation appeals ultimately to certain *isolable* elements in sense experience [e.g., 'This band of color lies between those two bands,' 'The end of this pointer coincides with that mark on the scale']. We search for such elements because concerning them universal agreement among all people is obtainable," and go on to claim that "what is believed to be a fact" depends ultimately upon such isolable elements "together with some assumed universal connection between them" (1934:217–218).

[5] Regarding the assertions of connections between properties that constitute "extraordinary things" like electrons and "ordinary things" like human beings, trees, and rain, Quine says "The positing of . . . extraordinary things is just a vivid analogue of the positing or acknowledging of ordinary things: vivid in that the physicist audibly posits them for recognized reasons, whereas the hypothesis of ordinary things is shrouded in prehistory (1960:22).

Now for at least two reasons it seems fair to say that that association of properties, that constitution of "things," is not something given in the structure of events independently of observers, but is something accomplished by the structure of observers[6] (the latter regarded, however, and paradoxically, as parts of the structure of the very events which their observation composes). First, the evidences we already have of the existence of properties that we are not equipped to sense directly (for example, the plane of visible light polarization, electromagnetic radiation such as radio waves and X-rays whose wavelengths lie outside the narrow range of visible light, the amount and polarity of magnetization, all the properties of subatomic particles) suggest that there may well exist other properties—and all the "things" which may be constituted by associating those properties—that lie forever beyond our ability to sense at all, whether directly or indirectly. Second, evidences of hallucination, misperception, and genetic, age, and cultural differences in perception suggest that we may bring even a given set of properties that we *are* able to sense directly into different associations and thereby constitute different "things" from the same properties. As Simmel says,

> reality . . . is given to us as a complex of images, as a surface of contiguous phenomena. We articulate this datum—which is our only truly primary datum—into something like the destinies of individuals. . . . Clearly . . . there occurs a process which *we* inject into reality, an *ex post facto* intellectual transformation of the immediately given reality (1950:8).

Similarly, Powers argues that

> The brain may be full of many perceptual signals, but the relationship between those signals and the external reality on which they depend seems utterly arbitrary. At least we have no assurance that any given perception has significance outside of a human brain. It could be that none of them have, not even the first-order perceptions. . . . This means that we would be much safer in general to speak of sensation-*creating* input functions rather than sensation-*recognizing* functions (1973:37, 114).[7]

Polanyi says

---

[6] Mead, however, insists that the connection is not created by the perceiver but is "objectively there . . . it is not a psychical addition to that act and it is not an 'idea' as traditionally conceived" (1934:76).

[7] Quite inexplicably, however, Powers suspends that skepticism when he exempts physics from sensation-creating and assigns it to sensation-recognizing: "when one acts to affect reality, he is acting so as to affect [the brain's] model, and he has no inkling, *save for physics,* of what he is really doing to the external world in the process of making his brain's model behave in various ways" (1973:152, emphasis added). In the same vein, Powers argues that "system concepts such as Society or Culture are not to be found in the world represented by physical models of the universe. They are elements of psychological models of the universe. . . . To ask the *physical* significance of [society and culture] is merely to mix one model with another. A society is a perception. That is its physical nature" (1973:173).

The boundless variety of raw experiences is devoid of all meaning, and our perceptive powers can render it intelligible only by identifying very different appearances as the same objects and qualities. Snow at dusk throws less light into our eyes than a dinner jacket in sunshine, and if you look at the surface of these objects through a blackened tube, snow may appear dark and the black cloth light. But when we look at them in the usual way, snow will always be seen to be white, and a dinner jacket to be black. . . . Such is the function of peripheral impressions when used as clues, and it is our powers of comprehension that bring them into action by looking at them with a bearing on the object of our attention. It is this art, the art of seeing infinite varieties of clues in terms of relatively few and enduring objects, by which we make sense out of the world (1969:114–115).

In short, "There is more to seeing than meets the eyeball" (Norwood Hanson, quoted in Kaplan, 1964:131).

It should be noted that although the generic definition of social phenomena (set forth in Chapter 2) refers only to certain *properties* that we require to be associated before constituting an observation on a social phenomenon, the special definitions of certain kinds of social phenomena set forth in Chapters 3 and 4 refer to *effects* that we must infer before we can identify those kinds. For example the "economy" of a society was regarded as a social phenomenon that has certain effects (namely, production, distribution, and consumption) on certain objects (namely, goods and services). It was argued (especially in Chapter 3) that this reliance on effect criteria seems due to the relative underdevelopment of the instruments with which we make sociological observations, which is, in turn, related to the characteristically sociological emphasis on field rather than laboratory research.[8]

EMPIRICAL GENERALIZATIONS

Every empirical definition (that is, every definition of an observable phenomenon) whether relying on the epistemic, generic, or functional criterion, is intrinsically classificatory and generalizing: we define not a single, unique, event but a type or class of event—a class that includes an unknown number of individual, unique, instances. In order to come within the purview of natural science, we normally[9] require observations on two or more such instances, believing, as someone has said, that "Once is an accident, twice is a coincidence, but three times is

[8] Of course, we are not alone in relying on effect criteria: Astronomers infer the existence of entities that do not emit or reflect enough radiation (e.g., planets, moons, interstellar dust, black holes)—and whose dimensions are therefore not directly measurable—from what are presumed to be the effects of these bodies on other entities that do emit or reflect radiation.

[9] "Normally," because at least one discipline, cosmology, so far has only one instance to observe—although there are theoretical claims that others exist.

a conspiracy." Indeed, scientific observations are generally required to be *doubly* multiple—that is, multiple analysts should each make observations of multiple instances. Thus, Popper claims

> We do not take even our own observations quite seriously, or accept them as scientific observations, until we have repeated and tested them. Only by such repetitions can we convince ourselves that we are not dealing with a mere isolated "coincidence," but with events which, on account of their regularity and reproducibility, are in principle intersubjectively testable (1961:45).

Hempel argues that

> When an individual event *b* is said to have been caused by another individual event *a, . . .* this claim cannot be taken to mean that whenever *a* recurs then so does *b;* for *a* and *b* are individual events at particular spatiotemporal locations and thus occur only once. Rather, *a* and *b* must be viewed as particular events of certain *kinds* (such as heating or cooling of a gas, expansion or shrinking of a gas) of which there may be further instances (1965:349; see also 423).

For this reason, almost every science requires empirical generalizations across multiple observations. The process of constructing such generalizations begins with the act of measurement—as Popper indicates when he says

> Measurement should be described in the following terms. We find that the point of the body to be measured lies between two gradations or marks on the measuring-rod or, say, that the pointer of our measuring apparatus lies *between* two gradations on the scale. . . . Thus an interval, a range, always remains (1961:125).

To this most fundamental and unavoidable generalization, Nagel adds sample summarization:

> In measuring the velocity of sound in a given gas, different numerical values are in general obtained when the measurement is repeated. Accordingly, if a definite numerical value is to be assigned to the velocity, these different numbers must be "averaged" in some fashion, usually in accordance with an assumed law of experimental error (1961:82).

The next generalizing step is parameter estimation. Because every science seeks universal truths (statements that are expected to hold across all observations on given phenomena), merely summarizing or "averaging" the scale values obtained by measuring a sample of observations is insufficient because the sample may be unrepresentative of all observations that could be made on that phenomenon.

Parameter estimation—whether employing essentially deductive techniques aimed at detecting nonrandom sample bias, or techniques of statistical inference aimed at detecting random sample variation, or "seat-of-the-pants," "gut-feeling," procedures aimed at both detections—therefore becomes an essential way of controlling the further transformation of individual observations into empirical generalizations. In this way, we seek to estimate the range and central tendency of different observations made on given samples of what we believe, a priori, to be the same phenomenon (e.g., What is the redness range and central tendency of all flowers whose plants have a thorny green flexible stem, pinnate leaves, etc., or what is the median income range and central tendency of all societies?).

It is through applying the measurement, sample summarization, and parameter estimation procedures just mentioned that many or few individual observations are transformed into an empirical generalization. Braithwaite defines such a generalization as "a proposition asserting a universal connection between properties," and adds that

> The generalization may assert a concomitance of properties in the same thing or event . . . or it may assert that of every two events or things of which the first has the property A and stands in the relation R to the second, the second has the property B. . . . Or it may make more complicated but similar assertions about three or four or more things. The relationship between the things may be a relationship holding between simultaneous events in the things, or it may hold between events in the same thing or in two or more things which are not simultaneous (1960:9).

The logic whereby observations are transformed into empirical generalizations (or, as Braithwaite puts it, "the inference of an empirical generalization from its instances" [1960:257n]) is often referred to as induction. Braithwaite describes two types of "inductive principles":

> There are, first, principles of induction by simple enumeration according to which an inductive hypothesis is to be treated as being well established if it has not been refuted by experience and has been confirmed by not fewer than n positive instances. . . . There are secondly, principles of elimination according to which an inductive hypothesis is taken to be well established if, while it has not been refuted by experience, alternative hypotheses have been so refuted (1960:260).

Wartofsky notes that form of induction which is most familiar to sociologists: namely, "statistical generalization," when he argues that "A statistical generalization makes the inductive inference that [a ratio of relative frequency of some property or some relation among properties] will continue to be observed as the total number of observations continues to grow" (1968:234).

Thus, generalizations like "All societies are stratified by income"; "The correlation between income and education is such-and-such"; "Businesses of the same type (e.g., gas stations, banks, doctors' offices, movie houses) tend to cluster in distinctive spatial areas of cities"; "Recreational activities tend to be concentrated during the last hours of the day and the last days of the week" are the final products of sociological descriptive analysis, and it is on this product that the next, explanatory, phase goes to work to find out why these generalizations are true.[10]

Setting the Stage for Explanation

Before examining explanation per se, however, let us note how powerfully empirical generalization predisposes explanation. Any given concrete event, having an infinite number of different properties, can yield an infinite number of different observations and therefore an infinite number of different empirical generalizations can be made about that type of event. Which properties, observations, and empirical generalizations we choose to make on the event in question is a crucial matter for subsequent analytic procedure because that choice determines the kind of explanatory factors which may legitimately be applied to the event. For example, if we describe society in terms of individual organisms only, without describing any intermediate subgroups, then only those influences that impinge on the whole society or on individuals are permissible explaining causes. However, the more intermediate subgroups we describe the more we permit influences impinging on them, as well as on the whole society and on individuals, to explain society. In more general terms, by describing a phenomenon we want to explain in one way rather than another we specify the accesses which potential explanatory causes may and may not have to it and the paths that these causes may and may not take within it. Descriptions thus set the stage on which the explanatory drama is to be played. They locate entrances and exits to the set and locate furniture that must be negotiated by causal forces moving through that set. Dispensing with metaphor, Hempel's illustration is apt:

> [R]equests for an explanation of the aurora borealis, of the tides, of solar eclipses in general or of some individual solar eclipse in particular, or of a given influenza epidemic, and the like have a clear meaning only if it is understood what aspects of the phenomenon in question are to be explained (1965:334).

[10] This implies that we can only understand and control events in their repeatable aspects—however much we may appreciate them, aesthetically and ethically, in their unique aspects.

It follows, then, that good descriptions make good explanations—but the converse is also true: the explanations we already have in mind before starting to make a given description strongly influence that description; good explanations thus make good descriptions. Indeed, as Popper says,

> The naive empiricist . . . thinks that we begin by collecting and arranging our experiences. . . . But if I am ordered: "Record what you are now experiencing" I shall hardly know how to obey this ambiguous order. Am I to report that I am writing; that I hear a bell ringing; a newsboy shouting; a loudspeaker droning; or am I to report, perhaps that these noises irritate me?. . . . A science needs points of view, and theoretical problems (1961:106).

And again:

> at no stage of scientific development do we begin without something in the nature of a theory, such as a hypothesis, or a prejudice, or a problem—often a technological one—which in some way *guides* our observations, and helps us select from the innumerable objects of observation those which may be of interest (Popper, 1973:71).

This interdependence between description and explanation, however, is saved from being entirely tautological by three things: First, the explanations of phenomena that we have already described are generally different from (e.g., of broader scope or greater detail and specificity than) the "points of view," "theoretical problems," and "[matrices] of relevance," on which the descriptions are predicated—thereby giving credence to the notion of scientific "progress" mentioned in Chapter 13. Second, partly as a result of this difference, explanations that account for specific descriptions are apt to carry more intersubjective verification than the explanations on which the descriptions are predicated because the verification required to establish the former is added on to that which is required to establish the latter. Third, that part of the untestable premises of natural science (see Chapter 16) that takes for granted the existence of a world "out there," independent of our observations but observable, in some part, by us, permits us to believe that that world may exert an independent influence over the observations we construct in order to test our explanations in ways that need not confirm these explanations but may disconfirm them.

EXPLANATIONS

Explanations have two distinct, but interdependent, aims: they explain phenomena (i.e., more precisely, of course, generalizations across two or more observations), and they explain relationships between phenomena. These two aims follow from the general natural science principle that all phenomena both contain, and are contained by, hierarchic structure. This principle was examined more closely (and applied specifically to social phenomena) in Chapter 6 and may be summarized now as asserting that every phenomenon may be treated as (1) an aggregate of "smaller" phenomena, and also (2) as a component of an aggregate constituting some "larger" phenomenon. For example, a business firm is an aggregate of "departments" and other subgroups, and one business firm, when appropriately aggregated with others, constitutes a sector of the national economy.

The manner in which this principle is manifested in scientific explanations may be exemplified as follows. Suppose we wanted to explain why billiard balls change the speed and direction of their motion. We would say collision (i.e., an exchange of causal influence) with other bodies—say, other billiard balls, for example—explains this. Suppose, however, that we wanted to explain why collision between billiard balls produces changes in their speed and direction; we would say Newton's first and second laws explain this—and so on, up the hierarchy of scientific laws to whatever may be its highest and most general laws and principles.[11] The two kinds of explanation are often called "causal" and "theoretical."

Thus, in describing the first, *causal,* aim of explanation, Hempel says "The explanation of the occurrence of an event of some specific kind E at certain times and place consists, as it is usually expressed, in indicating the causes or determining factors of E," and asserts that "the main function of general laws in the natural sciences is to connect events in [such] patterns" (1965:232). In pointing out the second, *subsumption,* aim of explanation, Hempel claims that

> empirical science raises the question "Why?" also in regard to the uniformities expressed by empirical laws and often answers it again, by means of [an] explanation, in which the uniformity in question is subsumed under more inclusive laws or under theoretical principles (1965:343),

and then underscores the difference: "the explanation of a general law by subsumption under theoretical principles is clearly not an explanation by causes" (1965:352).[12]

---

[11] Braithwaite says "A scientific theory is a deductive system consisting of a set of propositions . . . from which all the other propositions . . . follow according to logical principles" (1960:22), and Kaplan says "A hierarchical theory is one whose component laws are presented as deductions from a small set of basic principles. A law is explained by the demonstration that it is a logical consequence of these principles" (1964:298).

[12] I would add that inasmuch as any relationship between events may be regarded as constituting a single event and any single event may be regarded as constituted by a relationship between events, the distinction just made between two aims of explanation applies only after the analyst has decided, arbitrarily or by disciplinary convention, what to regard as an event. Each scientific discipline, of course, has its own conventions in this respect; perhaps the chief difference between chemistry and physics, for example, is that the latter takes as relationships between events what the former takes as whole events. But there may also be differences within disciplines (e.g., broadly speaking, microso-

Hempel is also at pains to show how the subsumption argument contributes to the causation argument (asserting that causal explanation of a phenomenon presupposes "general laws which connect 'cause' and 'effect' " [1965:348], and that "it is just this implicit claim of covering uniform connections which distinguishes the causal attribution [made in explanation] from a mere sequential narrative" [1965:360–361]). Unfortunately (in my judgment), however, Hempel does not take equal pains to show how the reverse is also true, namely, that the causation argument contributes to the subsumption argument and that the two are therefore not only different but complementary.[13] What is meant by that conclusion is discussed below.

Causation and Subsumption Explanatory Arguments

By causation I mean an energetic relationship attributed to the phenomena under analysis—specifically, a regular, temporally one-way (past-toward-future) propagation of energy at a vanishing distance in time and space.[14] This is the criterion Braithwaite describes as involving "regular sequences" of "action" in which the interval between successive members of the sequence can be filled in with a spatiotemporally continuous chain of events (see Braithwaite, 1960:309–310; see also Feigl, 1953:408–418; and Nagel, 1961:74). Nagel emphasizes the persistence of the idea of causality:

> It is beyond serious doubt that the term "cause" rarely if ever appears in the research papers or treatises currently published in the natural sciences, and the odds are heavily against any mention in any book on theoretical physics. Nonetheless, though the *term* may be absent, the *idea* for which it stands continues to have wide currency. It not only crops up in everyday speech, and in investigations into human affairs by economists, social psychologists, and historians, it is also pervasive in the accounts natural scientists give of

---

ciologists take as relationships between events what macrosociologists take as whole events—see Chapter 6). It follows that what is a causal argument for one analyst may be a subsumption argument for another, but for all analysts causation is taken to operate only *within* levels of generality (i.e., between events), whereas subsumption operates only *between* levels of generality (i.e., between relationships)— no matter how events and relationships are defined.

[13] Homans emphasizes the difference more than the complementarity (see Homans, 1980:18).

[14] I say "attributed" because causation, by this definition, can never be directly observed. Being finite and relying on finite instruments and indicators, we cannot focus down to that "vanishing"— ultimately, infinitely small—distance in time and space across which causal influence is assumed to be propagated. As a result, we cannot be certain that some other, unknown, factor does not in that infinitely small and unobservable—but utterly crucial—distance shoulder aside whatever causal influence we have been tracking up to that point and substitute itself. As Keyfitz says, "Observed uniformities make us *think* that one element has the power to cause another, but that is subjective, for the power in question can never be observed" (1980:184–185).

their laboratory procedures, as well as in the interpretations offered by many theoretical physicists of their mathematical formalism. . . . In short, the idea of cause is not as outmoded in modern science as is sometimes alleged (1965:12).

The reasons for this persistence do not seem hard to find: We only know the difference between past and future by observing causal irreversibility—that is, by learning that you can't go home again; that all the king's horses and all the king's men couldn't put Humpty Dumpty together again; that the moving finger writes and having writ, moves on. And we only know the difference between one place and another or between one thing and another by observing that causal relations differ between these loci—for example, between land and sea or house and highway.

By subsumption, on the other hand, I mean an ideational or logical relationship attributed not to the *phenomena* but to *propositions about* the phenomena. In such a relationship, we regard one proposition as being a special case included by another more general proposition, as we pursue the impossible dream of one supremely inclusive hierarchy of natural laws expressing the single simplest human understanding of the world—and "simplicity," says Quine, "engenders good working conditions for the continued activity of the creative imagination, for, the simpler a theory, the more easily we can keep relevant ideas in mind" (1960:20; see also Popper, 1961:142).

Here, then, seems to be the fundamental complementarity between subsumption and causation: subsumption enables us to entertain hopes of understanding all the variegated things in the world as expressions of one single super-general law; and causation infuses each level in this hierarchy of scientific laws with the import of history, the ineluctability and irreversibility of time, on which rest not only our fears of death and the world's end but all our hopes to improve our lives and to make of the world a humanly more habitable place.

Now let us see how these two principles—causation and subsumption—are combined in the explanatory and predictive procedures of natural science.

EXPLANATORY AND PREDICTIVE PROCEDURES

In Fig. 14.1 are represented explananda[15] (i.e., the variables we wish to explain; roughly speaking, effects, dependent variables) and explanantes (i.e., the variables we claim do the explaining; roughly speaking, causes, independent vari-

---

[15] I adopt Hempel's terms, "explanandum" and "explanans" (1965:247) here, rather than Braithwaite's "explicandum" and "explicans" (1960:320), in keeping with my references to scientific "explanation" rather than "explication."

General law level

Special law level

Individual generalization level

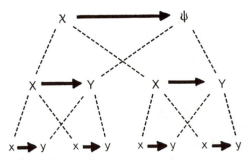

Figure 14.1. Explanation and prediction by causation and subsumption arguments. (Arrows represent causation arguments; dotted lines represent subsumption arguments.)

ables) at three levels of propositional generality. At the lowest level we refer to individual generalizations, such as when we claim that the change in motion of billiard balls is explained by their collisions with other billiard balls. The appropriate aggregation of two or more low-level generalizations (pertaining, say, to feathers, lumps of iron, and so on) may produce a higher-level, more encompassing, generalization or "special law," for example, we may claim that changes in motion of any and all material objects may be explained by their collision with other material objects (i.e., Newton's first law). The appropriate aggregation of two or more such special laws, in turn, may produce a still more encompassing "general law," for example, Einstein's special relativity theory, etc.

Note that although for the sake of simplicity only three levels of propositional generality are shown here, the hierarchy of levels remains inevitably open at both ends. Thus, whatever is treated as a single unitary phenomenon for one purpose or at one time in the history of a given science may be treated as composed of several parts for another purpose or at another time or by another science. Similarly, whatever is regarded as the most general level of scientific law in one analysis may be regarded as subsumed by some more general laws in another analysis. As Popper says

> Theories of some level of universality are proposed, and deductively tested; after that, theories of a higher level of universality are proposed, and in their turn tested with the help of those of the previous levels of universality, and so on. The methods of testing are invariably based on deductive inferences from the higher to the lower level; on the other hand, the levels of universality are reached, in the order of time by proceeding from lower to higher levels (1961:277).[16]

[16]There is ambiguity in usages of the term "theory." Sometimes it refers to the entire causal-deductive structure shown in Fig. 14.1, and sometimes, as in this quotation from Popper, it refers to a single proposition or law within such a structure. Note that Popper goes on here to picture "metaphysics" not in absolute or permanent terms but in relative and historical terms: "Those theories which are on too high a level of universality, as it were (that is, too far removed from the level reached by

Now let us trace the procedures of explanation and prediction in Fig. 14.1. Suppose we have developed a description of some social phenomenon (y) that we wish to explain. Reasoning inductively, we see if we can subsume y under the explanandum (Y) of at least one well-established special law. If we can do so, we then note the explanans (X) identified by that law and reason deductively from X to one or more conditions (x) which we then accept (without further empirical test, since the special law in question is an established one) as explaining y, on the ground that whatever is unexceptionably true for the general class of phenomena (Y) to which the particular explanandum (y) belongs must also be true for that explanandum itself. Thus, in sum, the explanatory inference procedure starts with inductive reasoning (from y and Y), ends with deductive reasoning (from X to x), and its net result is to subsume the entire causal relation $x \rightarrow y$ under $X \rightarrow Y$.

For example, suppose we wanted to explain the empirical generalization that the leadership of mass membership voluntary associations is consistently in the hands of only a few individuals in each association, despite the fact that such associations hold regular elections, and suppose Michels' "iron law of oligarchy" (1958:417–425) were an established special law in sociology (which, as stated by Michels, it is not—see Lipset et al., 1957). Then we might notice that our description of mass membership voluntary associations was subsumed by Michels' description of "organizations" in general; that our description of consistent leadership control by a few individuals was also subsumed by his description of "oligarchy"; and on this basis we would identify the "iron law" as a relevant special law. Next, we would note the explanantes specified by that law (i.e., the indispensability of expert leadership, the leaders' need for security, the gratitude of the led toward their leaders, and the passivity of the masses), and deduce that particular instances of these explanantes account for the consistent leadership control we started out to explain. At that point, the original relationship, whose explanandum has been observed and described empirically and whose explanantes have been logically inferred, becomes subsumed by the "iron law" as one of its instances and thereby explained.

In making a scientific prediction, the above process is reversed: whereas explanation seeks a cause given an effect (or more generally, an explanans given an explanandum), prediction seeks an effect given a cause. Therefore (still using the example drawn from Michels), we begin with an empirical generalization regarding certain conditions within a particular mass membership voluntary association (i.e., the indispensability of expert leadership, the leaders' need for security, the gratitude of the led toward their leaders, and the passivity of the masses), and ask "What leadership control situation may be predicted from these conditions?" No-

---

the testable science *of the day*) give rise, perhaps, to a 'metaphysical system' " (1960:277, emphasis added). Such relativity and historicity is clearly missing from Alexander's more fixed picture of "the metaphysical world" as simply "nonempirical" (1982:2).

ticing that the latter are subsumed by the explanantes specified in Michels' "iron law," we would then note that law's explanandum, namely, "oligarchy," and deduce that oligarchy is the predicted outcome of the described conditions. Again, at that point the entire original relation—whose explanantes have been observed and described empirically and whose explanandum has been logically inferred—becomes subsumed by the "iron law" as one of its instances.

Having thus considered the degree to which the subsumption and causation principles are interdependent in explanatory and predictive procedures, let us consider also the degree to which they are independent. Thus, a given scientific statement can be supported mainly by causal evidence, with relatively few deductive (subsumptive) connections to more general statements, or mainly by deductive connection to more general statements, with relatively little causal evidence. This distinction seems to be what Merton has in mind when he defines an "empirical generalization" as "an *isolated* proposition summarizing observed uniformities or relationships between two or more variables," and expressly reserves the term "scientific law" for "a statement of invariance *derivable from a theory*" (1957:95, 96, emphases added).[17] Braithwaite mentions both types of support but emphasizes the first when he refers to "generalizations which have been established by direct induction without any indirect hypothetico-deductive support" (1960:322). Nagel argues that

> The evidence on the strength of which a statement L is called a law can be distinguished as either "direct" or "indirect". . . . For example, direct evidence for the law that copper expands on heating is provided by lengths of copper wire which expand on heating. . . . The evidence for L may [also be] that L is jointly derivable with other laws L_1, L_2, etc., from some more general law (or laws) M, so that the direct evidence for these other laws counts as (indirect) evidence for L (1961:64–65).

Scientific analysis, of course, always strives to provide maximal evidential support for every proposition and also to subsume every proposition under more general laws. But it should be re-emphasized that the total corpus of scientific understanding seems bound to remain poorly articulated internally as well as open at both ends, so that the desired complete and closed subsumption of all scientific propositions is an ideal—certainly irresistible to such simplistic minds as ours, but forever beyond our grasp. Similarly, empirical support is always only tentative, such that

---

[17] This seems to parallel another of Merton's distinctions—namely, that between serendipitous and nonserendipitous findings; a serendipitous finding is one that is not *predicted* by an available theory, whereas an empirical generalization (according to Merton's definition) is one that is not *explained* by an available theory (see Merton, 1957:103–108). See also Kaplan's discussion of "cryptic data" as those that "not uncommonly . . . provide a point of departure for significant theoretical advance" (1964:134).

the basic standards of scientific inquiry demand that an empirical statement, however well supported, be . . . admitted to membership in [the class of all statements asserted or accepted by empirical science at time t] only tentatively, i.e., with the understanding that the privilege may be withdrawn if unfavorable evidence should be discovered (Hempel, 1965:396, see also 379).

Thus, every such empirical statement may be struck down at any moment by newly discovered (or newly appreciated) anomalous cases: the first person who emerges unscathed and smiling after actually having been sawn in half will falsify innumerable scientific laws—indeed, the tantalizing possibility that we may someday see such a thing creates a large part of the fascination of the trick and makes us, as all magicians know, want to believe.

Now, having introduced the main ideas surrounding explanation and prediction, let us consider three important elaborations on these ideas: first, the role of the subsumption and causation explanatory-predictive principles in discriminating between theories and models; second, their roles in "normal" and "crisis" developmental phases of a science; and, third, their roles in extending the scope of explanations and predictions.

Theories and Models

Figure 14.1 permits us to describe a theory most economically as at least two lower-level propositions subsumed under a higher. A theory, then requires *both* causal and deductive structures—explanations do not require both; they may rest on either. The specification that both structures are required for a theory rejects Kaplan's identification of two "types of theories"—"concatenated" (causal) and "hierarchical" (deductive) (see 1964: 298–300), but accords with and explicates Blalock's definition of a theory as containing "lawlike propositions that interrelate . . . concepts or variables two or more at a time . . . [plus] additional propositions enabling one to make deductive statements connecting these . . . propositions" (1969:2; see also Popper, 1961:60; Brodbeck, 1959:378; and Merton, 1957:39).

By contrast with a theory, a

model is conceived as a structure of symbols interpreted in a certain way, and what it is a model of is the subject-matter specified by the interpretation. Relations among the symbols are presumed to exhibit corresponding relations among the elements of the subject-matter. . . . [I]n general, we learn something about the subject-matter *from* the theory, but not by investigating properties *of* the theory. The theory *states* that the subject-matter has a certain structure but [unlike the model,] the theory does not . . . necessarily *exhibit* that structure in itself (Kaplan, 1964:264–265).

A model, then, is a symbolic (or physical) representation of causal relations between two or more variables, all at the same deductive level—a view that may be contrasted with Alexander's unexplicated placement of models near the "metaphysical . . . (nonempirical)" end of his "continuum of scientific thought," while "complex and simple propositions" and "correlations" are placed (equally without explication) near the "physical . . . (empirical)" end (1982:3, 40). While not *being* theories themselves, however, models have at least two properties that enable them to help *generate* theories—that is, multi-leveled propositional structures. First, "Since the model is easy to manipulate, this may help discovery of the principles by which it works, if these are not already known" (Brodbeck, 1959:375). That is, by freely manipulating the model's symbols and relations in ways whose costs when applied to the subject matter itself might be prohibitive, we may learn something about the more general propositions of which the observable subject matter may present a misleadingly narrow range of instances. Second,

> Suppose that one [substantive] area . . . , for which a well-developed theory is at hand, is said to be a model for another area, about which little is as yet known. The descriptive terms in the theory of the better-known area are put into one-to-one correspondence with those of the "new" area. . . . [and] the laws of one area are "translated" into laws of the other area. . . . This replacement results in a set of laws or hypotheses about the variables of the new area. . . . For example, suppose it is wondered whether rumors spread like diseases. That is, can the laws of epidemiology, about which quite a bit is known, be a model for a theory of rumor-transmission? (Brodbeck, 1959:379).

Thus, both theories and models explain (and predict), but the first do so both deductively and causally whereas the second do so only causally—although each can be used to generate the other.

Explanatory-Predictive Procedures in "Normal" and "Crisis" Phases of Pure Science

Kuhn says:

> Mopping-up operations are what engage most scientists throughout their careers. They constitute what I am here calling normal science. Closely examined, that enterprise seems an attempt to force nature into the preformed and relatively inflexible box that the [established] paradigm supplies. No part of the aim of normal science is to call forth new sorts of phenomena; indeed those that will not fit the box are often not seen at all (1970:24).

"The very nature of normal research," however,

> ensures that novelty shall not be suppressed for very long. . . . And when
> . . . the profession can no longer evade anomalies that subvert the existing
> tradition of scientific practice—then begins the extraordinary investigations
> that lead the profession at last to a new set of commitments, a new basis for
> the practice of science. [These] extraordinary episodes . . . are the ones known
> in this essay as scientific revolutions (Kuhn, 1970:5–6).[18]

In the "crisis" phase of "extraordinary investigations," the scientist "will, in the first place, often seem a man searching at random, trying experiments just to see what will happen, looking for an effect whose nature he cannot quite guess" (Kuhn, 1970:87; see also 13, 15, 47). This difference between scientific procedures during normal and crisis phases seems at least partly due to differences between the procedural requirements of the subsumption and causation explanatory-predictive principles discussed above.

Thus, in a normal phase, the availability of one or more relevant and well-established laws permits analysts to explain deductively—that is, by showing through argument alone that the phenomenon they want to explain may be deduced from (or is subsumed by) one of these laws. Under crisis circumstances, when no such law is available, analysts must first engage in difficult, slow, costly, empirical research in which many rival predictions are tested and compared and crucial studies are replicated intersubjectively, with all their substantive and methodological virtues and shortfalls being laboriously argued out. Beginning with an empirical generalization-to-be-explained like "the leadership of mass membership voluntary associations is consistently concentrated in only a few hands," we might construct, test, and reject any number of hypotheses, for example, "Whenever voluntary associations have predominantly rural memberships, their leadership is consistently concentrated in only a few hands," or "Whenever voluntary associations have more than 10,000 members, their leadership is consistently concentrated in only a few hands," and so on—until we finally conceptualized something approximating Michels' hypothesis. Then, as this (or some other) hypothesis gained more intersubjective verification than its rivals,[19] it would come to be called an established scientific "law" and would serve as a subsuming premise with which

---

[18] Habermas notes that "Historical materialism has always tended to identify linear progress with the expansion of productive forces and to apply dialectical modes of analysis to the development of the relations of production" (1981:275). Kuhn, however, may be said to apply dialectical analysis (see Chapter 12) to the development of pure science—the principal driving force, according to Marx and Engels, behind the modern expansion of productive forces.

[19] Braithwaite makes the idea of competition between rival propositions crucial when he claims that "an inductive hypothesis is taken to be well established if, while it has not been refuted by experience, alternative hypotheses have been so refuted" (1960:260). Braithwaite also expresses a philosophically valid caution, but one which is entirely outside the bounds of science when he warns: "we may fall into the . . . error that, when there are a limited number of competing mutually exclusive hypotheses of the same type . . . the rejection of all of these hypotheses save one requires the acceptance of this one—forgetting that no hypothesis of this type may hold, or indeed that the phenomenon in question may fall under no general law whatever" (1960:256).

other empirical generalizations could be explained deductively and with relative ease.

This is why the establishment of one or more laws within a scientific discipline (and all the more so an entire theory) is always revolutionary in some degree, always a breakthrough into a new phase of normal science: Established laws are simply tremendous time-saving, money-saving, and labor-saving devices and their availability shifts a scientific discipline into high gear.

A second revolutionary impact of an established law is that it enables correction of the observations and empirical generalizations it subsumes. Hempel notes that Newton's law of gravitation "enables the astronomer to compute the deviations of the planets from the elliptic orbits Kepler had assigned to them" (1965:344), and that, more broadly,

> the generalizations previously accepted as correct statements of empirical reg- ularities will normally appear as approximations only of certain lawlike state- ments implied by the explanatory theory, and to be very nearly satisfied only within a certain limited range. And in so far as tests of the laws in their earlier formulations were confined to cases in that range, the theoretical ac- count also indicates why those laws, though not generally true, should have been found confirmed (1965:345).

Thus, the establishment of laws helps make more precise the past discoveries of a scientific discipline as well as propelling it more rapidly toward new discoveries. For the establishment of laws in any scientific field, however, the first requisite seems to be the establishment of standard units in terms of which observations, descriptions, explanations, and predictions may be made, communicated, repli- cated, and critically evaluated throughout the discipline at any given time and from generation to generation across time. Without standard units in which the variables of a given law may be measured by any and all analysts, no such law can become established. For example, unless one specifies the units in which energy, mass, and the speed of light are to be measured (and specifies also the procedural meaning of "multiplication," "squaring," and "equivalency"), $E = mc^2$ can have no sense-based, intersubjectively verifiable meaning whatever. It is toward an eventual working solution of this problem of standard units that Parts I and II of this book are aimed—although the steps taken there are indeed only elementary.

Extensions of Explanatory and Predictive Scope

I have argued, with the aid of Fig. 14.1, that explanation seeks *an* explanans and that prediction seeks *an* explanandum. I must now amend that argument to show how *other* explanantes and *other* explananda come within the scope of the same explanation or prediction. Consider first the extensions of scope which are made possible by the converse of subsumption under general laws, namely deduction from general laws.

EXTENSIONS OF SCOPE BY LOGICAL DEDUCTION

Every scientific law purports to be universal in scope and not limited to the original empirical generalizations on which the law is founded; that, indeed, is the sense in which the latter is more "general" than the former. This means that general laws extend their claimed scope to endlessly more of the *original* kind of empirical generalizations, and also to endlessly *other* kinds of empirical generalizations whose relations to the original kind might not otherwise be suspected. For example, not only does the claimed scope of Newton's theory extend to every apple that might ever bop anyone on the head, but, as Hempel points out, the theory claims to govern all kinds of objects in "free fall not only on the earth but also on other celestial bodies; and not only planetary motions, but also the relative motions of double stars, the orbits of comets and of artificial satellites, the movement of pendulums, certain aspects of the tides, and many other phenomena" (1965: 345).

These extensions of scope are two means whereby a scientific law directs attention toward *replicative* tests of the law on more of the *same* kind of empirical generalizations that gave rise to it, and toward what might be called *applicative* tests of the law on *other* kinds of empirical generalizations.

Through these deductive extensions of scope, scientific laws enable us to become aware of and observe more and more of the world—vastly more than we ever could without them—and the more scientific laws the more we can observe. Without certain scientific laws no one might yet have observed the planet Pluto, or the microorganisms that cause disease, or molecules, atoms, protons, or any of countless other phenomena of all kinds. Without those laws we would simply not have known where, or when, or how to look and what to see when we looked. Therefore, just as the logical subsumption involved in explanation and prediction reaches "upward" (to use the imagery of Fig. 14.1), toward more and more general propositions, the logical deduction involved in extensions of explanatory and predictive scope reaches "downward" toward more and more specific observations.

In this view, every pure natural science is both "generalizing" and "specifying"—and it is just as one-sided to identify the discovery of general laws as the ultimate goal of such sciences as it is to identify the discovery of individual phenomena as their ultimate goal.

EXTENSIONS OF SCOPE BY CAUSAL EQUIFINALITY AND EQUIORIGINALITY[20]

The extensions of scope implied by the subsumption-deductive argument for explanation and prediction have counterparts in two extensions implied by the causation argument. The first extension derives from the proposition that any given effect may be produced by at least two alternative causes, and the second extension derives from the complementary proposition that any given cause may produce at least two alternative effects.

The idea that alternative causal paths may lead to the same effect has been called "equifinality" (Heider, 1958; von Bertalanffy, 1968)[21] and the converse idea that alternative effects may flow from the same cause has been called "multifinality" by Buckley ("similar initial conditions may lead to dissimilar end-states" [1967:60]). For terminological symmetry with "equifinality," however, I shall use "equioriginality" inasmuch as the former term indicates *equivalent alternative effects* rather than *multiple coexisting causes* (and its root word is therefore "equi-" rather than "finality"). Speaking colloquially, the concept of equifinality is expressed when we say "There is more than one way to skin a cat," "All fates become one fate," "All roads lead to Rome," and the like, while the concept of equioriginality is expressed when we say we have come to a "fork in the road," a "turning point," or a "crisis" from which alternative consequences may flow.[22]

It should be noted that the principles of equifinality and equioriginality hold that alternative causes and alternative effects *may* prevail; they do not hold that such alternatives *must* prevail: Some towns may have only one road leading to them; some animals may be skinned in only one way; some turning points are merely bends in a single path. The principles alert us to the possibilities; the actualities are matters for empirical investigation. Note also that the causes and effects in question are held to be alternative or mutually exclusive rather than simultaneously contributory or "multiple." That is, among several contributory causes no single one is sufficient in itself to produce the effect in question, but

---

[20] See also the discussion of convergence and divergence causal models in Chapter 12.

[21] Heider defines equifinality as "the invariance of the end and the variability of the means" (1958:101), and von Bertalanffy calls it the ability to "attain a time-independent state independent of initial conditions and determined only by the system parameters" (von Bertalanffy, 1968:18). Braithwaite implies this idea when he says "It may be the case that [a given effect] can be produced in other ways, that it has a 'plurality of causes' (to use Mill's language)" (1960:313).

[22] Of course, no one believes any two causes or any two effects can be literally identical (obviously not; otherwise they would be only one cause or one effect), but the two may remain undifferentiated— and, in the extreme case, undifferentiable—according to some given measure or for some given purpose. Different roads, of course, lead to different Romes insofar as they approach from different directions but when we say "All roads lead to (the same) Rome" we simply disregard that differentiation in favor of emphasizing their substitutability as far as bringing us somewhere within the Roman city limits is concerned.

among several equifinal causes each single cause is sufficient—even though two or more of them may be operating simultaneously. Similarly, among multiple effects no single effect represents the total outcome of the cause in question, but among equioriginal effects each single effect does represent that total outcome.

These two explanatory-predictive principles—equifinality and equioriginality—are of such pivotal importance to all the procedures of natural science (including those of its applied phase), that it seems worthwhile to illustrate their various and often unself-conscious expressions rather fully.

Durkheim relies on the principle of equifinality when he says "There are always several routes that lead to a given goal," and on that of equioriginality when he says "It is . . . a proposition true in sociology, as in biology, that the organ is independent of the function—in other words, while remaining the same, it can serve different ends" (1938:48, 91). His study of suicide (1951) also relies on equifinality insofar as it specifies four alternative causes (anomie, egoism, fatalism, and altruism) of the same event—namely, suicide.[23]

When Merton proposes, as "a major theorem of functional analysis," that "just as the same item may have multiple functions, so may the same function be diversely fulfilled by alternative items" (1957:33–34; emphasis removed), the idea that "the same function [may] be . . . fulfilled by *alternative* items" clearly expresses equifinality, but the idea that "the same item may have *multiple* functions" is only ambiguously expressive of equioriginality. Merton's concept of "functional alternatives," then, relies on equifinality insofar as it "focuses attention on the range of possible variation in the items which can . . . subserve a functional requirement" (1957:52), and Schneider's complementary concept of "cultural alternatives" implies equioriginality insofar as it argues that the same intention may be expressed in different ways (see 1973:135).

Eisenstadt raises first an equioriginal question ("whether social movements with seemingly similar characteristics . . . may give rise, in different societies or historical settings to different structural outcomes"), and then an equifinal question (whether "the true revolution is not the only natural way of 'real,' 'systemic' change, but just one of several ways" [1978a:85, 89; see also 1978b:9–10]). Lumsden and Wilson have equifinality in mind when they refer to "the ease with which [a given] pattern alteration can be initiated by different causes and reached along separate pathways" (1981:20).

Feuer offers a hypothetical illustration of equioriginality:

> Let us imagine . . . that some primitive society has been making its living through some form of hoe culture. Over a period of years, its population has come to exceed its output of subsistence. A social crisis then confronts the

[23] On the other hand, however, Durkheim inexplicably rejects equifinality when, after criticizing John Stuart Mill's acceptance of it, he argues that "this supposed axiom of the plurality of causes [leading to the same effect] is, in fact, a negation of the principle of causality" (1938:127).

group. What shall be its response? . . . The society may revise its values to allow for infanticide, or it may decide to destroy its old, or it may embark upon cannibalism. . . . A society in crisis is in unstable equilibrium; some fortuitous occurrence may then be decisive in determining which of several possible outcomes will be realized (1965:205–206).

Buckley, also illustrating equioriginality, says "two cultures developing in very similar ecological environments may end up with very different sociocultural systems" (1967:60).

Stinchcombe offers several illustrations of equifinality; one of them argues that

In most social groups there are some roles or positions into which a youth is never admitted without previous training. . . . But in some social groups this socialization is mostly done by the family, in some by schools and universities, in some by a "basic training" period in which one deals with simulated environments . . . in some by apprenticeship, in some by a group of future peers (e.g., fraternities) (1968:81–82).

Campbell provides another illustration of equifinality:

A convergent evolution on a complex pattern of social coordination that we may call "urban" has repeatedly occurred. In such "urban" social life there occur these features: an apartmenthouse mode of residence, a nonperishable food produced and stored in surplus, a full-time division of labor, including members who do no food producing themselves, being fed by others, and with one of the first occupational specialities being professional soldiers. Such urban civilizations have apparently arisen independently several times in the course of human history. . . . [And if] we keep the list of common features at this minimum level, the convergence repeatedly occurs among the social insects (1965b:297–298).

Now, having specified and illustrated the empirical referents of the principles of equifinality and equioriginality, let us see what effects these principles have on the scope of scientific explanations and predictions. Briefly, the principle of equifinality extends the range of phenomena to which a given explanation applies by calling upon the analyst, after having causally accounted for the event in question with one explanans, to seek *other* explanantes which can account for the same event. Similarly, the principle of equioriginality extends the range of phenomena to which a given prediction applies by calling upon the analyst, after having causally predicted one explanandum from the event in question, to seek *other* explananda which can be predicted from the same event.

However, an important question arises when, after granting that "There is more than one way to skin a cat," and "There is more than one way to go from a fork in the road," we ask, What constitutes "a way" different from other ways? Clearly, at the highest level of generality, there are *no* differences at all: all ways of skinning a cat are the same, and all roads are the same; but on the other hand, at the highest level of specificity, there are *only* differences: any specific skinning of any specific cat can only occur once and must therefore be different from all other skinnings of all other cats. What justifies our stopping at one level of generality rather than another? The answer, it seems to me, is *nothing:* we are not justified in stopping at *any* given level in our pursuit of understanding insofar as complete understanding means understanding of *all* such levels. Thus, we are required always to move inductively toward maximum generality, and also deductively toward maximum specificity, no matter at what level our minds happen momentarily to be focused.

In this context, then, what the principles of equifinality and equioriginality tell us is that at *any* level of generality there may be alternative causes of the same explanandum and there may be alternative effects of the same explanans. Meanwhile, the principle of induction tells us to subsume any such alternatives that we do find under some more general rubric, if we can. Thus, we must conclude that we need—not "either," but *both*—the understandings referred to by Inkeles: "What we need is either a set of more explicit propositions indicating all the different conditions which can independently bring about [a given effect], or a more general theory which uncovers what may be common to [all such different conditions]" (1974:306).

TESTS

As we shall see in Chapter 15, applied science is always interested in predictions for their own sakes, as direct prerequisites for its future manipulations of the world. Pure science, however, is interested in predictions not for their own sakes but as indirect checks on its present understanding of the world. That is to say, not being able to test the truth of our explanations directly, because they rest on observations and empirical generalizations that have already been made and cannot be made again, we do the next best thing: we test that truth indirectly through predictions of observations and empirical generalizations that can be made in the future.

Logically speaking, however, this is not as straightforward an adjustment to necessity as it may seem, because: What if the future should be fundamentally different from the past and obey entirely different laws—or no laws at all? What if the universe should turn out to be discontinuous across time and space rather than continuous? If that were so (and, never knowing for sure what the future will bring or what goes on outside the reach of our perceptions, it *could* be so), then indirect as well as direct tests of explanations would be blocked and we could never be confident that we possess any understanding of the world at all. Against the utter hopelessness that contemplation of that possibility brings we protect ourselves, as well as we can, with a leap of faith called the "principle of the uniformity of nature" (Popper, 1961:252). This principle, discussed more fully in Chapter 16, asserts that the universe proceeds in fundamentally the same way at any two points in time and/or space (for example, astrophysicists assume that electromagnetic radiation and gravitational force are the same across the farthest and oldest reaches of the universe as they are here and now).

It is this principle that sustains the most fundamental premise of experimental hypothesis-testing, namely, that scientific confidence in the validity of an explanation developed on the basis of *past* events rightfully depends on data collected on *future* events—the premise which underlies Hempel's claim that "an explanation . . . is not complete unless it might as well have functioned as a prediction" (1965:234).[24] Once we accept this principle, the way stands clear to testing explanations by testing predictions.[25] Then, whatever data we find in the future that agrees with the prediction adds to our confidence in the explanation from which it was derived, and whatever does not agree with it calls for either (1) throwing the data out as spurious, or (2) throwing the explanation out as having been disproved, or (3) devising a more general explanation that subsumes and thereby reconciles both data and explanation.[26] Nature may abhor a vacuum (which seems doubtful,

---

[24] Given the general symmetry between his views of explanation and of prediction, one expects Hempel to argue the converse of this statement also, namely, "a prediction . . . is not complete unless it might have functioned as an explanation," but he does so far more hesitantly. He regards this as "an open question" (1965:376) for reasons that appear to be related to the distinction he draws between deterministic and probabilistic laws and his claim that predictions made on the basis of the latter will have less explanatory precision than predictions made on the basis of the former (see 1965:408). But the converse also seems true—that is, probabilistic explanations have less predictive precision than do deterministic ones (as may be seen from Hempel's own discussion of what he calls "inductive-statistical explanation" [1965:381ff], from reversing the causal arrows in his diagram of probabilistic and deterministic relations [1965:408], and also more comprehensively from Costner and Leik [1964]). It follows that the complementarity of explanation and prediction seems symmetrical at constant levels of explanatory or predictive power—as Fig. 14.1 implies.

[25] It should be noted that predictions need not pertain to future *events* but they always pertain to future *observations*—whether these are made on traces of past events (as in paleontology, geology, and astronomy) or on future events (as in the experimental sciences, properly so-called, like chemistry and physics). Thus, in order to provide justification for prediction as a test of explanation in the sciences whose subject matter belongs exclusively to the past we should refer to the "principle of the uniformity of the *traces* of nature"—whether these traces are those of future or past nature.

[26] Popper holds that disagreement between prediction and data is a far more crucial result of a test than agreement:

> the method of science is . . . to look out for facts which may refute the theory. This is what we call testing a theory—to see whether we cannot find a flaw in it . . . [facts] confirm the theory only if they are the results of unsuccessful attempts to overthrow its predictions, and therefore a telling testimony in its favor (1950:444).

It may be argued, however, that theories which resist verification just as much as they resist falsification (e.g., theories of the supernatural or of universes adjacent to our own) are not at all likely to be regarded as empirically confirmed. So when Popper says "the discovery of instances which confirm a theory means

since it has produced so much of it in 12 billion years), but science most certainly abhors a discrepancy.

Between a prediction and its test against empirical data, however, there are many procedural bridges to cross—including those pertaining to the testability and interpretation of the prediction, the sampling, instrumentation, and scaling of the data, and finally the actual test comparison and its analytic consequences. Let us very briefly survey all of these.

Testability

Predictions vary widely in the extent to which they can be tested, both in principle and in practice, and this variability goes far to distinguish scientific predictions from nonscientific ones. A prediction is testable in principle if it claims that at least one logically possible empirical generalization will not be found to be true in fact; and the more such predictions it makes or implies, the more readily testable it is. In other words, a prediction is highly testable in principle when it can be shown to be false by any of a large number of logically possible empirical findings and when only one or a few such findings can confirm it. For example, the prediction that "all human groups will be found to be either stratified or not stratified" is untestable in principle because it does not rule out any logically possible empirical findings. The prediction that "all human groups will be found to be stratified," however, is testable because it asserts that the discovery of an unstratified human group, though logically possible, will not in fact occur. Further, the prediction that "all human groups will be found to be stratified according to prestige rank" is still more testable, since it rules out and can be falsified by even more logically possible findings—that some human groups are not stratified at all, or that some are stratified but not according to prestige rank.[27]

very little if we have not tried, and failed, to discover refutations" (1973:70), it also seems true that the discovery of instances which refute a theory means very little if we have not tried, and failed, to discover confirmations. In a word, it is the *net balance* between test results that confirm, and test results that refute, a theory—that is, "the weight of the evidence"—that matters. I believe that despite himself Lakatos implies this probabilist (but *subjective* probabilist) view. Thus, on the one hand, Lakatos ridicules probabilists as hoping that "a machine could flash up instantly the value . . . of a theory, given the evidence," and lumps them together with "justificationists" and "naive falsificationists" as hoping for "instant rationality" (1978:89). But, on the other hand, he says "Now, how do scientific revolutions come about? If we have two rival research programmes, and one is progressing while the other is degenerating, scientists tend to join the progressive programme" (Lakatos, 1978:6), and this seems clearly to indicate that scientists act on their subjective estimates of the *balance* of present evidence and future promise. Indeed, Lakatos, in an unfortunately incongruous comparison of the criteria of failure with the criteria of success, speaks of such a balance when he argues that "so-called 'refutations' are not the hallmark of empirical failure [in a theory]. . . . What really count are dramatic, unexpected, stunning predictions: a few of them are enough to tilt the balance" (1978:6).

[27] See Popper (1961:112–113) for discussion of this general point.

Assuming that a prediction is testable in principle, it is testable in practice if the requisite observations, empirical generalizations, and comparisons can actually be made, given the nature of the phenomena to be investigated, and given a particular available scientific methodology and technology.

Blalock addresses some testability problems encountered in sociology, where it is extremely difficult to isolate any given system of variables from disturbances originating outside that system and where predictions are therefore often phrased in "tendency" or probabilistic terms. Accordingly, Blalock points out that

> When we state laws in statistical terms, allowing for large amounts of unexplained variation, it becomes much more difficult to develop deductive systems. For example, the simple line of reasoning, if A then B, if B then C, therefore if A then C becomes translated into if A then usually B, if B then usually C, therefore if A then sometimes C. Such a theory no longer has much predictive value, unless precise values can be supplied for the probability of B given A, and so forth (1968:156).

Confronted with this difficulty, Blalock examines the possibility of testing deterministic propositions in the laboratory and in "natural systems that are for all practical purposes effectively isolated from outside influences" but believes that "future sociologists will seldom find it possible to test theories under any such ideal conditions" (1968:157). He concludes that

> It remains possible that the best strategy is to formulate rather precise deductive theories but to be satisfied with very crude tests of such theories. Another alternative . . . is to construct deductive theories that allow for unexplained variation. . . . But as soon as we begin to allow for such disturbances, we must make certain simplifying assumptions about *how* they are related to the other variables. Otherwise . . . testable predictions cannot be made (1968:157).

Regarding such simplifying assumptions, Blalock notes that

> the scientist is always confronted with the dilemma of how much to oversimplify reality. On the one hand, simple theories are easier to construct and evaluate. On the other hand, the more complex ones may stand a better chance of conforming to reality (1968:159).

Interpretation

Because every explanation and prediction—whether simple or complex—is a statement that employs words or other symbols, there is always doubt as to exactly which observations are indicated by those symbols. The procedure for resolving this doubt is called, in science as in everyday life, interpretation. Of this procedure, Zetterberg says

> Suppose that we are interested in the verification of the hypothesis: *The greater the division of labor is in a society, the less the rejection of deviates in the same society.* For its verification we first need to interpret the nominal definitions of an hypothesis into terms more acceptable for research. We may, for example, select the number of occupations to stand for the division of labor. And we may select the proportion of laws requiring the death penalty, deportation and long prison terms (but not fines) to stand for the degree of rejection of deviates from society norms (1954:29–30).

When interpretation specifies the observables referred to by predictions in terms of outcomes of certain operations (called applied science "implementations" in Figure 13.1) on the world, it is called operationalization:

> For example, the term "harder than" might be operationally defined by the rule that a piece of mineral, x, is to be called harder than another piece of mineral, y, if the operation of drawing a sharp point of x across the surface of y results in a scratch mark on the latter (Hempel, 1965:123).

It follows that each test examines the prediction (and the explanation from which it was derived) not in its more or less unique conceptual form but only in one of its many possible interpretations. Each test of a given prediction is, in short, a sample drawn from the universe of all possible tests, and as with any sample, its representativeness is crucial. However, because we know nothing about the distribution of possible interpretations of any given prediction, our sampling from that distribution is largely purposive and opportunistic. It is nevertheless on the basis of such inevitably unsystematic sampling of tests of a given prediction that we say evidence "accumulates," becomes "persuasive," and then "overwhelming" either in favor of the prediction and the explanation from which it was derived, or against them. One reason why "every scientific statement must remain *tentative forever*" (Popper, 1961:280) then, is that we can probably always come up with a new interpretation of any given prediction and there can be no guarantee that a test of the prediction under the new interpretation will show the same results as previous tests.

Once an interpretation is put forward in a given research, the resultant "test" prediction must be instrumented, and a measurement scale and sampling procedure fitted to it. To use Zetterberg's illustration regarding the division of labor and the rejection of deviates, this means that the analyst may decide to make observations on "the number of occupations" and, say, "the proportion of laws requiring the death penalty, deportation, and long prison terms" by interviewing or by mailing questionnaires to, or reading the publications of, persons designated as competent judges (for example, census officials and officials in the legal system); or by directly observing social actors as they carry out their occupational and legal role-performances in the field; or by setting up an experimental situation in which the occupations and laws to which subjects can respond are rigorously controlled; or by devising a simulation in which occupations and laws are represented by inputs into a computer, or in any number of other ways. Each way will involve its own distinctive sample of observations, observational instruments, and scales.

Sampling

Having decided the kinds of observations which are to enter the test, the analyst must next select the population on which these observations will be made (for example, in studying the division of labor in society, which "society" or "societies" should be observed—the United States, Japan, Nigeria, the U.S.S.R.?); decide whether to make statistically representative or purposive observations; and decide how many observations to make. It should be clear that all these decisions depend on how the prediction to be tested is interpreted, for certain kinds of observations can be made on certain populations and not others, certain observations lend themselves to purposive rather than representative samples (given the analyst's inevitably limited resources), and certain observations can be made only once or a few times before the observation process itself begins significantly to affect the events being observed.

Instrumentation

Augmentation of the senses through physical instruments seems general in all sciences, as we seek, more and more, to make observations on phenomena that are not immediately available to an observer's senses (for example, values and attitudes) and to raise the precision of all our observations. The price paid for this additional scope and precision is chiefly in the observational error introduced by the indirectness of instrumentally augmented observation. For example, light passes through manufactured lenses (and often onto a photographic plate, etc.) before reaching the astronomer's eye; and a respondent's age or occupation or attitude passes through his/her own and the interviewer's sometimes-censoring (or simply mistaken) consciousness and often hard-to-read writing or hard-to-understand tape recording before reaching the survey analyst's eye or ear. Thus, although one can see "farther" with a telescope than with the naked eye, and one can collect more information more quickly from a questionnaire than from direct observation of a respondent, the images projected by telescope and questionnaire may be more distorted (and are certainly differently distorted) than those built up by technologically unaugmented observation.

Scaling

All observational instruments (including the eyes and ears with which we are born) consist of some mechanism for receiving signals (such as light, sound, verbal and nonverbal gestures) and a scale against which these signals are compared (for example, sensory reaction thresholds, a calibrated dial, an interviewer's list of questions); the comparison of signal against scale constitutes "taking a measurement" or "making an observation." It should be noted that the scale used in making a given observation generally depends on the prediction being tested, the available instrumentation, and so on, rather than any intrinsic characteristics of the signal itself. Thus, colors may be measured by their names (nominal scale) or by their wavelengths (ratio scale); occupational prestige may be measured by a "high-medium-low" ordinal scale or by the Duncan interval scale; and so on (see Stevens, 1946).

Test Procedure

Most research papers may be regarded as reports of procedures followed by the analyst in putting some prediction (sometimes called a "hypothesis," "hunch," "idea," "belief," "perspective," and so forth) to an empirical test. Thus, in the "statement of the problem" and "review of the literature" we are apt to find the originating explanation, its prior empirical and deductive support, and the manner in which the prediction to be tested was derived. In the "methods" section we find the interpretation, sampling, instrumentation, and scaling procedures that were used. Three other prerequisites are also usually found (or implied) in the "methods" section: (1) a proposed measure of fit between prediction and data, (2) a set of rules for taking that measurement, and (3) a criterion level to which a measured fit must come up in order to justify calling the test a "confirmation" of the prediction and explanation (and/or a criterion level below which the fit must fall in order to justify calling the test a "disconfirmation").

Then, in the "results" sections, the analyst presents the actual comparison of prediction and empirical data, the actual measure of fit, and his/her verdict of confirmation or disconfirmation.

Test Consequences

Finally, in the "conclusions" section, we come to the analyst's assessment of the difference the test makes for the original prediction and explanation, and for the observations gathered to test the prediction. As indicated earlier here, whenever the fit is judged satisfactory, the prediction as well as the explanation from which the prediction was derived is believed confirmed. However, whenever that fit is unsatisfactory, we have three alternatives: either to throw out the data, throw out the prediction (and with it the explanation), or invent a more general explanation that reconciles the old explanation and the new data. Nagel, Lakatos, and Quine offer related explications of considerations entering into our choice among these alternatives. Nagel says

> some apparent exceptions to L [a scientific law] are encountered. We may nevertheless be most reluctant to abandon L despite these exceptions, and for at least two reasons. In the first place, the combined [deductive and inductive] confirmatory evidence for L may outweigh the apparently negative evidence. In the second place, in virtue of its relations to other laws and to the evidence for the latter, L does not stand alone, but its fate affects the system of laws to which L belongs. In consequence, the rejection of L would require a serious reorganization of certain parts of our knowledge. However, such a reorganization may not be feasible because no suitable replacement is momentarily available for the hitherto adequate system; and a reorganization may perhaps be avoided by reinterpreting the apparent exceptions to L, so that these latter are construed as not "genuine" exceptions after all (1961:65).

Lakatos, like Nagel, argues that no scientific law stands (or falls) alone, but Lakatos notes that the relationships of any two laws to other laws in the same substantive area may be different. Thus within a given "scientific research programme," some laws are part of its "hard core" and some are parts of its "protective belt" of "auxiliary, 'observational' hypotheses and initial conditions" which "has to bear the brunt of tests and gets adjusted and readjusted, or even completely replaced, to defend . . . the core" (1978:48). Lakatos concludes that

> We may rationally decide not to allow "refutations" to transmit falsity to the hard core as long as the corroborated empirical content of the protecting belt of auxiliary hypotheses increases. . . . [But] if and when the programme ceases to anticipate novel facts, its hard core might have to be abandoned (1978:49).

Quine also employs the center-and-periphery metaphor:

> The totality of our so-called knowledge or beliefs . . . is a man-made fabric which impinges on experience only along the edges. . . . A conflict with

experience at the periphery occasions readjustments in the interior of the field. . . . But the total [fabric] is so underdetermined by its boundary conditions, experience, that there is much latitude of choice as to what statements to reevaluate in the light of any single contrary experience. . . . Any statement can be held true come what may, if we make drastic enough adjustments elsewhere in the system. Even a statement very close to the periphery can be held true in the face of recalcitrant experience by pleading hallucination or by amending certain statements of the kind called logical laws (1963:42–43).

The choice of which statement to reevaluate, says Quine, is guided by two human tendencies which he regards as "natural" to our species, namely, the tendency to conserve and the tendency to simplify. Thus, Quine argues that we have a "vaguely pragmatic inclination to adjust one strand of the fabric of science rather than another in accommodating some particular recalcitrant experience. Conservatism figures in such choices, and so does the quest for simplicity" (1963:46). When Popper says "What ultimately decides the fate of a *theory* is the result of a test" (1961:109, emphasis added), it seems equally clear that the result of a test can decide the fate of observations as well.

And to all this, it is essential to add the element of chance or near-chance: "The best laid plans of mice and men. . . ." While assiduously collecting observations relevant to one empirical generalization, we may stumble upon an observation that, while anomalous in this respect, strikes the alert and prepared mind as the start of a new and different empirical generalization. When constructing a given explanation for an empirical generalization we may hit on a different explanation, or find that the explanation we are constructing pertains to a different empirical generalization—and so on. This is what Merton has in mind (and the general point applies to every information element shown in the applied as well as pure sides of Fig. 13.1) when he says

Fruitful empirical research not only tests theoretically derived hypotheses; it also originates new hypotheses. This might be termed the "serendipity" component of research, i.e., the discovery, by chance or sagacity, of valid results which were not sought for. . . . The serendipity pattern refers to the fairly common experience of observing an *unanticipated and strategic* datum which becomes the occasion for developing a new theory or for extending a different theory (1957:103, 104).

SUMMARY

This chapter has comprised my discussion of procedures associated with pure science. The discussion opened by examining observations and empirical generalizations and what it takes to construct them. The claim was emphasized that even the most elementary observations are constructions made by the observer and that in these constructions we may use property, cause, or effect criteria for identifying and differentiating any given phenomenon. No matter which of these criteria is used, however, individual observations must be aggregated into empirical generalizations before they can become liable to scientific explanation and prediction.

It was emphasized that, in principle, there exists an infinite number of ways in which a given phenomenon may be observed, measured, and described, and that the particular way chosen by the analyst crucially sets the stage for explanation by determining which explanations may and may not be applied to it. We can, in short, describe a given phenomenon in part only and it is only this highly selective description, never the phenomenon itself, that we then seek to explain.

Turning to explanations and predictions, it was argued that these are complementary procedures, both of which rely on the principles of causation and subsumption. It was also argued that when the weight of explanatory argument rests on subsumption, a "normal" stage of scientific development may be identified; and that when the weight rests on causation, a "crisis" stage may be identified. Extensions of explanatory and predictive scope occur through applying principles of logical deduction and of causal equifinality and equioriginality.

The general procedures for performing intersubjectively verifiable tests of predictions derived from explanations (i.e., interpretation, sampling, instrumentation, and scaling) were discussed, as were problems of propositional testability. In discussing the consequences of a failed test, some emphasis was given to the analyst's choice between blaming the explanation that gave rise to the prediction or blaming the observations against which the prediction was compared.

15

Applied Science

The preceding chapter has examined the procedures of pure science, in which the object is understanding; the present chapter examines the procedures of applied science, in which the object is control.

Here, briefly, are the procedures involved in applied science: The desire to assure, enhance, accelerate, prevent, mitigate, inhibit, focus, disperse, redirect, or otherwise influence some predicted event determines whether or not we initiate planning for it. And behind such a desire, ultimately, there stands an ethical or aesthetic value. As Mills says, "To detect practical problems is to make evaluations" (1959:90), and Freeman and Sherwood agree: "the setting of social policy [regarding, say, the goal of eliminating illiteracy] assumes certain basic societal values concerning education and the importance of literacy" (1970:4). Ultimately, as Chapter 16 will argue, this means justification for the desire to exert control over any given thing is beyond the reach of science to determine or confirm. The effect of that desire upon scientific procedure, however, is immediate: it transforms an explanandum of pure scientific analysis into a desideratum for applied scientific analysis. Planning describes and evaluates alternative ways of exerting control over that desideratum; decision selects one or more of these ways; implementation puts the chosen way or ways into effect such that outcomes are produced; evaluation compares these actual outcomes (which may also be seized upon by our desire for understanding as new observations for pure science) with the outcomes anticipated in the original decision and feeds the results of this comparison back to implementation and plans. (For other, similar sketches of procedure in applied science—especially applied social science—see Lasswell, 1971; Bauer, 1968:2; Mack, 1971:9, 136–137; Caro, 1971:3; and Freeman and Sherwood, 1970:3.)

Now, against the background of these general considerations, let us draw near to the first stage in applied science, namely, planning. I divide it into two parts: in the first part (feasibility assessment), the problem is to identify and describe alternative ways through which control over a given phenomenon can be achieved; in the second part (cost-benefit estimation), the problem is to evaluate or rank these alternative ways so that a decision can then be made to select one or a few and reject the others.[1]

PLANS

Feasibility Assessment[2]

A point made in Chapter 13 bears restatement: the first prerequisite of control is foresight or prediction.[3] For example, control of the temperature inside a house with thermostats hooked up to furnace and air conditioner is based on a prediction that the temperature inside will normally approximate the temperature outside the house—normally, that is, unless heat is added to or removed from the house. Obviously, it is that prediction and only that prediction which justifies starting up the furnace when the house cools past a certain point (because we predict that normally it will continue to cool down if the outside temperature is low) and starting up the air conditioner when the house heats up past a certain point. Without a relevant prediction, we simply would not know what to tell the ther-

---

[1] Etzioni goes so far as to identify policy research in its entirety with feasibility assessment and cost-benefit estimation (i.e., planning) when he describes it as "concerned with mapping alternative approaches and with specifying potential differences in the intent, effect, and cost of various programs" (1971:8). Freeman and Sherwood, however, distinguish "planning" from "program development": "Program development refers to the design of specific interventions and ameliorative activities based on the information, analyses, decisions, and recommendations produced in the planning phase. Practicality and feasibility are important considerations in the transition from the broader, more general, value-oriented planning stage" (1970:6).

[2] I refer here to *physical* feasibility (i.e., what *can* be done), not *political* feasibility (i.e., what *may* be done, given a certain balance and bargaining of power between interest groups).

[3] Merton draws a distinction between "predicting" and "forecasting": "concrete forecasts in applied science differ significantly from abstract predictions in basic science. Basic research typically deals with 'abstract predictions,' i.e., with predictions in which a large number of 'other factors' are, conveniently enough, assumed to remain constant. . . . *Ceteris paribus* is an indispensable concept in basic research" (1949:176). According to this view, however, a forecast should be regarded as a kind of prediction (i.e., a more robust one—one that does not assume that "a large number of 'other factors' " remain constant). "Prediction" is therefore the generic term and is used as such here. It should be emphatically noted, in addition, that *ceteris paribus* is no less an indispensable concept in applied research than in pure research.

mostat to do about any given change in house temperature. Accordingly, Pressman and Wildavsky say "Policies imply theories [and theories imply predictions—ed.]. Whether stated explicitly or not, policies point to a chain of causation between initial conditions and future consequences. If X, then Y" (1973:xv).[4] Becker and Horowitz agree:

> The sociological analysis of causes has practical importance. When some object or action is labeled as the cause of the event or the situation, the analysis suggests what would have to be influenced or altered in order to make a significant change in that event or situation (1972:58).

MacRae also agrees:

> [M]ost major policy choices involve ethical principles that call for the prediction of consequences. The prediction of consequences of alternative policies also requires maximal use of the rigor and methods that the social sciences have developed. . . . And even when we cannot aspire to know *all* these consequences . . . social science may nevertheless reduce our disagreements and our waste of resources in fruitless projects (1976:279).

So a prediction is the first informational requisite for control[5]—although, or course, prediction alone is not sufficient for control (MacRae notes that "prediction may lead not to control but to fatalism and indifference" [1976:284])—and therefore, as Mannheim puts it, "the significance of social knowledge grows proportionately with the increasing necessity of regulatory intervention in the social process" (1949:1).

The second informational requisite is the identification of at least one humanly

---

[4] Merton identifies six "types of research problems in applied social science," including

(1) *Diagnostic:* determining whether action is required. Magnitude and extent of problems; changes and trends since last appraisal of situation (e.g., changes in level of race tensions); differentials in affected groups, areas, institutions. (2) *Prognostic:* Forecasting trends to plan for future needs. . . . (3) *Differential Prognosis:* Determining choice between alternative policies; (e.g., public reaction to rent control or rationing). (4) *Evaluative:* Appraising effectiveness of action program. . . . (5) *General Background Data:* Of general utility or serving diverse purposes (e.g., censuses of population, housing, business, manufacturing). (6) *"Educative" Research:* Informing publics upon pertinent data and particularly countering misconceptions (1949:174).

All except (4) are subsumed by "predictions" once we note that descriptions of past observations—as in (1), (3), (5), and (6)—are relevant to applied social science only to the extent that we assume, *ceteris paribus,* that they or their extrapolations will hold in the future. What Merton calls the "evaluative" research problem will be discussed later in this chapter.

[5] Although Moore says he does not "believe that prediction is really the proper task for the social scientist," he nevertheless urges the same social scientists to do what is certainly tantamount to making predictions—namely,

present some rough outline of the inherent trends and possibilities in given situations, the probabilities of various types of change, the obstacles to them, and some of the probable costs in human suffering (1972:150).

manipulable factor in the causal production or inhibition of the predicted event. We must, in short, believe we can influence the event, whether directly or indirectly, if it is to become a target for applied science. For this reason, Freeman and Sherwood say "the planning process should also include some ideas about potentially successful means of moving in the desired direction" (1970:5), and Spector and Kitsuse go so far as to claim that "People do not define as problems those conditions they feel are immutable, inherent in human nature, or the will of God" (1977:84).[6]

Obviously, not all theories contain humanly manipulable factors nor do all theorists pursue such theories. Feuer, therefore, distinguishes

> Two modes of analysis, which I shall call the *interventionist* and the *necessitarian*. The interventionist social scientist believes that men can intervene in social situations to change conditions and determine, in significant measure, the direction of trends. The necessitarian believes, on the contrary, that social science can never be used to deflect the lines of evolution, that men's decisions are perturbations in irresistible movements. . . . From the logical standpoint, what characterizes necessitarian laws is that their independent variables are . . . inaccessible. Michel's [iron law of oligarchy], for instance, holds that . . . [o]ligarchical structure is . . . a function of time, and nothing can be done by human intervention to arrest the passage of time. . . . Interventionist models of causal law, on the other hand, are characterized by the quest for independent variables which will be, in large part, accessible. If oligarchical trends can be shown to depend on certain specific psychological traits, then intervention on the level of basic personality structure may avail to counteract them . . . through the controls of infant care and child rearing (1965:191, 193–194).

In the same vein, Coleman asserts that "for policy research, it is necessary to treat differently policy variables which are subject to policy manipulation, and situational variables which are not" (1972:5).[7] Similarly, Riecken warns that

---

[6] It seems extreme, however, to claim that people do not define immutable conditions as problems at all—if we accept that "problems" need only be perceived as presenting difficulty, causing discomfort, eliciting avoidance-wishes (whether "realistic" or not). Aversive conditions thought to be immutable present "inevitable" problems; as soon as a humanly manipulable factor pertaining to such conditions is identified, however, the conditions present "practical" problems.

[7] MacRae stresses the dependence of manipulable variables on nonmanipulable variables, arguing that it is often the case that "some act under consideration—sending a [propaganda] message, going outdoors, planting crops—will have different valued consequences, depending on the value of a nonmanipulated variable [like national character or the weather]. In this case, the consequences of policy choice or of action depend in an *interactive* fashion on manipulated and nonmanipulated variables" (1976:283). I include such interaction in my reference to manipulable variables on the ground that no manipulable variable (or any other variable, for that matter) can operate except in one or another interaction with nonmanipulable variables (e.g., gravity); MacRae's observation applies to *all* cases and not just the ones he cites.

> By fixing attention upon variables about which no action can be taken, most sociologists provide theoretical and explanatory statements that have neither interest nor promise for the social problem solver because he cannot use them as handles or levers (1969:110).

It should be emphasized that insofar as pure science (and physics in particular) assures us that everything in the universe is connected to everything else, everything in the universe should be regarded as humanly manipulable in principle and to some degree—but always, of course, within the limits that entropy and the speed of light impose on the propagation of all known causal influences. In this sense, the answer to the question of the *possibility* of human manipulation of future and spatially nearby phenomena is affirmative. Having established the answer to this primary question, a host of secondary questions swarm around every phenomenon that we might consider manipulating, and the answers to them are far less clear: In which direction and to what degree is the phenomenon manipulable? How effective and how efficient can that manipulation be? What manipulation procedure is required?

Insofar as all such questions call for predictions of the future based on experiences with the past, pure science provides the most intersubjectively verified answers. Not only that, but the principles of equifinality and equioriginality (discussed in Chapter 14) imply that pure science can usually identify more than one means to a given end (i.e., more than one way of accomplishing a given desideratum) and also more than one end that a given means can serve. The upshot of such identification of alternatives is that benefits and costs of achieving any given end and of using any given means may be apportioned in different ways among members of society. It is just at this point that political decision-making and economic budgeting play their crucial parts in determining which of these different apportionments are actually carried out—as we shall see later in this chapter. Cohen illustrates from the field of medicine:

> a thorough knowledge about the determinants of a disease always involves a number of factors. If one wants to "do something" about the disease, this knowledge suggests a number of different possible points of intervention. Should we, for example, concentrate on building up resistance or immunity, on treatment of the sick, on educating the public in how to avoid exposure, on compulsory segregation of carriers until they are deemed safe, on massive campaigns to eliminate the agent? Such decisions depend on our command of the necessary techniques and on their respective costs, all of which involves a complex balancing of values (1966:38).

Thus, applied science, although it depends on nonscientific sources for the values that identify its goals, depends for the identification of its means on two types of predictions made by pure science. First, a prediction of the "normal" course of events is required—a course which, when evaluated as good or bad, beautiful or ugly, is regarded as worth preserving or changing in some way. Second, a prediction is required that one or more phenomena which human action can deliberately manipulate will affect that normal course in the desired manner. It is this reliance of applied science on the predictions of pure science that Merton documents when he notes that "Throughout much of their work . . . [the Presidential Commissions on population, pornography, and crime] focused on [predicted] consequences: the consequences of existing practices and structures and the consequences anticipated from putting proposed policies into effect" (1976:171).

Figure 13.1 portrays this reliance of applied science on pure science by the arrow from predictions to plans—a transformation regulated by the "desire for control," that is, the identification of a given predicted event as desirable or undesirable and worth creating, terminating, preserving, or changing. Through this identification, the event in question becomes, as I have said, a desideratum for applied science. At that point, every pure science proposition in which that event plays a part, whether as explanandum or explanans, becomes pertinent to the first step toward controlling the event, namely, assessing the feasibility of such control.

Indeed, a feasibility assessment may best be described as an assembly of all these propositions—an assembly that, ideally, brings together everything known at that moment about all the causes and consequences (alternative and multiple, proximate and long-run) of the desideratum. Speaking of the importance of assembling not just one but many propositions of this kind, Keyfitz says any given proposition (he calls it a "model") presents

> a condition—say, that ignorance of contraception is what keeps the birth rate high, and this in turn holds up development—in a formal and relatively abstract way that leads to a clear-cut policy indication: in this case, provide contraception to poor countries. Such a model may indeed fit the reality, and hence the policy drawn from it may be effective, but we cannot know that without contrasting it with other models (for instance, that poor people have many children because they want helpers in the home and in the fields) that lead to very different policies. Any proposer has an obligation to compare his model with alternatives and to gather data that would ascertain which is the better fit (1980:179).

Of course, feasibility assessments will vary, not only in the extent to which they are the result of comparing many alternative predictions (or explanatory models) of the same desideratum, but in their completeness, determinateness, intersubjective verification, and complexity:[8]

[8] Powers, speaking of the individual organism, says "I think dreaming can be thought of, at least in part, as *feasibility testing* . . . [wherein one] is concerned with discovering and repairing basic design defects in the control systems themselves" (1973:225).

For some types of projects, fairly simple analyses . . . are all that is needed to determine that *no* possible version of the project is likely to be successful. For more complex projects . . . a good deal of work will be needed to determine . . . which one of many potential packages of resources will make most sense. At this stage, a team of specialists covering a range of disciplines (typically engineers, scientists [sic], economists, and more recently sociologists) will need to work together (Irvin, 1978:3, emphasis removed).

In any case, however,

research bearing upon general policies dealing with socially defined problems in and of society *must* focus on [i.e., predict—ed.]multiple functional and dysfunctional consequences of alternative causes of action for a variety of social units (e.g., varied groups, strata, regions) and the more comprehensive social systems. This is the case even though no scientific calculus of cause exists for assessing, choosing among, and integrating such diverse consequences (Merton, 1976:171).

Figure 15.1 portrays the general form that a feasibility assessment may take.

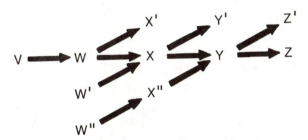

Figure 15.1. Predictions and explanations entering into feasibility assessment. Y = desideratum; X = proximate cause; W = manipulable cause; V = cause of manipulable cause; Z = long-run main effect; Z' = long-run side effect; X' = side effect of manipulable cause; Y' = side effect of proximate cause; W' = alternative manipulable cause; $W'' \rightarrow X''$ = alternative manipulable-proximate causal chain.

We assume here that a simple probabilistic prediction has been produced by pure science: $X \rightarrow Y$. Once Y becomes regarded as a desideratum, feasibility assessment asks of pure science: Does the causal production of X contain a humanly manipulable factor of reliable and significant influence on the desideratum?—a question often phrased as Can anything be done about it, and if so, what and how? Assuming such a factor (W) is identified, the next question is "What humanly manipulable causes can bring about W?"—a question often phrased as "What (and whom) will it cost (V)?" The next feasibility questions are "What will be the long-run effects and side effects (Z, Z') of realizing the desideratum,"[9] and "What will be the side effects (X', Y') of activating the manipulable cause and thus the proximate cause?" The answers to these questions are included among costs if negatively valued and among benefits if positively valued. Finally, feasibility assessment inquires into alternative manipulable causes of the main proximate cause (W'), and alternative causal chains (W", X") that can yield the desideratum—a question often phrased as Can we do the same thing in a better way?

It should be emphasized that the variables entering into any given feasibility assessment may come from any combination of disciplines. Thus MacRae points out the importance of connecting "policy variables that derive from various disciplines or professions and that are means to related ends" (1976:282), and Horowitz asserts that

> Policy problems do not come in neat discipline-defined packages, but rather require the simultaneous consideration of issues that traditionally have been regarded as the province of several social science disciplines (1971:3).

In order to clarify this overall picture of feasibility assessment before closing in on some of its details, here are four alternative formulations of the problems it seeks to systematize. First, Weber's classic remarks:

> The question of the appropriateness of the means for achieving a given end is undoubtedly accessible to scientific analysis. Inasmuch as we are able to determine (within the present limits of our knowledge) which means for the achievement of an appropriate end are appropriate or inappropriate, we can in this way estimate the chances of attaining a certain end by certain available means. . . . Furthermore, when the possibility of attaining a proposed end appears to exist, we can determine (naturally, within the limits of our existing knowledge) the consequences which the application of the means to be used will produce in addition to the eventual attainment of the proposed end, as a result of the interdependence of all events. We can then prepare the acting person with the ability to weigh and compare the undesirable as over against the desirable consequences of his action. Thus, we can answer the question: what will the attainment of a desired end "cost" in terms of the predictable loss of other values? Since, in the vast majority of cases, every goal that is striven for does "cost" or can "cost" something in this sense, the weighing of the goal in terms of the incidental consequences of the action which realizes it cannot be omitted from the deliberation of persons who act with a sense of responsibility (1949:52–53).

---

[9] Speaking of long-run consequences, Merton says

Short-run rationality often produces long-run irrationality. Public health measures may go awry; financial incentives may lead to decline rather than an increase in production; intensified punishment may aggravate rather than curb crime (1976:184).

Second, although Caro uses the term "evaluative research" for what I refer to here as "feasibility assessment" his argument is very much like my own:

> Basic research proceeds to test the "validity" of [a hypothesis like "the more *a*, the more *b*"] and to elaborate upon the control variables which account for or modify the relationship of *a* to *b*. The same basic logic applies to evaluative research. . . . However, unlike basic or nonevaluative research, value becomes attached to *b* as something desirable, while *a* becomes the object of deliberate, planned intervention. The nonevaluative hypothesis "the more *a*, the more *b*" becomes the evaluative hypothesis, "by changing *a* (through a planned program), the probability of *b* (which I judge to be desirable) increases (1971:45, emphasis removed).

Third, another variety of what I refer to here as feasibility assessment is the predecision half of "social indicator" research (I include its postimplementation half under evaluation research—discussed later in this chapter). Thus, Land argues that "a social indicator model can be analyzed to determine if the desired social state is feasible and, if so, what policy manipulations will be most likely to achieve this goal" (1975:20). Land also differentiates "policy instrument" indicators (measures of manipulable variables), "nonmanipulable" indicators (measures of nonmanipulable variables), "end-product" indicators (measures of the desideratum), and "side-effect" indicators (measures of effects other than the end products).[10] Moore and Sheldon emphasize that social indicators may conceivably provide continuous feasibility monitoring—for the feasibility of a given attempt at control will certainly change as the situation changes in which that attempt will take place. Thus, social indicators

> would give a reading both on the current state of some segment of the social universe and on past and future trends, whether progressive or regressive, according to some normative criteria. The notion of social indicators leads directly to the idea of "monitoring" social change (Moore and Sheldon, 1968:4).

Finally, Freeman and Sherwood argue that "the development of an impact model and the selection of a target population" are essential to "program development"; that "the impact model must include a statement concerning the stimulus or in-

---

[10] Land also refers to "analytic" indicators, and defines them as "components of explicit conceptual models of the social processes which result in the values of the output indicators." Land goes on to say that these components "might be viewed as indirectly policy related, for in the long run it will be these measurements and models [plus others] that will provide guidance for social intervention" (1975:17). But Land's "analytic" indicators must be included among his "policy instrument" and "nonmanipulable" indicators insofar as the latter seem logically to exhaust measures of "the social processes which result in the values of the output indicators."

put, an hypothesis about what changes the input will produce, and a theory or proposition about how that change will affect the behavior or condition the policy maker is seeking to modify"; and that "the selection of target populations is closely associated with the development of an impact model. In theory, the identification of the target population should precede the development of the impact model . . . [but the] usual procedure is to revise [each in light of knowledge about the other]" (1970:7, 8, 10).

Now let us consider some of the details of Fig. 15.1. First, we show the manipulable causes (W, W', W'') impacting on proximate causes (X, X'') of the desideratum rather than directly on the desideratum. Caro supports this point:

> in very few cases do action or service programs directly attack the ultimate objective. Rather they attempt to change the intermediate process which is "causally" related to the ultimate objective. . . . For example, the evaluation of an obesity clinic may show whether attendance leads to a loss of weight, but whether such a loss of weight decreases the incidence of heart disease is a question for nonevaluative medical research. Similarly, a project Head Start may succeed in increasing the curiosity of culturally deprived preschoolers, but whether increased curiosity leads to higher educational aspirations is a matter of . . . nonevaluative research (1971:47).

Note how this argument points to potential shortcomings in pure as well as applied social science when Caro concludes, "there are two possible sources of failure [in an action program] (1) the inability of the program to influence the 'causal' variable, or (2) the invalidity of the theory linking the 'causal' variable to the desired objective" (1971:47). Specifically regarding shortcomings in pure social science, Rossi says "A large part of the problem presented by broad aim programs lies in the absence of reasonable social science theories which could serve as a guide to the design of social action programs" (1972b:42).

Two other crucial features of Fig. 15.1 are its emphases on side effects $(W \rightarrow X;$ $X \rightarrow Y', Y \rightarrow Z')$, and on long-run effects $(Y \rightarrow Z, Y \rightarrow Z')$—that is, on ramifications. A classic reference to the importance of such effects is Weber's remark that "in numerous instances the attainment of 'good' ends is bound to the fact that one must be willing to pay the price of using morally dubious means or at least dangerous ones—and facing the possibility or even the probability of evil ramifications" (1958a:121).

Regarding the matter of responsibility for such ramifications, Weber says

> there is an abysmal contrast between conduct that follows the maxim of an ethic of ultimate ends—that is, in religious terms, "The Christian does rightly and leaves the results with the Lord"—and conduct that follows the maxim of an ethic of responsibility, in which case one has to give an account of the foreseeable results of one's action. [In an ethic of ultimate ends, if] an action

of good intent leads to bad results, then, in the actor's eyes, not he but the world, or the stupidity of other men, or God's will who made them thus, is responsible for the evil. However a man who believes in an ethic of responsibility . . . does not feel in a position to burden others with the results of his own actions so far as he was able to foresee them; he will say: these results are ascribed to my action (1958a: 120–121).

All these considerations seem clearly to set the stage for the importance to applied science of Merton's conceptualization of "latent" functions and dysfunctions (i.e., "objective consequences . . . which are neither intended nor recognized" [1957:51]):

[A]rmed with the concept of latent function, the sociologist . . . considers, for example, the consequences of the new wage plan for, say, the trade union in which the workers are organized or the consequences of a propaganda program, not only for increasing its avowed purpose of stirring up patriotic fervor, but also for making large numbers of people reluctant to speak their minds when they differ with official policies, etc. In short, it is suggested that the distinctive intellectual contributions of the sociologist are formed primarily in the study of unintended consequences (among which are latent functions) of social practices (1957:66).

Rossi also notes the importance of side effects, including long-run side effects, when he asserts that "a proposed program to reduce fertility may have indirect effects on the demand for education, which in turn may affect the publishing industry through changes in the levels of demand for textbooks, and so on" (1972b:24).

Regarding long-run effects, Merton supports concern for them in his distinction between eufunctions, dysfunctions, and nonfunctional consequences—that is, respectively, "observed consequences which make for the adaptation or adjustment of a given system," which "lessen the adaptation or adjustment of the system," and which "are simply irrelevant to the system" (1957:51). Merton's repeated reference here to consequences for the entire "system," rather than just for the most immediate target of a given act, highlights the role of long-run effects in feasibility assessment.

Finally, Fig. 15.1 stresses alternative causal routes to the same desideratum ($W \rightarrow X \rightarrow Y$, $W' \rightarrow X \rightarrow Y$, $W'' \rightarrow X'' \rightarrow Y$). Merton also exemplifies this feature when he proposes functional alternatives, a concept which, he says, "focuses attention on the range of possible variation in the items which can, in the case under examination, subserve a functional requirement" (1957:52). More generally, of course, there can be no possibility of human control and therefore no possibility of applied science at all where there are no causal alternatives. Freedom appears to be not the recognition of necessity but the recognition of alternatives—which brings us to the principles of equifinality and equioriginality again but this time, in their relevance to applied science.

Equifinality and Equioriginality in Applied Science

The central role of the principles of equifinality and equioriginality in applied science is suggested by Weber's distinction between "technical" and "economic" questions. Thus, when Weber asserts that "The presence of a 'technical question' always means that there is some doubt over the choice of the most efficient means to the end" (1947:161), he invokes the principle of equifinality insofar as the existence of alternative means to (causes of) the same end (effect) is assumed. When he asserts that an economic question "always takes the form of asking what would be the effect on the satisfaction of other wants if this particular means were not used for satisfaction of one given want" (1947:162), he invokes the principle of equioriginality insofar as the existence of alternative satisfactions (effects) that the same means (cause) could bring about is assumed (also see Chapter 10).

The two principles appear side by side, and explicitly as each other's direct and necessary complement, in Rothenberg's discussion of "substitutability"—which, he says,

> takes a number of forms. On the consumption side, for any one individual, his behavior indicates that when faced with scarcity he is willing to substitute fulfillment of one set of wants for that of a different set. . . . Thus, wants are substitutable for overall satisfaction; commodities are substitutable for specific satisfactions. On the production side, a given commodity can be produced alternatively by more than one set of resource inputs. Moreover, for any set of resource inputs the same commodity can be produced by a variety of different techniques: resources and techniques are substitutes in producing any combination of commodities. With all these forms of substitutability in the presence of scarcity, the target of overall best use of resources involves nontrivial choice: which resources shall be used to produce which commodities, by which techniques, and who shall receive them? (1975:59).

Not only do the principles of equifinality and equioriginality play essential roles in applied science (especially in its planning phase), but so does the different but related principle of multiple causation—that is, the principle that every effect may have multiple contributory (nonalternative) causes and every cause may have multiple coexistent (nonalternative) effects. It is this latter principle that underlies Merton's concept of manifest and latent functions (see above) as well as the concept which is implicit in it—namely, that of manifest and latent structures, when functions are defined as effects and structures are defined as causes (see Chapter 9).

Certainty and Uncertainty

Now it need hardly be added that feasibility assessment, as pictured in Fig. 15.1, must involve not only the identification of variables (e.g., desideratum, proximate and manipulable causes, main effects, and side effects) but the assignment of probabilities and their confidence limits to relationships between these variables. This assignment has important consequences for decision-making, for it determines the degree of certainty and uncertainty with which the decision-making body can approach its task. Thus, March and Simon identify three degrees of certainty and the theories of decision-making that are dependent on them:

> (a) *Certainty:* theories that assume the decision maker has complete and accurate knowledge of the consequences that will follow on each alternative. (b) *Risk:* theories that assume accurate knowledge of a probability distribution of the consequences of each alternative. (c) *Uncertainty:* theories that assume that the consequences of each alternative belong to some subset of all possible consequences, but that the decision maker cannot assign definite probabilities to the occurrence of particular consequences (1958:137).

Certainty or risk define well-structured decision problems:

> The business problems of inventory and quality control and of production scheduling fall in this group. Analogous well-structured decision problems appear in government. . . . Methods built on mathematical development of probability theory were used to expedite quality control in munitions manufacture; the optimal design of naval convoys was another famous example (Mack, 1971:2).

Of course, the vast majority of decision problems in the realm of applied social science is characterized by uncertainty, such that "targets may be hard to describe, alternative actions almost infinite in number, results of each very difficult to foresee, chances of a specified occurrence almost impossible to estimate" (Mack, 1971:2).

One way of making decisions under uncertainty is to modify the goal of the decision from *maximizing or optimizing* the desideratum (because a high degree of certainty must be associated with every feasible alternative in order to select the single one which is best), to *satisfying* some minimal level of the desideratum (because only enough certainty is needed to know whether a given feasible alternative falls at or above some minimal level or not). On this point, March and Simon argue that

> An alternative is *optimal* [or maximal—ed.] if (1) there exists a set of criteria that permits all alternatives to be compared, and (2) the alternative in question is preferred, by these criteria, to all other alternatives. An alternative is *satisfactory* if: (1) there exists a set of criteria that describes minimally satisfactory alternatives, and (2) the alternative in question meets or exceeds all these criteria. Most human decision-making, whether individual or organizational, is concerned with the discovery and selection of satisfactory alternatives; only in exceptional cases is it concerned with the discovery and selection of optimal [or maximal—ed.] alternatives (1958:140–141).

Now this distinction between optimization (or maximization) versus satisficing as alternative goals of decision-making is associated with a parallel distinction between the "rational" or "economic" versus the "natural" or "administrative" as alternative qualities of the decision maker, and both distinctions seem related to a further distinction between sources of uncertainty in the planned alternatives among which the decision is to be made: One possible source of that uncertainty is the world which the analyst seeks to understand and control, but another possible source is the analyst him/herself.

Thus, given the attribution of uncertainty mainly to the *world* rather than to the analyst, we have an image of the ideally "rational" or "economic" decision maker who seeks, perhaps through application of statistical decision theory, to optimize or maximize a given desideratum by selecting the single best alternative. Accordingly, Mack regards statistical decision theory as

> confined to the uncertainty inherent in a decision situation in which a choice is made when goals are clear and expected consequences . . . are accessible to quantification. . . . [Such theory] adopts the classic economic figment of "rational" man, who is receptive to and capable of manipulating all relevant information (Mack, 1971:9, 17).

For such a decision maker,

> In the case of *certainty*, the choice is unambiguous. In the case of *risk*, rationality is usually defined as the choice of that alternative for which the expected utility is greatest. . . . In the case of *uncertainty*, the definition of rationality becomes problematic. One proposal . . . is the rule of "minimax risk": consider the worst set of consequences that may follow from each alternative, then select the alternative whose "worst set of consequences" is preferred to the worst sets attached to other alternatives (March and Simon, 1958:137–138).

By contrast, if we attribute uncertainty mainly to the *analyst* rather than the world, we have an image of the "natural" or "administrative" decision maker who through lack of time, or energy, or money, or information, or whatever, seeks to find any alternative yielding a satisfactory measure of the desideratum. For this decision maker,

> Choice is always exercised with respect to a limited, approximate, simplified "model" of the real situation. . . . [And such models] are themselves the outcome of psychological and sociological processes, including the chooser's own activities and the activities of others in his environment (March and Simon, 1958:139).

Whatever their sources, however, both certainty and uncertainty seem functional, if not necessary, for human decision-making. Consider an individual person who is making a decision. Such an individual needs enough certainty to enable him/her to decide at all, because too much uncertainty creates unresolvable ambivalence and paralyzes the decision maker. But some degree of uncertainty helps to motivate the decision, for

> Could anyone face a life of certainty? Success preknown would be tasteless; defeat and grief known to lie ahead would erode the pleasures of today . . . no need for experiment, no open end to learning (Mack, 1971:3).[11]

Now consider a social group as decision maker. Here again, what is needed is enough certainty to make decision possible by avoiding paralysis and confusion on the part of each participant in the decision, but enough uncertainty to facilitate bargaining among participants:

> I wonder how often people would agree on a course of action if everyone knew precisely what they were agreeing on. [Uncertainty] . . . can provide the leeway for a rearrangement of fact and emphasis which makes coalition possible and a strategy of achieving consensus effective (Mack:1971:6).[12]

[11] Similarly, Mannheim implies that the disappearance of uncertainty "would lead us to a 'matter-of-factness' which ultimately would mean the decay of the human will" (1955:262).

[12] In a related view, Rule asks "Is ignorance the worst enemy of mankind, the source of most social ills, or is the enemy mankind itself? Will increased understanding of social life provide people with the tools necessary to control the social miseries which plague them? Or will such understanding simply sharpen the contests which pass as 'social problems'?" (1978:65). (Pogo says "We have met the enemy, and they is us.") Note, however, that Rule counterbalances the tentative cynicism implied here with a more definite (and blithe) optimism: "Happily, most people, most of the time, would probably endorse a redefinition of [each other's] interests to favor mutual survival over some more parochial political or religious interest" (1978:187).

Thus, from the standpoint of individuals as well as collectivities, some degree of uncertainty or risk associated with each alternative in pursuit of a given desideratum appears to be not only unavoidable but a good thing.

In summary, then, at least four assumptions underlie feasibility assessment: (1) the principles of equifinality and equioriginality (including consumption and production substitutabilities, and functional and structural alternatives); (2) the principle of multiple-factor causation (including manifest and latent effects and causes); (3) the possibility of human effectiveness in manipulating—and not merely contemplating—the world; and (4) the possibility of estimating the chances of successful manipulation.

The same assumptions underlie the second phase of planning but a further assumption is added, namely, that whatever is beneficial to human beings and whatever is injurious or costly to them can be estimated and compared.

Cost-Benefit Estimation

Weber urges us to study the distribution of benefits and costs in society:

> Only one thing is indisputable: every type of social order, without exception, must, if one wishes to evaluate it, be examined with reference to the opportunities which it affords to *certain types of persons* to rise to positions of superiority through the operation of the various objective and subjective selective factors (Weber, 1949:27).

Marx and Engels assert that that distribution has repeatedly led to the formation of antagonistic classes:

> The history of all hitherto existing society is the history of class struggles. Freeman and slave, patrician and plebeian, lord and serf, guild-master and journeyman, in a word, oppressor and oppressed, stood in constant opposition to one another . . . (1978:473–474).

Blau, who rephrases the first sentence in this quotation from Marx and Engels in more abstract terms when he says "The dynamics of organized social life has its source in opposition forces" (1964:334), implies that the superordination to which Weber refers may, but need not always, lead to the opposition to which Marx and Engels refer:

> Collective approval of power legitimates that power. People who consider that the advantages they gain from a superior's exercise of power outweigh the

> hardships that compliance with his demands imposes on them tend to com-
> municate to each other their approval of the ruler. . . . Collective disap-
> proval of power [however,] engenders opposition. People who share the ex-
> perience of being exploited by the unfair demands of those in . . . power,
> and by the insufficient rewards they receive for their contributions, are likely
> to communicate [these feelings] to each other (1964:23).

What matters in determining compliance or rebellion, then, is the distribution
of perceived benefits and costs of a given program. It is the aim of the second
planning step—namely, cost-benefit estimation—to anticipate the distribution in
question for every alternative manipulation outlined by feasibility assessment and
then to make both the feasibility assessment and the cost-benefit estimation available for decision-making. Thus, Zeckhauser and Schaeffer say "There are two elements in an act of choice: the set of alternatives from which the choice is to be
made, and the set of preferences according to which the chooser ranks these alternatives" (1968:28). Mack notes that construction of a decision matrix requires
deciding "the probability that each event will obtain," and "the utility each act is
expected to generate under each possible event" (1971:18). Further, Rothenberg
indicates that the assumptions on which cost-benefit estimation rests include a
prior feasibility assessment:

> Most cost-benefit studies assume that in each choosing situation the relevant
> set of alternatives is not problematic and is known. Similarly, with a given
> set of alternatives it is assumed that the consequences are in principle know-
> able, and can be derived from positive economic [more generally, scientific—
> ed.] analysis (1975:58, see also 76).

Cost-benefit estimation, therefore, sets out "a procedure for judging the relative
desirability of different social actions, a procedure that can be used either by agents
of the society in preparing its own actions, or by observers who seek to advise or
criticize the society on its policies" (Rothenberg, 1975:56, emphasis added).[13]
Moore notes that

> With the proviso that it is always necessary to ask *cost for whom,* the concep-
> tion of varying costs . . . [tells us that instead] of asking whether or not a

---

[13] Rossi asserts that "Cost-benefit analysis places itself squarely in the center of policy making.
Indeed, in an ideal sense . . . cost-benefit analysis is synonymous with good decision-making, since a
properly conducted cost-benefit analysis should yield a rank ordering of policy alternatives in terms of
their yield for the public good" (1972b:41). Rothenberg concurs: "As a broad emphasis on the importance of carefully sifting out the balance of desirable and adverse consequences of an explicitly formulated set of mutually exclusive alternatives [cost-benefit analysis] is unexceptionable" (1975:87). As
does Mack: "Benefit-cost analysis, broadened to cover all significant advantages and disadvantages, is
simply another name for comprehensive rational analysis" (1971:76).

particular social arrangement or practice (such as, for example, war) is somehow inevitable or determined, one tries to ascertain the conditions under which it does and does not occur. If one opposes the practice, one tries to learn from these conditions something about the probable costs and benefits of changing matters, and what the prospects for getting support for this change are (1972:10).

As its name implies, cost-benefit estimation (or analysis) seeks to rank alternative routes in pursuit of a given desideratum according to their utilities (i.e., benefits-minus-costs [see Rothenberg, 1975:77–78]), and thereby to facilitate decision-making or choice among such alternatives.[14] "Typical applications," says Rothenberg, "would be to ask whether government should enact a certain piece of legislation, or which of a number of different expenditure projects should a particular agency of the government adopt" (1975:55). The principles of equifinality, equioriginality, multiple causation, and multiple effects all enter cost-benefit estimation in ways which help illuminate its logic.

Equioriginality appears as the resource-allocation idea that any given means (say, a given amount of money) may be used in the furtherance of different, alternative, ends. Therefore, to use those means toward one end precludes using them toward other ends, and from this it follows that every allocation of means entails benefits to some ends and costs to others.[15] Equifinality appears as the idea that any given end (say, a particular birth rate, literacy rate, or crime rate) may be pursued through a variety of alternative, mutually substitutable means, and each means will entail different costs and benefits to a given social group. And essential to the possibility of the exchange, bargaining, and trade-off of costs and of benefits is the conceptual abstraction called "value," which, as Simmel implies (see 1955:115; quoted in Chapter 10), manifests equifinality insofar as any given value quantum may be generated in a variety of ways, and also manifests equioriginality insofar as the same value quantum may be exchanged for a variety of objects.

In addition to relying on the likelihood of alternative causes and alternative effects, cost-benefit estimation also relies on the likelihood of multiple causes and multiple effects (especially the latter) when it takes into account "externalities"— that is, costs and benefits of a given transaction or program which accrue to individuals and groups other than its direct participants. Rothenberg argues that "The keynote of the [cost-benefit] approach is that each change, regardless of where it has its first direct impact, will typically lead to a variety of ramifying indirect

---

[14] MacRae says: "The economist conducting cost-benefit analysis . . . typically considers not only the costs and benefits of the project, but also the alternative uses to which resources might have been put. This approach calls to our attention the alternative acts with which a given act must be compared" (1976:134).

[15] Rothenberg puts it this way: "Every decision about the use of scarce resources precludes all mutually exclusive ways in which these same resources could have been used. Thus, it gives rise to benefits, but to costs as well" (1975:60).

impacts whose significance may far exceed that of the direct one" (1975:66); and that externalities

> are especially likely to be important in areas where public policies are considered. Indeed, often it is the large-scale presence of externalities that makes collective action justifiable. Hence, in measuring costs and benefits, the analyst must not be satisfied to enumerate solely the outcomes for direct participants. Victims or beneficiaries of externalities must have their net spillover impacts added up as well (1975:70).

Types of Costs and Benefits

MacRae argues that we should take account of different kinds of costs and different kinds of benefits:

> we must separate three conceptually distinct bases for ranking states of affairs in relation to any individual: a. His *preferences* for these states, as regards his anticipated personal satisfaction . . . b. His *personal welfare* resulting from these states . . . c. His *judgment* as to the furthering of the *general welfare,* or the public interest, or the welfare of some collectivity, corresponding to the states of affairs being compared (1976:143–144).

Employing MacRae's own preference-versus-welfare distinction, and applying it to his reference to collectivity as well as individual, one might deduce not three but four types of possible benefits and costs: (1) benefits and costs to an individual's subjectively preferred personal satisfactions, (2) benefits and costs to his/her objective personal welfare,[16] (3) benefits and costs to the cultural preferences of others (including collectivities) whom he/she values, (4) benefits and costs to the objective welfare of those others.

This, of course, vastly complicates the problems of cost-benefit estimation because a benefit to one preference or welfare may entail costs to others and the trade-offs can become intricate. In particular, costs and benefits of the third and fourth kinds—which involve individuals other than the direct participant—are included among the "externalities" which Rothenberg refers to above. Since such externalities stress the social setting in which costs and benefits occur, let us consider some implications of that setting.

---

[16] By the individual's "objective" personal welfare I mean nothing more than the preferences that other, professionally "expert," "unbiased," and "disinterested" individuals (e.g., physicians, teachers) have for that individual—regardless of what these preferences may be or how the individual or anyone else may judge them.

Social Costs and Benefits

As long as cost-benefit estimation refers to only one individual—that is, the same individual who reaps the benefits also pays the costs—the analysis is made relatively simple by two assumptions.

First, every individual is assumed to operate an internal calculus that transforms radically different kinds of values into a common, subjective metric. Such different experiences as social prestige, money, political power, sexual gratification, aesthetic pleasure, food and drink, sleep, physical work, mental work, death, loyalty, revenge, personal freedom, security, new experience, and so on, are assumed comparable within each individual (provided he/she is already familiar with them, either directly or vicariously), so that an individual can generally say whether a given quantity and quality of one is substitutable for, or "worth," a given quantity and quality of another to him/her. Second, it is assumed that no one freely and knowingly chooses to lose; that individuals only make voluntary trade-offs of one value for another when they believe it will somehow yield a net benefit in their favor.[17]

Together, these assumptions enable us to regard each individual as capable of comparing apples and oranges, so to speak, with subjective validity and precision, and to regard all individuals as applying the same decision criterion to whatever alternatives they may face. This standardizing view of individuals, in turn, focuses attention on their choices as functions of only two variables: the alternatives that are objectively presented to individuals, and the subjective interpretations of self-interest that are genetically inherited and/or socially learned by individuals.

However, when the estimation of costs and benefits refers to two or more individuals—some of whom bear the main costs while others reap the main benefits—matters become much more complicated because social analogs of individual value-comparing calculi and individual self-interest have not been easy to find. Let us consider some proposals in this regard.

The nearest thing we have, so far, to a calculus that standardizes different values between different individuals, is, of course, money. However, money fails to mea-

---

[17] Zeckhauser and Schaeffer express both assumptions when they say "Most theories of rational individual decision-making under conditions of certainty require that the decision maker behave in accord with some ordinal ranking of the available alternatives. . . . The decision maker chooses that alternative with the highest [rank]; he maximizes his utility" (1968:29). Both assumptions, of course, are questionable. The value-comparison calculus assumption does not take into account that individuals may voluntarily make trade-offs of values which are noncomparable to them by some method analogous to tossing a coin. The self-interest assumption suffers from lack of a measure of subjective self-interest beliefs which is independent of objective acts of preference. Thus, no matter what an individual chooses—including what an observer would regard as pain as against pleasure for him/herself (masochism), or pain for him/herself as against pain for others (altruism)—we are apt to regard it as expressive of his/her believed self-interest. In short, self-interest may merely be another name for whatever an individual objectively chooses, not his/her subjective motivation for choosing it.

sure the social costs and benefits of many programs one might be interested in, as
Levin points out:

> the objectives of many, if not most, social programs often have no market
> counterpart. If a program is designed to improve the environment, how do
> we obtain a market price for the reduction of hydrocarbons and visible parti-
> cles in the air or the reduction of pollution in water? While it is true that
> some of the benefits of such an action would be reflected in reduced medical
> costs and the added value of human lives saved, as well as in decreases in
> pollution-related deterioration of property, it is difficult to quantify the psychic
> benefits of clean air and water. How do we obtain a price for the aesthetics
> of open space or of conserving a rare species of bird or animal? What is the
> market price that will help us assess the benefits of increase in the self-con-
> cept, reading level, or music appreciation of a youngster? In each of these
> instances it is difficult to express outcomes in terms of their market values
> because a market does not exist for such services (1975:92).

This means we cannot compare the costs of such programs with their benefits. In
Rothenberg's words, "An especially likely situation is that different individuals
possess and/or reveal different trade-offs [i.e., different definitions of costs and
benefits—ed.], so the requirements for a correct measurement of the aggregate of
trade-offs become practically unfeasible" (1975:69), and, as a result,

> most cost-benefit analyses . . . typically list only the outcomes that *are* sus-
> ceptible to monetary expression, aggregate these, and call the reader's atten-
> tion to the existence of so-called unmeasurable types of impacts that have had
> to be perforce omitted from the analysis (1975:69).

However, we do have a useful modification of cost-benefit analysis when costs
are expressed in their own metric (say, money) and benefits are expressed in theirs:
We can then compare the benefits promised by alternative programs whose estimated costs are the same, and we can separately compare the costs estimated for
alternative programs whose promised benefits are the same. Both these modifications have been called "cost-effectiveness analysis," [18] and writing of the second,
more frequently used, variety, Levin says

> When the effectiveness of programs in achieving a particular goal (rather than
> their monetary values) is linked to costs, the approach is considered to be a

---

[18] Dasgupta and Pearce describe cost-effectiveness analysis as *both* "maximizing physical benefits
subject to a cost constraint," and "minimizing costs for a desired level of physical benefits" (1972:114);
Anderson and Settle describe it as being "useful when it has been decided to achieve certain *benefits* and
the only criterion is to obtain them at the lowest possible cost" (1977:16, emphasis added); Rothenberg
(1975:78), and Levin (1975) agree with this; but Mack claims it asks "At the same *cost,* which of the
alternatives would yield the most advantage?" (1971:110, emphasis added).

cost-effectiveness rather than a cost-benefit analysis. For example, one might examine various alternatives for raising the literacy level of a population, for reducing hydrocarbons in the air, for reducing infant mortality, and so on. In this context, cost-effectiveness analysis enables us to examine the costs of alternative programs for achieving particular types of outcomes, but . . . we cannot ascertain whether a particular program is "worth it" in the sense that benefits exceed costs, because the latter are generally expressed in monetary units while the former are rendered in units of effectiveness for achieving a particular impact (1975:93).

Levin concludes that "the results of policy-oriented experiments or quasiexperiments lend themselves naturally to cost-effectiveness comparisons" (1975:93) and that "to the degree that the [benefits] can also be translated later into [the same metric as costs], a cost-benefit framework can be applied at a second stage" (1975:93).

The search for a social analog of individual self-interest has been no less difficult and no more fruitful than that for a social analog of individual value-standardization. Among the proposed solutions are Pareto optimality[19] with and without compensation to those who bear the costs of given social programs ("an increase in traffic safety will not satisfy the Pareto criterion [of not making anyone worse off] unless compensation is paid to body shops"), and social welfare functions with and without concern for how they are chosen ("Although they may differ over what decision should be made, individuals normally agree on who should make it: this is a persuasive justification for taking as a social welfare function the ranking of the decision makers chosen by the members of society" [Zeckhauser and Schaeffer, 1968:51]). None of these solutions seems satisfactory, however, and, as Merton says, "one of the enduring problems facing sociologists is that of clarifying and working out some way of analyzing 'the aggregate of humanly relevant consequences' " (1976:172).

Somehow, however, despite all these scientifically still-unresolved difficulties, planning for a given desideratum results in what may be thought of as a variably systematic, variably detailed, variably conscious decision-flow diagram, or decision "tree," wherein is depicted "in chronological order the alternative actions that are available to you as the decision maker and the information that you acquire as you move through its various paths" (Raiffa, 1968:14), as well as the intermediate and final costs and benefits of each alternative action. The next step in applied sci-

---

[19] Rothenberg says: "The criterion of cost-benefit evaluation is that the addition of the public sector . . . with powers of regulation, control, and direct use of productive resources, should increase the *total* of private net advantages to the greatest extent possible" (1975:65, emphasis changed); and to this end, "Some legislation attempts to compensate some losers for some of their losses, especially when glaring damage is done. However, there probably never has been an explicit attempt in real-world public policy to guarantee that *no one* will end up losing" (1975:72). Such an attempt would be in accord with Pareto optimality—which defines a net beneficial social action as one that benefits at least one person without injuring any person.

ence—namely, decision—threads one course at a time through these alternatives in determining how the desideratum shall actually be pursued.

DECISIONS

Suppose we have produced a feasibility assessment and a cost-benefit estimation—that is, a plan—as outlined above. The next step is to decide whether to implement at all, and if so, which feasible alternative to pursue first. This is a crucial step in applied science because even if all social participants agree on the desideratum, the differential distribution of perceived costs and benefits for each alternative will generate different opinions among participants with respect to the choice among those alternatives. Let us see how these differences may be resolved to the extent of reaching a decision (whether or not it is subsequently changed) to implement one alternative and not others.

Politics

The reaching of a single, collectively (however temporarily) binding decision in the presence of differences regarding that decision is politics. Weber says "What do we understand by politics? The concept is extremely broad and comprises any kind of independent leadership in action. . . . [Specifically, we] wish to understand by politics only the leadership, or the influencing of the leadership . . . of a state" (1958a:77, emphasis removed), and Lasswell says "The study of politics is the study of influence and the influential" (1971:295). In other words, assuming initial differences (whether actual or potential) among decision makers regarding any given decision, politics is the process whereby one decision maker "influences" others—and is influenced by others—toward the elimination or neutralization of those differences.

Although Weber is not altogether cogent and explicit on the matter, he provides the basis for my regarding politics as encompassing variable mixes of two kinds of influence, or, to use Weber's term, two kinds of "power": (1) physical (social structural) force applied to one decision maker by another, and (2) psychical (cultural structural) attitudes appealed to by one decision maker in another. Here is what I mean.

Weber says " 'Power' is the probability that one actor within a social relationship will be in a position to carry out his own will despite resistance, *regardless of the basis on which this probability rests*" (1947:152, emphasis added; see also 1958a:180), and "He who is active in politics strives for power" (1958a:78).

Weber implicitly locates the source of this "power," this influence over other decision makers, in two kinds of behavior—psychical and physical—when he asks: "When and why do men obey? Upon what *inner justifications* and upon what *external means* does this domination rest?" (1958a:78, emphasis added). Of the "external means" upon which "domination" may rest, Weber says "the use of physical force" is "peculiar . . . to every political association," although he immediately narrows "every political association" to "the state": "force is a means peculiar to the state . . . a state is a human community that (successfully) claims the monopoly of the legitimate use of physical force within a given territory" (1958a:78, emphasis removed). Of the "inner justifications" upon which "domination" may also rest, he says "there are three inner justifications, hence basic legitimations of domination . . . [and these are] 'traditional,' 'charismatic,' and 'legal' " (Weber, 1958a:78–79, emphasis removed). Thus, "Action, especially social action which involves social relationships may be oriented by the actors to a belief in the existence of a legitimate order . . . [such that] disobedience [to the rules of that order] . . . would be abhorrent to the sense of duty, which, to a greater or lesser extent, is an absolute value to him" (1947:124).

In a word, then, politics means physically putting actual dissenters to death—or, short of that, putting them in prison, in chains, under house-arrest, shunning them, sending them into exile, fining them, and so on—while letting consenters go free; and politics also means inculcating in potential dissenters psychical predispositions (e.g., legitimacy, justice, loyalty, right, duty, obligation, honor) and appealing to those predispositions in order to prevent potential dissent from turning into actual dissent. Both techniques influence different decision makers to converge on a single, collective, decision and to remain bound by it. The two techniques may also be combined in especially potent ways, as when the state (i.e., politicians-in-power) not only physically applies force to dissenters but, as Weber puts it, claims the monopoly of the psychically *legitimate* use of force and secures that claim by requiring that it be taught to all new recruits to its domain through their compulsory education.

Now as indicated above, the making of a collective decision (no matter what physical-psychical mix is employed) is the next step—after planning itself—in determining how the anticipated costs and benefits of a given implementation will be distributed among different social participants. Such distribution is an issue because, as Rule points out,

> few "social problems" in America today represent conditions equally undesirable from all political and social standpoints. Quite the opposite: conditions like pollution, racism, poverty, and the like are basically oppositions of interest—not social problems but social conflicts, overt or concealed. . . . [And therefore, we] can hardly imagine any "solution" to problems such as pollution, racism, or poverty which does not favor some interests at the expense of others (1978:25, 18, 140; see also Bauer, 1968:14).

Accordingly, Habermas criticizes representative democracy for delegating applied science decisions to a small group of legislators ("At best these decision-makers legitimate themselves before the public. Decisions themselves, according to [this] view, must remain basically beyond public discussion" [1970a:67]), and calls for a more thoroughly participatory democracy:

> the discussion that has begun in the offices of scientific consultants to government agencies basically has to be transferred to the broader political forum of the general public. . . . The question is . . . whether a productive body of knowledge is merely transmitted to men engaged in technical manipulation for purposes of control or is simultaneously appropriated as the linguistic possession of [all] communicating individuals (1970a:79–80).

Along these lines, it should be emphasized that although Fig. 13.1 only cites "politics" once—as the crucial technique controlling the transformation of plans into decisions—politics actually enters into control of *all* the information transformations shown in that figure. Thus, "sample summarization and parameter estimation," "causal and deductive arrangement of empirical generalizations," "tests," and so forth, in the pure phase, as well as "economics," "administration, operation," "evaluations," and so forth, in the applied phase, are all profoundly subject to politics. Indeed, we adhere to "causal and deductive arrangement of empirical generalizations," for example, only to the extent that we regard this as a legitimate technique and/or to the extent that we are forcefully compelled to adhere to it. And that attitudes of legitimacy, and physical force, have often changed the techniques regarded as "scientific" at given times and places seems well-documented by the history of science from the Inquisition to Nazi Germany. My limited citation of the role of politics here is meant to indicate only its most *distinctive* role in the entire process of scientific analysis—not its exclusive role. The same is true of the role of economics—to which we turn next.

Economics

Once a policy decision has been made—regardless of who makes it and regardless of the procedures used—the next step is physically to implement that decision. For present purposes, economics may be defined as the production and distribution of physical resources for implementing human decisions, and at an organizationally more specific level, budgeting may be defined as the allocation of such resources among the several components and phases of the implementation. Thus, Weber says " 'Economic action' . . . is a peaceful use of the actor's control over resources" (1947:158; see also 1958a:181), and Wildavsky says

> Budgeting is translating financial resources into human purposes. . . . Budgets, therefore, must be plans; they try to determine future states of affairs through a series of current actions. . . . Compared to party platforms and most legislative laws, inclusion in the budget carries a higher probability of concrete action. . . . If politics is regarded as conflict over whose preferences are to prevail in the determination of policy, then the budget records the outcome of this struggle (1975:2–3, 4:5).

Actually, one might prefer to say the budget records the *second* outcome of the political struggle—the first outcome being the programmatic decision, the legislation, or the judicial order, itself. And the arena for the political struggle over budgeting is significantly different from the arena of struggle over programmatic decision. Thus, whereas the latter tends to take place between political parties in the more public political arena, the former is apt to occur between "guardian" and "advocate" agencies in the more formally constituted and less public governmental arena:

> Administrative agencies act as advocates of increased expenditure, and central control organs function as guardians of the treasury. Each expects the other to do its job; agencies can advocate, knowing the center will impose limits, and the center can exert control, knowing that agencies will push expenditures as hard as they can. . . . The interaction between spending and cutting roles makes up the component elements of budgeting systems (Wildavsky, 1975:7).

The need to win two separate struggles in different arenas—one for programmatic decision and one for budgetary allocation— means that whichever party wins the first is still a long way from final victory, but once the second has been won and resources have been produced and allocated, applied science moves into its next phase, namely, implementation.

IMPLEMENTATIONS

Pressman and Wildavsky point out that "Legislation has to be passed and funds committed before implementation takes place to secure the predicted outcome" (1973:xiv), and they therefore view implementation "as a process of interaction between the setting of goals and actions geared to achieving them" (1973:xv). It is especially important to emphasize the word "interaction" here, since Pressman and Wildavsky call attention to the large measure of backing up and readjusting between the applied science steps which Fig. 13.1 summarily represents as comprising a net one-way process:

> Considered as a whole, a program can be conceived of as a system in which each element is dependent on the other. . . . A breakdown at one stage must be repaired . . . before it is possible to move on to the next. . . . The study of implementation requires understanding that apparently simple sequences of events depend on complex chains of reciprocal interaction. Hence, each part of the chain must be built with the others in mind. The separation of policy design from implementation is fatal (1973:xv, xvii).

Thus, in explaining implementation failures, Pressman and Wildavsky emphasize contingencies which create that fatal separation—contingencies like the sheer number of agreements that must be obtained for a given implementation, the wide variation among the actors who must give these agreements with respect to the direction and intensity of their preferences and their resources for influencing the implementation, and the inevitable tendency of such agreements to erode after they have been secured. ("Allow enough time to elapse in a rapidly changing external world and it is hard to imagine any set of agreements remaining firm" [Pressman and Wildavsky, 1973:92].)

Elaborating on Pressman and Wildavsky, Bardach says that because the numerous and diverse elements of any given implementation are initially "in the hands of many different parties, most of whom are in important ways independent of each other," persuasion and bargaining—politics, again—play an essential role in implementation, but

> it is a form of politics in which the very existence of an already defined policy mandate . . . affects the strategy and tactics of the struggle. The dominant effect is to make the politics of the implementation process highly defensive. A great deal of energy goes into maneuvering to avoid responsibility, scrutiny, and blame. . . . [But at the same time, some of the same politics of] the policy-adoption process carries over into the policy-implementation process. Die-hard opponents of the policy . . . seek, and find, means to continue their opposition when, say, administrative regulations and guidelines are being written. Many who supported the original policy proposal did so only because they expected to be able to twist it in the implementation phase. . . . They too seek a role in the administrative process (1977:37–38).

SCIENTIFIC AUTHORITARIANISM

One way to overcome all the obstacles to smooth implementation mentioned by Bardach as well as by Pressman and Wildavsky is simply to concentrate power in the hands of a single implementing authority (conceivably, decision-making power could continue dispersed). Thus, Scott and Shore argue that

In order to create optimal conditions for applying scientific knowledge to social policy [one would need] a strong, centralized, enlightened authority with enough power to . . . plan and carry out regional and national policies even in the face of regional and other kinds of resistance. . . . [The form of such a system] would almost certainly deviate in important ways from the concept of a representative democracy (1979:161; see also Pressman and Wildavsky, 1973:143).

Indeed, Comte, Marx, and Weber also reach this conclusion: authoritarian political systems (whether called positivism, the dictatorship of the proletariat, or bureaucracy) offer the possibility of smooth implementations by "coordinating" all the agreements required for them—and, as Pressman and Wildavsky remind us, "If we . . . admit the possibility (indeed the likelihood) of conflict over goals, then coordination becomes another term for coercion. . . . Achieving coordination means getting your own way" (1973:133, 135).

Even Campbell, who asserts that "the experimenting society" will be "a voluntaristic society, providing for individual participation and consent at all decision-levels possible" (1971:5), also admits that

true experiments involving randomization . . . present special moral problems which we will have to consider. True experiments are best done where those designing and directing the study have most complete and arbitrary control over the people participating in the study. . . . One needs optimally to be able to randomly assign persons to experimental treatments and to enforce 100% participation in these treatments. To avoid reactive arrangements, the participants should be unaware of the experiment, unaware that other people are deliberately being given different treatments (1971:14–15; see Coleman, 1978:686).

Bell, too, after praising "Technical decision-making . . . [as] the diametric opposite of ideology: the one calculating and instrumental, the other emotional and expressive," and praising "The goal of the new intellectual technology [in particular, systems analysis, as] neither more nor less, to realize a social alchemist's dream: the dream of 'ordering' the mass society," must admit that "When men have different valuations, how does one choose? For this the technocratic view has no answer" (1973:34, 33, 358).

A further tendency toward authoritarian coordination of implementation comes from the fact that having defined the pursuit of understanding as an effort to create a constantly improved "fit" between our theories and the world, this can be accomplished by making the world fit our theories better as well as by making our theories fit the world better. Thus, Scott and Shore point out that

> Some proportion of what is called "economic policy" involves the creation of restraints on the national economy so that over time this unit will begin to acquire artificially features that will then make intervention, control, and prediction possible. Economists have recognized that problems raised by the robustness of a theoretical model can be handled in one of three ways: by changing the model, by modifying the situations to which one applies it, or by some combination of the two (1979:229).

Put more generally, and to reiterate a point made in Chapter 13, every new control over the world can lead to enhanced understanding of the world and every new understanding of the world can lead to enhanced control over the world. Thus, insofar as the achievement of control requires implementation of some kind, both pure science and applied science have a stake in smooth implementation and therefore a stake in whatever may facilitate such implementation—including authoritarianism. For this reason, no scientific laboratory has even been run democratically—such that experimenters and subjects have equal voice in the experiment—and authoritarianism would conveniently make of the entire world a laboratory for controlled experimentation.

SCIENTIFIC AUTHORITARIANISM AND ETHICAL EGALITARIANISM

Now of course it is true that although one's role-expectation as scientist tends inevitably to favor authoritarian coordination of power, one's role-expectation as citizen may well favor a more democratic dispersal of power—a discrepancy made possible by the independence of ethical and empirical questions (see Chapter 16). One resolution of the dilemma is to make the citizen role dominant in the scientific arena—as Merton and Lerner suggest:

> the American social scientist has seen too many examples in recent history of the intellectual committing moral suicide by allowing himself to be routinized in the service of the directive-giving state. . . . It has become apparent that the first condition which social scientists must observe . . . is to retain their own freedom of choice—among goals and values, among policies and decisions, among ways and means (1951:306).

In a related vein, MacRae (1976) argues that the analyst must not only make his/her own judgment about valuation but must participate importantly in efforts to set collective valuations.

A second solution is to abandon any role in preimplementation planning and decision-making that the scientist might have and limit one's attention to post-implementation evaluation. Thus, Moynihan's belief is that "the role of social science lies not in the formation of policy, but in the measurement of its results" (1969:193), and Campbell's advice is similar:

> What I recommend to social scientists is a servant role, not a leadership role, that they participate as methodologists in evaluating the innovations which the political process produces, foregoing their theoretical interests for practical purposes (1972:164).

Let us therefore see what is involved in such evaluation research.

OUTCOMES AND EVALUATIONS

There is a complementarity between planning and evaluation: planning assesses, *before* implementation, ideas about how control over a given phenomenon may be accomplished; evaluation assesses, *after* implementation, the extent and manner in which that control has actually been accomplished.[20] Thus, evaluation tests the fit between actual outcomes and the outcomes projected in the original decision, and reflects the results of that test back to implementation and/or planning so as to guide them toward producing a better fit, maintaining the present fit, or abandoning the effort to achieve a fit at all.

Freeman and Sherwood distinguish between evaluating two kinds of outcomes of implementation, namely, its adherence to "proper" standards of procedure, and its production of projected impacts on the desideratum—and they warn that these require different procedures:

> It is often believed . . . that if a program is run properly it can also be assumed that the desired changes are taking place and that these changes are due to the program. . . . [But assessment of the conduct of a program] cannot substitute for the experimental measurement of [its] impact. Impact can only be assessed through systematic, empirical research, either through

---

[20] Williams defines "policy analysis" (i.e., planning) as "a means of synthesizing information to draw from it policy alternatives and preferences stated in comparable, predicted quantitative and qualitative terms as a basis or guide for policy decisions," and defines "outcome evaluations" (i.e., evaluation) as efforts to "assess the effects of an organization's existing projects or programs" (1972a:5,4). Rossi uses similar terms and conveys the same distinction when he says: "policy analysis [is] concerned with working out ways of making informed and intelligent decisions among alternative social policies," while "evaluation [is concerned with] determining the . . . extent to which the policies accomplish intended effects" (1972b:16).

the planned, experimental manipulation of events or behavior, or through the systematic observation of natural occurrences (1970:13).

Freeman adds: "for purposes of policy determination, as well as for contributions to basic social science knowledge, the most appropriate evaluation is one that includes both process and impact" (1975:146).

More inclusively, we may say that the aim of evaluation research is to discover whether a given implementation is (1) *legitimate,* in the sense of being no less procedurally in accord with the letter and spirit of its enabling legislation than alternative implementations; (2) *effective,* in the sense of bringing about no smaller portion of the desired effect than alternative implementations; (3) *efficient,* in the sense of not costing any more than alternative implementations; (4) *dependable,* in the sense of eliciting the desired effect not less regularly than alternative implementations; and (5) *clean,* in the sense of having no more undesired side effects and long-run effects than alternative implementations.

Needless to say, this is a tall order, with the result that the evaluation of implementations is very often unscientific, informal, hidden from public scrutiny, unrecorded, easily forgotten, perhaps even unconscious. Pressman and Wildavsky point out that when we look back at long-established implementations,

It is easy to forget (perhaps because we never knew) about their initial difficulties. The years of trial and error that led to the present state of operation are lost from view. The huge amount of resources that may have been poured into different alternatives before one caught on is conveniently part of past history for which we are not responsible (1973:116).

But very much like planning, whether evaluation of the results of implementation is conscious or unconscious, remembered or forgotten, sophisticatedly systematic or crudely seat-of-the-pants, it is always present in every applied science.

Now it frequently happens that the evaluation of a given implementation involves comparing particular outcomes to generalized decisions—in contrast to tests in pure science, which involve comparing empirical generalizations to equally generalized predictions. The reason for this is the potential cost to mortal humans of a single outcome that fails to implement a given decision, and the potential benefit of a single outcome that succeeds. Thus, a single nuclear power plant failure, or a single misuse of administrative prerogative may be evaluated as so costly that the decision maker abandons further implementation along these lines, thereby obviating any possible convergence of different outcomes toward a general average. Similarly, a single grandly successful outcome—the 100-to-one shot that romps home, the million dollar lottery ticket, the windfall, the stock market "killing"—can be evaluated as so beneficial as to warrant new plans, a new decision, a new implementation. Popper puts the difference between pure science hypothesis-testing and applied science outcome-evaluation as follows:

> in the case of the so-called theoretical or generalizing [i.e., pure] sciences we are predominantly interested in the universal laws or hypotheses. . . . In the case of applied sciences, our interest is different. The engineer who uses physics in order to build a bridge is predominantly interested in a prognosis: whether or not a bridge of a certain kind . . . will carry a certain load. For him, the universal laws are means to an end and taken for granted. Accordingly, pure and applied generalizing sciences are respectively interested in testing universal hypotheses, and in predicting [and evaluating—ed.] specific events (1950:447).

Experimentation

Partly because the cost of mistakes can be so high, and partly in order to restrict overtly authoritarian implementation to special occasions within a democracy, social experiments (and their poor relations, "demonstration projects") have gained currency—as already illustrated by the discussion in Chapter 13 of Berk et al. (1980). Through experimentation, "proposed courses of social action or social policy [can be scientifically evaluated] before they are adopted more widely" (Scott and Shore, 1979:44; see also Williams, 1972a:4)—thereby combining unknown risk and authoritarianism within the experimental locus with known risk and more democratic procedures outside that locus. Thus, Campbell argues that

> The United States and other modern nations should be ready for an experimental approach to social reform. . . . The political stance would become: "This is a serious problem. We propose to initiate Policy A on an experimental basis. If after five years there has been no significant improvement, we will shift to Policy B" . . . [thereby] making explicit that a given problem solution was only one of several that the administration or party could in good conscience advocate (1975:71, 73).

One other experimental technique should be mentioned, and that involves employing nonhuman stand-ins for human subjects. It is conceivable that nonhuman animal social groups like termites, honeybees, prairie dogs, chimpanzees, and perhaps others might perform this function for certain limited experimental purposes, but more likely is computer simulation:

With the growing sophistication of simulation procedures through the use of computers—simulations of economic systems, of social behavior, of decision problems—we have the possibility, for the first time, of large-scale "controlled experiments" in the social sciences (Bell, 1973:344).

Monitoring

When evaluation is repeated periodically we call it "monitoring," and when it is also fed back immediately into implementation and planning (and thence into decision), we have what Bauer calls the "cybernetic model":

> the cybernetic model demands an active information system with sensors to determine the consequences of actions. In addition, it demands provision for feeding this information back to decision centers and readiness to change one's behavior in response to signals of errors being committed. Thus a sophisticated approach to planning shares some of the characteristic features of "muddling through," which has long been regarded as the extreme of not planning (1966:8; quoted in Schoettle, 1968:178).

Pressman and Wildavsky, defending such a cybernetic model for social programs, point out that

> People who regularly deal with inanimate objects such as computer programs would never expect a new one to run the first time. "Debugging" is not something done on the rare occasion when things go wrong but is an expected part of making a program work. Numerous iterations, extending over long periods of time, may be required before the new program works adequately (1973:113).

Caro says that "The planning-action-evaluation cycle may be repeated indefinitely until objectives are realized or until problems and objectives are redefined" (1971:3–4). Finally, without explicitly mentioning iterated decisions, implementations, and evaluations, note that MacRae implies them all when he argues that

> Applied social science . . . requires *repeated measurement over time*. Such measurements are involved in the scientific study of systems in motion, from astronomy to electronics. They are also available to economists. . . . But in the other social sciences, either basic or applied, they are less generally available. . . . The use of this approach for economic indicators has led to increasing discussion of analogous "social indicators" (1976:287–288).

Social and Cultural Indicators

Viewed in this light, social indicators provide repeated measurements of certain outcomes of the society as a whole (conceiving of the latter as a complex implementation of complex decisions), thereby facilitating evaluation of that implementation and of its several contributory implementations—evaluations which may then feed into new planning, decision, implementation, outcomes, and so on. Thus, Moore and Sheldon argue that

> The notion of social indicators leads directly to the idea of "monitoring" social change. If an indicator can be found that will stand for a set of correlated changes, and if intervention can be introduced (whether on the prime, indicative, variable or on one of its systemic components), then the program administrator may have been given a powerful analytical and policy tool (1968:4).

Land cites, as the first type of "social indicators measuring social conditions," "output descriptive indicators [which] are measures of the end products of social processes and are most directly related to the appraisal of social problems and social policy" (1975:17).

And, here is Bell, who argues that

> What we need, in effect, is a System of Social Accounts which would broaden our concept of costs and benefits, and put economic accounting into a broader framework. . . . A System of Social Accounts . . . would move us toward measurement of the utilization of human resources in our society in four areas: (1) the measurement of social costs and net returns of innovations (2) the measurement of social ills (e.g., crime, family disruption); (3) the creation of "performance budgets" in areas of defined social needs (e.g., housing, education); and (4) indicators of economic opportunity and social mobility (1973:326, see also Merton, 1957:261–262).

Finally, in this connection, here is Gerbner's proposal that a set of "cultural indicators" can usefully monitor certain basic levels of collective thought within a given society:

> We need to know what general terms of public [thought and discourse] about existence, priorities, values, and relationships are given in collectively shared public message systems before we can reliably interpret facts of individual and social response. . . . [Thus,] interpretations of public opinion (that is, responses to questions elicited in specific cultural contexts), and of many social and cultural policy matters, require the background knowledge of general

"cultural indicators" similar to the economic indicators compiled to guide economic policy and the social indicators proposed to inform social policy making (1969:126).

Feedback of Outcomes to Pure Science

Shaver and Staines point out that "Although experimental reforms are primarily applied ventures from the social scientist's point of view, they can, if designed and evaluated properly, generate data of major theoretical significance" (1972:162). Thus, any outcome of any implementation may serve as grist for the pure science mill since an outcome of human manipulation of the world may be no less an observation of the world's working than anything else—and may, indeed, be an informationally more valuable observation of the world's working when that manipulation is part of an experimental design.

SUMMARY

With this chapter, tracing the procedures of applied science, my explication of Fig. 13.1 comes to an end. The chapter began by addressing planning, wherein alternative ways of exerting control over some phenomenon (called here the desideratum) are described and measured with respect to their physical feasibility, and their costs and benefits to various parts of society.

The role of politics in decision-making was examined, as were some elementary aspects of decision-making itself. Similarly, the role of economics in program implementation was discussed, and some attention was paid to the authoritarian demands of applied science and the problems of balancing these demands against ethical egalitarianism. Next, evaluation research and monitoring (including social indicators) were discussed, and a final word was said concerning the feedback of information from applied science to pure science.

16

Premises of Scientific Procedure, and Objections to Employing that Procedure in Sociology

In introducing Part III, Chapter 13 claimed that natural science analysis is commonsensical curiosity and coping gone public—that is, made social by virtue of each participant's requirement that other participants verify his/her conclusions. Let us now ask two questions of that claim. (1) On what premises does it rest? That is, What assumptions can justify making our personal confidence in our *own*, direct, experiences of the world dependent on what others tell us about *their* experiences of the world? (2) To what extent can procedures and premises of natural science be applied specifically to the discipline of sociology—What objections have been raised, so far, against that application and what rebuttals to those objections should be considered?

If we define a "premise" as an empirically untestable faith about the nature of some aspect of existence—untestable, because any test would have to take the premise for granted and thereby render itself tautological—then the fundamental premises of natural science procedure seem to fall into two categories. (And note that the idea that such premises are empirically untestable faiths contrasts sharply with Alexander's unexplicated placement of the "methodological assumptions" of science near the "empirical" rather than the "nonempirical," "metaphysical" end of his "continuum of scientific thought" [1982:3, 40].) The first category of premises concerns the *objects* we seek to understand and control, and the second contains premises concerning the *subjects*—ourselves—who seek that understanding and con-

458

trol (and, of course, when it is ourselves that we seek to understand and control, the two categories overlap—a point emphasized by certain objections to regarding sociology as a natural science which will be examined later). Let us consider these two kinds of premises in order.

OBJECT PREMISES

Whitehead argues that the task of science

> is the discovery of the relations which exist within the flux of perceptions, sensations, and emotions which form our experience of life. The panorama yielded by sight, sound, taste, smell, touch, and by more inchoate sensible feelings, is the sole field of activity (1967:106).

According to this view, each of us can only know his/her own individual, subjective experiences. Quine argues that from these experiences, in response to what he regards as the "natural" human tendency to follow "the rule of simplicity," each of us then constructs a so-called objective, "physical," world external to our experiences to which we believe those experiences correspond:

> Imagine . . . that we have devised the most economical set of concepts adequate to the play-by-play reporting of immediate experience. The entities under this scheme . . . are, let us suppose, individual subjective events of sensation or reflection. We should still find, no doubt, that a physicalistic conceptual scheme, purporting to talk about external objects, offers great advantages in simplifying our over-all reports. By bringing together scattered sense events and treating them as perceptions of one object, we reduce the complexity of our stream of experience to a manageable conceptual simplicity. The rule of simplicity is indeed our guiding maxim in assigning sense data to objects: we associate an earlier and a later round sensum with the same so-called penny, in obedience to the demands of maximum simplicity in our total world-picture. . . . [Therefore,] from a phenomenalistic point of view, the conceptual scheme of physical objects is a convenient myth, simpler than the literal truth and yet containing that literal truth as a . . . part (1963:17–18).

Note, however, that if we adopt Quine's view, *my* subjectively constructed, "mythical," world of physical objects presumably includes *you,* another human being, to whom I then must look—according to the argument set forth in Chapter 13—for verification of my world's objectivity. Even in the very act of your verification, however, you (and in the end, indeed, also I, insofar as I am a physical object to myself) must remain for me only a product of my own subjective construction of a "mythical" physical world. What then can possibly be the justification for my acceptance of "your" verification of that world's objectivity? In what sense can that verification be considered independent and not the most transparently tautological circle wherein my world verifies itself?

There seems to be no way out of this circularity without giving the physicalistic and antisolipsistic assumption—that is, that a world does exist outside and independent of my experience, a world which includes you, a world which I am capable of picturing and also influencing—equal footing with the phenomenalistic assumption mentioned above. Perhaps the best defense of physicalism is not the predictability and controllability of the world but, on the contrary, the obdurate *un*predictability and *un*controllability of the world. Thus, it is not my occasional and always partial successes with the world but my persistent *failures* there which convince me that the world is really beyond me; that the world is not merely a figment of my imagination but an objectivity existing independently, in part, of me. Only an omniscient and omnipotent being could justifiably look upon the world as having no independent existence—as, indeed, in that case it would have none. Seen in this light, all human efforts (including the scientific one) to understand and control the world seek (however futilely) to abolish the world as an independent reality and to enable someone ultimately and justifiably to say not merely "The world is mine," but "The world is *me*."

So long as none of us is fully successful in this effort, so long as we continue to fail and continue to report our failures to each other, we confirm in each other our belief in the world's continuing reality—including, not least of all, each other's reality. I therefore conclude here, with Quine, that

> Here we have two competing conceptual schemes, a phenomenalistic one and a physicalistic one. Which should prevail? Each has its advantages; each has its special simplicity in its own way. Each, I suggest, deserves to be developed. Each may be said, indeed, to be the more fundamental, though in different senses: the one is epistemologically, the other physically, fundamental (1963:17).

This conviction that both phenomenalistic and physicalistic presuppositions are needed for science is, perhaps, what Marcuse, too, has in mind when he says

> No concept can be valid which defines its objects by properties and functions that do not belong to the object. . . . However, matter confronts the subject in a historical universe, and objectivity appears under an open historical horizon; it is changeable . . . [and therefore] the interaction between a collec-

tive subject and a common world persists and constitutes the objective validity of the [concepts] (1964:218, 217).

It seems to be only the pairing of phenomenalistic and physicalistic assumptions that permits us not only to associate, as Quine says, "an earlier and a later round sensum [experienced by the *same* human being—ed.] with the same so-called penny," but even more crucially for science, to associate the round sensa experienced by *different* human beings with the same so-called penny.

Now what can we say about this so-called penny—more generally, what can we say about the whole so-called world of objects? Two premises here seem crucial to natural science. First, whatever nature "really" is, we assume that it presents itself in precisely the same way to the same human observer standing at different points in time and space; and second, we assume that it also presents itself in precisely the same way across different human observers standing at the same point in time and space. Note that both assumptions refer to constancies in the way *nature presents* itself, not to constancies in the way *humans observe and manipulate* that presentation; the latter are the foci of the subject premises examined later here.

Regarding the first premise above, Popper asserts that

> regularities which are directly testable by experiment do not change. Admittedly it is conceivable, or logically possible, that they might change; but this possibility is disregarded by empirical science and does not affect its methods. On the contrary, scientific method presupposes the immutability of natural processes, or the "principle of the uniformity of nature." . . . [This principle] expresses the metaphysical faith in the existence of regularities in our world (a faith . . . without which practical action is hardly conceivable) (1961:252).

The premise that nature is *uniform,* then, declares that no matter where or when a given human being is located, the fundamental natural processes present themselves in the same way. Thus, as indicated in Chapter 14, astrophysicists assume that the same atomic processes (whether these processes are known or not) that prevail now and here on Earth prevail throughout the cosmos and throughout all past and future time, and, similarly, sociologists assume that the same processes (again, whether known or not) prevail across all societies, past, present, and future.

Regarding the second premise, Kaplan says "nature plays no favorites, but exposes herself promiscuously" (1964:128)—a faith that stands in sharpest contrast with the mystical faith expressed in Don Juan's claim "that there were no exact steps to knowing Mescalito; therefore no one could teach about him except Mescalito himself. This quality made him a unique power; he was not the same for every man" (Castaneda, 1968:52). The premise that nature is *universalistic,* then, declares that no matter which human being is standing in a given place and time, the fundamental natural processes present themselves in the same way.

These two assumptions about the object of natural science—that nature presents itself in perfectly uniform ways to each human, and in perfectly universalistic ways across different humans—constitute one side of our justification for scientific procedure as set forth in the preceding three chapters. The other side of this justification, of course, pertains to us, the observers and manipulators of that presentation.

SUBJECT PREMISES

Scientific assumptions about the nature of human beings are divisible into two classes: those pertaining to the cognitive and motor capabilities of humans, and those pertaining to their valuational capabilities.

Cognitive and Motor Capabilities

Here we have two assumptions. First is the faith that all human beings are created interchangeable with respect to their cognitive and motor capabilities and that it is only circumstance which prevents that intrinsic interchangeability from being manifest. In other words, we assume that if *any*[1] two human individuals

[1] This view should be sharply distinguished from Polanyi's ("Naturally, only fellow scientists working in closely related fields are competent to exercise authority over each other" [1969:85]), and Mulkay's ("trustworthy assessments of the quality of a given piece of work can only be made by those who are working on the same or similar problems and are known to be capable of producing results of at least the same level of quality" [1977:107]). Some of the logical difficulties to which Polanyi's and Mulkay's position leads seem exemplified in Polanyi's unresolved ambivalence between (1) his claim that science is and ought to be a "republic" in which "the authority of scientific opinion . . . is established *between* scientists, not above them," and—goaded by the belief that "only a strong and unified scientific opinion imposing [sic] the intrinsic [sic] value of scientific progress on society at large can elicit the support of scientific inquiry by the general public"—(2) his call for "a strong and effective scientific authority to reign over this republic" (1969:56, 57–58, 65). Gouldner's view is more congenial to my own, but still stops short of the mark: "in the last analysis, the [scientific] group must win acceptance of its procedures and conclusions from some *larger* group. The scientist's actions must be deemed reasonable by the larger community of *non*specialist scholars" (1976:20). I believe Garfinkel, however, is exactly right here when he claims that "The 'relevant other persons' [capable of confirming or refuting his/her conclusions] for the scientific theorizer are universalized 'Anymen' " (1967:275). In this view, *every* human being's sense-based conclusions about the nature of the world enter into scientific conclusions. This is not to say, of course, that all human beings' conclusions have equal weight (see Merton, 1973:446; Gouldner, 1976:21; Polanyi, 1969:56; Mulkay, 1977:107), but only that they all have *some* weight and that that universality is specifically acknowledged in the several interchangeability premises of natural science. Note that the idea that all human beings are implicated in the sense-based

could stand precisely in each other's places, each would experience (i.e., observe and manipulate) the world precisely as the other does. Thus, Schutz says

> I take it for granted—and assume my fellowman does the same—that if I change places with him so that his "here" becomes mine, I would be at the same distance from things and see them in the same typicality that he does; moreover, the same things would be in my reach which are actually in his (1953:8);

Popper says that when we "understand actions in an objective sense" we mean "had I been placed in [the actor's] situation . . . then I, and presumably you too, would have acted in a similar way to him" (1976:103); and Kaplan says "A scientific observation could have been made by any other observer so situated" (1964:128).

Obviously, the *manifest* cognitive and motor capabilities of observer-manipulators vary widely from one individual to the next. That is, in actual observable fact one individual is apt to be more intelligent, or more "verbal" or more "quantitative" than another; one individual is apt to have more physical strength, or dexterity, or stamina than another, or better eyesight and hearing than another—and so on. Under the assumption that all humans are *intrinsically* identical in these respects, we regard all these *manifest* differences as trivial epiphenomena—"noise" which needs to be filtered out or otherwise remedied in order to permit the presumed intrinsic identity to come through.

Over the millennia of human history a twofold remedy has been constructed; it is scientific "method" and scientific "instrumentation." By training each new recruit to scientific "discipline" in the same method (including the general procedures discussed in Chapters 13, 14, and 15, but extending to the much more detailed techniques current in specialized fields and subfields), and by making the same observation-making, data-processing, and world-manipulating instruments (e.g., eyeglasses, microscopes, interview schedules, microphones, computers, and, on the applied science side, lasers, tractors, cranes, guns, television sets, books) available to them all, we strive to remove as much circumstantial differences from their cognitive and motor capabilities as possible—thereby making them as nearly identical and interchangeable in these respects as possible.

The second assumption of natural science pertaining to human cognitive and motor capabilities recognizes that we cannot *directly* know each other's experiences of the world but can only know them indirectly, through what we *tell* each other.

intersubjective verification of scientific propositions differs sharply from Habermas' "notion of permanent communication between the sciences, *considered in terms of their political relevance,* and informed public opinion," (1970a:69, emphasis added), because Habermas has reference to scientifically informed public participation in deciding how already established scientific propositions are to be used in applied science, not in establishing (or overturning) such propositions in the first place.

Consequently, natural science assumes that we are intrinsically perfect communicators and that, again, only circumstances (e.g., differences in language, personal candor, personal attentiveness to detail, etc.) impede the manifestation of this intrinsic identity. Here again, the remedy is scientific method—especially its reliance on precise and universal terminology and on technical (i.e., non-ad hominem) public criticism. Thus, Kaplan says "The methodological question is . . . whether what is *reported* as an observation [i.e., not what *is* an observation—ed.] can be used in subsequent inquiry even if the particular observer is no longer a part of the context" (1964:128, emphasis added).[2]

The net result of reliance on scientific method and instrumentation, then, is that when two observer-manipulators who rely on this method ask each other "Do you see what I see?" and "Can you do what I can do?" they may be relatively sure (never absolutely sure, of course) that the cognitive and motor referents of these questions, and their answers, are the same for both of them.[3]

There remains one further subject premise on which different observer-manipulators' reliances on each other's reports depend, and this premise pertains not to their cognitive and motor capabilities but to their cathectic or valuational capabilities.

Valuational Capabilities

The slightest reflection tells us that we are impinged upon by far more stimuli (from inside as well as outside ourselves) than we can possibly collect and under-

---

[2] Note, however, that when Kaplan goes on to say "I ask 'Do you see what I see?' to help decide whether what I see is to be explained by self-knowledge or by knowledge of the presumed object" (1964:128), he overlooks that it is the other's verbal *answer* to that verbal question—and not the other's perception itself—that enters that decision. And note also that scientific method pertains directly to the *reporting* of observations, explorations, tests, plans, evaluations, and so forth, and only indirectly to the *making* of them. That is, we follow scientific method in making observations, explanations, tests, etc., only because when we do so we can report them in ways that "can be used in subsequent inquiry." To modify Popper's assertion somewhat, "The question, 'How did you first *find* your theory?' relates, as it were, to an entirely private matter, as opposed to the question 'How did you [*report*] *your theory?*' " (1973:71; Popper says "*test* your theory," but the scientific essence of a test, too, is in its report and only afterward, and only for this reason, in its performance). Similarly, Nisbet notes "the crucial difference between what may properly be called the logic of discovery and the logic of demonstration. The second is properly subject to rules and prescriptions; the first isn't" (1976:5, emphasis removed). It follows that a poorly reported (that is, poorly demonstrated-to-others) observation—and certainly an *un*reported one—almost always goes unnoticed in natural science, no matter how well-made the observation itself may have been; but a well-reported observation, no matter how poorly made (or even fraudulently made) the observation itself may have been, tends to be noticed—and being noticed, tends to be checked, replicated, and then verified or falsified intersubjectively.

[3] Luckmann seems to summarize the subject premises discussed above as "(1) The unity of experience among men in different societies throughout the course of history . . . [and] (2) The givenness and the possibility of communication" (1978:253).

stand at any given moment, and that we are able to act upon the world (including ourselves) in far more ways than we can carry out at any given moment. It follows that we must *select* the stimuli we actually do collect and *select* the acts we actually do perform. As Mead says, "The human is an attentive animal. . . . Our whole intelligent process seems to lie in the attention which is selective of certain types of stimuli. Other stimuli which are bombarding the system are in some fashion shunted off" (1934:25). But what are the mechanisms that perform that selection and shunting?

In part, of course, the human anatomy performs it, and in part human conceptual apparatuses perform it. Human *values* perform it too, and their role here is no less essential than those of anatomy and conceptualization. Thus, Comte, speaking of "affection," argues

> This element it is, and this only, which gives a stimulus and direction to the other two parts of our nature [i.e., thought and action], without it the one would waste its force in ill-conceived or, at least, useless studies, and the other in barren or even dangerous contention (1975:322);

Whitehead says "feeling is the agent which reduces the universe to its perspective for fact" (1938:13); Mannheim says "no interpretation of history can exist except in so far as it is guided by interest and purposeful striving" (1955:261); and Lynd agrees: "in the world of science there is no such thing as 'pure' curiosity. . . . Research without an actively selective point of view becomes the ditty bag of an idiot" (1946:183).

Thus, natural science, far from being *free* of values, absolutely *requires* values in order to direct its attention, and, as with the human cognitive and motor capabilities that science also requires, we assume that all human beings are created intrinsically interchangeable with respect to values. That is, natural science is premised on the notion that in precisely the same circumstances all human beings would desire the same things and would abhor the same things.[4]

But again, what we presume to be intrinsic value-interchangeability is not manifest. People vary widely in their actual values, and the result is that when one observer-manipulator asks another "Do you see what I see?" or "Can you do what I do?" the answer may not be trustworthy because the second observer-manipulator, although cognitively and motorically interchangeable with the first observer, *wants* something different and so looks in a different direction, pursues a different goal, marches to a different drummer. As Habermas says (though somewhat less plainly than one might wish), in order to trust someone else's word, we have to

---

[4] The various lists of "universal," "inalienable," and "human" rights (e.g., to life, liberty, and the pursuit of happiness, to freedom from want and fear, to freedom of information, of assembly, of speech, of religion, etc.) represent premises of this kind.

believe that his/her motivations in giving that word are what they seem to be, but this is not always the case:

> the "idealization" of the concept of the ideal speech situation . . . consists . . . of the supposition that. . . . the actual motivations of the actor [are] identical with the linguistically apprehensible intentions of the speakers. . . . Now we have reason enough to assume, however, that social action is not only—and perhaps not even primarily—controlled by motives which coincide with the intentions of the actor-speaker, but rather by motives excluded from public communication and fixed to a prelinguistic symbol organization (1970b: 373).

Now if, as we have seen above, scientific method is the preferred remedy for manifest differences in observer-manipulators' cognitive and motor capabilities, what remedies do we have for manifest differences in observer-manipulators' *values?*

There is far less agreement on any single remedy here than there is on scientific method and instrumentation, with the result that at least four proposals still seem to be very much in the running.[5] They urge, respectively, that natural science should be (1) value-determining, (2) value-free, (3) value-individuated, and (4) value-universal. Let us examine each in turn.

VALUE-DETERMINING SCIENCE

Here "value-determining" does not refer to natural science's unquestioned ability to identify values as they *actually* exist (or did exist or will exist) in a given population but to its supposed ability to identify the values that *should* exist there. Comte is a classical progenitor of this idea, insofar as he claims science can tell us which values we should hold by telling us which values can and cannot be realized and then appealing to prudence (But what can validate prudence?):

> [M]orals, and this is true even of practical morality, are objectively dependent on sociology . . . as determining the primary direction of all our tendencies without exception. . . . Is it not evident that those who have placed themselves in opposition to the course of civilization would not have adopted this attitude if its antagonistic character had been clearly demonstrated? No one

---

[5] Alexander indicates this lack of consensus when he says

> The basic question [in social science analysis] is not whether there is ideology, but what our attitude toward it should be. Do we welcome it and try to tailor our cognitive interest to meet these demands, or do we try to separate our values from our concepts in an analytic sense, knowing full well that any concrete statement will, nonetheless, be permeated with both? (1981:282).

is so foolish as knowingly to place himself in opposition to the nature of things (1975:443, 45).

And here are Lumsden and Wilson, more than a hundred years later, holding out the same vain hope for sociobiology:

> the deep scientific study of the epigenetic rules will . . . translate [their] commands into a precise language that can be understood and debated. Societies that know human nature in this way might well be more likely to agree on universal goals within the constraints of that nature. And although they cannot escape the inborn rules of epigenesis . . . societies can employ knowledge of the rules to guide individual behavior and cultural evolution to the ends upon which they agree (1981:359–360).

In similar manner, Durkheim scorns the belief that "science can teach us nothing about what we ought to desire" (1938:47), and after categorically asserting, instead, that "for societies as for individuals, health is good and desirable; disease, on the contrary, is bad and to be avoided," claims to "find an objective criterion, inherent in the facts themselves, which enables us to distinguish scientifically between health and morbidity in the various orders of social phenomena" (1938:49).[6]

Now at least two points regarding this proposed remedy for manifest value noninterchangeability should be made. First, to the extent that values refer to what is *ultimately* (not merely instrumentally) good and/or beautiful, bad and/or ugly, no science whatever can determine such values. Weber is especially eloquent here:

> Who—aside from certain big children who are indeed found in the natural sciences—still believes that the findings of astronomy, biology, physics, or chemistry could teach us anything about the *meaning* of the world? . . . [It cannot be] proved that the existence of the world which . . . [the] sciences describe is worth while, that it has any "meaning," or that it makes sense to live in such a world. . . . [And as for the historical and cultural sciences,] they give us no answer to the question, whether the existence of . . . cultural phenomena have been and are *worth while*. And they do not answer the further question, whether it is worth the effort required to know them (1958a:142, 144, 145).

---

[6] Durkheim claims to find such an "objective criterion" in the relative distribution of types: "we shall call 'normal' these social conditions that are the most generally distributed, and [we shall call] the others 'morbid' or 'pathological' " (1938:55), and defends this criterion by arguing that "It would be incomprehensible if the most widespread forms of organization would not at the same time be, *at least in their aggregate*, the most advantageous. How could they have maintained themselves under so great a variety of circumstances if they had not enabled the individual better to resist the elements of destruction?" (1938:58). "[G]reater frequency . . ." says Durkheim, "is, thus, a proof of . . . superiority" (1938:58).

Indeed, natural science cannot determine *any* ultimates at all—despite all talk about cosmic constants, ultimate components of matter, ultimate destiny of the universe, and the like. Even if we succeeded in observing and intersubjectively verifying something we named as "ultimate," we could never be sure that some future, equally verified observation would not come along to negate that conclusion—either because our present observations may be erroneous, or because the universe itself, not being completely subject to human control, may change without our permission or knowledge. It follows that "as soon as truly 'ultimate' problems are at stake for us . . . [we] come to the limits of science" (Weber, 1958a: 151), and therefore "any scientific statement must remain *tentative forever*" (Popper, 1961:280).

The second point follows from the first. The argument that science can determine the values which people should hold (and therefore the values to which science itself should be aimed) covertly, but necessarily, takes for granted at least one value as its own untestable premise. Thus, when Comte says "No one is so foolish as knowingly to place himself in opposition to the nature of things"; when Lumsden and Wilson say "Societies that know human nature . . . [will] be more likely to agree on universal goals within the constraints of that nature"; and when Durkheim says "health is good and desirable; disease . . . is bad and to be avoided"; each takes for granted that *survival,* continued *life*—and, as mentioned above, prudence in its pursuit—should be a universal human value. Thus, the remedy that proposes natural science can determine its own values rests, however tacitly, on an inevitably *assumed* value which it itself cannot determine.[7]

VALUE-FREE SCIENCE

Weber, cited above as insisting on the independence of values from natural science seems, prima facie, also to insist on the converse—namely, the independence of natural science from values:

[7] The claim that science cannot determine human values does not mean that science cannot *contribute* to values—their clarification, as well as their attainment. Weber himself notes that science is

in a position to help . . . to gain clarity. . . . If you take such and such a stand, then according to scientific experience, you have to use such and such a *means.* . . . Now, these means are perhaps such that you believe you must reject them. Then you simply must choose between the end and the inevitable means. . . . [Science] can also tell you that if you want such and such an end, then you must take into the bargain the subsidiary consequences which according to all experience will occur (1958a: 151).

More recently, Campbell advocates what he calls "a *science* of ethics" which, although it "could never prove that continued human existence in large cooperative groups was a desirable goal, nor prove any other ultimate goal," would, "for persons who had already made such a value choice, . . . provide sets of derived, mediational values which if adhered to would further the achievement of the chosen ultimate values" (1975:1109; see also Rule, 1978:123).

the investigator and teacher should keep unconditionally separate the establishment of empirical facts (including the "value-oriented" conduct of the empirical individual whom he is investigating) and *his* own . . . evaluation of these facts as satisfactory or unsatisfactory (1949:11; see also 1958a:145).

In short, the value-free remedy, viewed superficially, would purge scientific analysis of all values except those favoring an abstract, goal-free, understanding and control. Weber, however, is aware of the superficiality of this view—because of the impossibility of a goal-free understanding and control—as becomes clear when he notes that

There is no absolutely "objective" scientific analysis of culture—or . . . of "social phenomena" independent of special and "one-sided" viewpoints according to which . . . they are selected, analyzed, and organized for expository purposes. . . . To be sure, without the investigator's evaluative ideas, there would be no principle of selection of subject-matter and no meaningful knowledge of the concrete reality (1949:72, 82).

But if Weber does not intend to advocate a literally "value-free" science, what *does* he intend to advocate? The answer seems given when we combine Weber's insistence that the scientist should separate *"his* own . . . evaluation" (emphasis in the original) from the establishment of facts with the following argument:

How should a devout Catholic, on the one hand, and a Freemason, on the other, in a course on the forms of church and state or on religious history ever be brought to evaluate these subjects alike? This is out of the question. And yet the academic teacher must desire and must demand of himself to serve the one as well as the other by his knowledge and methods (1958a:146– 147).

It would appear, then, that while sharply closing science to the scientist's *personal* values, Weber opens science to *public,* universally consensual values such as are represented by whatever values "Catholics" and "Freemasons"—or any other contending *sub*cultures—share in common, for it can only be these values that enable science to "serve the one as well as the other." In short, Weber's advocacy of value-free science calls for freedom from values about which there is dissensus at a given time and place but subordination to values about which there is so much consensus that one is not even aware of them. Indeed, Weber almost says this when he tells us that "the historian and social research worker . . . must understand how to relate the events of the real world consciously or unconsciously to *universal* 'cultural values' and to select out those relationships which are significant for *us"* (1949:81–82, emphasis added).

VALUE-INDIVIDUATED SCIENCE

Gouldner argues that Weber's proposed separation of the individual scientist's personal values from his/her scientific work is impossible:

> If we assume, as we must, that social theorists are fundamentally like other men, then we must also assume that, whatever their professions of being "value-free," they too assign meanings to social objects not only in terms of their potency, but also in terms of their goodness (1970:485).

Having thus accepted the influence of values on scientific analysis as inevitable, Gouldner leaves untouched the question of what each analyst's values ought to be, but insists that whatever they are, they should be reflected upon and, presumably, made explicit and public. Thus, "the ultimate goal of a reflexive sociology is the deepening of the sociologist's own awareness, of who and what he is, in a specific society at any given time, and of how both his social role and his personal praxis affect his work as a sociologist" (1970:494).[8]

Note that Gouldner (unlike Habermas—discussed below—who also emphasizes "reflection") regards any given value as just as good as any other for the purposes of "Reflexive Sociology":[9] "men must accept their own unique talents, varying ambitions, and experience of the world, as authentic" (1970:505). Thus, by permitting every sociologist to hold and propound whatever values he/she wishes (provided he/she is aware of them), Gouldner implies a sociological discipline embracing, potentially, as many values as there are sociologists—and none of them interchangeable.

In summary, then, value-determining science, as proposed remedy for manifest value-noninterchangeability, fails because it inevitably rests on values which it cannot determine but must take for granted; value-free science fails because it is not value-free but must take some values for granted; and value-individuated science fails because it only acknowledges, but does not remedy, manifest value-noninterchangeability.

---

[8] Weber claims the whole discipline of sociology can perform a "reflexive" role for society-at-large: "If we are competent in our pursuit . . . we can force the individual, or at least we can help him, to give himself an account of the ultimate meaning of his own conduct" (1958a:152, emphasis removed).

[9] Admittedly, Gouldner calls "Reflexive Sociology" "radical," but its radicalness lies not in its embracing a particular ultimate goal (beyond "awareness"), such as the redistribution of power and wealth, but in the claim that "it would accept the fact that the roots of sociology pass through the sociologist as a total man" (1970:489), and that it resists "the irrationalities of those authorities met daily in eye-to-eye encounter" (1970:503–504). It would seem that Gouldner fits Colfax and Roach's description of "the professionally radical sociologist" more than that of "the politically radical sociologist" (see Colfax and Roach, 1971:14).

We are therefore left with what appears to be the only possible genuine remedy—namely, value-universal science.

VALUE-UNIVERSAL SCIENCE

In this remedy, we would strive systematically to remove all circumstantial impediments to value interchangeability, just as scientific method and instrumentation strive to remove circumstantial impediments to the manifestation of cognitive and motor interchangeability. Successful adoption of this remedy would mean that the explananda and desiderata of natural science—that is, the objects of its desired understanding and control—would be selected according to a single set of universally held values.

There seem to be two main approaches to this remedy. One approach directly seeks support for values having some particular substantive content—a content that its proponents assert matches that of what they believe to be the intrinsically universal human values. The second approach does not overtly claim to know what the intrinsic content is but propounds, instead, some particular method whereby that content can be discovered.

Lafargue attributes the first, specific-content, approach to Marx:

"Science must not be a selfish pleasure," he used to say. "Those who have the good fortune to be able to devote themselves to scientific pursuits must be the first to place their knowledge at the service of humanity." One of his favorite sayings was: "Work for humanity" (n.d.:72).

Following in this tradition, Horowitz asserts that

The task of a radical sociology is to . . . study the structure of social oppression and to bring this knowledge, and the power it conveys, to the powerless and exploited social majority (Horowitz, 1971:5; see also Colfax and Roach, 1971:3; and Nicolaus, 1971:58–59).

Friedrichs, perhaps not subscribing to the same set of values, and phrasing his personal advocacy as an empirical prediction, argues that sociology, as a discipline,

can be expected to continue to move toward a reclamation of its original prophetic understanding of itself and away from the exclusively priestly paradigm. . . . The sociologist as priest [views] his office as but a means by which *any* given social reality may be revealed to the layman. . . . On the other hand, the sociologist as prophet is consciously committed to *an* image of society that transcends any given social reality (1970:292, emphasis changed).

The "critical theorists" of the Frankfurt School (Institute for Social Research) are prominent among those adopting the second, general-method approach. In one sentence, their essential claim seems to be that through a method called "reflection," practised in an "ideal speech situation" (i.e., under conditions of "free and uncoerced discussion"), human beings can discover their "real interests"—interests which may then guide their efforts to understand and control the world "rationally." Let us see what this means.

First, note Horkheimer's underscoring of the critical theorists' focus on values[10]—a focus that seeks to penetrate beyond the categories in which values are usually put:

> The aim of [critical] activity is not simply to eliminate one or another abuse. . . . [I]ts purpose is not . . . the better functioning of any element in the structure. On the contrary, it is suspicious of the very categories of better, useful, appropriate, productive, and valuable, as these are understood in the present order, and refuses to take them as nonscientific presuppositions about which one can do nothing (1976:217).

What is it, however, that one *can* do? The critical theorists' answer is that we need not take values as presuppositions; we can identify those values which are intrinsically (instinctively) human if we employ a method of introspective contemplation called "reflection."[11]

Habermas believes this method (which Durkheim rejects and Weber accepts[12])

[10] In a similar description, Frisby says the critical sociology-positivism dispute is not a *"Methodenstreit"* but a *"Werturteilsstreit* [value-judgment dispute]" (1976:xxlx), and asserts that "It is the *aims* of the social sciences which have again been placed in question in the positivist controversy" (1976:xxlx–xxx, emphasis added).

[11] Adorno speaks for the critical theorists' belief in the superiority of the method of reflection over the scientific method:

> There are sociological theorems which, as insights into the mechanisms of society which operate behind the facade, in principle, even for societal reasons, contradict appearances to such an extent that they cannot be adequately criticized through the latter. Criticism of them is incumbent upon systematic theory, upon further reflection, but not, for instance, upon the confrontation with protocol [i.e., observation] statements (1976b:112).

See also Schutz's discussion of Husserl's notion of the phenomenological "epoché" as a method for returning "fundamentally to the original experience of the life-world in which the facts themselves can be grasped directly" (1978:124).

[12] Durkheim says "the group's conception . . . [cannot] be arrived at by simple introspection, since it does not exist in its entirety in any one individual," and, after defining "social facts" as "things," he argues that "Things include all objects of knowledge that cannot be conceived by purely mental activity, those that require for their conception data from outside the mind, from observations

unfailingly produces perfect knowledge of one's true interests, thereby revealing what one's values really should be and liberating one from worship of all false values—in a manner comparable, says Habermas, to Freudian psychoanalysis (see 1971:214–245). Armed with this faith, Habermas scorns "social interests that arise autochthonously out of the compulsion of the reproduction of social life without being reflected upon" (1970a:60); proclaims that reflection possesses a "redeeming power" (1970a:61) and an "emancipatory power . . . which the subject experiences in itself to the extent that it becomes transparent to itself in the history of its genesis" (1971:197); and most importantly, declares that

> It is no accident that the standards of self-reflection are exempted from the singular state of suspension in which those of all other cognitive processes require critical evaluation. They possess theoretical certainty (1971:314).

In the latter connection, it should be noted that although one may find congenial the particular interests which Habermas himself believes will emerge from self-reflection and which he would therefore exempt from critical evaluation ("The human interest in autonomy and responsibility is not mere fancy, for it can be apprehended a priori" [1971:314]), one can easily imagine more authoritarian and genocidal theorists claiming the same exemption for quite different interests.

But it seems very clear that no matter how unequivocally he proclaims the "redeeming" and "emancipatory" power of reflection (carried out, as it must be, within the privacy of each individual's own mind), Habermas does not trust different reflecting individuals privately to arrive at the same interests. Thus, instead of that spontaneous consensus which one might expect from individuals reflecting separately on interests that "can be apprehended a priori," Habermas proposes a consensus arrived at through discussion—thereby implying the likelihood of differences between individuals in the interests which their reflection will lead them to regard as a priori. Thus, Habermas says "the solution demands [an] unrestricted *communication* about the goals of life activity and conduct" (1970a:120, emphasis added)— thereby proposing an analog, in the realm of cathexis, for the demand of natural science for intersubjective verification in the realm of cognition.

There is an essential difference, however, between the demand for communication about the results of "reflection" and the demand for communication about the results of "observation." Both, admittedly, are mental apprehensions of phenom-

---

and experiments" (1938:xlvi–xlvii, xliii). Weber, however, says "Every science of psychological and social phenomena . . . seeks to 'understand' [human] conduct and by means of this 'understanding' to 'explain' it 'interpretatively,' " and claims that the methods of " 'understanding explanation' are . . . the conventional habits of the investigator and teacher in thinking in a particular way, and . . . his capacity to 'feel himself' empathically into a mode of thought which deviates from his own" (1949:40–41).

ena. But the phenomena apprehended by reflection are internal to the apprehender and those of observation are external.

As a result, observers can physically *point* directly at something in the outside world (thereby directing each other's attention relatively unambiguously) and ask "Do you see what I see?" with considerable confidence that they are talking about the same thing. Reflecting individuals, however, cannot point directly to their (or anyone else's) feelings and so cannot have that confidence. In order reasonably to ask another individual "Do you feel as I do?" we have first to find or construct some outward "sign," "symbol," "expression" or, more generally, indicator, of these feelings (for example, a grimace, gesture, word, or tone of voice). We then display (point at) this expression and say, in effect, "I feel like *this*. Do you feel like this too?" Clearly, such mediation of inward feeling by outward indicator renders communication about feelings much more problematic than communication about external referents, as may be suggested by comparing what we have to do in order to agree on how many lines a poem contains and on which feelings it elicits. In summary, then, the direct referents of communication about observation are equally available to all; the direct referents of communication about reflection, however, are *not* equally available to all,[13] thereby requiring indicators which *are* so available, but which introduce major problematics of correspondence between indicator and referent both within and between communicators.

Habermas steps over all these problematics, however, by asserting the existence of "dialogue-constitutive universals . . . [which make] mutuality of understanding possible" (1970b:369, see also Clynes, 1980:263), and thereby claiming an exact and unfailing correspondence between inward feeling and outward expression which would render the reliability of reflection-communication equal to that of observation-communication. Obviously, were that reliability assured, we would need only require that consensus in matters of reflection (as in matters of observation) be reached, ideally, under circumstances where each participant is perfectly free to express the results of his/her reflection and every such expression is perfectly equal in weight to every other such expression.[14] In Habermas' words,

> only in an emancipated society, whose members' autonomy and responsibility had been realized, would communication have developed into the nonauthor-

---

[13] Geuss points to this difference when he says

Scientific theories require empirical confirmation through observation and experiment; critical theories are cognitively acceptable if they survive a more complicated process of evaluation the central part of which is a demonstration that they are "reflectively acceptable" . . . [F]or most "scientific" theories the question of whether or not the "objects of research" would freely assent to the theory doesn't even arise; planets, genes, microscopic particles, etc. can't assent or dissent (1981:55–56, 79).

[14] This prerequisite is associated mainly with Habermas. More generally, Geuss argues that the critical theorists identify two prerequisites for reflection leading to knowledge of the real interests of human beings: (1) perfect knowledge of all the possible effects of all one's possible actions, and (2) optimal conditions of free choice among those possible actions. The "ideal speech situation" combines these prerequisites (see Geuss, 1981:47–54).

itarian and universally practised dialogue from which . . . our idea of true consensus [is] always implicitly derived (1971:314; see also 1973:12).

This, as Geuss says, is the " 'ideal speech situation' . . . a situation of absolutely uncoerced and unlimited discussion between completely free and equal human agents," and

> The "ideal speech situation" will serve Habermas as a transcendental criterion of truth, freedom, and rationality. Beliefs agents would agree on in the ideal speech situation are ipso facto "true beliefs," preferences they would agree on are "rational preferences," interests they would agree on are "real interests" (1981:65–66).

In addition to the critical theorists' method of "reflection" and free discussion among "communicatively competent" individuals in the "ideal speech situation" (a method which, it should be noted, combines instinctivistic, enculturistic, social structuralistic, and cultural structuralistic variables), at least three other methods seem currently available for arriving at value interchangeability. The first and certainly the most ancient method relies on force and threat of force, or coercion (social structuralistic, cultural structuralistic, and technologistic variables); the second, not quite so old, method relies on philosophical analysis and persuasion (cultural structuralistic variables); and the third, decidedly recent, method relies on modernization (technologistic and social structuralistic variables).

Thus, in an espousal of the method of coercion that seems altogether crazy—especially for any time since the Holocaust and Hiroshima—White asserts that

> The hope of the future . . . , and the salvation of mankind and civilization would seem to lie in the emergence from the next war of a victor—not merely a survivor—and one with sufficient power and resources to organize the whole planet and the entire human species within a single social system (1949:390).

In choosing the more pacific method of philosophical synthesis Gewirth argues that

> the drive toward unity of science is matched by the increasing communication and homogeneity of ethical standards among the peoples of the world, but also by the traditional concern of philosophers, in opposition to cultural relativism, to find underlying principles under which to organize and interrelate man's ethical ideals (1960:328).[15]

---

[15] Gewirth defines "ethics" as "a body of rules, ideals, and practices which enables us to get along with ourselves and with other people" (1960:323). This definition is much narrower in one respect than my own insofar as I would admit as equally "ethical" the ultimate goal of *not* "getting along with"—that is *destroying*—ourselves and/or others; and it is also much broader in another respect than my own insofar as I would limit ethics strictly to the identification of ultimate goals and regard the

Finally, Inkeles and Smith assert that modernizing institutions like formal education, the mass media, the factory system, and so forth, engender similar values in their participants: men in their six-country (Argentina, Chile, East Pakistan, India, Israel, and Nigeria) survey "developed values, attitudes, and behavior patterns analogous to the norms reflected in the organization and functioning of the modern institutions" (1974:308).

Now it may be that *no* effective remedy for manifest value noninterchangeability is possible that can operate across all human beings; Freud argues that what the critical theorists call the "real interests" of human individuals are irremediably contradictory within each individual, and Pareto argues they are irremediably contradictory between individuals. Nevertheless, it seems clear that the quest for such a remedy, whether it eventually succeeds or not, is irresistible. It seems irresistible that we should strive ceaselessly to transcend the brevity, brutishness, and punyness of our separate lives by identifying ourselves with all others of our species: not for nothing has it been said that "nothing human is alien to me." For purposes of doing science, it also seems irresistible that we should want to regard ourselves as mere parts of a single compound organism[16]—an organism equipped with a single cathexis, a single cognition and conation, a single body, and living a single lifetime already measured in millions of years—struggling to understand and control what we take to be a single World.

Is it reasonable to include sociology as one substantive specialty in this struggle? I believe so. As indicated in Chapter 1, I regard sociology as no less a natural science than physics, chemistry, or biology, and hold that only secondary (though certainly important) features like substantive content, techniques, instrumentation, societal support, accuracy, precision, parsimony, practical applications, degree of intersubjective verification, and the like, can distinguish one natural science from another, insofar as they all share the same premises and procedures. From this point of view, Popper says, "the methods [of the natural and the social sciences]

---

identification of instrumental "rules," "practices," and so forth, leading to a given goal as an empirical problem rather than an ethical one. It seems altogether striking that Gewirth, who holds that human will is an intrinsically *unpredictable* factor in the world should also propose what we might call an "ethics method" to parallel the scientific method—whose aim is always to increase the intersubjectively verified accuracy of our *predictions* about the world. It is as though Gewirth, and indeed all of us to one degree or another, may be pinioned by two fears whose cures run counter to one another. Fearing that we may create an interchangeability of human values (and with it, that *deadening* "matter-of-factness" against which Mannheim warns), we posit the human will as a permanently unpredictable (and therefore noninterchangeable) factor which allays that fear. But fearing also that when ethics are regarded as noninterchangeable and nonvaluable except through force and violence (Marx says "Between equal rights, force decides" [1978:364]), humankind risks increasingly *deadly* wars, we may then seek to substitute persuasion for coercion in resolving value disagreement—a method which, if it is to be an analog of the scientific method, must rest on effacing the very noninterchangeability which Gewirth's conceptualization of the will assures us is both ineluctable and desirable.

[16] This is the composite, flesh-and-blood organism, indeed, that represents *homo sapiens'* closest approximation to the indefinitely deployable fleet of robot sensors and manipulators commanded by a single indefinitely extendable and virtually immortal artificial intelligence that Jastrow, and Hogan, foresee as our evolutionary successor in science (see Chapter 11).

are fundamentally the same. . . . The methods always consist in offering deductive causal explanations and in testing them (by way of predictions)" (1973:68). Luckmann, speaking of "whatever it is that distinguishes social science from physical science," says

> It is not a matter of logical form. The logic of social science is the logic of science. . . . It is the constitution of the domain and the explanatory aims that are bound to it, rather than the logical form by means of which the domain is explained, that account for the difference between social and physical science (1978:242–243; see also 252).

At least five strong objections have been made to this viewpoint, so let us see to what extent they can be met. The first objection argues that even if a natural science of social phenomena (in which, as in all natural sciences, we would strive to establish general laws) were possible, we ought not interest ourselves in such a discipline but in a discipline devoted to comprehending each individual social phenomenon as an unique event. The remaining four objections argue that such a natural science is not even possible (so we should save ourselves the trouble of being interested in it) because the individual human beings who participate in social phenomena (a) possess too much free will, (b) are too reflexive, (c) are too unpredictable, and (d) are too complex.

OBJECTIONS TO APPLYING SCIENTIFIC PROCEDURE TO SOCIOLOGY

An Idiographic Rather than Nomothetic Discipline

The terms "idiographic" and "nomothetic" are Dilthey's:

> [W]e may say that the experiential sciences seek in the knowledge of reality either the general, in the form of laws of nature, or the particular, in the historically determined formation. . . . If we may be permitted to coin new artificial terms, scientific thought is *nomothetic* in the former case and *idiographic* in the latter. If we confine ourselves to the accustomed terminology, we could speak further in this sense of the opposition between natural scientific disciplines and historical disciplines (quoted in Plantinga, 1980:25).

For a detailed examination of this general view, however, let us turn to its restatement by Weber.[17]

[17] More recently, Hayek argues that

In most natural sciences the particular situation or event is generally one of a very large number of similar events, which as particular events are only of local and temporary interest. . . . In the

Weber asserts that

> [In the] science in which we are interested . . . [o]ur aim is the understand-
> ing of the characteristic *uniqueness* of the reality in which we move. We wish
> to understand on the one hand the relationships and the cultural significance
> of *individual* events in their contemporary manifestations and on the other the
> causes of their being historically so and not otherwise (1949:72, emphasis
> added).

In the "exact natural sciences," says Weber,

> Laws are important and valuable . . . in the measure that those sciences are
> *universally valid.* For the knowledge of historical phenomena in their historical
> concreteness, [however,] the most general laws, because they are most devoid
> of content are . . . the least valuable. . . . [Their abstractness leads us]
> away from the richness of reality (1949:80).

Weber admits that this

> does not imply that the knowledge of universal propositions, the construction
> of abstract concepts, the knowledge of regularities, and the attempt to for-
> mulate *"laws"* have no scientific justification in the social sciences. Quite the
> contrary, if the causal knowledge of the historians consists of the imputation
> of concrete effects to concrete causes, a *valid* imputation of any individual
> effect without the application of . . . knowledge of recurrent causal se-
> quences . . . would in general be impossible (1949:79).

Nevertheless, he argues insistently against the importance of such general laws in
the social (or "cultural") sciences (actually, Weber seems to argue both that such
laws are useful but insufficient, and, warming to his theme, that they are simply
useless):

---

social field, on the other hand, a particular or unique event is often of such general interest and
at the same time so complex and so difficult to see in all its important aspects, that its explanation
and discussion constitutes a major task requiring the whole energy of a specialist (1973:50).

Popper, too, defends "the view . . . that history is characterized by its interest in actual, singular, or
specific events, rather than laws or generalizations" (1973:77)—although he crucially modifies this
view:

And yet I feel that [the historicists' notions of the "spirits" of an age, nation, army, etc.,] indicate
. . . the existence of a lacuna, of a place which it is the task of sociology to fill. . . . We need
studies [note that Popper does not dare say "laws", but that is what he means—ed.], based on
methodological individualism, of the social institutions through which ideas may spread and cap-
tivate individuals, of the way in which new traditions may be created, of the way in which
traditions work and break down (1973:80).

> In the cultural sciences the knowledge of the universal or general is never valuable in itself. . . . [The] analysis of cultural events, which proceeds according to the thesis that the ideal of science is the reduction of empirical reality [to] "laws," is meaningless. It is not meaningless . . . because cultural or psychic events for instance are "objectively" less governed by laws. It is meaningless . . . because the knowledge of social laws is not knowledge of social reality but is rather one of the aids used by our minds for attaining this end; secondly, because knowledge of cultural events is inconceivable except on a basis of the significance which the concrete constellations of reality have for us in certain individual concrete situations (1949:80, emphasis removed).

Let us consider, first, Weber's reasons for claiming that the search for laws governing human social phenomena is "meaningless"—the most radically idiothetic of his arguments. Weber's assertion in this connection that "knowledge of social laws is not knowledge of social reality" may be discarded as trivially self-evident: with the single exception of self-referential statements,[18] *no* statement (including an idiographic one) should be mistaken for its referent, and knowledge of such a statement should therefore not be mistaken for knowledge of its referent. Further, Weber's claim that knowledge of social laws is merely "one of the aids used by our minds" as we seek to attain knowledge of social reality, while certainly true, in no way distinguishes *social* laws and *social* reality from any other scientific laws and any other reality. That is, it is in the very nature of *all* scientific laws (indeed, of all empirical statements, whether scientific and lawlike or not) to be merely aids used by our minds toward knowledge of reality. Incidentally (as the first part of this chapter, with Weber's own help, has argued), neither aids nor knowledge of *any* kind are conceivable except on the basis of the significance or value which the knower gives them, and such significance can only arise in individual (and repeated) concrete situations engendering the experience of curiosity, thirst, hunger, cold, heat, sexual desire, and other motivations to understand and control the world.

Thus, despite their apparent effort to do so, Weber's claims here do not distinguish between the social (or cultural) sciences on the one hand and the nonsocial (or noncultural) sciences on the other, and are therefore unacceptable as objections to applying the same procedure to both kinds of science—for better or worse in both cases.

Consider, then, Weber's less extreme claim that the search for laws governing human social phenomena, though valuable, "is never valuable in itself" because the goal of the social sciences is understanding "the characteristic uniqueness of the reality in which we move." But how, Weber asks, is such understanding possible when,

---

[18] For example, "This statement is a statement."

Even with the widest imaginable knowledge of "laws," we are helpless in the face of the question: how is the causal explanation of an individual fact possible—since a description of even the smallest slice of reality can never be exhaustive? The number and type of causes which have influenced any given event are always infinite and there is nothing in the things themselves to set some of them apart as alone meriting attention (1949:78, emphasis removed).

Weber's answer is as follows:

Order is brought into this chaos only on the condition that in every case only a part of concrete reality is significant to us, because only it is related to the cultural values with which we approach reality. Only certain sides of the infinitely complex concrete phenomenon . . . are therefore worthwhile knowing. They alone are objects of causal explanation. And even this causal explanation evinces the same character: an exhaustive causal investigation of any concrete phenomenon in its full reality is not only practically impossible—it is simply nonsense. We select only those causes to which are to be imputed in the individual case, the "essential" feature of an event (1949:78).

Once we grant the inevitability that Weber claims for this selection of *aspects* of effects and *aspects* of causes, what becomes of that "uniqueness," that "richness of reality," which Weber urges the kind of social sciences in which he is interested to grasp and whose absence he bemoans in general laws? The answer is that it irresistibly fades away: Weber ends, necessarily and unavoidably, by embracing (or being embraced by) the very same abstractness for which he so vehemently condemns general laws. This, in my opinion, is the main significance of his advocacy of "ideal types" in the study of social phenomena (see Weber 1949:89–97).

It is crucial to this interpretation that Weber describes ideal types both as "purely ideal limiting concept[s] with which the real situation or action is compared," and also as empirically based by virtue of having "taken certain traits . . . from the empirical reality" (1949:93, 91). Ideal types may thus be regarded as causal models in the sense discussed in Chapter 14; they consist of sets of interrelated laws at the same level of generality (and, of course, how well or poorly established these laws are is beside the point here). But further, to the extent that individual observations and empirical generalizations are deductively "compared" with ideal types we have tests of predictions; and to the extent that such tests are successful we have not only single-level models but rudimentary two-level theories—all in accord with the procedures of (pure) natural science as set forth in Chapter 14.

It must be admitted, however, that his embrace of the abstractness of general law is confused and self-contradictory, and Weber resists it to the last—claiming that the social sciences should concern themselves "with the question of the individual consequence which the working of [different] laws in an unique *configuration* produces, since it is these individual *configurations* which are significant for us" (1949:73, emphasis changed; see also 1949:78–79). Of course, this too is a goal of the natural sciences. True, such sciences infer general tendencies by observing individual events, but they then always explain individual events—in whatever degree of complexity these may be described—as unique confluences of two or more general tendencies. Consider, for example, how an individual solar eclipse is explained as the confluence of general laws of mechanics, gravity, and optics.

So here again Weber's claims fail to distinguish social from nonsocial sciences and are therefore unacceptable as objections to applying the same basic procedures to the former as to the latter.

Let us therefore turn to those objections which regard a natural science of human social phenomena, even if it were desirable, as impossible for reasons having to do with the nature of the human participant in such phenomena. Before doing so, however, it should be noted that no one, to my knowledge, objects to a natural science of social phenomena whose participants are nonhuman (i.e., sociobiology, as that term has been used here)—a fact that renders objections solely to a natural science of human social phenomena highly particularistic.

Human Free Will

Winch argues forcefully and unequivocally that

> the central concepts which belong to our understanding of social life are incompatible with concepts central to the activity of scientific prediction. When we speak of the possibility of scientific prediction of social developments . . . we literally do not understand what we are saying. We cannot understand it, because it has no sense (1958:94).

In support of this view, Winch makes two main, but jointly paradoxical, points: (1) that the regularities studied by the sociologist and those studied by natural scientists differ with respect to who may define these regularities, and (2) that the regularities studied by the sociologist are not really regularities at all and should not be defined as such by anyone.

In advancing the first point, Winch asserts that although both natural and social scientists understand phenomena "in relation to the rules governing . . . investigation," the situation is not the same for the latter as for the former,

> for whereas in the case of the natural scientist we have to deal with only [those rules] governing the scientist's investigation itself, here *what the sociologist is studying,* as well as his study of it, is a human activity and is therefore

carried on according to rules. And it is *these* rules, rather than those which govern the sociologist's investigation, which specify what is to count as "doing the same kind of thing" in relation to that kind of activity (1958:87), emphasis changed).

This argument echoes Schutz, who claims that social science analysis "refers *by necessity* to the subjective point of view, namely, to the interpretation of the action and its settings in terms of the actor. . . . [Any] social science aspiring to grasp 'social reality' *has* to adopt this principle" (1953:27, emphasis added). And, as we have already seen, Blumer enjoins us to "approach the study of group activity through the eyes and experience of the people who have developed the activity" (1956:689).

In contrast with Winch, Schutz, and Blumer, however, it seems quite conceivable to me that we might come to understand a given social phenomenon as a manifestation of the *absence* of rules and interpretations held by some or all of its participants, or as a manifestation of *incomplete* or *erroneous* rules and interpretations, or as a manifestation of the causal *overwhelming* of such participants' rules and interpretations by external constraints. In all these cases, the actor's rules and interpretations would prove unfruitful—to one degree or another—for the observer's (and perhaps also the actor's own) understanding and control of the social phenomenon in question. As Merton, in a different but related context, says,

> Determinants of social life—for an obvious example, ecological patterns and processes—are not necessarily evident to those directly engaged in it. In short, sociological understanding involves much more than the acquaintance-with of the Insider. It includes an empirically confirmable comprehension of the conditions and the often complex processes in which people are caught up without much awareness of what is going on (1973:133).

In many ways, however, Winch's second point, namely, that the regularities studied by sociology are not really regularities at all, is the more interesting. Here Winch claims that

> sometimes even if [the observer] knows with certainty the rule which [the actor] is following, he cannot predict with any certainty what [the actor] will do: where, namely, the question arises of *what is involved* in following that rule, e.g., in circumstances markedly different from any in which it has previously been applied (1958:92).

Thus, even if we agreed with Winch's claim that the sociologist must adopt the actor's rules regardless of what is being investigated, Winch confounds us by claiming that those rules may not help anyway because human behavior is intrinsically (albeit "sometimes") unpredictable.[19]

What can be the basis for this view of human behavior? Winch tells us it is not based on the possibility that some behavior which (according to his definition) is of sociological interest is carried on outside of rules: "all behavior which is meaningful . . . is ipso facto rule-governed"; and "social relations between men exist only in and through their ideas" (1958:52, 123). He also tells us it is not based on the possibility that some rules are not discoverable by the observer: "it is only in a situation in which it makes sense to suppose that somebody else could in principle discover the rule which I am following that I can intelligibly be said to follow a rule at all" (1958:30). And finally, Winch tells us it is not based on the possibility that "what is involved in following" the rule is not discoverable, for every pupil "has to acquire not merely the habit of following his teacher's example but also . . . the ability to apply a criterion; he has to learn not merely to do things in the same way as his teacher, but also *what counts* as the same way" (1958:59)—and the implication is clear that pupils (and therefore, presumably, sociologists) *can* learn all this. Why, then, should it be the case that "even if [the observer] knows with certainty the rule which [the actor] is following, he cannot predict with any certainty what [the actor] will do"?[20] Winch does not tell us.

However, examination of some of the views of Gewirth may cast some light on this question. Gewirth claims that "the laws of the social sciences cannot have the same fixity or permanence as the laws of the natural sciences" (1954:230). This appears, at first, to be a more moderate statement than Winch's—insofar as Gewirth implies that the laws of the social sciences have *some* fixity and permanence, whereas Winch implies they have no fixity at all.

Consider Gewirth's description of that fixity: "the telescope may be said to find rather than make stars. But if man can to any extent make his own history, then

---

[19] It should be noted that Winch expresses an extraordinary view of the nature of prediction when he argues that "to predict the writing of a piece of poetry or the making of a new invention would involve writing the poem or making the invention oneself" (1958:94) and claims that the prediction of either is therefore impossible. This argument, however, is either trivial or false, depending on the detail required in a given prediction. If we require the same perfect detail in a prediction that may be found in the phenomenon being predicted (as, in fact, no one ever does) then Winch's argument is trivial: Because the prediction and the predicted are then identical, of course it becomes meaningless to speak of a prediction per se. But if we require any less detail in the prediction than in the predicted (as, indeed, we always do) then Winch's argument is false. It is noteworthy that even Schutz, with whom Winch shares other views, argues that "It is not necessary that the 'same' projected action in its individual uniqueness, with its unique ends and unique means has to be pre-experienced and, therefore, known. If that were the case nothing novel could ever be projected" (1951:166). Whether trivial or false, however, Winch's argument does not in any way distinguish predicting a human artifact—say, a poem or an "invention" (as though a poem were not an invention)—from predicting a snowstorm or an eclipse.

[20] Blumer implies the same when he argues that "Interpretation is a formative or creative process in its own right. It constructs meanings which . . . are not predetermined or determined by the independent variable" (1956:687).

. . . the very correlation in which [his social laws] consist may be changed by men's decisions" (1954:235)—and these "decisions," Gewirth says, are "free": "Man creates laws . . . when, by means of his free decision and consequent action, he causes a correlation to exist which did not exist before," and "Insofar as social laws follow from men's free decisions, men may create social laws" (1954:234, emphasis removed).

Now the crucial question is "What does Gewirth mean by 'free' decisions?" Unfortunately, he does not give us an explicit definition, but he does clearly associate the term "free" with "purely spontaneous" (1954:236)—thereby suggesting the very same unpredictability (because no purely spontaneous act can be predictable, in any scientific sense) that Winch asserts,[21] and that Adorno also indicates ("Theoretical speculations on society cannot be confirmed by precisely corresponding sets of empirical data . . . [partly because there exists, in society,] the moment of spontaneity that cannot be captured by the law of averages" [1976a:238, 247]).[22] Although it is true that Gewirth qualifies this position when he argues that "To say that men create new social laws is by no means to say that the possibilities of such creation are limitless" (1954:235), he goes on largely to vitiate that qualification by asserting that "even if [limitations] do exist, it seems safe to say . . . that the rigidities imposed by [them] operate at a very high level of generality, within which there is a great deal of plasticity making possible [creative] changes in social laws" (1954:235–236)—thereby reinstating, albeit more ambiguously, the idea of spontaneity and unpredictability in the word "plasticity."

Thus, it seems fair to conclude that Gewirth, as well as Winch, assumes some degree of intrinsic unpredictability in human social phenomena and that although Winch does not say where this unpredictability resides, Gewirth does: it resides, he says, in the ineluctably "free" and "spontaneous" nature of human decisions. Thus, it appears that Gewirth holds, with Kant, that

> the will of every rational being [is] a universally legislative will. . . . Thus the will is not subject simply to the law, but so subject that it must be

[21] Gewirth also calls these decisions "new" when he argues that

men can generate or create *new* correlations of social variables by making *new* decisions which function as antecedent conditions from which *new* consequences follow. In the natural sphere, on the other hand, men cannot generate such new antecedent conditions but only *exchange* one set of conditions for another. (1954:236, emphasis added).

Although Gewirth does not make his definition of "new" explicit, one feels justified in believing he means without-antecedent, spontaneous, unpredictable, because his definition of "exchange" appears to cover cases where conditions under which *several* sets of laws obtain replace the conditions under which *one* set of laws obtains. Thus, others might call instances of the humanly decided correlation or combination of already-existing elements (as in the invention of glass, domesticated plants and animals, plastics, etc.) "new," but Gewirth apparently would not because all such instances constitute exchanges of one set of conditions for another.

[22] Adorno emphasizes the uniqueness not only of "the moment" but also of the individual organism ("The similarity to each other of the smallest units of society—individuals—cannot be asserted . . . with quite the same seriousness and stringency as in the case of physical or chemical matter" [1976a:248]), and both militate, in his view, against sociology as a natural science.

> regarded *as itself giving the law,* and on this ground only, subject to the law (of which it can regard itself as the author) (Kant, 1929:312);

a view opposed by Comte:

> [T]rue liberty is nothing else than a rational submission to the preponderance of the laws of nature in release from all arbitrary personal dictation. . . . We have to contemplate social phenomena as susceptible of prevision like all other classes [of phenomena], within the limits of exactness compatible with their higher complexity (1975:214, 222);

and by Simmel: "No human wish or practice can take arbitrary steps, jump arbitrary distances, perform arbitrary syntheses. They must follow the intrinsic logic of things" (1950:17); and by Durkheim:

> We tend to believe that all has been said and done when we attach such and such a fact, whose causes we are seeking, to a human faculty. But why should the human spirit, which is—to put it briefly—only a system of phenomena that are comparable in all ways to other observable phenomena, be outside and above explanation? We know that an organism is the product of a genesis; why should it be otherwise with our psychic constitution? (1973:158).

Human Reflexivity

Before examining the unpredictability objection directly, let us consider what may seem, at first glance, to be a more moderate alternative to it. Thus, it may be claimed that because humans can act on the basis of their knowledge, the prediction of human social phenomena (or other phenomena within human control) can contribute to achieving the very phenomena being predicted (thereby affirming the prediction), or to avoiding those phenomena (thereby negating the prediction)—eventualities which Gewirth calls, following Merton, 1957:421–436, including n. 1, page 423), the "self-fulfilling prophecy" and the "self-destroying prophecy," respectively. Friedrichs, echoing Winch echoing Schutz (both quoted earlier here), expresses this view as follows:

> The social scientist's perception of uniformities represents a new and unique event that by its very appearance must . . . operate to deny the full validity of the perceived sequence when he seeks to reconfirm at a later time the order apprehended earlier. . . . [This] means that the search for "laws" of human nature and for fundamental social processes that are in principle stable is ultimately destined to be futile (1970:180–181, emphasis removed).

The issue raised by this view, however, seems easily misconstrued: The question is not whether awareness can operate to deny a *particular* social uniformity but whether it can operate to deny *all* uniformities. The question, to put it differently, is not whether this or that social process is unstable—because the present conclusion of natural science is that *all* processes are to varying degrees unstable and that many of these are, in principle, susceptible to some degree of local manipulation. Indeed, as we have already seen in Chapter 15, applied science in all fields rests exactly on that assumption. The question, again, is whether literally *all* social processes are unstable and susceptible to manipulation; whether the search for *any* stable, unmanipulable, law of human social phenomena is "ultimately destined to be futile," and, most importantly, whether that search is any more futile in sociology and the other social sciences than is the search for such laws in any nonsocial science.

It is just at this point that what might have seemed a moderate question turns into the more extreme (and vastly more fundamental) question posed earlier here, namely, whether we should assume that there is any intrinsically irregular and unlawful—any *necessarily* unpredictable—element that is unique to human social phenomena, for only if one believes such an element exists can one believe that no fundamental social processes are stable; that the search for any sociological law is futile. Otherwise, whenever we find an unstable social process or an untrue sociological law we need only conclude (like the physicists who once regarded protons and electrons as fundamental elements) that we must search deeper, endlessly deeper, toward ever more stable processes and ever more unexceptionable laws.

Indeed, every natural science must regard this search as endless for it seems that no process known to us so far is or has been stable in the long run; not life, not Earth, not Sun, not matter, not energy, not space, not time. Thus, *every* science's search for absolutely stable laws is indeed "destined to be futile"—as Jeans says of physics: "our studies can never put us into contact with reality, and its true meaning and nature must be forever hidden from us" (1958:16). Ultimate futility, however, should not halt efforts to find always more and more stable laws, and in any case, that science-wide ultimate futility is obviously not what Friedrichs and the others have in mind; for reasons which remain unclear, they imagine the futility belongs to sociology and the other social sciences alone.

Human Unpredictability

Having considered its seemingly more moderate form, let us address directly the more extreme and more fundamental claim to which it reduces as put forward most explicitly in Winch's assertion that "When we speak of the possibility of scientific prediction of social developments . . . it has no sense." Note that this idea appears also in Gewirth's assertion that men's decisions are "free," "spontaneous," and that "men may create social laws," and also in Etzioni's claim that "social laws, unlike those of nature, can be flaunted and, above all, rewritten" (1968:2), and, of course, earlier, in Mead's claim that "the response of the 'I' is something that is more or less uncertain," and that "If [the individual] says he knows what he is going to do, even there he may be mistaken. He starts out to do something and something happens to interfere. The resulting action is always a little different from anything he could anticipate" (1934:176, 177).

In order fully to appreciate the significance of this claim, consider two fundamental working assumptions of natural science. The first is that everything coming within the scope of human experience (whether it be our experience of electrons, galaxies, mitosis, the fossil record, paranoia, artistic and scientific creativity, childbirth, philosophy, sociology, wars, modernization, suicide, home-cooking, or whatever) has regular, lawful, nonidiosyncratic, and nonspontaneous aspects and, therefore, in principle if not in practice, aspects which are understandable and controllable by the human species collectivity. Total freedom and total novelty in any phenomenon—that is, its entirely random or irregular, and entirely spontaneous or causeless, occurrence—are the archenemies of natural science (as, indeed, of everyday life). Routing these two demons of chaos becomes the first requisite of natural science, for only in that rout have we been able to construct any understanding of the world and any control over the world.

Thus, Comte reminds us that "the most terrible sensation we are capable of is that which we experience when any phenomenon seems to arise in violation of the familiar laws of nature," and concludes that "Disorder dreads the scientific spirit" (1975:89, 212)—although he might better have put the last the other way around. Whitehead reiterates this point when he says "Nothing is more interesting to watch than the emotional disturbance produced by an unusual disturbance of the forms of process. . . . [W]hen for human experience quick changes arrive, human nature passes into hysteria" (1938:130); similarly, Einstein is said to have been unable to believe that God plays dice with the universe; and Merton asserts that "random variation [is] a situation distasteful to the theorist whose task it is to perceive underlying uniformities amid such apparent disorder" (1957:252).

Clearly now, the logical consequence of the first working assumption is the second assumption, namely, that all the endlessly varied things coming within the scope of human experience are really only *one* thing; that is, all differences are, in the long run and in the broad scope, merely manifestations of the *same* regularity. On this working assumption every natural scientist is driven to subsume every particular observation under some regularity, and forever to make regular the differences between such regularities by showing that each of them manifests a single still more encompassing, more general (we are apt to call it "higher") regularity— as Newton claims that a falling apple and the rising sun both manifest the same "gravitation" regularity and as Merton and Rossi claim that the behavior of army replacement troops, when unlike that of both green and veteran troops, when unlike green troops but like veteran troops, and also when like green troops but unlike veteran troops, all manifest the same "reference group" regularity (Merton, 1957:252–257).

The doctrine of human unpredictability implies that humans are somehow exempt from such subsumption and, indeed, Gewirth explicitly asserts that exemption with respect to human knowledge (on which, human decision is, in part, based):

> The error [of thinking that "the operation of human knowledge is itself determined by social laws"] is that of viewing social laws as so all-inclusive that from a small number of them there follow *en bloc* all social phenomena, including knowledge. But if we view social laws as specific correlations of distinct phenomena, then the causal laws determining men's knowledge may well be different from those determining other social phenomena, and thus there is no impossibility in knowledge leading to action which reacts on and changes the latter phenomena (1954:238–239).

Thus, Gewirth asserts that "the causal laws determining men's knowledge" are not only *presently* unintegrated deductively (either among themselves or with other causal laws), they will *never* be so integrated. Their "difference" relegates them to a mere congeries of "specific correlations of distinct phenomena," a congeries whose subsuming nets are irremediably ragged enough to allow human knowledge always to slip through and go free of lawfulness and predictability. Clearly, to the extent that human knowledge is or becomes a dominant constituent of human social phenomena the unsubsumable freedom of the former renders the latter also free. To that extent, as Winch puts it, "the possibility of scientific prediction of social developments . . . [would have] no sense."

Now let me at once admit that human behavior seems almost certain to contain a humanly unpredictable factor—whether a supernatural factor like the Soul (about which science is permanently agnostic) or some natural factor lying forever beyond the reach of human knowledge although not necessarily beyond the reach of all knowledge—that is, knowledge held by other natural phenomena of greater-than-human cognitive capacity. I base this admission on two grounds. First, it seems likely that every entity (whether human or not) that makes a prediction finds *itself* unpredictable in some essential respects[23]—otherwise, it could, in principle, pre-

---

[23] Polanyi surely means to include this unpredictability when, in an essay entitled "The Unaccountable Element in Science," he refers to perception as "a secret trick which is unlikely ever to be revealed to our understanding" (1969:106). However, after himself elucidating these "secret tricks," Polanyi concludes that "We see a great deal can be known about [them], but we realize also that the better we know [them] the less [they appear] capable of definition by precise objective rules" (1969:115).

dict its own predictions and predict its own predictions of its own predictions[24] and thus fall into infinite regress.

This seems to apply, even, to the difference between the way an individual human is apt to view his/her own acts versus other humans' acts. On this, Jeans quotes Sidgwick as follows:

> We always explain the voluntary actions of all men except ourselves on the principle of causation by character and circumstances. We infer generally the future actions of those whom we know from their past actions; and if our forecast turns out in any case to be erroneous, we do not attribute the discrepancy to the disturbing influence of free will, but to our incomplete acquaintance with their character and motives (1958:207).

Jeans also notes that the "supposed freedom [of oneself] applies only to . . . present acts and not to the past; we see our own past lives as [we do] other men" (1958:207), and so explain our past acts without recourse to free will. Obviously, however, the subjective experience of personal and present unpredictability (as the quotation from Sidgwick indicates) does not rule out the possibility that others may find highly predictable the very behavior which we ourselves find most unpredictable. Thus, to say that human behavior seems almost certain to contain a factor that is not predictable by *humans* is not the same as saying it contains a factor which is *in principle* unpredictable. Second, it appears that *all* phenomena are in some ways and to some extent unpredictable by humans; human behavior is not at all unique in this respect.

More important than all this, however, are the obvious hypotheses that the predictability of human behavior varies (1) according to the behavior one is predicting, (2) according to the individuals one is examining, and (3) according to the setting in which the behavior is occurring—and that the effectiveness of human decisions to change human behavior varies, therefore, in the same way. As Feuer says, "It may be the case . . . that human decision counts for more in certain social systems than in others" (1965:203), and indeed this is the main significance of technological advance so far (see Chapter 11).

Having admitted, on such tentative principles alone, the likely existence of a humanly unpredictable factor in human behavior, it is essential to add that (1) we

---

[24] Gilbert and Berger argue persuasively that the scientific community can, in principle, predict its own predictions but their argument depends on the predictors forgetting their prediction immediately after making it (see 1975:107). Although Gilbert and Berger's logical reason for introducing this requirement is to rule out the possibility that knowledge of the prediction may causally fulfill the prediction, the empirical effect of the requirement is to make the predictors regard themselves as unpredictable (or at least unpredicted) at the time of the prediction's verification—which, having forgotten the prediction, they cannot recognize as a verification.

cannot ever identify that factor empirically, and (2) even if we could, the existence of unpredictability in each individual human's behavior does not necessarily mean that the coincidence of behaviors across two or more such individuals is also unpredictable. Let us consider these two points in turn.

Regarding the first—that we can never identify an unpredictable factor empirically—I mean that we can never distinguish between a factor which *is ultimately* unpredictable and a factor which only *temporarily seems* to be unpredictable; we can never know whether a factor which has stubbornly resisted a thousand million of our best attempts to formulate general laws of natural science under which it can be subsumed, resisted a thousand million of our best attempts to predict its occurrences, will not yield on the very next attempt. Since this seems just as true for predictions of the behavior of nonhuman, inanimate, phenomena as for predictions of human behavior, Popper concludes that "every scientific statement must remain *tentative forever.* . . . It is not his possession of knowledge, or irrefutable truth that makes the man of science but his persistent and recklessly critical *quest* for truth" (1961:280–281)—a view that echoes Weber:

> In science, each of us knows that what he has accomplished will be antiquated in ten, twenty, fifty years. That is the fate to which science is subjected; it is the very *meaning* of scientific work. . . . Every scientific "fulfillment" raises new "questions"; it *asks* to be "surpassed" and outdated. Whoever wishes to serve science has to resign himself to this fact. . . . We cannot work without hoping that others will advance further than we have. In principle, this progress goes on *ad infinitum* (1958a:138).

Therefore, even though we admit, on principle, the existence of a humanly unpredictable factor in human behavior, our permanent inability to identify that factor empirically argues for the pragmatic point I adopt here, namely, that we should behave as if the factor did *not* exist—because otherwise, we encourage every phenomenon that is merely difficult to predict to be written off from the start as impossible to predict. We would, in short, be giving up, excusing ourselves from pressing our understanding and control of the world to their limits when we have hardly begun. In contrast with that capitulation, Popper proposes that we adhere to

> the simple rule that we are not to abandon the search for universal laws and for a coherent theoretical system, nor give up our attempts to explain causally any kind of event we can describe (1961:61).

It is the second qualification above—namely, that unpredictability in each individual's behavior does not necessarily mean that behavior coincidences across individuals are also unpredictable—which alone endows the rule that Popper proposes with hope for success; and success, indeed, not only in the social sciences but in all natural sciences. Thus, Jeans points out how the coincidence of humanly unpredictable or "indeterminate" events at the subatomic level itself becomes predictable:

> No amount of calculation will tell [the physicist which atoms of radium will disintegrate at any given time]; we must rather picture Fate as picking out her atom, by methods undiscoverable by us. . . . [But] the indeterminism disclosed by the quantum theory is confined to the small-scale processes of nature, and . . . even these indeterminate events are governed by statistical laws. In all man-sized phenomena, billions of electrons and atoms are involved, and for the discussion of such phenomena as are perceptible to us, these may be treated statistically as a crowd. But these crowds obey statistical laws which now take control of the situation, with the result that the phenomena can be predicted with almost the same precision as though the future motion of each particle were known. In the same way, the statistician, knowing the birth rate, death rate, etc., of a population, can predict the future changes in the population as a whole, without being able to predict what each separate individual will do in the matter of births and deaths (1958:150, 151–152).

Accordingly, after Chapter 2 defined social phenomena as *inter*organism behavior regularities, Chapter 7 then argued that the organisms in question may behave irregularly and therefore unpredictably *as individuals* so long as the coincidence of their behaviors is regular—and it is only this regular, predictable, coincidence in which sociologists, as natural scientists, take interest.

Human Complexity

Finally, let us briefly consider that objection to regarding sociology as a natural science which rests on the belief that human behavior is too complex ever to be reduced to scientific laws. Wilson puts this idea as follows:

> We note that even if the basis of mind is truly mechanistic, it is very unlikely that any intelligence could exist with the power to predict the precise actions of an individual human being, as we might to a limited degree chart the path of a [flipped] coin or the flight of a honeybee. The mind is too complicated a structure, and human social relations affect its decisions in too intricate and variable a manner, for the detailed histories of individual human beings to be predicted in advance by the individuals affected or by other human beings. You and I are consequently free and responsible persons in this fundamental sense (1978:77).

Realizing that the pivotal terms in this statement are "precise" and "detailed"—
for surely the *general* actions of an individual human being, and the *general* histories
of individual human beings are predictable with great accuracy—Wilson himself
goes on to answer his own objection when he says

> If the categories of behavior are made broad enough, events can be predicted
> with confidence. The coin will spin and not settle on its edge, the bee will
> fly around the room in an upright position, and the human being will speak
> and conduct a wide range of social activities characteristic of the human spe-
> cies. Moreover, the statistical properties of *populations* of individuals can be
> specified . . . [and therefore] the statistical behavior of human societies might
> be predicted, given a sufficient knowledge of human nature, the histories of
> the societies, and their physical environment (1978:77–78).

And so, to me at least, it seems fair to say that neither the call for an idiographic sociology, nor the postulate of human free will, nor that of human reflexivity, nor that of human unpredictability, nor that of human complexity justifies
setting human social phenomena beyond the reach of scientific procedure—or, more
to the point, setting them any more beyond the reach of scientific procedure than
any other phenomena.

My guess, however, is that while they do not identify insuperable obstacles to
scientific sociology per se, the postulates of human free will, reflexivity, unpredictability, and complexity do spring from an accurate assessment of the very great
hindrances to any scientific sociology which is easy, simple, or inexpensive. In a
word, it is the practical *difficulty* of doing scientific sociology and not its principled
impossibility, to which these postulates point.

Thus, it may be inferred from Chapter 2 that a complete description of any
given social phenomenon is very difficult to achieve because it must implicate so
many different kinds of variables (and must select appropriate representatives of
each kind), and similarly, it may be inferred from Chapter 7 that a complete
explanation of such a phenomenon is very difficult to achieve because it too must
implicate so many different kinds of variables (and must also select appropriate
representatives of each kind).

In pursuing these completenesses, it seems to me that sociology has been ham-
strung so far by at least two major restrictions. First, we do not yet have standard
operationalizations (i.e., interpretation, sampling, instrumentation, scaling, and
measurement techniques) for most of the central concepts comprising sociological
description and explanation-prediction as outlined in Parts I and II. Instead, each
analyst has constructed his/her own operationalization virtually from scratch and
without strict comparability and cumulation between analyses.

Second, while, on the one hand, we are rightly prohibited from most of that
physically controlled (laboratory) experimentation with randomly assigned subjects

which other natural sciences have found most essential to their present stages of development, on the other hand, and at the same time we are also severely restrained from using the next best thing: most of our research is on far too small a scale to enable adequate substitution of statistical for physical control over the large number of extraneous variables that we know must be operating in and on any given social phenomenon of interest. As a result, we are almost always left with large amounts of unexplained variation.

One can hardly imagine a simple solution to these problems, but it seems essential to recognize them as *practical* problems and not problems that inhere, in principle, in either the objects or the subjects of sociological analysis because then, instead of throwing up our hands, we may begin to seek new ways of attacking them.

SUMMARY

This chapter examined natural science premises concerning the fundamental uniformity and universalism of nature, and concerning the fundamental interchangeability of human beings who seek to understand and control that nature. Remedies for manifest noninterchangeability were discussed. Finally, five leading objections to applying these premises to sociology, and to employing scientific procedure in sociology, were examined.

Concluding Remarks

Chapter 1 promised this book would try to explicate an already existing, but largely unrecognized, consensus in scientific sociology and to derive from that consensus a matalanguage which might serve as rules-of-the-game for all the controversies that rightfully characterize our discipline.

It should again be emphasized that in pursuing this objective, I have not claimed superior generality for any single substantive or procedural orientation in sociology; I have not argued that any given orientation should be regarded as the super-orientation to which all others should be subservient. My imperialism has been that of the eclectic rather than the partisan.

I have therefore ransacked and pulled apart the literature of sociology (and, to some extent, sociobiology) without much respect for the so-called "embeddedness" of specific substantive claims and procedural injunctions, or for the claimed "territory" of this or that school of thought. Indeed, I have regarded all such embeddednesses and territories as though they were largely the results of accidents so far—that is, accidental combinations of nonaccidental elements—in something like the ways twos, tens, sevens, fours, elevens, and so on, may be random rolls by crapshooters handling dice whose faces carry entirely nonrandom numbers in nonrandom relations.

It is in these nonrandom numbers and relations that I have been interested here, and, not being able directly to examine the dice for them, I have had to infer them from watching the rolls. That is to say, I have tried to deduce what few constant substantive and procedural elements and relations could have produced the spectacularly varied panoply of whole theories, whole procedures, whole specialties, whose researches, that the sociological (and sociobiological) literature now presents.

The result of this effort is a stock of broadly standard ideas whose details may be endlessly specified, and that may be almost endlessly combined and recombined into new analyses—and now in deliberate, purposefully directed, systematic, *non*-random ways. The result, in short, appears to be that metalanguage for scientific sociology which Chapter 1 identified as the prime objective of this book. Its adoption may conceivably free us from blind loyalty to this or that substantive or procedural orientation—and free us, not by turning us aimlessly "loose" but by binding us closely to a shared and systematic vocabulary and grammar which, like dictionaries of natural languages, may enable us to take a collective leap ahead both in creativity and communicability.

REFERENCES

Abel, Theodore
    1948   "The Operation Called *Verstehen*," *American Journal of Sociology*, Vol. 54, No. 3 (November): 211–218.

Aberle, D.F., A.K. Cohen, A.K. Davis, M.J. Levy, Jr., and F.X. Sutton
    1950   "The Functional Prerequisites of a Society," *Ethics* Vol. 60 (January): 100–111.

Adler, Franz
    1956   "The Value Concept in Sociology," *American Journal of Sociology*, Vol. 62 (November), 272–279.
    1960   "A Unit Concept for Sociology," *American Journal of Sociology*, Vol. 65 (January): 356–364.

Adorno, Theodor W.
    1976a   "Sociology and Empirical Research," in Paul Connerton (ed.), *Critical Sociology*. New York: Penguin Books.
    1976b   "On the Logic of the Social Sciences," in Theodor W. Adorno *et al.* (eds.), *The Positivist Dispute in German Sociology*. New York: Harper Torchbooks.

Alexander, Christopher
    1972   "The City as a Mechanism for Sustaining Human Contact," in Robert Gutman (ed.), *People and Buildings*. New York: Basic Books.

Alexander, Jeffrey C.
    1981   "Looking for Theory," *Theory and Society*, Vol. 10 (March): 279–292.
    1982   *Positivism, Presuppositions, and Current Controversies*. University of California Press.

Allee, W.C.
    1958   *The Social Life of Animals*. Boston: Beacon Press.

Allport, Gordon W.
    1968   "The Historical Background of Modern Social Psychology," in Gardner Lindzey and Elliot Aronson (eds.), *The Handbook of Social Psychology*. Reading, Mass.: Addison-Wesley.

Anderson, Lee G., and Russell F. Settle
   1977   *Benefit-Cost Analysis: A Practical Guide.* Lexington, Massachusetts: Lexington Books.
Archer, Dane, and Rosemary Gartner
   1976   "Violent Acts and Violent Times: A Comparative Approach to Postwar Homicide Rates,"
           American Sociological Review, Vol. 41 (December): 937–963.
Ashby, W. Ross
   1968   "Principles of the Self-Organizing System," in Walter Buckley (ed.), *Modern Systems Re-
           search for the Behavioral Scientist.* Chicago: Aldine.
Barber, Bernard
   1957   *Social Stratification.* New York: Harcourt, Brace.
Bardach, Eugene
   1977   *The Implementation Game,* Cambridge, Massachusetts: The MIT Press.
Barnard, Chester I.
   1948   *The Functions of the Executive.* Cambridge, Massachusetts: Harvard University Press.
Bartholomew, G.A.
   1959   "Mother-Young Relations and Maturation of Pup Behavior in the Alaska Fur Seal," *An-
           imal Behavior,* Vol. 7 (July–October): 163–171.
Bauer, Raymond A.
   1968   "The Study of Policy-Formation: An Introduction," in Raymond A. Bauer and Kenneth
           J. Gergen (eds.), *The Study of Policy Formation.* New York: Free Press.
Becker, Howard S.
   1973   *Outsiders.* New York: Free Press.
Becker, Howard S., and Irving Louis Horowitz
   1972   "Radical Politics and Sociological Research," *American Journal of Sociology,* Vol. 78 (July):
           48–66.
Becker, Howard S., and Anselm L. Strauss
   1956   "Careers, Personality, and Adult Socialization," *American Journal of Sociology,* Vol. 62
           (November): 253–263.
Bell, Daniel
   1973   *The Coming of Post-Industrial Society.* New York: Basic Books.
Benoit-Smullyan, Emile
   1944   "Status, Status Types, and Status Interrelations," *American Sociological Review,* Vol. 9
           (April): 151–161.
Berg, Alan
   1973   *The Nutrition Factor.* Washington, D.C.: The Brookings Institution.
Berger, Peter L.
   1969   *The Sacred Canopy.* Garden City, NY: Doubleday Anchor.
Berger, Joseph, M. Hamit Fisek, Robert Z. Norman, and Morris Zelditch, Jr.
   1977   *Status Characteristics and Social Interaction.* New York: Elsevier.
Berger, Peter L., and Thomas Luckmann
   1967   *The Social Construction of Reality.* Garden City, New York: Anchor Books.
Berk, Richard A.
   1974   "A Gaming Approach to Crowd Behavior," *American Sociological Review,* Vol. 39 (June):
           355–373.
Berk, Richard A., Kenneth J. Lenihan, and Peter H. Rossi
   1980   "Crime and Poverty: Some Experimental Evidence from Ex-Offenders," *American Sociolog-
           ical Review,* Vol. 45 (October): 766–786.

Blake, Judith, and Kingsley Davis
    1964   "Norms, Values, and Sanctions," in Robert E.L. Faris (ed.), *Handbook of Modern Sociology.* Chicago: Rand McNally.

Blalock, Hubert M., Jr.
    1968   "The Measurement Problem: A Gap Between the Languages of Theory and Research," in H.M. Blalock and Ann B. Blalock (eds.), *Methodology in Social Research.* New York: McGraw-Hill.
    1969   *Theory Construction.* Englewood Cliffs, New Jersey: Prentice-Hall.
    1979   "The Presidential Address: Measurement and Conceptualization Problems: The Major Obstacle to Integrating Theory and Research," *American Sociological Review,* Vol. 44 (December): 881–894.

Blau, Peter M.
    1957   "Formal Organizations: Dimensions of Analysis," *American Journal of Sociology,* Vol. 63 (July): 58–69.
    1964   *Exchange and Power in Social Life.* New York: Wiley.
    1974   "Parameters of Social Structure," *American Sociological Review,* Vol. 39 (October): 615–635.
    1975   "Introduction: Parallels and Contrasts in Structural Inquiries," in Peter M. Blau (ed.), *Approaches to the Study of Social Structure.* New York: Free Press.
    1977   *Inequality and Heterogeneity.* New York: Free Press.

Blau, Peter M., and W. Richard Scott
    1962   *Formal Organizations.* San Francisco: Chandler.

Blumer, Herbert
    1946   "Collective Behavior," in Alfred McClung Lee (ed.), *New Outline of the Principles of Sociology.* New York: Barnes & Noble.
    1956   "Sociological Analysis and the 'Variable,' " *American Sociological Review,* Vol. 21 (December): 683–690.
    1957   "Collective Behavior," in Joseph B. Gittler (ed.), *Review of Sociology.* New York: Wiley.
    1962   "Society As Symbolic Interaction," in Arnold M. Rose (ed.), *Human Behavior and Social Processes.* Boston: Houghton Mifflin.

Bonner, John T.
    1980   *The Evolution of Culture in Animals.* Princeton: Princeton University Press.

Boocock, Sarane Spence
    1980   *The Sociology of Education: An Introduction.* Boston: Houghton Mifflin.

Booth, Alan, and John N. Edwards
    1976   "Crowding and Family Relations," *American Sociological Review,* Vol. 41 (April): 308–321.

Bottomore, Tom
    1975   "Structure and History," in Peter M. Blau (ed.), *Approaches to the Study of Social Structure.* New York: Free Press.

Boulding, Kenneth E.
    1962   *Conflict and Defense.* New York: Harper Torchbooks.
    1968   "General Systems Theory—The Skeleton of Science," in Walter Buckley (ed.), *Modern Systems Research for the Behavioral Scientist.* Chicago: Aldine.

Bourdieu, P.
    1981   "Men and Machines," in K. Knorr-Cetina and A.V. Cicourel (eds.), *Advances in Social Theory and Methodology.* Boston: Routledge & Kegan Paul.

Braithwaite, Richard Bevan
　　1960　*Scientific Explanation.* New York: Harper Torchbooks.
Bredemeier, Harry
　　1978　"Exchange Theory," in Tom Bottomore and Robert Nisbet (eds.), *A History of Sociological Analysis.* New York: Basic Books.
Brillouin, L.
　　1968　"Life Thermodynamics, and Cybernetics," in Walter Buckley (ed.), *Modern Systems Research for the Scientist.* Chicago: Aldine.
Brim, Orville G., Jr.
　　1966　"Socialization Through the Life Cycle," in Orville G. Brim, Jr. and Stanton Wheeler (eds.), *Socialization After Childhood: Two Essays.* New York: Wiley.
　　1968　"Adult Socialization," in John A. Clausen (ed.), *Socialization and Society.* Boston: Little, Brown.
Brodbeck, May
　　1959　"Models, Meaning, and Theories," in Llewellyn Gross (ed.), *Symposium on Sociological Theory.* New York: Harper & Row.
　　1973a　"On the Philosophy of the Social Sciences," in John O'Neill (ed.), *Modes of Individualism and Collectivism.* New York: St. Martin's Press.
　　1973b　"Methodological Individualisms: Definition and Reduction," in John O'Neill (ed.), *Modes of Individualism and Collectivism.* New York: St. Martin's Press.
Broom, Leonard
　　1959　"Social Differentiation and Stratification" in Robert K. Merton, Leonard Broom, and Leonard S. Cottrell, Jr. (eds.), *Sociology Today.* New York: Basic Books.
Broom, Leonard, and Philip Selznick
　　1963　*Sociology* (Third Edition). New York: Harper & Row.
Brown, Roger
　　1965　*Social Psychology.* New York: Free Press.
Buckley, Walter
　　1957　"Structural-Functional Analysis in Modern Sociology," in Howard Becker and Alvin Boskoff (eds.), *Modern Sociological Theory.* New York: Dryden.
　　1967　*Sociology and Modern Systems Theory.* Englewood Cliffs, New Jersey: Prentice-Hall.
Burgess, Ernest W.
　　1961　"The Growth of the City: An Introduction to a Research Project," reprinted in George A. Theodorson (ed.), *Studies in Human Ecology.* Evanston, Illinois: Row, Peterson.
Burgess, Ernest W., and Harvey J. Locke
　　1953　*The Family.* New York: American Book.
Callon, Michel, and Bruno Latour
　　1981　"Unscrewing the Big Leviathan: How Actors Macro-Structure Reality and How Sociologists Help Them To Do So," in K. Knorr-Cetina and A.V. Cicourel (eds.), *Advances in Social Theory and Methodology.* Boston: Routledge & Kegan Paul.
Campbell, Donald T.
　　1957　"Factors Relevant to the Validity of Experiments in Social Settings," *Psychological Bulletin,* Vol. 54: 297–312.
　　1958　"Common Fate, Similarity, and Other Indices of the Status of Aggregates of Persons as Social Entities," *Behavioral Science,* Vol. 3, No. 1 (January): 14–25.
　　1965a　"Ethnocentric and Other Altruistic Motives," in D. Levine (ed.), *Nebraska Symposium on Motivation,* Vol. 13. Lincoln: University of Nebraska Press.
　　1965b　"Variation and Selective Retention in Socio-Cultural Evolution," in Herbert R. Barringer et al. (eds.), *Social Change in Developing Areas.* Cambridge, Massachusetts: Schenkman.

1969   "Reforms as Experiments," *American Psychologist,* Vol. 24, No. 4 (April): 409–429.

1971   "Methods for the Experimenting Society." Unpublished Manuscript.

1972   "Comments on the Comment by Shaver and Staines," *American Psychologist,* Vol. 27 (February): 164.

1975a   "Assessing the Impact of Planned Social Change," in Gene M. Lyons (ed.), *Social Research and Public Policies.* Hanover, New Hampshire: Public Affairs Center, Dartmouth College.

1975b   "On the Conflicts Between Biological and Social Evolution and Between Psychology and Moral Tradition," *American Psychologist,* Vol. 30 (December): 1103–1126.

Campbell, Donald T. and Donald W. Fiske

1959   "Convergent and Discriminant Validation by the Multitrait-Multimethod Matrix," *Psychological Bulletin,* Vol. 56 (March): 81–105.

Caplow, Theodore

1968   *Two Against One.* Englewood Cliffs, New Jersey: Prentice-Hall.

Cardwell, D.S.L.

1972   *Turning Points in Western Technology.* New York: Science History Publications.

Caro, Francis G.

1971   "Evaluation Research: An Overview," in Francis G. Caro (ed.), *Readings in Evaluation Research.* New York: Russell Sage Foundation.

Castaneda, Carlos

1968   *The Teachings of Don Juan: A Yaqui Way of Knowledge.* New York: Pocket Books.

Chen, S.C.

1969   "Social Modification of the Activity of Ants in Nest-Building," in Robert B. Zajonc (ed.), *Animal Social Psychology.* New York: Wiley.

Cicourel, Aaron V.

1974   *Cognitive Sociology.* New York: Free Press.

1981   "Notes on the Integration of Micro- and Macro-Levels of Analysis," in K. Knorr-Cetina and A.V. Cicourel (eds.), *Advances in Social Theory and Methodology.* Boston: Routledge & Kegan Paul.

Clark, Kenneth B.

1967   *Dark Ghetto.* New York: Harper Torchbooks.

Cloward, Richard A.

1959   "Illegitimate Means, Anomie, and Deviant Behavior," *American Sociological Review,* Vol. 24 (April): 164–176.

Cloward, Richard A. and Lloyd E. Ohlin

1960   *Delinquency and Opportunity.* New York: Free Press.

Clynes, Manfred

1980   "The Communication of Emotion: Theory of Sentics," in Robert Plutchik and Henry Kellerman (eds.), *Emotion: Theory, Research, and Experience.* New York: Academic Press.

Cohen, Albert K.

1959   "The Study of Social Disorganization and Deviant Behavior," in Robert K. Merton et al. (eds.), *Sociology Today.* New York: Basic Books.

1966   *Deviance and Control.* Englewood Cliffs, New Jersey: Prentice-Hall.

Cohen, Morris R., and Ernest Nagel

1934   *An Introduction to Logic and Scientific Method.* New York: Harcourt Brace & World.

Coleman, James S.

1955   *Community Conflict.* Glencoe: Free Press.

1972   *Policy Research in the Social Sciences.* Morristown, New Jersey: General Learning.

1974   *Power and the Structure of Society.* New York: Norton.

1976   "The Emergence of Sociology As a Policy Science, in Lewis A. Coser and Otto N. Larsen (eds.), *The Uses of Controversy in Sociology*. New York: Free Press.

1978   "Sociological Analysis and Social Policy," in Tom Bottomore and Robert Nisbet (eds.), *A History of Sociological Analysis*. New York: Basic Books.

Coleman, James S., Elihu Katz, and Herbert Menzel

1957   "The Diffusion of an Innovation Among Physicians," *Sociometry*, Vol. 20 (December): 253–270.

Colfax, J. David, and Jack L. Roach

1971   "Introduction—The Roots of Radical Sociology," in J. David Colfax and Jack L. Roach (eds.), *Radical Sociology*. New York: Basic Books.

Collins, Randall

1975   *Conflict Sociology*. New York: Academic Press.

1981   "Micro-Translation as a Theory-Building Strategy," in K. Knorr-Cetina and A.V. Cicourel (eds.), *Advances in Social Theory and Methodology*. Boston: Routledge & Kegan Paul.

Comte, Auguste

1975   *Auguste Comte and Positivism* (ed. by Gertrud Lenzer). New York: Harper Torchbooks.

Coser, Lewis

1956   *The Functions of Social Conflict*. Glencoe: Free Press.

1975   "Structure and Conflict," in Peter M. Blau (ed.), *Approaches to the Study of Social Structure*. New York: Free Press.

1977   *Masters of Sociological Thought* (Second Edition). New York: Harcourt Brace Jovanovich.

1978   "American Trends," in Tom Bottomore and Robert Nisbet (eds.) *A History of Sociological Analysis*. New York: Basic Books.

Costner, Herbert L. and Robert K. Leik

1964   "Deductions from 'Axiomatic Theory,' " *American Sociological Review*, Vol. 29, No. 6 (December): 819–835.

Cottrell, Fred

1955   *Energy and Society*. New York: McGraw-Hill.

Dahrendorf, Ralf

1958   "Out of Utopia," *American Journal of Sociology*, Vol. 64 (September): 115–127.

1959   *Class and Class Conflict in Industrial Society*. Stanford, California: Stanford University.

Dasgupta, Ajit K., and D.W. Pearce

1972   *Cost-Benefit Analysis*. New York: Barnes & Noble.

Davis, Kingsley

1949   *Human Society*. New York: Macmillan.

1959   "The Myth of Functional Analysis as a Special Method in Sociology and Anthropology," *American Sociological Review*, Vol. 24 (December): 757–772.

1976   "The World's Population Crisis," in Robert K. Merton and Robert Nisbet (eds.), *Contemporary Social Problems* (Fourth Edition). New York: Harcourt Brace Jovanovich.

Douglas, Mary

1969   *Purity and Danger*. London: Routledge & Kegan Paul.

Dubin, Robert

1959   "Deviant Behavior and Social Structure," *American Sociological Review*, Vol. 24 (April): 147–164.

Duncan, Otis Dudley

1964   "Social Organization and the Ecosystem," in Robert E.L. Faris (ed.), *Handbook of Modern Sociology*. Chicago: Rand McNally.

Durkheim, Emile

1933   *The Division of Labor in Society*. Glencoe: Free Press.

1938   *The Rules of Sociological Method.* Glencoe: Free Press.

1951   *Suicide.* Glencoe: Free Press.

1956   *Education and Sociology.* Glencoe: Free Press.

1965   *The Elementary Forms of the Religious Life.* New York: Free Press.

1973   *On Morality and Society.* Chicago: University of Chicago Press.

1978   *On Institutional Analysis* (ed. by Mark Traugott). Chicago: University of Chicago Press.

Duster, Troy

1981   "Intermediate Steps Between Micro- and Macro-Integration: The Case of Screening for Inherited Disorders," in K. Knorr-Cetina and A.V. Cicourel (eds.), *Advances in Social Theory and Methodology.* Boston: Routledge & Kegan Paul.

Eisenstadt, S.N.

1978a   "The Social Framework and Conditions of Revolution," *Research in Social Movements, Conflicts and Change,* Vol. I, pp. 85–104.

1978b   *Revolution and the Transformation of Societies.* New York: Free Press.

Eisenstadt, S.N. and M. Curelaru

1976   *The Forms of Sociology—Paradigms and Crises.* New York: Wiley.

Ekeh, Peter P.

1974   *Social Exchange Theory.* London: Heinemann.

Engels, Frederick

1968   "The Part Played by Labour in the Transition from Ape to Man," in *Karl Marx and Frederick Engels Selected Works.* New York: International Publishers.

Erikson, Kai T.

1966   *Wayward Puritans.* New York: Wiley.

1976   *Everything in Its Path.* New York: Simon & Schuster.

Etkin, William

1964a   "Co-operation and Competition in Social Behavior," in William Etkin (ed.), *Social Behavior and Organization Among Vertebrates.* Chicago: University of Chicago Press.

1964b   "Reproductive Behaviors," in Willam Etkin (ed.), *Social Behavior and Organization Among Vertebrates.* Chicago: University of Chicago Press.

Etzioni, Amitai

1968   *The Active Society.* New York: Free Press.

1971   "Policy Research," *The American Sociologist,* 6 (Supplementary Issue: June, entitled "Sociological Research and Public Policy"): 8–12.

Etzioni, Amitai, and Richard Remp

1973   *Technological Shortcuts to Social Change.* New York: Russell Sage Foundation.

Fanon, Frantz

1963   *The Wretched of the Earth.* New York: Grove.

Feigl, Herbert

1953   "Notes on Causality," in Herbert Feigl and May Brodbeck (eds.), *Readings in the Philosophy of Science.* New York: Appteton-Century-Crofts.

Festinger, Leon

1972   "Architecture and Group Membership," in Robert Gutman (ed.), *People and Buildings.* New York: Basic Books.

Festinger, Leon, Stanley Schachter, and Kurt Back

1950   *Social Pressure in Informal Groups.* New York: Harper.

Festinger, Leon, Henry W. Riecken, and Stanley Schachter

1964   *When Prophecy Fails.* New York: Harper Torchbooks.

Feuer, Lewis S.

1965   "Causality in the Social Sciences," in Daniel Lerner (ed.), *Cause and Effect.* New York: Free Press.

Fine, Gary Alan
  1979 "Small Groups and Culture Creation: The Idioculture of Little League Baseball Teams," *American Sociological Review,* Vol. 44 (October): 733–745.
Fine, Gary Alan, and Sherryle Kleinman
  1979 "Rethinking Subculture: An Interactionist Analysis," *American Journal of Sociology* (July): 1–20.
Firestone, Shulamith
  1970 *The Dialectic of Sex.* New York: William Morrow.
Fishman, J.A.
  1972 "The Sociology of Language," in Pier Paolo Giglioli (ed.), *Language and Social Context.* Baltimore: Penguin Books.
Freeman, Howard E.
  1963 "The Strategy of Social Policy Research," *Social Welfare Forum.* New York: Columbia University Press for the National Conference on Social Welfare.
  1975 "Evaluation Research and Public Policies," in Gene M. Lyons (ed.) *Social Research and Public Policies.* Hanover, New Hampshire: Public Affairs Center, Dartmouth College.
Freeman, Howard E., and Clarence C. Sherwood
  1970 *Social Research and Social Policy.* Englewood Cliffs, New Jersey: Prentice-Hall.
Freire, Paulo
  1972 *Pedagogy of the Oppressed.* New York: Herder and Herder.
Freud, Sigmund
  1962 *Civilization and Its Discontents.* New York: Norton.
Friedrichs, Robert W.
  1970 *A Sociology of Sociology.* New York: Free Press.
Frisby, David
  1976 "Introduction to the English Translation," in Theodor W. Adorno et al., *The Positivist Dispute in German Sociology.* New York: Harper Torchbooks.
Gagnon, John H. and William Simon
  1973 *Sexual Conduct.* Chicago: Aldine.
Garfinkel, Harold
  1956 "Conditions of Successful Degradation Ceremonies," *American Journal of Sociology* Vol. 61 (January): 420–424.
  1967 *Studies in Ethnomethodology.* Englewood Cliffs, New Jersey: Prentice-Hall.
Geertz, Clifford
  1973 *The Interpretation of Cultures.* New York: Basic Books.
Gellner, E.A.
  1973 "Explanations in History," in John O'Neill (ed.), *Modes of Individualism and Collectivism.* New York: St. Martin's Press.
Gerbner, George
  1969 "Toward 'Cultural Indicators': the Analysis of Mass Mediated Public Message Systems," in George Gerbner, Ole R. Holsti, Klaus Krippendorff, William S. Paisley, and Philip J. Stone (eds.), *The Analysis of Communication Content.* New York: Wiley.
Geuss, Raymond
  1981 *The Idea of a Critical Theory.* Cambridge, Massachusetts: Cambridge University Press.
Gewirth, Alan
  1954 "Can Men Change the Laws of Social Science?," *Philosophy of Science,* Vol. 21, No. 3 (July): 229–241.
  1960 "Positive 'Ethics' and Normative 'Science,' " *The Philosophical Review,* Vol. LXIX, No. 3 (July): 311–330.
Gibbs, Jack P.

1965   "Norms: The Problem of Definition and Classification," *American Journal of Sociology,* Vol. 70 (March): 586–594.

1968   "The Study of Norms," in David L. Sills (ed.), *International Encyclopedia of the Social Sciences,* Vol. 11. New York: Macmillan and Free Press.

1972   *Sociological Theory Construction.* Hinsdale, Illinois: Dryden Press.

1981   *Norms, Deviance, and Social Control.* New York: Elsevier.

Giddens, Anthony

1973   *The Class Structure of the Advanced Societies.* New York: Harper Torchbooks.

1974   "Introduction," in Anthony Giddens (ed.), *Positivism and Sociology.* London: Heinemann.

1979   *Central Problems in Social Theory.* London: The Macmillan Press.

1981   "Agency, Institution and Time-Space Analysis," in K. Knorr-Cetina and A.V. Cicourel (eds.), *Advances in Social Theory and Methodology.* Boston: Routledge & Kegan Paul.

Gilbert, Margaret, and Fred R. Berger

1975   "On an Argument for the Impossibility of Prediction in the Social Sciences," *American Philosophical Quarterly,* Monograph No. 9, Oxford: 99–111.

Glassner, Barry, and Bruce Berg

1980   "How Jews Avoid Alcohol Problems," *American Sociological Review,* Vol. 45 (August): 647–664.

Goetsch, Wilhelm

1957   *The Ants.* Ann Arbor, Michigan: University of Michigan Press.

Goffman, Erving

1959   *The Presentation of Self in Everyday Life.* Garden City, New York: Doubleday Anchor.

1961   *Asylums.* Garden City, New York: Doubleday Anchor Books.

1962   "On Cooling the Mark Out: Some Aspects of Adaptation to Failure," in Arnold M. Rose (ed.), *Human Behavior and Social Processes.* Boston: Houghton Mifflin.

1971   *Relations in Public.* New York: Harper Colophon.

Goode, William J.

1960a   "A Theory of Role Strain," *American Sociological Review* Vol. 25 (August): 483–496.

1960b   "Norm Commitment and Conformity to Role-Status Obligations," *American Journal of Sociology,* Vol. 66 (November): 246–258.

1973   *Explorations in Social Theory.* New York: Oxford University Press.

1975   "Homans' and Merton's Structural Approach," in Peter M. Blau (ed.), *Approaches to the Study of Social Structure.* New York: Free Press.

Goody, J. and I. Watt

1972   "The Consequences of Literacy," in Pier Paolo Giglioli (ed.) *Language and Social Context.* Baltimore: Penguin Books.

Goslin, David A.

1969   "Introduction," in David A. Goslin (ed.), *Handbook of Socialization Theory and Research.* Chicago: Rand McNally.

Gould, James L.

1979   "Do Honeybees Know What They Are Doing?", *Natural History,* Vol. 88 (June–July): 66–75.

Gouldner, Alvin W.

1954   *Patterns of Industrial Bureaucracy.* Glencoe: Free Press.

1959   "Organizational Analysis" in Robert K. Merton et al. (eds.), *Sociology Today.* New York: Basic Books.

1960   "The Norm of Reciprocity," *American Sociological Review,* Vol. 25 (April): 161–178.

1970   *The Coming Crisis of Western Sociology.* New York: Basic Books.

1976   *The Dialectic of Ideology and Technology.* New York: Seabury.

Gove, Walter, Michael Hughes, and Omer R. Galle

1979   "Overcrowding in the Home: An Empirical Investigation of its Possible Pathological Consequences," *American Sociological Review*, Vol. 44 (February), 59–80.

Graham, Hugh Davis and Ted Robert Gurr

1969   *The History of Violence in America*. New York: Bantam Books.

Granovetter, Mark S.

1973   "The Strength of Weak Ties," *American Journal of Sociology*, Vol. 78 (May): 1360–1380.

Grobstein, Clifford

1969   "Hierarchical Order and Neogenesis" in Lancelot Law Whyte et al. (eds.), *Hierarchical Structures*. New York: Elsevier.

Gross, Neal, Ward S. Mason, and Alexander W. McEachern

1958   *Explorations in Role Analysis*. New York: Wiley.

Gutman, Robert

1975   "The Place of Architecture in Sociology," Working Paper 17, Princeton, New Jersey: Research Center for Urban and Environmental Planning, Princeton University.

Guttentag, Marcia (estate), and Paul F. Secord

1983   *Too Many Women*. Beverly Hills, California: SAGE.

Habermas, Jürgen

1970a   "Towards a Theory of Communicative Competence," *Inquiry* 13 (Winter): 360–375.

1970b   *Toward a Rational Society*. Boston: Beacon Press.

1971   *Knowledge and Human Interests*. Boston: Beacon Press.

1973   *Theory and Practice*. Boston: Beacon Press.

1975   *Legitimation Crisis*. Boston: Beacon Press.

1976   "The Analytical Theory of Science and Dialectics," in Theodor W. Adorno et al., *The Positivist Dispute in German Sociology*. New York: Harper Torchbooks.

1979   *Communication and the Evolution of Society*. Boston: Beacon Press.

1981   "Toward a Reconstruction of Historical Materialism," in K. Knorr-Cetina and A.V. Cicourel (eds.), *Advances in Social Theory and Methodology*. Boston: Routledge & Kegan Paul.

Hall, Edward T.

1959   *The Silent Language*. Garden City, New York: Doubleday.

1972   "Silent Assumptions in Social Communication," in Robert Gutman (ed,), *People and Buildings*. New York: Basic Books.

Hamilton, V. Lee, and Steve Rytina

1980   "Social Consensus on Norms of Justice: Should the Punishment Fit the Crime?," *American Journal of Sociology*, Vol. 85 (March): 1117–1144.

Harlow, Harry F.

1965   "Sexual Behavior in the Rhesus Monkey," in Frank A. Beach (ed.), *Sex and Behavior*. New York: Wiley.

Harré, Rom

1981   "Philosophical Aspects of the Micro-Macro Problem," in K. Knorr-Cetina and A.V. Cicourel (eds.), *Advances in Social Theory and Methodology*. Boston: Routledge & Kegan Paul.

Hart, Hornell

1957   "Acceleration in Social Change," in Francis R. Allen et al. (eds.), *Technology and Social Change*. New York: Appleton-Century-Crofts.

Hauser, Philip and Otis Dudley Duncan

1959   "Overview and Conclusions," in Philip Hauser and Otis Dudley Duncan (eds.), *The Study of Population*. Chicago: University of Chicago Press.

Hawley, Amos

1944   "Ecology and Human Ecology," *Social Forces*, Vol. 22 (May): 398–405.

1950   *Human Ecology*. New York: Ronald Press.

| 1971 | *Urban Society: An Ecological Approach*. New York: Wiley. |

1978   "The Presidential Address: Cumulative Change in Theory and in History," *American Sociological Review*, Vol. 43 (December): 787–796.

1979   "Cumulative Change in Theory and in History," in Amos H. Hawley (ed.), *Societal Growth*. New York: Free Press.

Hayek, F.A.

1973   *"From* Scientism and the Study of Society," in John O'Neill (ed.), *Modes of Individualism and Collectivism*. New York: St. Martin's Press.

Hechter, Michael, and William Brustein

1980   "Regional Modes of Production and Patterns of State Formation in Western Europe," *American Journal of Sociology*, Vol. 85 (March): 1061–1094.

Heider, Fritz

1958   *The Psychology of Interpersonal Relations*. New York: Wiley.

Hempel, Carl G.

1952   "Methods of Concept Formation in Science," in *International Encyclopedia of Unified Science*. Chicago: University of Chicago Press.

1965   *Aspects of Scientific Explanation*. New York: Free Press.

1967   "Scientific Explanation," in Sidney Morganbesser (ed.), *Philosophy of Science*. New York: Basic Books.

Hess, E.H.

1962   "Imprinting and the 'Critical Period' Concept," in E.L. Bliss (ed.), *Roots of Behavior*. New York: Harper & Row.

Hewitt, John P., and Randall Stokes

1975   "Disclaimers," *American Sociological Review*, Vol. 40 (February): 1–11.

Himes, Joseph

1980   *Conflict and Conflict Management*. Athens, Georgia: University of Georgia Press.

Hobbes, Thomas

1955   *Leviathan*. Oxford: Basil Blackwell.

Hochschild, Arlie Russell

1975   "The Sociology of Feeling and Emotion: Selected Possibilities," in Marcia Millman and Rosabeth Moss Kantor (eds.), *Another Voice*. New York: Anchor Press.

1979   "Emotion Work, Feeling Rules, and Social Structure" *American Journal of Sociology* Vol. 85 (November): 551–575.

Hogan, Dennis P.

1978   "The Variable Order of Events in the Life Course," *American Sociological Review*, Vol. 43 (August): 573–586.

Hogan, James P.

1979   *The Two Faces of Tomorrow*. New York: Ballantine Books.

Hollander, Edwin P.

1976   *Principles and Methods of Social Psychology*. New York: Oxford University Press.

Homans, George Caspar

1950   *The Human Group*. New York: Harcourt Brace Jo 'anovich.

1961   *Social Behavior: Its Elementary Forms*. New York: H rcourt Brace & World.

1964   "Bringing Men Back In," *American Sociological Review*, Vol. 29 (December): 809–818.

1974   *Social Behavior: Its Elementary Forms* (revised). New York: Harcourt Brace Jovanovich.

1975   "What Do We Mean by Social 'Structure'?," in Peter M. Blau (ed.), *Approaches to the Study of Social Structure*. New York: Free Press.

1980   "Discovery and the Discovered in Social Theory," in Hubert M. Blalock, Jr. (ed.), *Sociological Theory and Research*. New York: Free Press.

Hooker, Barbara I.
1968 "Birds," in Thomas A. Sebeok (ed.), *Animal Communication*. Bloomington, Indiana: Indiana University Press.

Horkheimer, Max
1972 "Traditional and Critical Theory," in Paul Connerton (ed.), *Critical Theory*. New York: Herder and Herder.

Horowitz, David
1971 "General Introduction," in David Horowitz (ed.), *Radical Sociology*. San Francisco: Canfield Press.

Hutt, Corinne
1972 *Males and Females*. Baltimore: Penguin Books.

Ibn Khaldun
1967 *The Muqaddimah*. Princeton: Princeton University Press.

Inbar, Michael
1979 *Routine Decision-Making*. Beverly Hills, California: SAGE.

Inkeles, Alex
1964 *What is Sociology?* Englewood Cliffs, New Jersey: Prentice-Hall.
1969 "Social Structure and Socialization," in David A. Goslin (ed.), *Handbook of Socialization Theory and Research*. Chicago: Rand McNally.
1980 "Personal Development and National Development: A Cross-National Perspective," in Alexander Szalai and Frank M. Andrews (eds.), *The Quality of Life: Comparative Studies*. London: SAGE.
1981 "Convergence and Divergence in Industrial Societies," in Mustafa O. Attir, Burkart Holzner, and Zdenek Suda (eds.), *Directions of Change: Modernization Theory, Research and Realities*. Boulder, Colorado: Westview.

Inkeles, Alex, and David H. Smith
1974 *Becoming Modern*. Cambridge, Massachusetts: Harvard University Press.

Irvin, George.
1978 *Modern Cost-Benefit Methods*. New York: Barnes & Noble.

Jacobs, Robert C., and Donald T. Campbell
1961 "The Perpetuation of an Arbitrary Tradition Through Several Generations of a Laboratory Microculture," *Journal of Abnormal and Social Psychology*, Vol. 62 (May): 649–658.

Jastrow, Robert
1981a "The Post-Human World," *Science Digest*, Vol. 89 (January–February): 89–91, 144.
1981b *The Enchanted Loom*. New York: Simon & Schuster.

Jeans, Sir James
1958 *Physics and Philosophy*. Ann Arbor, Michigan: University of Michigan Press.

Johnson, Barclay D.
1965 "Durkheim's One Cause of Suicide," *American Sociological Review*, Vol. 30 (December): 875–886.

Johnson, Norris R., and William E. Feinberg
1977 "A Computer Simulation of the Emergence of Consensus in Crowds," *American Sociological Review*, Vol. 42 (June): 505–521.

Jonas, Doris, and David Jonas
1978 *Other Senses, Other Worlds*. New York: Stein & Day.

Jones, Nicholas G. Blurton, and Robert H. Woodson
1979 "Describing Behavior: The Ethologist's Perspective," in Michael E. Lamb et. al. (eds.), *Social Interaction Analysis*. Madison, Wisconsin: University of Wisconsin Press.

Kant, Immanuel
1929 *Kant Selections*. New York: Scribner.

Kaplan, Abraham
  1964   *The Conduct of Inquiry*. San Francisco: Chandler.
Kasarda, John D.
  1974   "The Structural Implications of Social System Size: A Three-Level Analysis," *American Sociological Review*, Vol. 39 (February): 19–28.
Katz, Fred E.
  1976   *Structuralism in Sociology*. Albany, New York: State University of New York Press.
Keller, Suzanne
  1971   "Does the Family Have a Future?" *Journal of Comparative Family Studies*, II (Spring), pp. 1–14.
Keyfitz, Nathan
  1980   "Explanation in Demography and History," in Hubert M. Blalock, Jr. (ed.), *Sociological Theory and Research*. New York: Free Press.
Killian, Lewis M.
  1980   "Theory of Collective Behavior: The Mainstream Revisited," in Hubert M. Blalock, Jr. (ed.), *Sociological Theory and Research*. New York: Free Press.
Kitsuse, John I.
  1962   "Societal Reaction to Deviant Behavior: Problems of Theory and Method," *Social Problems*, Vol. 9 (Winter): 247–256.
Kleck, Gary
  1979   "Capital Punishment, Gun Ownership, and Homicide," *American Journal of Sociology*, Vol. 84 (January): 882–910.
Klopfer, Peter H.
  1962   *Behavioral Aspects of Ecology*. Englewood Cliffs, New Jersey: Prentice-Hall.
Klopfer, Peter H., and Jack P. Hailman
  1967   *An Introduction to Animal Behavior*. Englewood Cliffs, New Jersey: Prentice-Hall.
Kluckhohn, Clyde, and others.
  1951   "Values and Value-Orientations in the Theory of Action," in Talcott Parsons and Edward A. Shils (eds.), *Toward a General Theory of Action*. New York: Harper Torchbooks.
Knorr-Cetina, Karin
  1981   "Introduction: The Micro-Sociological Challenge of Macro-Sociology: Towards a Reconstruction of Social Theory and Methodology," in K. Knorr-Cetina and A.V. Cicourel (eds.), *Advances in Social Theory and Methodology*. Boston: Routledge & Kegan Paul.
Krech, David, Richard S. Crutchfield, and Egerton L. Ballachey
  1962   *Individual In Society*. New York: McGraw-Hill.
Kroeber, A.L., and Clyde Kluckhohn
  1963   *Culture*. New York: Vintage.
Kroeber, A.L., and Talcott Parsons
  1958   "The Concepts of Culture and of Social System," *American Sociological Review*, Vol. 23 (October): 582–583.
Kuhn, Thomas S.
  1970   *The Structure of Scientific Revolutions* (Second Edition, Enlarged). Chicago: University of Chicago Press.
Kuper, Leo
  1969   "Plural Societies: Perspectives and Problems," in Leo Kuper and M.G. Smith (eds.), *Pluralism in Africa*. Berkeley, California: University of California Press.
Lafargue, Paul
  n.d.   "Reminiscences of Marx," in (no editor) *Reminiscences of Marx and Engels*. Moscow: Foreign Languages Publishing House.
Lakatos, Imre

1978   *The Methodology of Scientific Research Programmes* (Vol. I). Cambridge: Cambridge University Press.

Land, Kenneth C.
1975   "Social Indicator Models: An Overview," in Kenneth C. Land and Seymour Spilerman (eds.), *Social Indicator Models*. New York: Russell Sage Foundation.

Lasswell, Harold D.
1966   "The Structure and Function of Communication in Society," in Bernard Berelson and Morris Janowitz (eds.), *Reader in Public Opinion and Communication*. New York: Free Press.
1971   *A Preview of Policy Sciences*. New York: Elsevier.

Laumann, Edward O., and Franz U. Pappi
1976   *Networks of Collective Action*. New York: Academic Press.

Lazarsfeld, Paul F., William H. Sewell, and Harold L. Wilensky
1967   "Introduction," in Paul F. Lazarsfeld, William H. Sewell, and Harold L. Wilensky (eds.), *The Uses of Sociology*. New York: Basic Books.

Leach, Edmund R.
1968   "Social Structure: The History of the Concept," in David L. Sills (ed.), *International Encyclopaedia of the Social Sciences, Vol. 14*. New York: Free Press.

Leavitt, Harold J.
1958   "Some Effects of Certain Communication Patterns on Group Performance," reprinted in Eleanor Maccoby et al. (eds.), *Readings in Social Psychology* (Third Edition). New York: Holt, Rinehart and Winston.

LeBon, Gustave
1960   *The Crowd*. New York: Viking Press.

Lenski, Gerhard E.
1954   "Status Crystallization: A Non-Vertical Dimension of Social Status," *American Sociological Review*, Vol. 19 (December): 405–413.
1970   *Human Societies*. New York: McGraw-Hill.
1975   "Social Structure in Evolutionary Perspective," in Peter M. Blau (ed.), *Approaches to the Study of Social Structure*. New York: Free Press.

Lever, Janet
1978   "Sex Differences in the Complexity of Children's Play and Games," *American Sociological Review*, Vol. 43 (August): 471–483.

Levin, Henry M.
1975   "Cost-Effectiveness Analysis in Evaluation Research," in Marcia Guttentag and Elmer L. Struening (eds.), *Handbook of Evaluation Research*. Beverly Hills, California, SAGE.

Lévi-Strauss, Claude
1956   "The Family," in Harry L. Shapiro (ed.), *Man, Culture, and Society*. New York: Oxford University Press.
1963   *Structural Anthropology*. New York: Basic Books.

Levy, Marion J., Jr.
1952   *The Structure of Society*. Princeton: Princeton University Press.
1968   "Structural-Functional Analysis," in David L. Sills (ed.), *International Encyclopedia of the Social Sciences*, Vol. 6, New York: Macmillan and Free Press.
1972   *Modernization: Latecomers and Survivors*. New York: Basic Books.

Leyhausen, Paul
1965   "The Communal Organization of Solitary Animals," in P.E. Ellis (ed.), *Social Organization of Animal Communities* (Symposia of the Zoological Society of London, No. 14). London: Zoological Society of London.

Linton, Ralph
1936   *The Study of Man*. New York: Appleton-Century.

Lipset, Seymour Martin

    1964   "The Political Process in Trade Unions: A Theoretical Statement," in Morroe Berger, et al. (eds.), *Freedom and Control in Modern Society*. New York: Octagon.

    1975   "Social Structure and Social Change" in Peter M. Blau (ed.), *Approaches to the Study of Social Structure*. New York: Free Press.

Lipset, Seymour Martin, Martin A. Trow, and James S. Coleman

    1957   *Union Democracy*. Glencoe: Free Press.

Luckmann, Thomas

    1978   "Philosophy, Social Sciences and Everyday Life," in Thomas Luckmann (ed.), *Phenomenology and Sociology*. New York: Penguin Books.

Luhmann, Niklas

    1981   "Communication About Law in Interaction Systems," in K. Knorr-Cetina and A.V. Cicourel (eds.), *Advances in Social Theory and Methodology*. Boston: Routledge & Kegan Paul.

Lukes, Steven

    1975   *Emile Durkheim: His Life and Work*. New York: Penguin Books.

    1978   "Power and Authority," in Tom Bottomore and Robert Nisbet (eds.), *A History of Sociological Analysis*. New York: Basic Books.

Lumsden, Charles J. and Edward O. Wilson

    1981   *Genes, Mind, and Culture*. Cambridge, Massachusetts: Harvard University Press.

Lynd, Robert S.

    1946   *Knowledge for What?* Princeton: Princeton University Press.

Maccoby, Eleanor Emmons, and Carol Nagy Jacklin

    1974   *The Psychology of Sex Differences*. Stanford: Stanford University Press.

McCorduck, Pamela

    1979   *Machines Who Think*. San Francisco: Freemen.

McDougall, William

    1914   *An Introduction to Social Psychology*. Boston: John W. Luce.

McGranahan, David A.

    1980   "The Spatial Structure of Income Distribution in Rural Regions," *American Sociological Review*, Vol. 45 (April): 313–324.

Machiavelli, Niccolo

    1940   *The Prince and The Discourses*. New York: Modern Library.

Mack, Raymond W. and Richard C. Snyder

    1957   "The Analysis of Social Conflict—Toward an Overview and Synthesis," *The Journal of Conflict Resolution*, Vol. I (June): 212–248.

Mack, Ruth P.

    1971   *Planning on Uncertainty*. New York: Wiley-Interscience.

MacRae, Duncan, Jr.

    1976   *The Social Function of Social Science*. New Haven: Yale University Press.

Malinowski, Bronislaw

    1944   *A Scientific Theory of Culture*. Chapel Hill, North Carolina: University of North Carolina Press.

    1961   *The Dynamics of Culture Change*. New Haven: Yale University Press.

    1963   "Parenthood—The Basis of Social Structure," reprinted in Marvin B. Sussman (ed.), *Sourcebook in Marriage and the Family*. Boston: Houghton Mifflin.

Malthus, Thomas R.

    1933   *An Essay on Population*. New York: Dutton.

Mandelbaum, Maurice

    1973a   "Societal Facts," in John O'Neill (ed.), *Modes of Individualism and Collectivism*. New York: St. Martin's Press.

1973b   "Societal Laws," in John O'Neill (ed.), *Modes of Individualism and Collectivism.* New York: St. Martin's Press.

Mannheim, Karl
1955   *Ideology and Utopia.* New York: Harvest Books.

March, James G., and Herbert A. Simon
1958   *Organizations.* New York: Wiley.

Marcuse, Herbert
1964   *One Dimensional Man.* Boston: Beacon Press.

Marler, Peter
1964   "Developments in the Study of Animal Communication," in P.R. Bell (ed.), *Darwin's Biological Work.* New York: Science Editions.

Marler, Peter, and Andrew Gordon
1968   "The Social Environment of Infant Macaques," in David C. Glass (ed.), *Biology and Behavior: Environmental Influences.* New York: Rockefeller University Press and Russell Sage Foundation.

Marx, Gary T.
1980   "Conceptual Problems in the Field of Collective Behavior," in Hubert M. Blalock, Jr. (ed.), *Sociological Theory and Research.* New York: Free Press.

Marx, Karl, and Frederick Engels
1947   *The German Ideology.* New York: International.
1978   *The Marx-Engels Reader* (Second Edition), Robert C. Tucker (ed.). New York: Norton.

Mason, William A.
1969   "The Effects of Social Restriction on the Behavior of Rhesus Monkeys," in Robert B. Zajonc (ed.), *Animal Social Psychology.* New York: Wiley.

Matza, David
1964   *Delinquency and Drift.* New York: Wiley.

Mead, George Herbert
1934   *Mind, Self, and Society.* Chicago: University of Chicago Press.

Mechanic, David
1978   *Medical Sociology* (Second Edition). New York: Free Press.

Melbin, Murray
1978   "Night as Frontier," *American Sociological Review,* Vol. 43 (February): 3–22.

Melzack, Ronald
1967   "Brain Mechanisms and Emotion," in David C. Glass (ed.), *Neurophysiology and Behavior.* New York: Rockefeller University Press and Russell Sage Foundation.

Merton, Robert K.
1948   "The Position of Sociological Theory: Discussion," *American Sociological Review,* Vol. 13 (April): 164–168.
1949   "The Role of Applied Social Science in the Formation of Policy: A Research Memorandum," *Philosophy of Science,* Vol. 16 (July): 161–181.
1957   *Social Theory and Social Structure* (revised and enlarged). Glencoe: Free Press.
1959   "Social Conformity, Deviation, and Opportunity Structures," *American Sociological Review,* Vol. 24 (April): 177–189.
1963   "Basic Research and Potentials of Relevance," *American Behavioral Scientist,* Vol. 6 (May): 86–90.
1973   *The Sociology of Science* (ed. by Norman W. Storer). Chicago: University of Chicago Press.
1975   "Structural Analysis in Sociology," in Peter M. Blau (ed.), *Approaches to the Study of Social Structure.* New York: Free Press.
1976   *Sociological Ambivalence.* New York: Free Press.

1981 "Foreword: Remarks on Theoretical Pluralism," in Peter M. Blau and Robert K. Merton (eds.), *Continuities in Structural Inquiry.* Beverly Hills, California: SAGE.

Merton, Robert K. and Daniel Lerner

1951 "Social Scientists and Research Policy," in Daniel Lerner and Harold Lasswell (eds.), *The Policy Sciences.* Stanford: Stanford University Press.

Mesarovic, M.D., and D. Macko

1969 "Foundations for a Scientific Theory of Hierarchical Systems," in Lancelot Law Whyte et al. (eds.), *Hierarchical Structures.* New York: Elsevier.

Michels, Robert

1958 *Political Parties.* Glencoe: Free Press.

Miller, George A., Eugene Galanter, and Karl H. Pribam

1960 *Plans and the Structure of Behavior.* New York: Holt, Rinehart and Winston.

Mills, C. Wright

1940 "Situated Actions and Vocabularies of Motive," *American Sociological Review,* Vol. 5 (December): 904–913.

1959 *The Sociological Imagination.* New York: Oxford University Press.

Minsky, Marvin Lee

1979 "The Society Theory of Thinking," in Patrick Henry Winston and Richard Henry Brown (eds.), *Artificial Intelligence: An MIT Perspective,* Vol. I. Cambridge, Massachusetts: MIT Press.

Mitchie, Donald

1974 *On Machine Intelligence.* Edinburgh: Edinburgh University Press.

Montesquieu, Baron de.

1949 *The Spirit of the Laws.* New York: Hafner.

Moore, Barrington, Jr.

1966 *Social Origins of Dictatorship and Democracy.* Boston: Beacon Press.

1972 *Reflections on the Causes of Human Misery.* Boston: Beacon Press.

Moore, Mary E.

1968a "The Nature of Aging," in Matilda White Riley and Anne Foner (eds.), *Aging and Society, Volume One.* New York: Russell Sage Foundation.

1968b "Behavioral Changes," in Matilda White Riley and Anne Foner (eds.), *Aging and Society, Volume One.* New York: Russell Sage Foundation.

Moore, Wilbert E.

1959 "Sociology and Demography," in Philip M. Hauser and Otis Dudley Duncan (eds.), *The Study of Population.* Chicago: University of Chicago Press.

1963a *Man, Time, and Society.* New York: Wiley.

1963b *Social Change.* Englewood Cliffs, New Jersey: Prentice-Hall.

1978 "Functionalism," in Tom Bottomore and Robert Nisbet (eds.), *A History of Sociological Analysis.* New York: Basic Books.

Moore, Wilbert E., and Eleanor Bernert Sheldon

1968 "Monitoring Social Change in American Society," in Eleanor Bernert Sheldon and Wilbert E. Moore, *Indicators of Social Change.* New York: Russell Sage Foundation.

Morley, Derek Wragge

1953 *The Ant World.* London: Penguin Books.

Morris, Richard T., and Raymond J. Murphy

1959 "The Situs Dimension in Occupational Structure," *American Sociological Review,* Vol. 24 (April): 231–239.

Moynihan, Daniel Patrick

1969 *Maximum Feasible Misunderstanding.* New York: Free Press.

Mulkay, Michael
   1977   "Sociology of the Scientific Research Community," in Ina Spiegel-Rösing and Derek de
           Solla-Price (eds.), *Science, Technology, and Society*. Beverly Hills, California: SAGE.
   1979   *Science and the Sociology of Knowledge*. London: Allen and Unwin.
Murphy, Raymond J., and Richard T. Morris
   1961   "Occupational Situs, Subjective Class Identification, and Political Affiliation," *American
           Sociological Review* Vol. 26 (June): 383–392.
Murray, Henry A., and Clyde Kluckhohn
   1961   "Outline of a Conception of Personality," in Clyde Kluckhohn and Henry A. Murray
           (eds.), *Personality in Nature, Society, and Culture*. New York: Knopf.
Nadel, S.F.
   1957   *The Theory of Social Structure*. Glencoe: The Free Press.
Nagel, Ernest
   1961   *The Structure of Science*. New York: Harcourt, Brace.
   1965   "Types of Causal Explanation in Science," in Daniel Lerner (ed.), *Cause and Effect*. New
           York: Free Press.
Newton, George D. and Franklin E. Zimring
   1969   *Firearms and Violence in American Life*. Washington, D.C.: U.S. Government Printing
           Office.
Nicolaus, Martin
   1971   "The Professional Organization of Sociology: A View from Below," in J. David Colfax
           and Jack L. Roach (eds.), *Radical Sociology*. New York: Basic Books.
Nietzsche, Friedrich Wilhelm
   1954   *The Portable Nietzsche* (Walter Kaufmann, ed.). New York: Viking Press.
Nisbet, Robert
   1966   *The Sociological Tradition*. New York: Basic Books.
   1969   *Social Change and History*. New York: Oxford University Press.
   1976   *Sociology as an Art Form*. New York: Oxford University Press.
Northrop, F.S.C.
   1959   *The Logic of the Sciences and the Humanities*. New York: Meridian Books.
Nowak, Stefan
   1977   *Methodology of Sociological Research*. Boston: D. Reidel.
Ogburn, William Fielding
   1933   *Social Change*. New York: Viking Press.
   1957a   "The Meaning of Technology," in Francis R. Allen et al. (eds.), *Technology and Social
           Change*. New York: Appleton-Century-Crofts.
   1957b   "How Technology Causes Social Change," in Francis R. Allen et al. (eds.), *Technology
           and Social Change*. New York: Appleton-Century-Crofts.
Ogles, Richard H., Marion J. Levy, Jr., and Talcott Parsons
   1959   "Culture and Social System: An Exchange," *American Sociological Review*, Vol. 24 (April):
           246–250.
Ong, Walter J.
   1971   *Rhetoric, Romance, and Technology*. Ithaca: Cornell University Press.
   1974   "Agonistic Structures in Academia: Past to Present," *Interchange*, Vol. 5, No. 4: 1–12.
   1978   "Literacy and Orality in Our Times," Association of Departments of English (ADE) Bul-
           letin, No. 58 (September): 1–7.
Oppenheimer, Valerie Kincade
   1973   "Demographic Influence on Female Employment and the Status of Women," *American
           Journal of Sociology*, Vol. 78 (January): 946–961.

Pareto, Vilfredo
　　1935　*The Mind and Society*. New York: Harcourt, Brace.
Park, Robert Ezra
　　1961　"Human Ecology," reprinted in George A. Theodorson (ed.), *Studies in Human Ecology*. Evanston, Illinois: Row, Peterson.
　　1972　*The Crowd and the Public*. Chicago: University of Chicago Press.
Park, Robert E., and Ernest W. Burgess
　　1921　*Introduction to the Science of Sociology*. Chicago: University of Chicago Press.
Parkin, Frank
　　1978　"Social Stratification," in Tom Bottomore and Robert Nisbet (eds.), *A History of Sociological Analysis*. New York: Basic Books.
Parsons, Talcott
　　1937　*The Structure of Social Action*. Glencoe: Free Press.
　　1951　*The Social System*. Glencoe: Free Press.
　　1954　*Essays in Sociological Theory* (revised). Glencoe: Free Press.
　　1957　"Malinowski and the Theory of Social Systems," in Raymond Firth (ed.), *Man and Culture*. London: Routledge & Kegan Paul.
　　1959　"An Approach to Psychological Theory in Terms of the Theory of Action" in Sigmund Koch (ed.) *Psychology: A Study of a Science*. New York: McGraw-Hill.
　　1960　"Pattern Variables Revisited: A Response to Robert Dubin," *American Sociological Review*, Vol. 25 (August): 467–483.
　　1961a　"An Outline of the Social System," in Talcott Parsons, Edward Shils, Kaspar D. Naegele, and Jesse R. Pitts (eds.), *Theories of Society*. New York: Free Press.
　　1961b　"The General Interpretation of Action," in Talcott Parsons, Edward Shils, Kaspar D. Naegele, and Jesse R. Pitts (eds.), *Theories of Society*. New York: Free Press of Glencoe.
　　1965　"Full Citizenship for the Negro American? A Sociological Problem," *Daedalus*, Vol. 94 (Fall): 1009–1054.
　　1966　*Societies*. Englewood Cliffs, New Jersey: Prentice-Hall.
　　1967　*Sociological Theory and Modern Society*. New York: Free Press.
　　1968a　"An Overview," in Talcott Parsons (ed.) *American Sociology*. New York: Basic Books.
　　1968b　"On the Concept of Value-Commitments," *Sociological Inquiry*, Vol. 37 (Spring): 135–160.
　　1970　"Some Problems of General Theory in Sociology," in John C. McKinney and Edward A. Tiryakian (eds.), *Theoretical Sociology*. New York: Appleton-Century-Crofts.
　　1973　"Culture and Social Structure Revisited," in Louis Schneider and Charles Bonjean (eds.) *The Idea of Culture in the Social Sciences*. Cambridge: Cambridge University Press.
Parsons, Talcott and Robert F. Bales
　　1953　"The Dimensions of Action Space," in Talcott Parsons, Robert F. Bales, and Edward A. Shils, *Working Papers in the Theory of Action*. Glencoe: Free Press.
　　1955　*Family, Socialization, and Interaction Process*. New York: Free Press.
Parsons, Talcott and Edward A. Shils
　　1951　"Values, Motives, and Systems of Action," in Talcott Parsons and Edward A. Shils (eds.), *Toward a General Theory of Action*. New York: Harper Torchbooks.
Parsons, Talcott and Neil Smelser
　　1956　*Economy and Society*. Glencoe: Free Press.
Parsons, Talcott, et al.
　　1951　"A General Statement," in Talcott Parsons and Edward A. Shils (eds.), *Toward A General Theory of Action*. New York: Harper Torchbooks.
Pattee, Howard H.

1973 "The Physical Basis and Origin of Hierarchical Control," in Howard H. Pattee (ed.), *Hierarchy Theory*. New York: Braziller.

Peterson, Richard A., and David G. Berger
1975 "Cycles in Symbol Production: The Case of Popular Music," *American Sociological Review*, Vol. 40 (April): 158–173.

Phillips, David P.
1974 "The Influence of Suggestion on Suicide: Substantive and Theoretical Implications of the Werther Effect," *American Sociological Review*, Vol. 39 (June): 340–354.
1979 "Suicide, Motor Vehicle Fatalities, and the Mass Media: Evidence Toward a Theory of Suggestion," *American Journal of Sociology*, Vol. 84 (March): 1150–1174.

Plantinga, Theodore
1980 *Historical Understanding in the Thought of Wilhelm Dilthey*. Toronto: University of Toronto Press.

Polanyi, Michael
1969 *Knowing and Being*. Chicago: University of Chicago Press.

Popper, Karl R.
1950 *The Open Society and Its Enemies*. Princeton: Princeton University Press.
1961 *The Logic of Scientific Discovery*. New York: Science Editions.
1973 "From *The Poverty of Historicism*," in John O'Neill (ed.), *Modes of Individualism and Collectivism*. New York: St. Martin's Press.
1976 "The Logic of the Social Sciences," in Theodor W. Adorno et al., *The Positivist Dispute in German Sociology*. New York: Harper Torchbooks.

Powers, William T.
1973 *Behavior: The Control of Perception*. Chicago: Aldine.

Pressman, Jeffrey L., and Aaron Wildavsky
1973 *Implementation*. Berkeley, California: University of California Press.

Quine, Willard Van Orman
1960 *Word and Object*. Cambridge, Massachusetts: M.I.T. Press.
1963 *From a Logical Point of View*. New York: Harper Torchbooks.

Quinn, James A.
1939 "The Nature of Human Ecology: Reexamination and Redefinition," *Social Forces*, Vol. 18 (December): 161–168.

Radcliffe-Brown, A.R.
1965 *Structure and Function in Primitive Society*. New York: Free Press.

Raiffa, Howard
1968 *Decision Analysis*. Reading, Massachusetts: Addison-Wesley.

Riecken, Henry
1969 "Social Science and Social Problems," *Social Science Information* (February): 101–109.

Riley, Matilda White
1963 *Sociological Research*. Harcourt Brace & World.

Riley, Matilda White, and Joan Waring
1976 "Age and Aging," in Robert K. Merton and Robert Nisbet (eds.), *Contemporary Social Problems* (Fourth Edition). New York: Harcourt Brace Jovanovich.

Riley, Matilda White, Anne Foner, and Marilyn Johnson
1972 "Age Strata in the Society," in Matilda White Riley, Anne Foner, and Marilyn Johnson (eds.), *Aging and Society, Volume Three*. New York: Russell Sage Foundation.

Rose, Arnold M.
1962 "A Systematic Summary of Symbolic Interaction Theory," in Arnold M. Rose (ed.), *Human Behavior and Social Processes*. Boston: Houghton Mifflin.

Rosenberg, Morris, and Leonard I. Pearlin

950   "A Consideration of Some Problems in the Ontogeny of Family Life and Social Adjustment in Various Infrahuman Animals," in Milton Senn (ed.), *Problems of Infancy and Childhood*. New York: Josia Macy Jr. Foundation.

ettle, Enid Curtis Bok

1968   "The State of the Art in Policy Studies," in Raymond A. Bauer and Kenneth J. Gergen (eds.), *The Study of Policy Formation*. New York: Free Press.

rödinger, Erwin

1968   "Order, Disorder, and Entropy," in Walter Buckley (ed.), *Modern Systems Research for the Behavioral Scientist*. Chicago: Aldine.

chutz, Alfred

1951   "Choosing Among Projects of Action," *Philosophy and Phenomenological Research,* Vol. XII, No. 2 (December): 161–184.

1953   "Common-Sense and Scientific Interpretation of Human Action," *Philosophy and Phenomenological Research,* Vol. XIV, No. 1 (September): 1–37.

1978   "Phenomenology and the Social Sciences," in Thomas Luckmann (ed.), *Phenomenology and Sociology*. New York: Penguin Books.

Scott, John Finley

1971   *Internalization of Norms*. Englewood Cliffs, New Jersey: Prentice-Hall.

Scott, Robert A.

1969   *The Making of Blind Men*. New York: Russell Sage Foundation.

Scott, Robert A., and Arnold A. Shore

1979   *Why Sociology Does Not Apply*. New York: Elsevier.

Sebeok, Thomas A.

1968   "Communication in Animals and Men; Three Reviews," in Joshua A. Fishman (ed.), *Readings in the Sociology of Language*. The Hague: Morton.

Secord, Paul F., and Carl W. Backman

1974   *Social Psychology*. New York: McGraw-Hill. Second Edition.

Selznick, Philip

1948   "Foundations of the Theory of Organization," *American Sociological Review,* Vol. 13 (February): 25–35.

Shaver, Phillip, and Graham Staines

1972   "Problems Facing Campbell's Experimenting Society," *American Psychologist,* Vol. 27 (February): 161–163.

Shott, Susan

1979   "Emotion and Social Life: A Symbolic Interactionist Analysis," *American Journal of Sociology,* Vol. 84 (May): 1317–1334.

Simmel, Georg

1950   *The Sociology of Georg Simmel*. Glencoe: Free Press.

1955   *Conflict and the Web of Group-Affiliations*. New York: Free Press of Glencoe.

Simon, Herbert A.

1965   "The Architecture of Complexity," in *General Systems: Yearbook of the Society for General Systems Research,* Vol. X, 63–76.

1973   "The Organization of Complex Systems," in Howard H. Pattee (ed.), *Hierarchy Theory*. New York: Braziller.

Singer, Milton

1968   "The Concept of Culture," in David L. Sills (ed.). *International Encyclopedia of the Social Sciences,* Vol. 3. New York: Free Press.

Sjoberg, Gideon

1969   "Disasters and Social Change," in George W. Baker and Dwight W. Chapman (eds.), *Man and Society in Disaster*. New York: Basic Books.

Skocpol, Theda

1979   *States and Social Revolutions*. Cambridge, Massachusetts: Cambridge University Press.

REFERENCES

1978   "Social Class and Self-Esteem Among Children and Adult.
         Vol. 84 (July): 53–77.

Rossi, Alice
     1977   "A Biosocial Perspective on Parenting," *Daedalus,* Vol. 106 (

Rossi, Peter H.
     1971   "Evaluating Social Action Programs," in Francis G. Caro (ed.
           Research. New York: Russell Sage Foundation.
     1972a   "Observations on the Organization of Social Research," in Peter
           Williams (eds.), *Evaluating Social Programs.* New York: Seminar Pre
     1972b   "Testing For Success and Failure in Social Action," in Peter H. Ro
           liams (eds.) *Evaluating Social Programs.* New York: Seminar Press.
     1975   "Field Experiments in Social Programs: Problems and Prospects," in
           (ed.), *Social Research and Public Policies.* Hanover, New Hampshire: Publi
           Dartmouth College.
     1980   "The Presidential Address: The Challenge and Opportunities of Applied So
           American Sociological Review, Vol. 45 (December): 889–904.

Rostow, W.W.
     1960   *The Stages of Economic Growth.* New York: Cambridge University Press.

Rothenberg, Jerome
     1975   "Cost-Benefit Analysis: A Methodological Exposition," in Marcia Guttentag an
           L. Struening (eds.), *Handbook of Evaluation Research,* Beverly Hills, California: SA

Rule, James B.
     1978a   *Insight and Social Betterment.* New York: Oxford University Press.
     1978b   "Models of Relevance: The Social Effects of Sociology," *American Journal of Sociology,*
           84 (July): 78–98.

Ryder, Norman B.
     1964   "Notes on the Concept of a Population," *American Journal of Sociology,* Vol. 69 (March)
           447–463.
     1965   "The Cohort as a Concept in the Study of Social Change," *American Sociological Review,*
           Vol. 30 (December): 843–861.
     1980   "Where Do Babies Come From?," in Hubert M. Blalock, Jr. (ed.), *Sociological Theory and
           Research.* New York: Free Press.

Sarbin, Theodore R.
     1968   "Role: Psychological Aspects," in David L. Sills (ed.), *International Encyclopaedia of the
           Social Sciences,* Vol. 13. New York: Free Press.

Scarr, Sandra, and Richard A. Weinberg
     1978   "The Influence of 'Family Background' on Intellectual Attainment," *American Sociological
           Review,* Vol. 43 (October): 674–692.

Schatz, Gerald S.
     1982   "Factory-Automation in Japan and in Western and Eastern Europe," *News Report,* Vol.
           XXXII (April): 3–11.

Scheff, Thomas J.
     1966   *Being Mentally Ill.* Chicago: Aldine.

Schneider, Louis
     1973   "The Idea of Culture in the Social Sciences," in Louis Schneider and Charles M. Bonjean
           (eds.), *The Idea of Culture in the Social Sciences.* Cambridge, Massachusetts: Cambridge
           University Press.

Schneirla, T.C.
     1946   "Problems in the Biopsychology of Social Organization," *Journal of Abnormal and Social
           Psychology,* Vol. 41 (October): 385–402.

Smelser, Neil
    1962   *Theory of Collective Behavior.* New York: Free Press.
    1968   *Essays in Sociological Explanation.* Englewood Cliffs, New Jersey: Prentice-Hall.
    1980   "Biography, the Structure of Explanation, and the Evaluation of Theory in Sociology," in Hubert M. Blalock, Jr. (ed.), *Sociological Theory and Research.* New York: Free Press.

Smith, Cyril Stanley
    1969   "Structural Hierarchy in Inorganic Systems," in Lancelot Law Whyte, et al. (eds.), *Hierarchical Structures.* New York: Elsevier.

Sopher, David
    1973   "Place and Location: Notes on the Spatial Patterning of Culture," in Louis Schneider and Charles M. Bonjean (eds.), *The Idea of Culture in the Social Sciences.* Cambridge: Cambridge University Press.

Sorel, Georges
    1950   *Reflections on Violence.* Glencoe: Free Press.

Sorokin, Pitirim A.
    1937–
    1941   *Social and Cultural Dynamics.* New York: American Book.
    1947   *Society, Culture, and Personality.* New York: Harper and Row.

Spector, Malcolm, and John I. Kitsuse
    1977   *Constructing Social Problems.* Menlo Park, California: Cummings.

Spencer, Herbert
    1898   *The Principles of Sociology.* New York: Appleton.
    1967   *The Evolution of Society: Selections From "Principles of Sociology."* Chicago: University of Chicago Press.
    1972   *On Social Evolution: Selected Writings.* Chicago: University of Chicago Press.

Spilerman, Seymour
    1976   "Structural Characteristics of Cities and the Severity of Racial Disorders," *American Sociological Review* (October): 771–793.

Starr, Paul
    1982   *The Social Transformation of American Medicine.* New York: Basic Books.

Stehr, Nico
    1978   "The Ethos of Science Revisited: Social and Cognitive Norms," in Jerry Gaston (ed.), *Sociology of Science,* San Francisco: Jossey-Bass.

Stevens, S.S.
    1946   "On the Theory of Scales of Measurement," *Science,* Vol. 103, No. 2684: 677–680.

Stinchcombe, Arthur L.
    1968   *Constructing Social Theories.* New York: Harcourt, Brace and World.

Stouffer, Samuel
    1962   *Social Research to Test Ideas.* New York: Free Press.

Stryker, Sheldon
    1980   *Symbolic Interactionism.* Menlo Park, California: Benjamin/Cummings.
    1982   "Editor's Comment," *American Sociological Review,* Vol. 47 (February), iii.

Suchman, Edward A.
    1968   "Sociocultural Factors in Nutritional Studies," in David C. Glass (ed.), *Biology and Behavior: Environmental Influences.* New York: The Rockefeller University Press and Russell Sage Foundation.

Sykes, Gresham M.
    1965   *The Society of Captives.* New York: Atheneum.

Sztompka, Piotr
    1974   *System and Function: Toward a Theory of Society.* New York: Academic Press.

1979 *Sociological Dilemmas.* New York: Academic Press.

Tarde, Gabriel
1968 *On Communication and Social Influence* (Terry N. Clark, ed.). Chicago: University of Chicago Press.

Taton, R.
1962 *Reason and Chance in Scientific Discovery.* New York: Science Editions.

Taylor, Howard F.
1980 *The IQ Game.* New Brunswick: Rutgers University Press.

Thomas, Lewis
1977 "On the Science and Technology of Medicine," *Daedalus,* Vol. 106 (Winter): 35–46.

Thomas, W.I.
1961 "The Four Wishes and the Definition of the Situation," in Talcott Parsons, et al. (eds.), *Theories of Society.* New York: Free Press.

Thomas, William I., and Dorothy Swaine Thomas
1928 *The Child in America.* New York: Knopf.

Thompson, James D. and Robert W. Hawkes
1969 "Disaster, Community Organization, and Administrative Process," in George W. Baker and Dwight W. Chapman (eds.), *Man and Society in Disaster.* New York: Basic Books.

Tilly, Charles
1975 "Revolutions and Collective Violence," in Fred I. Greenstein and Nelson Polsby (eds.), *Handbook of Political Science Vol. III.* Reading, Massachusetts: Addison-Wesley.
1978 *From Mobilization to Revolution.* Reading, Massachusetts: Addison-Wesley.

Tiryakian, Edward
1970 "Structural Sociology," in John C. McKinney and Edward A. Tiryakian (eds.), *Theoretical Sociology.* New York: Appleton-Century-Crofts.

Toby, Jackson
1980 "Where Are the Streakers Now?," in Hubert M. Blalock, Jr. (ed.), *Sociological Theory and Research.* New York: Free Press.

Tönnies, Ferdinand
1963 *Community and Society.* New York: Harper Torchbooks.

Torgerson, Warren S.
1958 *Theory and Methods of Scaling.* New York: Wiley.

Tumin, Melvin M.
1967 *Social Stratification: The Forms and Functions of Inequality.* Englewood Cliffs, New Jersey: Prentice-Hall.

Turner, Jonathan H. and Alexandra Maryanski
1979 *Functionalism.* Menlo Park, California: Benjamin/Cummings.

Turner, Ralph, H.
1962 "Role-Taking: Process versus Conformity," in Arnold M. Rose (ed.), *Human Behavior and Social Processes.* Boston: Houghton Mifflin.
1964 "Collective Behavior," in Robert E.L. Faris (ed.), *Handbook of Modern Sociology.* Chicago: Rand McNally.
1976 "The Real Self: From Institution to Impulse," *American Journal of Sociology,* Vol. 81 (March): 989–1016.
1978 "The Role and the Person," *American Journal of Sociology,* Vol. 84 (July): 1–23.

Turner, Ralph H., and Lewis M. Killian.
1957 *Collective Behavior.* Englewood Cliffs, New Jersey.

Udy, Stanley H., Jr.
1968 "Social Structure: Social Structural Analysis," in David L. Sills (ed.), *International Encyclopedia of the Social Sciences, Vol. 14.* New York: Free Press.

van den Berghe, Pierre L.

1963   "Dialectic and Functionalism: Toward a Theoretic Synthesis," *American Sociological Review,* Vol. 28 (October): 695–705.

1974   "Bringing Beasts Back in: Toward a Biosocial Theory of Aggression," *American Sociological Review,* Vol. 39 (December): 777–788.

1975   *Man in Society.* New York: Elsevier.

von Bertalanffy, Ludwig

1968   "General System Theory—A Critical Review," in Walter Buckley (ed.), *Modern Systems Research for the Behavioral Scientist.* Chicago: Aldine.

Wallace, Walter L.

1966   *Student Culture.* Chicago: Aldine.

1968   "Toward a Theoretic Synthesis in Sociology," *The Sociological Quarterly,* Vol. 9 (Autumn): 440–478.

1969   "Overview of Contemporary Sociological Theory," in Walter L. Wallace (ed.), *Sociological Theory.* Chicago: Aldine.

1971   *The Logic of Science in Sociology.* Chicago: Aldine.

1975   "Structure and Action in the Theories of Coleman and Parsons," in Peter M. Blau (ed.), *Approaches to the Study of Social Structure.* New York: Free Press.

1981   "Hierarchic Structure in Social Phenomena," in Peter M. Blau and Robert K. Merton (eds.), *Continuities in Structural Inquiry.* London: SAGE Publications.

Wallerstein, Immanuel

1974   *The Modern World-System.* New York: Academic Press.

1979   *The Capitalist World-Economy.* Cambridge: Cambridge University Press.

Wallis, D.I.

1965   "Division of Labour in Ant Colonies," in P.E. Ellis (ed.), *Social Organization of Animal Communities* (Symposia of the Zoological Society of London, No. 14). London: Zoological Society of London.

Waring, Joan M.

1976   "Social Replenishment and Social Change," in Anne Foner (ed.), *Age in Society.* Beverly Hills, California: SAGE.

Warner, Robert

1982   "Metamorphosis," *Science 82,* Vol. 3 (December): 42–46.

Warriner, Charles K.

1956   "Groups Are Real: A Reaffirmation," *American Sociological Review,* Vol. 21 (October): 549–554.

1981   "Levels in the Study of Social Structure," in Peter M. Blau and Robert K. Merton (eds.), *Continuities in Structural Inquiry.* Beverly Hills, Califorani: SAGE.

Wartofsky, Marx W.

1968   *Conceptual Foundations of Scientific Thought.* New York: Macmillan.

Watkins, J.W.N.

1973a   "Ideal Types and Historical Explanation," in John O'Neill, (ed.), *Modes of Individualism and Collectivism.* New York: St. Martin's Press.

1973b   "Historical Explanation in the Social Sciences," in John O'Neill (ed.), *Modes of Individualism and Collectivism.* New York: St. Martin's Press.

1973c   "Methodological Individualism: A Reply," in John O'Neill (ed.), *Modes of Individualism and Collectivism.* New York: St. Martin's Press.

Weber, Max

1947   *Theory of Social and Economic Organization.* Glencoe: Free Press.

1949   *The Methodology of the Social Sciences.* Glencoe: Free Press.

1958a   *From Max Weber: Essays in Sociology* (ed. by H.H. Gerth and C. Wright Mills). New York: Oxford.

1958b   *The Protestant Ethic and the Spirit of Capitalism.* New York: Scribner.

1968   *Economy and Society*. Berkeley: University of California Press.

Weiss, Carol H., and Michael J. Bucuvalas

1980   "Truth Tests and Utility Tests: Decision-Makers' Frames of Reference for Social Science Research," *American Sociological Review*, Vol. 45 (April): 302–313.

Wellman, Barry

1979   "The Community Question: The Intimate Networks of East Yorkers," *American Journal of Sociology*, Vol. 84 (March): 1201–1213.

Westoff, Charles F., and Ronald R. Rindfuss

1974   "Sex Preselection in the United States: Some Implications," *Science*, Vol. 184 (May 10), 633–636.

White, Leslie

1949   *The Science of Culture*. New York: Grove.

Whitehead, Alfred North

1938   *Modes of Thought*. New York: Capricorn.

1967   *The Aims of Education*. New York: Free Press.

Wildavsky, Aaron

1975   *Budgeting*. Boston: Little, Brown.

Williams, Robin M., Jr.

1968a   "The Concept of Norms," in David L. Sills (ed.), *International Encyclopedia of the Social Sciences, Vol. 11*. New York: Macmillan and Free Press.

1968b   "Values," in David L. Sills (ed.), *International Encylopedia of the Social Sciences, Vol. 16*. New York: Macmillan and Free Press.

1976   "Conflict and Social Order: A Research Strategy for Complex Propositions," in Marcello Truzzi and Philip B. Springer (eds.), *Solving Social Problems*. Pacific Palisades, California: Goodyear Publishing.

Williams, Walter

1972a   "The Organization of the Volume and Some Key Definitions," in Peter H. Rossi and Walter Williams (eds.), *Evaluating Social Programs*. New York: Seminar Press.

1972b   "The Capacity of Social Science Organizations to Perform Large-Scale Evaluative Research," in Peter H. Rossi and Walter Williams (eds.), *Evaluating Social Programs*. New York: Seminar Press.

Wilson, Albert.

1969   "Closure, Entity, and Level," in Lancelot Law Whyte et al. (eds.), *Hierarchical Structures*. New York: Elsevier.

Wilson, Edward O.

1971   *The Insect Societies*. Cambridge, Massachusetts: Belknap Press/Harvard University Press.

1975   *Sociobiology*. Cambridge, Massachusetts: Belknap Press/Harvard University Press.

1978   *On Human Nature*. Cambridge, Massachusetts: Harvard University Press.

Winch, Peter

1958   *The Idea of a Social Science and Its Relation to Philosophy*. London: Routledge & Kegan Paul.

Winch, Robert F.

1963   *The Modern Family*. New York: Holt, Rinehart and Winston.

Wrong, Dennis H.

1961   "The Oversocialized Conception of Man," *American Sociological Review*, Vol. 26 (April): 183–193.

Wyer, Robert S., Jr., and Donal E. Carlston

1979   *Social Cognition, Inference, and Attribution*. Hillsdale, New Jersey: Lawrence Erlbaum Associates.

Wynne-Edwards, V.C.

1962   *Animal Dispersion in Relation to Social Behaviour*. Edinburgh: Oliver and Boyd.

1968   "Population Control and Social Selection in Animals," in David C. Glass (ed.), *Biology and Behavior: Genetics*. New York: The Rockefeller University Press and Russell Sage Foundation.

Zeckhauser, Richard, and Elmer Schaeffer

1968   "Public Policy and Normative Economic Theory," in Raymond A. Bauer and Kenneth J. Gergen (eds.), *The Study of Policy Formation*. New York: Free Press.

Zetterberg, Hans L.

1954   *On Theory and Verification in Sociology*. Stockholm: Almqvist and Wiksell.

1963   *On Theory and Verification in Sociology* (Second Edition). Totowa, New Jersey: Bedminster Press.

Zinsser, Hans

1967   *Rats, Lice and History*. New York: Bantam Books.

Zorbaugh, Harvey

1961   "The Natural Areas of the City," in George A. Theodorson (ed.), *Studies in Human Ecology*. Evanston, Illinois: Row, Peterson.

Name Index

Numbers in italics indicate pages where complete references are given.

523

524

Subject Index

Action, 198, 282, 308, 446
  collective, 125, 323
  frame of reference, 99
  rational and nonrational, 285n
  social, *see* Social action
Activity, 68
Actor, 20, 94, 198
Actor expectation, normative, 97–115, 130–131, 228
Administration, *see* Social structure; Social structuralism
Adolescence, 224n
Affectual orientation, 220, 282, 286; *see also* Orientation, cathectic
Age
  cohorts, 244
  distribution, 240, 243–244, 247
  of individuals, 211, 213, 214, 244
Aggression, 218, 222, 222n, 233
Alienation, 313, 337
Altruism, 196, 196n–197n, 249, 269n–270n, 329, 345–347, 360, 363
Anomie, 196, 196n, 249, 329, 345–347, 361, 363
Architecture, *see* Housing
Artificial
  intelligence, 314–315
  reproduction, 317
Attitudes, 128; *see also* Norms

Authority, 183–184, 292
Automation, 311n, 313

Bank wiring room, 30–31, 68, 211
Behavior, individual
  definition, 14n
  physical, 21–22, 26–28, 57–87, 342
    aggregates of, 72–80
    coincidences between, 80–87, 160
    direction and object of effect, 57–58
    types, 58–60, 63–72, 77–78, 80
  psychical, 21–22, 26–28, 89–127, 342
    aggregates of, 97–124
    coincidences between, 124–127
    mode and referent of orientation, 90–96
    types, 96–97; *see also* Orientation
Behavioral organism, 328
Biological reproduction, 70–71, 312
Birth-death ratio, 240
Blindness, 215
Brain, 200, 203, 217
Budgeting, 362, 427, 448
Bureaucracy, 285n, 289, 313–314, 450

Capital, 310
Categories of the understanding, 350
Cathexis, *see* Orientation